1978

Medical and Health Annual

Encyclopædia Britannica, Inc.

CHICAGO · LONDON · TORONTO · GENEVA · SYDNEY · TOKYO · MANILA · SEOUL

1978 Medical and Health Annual

Editor	Douglas C. Benson
Assistant Editor	Linda Tomchuck
Contributing Editors	David Bracey, Robert Rauch, Christine Timmons
Consulting Editor	Richard Pope
Medical Editor	Richard H. Kessler, M.D. Professor of Medicine and Associate Dean Northwestern University Medical School
Art Director	Cynthia Peterson
Design Supervisor	Ron Villani
Senior Picture Editor	Barbara M. Epstein
Picture Editor	Roberta J. Homan
Picture Staff	Holly Harrington, Julie A. Kunkler
Layout Artist	Richard Batchelor
Illustrator	John L. Draves
Art Production	Richard Heinke
Art Staff	William W. Karpa, Miguel Rodriguez
Editorial Production Manager	J. Thomas Beatty
Production Coordinator	Anita K. Wolff
Production Staff	Kathryn Blatt, Elizabeth Chastain, Laura Grad, Juanita L. Murphy, John Park, Nancy W. Pask, Julian Ronning, Melinda Shepherd, Cheryl W. Trobiani, María Dolores del Valle, Joyce P. Walker, Coleen Withgott
Copy Control	Mary C. Srodon, *Supervisor* Mayme R. Cussen
Computer Typesetting Services	Robert Dehmer, *Supervisor* Ronald J. Laugeman, Melvin E. Stagner, Gilberto Valle, Elaine V. Yost
Index	Frances Latham, *Supervisor* Rosa E. Casas, *Assistant Supervisor* Judith Anderson, Mary Neumann, Helen Peterson, Mary L. Reynolds
Librarian	Terry Miller
Assistant Librarian	Shantha Channabasappa
Manuscript Typist	Eunice L. Mitchell
Secretary	Marie Lawrence

Editorial Administration

Managing Editor, Encyclopædia Britannica, Inc.
Margaret Sutton

Director of Budgets
Verne Pore

Encyclopædia Britannica, Inc.

Chairman of the Board	Robert P. Gwinn
President	Charles E. Swanson
Vice President, Editorial	Charles Van Doren

Contents

Consultants and Contributors to The World of Medicine

Francois Alouf, M.D. *Human Sexuality Special Report: Sex and Pregnancy* (in part). Associate Professor of Psychiatry, and Director of Education, Department of Psychiatry, Northwestern University Medical School, Chicago.

Charles E. Alverson, B.A. *World Medical News: Great Britain.* Medical Writer, Cambridge, England.

Edward Russell Ames, D.V.M., Ph.D. *Veterinary Medicine.* Director, Continuing Education, American Veterinary Medical Association, Chicago.

Edward Leon Applebaum, M.D. *Ear Diseases and Hearing Disorders.* Assistant Professor, Department of Otolaryngology and Maxillofacial Surgery, Northwestern University Medical School, Chicago.

Peter Barglow, M.D. *Human Sexuality Special Report: Sex and Pregnancy* (in part). Head, Psychosomatic Medicine Section, Prentice Women's Hospital and Maternity Center of Northwestern Memorial Hospital; Associate Professor, Department of Psychiatry, Northwestern University Medical School, Chicago.

Nathaniel Isaac Berlin, M.D. *Cancer; Cancer Special Report: The National Cancer Program.* Director, Cancer Center, and Teuton Professor of Medicine, Northwestern University, Chicago.

Benjamin Boshes, M.D., Ph.D. *Aging; Death.* Professor Emeritus, Neurology and Psychiatry, Northwestern University Medical School, Chicago.

Edward P. Cohen, M.D., Ph.D. *Allergy and Immunology; Infectious Diseases; Lymphatic System Diseases; Microbiology.* Associate Professor, La Rabida-University of Chicago Institute, Chicago.

Theodore Miller Cole, M.D. *Physical Medicine and Rehabilitation.* Professor and Chairman, Department of Physical Medicine and Rehabilitation, University of Michigan Medical School, Ann Arbor.

Morris Frank Collen, M.D. *Health Care Costs Special Report: Outpatient Health Care.* Director, Medical Methods Research, Kaiser-Permanente Medical Care Program, Oakland, Calif.

Grace A. Cordts, B.S.N. *Stress* (in part). Teacher, Oncology Nursing Program, School of Nursing, and Lecturer, Health Activation Program, Division of Continuing Education—Nursing, Georgetown University, Washington, D.C.

Patricia Dragisic, M.S. *Surgery.* Free-lance Writer and Health Columnist, *The Spokeswoman,* Chicago.

Nancy Ethiel, B.A. *Health Care Special Report: The Laetrile Controversy.* Free-lance Writer and Editor; formerly Associate Editor, *Modern Healthcare,* Chicago.

Casimir F. Firlit, M.D., Ph.D. *Urology.* Associate Professor, Urology and Physiology, Northwestern University Medical School; Head, Pediatric Renal Transplantation, and Attending Pediatric Urologist, Children's Memorial Hospital, Chicago.

Jeanne P. Goldberg, M.Ed., R.D. *Diet and Nutrition.* Nutritionist and Free-lance Writer, West Hartford, Conn.

Solomon G. Hershey, M.D. *Anesthesiology.* Professor of Anesthesiology, and Director, Office of Continuing Medical Education, Albert Einstein College of Medicine, New York City.

Joan Hollobon. *World Medical News: Canada.* Medical Reporter, *Globe and Mail,* Toronto, Ont.

John F. Horty, L.L.B. *Health Care Law* (in part). Partner, Horty, Springer, and Mattern; Editor, *Action-Kit for Hospital Law,* Pittsburgh, Pa.

John William Huffman, M.D. *Birth Control.* Professor Emeritus of Obstetrics and Gynecology, Northwestern University Medical School, Chicago.

Eric R. Hurd, M.D. *Connective Tissue Diseases; Muscle Diseases.* Associate Professor of Internal Medicine, University of Texas Southwestern Medical School, Dallas, Texas.

Ted Isaacman, M.S. *Health Care Law* (in part). Managing Editor, *Action-Kit for Hospital Law,* Pittsburgh, Pa.

Thomas Killip, M.D. *Cardiovascular System Diseases.* Professor of Medicine, and Associate Dean, Northwestern University Medical School, Chicago; Chairman, Department of Medicine, Evanston Hospital, Evanston, Ill.

Resa W. King. *Health Care Costs.* Correspondent, *Business Week,* New York City.

Hau Cheong Kwaan, M.D. *Blood Diseases.* Professor of Medicine, Northwestern University Medical School; Chief, Hematology Section, Veterans Administration Lakeside Hospital, Chicago.

Lynne F. Lamberg, M.A. *Psychiatry* (in part); *Skin Diseases* (in part); *Taste and Smell Disorders.* Free-lance Medical Journalist, Baltimore, Md.

Stanford I. Lamberg, M.D. *Skin Diseases* (in part). Associate Professor, Johns Hopkins University School of Medicine; Chief of Dermatology, Baltimore City Hospitals, Baltimore, Md.

Albert W. Lang, M.D. *Psychiatry Special Report: Community Psychiatry.* Private practice; Consultant, outpatient psychiatric programs and agencies for children and families, Northfield, Ill.

Marvin E. Lehrman, M.S.W. *Human Sexuality.* Assistant Director of Social Work, Rehabilitation Institute of Chicago; Instructor, Health Sciences and Arts, Northwestern University Medical School, Chicago.

Bernard Levin, M.D. *Digestive System Diseases.* Assistant Professor of Medicine, Pritzker School of Medicine, The University of Chicago; Director, Gastrointestinal Oncology Clinic, The University of Chicago Hospitals and Clinics.

Nathan W. Levin, M.D. *Transplantation.* Chief, Division of Nephrology, Henry Ford Hospital, Detroit; Clinical Associate Professor of Medicine, University of Michigan Medical School, Ann Arbor.

Mortimer B. Lipsett, M.D. *Hormones and Prostaglandins.* Director, Clinical Center, National Institutes of Health, Bethesda, Md.

Nicholas Lloyd. *World Medical News: Australia.* Director of Communications, Australian Medical Association, Glebe, New South Wales.

James McDonald, B.S. *Pain.* Editor and Hospital Medical Staff Advocate, American Medical Association, Chicago.

M. Kathleen McIntyre, M.S.N. *Stress* (in part). Assistant Professor, School of Nursing, Faculty, Oncology Nursing Program, and Lecturer, Health Activation Program, Division of Continuing Education — Nursing, Georgetown University, Washington, D.C.

Walter Modell, M.D. *Drugs.* Editor, *Clinical Pharmacology & Therapeutics;* Emeritus Professor of Pharmacology, Cornell University Medical College, Larchmont, N.Y.

Joseph T. Nocerino, M.S. *Health Care Technology.* National Coordinator, Health Activation Network, Vienna, Va.

Barbara Peterson. *Osteopathic Medicine.* Executive Editor, American Osteopathic Association, Chicago.

Keith D. Peterson, D.O. *Osteopathic Medicine Special Report: An Osteopathic Approach to Sports Medicine.* Founder and Executive Director, the Sports Medicine Clinic, Seattle, Wash.

Robert E. Rakel, M.D. *Family Practice.* Professor and Head, Department of Family Practice, University of Iowa College of Medicine, Iowa City, Iowa.

Robert E. Rogers, M.D. *Obstetrics and Gynecology.* Professor of Obstetrics and Gynecology, Indiana University School of Medicine, Indianapolis.

Peter Rosen, M.D., F.A.C.S. *Emergency Medicine.* Director of Emergency Medical Services and Program Director, Denver General Hospital / St. Anthony Hospital Systems Emergency Medicine Residency Program, Denver, Colo.

Leon D. Rosenfeld, D.D.S., M.S.D. *Dentistry; Periodontal Disease.* Professor, Department of Periodontics, Northwestern University Dental School, Chicago.

David A. Ross, M.D. *Plastic Surgery.* Attending Plastic and Reconstructive Surgeon, Michael Reese Hospital, Chicago.

Joel G. Sacks, M.D. *Eye Diseases and Visual Disorders.* Associate Professor of Ophthalmology and of Neurology, Northwestern University Medical School, Chicago.

Stephen L. Seagren, M.D. *Radiology.* Assistant Professor of Medicine and Radiology, University of California at San Diego.

Solomon Halbert Snyder, M.D. *Psychiatry* (in part). Professor of Psychiatry and Pharmacology, Johns Hopkins University School of Medicine, Baltimore, Md.

Naomi S. Suloway, M.S. *Toxicology Special Report: Gardening May Be Hazardous to Your Health.* Account Executive, Frank C. Nahser, Inc., Chicago, Ill.

Linda F. Tomchuck, B.A. *Toxicology; World Medical News: South Africa.* Associate Editor, Encyclopaedia Britannica, Inc., Chicago.

Robert W. Veatch, Ph.D. *Medical Ethics.* Senior Associate, Institute of Society, Ethics and Life Sciences, Hastings-on-Hudson, N.Y.

Edward Wasserman, M.D. *Psychosomatic Medicine.* Coordinator, Psychiatry Consultation-Liaison Service, Institute of Psychiatry, Northwestern University Medical School, Chicago.

Jordan Wilbur. *Pediatrics Special Report: Treating Cancer in Children.* Chief of Pediatric Oncology, Presbyterian Hospital of Pacific Medical Center, San Francisco, Calif.

Asclepius   *Hygieia*

From a 5th-century A.D. *ivory diptych in the Liverpool City Museum;
photograph, The Cooper-Bridgeman Library, London*

Foreword

We are proud to present the 1978 issue of the Britannica *Medical and Health Annual*. In this second issue our goal is basically the same as in the first—to produce an informative and readable book, by experts, for laymen. The contents are similarly arranged. This issue differs from the first, however, in one important respect—in possessing an underlying philosophical approach that transcends the boundaries of the book's individual sections and becomes a unifying theme. This theme is the concept of the *health partnership*, of physician and patient working together to maintain health and, when necessary, to treat disease. Preventive medicine is not a new idea, but the rapidly escalating costs of medical treatment and the recent discoveries of the association between disease, life-style, and environment have given the notion of prevention renewed urgency. Furthermore, preventive, medicine is no longer viewed as a service to be dispensed by the physician or other health professional to a passive, helpless patient. Increasingly it is recognized that the individual must take an active and responsible part in maintaining his own health—and that if he abrogates this responsibility, no amount of professional attention can compensate for his neglect. "Patient activation," "self-care," "healthful life-styles," and "individual responsibility" are phrases that reappear throughout this volume, in a variety of different contexts and in the contributions of numerous practitioners.

Among the "Features" in this book is the second in a series of symposia. This one poses the question "What Is Medicine?" and the three-part discussion examines the history and nature of medical controversy, the psychological intricacies of the doctor-patient relationship, and the necessary balance between medical intervention in disease and individual responsibility in promoting health. There are also a historical article on the search for safe surgical anesthetics, one on contemporary anesthesiology, and two articles in the series of in-depth studies of common conditions that affect health: the one on alcoholism and the other on aging. An interesting study of Kaiser-Permanente, the pioneering prepaid medical care plan, is included, and also a brilliant photo essay by the internationally known portrait photographer Yousuf Karsh, featuring some of the giants of 20th-century medicine.

The "World of Medicine" section provides a summary of important recent developments in the major medical specialties, intended to serve as a reference point in answering your questions about current theory and practice.

The series of "Health Education Units" is continued. The 18 units focus on some common health problems from asthma to stroke, helping to further individual understanding of health maintenance.

Finally, the "First Aid Handbook" is again included, but in revised form. It should be kept at hand and thoroughly read and reviewed *before* it is needed.

We emphasize again that this book is not meant to be a guide for self-diagnosis or self-treatment and certainly is not a substitute for the advice and care of your physician. We hope, rather, that it will help to increase your interest in the care of your own and your family's health as at the same time it helps you to become more knowledgeable about how and when to seek professional help.

The Editors

The Conquest of Surgical Pain

by Estrellita Karsh

All pain's one malady with many names.
—Antiphanes (Fragment from The Doctor*)*

Pain seems to be part of the price man has always paid for the gift of life. Throughout history, all humans have been subject to pain's agonies, from the lowliest slaves to kings and queens. When archaeologists explored the ancient city of Nippur, they found on a clay tablet the prayer of a king's daughter—the first recorded cry of human anguish: "Pain has seized my body. May God tear this pain out."

To the pains originating from within the body, man himself added a new pain from without—that of the surgeon's knife. The story of the "greatest single gift ever made to suffering humanity"—freedom from the pain of surgery—is an account of missed opportunities, ironic twists of fate, and distressingly human frailties. It is also a tale of brilliant insights, culminating in the first successful public demonstration of ether anesthesia by 27-year-old William Thomas Green Morton at the Massachusetts General Hospital in Boston on Oct. 16, 1846.

The dawn of anesthesia

It was natural that Paleolithic (Stone Age) man would seek pain relief in the world around him; herbs and leaves provided the earliest narcotics. Among the first anesthetists may have been the South American witch doctor who, a millennium before the arrival of Christopher Columbus, chewed coca leaves (the source of cocaine) and spat the crude drug onto the open incision made by the priest-surgeon.

Greek and Roman antiquity witnessed the dawn of anesthesia, but it was a "strange dawn with twilight shadows," more efficacious poetically than scientifically. "There are drugs," the Roman poet Ovid wrote, evoking the essence of anesthesia, "which induce deep slumber, and steep the vanquished eyes in Lethean night."

Estrellita Karsh *is a writer with a special interest in the history of medicine; her article "The Doctor-Patient Relationship Through the Ages" appeared in the 1977* Medical and Health Annual.

(Facing page) "Paradise" by Lucas Cranach the Elder (1472–1553); Courtesy, the Kunsthistorisches Museum, Vienna.

8

(Top, right) Courtesy, the Musée Guimet, Paris (MG 8440); photograph, Cliché Musées Nationaux; (top, left) Courtesy, the Biblioteca Vaticana, Rome, (MS. Barb. Lat. 241, fol. 13V); photograph, Madeline Grimoldi

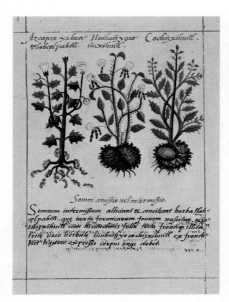

The Aztec people had extensive knowledge of herbal medicine. The Badianus Manuscript, named for Johannes Badianus who translated the work into Latin, is an herbal composed in 1552 by the Aztec physician Martinus de la Cruz. One page (above) shows three plants valued for their narcotic properties. A Hindu picture (right) depicts the legendary origin of hashish, said to have been derived from the hairs of the tortoise. Opium smoking, known since ancient times, is illustrated in a Persian miniature (opposite) from the collection of the Free Public Library of Philadelphia.

Of the drugs known to the ancients, only five were significant: mandrake, or mandragora; its botanical cousin henbane, or hyoscyamus; cannabis (hashish or Indian hemp); opium; and alcohol. These early drugs gave but a "bare hint, an unfulfilled promise" of surgical anesthesia because the ancients did not know that the alkaloids hidden in the drugs were what produced the sleepiness or narcosis, and thus they could not regulate dosage. They did not know which part of an herb they could safely swallow nor whether it would produce drowsiness or the ultimate sleep, death. Not until the Muslims gave us distillation in the 9th century could medieval alchemists separate the useful from the harmful part of the plant and turn the base metal of the crude drug into the gold of its alkaloids.

10

Of the ancient narcotics, mandragora, or mandrake, was the most mysterious and most widely used. More legends surround this drug than any other. The manlike two-legged form of the root itself, of which fanciful artistic renditions adorn Renaissance herbals, suggested to the Greeks that an evil—and sexual—spirit dwelt in the plant. It was thought unsafe to uproot mandrake because it would utter shrieks so frightful that no mortal, hearing them, could live. "To gather the mandrake," reads a later medieval herbal and how-to booklet, "Take the dogge and tye hym to the mandrake . . . then leave the dogge. He wille teare up the roote, which by its dreadfull cryes will kyll the animal."

Using mandrake roots and the exact ancient formulations, Victorian-era physician Sir Benjamin Ward Richardson produced an anesthetic state in small animals. Today, however, we would classify mandragora as a mild narcotic, a "faint and fading memory in medicine."

The effects of hashish, opium, and alcohol, however, have earned those drugs a more important place in history. "The Scythians howl for joy in the vapor-bath," says Herodotus, describing the ancient counterpart of a modern pot party. "Creeping under the rugs," gleefully crows this usually staid historian, "the Scythians take the hemp . . .

11

throw it on hot stones and the mind is filled by a delicious sensation of pleasant ideas!"

The most important ancient narcotic was opium, used for centuries before the birth of Christ. About 1500 B.C. the Egyptian architect Cha was buried with a tiny jug of ointment. Not until 1927 did an Italian archaeologist and pharmacologist find that this ointment behaved like opium's alkaloid, morphine.

Alcohol helped the ancients, as it does us, to forget the pain of reality: "If a man is led forth to death, he is given a cup of spiced wine to drink, whereby his soul is wrapped in night," says the Talmud. Alcohol was used until well into the 19th century not only to prepare patients for surgery but also to fortify the apprehensive surgeon, who often would enter the operating theater with one bottle of rum in each hand, one for the patient and one to steel himself.

The dark ages of pain

Although in ancient Greece no distinction existed between physician and surgeon, by the Middle Ages the status of surgery was in decline and remained so into the 18th century. Many qualified medieval physicians would not perform operations, believing the bloody practice beneath their dignity; surgery was largely carried out by untrained barbers. Medieval theologians did not help in man's fight against pain. Pain entered life with the Fall of Man and must be endured. "To die of a long illness bravely borne" was deemed more worthy in God's eyes than to survive — and especially to survive without pain!

One could not blame the medieval patient for often preferring to heed Church teaching rather than place himself in the unskilled hands of the barber surgeon. To the medieval mind, the torture chamber and the operating room were synonymous. Illness, however terrible, was preferable to the agony — or death — resulting from surgery performed under unpredictable sleep-producing drugs.

Medieval physicians did have a prescription for the pain of surgery, the sleeping sponge invented by Hugh of Lucca. Hugh's son, Theodoric, gives us the recipe for this preparation, which contained all the well-known drugs of antiquity, in his 13th-century surgical book, *Chirurgia:* First, take an ounce each of opium, juices of unripe mulberry, hyoscyamus (henbane), hemlock, mandragora, wood ivy, and of the seeds of dock, lettuce, and water hemlock. Then, "mix all these in a brazen vessel, and then place in it a new sponge." Finally, "let the whole boil, as long as the sun lasts on the dog-days, until the sponge consumes it all." To use the sponge: "As oft as there shall be need of it, . . . let it be applied to the nostrils of him who is to be operated on, until he has fallen asleep, and so let the surgery be performed."

The sleeping sponge notwithstanding, medieval surgeons relied more on the safer and less complicated method of inducing sleep — "drugged wine and plenty of it." And no wonder. A modern pharmacologist evaluated Theodoric's recipe and concluded, "It won't even make a guinea pig nod." We who have never known the pain of major

surgery may, at the safe distance of centuries, view Theodoric's stew as quaint. Such remedies for relief of pain were, however, a sobering indication of medieval desperation. How little anesthesia had really progressed from the practices of the ancients is pitifully revealed in William Bullein's "Bulwarke of Defence againste all Sicknes." The first known English medical reference to an anesthetic in surgery resurrects an ancient friend: "The juice of this herbe mandragora. . .bryngeth slepe, it casteth men into a trauns on a depe tirrible dreame," Bullein wrote in 1562; the same might have been written in A.D. 400!

While some 13th-century surgeons were using Hugh of Lucca's inadequate sleeping sponge, the alchemist Raymond Lully discovered a "white fluid" that he called sweet vitriol. Two centuries later, the most controversial of the Renaissance quasi-physicians, Paracelsus, whom Sir William Osler called the Father of Medicine, rediscovered Lully's fluid. Of the heated alcohol and sulphuric acid, he made an observation that nearly entitled him to be called the Father of Anesthesia as well:

Disease and its inevitable companion, pain, have always been a part of human life. "Job Smote by Boils" is a watercolor illustration painted by English artist William Blake (1757–1827) for an edition of The Book of Job.

13

Understanding the physiological processes involved in respiration was a necessary forerunner to the development of inhalation anesthesia. In the late 18th century several scientists engaged in experiments that attempted to identify the gaseous components of air and to explain their part in the process of respiration. Observation of small animals—often birds or guinea pigs—breathing in confined spaces was essential to this research. "The Air Pump," painted in 1768 by English artist Joseph Wright of Derby, shows one such experiment.

"This sulfur . . . has . . . such a sweetness . . . it quiets all suffering without any harm and relieves all pain."

Paracelsus' charismatic personality attracted to him brilliant young Valerius Cordus, who traveled with his flamboyant mentor much as James Boswell traveled with Samuel Johnson. A precocious chemical investigator, Valerius Cordus described how sweet vitriol might be used in "pleurisy, peripneumonia and hacking cough." In 1542, the year after Paracelsus' death, Valerius Cordus sold all of his notes of Paracelsus' prescriptions to the senate fathers of Nuremberg for 100 ducats—and sweet vitriol became a "dead letter in a dusty pharmacopaeia." Some 250 years later, the German apothecary Frobenius, in tribute to its alchemical origin, would give it the name more familiar to us—ether. Used according to Valerius Cordus' clinical recommendations in cough mixtures, ether's greater anesthetic properties would go unrecognized until the middle of the 19th century.

Meanwhile, both patients and the medical establishment began to distrust mandrake and the other herbal painkillers. By the middle of the 17th century, so many patients had died that these drugs had become thoroughly discredited, and Nicolas Bailly, a French barber-surgeon who administered them, was fined for practicing witchcraft. After that, anesthesia by herbal means was forbidden.

14

The chemical revolution

In the 18th century, profound sleep was finally found in the new world of chemistry. Of the chemists who were central to the search for the surcease of pain—who came close but did not realize the significance of their discoveries—the first was Joseph Priestley, the son of a Nonconformist cloth dresser. During the long English weekends Priestley, living in Lord Shelburne's castle as resident curiosity and wonder boy, provided amusement for his patron's bored houseguests—and changed the history of chemistry and anesthesia. He discovered oxygen, experimented with its use in the living body, and chanced upon nitrous oxide, a gas that produces both giddy laughter and insensibility to pain. Ironically, because he was highly sensitive to nitrous oxide Priestley could not continue his research into its properties. After a mob opposed to Priestley's political views burned down his laboratory he fled to America, never dreaming that here was the land where both his nitrous oxide and Paracelsus' ether would end the search for the relief of surgical pain.

The chemical revolution found its way to the picturesque town of Penzance in Cornwall where, the story goes, young Humphry Davy's genius was discovered while Davy was swinging on a gate, talking with a visiting scientist. This "short, slight round-shouldered lad with a painfully shrill voice which gave forth some remarkable ideas," was soon ensconced as superintendent of Thomas Beddoes' Pneumatic Institution, where the effect of the inhalation of these newly discovered gases was being tried on asthmatic and consumptive patients. The warmhearted Beddoes, with his altruistic schemes for the improvement of the world, might have stepped from the pages of "The Pickwick Papers." Among Beddoes' patrons was Josiah Wedgwood, and among his friends were the poets William Wordsworth, Robert Southey, and Samuel Taylor Coleridge.

From America, where Priestley had found sanctuary, came harsh criticism of nitrous oxide. America's arbiter of science, Samuel Latham Mitchill, railed against the gas as a "diabolic septon" causing fever, cancer, and terrible disasters when inhaled. Young Davy, combining the spirit of scientific inquiry with youthful rebellion, of course proceeded to inhale the gas. This was no "diabolic septon"; not only did it relieve the pain of his emerging wisdom teeth, but he felt light-headed—and could not stop himself from laughing. Coleridge, Southey, and Wedgwood soon joined Davy in nightly frolics, experiencing "the most voluptuous sensations, the most entrancing visions." Even Beddoes' asthmatic patients rejoiced, for they could laugh away their shortness of breath.

In Davy's book on his nitrous oxide experiments he left one of the most important passages in the history of medical observation: "As nitrous oxide . . . appears capable of destroying physical pain, it may probably be used with advantage during surgical operations."

Michael Faraday comes to light as a bookbinder's assistant committing to memory the chemistry text of his hero, Davy. The brilliant Fara-

An 18th-century engraving by Martin Engelbrecht depicts a surgeon of the period brandishing the tools of his trade. In addition to the requisite saws, drills, and scissors hanging from his belt are a pan and pitcher, used in the preparation of salves, and a barber's plate, hanging from a cord around his neck. Adorning his head is an elevatory, an instrument used for raising the patient's head.

Courtesy, the Library of Decorative Arts, Paris; photograph, Jean-Loup Charmet

Before its application to anesthesiology, nitrous oxide—or laughing gas, as it was called—was used for amusement, as a source of pleasant intoxication. The 1808 drawing of two gentlemen getting "high" on the gas (right) was later used by a medical student to illustrate "A Dissertation on the Chemical Properties and Exhilirating Effects of Nitrous Oxyd Gas." A detail from an English drawing dating from 1830 entitled "Prescription for Scolding Wives," suggests that nitrous oxide might be employed to promote domestic tranquility.

day applied to Davy for employment and was soon working as Davy's laboratory assistant—and shining shoes for Davy's arrogant heiress-wife, who regarded Faraday as a "low class upstart." When Faraday was not performing menial tasks for the ferocious Lady Davy, he investigated Paracelsus' 16th-century work on ether. In 1818 he discovered ether's anesthetic property and made an offhand reference to it in the *Quarterly Journal of Science and the Arts.* Doctors who might have recognized the significance of Faraday's work probably never saw it. Both Davy and Faraday, seeking new chemical compounds, were unknowingly on the threshold of magnificent accomplishment but failed (as did Beddoes, who died without realizing he had anticipated the inhalation therapy of today's anesthesia). Their brilliant observations found no congenial soil in which to germinate and so went unheeded, while millions continued to suffer. Had the two continued their work, mankind might have had surgical anesthesia 50 years sooner.

While Davy and Faraday were experimenting, surgery and suffering were still inseparable, but no longer was it beneath the dignity of a physician to perform surgery. (Before 1731 in France, when the Academy of Surgery was founded, and 1745 in England, an important duty of a military surgeon—besides operating—had been to shave the beards of both enlisted men and officers.) Even with the degrading association of barbers and surgeons abolished, physicians who urged a union with surgeons lost caste with their colleagues. (The cultural remnant of this attitude has lingered in England, where surgeons are still addressed as "Mister.")

Henry Hill Hickman was born in Bromfield, England, in 1800, the year Davy published his conclusions about nitrous oxide. Hickman, too, might have been acclaimed the discoverer of surgical anesthesia. Appalled by the inhumane medical practices of his day, he experimented

on animals with carbon dioxide and succeeded in producing insensibility to pain. Hickman desperately tried to bring his pleas for further investigation into the principles of inhalation to the attention of Sir Humphry Davy. But even writing to Davy's closest friend, Thomas Andrew Knight, at whose castle the now insufferably snobbish baronet was a frequent guest, produced no results; Davy repudiated completely his youthful excursions into the intoxicating regions of laughing gas. The words Hickman used for the state he had induced in his animals —"suspended animation"—frightened doctors; they conjured up the ancient brutal practice of pressing on the carotid artery in the neck to produce insensibility.

In 1828 Hickman journeyed to Paris where he appealed to Charles X for help. His letter to the king was passed on to the French Academy of Medicine. "Innovators and discoverers have learned from history," comments medical historian Victor Robinson, "that the silence of official committees is a frequent fate of the pioneer." Only one man in the Academy of Medicine, Napoleon's surgeon-general, Baron Dominique-Jean Larrey, who knew firsthand the horrors of battlefield surgery, offered himself as a subject for Hickman's experiments but was voted down by his colleagues. Hickman returned to England defeated and in despair. In 1928 Hickman's experiments were finally evaluated. His conclusions were found to be correct.

Surgery before anesthesia

As Victor Robinson has noted, "All those who sought release from disease at the point of the knife, prior to the introduction of anesthesia,

An illustration from the collection of the Bibliothèque de l'Arsenal, Paris, depicts the death of Roland at the Battle of Roncesvalles (A.D. 778), as recounted in the 12th-century French epic poem The Song of Roland. *The rudimentary nature of anesthesia in medieval times severely limited the scope of the battlefield surgeon and provided scant relief for his patients.*

17

Although herbal and alcoholic preparations were employed to dull consciousness and reduce pain, a surgical operation during the Middle Ages usually required the participation of three persons: the surgeon, the patient, and someone—preferably large and muscular —to restrain the patient. These illustrations are from a 14th-century manuscript of the Chirurgia *of Theodoric of Cervia.*

were first compelled to pay homage to Pain''—whether the surgeon's scalpel was a sharpened flint stone and the operating room a cave, or the scalpel tempered steel and the location a dubiously comfortable 19th-century operating chair. By the beginning of the 19th century, ''liquor and laudanum—and brute force'' were the means to prepare patients for surgery.

The mental attitude of patients about to undergo pre-anesthetic surgery was one of terrified apprehension. Most people could not emulate the veterans of the Napoleonic campaign who ''lay motionless under the knife.''

The Boston surgeon who performed the first operation under ether anesthesia, John Collins Warren, writes with sympathetic insight of the preoperative patient: ''. . . condemned to the knife, what terrors does his imagination inflict? How many sleepless nights and horrible dreams and sinking of the heart. What apprehension of . . . sudden death does he paint to himself?'' To imagine what surgery must have been like, we need only read excerpts from the ghastly account of a leg amputation on a 15-year-old boy, written by an anonymous reporter in the *New York Herald* of July 21, 1841. The shocked writer describes the sickening sights, the screaming, the sound of the bone as it was crushed by the ''long, glittering knife,'' and the ''boy's eyes fastened on the instruments with glazed agony.'' Only five years before ether anesthesia was introduced ''an operation was attended with almost the formality of an execution.''

If the patient survived, there was always severe nervous shock, and a long, painful convalescence, accompanied by depression. One who had himself experienced amputation wrote: ''The blank whirlwind of emotion, the horror of great darkness, and the sense of desertion by God and man, bordering close upon despair which overwhelmed my heart, I can never forget, however gladly I would do so . . . for a long time they haunted me.''

The surgeon's very appearance no doubt intensified the patient's sense of terror. The pre-anesthetic period was also pre-antisepsis; knowing nothing of the role of germs in creating infection, surgeons washed neither their hands, their instruments, nor their dressings, and they operated in their street clothes. ''A surgeon's experience could be measured by his coat, the stiffer the coat, the more experienced the surgeon.'' The operating theater was often placed over the dead house (morgue), with its accompanying sickening stench, or as in the Massachusetts General Hospital, in the dome (now called the Ether Dome) so that, it was said, the screams of the patients could not be heard.

Through the ages, surgeons themselves were not insensitive to the torture they had to inflict, from the resolute Celsus in the first century, who would have surgeons ''ignore cries and pleadings,'' to John Hunter, who in the 18th century counseled, ''No surgeon should approach surgery without a sacred dread and reluctance.'' It was the illustrious 19th-century surgeon Valentine Mott who remained loyal to William Morton during the bitter years of the ether controversy, who

expressed most eloquently the terrible ordeal of the surgeon and his awareness of his fearful responsibility:

How often when operating in some deep, dark wound . . . have I dreaded that some unfortunate struggle of the patient would deviate the knife a little from its proper course, and that I, who fain would be the deliverer, should involuntarily become the executioner, seeing my patient perish in my hands by the most appalling form of death.

Surgeons' emotional reactions to the operating room were far from stoic. The great surgeon William Cheselden could not sleep the night before surgery, and the equally illustrious John Abernethy regarded amputation with repulsion. Guillaume Dupuytren, the ablest French surgeon of his day, tersely expressed the sentiments of his colleagues: "Pain kills like hemorrhage."

There was, incredibly, a small minority of the medical profession who, even after surgical anesthesia became available, believed pain was a human inevitability. One asserted, "Men should not be prevented from passing through what God intended them to endure." And even after ether anesthesia was introduced in 1846, there was still a hospital

Even as late as the 17th century, anesthesiology was still in a primitive stage and surgery an ordeal to be endured. "The Operation," by Flemish painter Adriaen Brouwer, conveys the atmosphere of the surgeon's office in 17th-century Flanders.

19

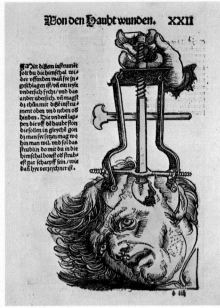

*Trephination, the perforation of the skull
with an instrument such as a drill or
chisel, is a process known since
prehistoric times. During the Middle Ages
it was used to relieve inflammations of the
brain and skull as well as to treat certain
mental disorders. A 16th-century
illustration from the* Feldtbuch der
Wundartzney *("Field-Book of Wound
Surgery")* by Hans von Gersdorff *(above)
explains how the procedure may be used
to alleviate pressure on the brain caused
by a skull injury. A picture from a
14th-century French manuscript (opposite)
shows a similar operation; in this case the
patient's head has been shaved.*

in Philadelphia that did not use it for a year. It was said that it was
unworthy to try "by artificial sleep, to transform the body into an insensitive cadaver." But the most skillful surgeons were prevented by the
lack of this artificial sleep from fulfilling the greatest possibilities of
surgery, which they knew existed from experimentation with cadavers.
They apologized for their profession. Robert Liston spoke of surgery as
"this narrowing field" that had no real place in science, and as "an
inferior part of our professional duties."

Liston was right—surgery had made no real progress in hundreds of
years. Most 19th-century operations were actually ancient or Renaissance procedures: Paleolithic surgeons had performed trephining
(opening a hole) of the skull; Hippocrates had drained for lung abscess;
Ambroise Paré in the 16th century had reduced fractures and dislocations. Liston and his contemporaries generally confined their surgical
attentions to the surface of the body, to amputations and some plastic
operations.

The lack of anesthesia made lengthy or delicate surgery impossible,
since a conscious patient could not survive for more than about 15
minutes. Speed, manual dexterity, and anatomical knowledge—and a
strong stomach—thus were required of the surgeon. Sir Thomas Clifford Allbutt, whose life spanned the periods before and after the inception of anesthesia, recalls: "When I was a boy, surgeons operating upon
the quick were pitted one against the other like runners on time."
Dominique-Jean Larrey, Napoleon's surgeon, is said to have performed
200 amputations in one night; it could be done if each amputation took
but 28 seconds! Robert Liston performed an appendectomy in less than
one minute. John Collins Warren chafed against this necessary but
harrowing speed when he rebuked a time-conscious student: "You may
put up your watch; I do not operate by time."

For 40 years, John Collins Warren performed all the operations for
bladder stones in Boston—25 cases! In England, Liston's operations in
1844 and 1845 included only 5 lithotomies (bladder stone removal), 4
herniotomies (hernia repair), and 10 amputations—and this from one of
the world's busiest surgeons. Following the introduction of ether the
number of operations trebled, many of them elective—probably for the
first time in history. Today, with asepsis and anesthesia keeping the
mortality rate low, 20,000 operations a year are performed at the Massachusetts General Hospital. With anesthesia, the quest for technical
perfection, and not speed, became the surgical ideal. The scalpel could
now reach the abdomen, and eventually the chest and the heart itself.

An alternative to chemistry: mesmerism

While other 18th-century investigators sought to unlock the chemical
secrets of anesthetic sleep, Franz Anton Mesmer was experimenting in
Vienna with Paracelsus' ideas on the curative powers of the magnet. His
techniques can now be seen as the forerunners of the modern practice
of hypnotism. Mesmer established a reputation as a man who could
relieve symptoms and cure sickness painlessly. It wasn't long before

20

the ladies and gentlemen of Vienna opened wide their elegant salons —and their purses—to Anton Mesmer and his theory of "animal magnetism," a cosmic healing fluid whose properties could be transferred to the sick by stroking. But while Mesmer's clients may have been impressed by his methods and successes, orthodox physicians were not; accusing him of practicing magic, they forced him to leave Vienna. Settling in Paris, Mesmer again established a lucrative practice and a sumptuous clinic. Clad in an embroidered violet robe, holding a rod he

21

Hypnotism was used to allay surgical pain in the 19th century. A French caricature, dated 1826, shows a woman undergoing hypnosis.

had invested with "magnetic energy," Mesmer resurrected the medieval healing power of touch. Though Mesmer believed he had found a great new truth, he had in fact rediscovered an *old* truth which was of significance for pain: the therapeutic effect of suggestion. His patients got better not because he willed it, but because they did.

Nevertheless, it did not take long for doctors to recognize that Mesmer's techniques might be used to allay pain. It was in Edinburgh that mesmeric surgery found its greatest adherents, chief among them John Elliotson and, in India, James Esdaile. Elliotson's journal of mesmerism and phrenology, *The Zoist,* found greater acceptance in America than Britain; cases were reported from as far away as Illinois and Missouri. Elizabeth Blackwell, America's first woman doctor, wrote to her mother, "I have just performed my first professional cure . . . mesmerized away a severe headache that afflicted Miss O'Heara."

The quest for anesthesia moves to the U.S.

Mesmeric surgery had captured the attention of American physicians, but one wonders how long the anesthetic properties of laughing gas or ether might have gone unnoticed had they not been used in a most unexpected place: traveling carnivals. In the 1830s, especially in New England, strict Puritan parents could frown on wordly delights, but hardly on the "highly instructive lectures" given by a professor, his laboratory on a handcart, who first inhaled the gas and then encouraged members of his audience to partake—scientifically, of course!

In the United States, private laughing gas and ether parties had already become the vogue, as in Jefferson, Georgia, where the resourceful young Crawford Williamson Long, of the South's old cotton aristocracy, would prepare ether for the frolics of his friends. What was for them an evening of hilarity was for Long one of medical observation when he noticed that his etherized friends "received falls and blows which I believed were sufficient to produce pain on a person not in a state of anaesthesia." On March 30, 1842, he removed a tumor from the back of the neck of James M. Venable, using ether administered on a towel. "The patient . . . seemed incredulous, until the tumor was shown him. He gave no evidence of suffering during the operation, and assured me . . . that he did not suffer the slightest degree of pain." For centuries, the world had waited for just such a momentous communication, but Long confined his record of the occasion to his ledger: "James Venable, 1842. Ether and excising tumor, $2.00." Long had accomplished what Hickman had sought in vain. He did not announce or write about his discovery until 1849, even though he had performed several similar operations, because, as he admitted in 1852 before the Georgia Medical and Surgical Association, he had not understood the enormous significance of what had transpired. During the Civil War, fleeing his home to escape the Union Army, Long carried with him papers constituting "my proofs of the discovery of ether anesthesia." He died in obscurity in 1878 after delivering a baby—whose mother he had first anesthetized.

22

Photographs, Jean-Loup Charmet; (bottom) courtesy, the Musée Carnavalet, Paris

Horace Wells and William Thomas Green Morton, tragically associated in the quest for painless surgery, were not surgeons but dentists. Why would the impetus for surcease of pain come from a poor craft regarded as a sideline of medicine, its status akin to that of the medieval barber-surgeon? (Dentistry only began to achieve professional respectability in 1840, with the founding of the Baltimore College of Dental Surgery.) Richard Shryock wryly suggests that 19th-century surgeons were "once-ers"—but to dentists, who had to inflict pain daily, it was crucial that patients return.

Horace Wells began his association with William Morton as Morton's teacher; later, they joined forces in a short-lived partnership in Boston, then the medical center of New England. The partnership was formed to exploit Wells's invention of a dental solder. Of the two men, Morton was the more aggressive and materialistic, and he hoped to fulfill his original desire to become a physician. Wells was the more artistic, interested in birds, shells, and engravings; and, by the standards of the time, he was a splendid dentist. The young dentists' first encounter with Charles T. Jackson, to obtain an endorsement for the solder, was so successful that Morton was soon living as student-boarder in Jackson's Somerset Street home. Jackson, who was to become Morton's mortal enemy after his ether demonstration in 1846, first received him as an intimate of the family. Wells and Morton were aware of Jackson's impeccable professional and social credentials as a Harvard-trained chemist, pioneer geologist and mineralogist, and brother of the wife of Ralph Waldo Emerson. They could not have known that Jackson's feelings about the accomplishments of others bordered on the psychotic. Obsessed with corrosive jealousy, he laid claim to new scientific developments clearly not his own. He declared himself the inventor of the telegraph after a brief shipboard meeting with Samuel F. B. Morse, and the resultant litigation went on for years. The harassed Morse characterized Jackson's later dealings with Morton when he said, "There was never a more finished specimen of wholesale lying. . . . He is certainly a monomaniac." But vendetta was years in the future; Morton and his bride were to live with the Jacksons after their marriage in 1844.

Wells and Morton dissolved their partnership in October 1844. The pioneer anesthesiologist Henry K. Beecher speculates on what a rich chapter one could write on the history of anesthesia had they continued their association. "Nothing could have proved more unfortunate to their future lives than their estrangement."

Wells returned to Hartford to the bizarre stage of his great discovery, "Professor" Gardner Q. Colton's traveling nitrous oxide show, whose newspaper advertisement was strangely premonitory: "The entertainment is *scientific* to those who *make* it scientific." On Dec. 10, 1844, Horace Wells attended, inhaled nitrous oxide, and noticed that a fellow citizen, Samuel Cooley, had severely injured his knees after inhaling the gas—and felt no pain! Genius is the gift of perception, and Horace Wells made the great leap; unlike Crawford Long, he knew what he was witnessing. Early the next morning, Wells's student Riggs removed

In the United States some of the pioneering experiments in inhalation anesthesia were conducted not by physicians but by dentists, whose daily practice almost inevitably involved the infliction of pain. Two European caricatures of 18th- and 19th-century dentists at work indicate that surgeons were not the only practitioners whose patients had to be forcibly restrained.

23

Wells's wisdom tooth under nitrous oxide prepared by Colton. Riggs's account tells us how little was known of the behavior of the gas. "Our agreement . . . was, to push the administration to a point hitherto unknown. We knew not whether death or success confronted us. It was *terra incognito* . . . but the great law of Nature, hitherto unknown, was kind to us and a grand discovery was born into the world."

Wells journeyed to Boston to seek Jackson's advice: Jackson is supposed to have thought the experiment of no consequence. Wells prevailed upon Morton, now attending lectures at Harvard Medical School, to arrange for him to demonstrate nitrous oxide in a capital (major) operation. No patient was scheduled for capital surgery, but Morton lent Wells his forceps and accompanied him to the demonstration of a tooth extraction, the patient a volunteer medical student with an aching molar. "They (the medical students) were preparing to inhale that very evening for sport," Morton was later to write.

The demonstration was a fiasco. The patient cried out; the students hissed and cried "Humbug" and, to their catcalls, the overwrought Wells fled the room. The bitter irony of this unsuccessful demonstration is that, as Wells explained in a letter, the gas bag had been withdrawn before the patient was fully anesthetized; the patient later said he had felt some pain, but not as much as usually attended an extraction. Thus, the first public demonstration of the safest of the anesthetic gases, which has now supplanted ether, was a bitter failure. Wells's advice to the class, that it was their attitude that determined the difference between hilarity or sleep, was to become one of the basic requirements for reassuring patients and inducing anesthesia.

Wells returned to Hartford a broken man, on the verge of a nervous collapse. Mrs. Wells was to write later that the whole affair had been "an unspeakable evil." Almost forgotten in the early days of the ensuing controversy between Morton and Jackson, Wells wrote four gentle letters about his work to the *Boston Medical and Surgical Journal.* He had a few moments of the joy of the discoverer when he was briefly lionized in Paris. Upon the urging of a friend in Paris he wrote a pamphlet, "History of the Discovery of the Application of Nitrous Oxide Gas, Ether, and other Vapors, to Surgical Operations," for which he was almost too well prepared. He had become hopelessly addicted to drugs.

After a shocking incident when, under the influence of drugs, he threw acid at two prostitutes and was imprisoned in the Tombs of New York, he wrote a last, tragic letter to his wife: "I feel I am fast becoming a deranged man. . . . I cannot live and keep my reason, and on this account God will forgive the deed. I can say no more. Farewell." He inhaled chloroform and severed the artery in his thigh. He was 33 years old. In the mail, unread, was a jubilant letter from a friend. The Paris Medical Society had accorded Wells "all the honor of having successfully discovered and successfully applied the use of vapors or gases whereby surgical operations could be performed without pain."

Wells's unsuccessful demonstration in 1845 made a great impression on the energetic Morton. Described as a "person of great ingenuity,

24

patience and pertinacity of purpose," Morton had already been experimenting, first with ether drops directly on the tooth, then inhaling ether himself. His original aim soon went beyond painless dentistry to "producing an extended artificial sleep so that surgeons might operate without pain." He journeyed to Hartford to question the despondent Wells; he talked to Wells's prize patient about her painless tooth extraction. He retired to the Mortons' little cottage at West Needham (later renamed "Etherton") and subjected goldfish, small animals, and even their spaniel, Nig, to ether inhalation. In answer to later detractors who said he did no experimenting at all, Mrs. Morton, writing in *McClure's Magazine,* described him as one possessed.

On the evening of Sept. 30, 1846, Morton went to consult Charles Jackson, with whom he had remained on precariously friendly terms. Jackson made a suggestion that Morton never denied—even at the height of later recriminations: that Morton use rectified (purified) ether. Of that evening, Jackson later claimed not only that he introduced Morton to ether but that *he* first discovered its use in 1842. He would also swear that Morton was but his agent at the decisive operation on Oct. 16, 1846, although Jackson attended neither that operation nor the second, to which he was invited. An unpublished letter from E. A. L. Peirson of Salem confirms that, the week of the ether demonstration, Jackson understood neither its magnitude nor its implications.

Later the same evening of September 30, after his decisive visit with Jackson, Morton was preparing again to experiment with ether. As he was about to use himself as guinea pig, the night bell rang and music teacher Eben H. Frost, with swollen face bandaged, appeared in the doorway, obviously in need of a tooth extraction. "He was afraid," later wrote Morton, "of the operation and asked if he could be mesmerized. I told him I had something better." Saturating his pocket handkerchief with the ether with which he was experimenting, Morton proceeded to anesthetize Frost and painlessly removed his tooth. (Subsequent attempts to administer ether in that fashion failed, so Morton set about designing a different apparatus.) From that moment, Frost's life was changed. He became Morton's "grateful shadow," telling to whoever would listen the story of his miraculous tooth extraction.

When Morton approached John Collins Warren about demonstrating ether in a capital operation, it was not the first request the 68-year-old senior surgeon had heard. Mesmerists, somnambulists, and cultists frequently claimed to have discovered the secret of release from pain. But there had been recent suicides at the Massachusetts General Hospital by surgical patients who feared the dread scalpel. Despite his years as a surgeon, "time had neither crystallized his mind, nor killed his hope," and Warren retained his humaneness and compassion. A founder of the Massachusetts General Hospital, and a member of a prestigious Boston medical family, he nevertheless listened to the claim of "only a dentist."

The operation was set for Oct. 16, 1846, in the new operating theater designed by Charles Bulfinch. Today a shrine of surgery, it is preserved

Hartford, Conn., dentist Horace Wells (1815–1848), a pioneer in medical anesthesia, was the first to use an anesthetic for dental surgery. This portrait of Wells was painted by Charles Noel Flagg.

25

as it was the day of the operation, its atmosphere early Victorian, its extraordinary decorations including a large plaster statue of Apollo Belvedere and two authentic Egyptian mummies. Pulley hooks in the ceiling are the only grim reminders of patients' restraints.

Washington Ayer of San Francisco, who was a Harvard medical student in 1846, gives an understated, moving eyewitness account of this landmark occasion. Ayer could not have known that Morton was late because he was perfecting his inhaler until the last minute.

The day arrived; the time appointed was noted on the dial, when the patient was led into the operating-room, and Dr. Warren and a board of the most eminent surgeons in the State were gathered around the sufferer. "All is ready —the stillness oppressive." It had been announced "that a test of some preparation was to be made for which the *astonishing* claim had been made that it would render the person operated upon free from pain." These are the words of Dr. Warren that broke the stillness.

Those present were incredulous, and, as Dr. Morton had not arrived at the time appointed and fifteen minutes had passed, Dr. Warren said, with significant meaning, "I presume he is otherwise engaged." This was followed with a "derisive laugh," and Dr. Warren grasped his knife and was about to proceed with the operation. At that moment Dr. Morton entered a side door, when Dr. Warren turned to him and in a strong voice said, "Well, sir, your patient is ready." In a few minutes he was ready for the surgeon's knife, when Dr. Morton said, "*Your* patient is ready, sir."

Here the most sublime scene ever witnessed in the operating-room was presented, when the patient placed himself voluntarily upon the table, which was to become the altar of future fame. Not that he did so for the purpose of advancing the science of medicine, nor for the good of his fellow-men, for the act itself was purely a personal and selfish one. He was about to assist in solving a new and important problem of therapeutics, whose benefits were to be given to the whole civilized world, yet wholly unconscious of the sublimity of the occasion or the part he was taking. . . .

The heroic bravery of the man who voluntarily placed himself upon the table, a subject for the surgeon's knife, should be recorded and his name enrolled upon parchment, which should be hung upon the walls of the surgical amphitheatre in which the operation was performed. His name was Gilbert Abbott. The operation was for a congenital tumor on the left side of the neck, extending along the jaw to the maxillary gland and into the mouth, embracing margin of the tongue. The operation was successful; and when the patient recovered he declared he had suffered no pain. Dr. Warren turned to those present and said, "Gentlemen, this is no humbug."

The "ether controversy" between Jackson and Morton began in earnest after the operation, as the reports of its successful administration were joyfully received in medical capitals of the world. The two men were involved in patent lawsuits in 1847—while Robert Liston, critic of mesmerism, performed the first amputation in Europe under ether anesthesia in his characteristic 28 seconds. When the patient was shown the severed limb, he fell back weeping in relief. "This Yankee dodge, gentlemen," said a relieved and astonished Liston, "beats mesmerism hollow!"

In 1848, while the blessings of ether and, later, of chloroform were benefiting surgical patients around the world, Wells's shocking suicide temporarily sobered both Morton and Jackson. In 1852, one year prior to Queen Victoria's receiving chloroform at the birth of her eighth child, Congress was about to award Morton $100,000 as compensation for his discovery when the honorable ghost of Horace Wells intervened, as a senator from Connecticut pressed Wells's claim. There were lies, intrigues, and Washington demonstrations; in 1854, a senator from Georgia introduced Crawford Long's name. Daniel Webster supported Morton; Horace Greeley supported Jackson. In 1863, after 17 debilitating years, when it was discovered that Morton had received funds from a convicted embezzler and Jackson tried to persuade Crawford Long to join his camp, Congress threw up its hands.

His health, his dental practice, and his model farm gone, Morton was an old man at the age of 48. He died of apoplexy in New York City. Jackson was placed in the McLean Asylum (for the mentally ill) where he died at the age of 75.

With Morton's triumph, the traditional role of Europe as America's medical mentor was reversed. For the first time, a major medical discovery traveled from the New World to the Old: from Boston to London —to Edinburgh—to Vienna, hitherto centers of study for American physicians. It was America that now "taught Europe the alphabet of anesthesia."

Benjamin Ward Richardson was a medical student in Glasgow in 1846 when the news arrived from America of successful etherization at the Massachusetts General Hospital. The next day an operation using ether was scheduled. Writing of witnessing the joy of the patient about to undergo anesthesia, the intent silence instead of screams in the operating theater, and the broad smiles of all concerned at the conclusion of the surgery, Richardson reminds us again that the magnitude of the contribution far outweighed the controversy:

The most treasured day in my life is that day when I witnessed for the first time the physical miracle of the abolition of pain during a surgical operation, the grand transformation of the phenomenon of agony into the phenomenon of sleep.

On Oct. 16, 1846, at the Massachusetts General Hospital, dental surgeon William T. Morton gave the first successful public demonstration of ether anesthesia. Some years later U.S. artist Robert Hinckley painted his own version of the memorable occasion that came to be known as "Ether Day."

RESTRICTED

·FLAMMABLE INHALATION ANESTHETICS·
STRICTLY PROHIBITED

ATTENTION

PLEASE DO NOT ENTER
UNLESS INVOLVED IN THE CASE

Anesthesiology Today

by James E. Eckenhoff, M.D., D.Sc.

photographs by Lee Balterman

Anesthesia must be listed as one of the major contributions of U.S. medicine to the world. Its significance lies not only in alleviating the patient's suffering during surgical procedures, but, equally important, in permitting increasingly complex operations on previously inaccessible organs and untreatable diseases. It is easy to forget with the passage of decades that in preanesthetic 1845, operations were performed only in dire emergencies as a last resort: that year only 37 operations were scheduled at the Massachusetts General Hospital, whereas today the hospital's annual total approaches 23,000. Medicine had to learn to grow with this new wonder: Which drugs could be used? How could they best be administered and by whom? What operations could be performed on anesthetized patients? Which patients could be safely anesthetized? Some lessons were learned quickly, others slowly. Neither anesthetic agents, techniques, nor the skill of administrators changed much over the next century, except that the nurse anesthetist was introduced in the late 1800s. The specialty of surgery rapidly outdistanced anesthesia in scope, complexity, and success.

In the operating room, where the surgeon was "captain of the ship," anesthesia was relegated to a minor role. Yet thoughtful physicians and surgeons realized the need for anesthesiologists, well-trained specialist physicians dedicating full time to anesthesia, who could extend surgical horizons by permitting operations only then dreamed of and by allowing applications of surgical principles to patients then considered too ill to withstand either anesthesia or operation. A few physicians were attracted by this opportunity early in the 20th century, and added impetus was gained from World War I, but it was not until the mid-1930s that the specialty was officially recognized with the establishment of the American Board of Anesthesiology for certifying appropriately trained physician anesthetists. Today, in nearly every medical school in the country, anesthesiology functions either as an autonomous academic department or as a division of surgery. There are approximately 2,300 physicians in training in some 160 anesthesiology residency programs throughout the country. The American Board of Anesthesiology has certified more than 8,000 specialists and is recognized as a leader among specialty boards in setting standards.

Anesthesiology originally concerned itself entirely with the administration of general anesthetics, and the anesthesiologist's activities were confined to the operating room. The advent of local anesthetics injected into the fluid surrounding the spinal cord broadened the methods available to provide relief of pain during an operation. The introduction into clinical anesthesia of drugs aimed specifically at relaxing muscles made the surgeon's job easier but deprived patients of the ability to breathe spontaneously, thus creating a need for artificial respiratory support during the operation. As a result, anesthesiologists became specialists in respiratory and circulatory physiology, as well as in devices used to support and monitor these systems and in drugs that act upon them. Increasingly complex operations were undertaken, and more critically ill patients, including the very young and the very elderly, were treated surgically. Because the individualized attention provided to patients in the operating room could not be terminated abruptly upon completion of an operation, recovery rooms, intensive care units, and respiratory care units became necessities. The anesthesiologist came to be a central figure in all of these areas.

Far from merely providing sleep in the operating room, today's anesthesiology is defined as a practice of medicine dealing with but not limited to (a) the management of procedures for rendering a patient insensible to pain and emotional stress during surgical, obstetrical, and certain medical procedures; (b) the support of life functions under the stress of anesthetic and surgical manipulations; (c) the clinical management of the unconscious patient, whatever the cause; (d) the management of problems in pain relief; (e) the management of problems in cardiac and respiratory resuscitation; (f) the application of specific methods of respiratory therapy; (g) the clinical management of various fluid, electrolyte, and metabolic disturbances.

The general anesthetics

More than 130 years after the first public demonstration of ether anesthesia, we still do not understand the mechanism of action of general anesthetics. Some of the best scientific minds of the period have attempted to unravel this mystery and a variety of theories have been propounded, but none is universally accepted. The site of action of the

James E. Eckenhoff, M.D., D.Sc., *is Professor of Anesthesia and Dean of the Northwestern University Medical School.*

Lee Balterman *is a Chicago photojournalist who has worked for Abbott Laboratories; his work has appeared in many Time Inc. publications.*

general anesthetics, so far as unconsciousness and analgesia (insensibility to pain) are concerned, is in the brain, to which the anesthetizing agent is delivered from the lungs via the arterial circulation. General anesthetics are either volatile liquids (halothane [Fluothane], enflurane [Ethrane], methoxyflurane [Penthrane], diethyl ether) or gases (nitrous oxide, cyclopropane, and ethylene, of which the latter two are seldom used today). For most of anesthesiology's first 100 years ether and chloroform were used principally. These volatile liquids were poured on gauze that was stretched over a wire frame or stuffed in a paper cone through which the patient breathed, inhaling unknown concentrations of vapor and accumulating carbon dioxide beneath the mask. The carbon dioxide together with the anesthetic vapor displaced oxygen, thus leading to hypoxia (oxygen deprivation) as well as anesthesia.

The anesthesia machine. Today, general anesthetics are universally administered via anesthesia machines, schematically represented in Figure 1. Gases, including oxygen and gas anesthetics, are delivered from tanks (A) or central sources, through reducing valves (B) to prevent exposure of patients to high tank pressures, and through calibrated flow meters (C) that permit delivery of accurate concentrations of agents. Anesthetics requiring vaporization are placed in chambers (D) constructed to maintain a reasonably constant temperature and to provide a large internal surface area for vaporization by a specially metered oxygen supply, thus delivering known concentrations of agents. Gases and anesthetic agents flow into a rubber reservoir bag (E) where they mix. The patient breathes the mixture from the bag via

One type of anesthesia machine (below). Figure 1 is a schematic representation of the anesthesia machine (see text).

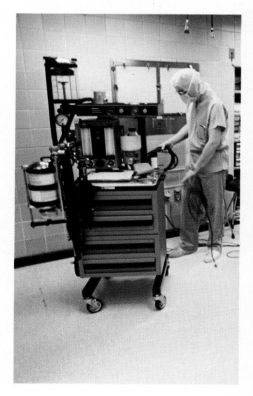

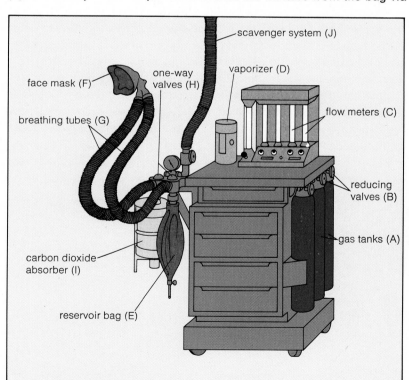

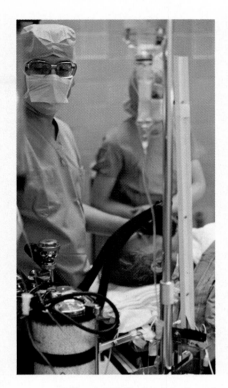

(Above) Initial administration of anesthetic gases. (Below) Figure 2: A schematic diagram of the uptake and distribution of a general anesthetic.

a mask (F) and breathing tubes (G) in which are incorporated unidirectional valves (H) that prevent rebreathing of the expired gases and assure their passage through a canister (I). The canister contains a dry, granular substance that absorbs carbon dioxide, assuring removal of this potentially toxic product of metabolism. The anesthetist may assist or control breathing by rhythmic compression of the reservoir bag. Excess or overflow gases are removed from the operating room atmosphere via a scavenger system (J).

Uptake and distribution of general anesthetics. Anesthetic gases and vapors breathed into the lungs pass from the air spaces (alveoli) through the pulmonary membranes into blood in the pulmonary capillaries in direct proportion to the partial pressures of the various gases in the air and in the patient's blood. Their concentration in the air is dependent upon the concentration of gas or vapor delivered from the machine and the mixing of the gas or vapor with air passing into and out of the lungs. In blood, gas concentration is dependent upon rate of blood flow through the lungs, upon passage of anesthetic gas from blood into tissues (again related to partial pressure differences), and upon the degree of concentration of the anesthetic agent remaining in the blood that returns to the lungs (Figure 2).

The varying solubility of agents in blood and tissues plays a part in rapidity of onset and duration of anesthesia; highly soluble agents require a longer time to produce anesthesia and last longer—ether is an example. Organs with a rapid blood flow, like the brain, develop high tissue concentrations of anesthetic most quickly, thus explaining the rapid loss of consciousness. In the athletic and robust patient and in the apprehensive patient, rapid blood flow in peripheral tissues (muscle and the like) soaks up anesthetics, making necessary larger quantities of the anesthetic to produce adequate anesthesia. The sedentary, elderly, critically ill, or traumatized patient may have poor peripheral circulation, thus requiring minimal anesthetic for deep anesthesia to develop. In general, a high concentration is delivered early, to establish the desired level of anesthesia, and then the concentration is reduced as tissues become saturated and uptake is diminished.

General anesthetics differ in their potency and in the completeness of the anesthetic state produced. Nitrous oxide is the weakest of the

Machine	Lungs	Circulation	Tissue		
ANESTHETIC DELIVERY	GAS EXCHANGE WITH BLOOD	MIX/CARRY ANESTHETIC TO TISSUES	UPTAKE OF ANESTHETIC		
Gases/Vapors	Diffusion	Solubilities	The Tissue Groups	% of Cardiac Output	% of Body Weight
		left heart	muscle group	20	55
fraction inspired minute volume of ventilation	fraction in alveoli	circulation ↔ vital organs	vessel-rich group brain heart visceral circulation kidney	75	7
	alveoli	right heart	vessel-poor group fat, bone, connective tissue, skin	5	38
Inspired Mixture	Ventilation	Blood Carriage			

frequently used agents. Barely causing unconsciousness in the healthy person when administered in maximum safe concentration (75–80%), nitrous oxide usually does not provide sufficient analgesia and does not relax muscles sufficiently for abdominal or thoracic operations. For this reason nitrous oxide is almost always given in conjunction with opiates (narcotic analgesics), muscle relaxants, intravenous barbiturates (thiopental [Pentothal]), or with the more potent volatile general anesthetics. At the other end of the spectrum are agents such as ether or methoxyflurane, highly soluble substances producing unconsciousness slowly but ultimately providing profound analgesia and effective muscle relaxation as depth of anesthesia increases. If continued in sufficiently high concentration, they would cause respiration to cease, resulting in circulatory failure and death. Ethrane and halothane, today's most commonly used volatile anesthetics, are not as soluble, cause unconsciousness more rapidly, are not as effective analgesics, and do not relax muscles until potentially dangerous levels of anesthesia are reached. Both agents are invariably used conjointly with nitrous oxide. Cyclopropane, not popular today, is relatively insoluble and causes rapid loss of consciousness; a good analgesic, it does not provide muscle relaxation. Cyclopropane fell into disuse because of its flammability and the frequency with which it caused irregularities of heart rhythm.

Nonanesthetic actions of general anesthetics. Ideally, the effects of an acceptable general anesthetic would be confined to the loss of consciousness and the production of analgesia and muscle relaxation. Unfortunately all anesthetics have other effects, some acceptable and some not. Cyclopropane was used in spite of its defects until something better came along, namely halothane and Ethrane. Ether likewise has essentially ceased to be used in modern clinical practice because of its flammability, slow onset and long duration of anesthesia, and high incidence of postoperative nausea and vomiting. Since ethylene is no more potent than nitrous oxide and is highly flammable, it no longer has advocates. Chloroform, the second general anesthetic used clinically, disappeared from appreciable use more than 40 years ago because of its toxic effects on the liver. Methoxyflurane, introduced only about 20 years ago, has come under a cloud because it has a toxic effect on the kidney tubules, an effect directly related to concentration of the agent and duration of anesthesia. Halothane, probably the most widely used volatile agent, has been suspect for about 15 of its 25 years of existence because of an alleged destructive action on cells of the liver. Its effect, however, is ill-defined and unpredictable; the effect is not a true toxicity phenomenon as compared with that of chloroform, is relatively uncommon, and cannot be reproduced experimentally. There are reasons to suspect that the liver damage is a sensitivity response either to the agent or to its metabolic breakdown products. Thus, for many specialists, the ease of administration and the smooth maintenance of anesthesia and of recovery make halothane the agent of choice. The remaining agent, Ethrane, has no major black marks

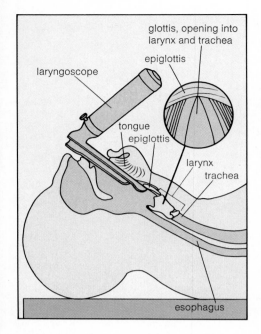

laryngoscope

glottis, opening into larynx and trachea

epiglottis

tongue
epiglottis

larynx
trachea

esophagus

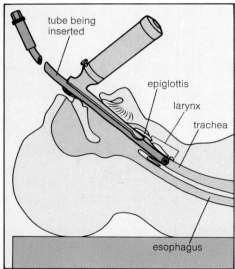

tube being inserted

epiglottis

larynx

trachea

esophagus

against it; aberrations may appear in the electroencephalogram, minor readily controllable muscle twitchings have been reported infrequently, and renal dysfunction has been noted in patients with previously existing renal disease. All general anesthetics have a depressant action on the heart, the effect worsening with depth of anesthesia and the severity varying with the agent.

Metabolism of general anesthetics. For 115 years of anesthetic practice, it was assumed that general anesthetics were inert substances that produced anesthesia when inhaled and later were eliminated unchanged from the body, primarily via the lungs. (An exception was trichloroethylene, a substance useful to produce analgesia but not advised for general anesthesia.) We now know this to be untrue; all anesthetics are metabolized to varying extents, some as much as 50%. Various drugs, for example, phenobarbital, may increase this percentage by stimulating the release of enzymes that metabolize anesthetics. The significance of this process is unknown, although there has been much investigation and speculation. Evidence has accumulated to show that chronic inhalation of anesthetics depresses the body's immune responses and the production of white blood cells and may adversely affect the early stages of pregnancy, leading to abortion, miscarriage, or genetic defects in the offspring. These conditions may even result from prolonged inhalation of subanesthetic concentrations, for instance by personnel working in an operating room where general anesthesia is being given. Investigation in this area is only beginning, but the early data have been convincing enough to prompt installation of scavenger systems to remove escaped anesthetic gases from the operating room environment.

Muscle relaxants

Curare, an Indian arrow poison, was known to 19th-century French physiologist Claude Bernard as a laboratory curiosity capable of blocking the junction between nerve and muscle (neuromuscular junction), resulting in total muscle flaccidity. Not until the early 1940s, however, was its clinical use considered; its introduction revolutionized anesthesia because it obviated the need for deep anesthesia to produce adequate muscle relaxation for intra-abdominal operations and made anesthesiologists turn their attention more rapidly to respiratory physiology and to the monitoring of vital functions. In the hands of the competent practitioner, it has increased the safety of anesthesia; when used by the incompetent or ill-informed it has increased the hazard. Unfortunately, blocking of the neuromuscular junction is only minimally selective; respiration is not spared and most morbidity and mortality associated with use of muscle relaxants come from respiratory inadequacy and oxygen lack.

Muscle relaxants produce neither analgesia nor unconsciousness; fully paralyzed individuals retain pain sensation and are conscious even though incapable of responding. Consequently, the relaxants must be used in conjunction with anesthetics, their value lying in elimi-

34

nating the need for other than minimal depths of anesthesia. A commonly used combination of anesthetic drugs today includes an intravenous barbiturate for rapid induction of anesthesia, a muscle relaxant, an opioid for analgesia, and nitrous oxide and oxygen for unconsciousness and control of ventilation.

There are two groups of relaxants in current clinical use, both of which prevent passage of impulses across the neuromuscular junction, resulting in loss of muscle tone. One group, called nondepolarizers, of which curare is the prototype, has an effect lasting 30–45 minutes; if block persists, antagonists to the drug action are available and effective, although in due course the action will wear off by itself. The second group, called depolarizers, of which the prototype is succinylcholine, is evanescent in action (3–4 minutes) and is rapidly metabolized. Under certain circumstances — usually hereditary in nature — the action is prolonged, possibly for hours. Antagonists are ineffective against this group of drugs.

Care of pulmonary ventilation. If the muscles of respiration are paralyzed, pulmonary ventilation must be assured by artificially assisting or controlling respiration, either by hand compression of the breathing bag or connection of the patient to a mechanical ventilator. Passage of air into the lungs is assured by insertion into the patient's trachea of an endotracheal tube (Figure 3), which is connected to the breathing tubes of the anesthesia machine. An airtight seal is provided by an inflatable balloon on the tracheal end of the tube. The balloon prevents aspiration of fluids from the patient's stomach and esophagus into the lungs and assures ease of inflation of the lungs. Because passage of endotracheal tubes and supervision of pulmonary ventilation is a daily function of anesthesiologists, it should be no surprise that these physicians are commonly in charge of cardiopulmonary resuscitation teams in hospitals, direct the activities of the inhalation therapy departments and respiratory care units, and supervise the instruction of civilians in emergency resuscitation measures.

Intravenous anesthetic agents

Three widely differing groups of drugs are employed intravenously to supplement or augment anesthesia: thiobarbiturates, opioids, and neuroleptic agents.

Thiobarbiturates are rapidly acting, highly fat-soluble barbituric acid derivatives. Pentothal is the popular prototype. Intravenous barbiturates are neither anesthetics nor analgesics. They are hypnotics, used for inducing sleep, and are intended only for induction of anesthesia to be followed by inhalation agents or for very brief surgical procedures not requiring muscle relaxation. Usually injected in fractionated doses into the tubing of a previously inserted intravenous infusion, thiobarbiturates produce drowsiness followed by sleep that appears within seconds to a minute depending upon the dose and speed of injection. The abundant cerebral circulation carries a large proportion of the drug to the brain, which explains the rapid onset of action, but if additional

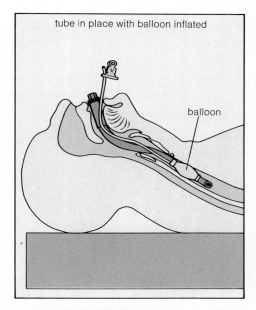

tube in place with balloon inflated

balloon

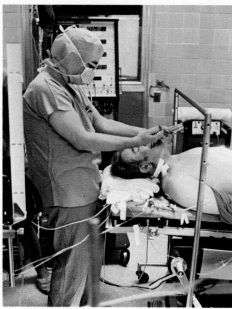

Figure 3: Illustrations opposite and above portray steps in the passage of a cuffed endotracheal tube through the mouth into the trachea. The anesthetist (above) begins insertion of endotracheal tube.

35

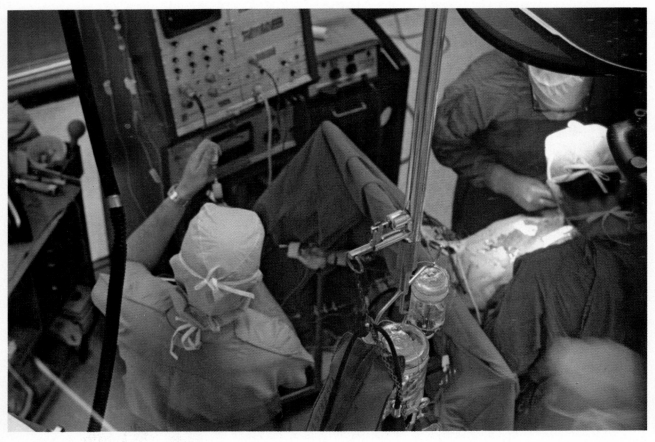

Anesthesiologist during open-chest operation, surrounded by anesthesia and monitoring equipment.

increments of drug are not given, redistribution occurs throughout the body, the concentration in the brain decreases, and the patient awakens. This phenomenon originally led to a mistaken description of these drugs as having "ultrashort" action. If enough thiobarbiturate is given over a sufficiently long interval, however, fat tissues within the body will store appreciable quantities and the patient may sleep for many hours, even a day, depending on the dose. The poor circulation in fatty tissues causes slow release of the drug, keeping the blood level high and metabolism of the drug proceeding slowly.

Opioids, opium alkaloids such as morphine and comparable synthetic substances, are analgesics. Usually employed in small dosage, they dull pain, thus making it tolerable. In higher doses, they may produce sleep, but, importantly, they also cause respiration to become depressed or even cease. Normally opioids have little effect on circulation if the patient remains supine. Because they offer the advantage of potent analgesia without circulatory depression, such drugs are often used for major surgical procedures in poor risk patients. Large doses are injected intravenously, relaxation is provided by muscle relaxants, and respiration is controlled with nitrous oxide and oxygen throughout the operation. When the surgical procedure is completed, the opioid action can be reversed by antagonists. The metabolism of the opioid is

36

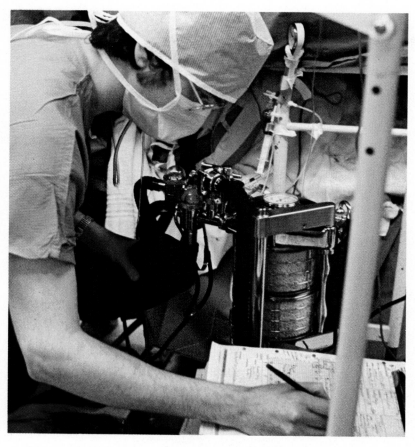

Recording minute-to-minute observations during the operation.

Oxygen and anesthetic gases of anesthesia machine.

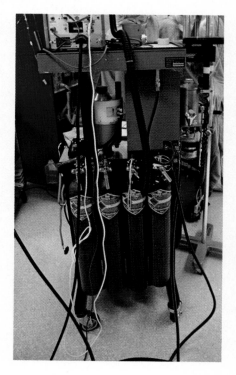

not hastened by the antagonist, however, and patients remain groggy for up to one or two days postoperatively. Opioid anesthesia has proven especially useful in cardiothoracic surgical procedures.

Neurolept anesthesia is a technique that combines the actions of two powerful groups of drugs to produce a state of analgesia in which the patient is detached from the environment. The most popular combination consists of a potent, brief-acting opioid, fentanyl, and a dissociative drug, droperidol. The drugs can be used separately as indicated clinically or in a premixed form, Innovar. As with other opioid analgesics, respiration is depressed and must be supported artificially. A patient may be operated upon while essentially awake but betraying no evidence of pain perception; automatic respiration will cease, but the patient will breathe if repeatedly instructed to do so. Again, muscle relaxation does not occur. In fact, muscle rigidity occasionally results from a relative overdose of the opioid. Today most anesthesiologists use neurolept agents in combination with muscle relaxants, nitrous oxide and oxygen, and controlled ventilation.

Local or regional anesthesia

Satisfactory anesthesia for some procedures can be provided by the injection of local anesthetics. These are weakly acid substances, which,

37

when placed in proximity to a nerve, prevent the propagation of an impulse along that nerve by blocking muscle activity between the point of injection and the periphery of the body and by blocking perception of pain sensation between the center of the body and the site of injection. The action is reversible, lasting from 40–50 minutes in the case of procaine (Novocaine) to a maximum of four to six hours with bupivacaine (Marcaine). All of the agents in use have the potential for causing convulsions if absorbed into the blood from the site of injection too rapidly; careful attention to concentration, site and rapidity of injection, and volume of local anesthetic injected are therefore important in preventing complications. Adrenaline is often added to the local anesthetic to constrict the blood vessels in the area, thereby delaying absorption of the agent and prolonging action. Local anesthetics may be infiltrated into the skin in or around the site of an incision; deposited in proximity to large nerve trunks (brachial plexus block of the arm is the most common such procedure); injected into the spinal fluid surrounding the spinal cord (spinal anesthesia); or injected into the space between the dura, a fibrous membrane that contains spinal cord and fluid, and the bony inner wall of the vertebra (caudal, epidural, or peridural anesthesia). Spinal and epidural anesthesia are among the most frequently used forms of local anesthesia.

Spinal anesthesia. The spinal cord, extending from the brain to the second lumbar vertebra, is bathed in a delicately balanced electrolyte fluid retained within the dura, which runs most of the length of the

Figure 4: A schematic representation of injection for spinal and epidural anesthesia.

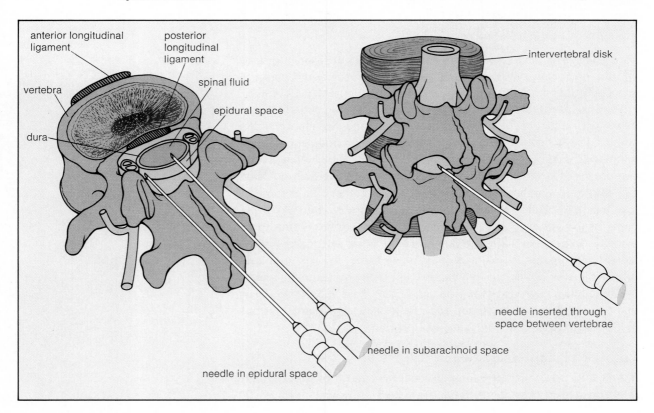

spinal column. Local anesthetics, usually tetracaine (Pontocaine) or procaine, injected into the spinal fluid anesthetize nerve fibers leaving and entering the spinal cord, causing a motor and sensory paralysis (Figure 4). After the skin and underlying tissue are anesthetized with a local anesthetic, a needle is inserted between the lower lumbar vertebrae, penetrating the ligaments, and entering the subarachnoid space (a fluid-containing space below the termination of the spinal cord). The level of anesthesia obtained may be altered by weighting the local anesthetic with a dextrose solution heavier than spinal fluid and tilting the operating table, thus causing the solution to run downward. Spinal anesthesia with tetracaine lasts one to two hours, but the duration can be doubled by adding adrenalin to the injected solution, which retards absorption of the anesthetic from spinal fluid into blood. A small plastic catheter can also be inserted allowing for additional periodic injections. Spinal anesthesia is most often used for lower abdominal, urologic, and lower extremity operations.

Epidural anesthesia. This technique differs only slightly from spinal anesthesia in that the local anesthetic is injected into the epidural space, that is, between the dura and the inner vertebral wall. Most often, a small plastic catheter is introduced through a needle; the tip of the catheter is threaded into the epidural space. Local anesthetics are injected through the catheter and spread through the space, blocking the nerves as they traverse it (Figure 4). The extent of spread is determined by the volume injected. This procedure can be used for thoracic or abdominal operations and is commonly employed for relieving the discomfort of birth by vaginal delivery. Since the volume of drug is larger than with spinal anesthesia, the potential for absorption and a reaction are greater. A related technique, caudal anesthesia, is similar to epidural anesthesia except that the epidural space is penetrated at its most distal point, therefore requiring a larger volume of local anesthetic for vaginal delivery.

Advantages of local or regional anesthesia. Local injection or nerve block is always preferable for an outpatient who will return home after a surgical or dental procedure. The patient retains full consciousness, judgment, and equilibrium—often not the case for several hours after general anesthesia. Further, one of the feared complications during general anesthesia, that of vomiting and aspiration of vomitus into the lungs, is avoided; the patient is awake and vomitus can be expelled, not inhaled. Brachial plexus block and local anesthesia are especially valuable following trauma to an arm or hand shortly after ingestion of food. Spinal and epidural anesthesia provide maximal analgesia and muscle relaxation, ideal conditions for lower abdominal and bladder operations. The patient can retain full control of respiration and does not lose consciousness. The maintenance of consciousness, ability to see the newborn immediately, and lack of depressant effect of general anesthetics on the baby during birth have made these the current techniques of choice for vaginal delivery. Spinal anesthesia is feared by some patients because of its potential for causing postoperative headache due to leakage of spinal fluid from the subarachnoid space, and the possibility of permanent paralysis, an extremely rare complication almost always due to improper administration. Regional anesthesia is important and has its own definite application.

The risk of anesthesia

Anesthetics and anesthesia have diverse effects upon the bodily systems; these effects vary depending upon the conditions at the time of anesthesia. There is a relationship between the patient's physical status or condition and the successful outcome of an anesthetic. In a healthy patient, regardless of age, death as a result of anesthesia should be rare; nevertheless, the physician cannot render patients unconscious and give substances that depress normal circulatory response and paralyze breathing without undertaking some risk.

The risk of anesthesia increases as the physical condition of the patient worsens. Thus, for elective surgery, a patient with hypertension or diabetes is at greater risk from anesthesia than is a healthy patient; likewise, a bedridden patient who has congestive heart failure or recent myocardial infarction is predictably more threatened by anesthesia.

Anesthesia and advancement of surgery

The improvement in anesthetic techniques, development of new anesthetics and adjuvants (substances that increase the effectiveness of anesthetics), and training of modern anesthesiologists and nurse anesthetists have led to vast changes in the scope of operations that can be performed and in the chances of patient survival during and after surgical procedures. Speed, once considered the mark of distinction of a surgeon, is no longer of appreciable importance; the surgeon is now free to perform the procedure with painstaking care, usually without concern for time or for the patient's condition. The abdominal, thoracic, cardiac, and cranial cavities are opened with relative frequency. Most large medical centers will commonly complete ten or more abdominal and several thoracic, cardiac, and cranial operations daily.

The muscle relaxation required for successful performance of major abdominal operations was provided through advances in anesthesia; anesthesia also provided the artificial control of ventilation that permitted surgeons to open the chest, to remove cancerous lungs, to correct the vascular defects of the "blue baby," or to repair an aneurysm of the aorta. Had it not been for anesthesia, heart-lung machines would never have come into common use, allowing defects of the valves of the heart to be corrected, occluded coronary arteries of the heart removed and replaced, and most spectacularly, whole hearts removed and replaced. Anesthesia has also made possible the correction of congenital defects in newborns. Anesthesiologists have developed a technique of lowering the blood pressure (deliberate hypotension) that can so reduce loss of blood at the operative site that the surgeon can better delineate tissues and control bleeding that is otherwise ungovernable; this technique made possible new lifesaving operations and improved the results of plastic surgical procedures. Perhaps of greatest importance is the increased willingness of surgeons to operate on the extremely ill patient, or the very young or elderly, all of whom would in the past have been turned away as unable to withstand the operation or anesthesia. Anesthesia has helped reduce maternal and fetal death rates; because of improved anesthesia, obstetricians are more willing to resort to cesarean sections rather than wait hours for difficult vaginal deliveries.

Modern surgery

In the past several decades modern operating theaters have changed in several important ways. The attending surgeon is no longer "captain of the ship" but is one of a team of physicians, nurses, and technicians, each of whom contributes to improved results and safety, each responsible for his or her job and actions. Today's surgeon does not direct the anesthesiologist's duties and indeed, with few exceptions, could not do so because of lack of training in a rapidly changing field. The anesthesiologist has a thorough acquaintance with the patient's medical history, the operation proposed, and the risks involved. Consultation with surgeons and referring physicians is held concerning the patient's disease; during these discussions, when appropriate, the anesthesiologist explains the stresses and risks of anesthesia. The anesthesiologist keeps the surgeon informed of the patient's condition throughout the operation and supervises the patient's postoperative recovery while the surgeon is engaged elsewhere. Sometimes technically simple operations are performed under trying anesthetic conditions, whereas at other times good anesthesia provides little challenge even in difficult and intricate operations. Patients are usually unaware of the relationship of anesthesiologist and surgeon because the former makes the principal contribution while the patient is unconscious, but the latter relates to the patient before, during, and after the operation.

Monitoring. Another change in the modern operating theater is the amount of monitoring equipment available, providing the signals that enable the anesthesiologist to guide the patient safely through the anesthetic experience. Usual standards provide that blood pressure, pulse, and respiration are recorded every few minutes by means of a cuff attached to the patient's arm and a stethoscope affixed to the chest, monitored by the anesthesiologist through an earpiece. Often, especially in major operations, a stethoscope is inserted into the esophagus, immediately behind the heart, allowing for minute-to-minute recording of heart and respiratory sounds. Electrocardiographic leads are attached to most anesthetized patients and the signals are displayed on an oscilloscope, thus providing a visual image of heart action for all to observe. Sometimes an audible signal indicating the heart rate is incorporated. In major operations, especially those in which there may be considerable blood loss, several other body functions are closely watched. The urinary output is continuously monitored via a catheter inserted into the bladder (a guide to adequacy of the patient's fluid balance); arterial pressure is continuously recorded via a short,

The operation completed, the surgeon leaves the operating room; the anesthesiologist remains to supervise care of the patient.

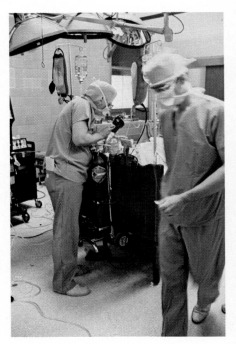

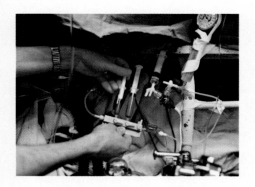

Monitoring: arterial monitor at right, withdrawing blood for blood gas analysis at left.

fine catheter placed into an artery at the wrist and connected to a monometer; central venous pressure is observed by means of a longer fine catheter inserted through the jugular vein into the chamber of the right ventricle of the heart or a similar catheter at mid-arm, again allowing estimate of the adequacy of the blood volume and action of the heart; and finally, an even longer catheter with a balloon at the end is inserted through the right heart chamber into the pulmonary artery and lodged into a smaller artery in the lung, providing an estimate of the action of the left auricle of the heart. In addition, blood samples may be removed at intervals and analyzed within minutes to inform the anesthesiologist of the oxygen and carbon dioxide tension and acid-base balance of the blood. All of these procedures provide the data that enable the critically ill and those undergoing complex major surgical procedures to survive. The monitoring continues throughout the operation and into the recovery room and intensive care unit.

The nurse anesthetist and anesthesiologists

Of the approximately 20 million anesthetics given each year in the United States, about half are administered by nonanesthesiologists. The public is often confused about the difference between nurse anesthetists and anesthesiologists; and, indeed, some wonder why the latter are needed. There are three basic differences: education, responsibility, and interests. The nurse anesthetist generally has completed high school and, usually, three years of nursing education to become a registered nurse, followed by two years of anesthesia training and a certifying examination to become a certified registered nurse anesthetist (CRNA). Anesthesiologists are physicians, usually with a college degree as well as an M.D.; they also have three or four years of specialty training in anesthesia, depending upon optional programs selected. Those who are qualified pass examinations to become diplomates of the American Board of Anesthesiology. In fact, however, either physician or nurse can administer anesthetics without specified training if a hospital will accept their credentials.

Nurse anesthetists are generally employees of a hospital or clinic, although a few engage in a private practice similar to that of physicians.

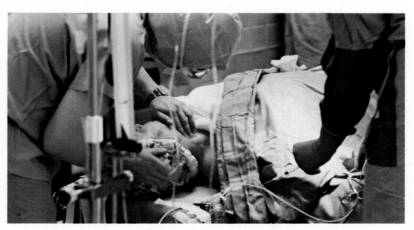

Application of monitoring devices: central venous catheter.

Their medicolegal liability is less than that of physicians because they are considered in the eyes of the law to function under the medical direction of physicians. Most nurse anesthetists confine their activities to the operating room, do not participate independently in pre- or postoperative care, and are not in a position to exercise medical judgment. Nurse anesthetists and physicians usually work in harmony, particularly in large hospital departments. It is unlikely, however, considering the growing worldwide needs of patients, that physicians will ever have a monopoly on anesthesia. As with midwives in obstetrics and nurse practitioners in pediatrics, the nurse anesthetist will always be needed to provide nonphysician support in anesthesia.

A unique specialty

Certain facts should emerge from this discussion. First, the mechanism by which anesthetics act is unexplained; it remains the subject of research that continues to challenge the scientific elite. Second, no other branch of medicine so crosses the lines between basic science, pharmacology, and clinical medicine as does anesthesiology. Knowledge of physiology, biochemistry, pharmacology, and clinical medicine are absolutely necessary to the competent anesthesiologist. Furthermore, anesthesiology is unique among medical specialties in its use of monitoring equipment and measures for accumulating data on body functions. No other area of medicine deliberately depresses the brain and the bodily systems as does anesthesia—with the tacit expectation of returning them to normality in minimum time without incident or complication. Finally, anesthesiologists rub elbows daily with more specialists in medicine and hospital administrators than perhaps do any other practitioners. Anesthesia has indeed come a long way since October 16, 1846, when surgeon John Collins Warren of the Massachusetts General Hospital turned to the audience after the first persuasive demonstration of ether anesthesia and said, "Gentlemen, this is no humbug!"

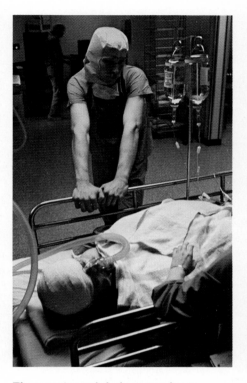

The operation ended, the patient lies in the recovery room. The anesthesiologist supervises and monitors the patient's condition.

FOR ADDITIONAL READING

Adriani, John. *The Chemistry and Physics of Anesthesia*. 2nd ed. Springfield, Ill.: C. C. Thomas Co., 1962.

Applebaum, Edward L., and Bruce, David L. *Tracheal Intubation*. Philadelphia: W. B. Saunders Co., 1976.

Bonica, John J. *Principles and Practice of Obstetric Analgesia and Anesthesia*. 2 vols. Philadelphia: F. A. Davis Co., 1967–69.

Dripps, Robert D.; Eckenhoff, James E.; and Vandam, L. D. *Introduction to Anesthesia*. 5th ed. Philadelphia: W. B. Saunders Co., 1977.

Eckenhoff, James E. *Anesthesia from Colonial Times*. Montreal and Philadelphia: J. B. Lippincott Co., 1966.

Greene, Nicholas M. *Physiology of Spinal Anesthesia*. 2nd ed. Baltimore, Md.: Williams and Wilkins Co., 1969.

Wylie, William D. and Churchill-Davidson, H. C. *A Practice of Anaesthesia*. 3rd ed. Chicago: Year Book Medical Publishers, 1972.

Rx for Athletes
by Allan J. Ryan, M.D.

Pictorial records show that human beings have enjoyed games and sports since the earliest times. Our knowledge of a particular relationship between medicine and sports, however, extends only to written records produced in Greece in the 5th century B.C. Certain Greek physicians known as "gymnastes" devoted themselves largely, if not entirely, to the supervision of the physical activities of young men (and in Sparta also of young women) and to the training of athletes. The first such practitioner whose name we know was Herodicus, reputed to have been a teacher of Hippocrates. Herodicus and his contemporaries practiced herbal medicine, not specifically tailored to particular illnesses and so only accidentally effective; surgery was primitive. Among these physicians treatment consisted mainly of recommending changes in diet or prescribing rest or therapeutic exercise for rehabilitation of the ill or injured.

Galen, a Greek physician to the Roman emperors who was born about A.D. 129, had an influence on medicine that was felt for 1,500 years. Considered the founder of experimental physiology, he discovered several important facts about the human body. Much of Galen's knowledge was derived from experience as a physician to professional athletes, including gladiators. From his examination of the wounds of athletes, Galen expanded his knowledge of human anatomy and developed skill, including surgical techniques, in treating different kinds of wounds. From the time of Galen to the Renaissance there were no significant advances in medicine that resulted from physicians' treatment of athletes. During the Renaissance, however, in addition to the establishment of the foundations of modern biomechanics, anatomy, and physiology, there was renewed emphasis on the value of regular physical exercise as a way of achieving and maintaining good health.

Allan J. Ryan, M.D., *has written numerous books and articles on health care and sports and is editor in chief of* The Physician and Sportsmedicine *in Minneapolis.*

Photograph, Joseph F. Viesti

44

Sports competition has grown tremendously in the 20th century, helping to create the need for modern sports medicine. Despite the best precautions, injuries to athletes (opposite) do occur. Treating injuries and rehabilitating athletes are important aspects of sports medicine.

In the early 19th century, chiefly as the result of the establishment of military requirements, physical education attained the status of a profession. While physical education was not a part of medical practice or exclusively controlled by physicians, the medical profession continued during this period to be actively interested in physical exercise and sports as a way of achieving and maintaining health. The advent of general anesthesia in the mid 1800s and discoveries in microbiology and immunology later in the century, however, turned the whole orientation of surgery and medicine away from physical well-being and toward the development of specific therapy for specific diseases.

The development and practice of modern sports medicine

The development of competitive sports on a mass scale in the 20th century has produced the modern science of sports medicine, in which physicians do play a major role. The structure of sports medicine began to take shape in 1928 when a group of physicians and specialists in physical education from 20 countries, meeting at the time of the Olympic games in Amsterdam, founded the Association Internationale Médico-Sportive. The organization's first constitution contained some important goals: (1) to inaugurate research in biology, psychology, and sociology related to sports; (2) to promote the study of medical problems encountered in physical exercise and sports in collaboration with international sports federations; and (3) to organize international con-

46

gresses on sports medicine. At the second congress held in Turin, Italy, in 1933, the name was changed to the Fédération Internationale de Médecine Sportive et Scientifique (FIMS). With the exception of a nine-year interruption during World War II, FIMS has held a congress every two years since. More than 60 countries currently belong to the federation, and there are numerous other sports medicine organizations throughout the world.

In some countries sports medicine is a certified specialty in which medical schools offer degrees. Physicians who qualify in sports medicine devote their practices exclusively to the specialty. In the United States, Canada, and Great Britain, however, sports medicine is an avocational interest for physicians. In these countries it has become a multidisciplinary field that involves not only physicians but also physical educators, coaches, athletes, trainers, physical therapists, and even psychologists, historians, and sociologists. Sports medicine in the United States includes four principal areas of interest and activity: (1) the medical supervision of athletes; (2) physical education and sports for the handicapped; (3) physical exercise to prevent disease; and (4) therapeutic exercise.

Physicians practicing sports medicine are concerned with the medical supervision of individual athletes and of teams. Medical supervision includes a wide range of concerns: physical examinations, tests for functional capacities, training and conditioning, nutrition, protective equipment, rules of sports and officiating, supervision of practice and competition, emergency treatment of illness and injury, follow-up definitive diagnosis and treatment, rehabilitation following injury and illness, supervision of the athlete's return to activity, psychological assessment and counseling, and research.

Examination of athletes is important to insure that there are no mental or physical factors that would expose them to greater than usual risks of injury or illness. It is important to identify physical defects that can be corrected before competition or to modify activities for athletes whose defects are not correctable. Examination should also provide a record of normal functions in the event that injury or illness later occurs. In some sports, classification of athletes by weight and size is necessary. In recent years physical examinations have also become important for legal reasons.

Physicians do not follow wholly consistent practices in examining athletes. Most physicians probably take a medical history from the athlete or family. Such a history should include any record of previous injury, its treatment, and the outcome. The choice of those parts of the body or bodily functions which are to be examined is generally determined by the nature of the sport, although an athlete's heart, lungs, and resting blood pressure are almost invariably assessed. The physician usually tests vision and hearing as well, and almost always inspects the athlete's throat. If the abdomen is examined, a test for inguinal hernia is made. The most commonly performed laboratory examination is a urine test; the second most common is a blood count, including

47

Photographs, Wally McNamee—Woodfin Camp

a hemoglobin estimate. Testing of functional capacities, including strength, endurance, coordination, agility, balance, and speed, should be a part of the examination.

To be effective, training and conditioning programs must not only be tailored to each sport but also to roles played in the sport and to individual needs. A swimmer, for example, must develop endurance and muscular flexibility, while an alpine skier's training is designed to produce quick reflexes and great leg strength. In a single sport, *e.g.,* football, a defensive tackle needs tremendous upper body strength, while a wide receiver's conditioning emphasizes speed and agility. Physicians historically have played active roles in developing programs aimed at meeting such specialized requirements. In the 19th century many physicians for private schools and colleges were also coaches and trainers. Today, most training and conditioning programs for athletes are developed by coaches and trainers, not by physicians, but physicians' advice is frequently sought. For example, the "duck waddle" has been largely eliminated in training and conditioning programs because physicians presented evidence that the exercise puts too much stress on the lateral ligaments of the knee. Athletic injuries like tennis elbow, and a similar problem among adolescent baseball players taught to throw too hard and fast for their muscular and skeletal development, further illustrate the importance of proper conditioning and training.

Athletes must have diets that are adequate for the demands of sports as well as for normal growth and metabolism. Exercise physiologists in Sweden have developed the concept of "carbohydrate loading" for events that require great endurance, such as long-distance running, swimming, skiing, or cycling. To prepare for an event, the athlete takes a strenuous workout one week beforehand, followed for three days by a diet high in fat and protein. The effect is to increase the system's demand for carbohydrates, which are the body's preferred energy source. The athlete then goes on a high-carbohydrate diet for three days. On the day of the event he eats a high-carbohydrate meal in a form that is readily assimilated. The chief problem with this regimen is that it can be used effectively only for a particular occasion. The diet cannot be used week after week and is of no help to the athlete who has to compete three times or more in a week or on consecutive days. Most sports physicians today advocate a balanced diet as best for athletes. Physicians should also counsel athletes not to use drugs or other toxic substances that are unnecessary to good athletic performance and are harmful to the body.

Because diet is important for athletes, research on diets is an important concern of sports medicine. Swedish researchers have developed a carbohydrate diet that can be useful for endurance events such as running, swimming, cycling, and skiing.

Proper conditioning and training are vital for athletes. Young baseball pitchers encouraged to throw beyond the limits of their strength can develop arm injuries.

Sports physicians have helped document types of injuries common in particular sports, which had led to rule changes in those games. Statistics on head and neck injuries in amateur football, for example, helped bring about a ban on certain uses of the head during play.

Protective equipment is necessary in many sports. The equipment must be designed not only to withstand maximum stress but also to function without hindering the athlete unduly. It must be durable without being unduly hazardous to other athletes. Equipment must also be properly fitted and worn, and replaced when it no longer protects adequately. Sports physicians influence the design of protective equipment principally through two agencies. The National Operating Committee on Standards for Athletic Equipment includes physicians among its members. The committee's work has included cooperation with manufacturers to improve and standardize testing procedures for football helmets. The American Society for Testing and Materials includes physicians on committees that work on safety standards for equipment for football, baseball, ice hockey, and other sports. Both organizations have been influenced by reports on sports injuries provided by physicians. The American Medical Association (AMA), for example, has recommended that equipment with hard plastic surfaces be padded to reduce injuries, a recommendation that, in mid 1977, had not been implemented. Reports of serious eye injuries by physicians in Canada and the United States led to requiring face protectors for all amateur hockey players in the United States and for amateur players below the top level of play in Canada beginning in 1977.

The rules of sports and officiating must also promote safety. The team of medical supervisors, including physicians, must assist in revising old rules and writing new ones as needed, and they must insist that the rules be enforced by properly qualified officials. A major rule change made largely as the result of pressure from the medical profession was the ban in 1976 on head blocking and tackling in amateur football in the United States. Physicians documented the increase in the number of serious and fatal head and neck injuries due to head blocking and tackling. The evidence was influential in persuading rule-making bodies in football to extend the ban that had previously applied only to "spearing," hitting with the top of the helmet with deliberate intent to injure.

Supervision of athletic practice is provided chiefly by coaches, and by trainers when they are available, but only rarely by physicians. Because the risks of injury are generally greater during competition, however, physicians, and often ambulances, are usually available during games. Special provisions may also be necessary for spectators, who for some events number in the hundreds of thousands. Emergency treatment of illness and injury among athletes may depend not only on a physician but also on the coach, the trainer, a person trained in first aid, or on special rescue teams such as ski patrols. The training of all emergency personnel in recognizing and treating injuries is an important part of sports medicine. Everyone involved should be taught to follow standard procedures and should be provided with the necessary first aid equipment.

Definitive treatment of injuries is solely the province of the physician. Because athletes are generally in good physical condition and are

50

Protective equipment must withstand the maximum stresses the athlete may be subjected to during play. Headgear design, for instance, varies widely from sport to sport. Furthermore, the equipment must function without hindering the athlete's ability to perform. In most cases, standard gear does the job, although some protective devices, such as Kareem Abdul-Jabbar's goggles (above), are designed specially for the individual athlete.

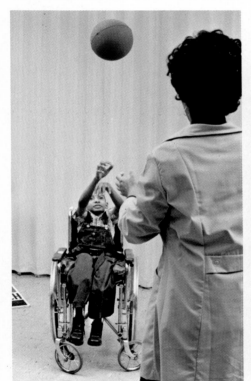

Exercise and sports can help the handicapped lead fuller lives: (top left) a skiing school for amputees; (bottom left) a handicapped boy receiving physical training; (top right) the first Intercollegiate Wheelchair Basketball Tournament, held in 1977; and (bottom right) the International Stoke-Mandeville Wheelchair Games.

highly motivated to make rapid recoveries, treating them can be easier than treating other patients. Treating athletes may be more exacting, however, since they want to return to normal function as quickly as possible. Rehabilitation of the ill or injured athlete is best accomplished by a team approach in which the physician, coach, trainer, therapists, the athlete himself, and even his family may be involved. The emphasis should be on preserving as much function as possible during recovery and on early restoration of strength, endurance, and range of motion. Psychological assessment and counseling may be especially helpful during rehabilitation. Return to activity should be accompanied by progressive retraining and by careful observation, reexamination, and testing.

Sports medicine and nonathletes

Because of urban life-styles and automation, particularly an almost total reliance on the automobile, people in most industrial societies today are threatened by poor physical conditioning. Many people fail to reach or maintain levels of physical fitness necessary to perform the tasks of daily living, let alone enjoy recreation or maintain reserve energy for an emergency. Poor physical conditioning increases the risk of progressive physical debility. It appears to increase susceptibility to chronic degenerative diseases, especially premature aging of the cardiovascular system. Regular and vigorous physical exercise is considered by those involved in sports medicine as the best way to achieve adequate conditioning and to help people reach reasonable levels of physical fitness. There are indications that physical exercise also retards the onset of chronic degenerative diseases that reduce physical ability in old age, and that exercise may actually prolong life.

Physical exercise and the opportunity to participate in sports are at least as important to handicapped people as to those who have normal body functions. Recognition of the importance of physical activity for such people has led to the development of a specialization in teaching physical education to the handicapped and to an international program of sports for the disabled. There are local, national, and worldwide organizations and competitions, such as the Association for Disadvantaged Sportsmen and the Special Olympics for retarded persons.

The success of physical education and sports programs for the handicapped depends on careful evaluation of their functional capacities, for example, distinguishing different levels of spinal paralysis. Exercises and sports for the handicapped, as well as training and conditioning, must be modified and adapted to their needs and capacities. Often, it is necessary to design special equipment and facilities. A successful program requires teamwork between physicians and the many other people involved in working with the handicapped.

As the ancient Greek physicians first noted and modern attempts to rehabilitate athletes have confirmed, exercise can be useful in reconditioning all people who have been ill or injured. Applied by therapists under the supervision of physicians, effective exercise can include

Being able to hail a taxi is a convenience of modern urban life, but the automobile has also contributed to the poor physical conditioning of many people.

Dale Ahearn—Sullivan Associates

53

To improve their physical conditioning, businessmen exercise on a treadmill in a company gym. There is evidence that good conditioning helps prevent cardiovascular and other diseases.

In a test of his body's ability to use oxygen, an athlete runs on a treadmill in a human performance research laboratory while a technician measures his pulse rate and blood pressure.

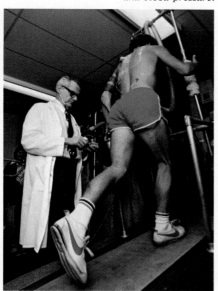

everything from passive manipulation to the actual playing of sports and games. Even in some cases of chronic disability in which functional capacities cannot be restored to normal, the degree of physical function can, nevertheless, be improved by exercise. Studies indicate that people suffering from emotional and mental disorders may benefit from exercise, although the matter has not been fully explored.

Research in sports medicine

Research that has influenced the practice of sports medicine has not always originated in the field itself, and it has often affected the athlete and nonathlete alike. Research has focused chiefly on four principal areas: (1) studies in the physiology of exercise; (2) technical innovations that can lead to improvements in performance; (3) the incidence of sports injuries; and (4) efforts to improve clinical treatment of sports injuries.

Research in exercise physiology has had applications to occupations as diverse as aerospace exploration and tunnel construction. The research has also been a fertile source of help for sports medicine practitioners. It has showed, for example, how to deal with the stresses of heat, humidity, cold, and high and low barometric pressures—factors that athletes are often subject to. In some cases, the interest of athletes and coaches itself has directly stimulated research, for example, to find the best means to develop such qualities as strength and endurance.

Research in performance techniques, not always medical in nature, has produced changes in hand positions and suit weights to cut swimming times, changes in body position in downhill skiing to reduce air resistance and drag, and different configurations of oars to increase the efficiency of the stroke in rowing. Improvements in many performances that are measured in time and distance are due as much to such technical discoveries as they are to medically related factors like greater size or speed or better nutrition.

With the exception of a few well-organized studies of such sports as football and skiing, most of sports medicine's information about injuries and fatalities in sports is anecdotal. The statistics are generally so inadequate that no definite conclusions can be drawn from them. Our knowledge about sports injuries has come largely from the personal experiences of sports physicians and from analyses of the nature of particular sports. There are several problems that prevent accurate compilation of thorough statistics: the tremendous number of athletes involved, the complexity of the uncontrolled variables in injury situations, and the lack of money and personnel to record the injuries and their associated factors.

Researchers and physicians have made substantial improvements in the management and treatment of sports injuries, particularly to joints, that have been applied to the treatment of nonathletes. Many of the surgical techniques for repair of knee and shoulder injuries that are commonly used by orthopedic surgeons today, for example, were derived from treatments originally developed for athletes. The use of cold for the immediate treatment of soft tissue injuries also resulted from treatments developed in sports medicine. Rehabilitative techniques developed for athletes, particularly for restoring strength, have also been used for nonathletes.

Research in sports medicine has been and likely will continue to be hampered by lack of money. Generally, the total amount of money for research in sports medicine has been very small. More than 80% of all medical research in the United States is funded by the federal government, chiefly through the National Institutes of Health. No money is appropriated specifically for sports medicine. Some financial support comes from manufacturers of sports equipment and medical supplies. Individual researchers have obtained grants from a variety of sources, chiefly for research related to the prevention or treatment of cardiovascular diseases. Many projects are supported by researchers themselves, who contribute their time and resources. The few centers of sports medicine research in the United States are located chiefly at universities and are typically called laboratories for human performance research. In Europe there are centers for sports research in many countries. East Germany, West Germany, and the U.S.S.R. probably have the greatest number of centers, and the most active ones.

There are many questions in sports medicine that need to be answered through further research. More investigation is needed regarding diets for athletes competing more than once a week. More needs to be known about the exact effects of regular vigorous exercise in preserving health and prolonging life as well as about effective motivation for establishing lifelong habits of regular exercise. Research should determine how frequently and at what intensity it is necessary to perform resistance exercise to improve or maintain a given level of strength. Research should determine the effects of very early sports training on the normal growth and development of children.

In a rehabilitation clinic an athlete exercises on a machine designed to build strength in the arms and back.

Although most athletes, who are highly motivated and who train under supervision, are able to exercise effectively alone, many nonathletes require a more structured program of exercise. The men (below right) are participating in a heart Parcours, a Swiss-developed jogging trail that includes exercise stations with specific instructions.

Michael D. Sullivan

Art Seitz

Organizations like Little League baseball have long promoted participation in sports by youngsters. Although it is generally agreed that sports are beneficial for young people, more research is needed on the specific effects of sports on the growing, developing body.

The future of sports medicine

As evidence of the interest in sports medicine, during the mid 20th century many sports medicine organizations, including several in the United States alone, have been formed. The American College of Sports Medicine was founded in 1954 as a multidisciplinary organization. It holds annual scientific meetings and has a number of regional chapters. The organization publishes a journal and a bulletin and in 1971 sponsored the publication of the *Encyclopedia of Sports Sciences and Medicine*. The AMA established a Committee on Injuries in Sports in 1954, which in 1959 became the Committee on the Medical Aspects of Sports. The committee sponsored a national congress, set standards for physical examinations of athletes, and cooperated actively with national organizations engaged in the control of sports and athletes. (The committee was disbanded in January 1977.) From 1964 to 1975, the AMA also had a Committee on Exercise and Physical Fitness.

A National Athletic Trainers Association was formed in the United States in 1938 but was dissolved in 1944. The association was revived in 1950 and is currently active with a large membership, a certification program, and a journal. The American Physical Therapy Association also has a section on Sports Medicine. An American Academy of Podiatric Sports Medicine was established in 1970, an American Orthopedic Society for Sports Medicine in 1972, and a Sports Safety and Health Care Society in 1976. There is also an American Osteopathic Academy of Sports Medicine, established in 1976.

The expansion of sports around the world promises even greater development of sports medicine in the future. Commitment to this special area of medicine will increase, although for the majority of physicians and other medical workers involvement will be only part

56

time. Part of the successful development of sports medicine will depend on support for research into basic, unanswered questions about the performance of the human body.

FOR ADDITIONAL READING:

Arnheim, Daniel D.; Auxter, David; and Crowe, Walter C. *Principles and Methods of Adapted Physical Education*. Saint Louis: C. V. Mosby Co., 1969.

Astrand, Per-Olaf, and Rodahl, Kaare. *Textbook of Work Physiology*. New York: McGraw-Hill, 1970.

Harris, Harold A. *Greek Athletes and Athletics*. Bloomington: Indiana University Press, 1966.

International Committee for the Standardization of Physical Fitness Tests. *Fitness, Health, and Work Capacity—International Standards for Assessment*. Edited by L. A. Larson. New York: Macmillan Publishing Co., 1974.

Larson, Leonard A., ed. *Encyclopedia of Sport Sciences and Medicine*. New York: Macmillan Publishing Co., 1971.

O'Donoghue, Don H. *Treatment of Injuries to Athletes*. 2nd ed. Philadelphia: W. B. Saunders Co., 1970.

O'Shea, John P. *Scientific Principles and Methods of Strength Fitness*. 2nd ed. Reading, Mass.: Addison-Wesley Publishing Co., 1976.

Paul, W. D., ed. *Fundamentals of Athletic Training*. 2nd ed. Chicago: American Medical Association, 1975.

Ryan, Allan J., and Allman, Fred L., Jr., ed. *Sports Medicine*. New York: Academic Press, 1974.

Taylor, Albert W., ed. *The Application of Science and Medicine to Sport*. Springfield, Ill.: Charles C. Thomas, 1975.

——.*The Scientific Aspects of Sports Training*. Springfield, Ill.: Charles C. Thomas, 1975.

Williams, J. G. P., and Sperryn, P. N., ed. *Sports Medicine*. London: Edward Arnold Publishers, 1976.

Wilson, P. K., ed. *Adult Fitness and Cardiac Rehabilitation*. Baltimore, Md.: University Park Press, 1975.

The following list is a selection of sports medicine periodicals.

The American Journal of Sports Medicine (formerly The Journal of Sports Medicine)

The Australian Journal of Sports Medicine

The British Journal of Sports Medicine (formerly the Bulletin of the British Association of Sport and Medicine)

The Canadian Journal of Applied Sport Sciences

The Journal of Sports Medicine and Physical Fitness

Medicine and Science in Sports

The Physician and Sportsmedicine

A Symposium

WHAT
IS
MEDICINE?

Controversy in Medicine

by Arnold S. Relman, M.D.

Medical controversy is by no means a new phenomenon. It is, in fact, as old as the practice of medicine itself. Physicians are not by nature less disputatious than other men, so they have always had disagreements about the way their profession ought to be practiced. But the past 150 years have seen a remarkable transformation in the style and significance of medical controversy. Now doctors disagree about quite different kinds of issues and in a very different manner than they did in the early 19th century. Furthermore, the reasons for medical controversy and the methods of resolution have also changed.

A brief account of this evolution can tell us much about the dramatic developments that have occurred in the medical profession since the beginning of the 19th century. Our story can be put into sharpest focus if we limit ourselves to a consideration of medical controversy in the United States. This is not because there is anything inherently unique about medical controversy in this country, but rather because the general significance of medical debate can be perceived most clearly when viewed against a familiar social and historical background.

We might begin with a look at some of the medical disputes that prevailed in this country at the beginning of the 19th century, before the advent of modern biological science. Medicine had changed relatively little during the preceding two or three hundred years, and in many ways was still enshrouded in medieval mysticism. Clinical teaching was based largely on dogma, on sweeping theories conceived *a priori* by their inventors to provide unified explanations of all forms of disease, but with little or no foundation in fact. Neither inductive reasoning from systematic observation of patients, nor the use of physical measurements in the study of disease, nor the quantitative analysis of objective data had yet begun to influence the education or the behavior of most physicians.

Benjamin Rush: eye of a storm

Probably the most famous American physician of that time was Benjamin Rush of Philadelphia (1746–1813), who was the professor of medicine at the University of Pennsylvania. In this post, as doyen at the leading medical school of its day, Rush attracted to his lectures hundreds of students from all over the country, and his prolific writings were widely read. No man had a greater influence on American medical practice of that time—nor was any practitioner more controversial.

Arnold S. Relman, M.D., *is Editor of the* New England Journal of Medicine *and Professor of Medicine, Harvard Medical School at the Peter Bent Brigham Hospital, Boston.*

(Overleaf) Center photograph from Photo Trends. Background illustration, woodcut by Hans Weiditz, title page of Spiegel der Artzney *by Laurentius Friesen, Strasbourg, 1532; courtesy, Philadelphia Museum of Art, The Smith, Kline and French Laboratories Collection; photograph, A. J. Wyatt.*

Rush was a product of his times, a doctrinaire theoretician who acted from first principles and had deep religious and political convictions. He believed and taught that almost all diseases were potentially curable and that their basic cause was increased tension in blood vessels. To eliminate a hypothetical poisonous substance thought to be responsible for this condition, Rush advocated bleeding, purging, sweating, and drawing the poison to the surface by blistering the skin with local irritants. These measures were necessary, he thought, because the body had few defenses of its own against serious illness.

Rush's favorite medication was a mixture of calomel (mercurous chloride) and jalap (an organic resin), which he used vigorously and repeatedly, to obtain a violent purgative effect. He was also convinced of the great therapeutic value of bleeding, which he used in the treatment of most diseases. Bleeding and purging were, of course, ancient remedies, certainly not invented by Rush. But he was their apostle in the New World, and he sanctified their use by offering a theoretical explanation that made them seem to be logical, even necessary, tactics in the struggle with disease. He supported his views with the force of his personality and the fervor and eloquence of his speech and writing, attributes that never failed to impress laity and physicians alike.

We know today that in the vast majority of cases bleeding and purging could not possibly have done any good, and in most instances succeeded only in further weakening an already debilitated patient. Furthermore, chronic overdosage with calomel often led to symptoms of severe mercury poisoning. Yet, as an apostle, Rush believed so deeply in the truth of his theories, and was so confident that he was in

"Physicians are not by nature less disputatious than other men, so they have always had disagreements about the way their profession ought to be practiced."

When Doctors three the Labour share, No wonder Death attends them there. "The Chamber War" from *The English Dance of Death* (1815–16); verse by William Combe, drawing by Thomas Rowlandson.

61

"Rush's heroic therapeutic approach was put to its most dramatic test in the summer and fall of 1793 when a great epidemic of yellow fever struck Philadelphia, then an overcrowded, mosquito-ridden river port of some 45,000 inhabitants."

"The City & Port of Philadelphia, on the River Delaware from Kensington," engraving by William Birch and son Thomas, 1800.

"Probably the most famous American physician of that time was Benjamin Rush of Philadelphia (1746–1813), who was the professor of medicine at the University of Pennsylvania. No man had a greater influence on American medical practice of that time—nor was any practitioner more controversial."

Portrait by James Sharples, c. 1975.

fact helping patients with his treatments, that he persuaded others to believe it, too.

Rush's heroic therapeutic approach was put to its most dramatic test in the summer and fall of 1793 when a great epidemic of yellow fever struck Philadelphia, then an overcrowded, mosquito-ridden river port of some 45,000 inhabitants. Many fled the city, but before the epidemic had run its course about 8,000 persons became ill and more than half of them died. At great personal risk, Rush and his young apprentices remained in the city, working ceaselessly in caring for the sick. Their treatment, of course, consisted of bleeding and purging, which Rush applied with what must have been almost fanatical zeal. Some of his patients recovered, but many died, yet Rush remained convinced that his methods were correct.

Even while the epidemic was raging, voices were raised in criticism. Several of Rush's medical colleagues in Philadelphia and elsewhere were publicly skeptical, and some were appalled by what they considered to be the harm caused by his draconian methods. It is not clear how much of the early criticism was directed at Rush for purely personal and political motives (he was an ardent Whig and an outspoken champion of many controversial causes) and how much for medical reasons. In any case, the criticism grew sharper and more public, even appearing in the newspapers. Rush's most aggressive opponent was a layman, a vitriolic young Englishman by the name of William Cobbett, who came to Philadelphia in 1794 and soon became a pamphleteer for the Federalist cause. Cobbett's bitter attacks on Rush's medical methods, as well as on his political views, finally drove Rush to sue him for libel in 1797. Rush won the suit in 1799, but did not thereby silence his other critics.

An atmosphere of skepticism

Throughout the remainder of Rush's life, and for several decades after his death, bleeding and purging continued to be widely used by American physicians, many of them his former students. Although his theory of disease upon which his therapeutics had been based was quickly discarded and forgotten, Rush's methods survived until the latter part of the 19th century. And throughout this same period the controversy over these methods continued to rage.

Advocates, mostly established physicians, were certain that these remedies, properly employed, saved lives and hastened recovery. The opposition was voiced by some of the lay public, who were openly critical of *all* doctors; by certain physicians, such as Oliver Wendell Holmes and Jacob Bigelow of Boston, who had begun to take a skeptical view of most forms of heroic therapy; and by the practitioners of the several new "irregular" medical sects that were gaining many adherents during the early decades of the 19th century. Greatly varied in their own philosophies of medicine, these sects were united in the belief that the orthodox practitioners, with their zeal for bleeding and purging, did more harm than good. They were right, of course, but no one on either side of the question could marshal convincing evidence for his position. It apparently never occurred to doctors in those days, as it had not occurred to Rush himself, that the issue might have been settled by what modern physicians would call a "controlled clinical trial," that is, by careful observation of results in comparable groups of treated and untreated patients.

The controversy was in that sense never "settled." Rush's methods were never put to a definitive clinical test. Instead, they were simply washed away by the slowly advancing tide of medical progress. In the latter half of the century the new scientific methods of pathology and bacteriology began to establish the numerous specific and varied causes of diseases, and it became increasingly apparent that Rush's monistic theory of disease did not fit with the new facts. No one form of treatment could possibly be effective in all kinds of disease. At that time it was recognized that many diseases were self-limited and would likely improve without resort to heroic therapy. Furthermore, with the rise of the science of physiology, a new appreciation of the deleterious physiological effects of hemorrhage and profuse diarrhea raised questions about the rationality of compounding the injury of a spontaneous disease with the iatrogenic insults of bleeding and purging. Added to all this was a growing and widespread lay resistance to the use of these frightening and unpleasant measures.

Long after all the heat had gone out of the controversy, however, and the issue was no longer debated, many physicians continued to employ bleeding occasionally as a nonspecific treatment. In the 1909 edition of his famous textbook of medicine, Sir William Osler still recommended bloodletting as a useful form of symptomatic therapy in lobar pneumonia. Modern physicians have long since abandoned this practice and now reserve venesection only for those few conditions in which there

"Rush's favorite medication was a mixture of calomel and jalap, which he used vigorously and repeatedly, to obtain a violent purgative effect."
"Taking a Physick," engraving by James Gillray.

"Cobbett's bitter attacks on Rush's medical methods . . . finally drove Rush to sue him for libel in 1797."

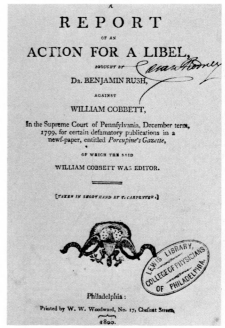

*"The two most important sects of the
period were the so-called botanical
practitioners, followers of a nature healer
and herbalist named Samuel Thomson,
and the homeopathic physicians, who
practiced a system of therapy expounded
by a German physician named
Samuel Hahnemann."*

Samuel Thomson (above), engraving
from *A Narrative, of the Life and
Medical Discoveries of Samuel Thomson*
written by himself, Boston, 1822; Samuel
Hahnemann (below), engraving by Anton
Wachsmann, *c.* 1812.

is a demonstrated excess of red blood cells in the circulation or an
excessive accumulation of iron in the body. They never use calomel
purgatives or the old technique of blistering.

19th-century movements: herbalism and homeopathy

The controversy over Rush's therapeutics lasted for more than half a
century, during the most discordant period in the history of American
medicine. In the early and mid 19th century the entire profession was
divided and quarrelsome. Educational and licensing standards were
lax. Medical cultists of all types and just plain quacks competed with
traditional practitioners for the public's trust, because orthodox medicine was, in fact, unable to generate much popular confidence.

The two most important sects of the period were the so-called botanical practitioners, followers of a nature healer and herbalist named
Samuel Thomson, and the homeopathic physicians, who practiced a
system of therapy expounded by a German physician named Samuel
Hahnemann. The Thomsonians were relatively uneducated healers
who believed in the curative and preventive powers of a variety of
harmless herbs and natural foods. Homeopaths, on the other hand,
were trained physicians who were convinced that diseases could be
cured by the use of infinitesimally small doses of certain drugs. By
modern standards, neither of these therapeutic approaches had the
slightest scientific rationale, but they did have the virtue of being essentially harmless. Hahnemann and his followers in fact made an important contribution in emphasizing that many patients recover from
even serious, acute illness merely with bed rest, fresh air, and proper
diet. Given the deplorable state of the orthodox medical practice of the
day, the *absence* of therapy was probably better than any of the measures usually employed by the traditional physicians.

The Thomsonian and homeopathic movements were in effect a rebellion against the regular profession, and the "regulars" reacted in a
predictably hostile way. Denunciations in the public and professional
press, legal sanctions, and expulsion from regular medical societies
were all part of the campaign. Competition and conflict with many other
types of unorthodox practitioners, as well as unethical behavior within
the ranks of the regulars themselves, added still further to the conten-
tiousness that divided the profession in the mid 19th century. Public
controversy was the order of the day. The basic reason, of course, was
the unscientific nature of medical practice, which made it impossible
to prove the value of any proposed treatment.

The era of scientific medicine

This age of discord was brought to a close by the rise of medical
science in the latter half of the 19th century and by the subsequent
social reform of the medical profession that was stimulated by scientific developments. The new sciences of physiology, biochemistry,
pathology, bacteriology, and pharmacology began to generate information profoundly significant to the understanding and treatment of

disease. Gradually it was recognized that to be effective medical practice would have to be based on science rather than belief. While physicians themselves might not be scientists (although a few were), they would increasingly need a sound scientific education and would have to learn to apply scientific principles in their clinical practices.

Another consequence of the rise of medical science was the extensive reform of the medical profession that took place in the late 19th and early 20th centuries. State and national medical societies were strengthened, codes of ethical behavior were adopted, and licensing and educational standards were improved. The homeopaths were for the most part absorbed into the regular profession, and most of the sects that had flourished in the 19th century were heard from no more. Quackery was brought under better legal control, although it was never entirely eliminated.

By the end of the first two decades of this century, medicine had firmly established itself as a rational discipline. The medical profession was strictly regulated not only by legal and ethical codes, but more importantly by the methods of natural science. Bitter public controversies about principles and theories of practice were no longer necessary because it had become possible to answer specific questions by scientific observation and experimentation. To the lay public, therefore, it might have seemed as if the doctors were at last in accord on most matters and that controversy would disappear from the medical scene.

Science and controversy: inseparable companions

Controversy did not disappear with the emergence of scientific medicine, however. It simply became more muted, less visible to the public, and concerned largely with technical and scientific questions that were of interest only to the profession. Controversy continued to exist—and exists today—because it is inherent in the scientific method upon which medicine is based. Science and controversy are, in fact, inseparable companions. It is worth noting briefly why this should be so.

There are no absolute truths in any natural science, only hypotheses

"*Hahnemann and his followers in fact made an important contribution in emphasizing that many patients recover from even serious, acute illness merely with bed rest, fresh air, and proper diet.*"

Lithograph from the School of Daumier satirizing the controversy between regular physicians (allopaths) and homeopaths in the 19th century: Homeopath: *If you take me you'll die of the disease.* Allopath: *If you take me you'll die of the cure.* Patient: *It's all the same to me.*

"*The Thomsonians were relatively uneducated healers who believed in the curative and preventive powers of a variety of harmless herbs and natural foods.*"

that are more or less satisfactory and therefore more or less durable. Hypotheses that cannot be tested or challenged are not useful, and the advance of scientific knowledge involves a continual reshaping of ideas to conform with the experimental and clinical data. Controversy arises inevitably when there are hypotheses but insufficient data—that is to say, when there are questions without factual answers. Under these circumstances different and often conflicting interpretations of data will be offered, which can only be resolved by the accumulation of more data.

Controversy in the present era of scientific medicine is in this sense a manifestation of ignorance, just as it was in the prescientific era. But the difference is that contemporary scientific controversies usually lead to their own resolution, whereas the controversies of the previous era were essentially unresolvable. Scientific controversies act as a guide and stimulus to research aimed at obtaining new data that will settle the question at issue. Viewed in this perspective, controversy is a powerful motivating force in research, probably no less important than curiosity itself. Controversy in medicine is a healthy sign, a reflection of the ongoing process of self-criticism and reevaluation through which physicians are kept abreast of new information.

During the past decade or two the public has once again become aware of disagreement within the medical profession. This awareness may in part be explained by a generally heightened level of public interest in and understanding of medical matters. To judge from the attention accorded to medical items in the lay press and other communications media, medicine has become big news.

Not only has the public become more avid for news about issues and developments in medicine, but the medical profession has become more willing to communicate with the public. There is an increasing recognition by physicians that they have a responsibility to explain to the public what they are doing and why. Health care is now an enormous industry in this country; it consumes 8% of our gross national product and receives only slightly more support from private than from public funds. Medical controversies now often involve questions of great social concern. Doctors need the understanding and support of the public in dealing with these issues. The public, in turn, has increasingly indicated that it *expects* the medical profession to be more communicative and more responsive to public needs. The net result is that patients, government, and the public at large are now interested in questions that were formerly the exclusive domain of physicians.

Current focuses of debate

Important, unresolved—and therefore controversial—scientific and technological questions abound in medicine, and most involve one or all of three basic aspects: the scientific and technological, the economic, and the ethical or philosophical. A few detailed examples of specific issues will serve to illustrate how modern controversies arise and how they are being dealt with. Some of the most urgent of the

66

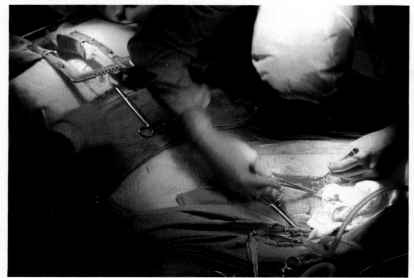

unsolved medical problems concern the treatment of choice for coronary artery disease, which is the most common cause of death in the
U.S., the most effective means of managing diabetes, and the highly
publicized debate over the possible hazards of mammography.

In the case of coronary artery disease, the controversy revolves
around the alternatives of coronary bypass surgery or medical management of the condition. While it is known that the bypass operation
relieves the pain of angina pectoris, there is no proof that the procedure
is effective in preventing heart attack or prolonging the survival of
patients with severe coronary artery disease. Since its development
about 10 years ago, the operation has become increasingly popular. At
present about 70,000 such procedures are being performed annually in
the U.S. — at a total estimated cost of nearly $1 billion. Is the relief of
pain a sufficient reason for subjecting a patient to the risks, discomfort,
and expense of such an operation? How can it be determined if the
surgery is effective in prolonging the survival of coronary patients?
Surely, one might think, it ought to be easy enough to determine
whether an operation really saves lives. Unfortunately, the only way to
demonstrate beyond reasonable doubt the effectiveness of a surgical
procedure is to carry out a full-scale prospective clinical trial — that is,
to observe the course of the disease in two comparable groups of
patients, one treated surgically and the other medically.

Another major controversy in medicine today concerns the best
method of treating diabetes. Not only do physicians disagree over the
management of blood sugar levels for patients taking insulin, they also
disagree over the efficacy and safety of the oral antidiabetic pills that
are often used for patients with only mild diabetes. Surprisingly, most
diabetics now die not as a result of acidosis or high blood sugar, but
rather as the long-term result of the peripheral vascular diseases to
which they are particularly vulnerable. Even more surprising is the fact
that physicians do not yet know whether close regulation of the blood

*"In the case of coronary artery disease,
the controversy revolves around the
alternatives of coronary bypass surgery or
medical management of the condition."*

67

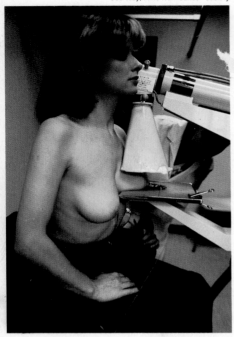

"The issue is far from resolution because precise information about both risks and benefits of mass screening by mammography has yet to be obtained."

sugar level can prevent these vascular complications. Furthermore, an additional controversy has developed concerning the side effects of antidiabetic pills, based on recent evidence that suggests that oral hypoglycemic agents may actually increase the incidence of vascular disease. Again, only a properly designed and controlled clinical trial — a lengthy and expensive project — can resolve this question. A further difficulty, related also to the problem of coronary artery disease, is that modern medical science remains ignorant of the basic biological processes involved in vascular diseases. Such knowledge can come only from laboratory research of a relatively fundamental kind. Like controlled clinical trials, basic research is costly and takes many years to produce conclusive findings.

A final and particularly interesting example of medical controversy is the debate over the use of mammography for early detection of breast cancer. This disease, the most common malignant tumor in women, is responsible for about 34,000 deaths per year in the U.S.; 90,000 new cases are discovered annually. Breast cancer has always provoked attention and produced fear, but the announcement in 1974 that both Betty Ford and Happy Rockefeller had — within a few weeks of each other — undergone surgery for cancer of the breast led to what can only be described as a public panic. Women sought breast examinations in such numbers that diagnostic facilities were swamped.

This event served to focus public attention on a medical controversy that had been simmering for some time: Is routine periodic X-ray examination of the breasts (mammography) a safe and reliable method of detecting early cancerous lesions? Mammography had been highly recommended during the 1960s, advocated both for the evaluation of lumps detected during physical examination of the breasts and for routine screening for early cancer in asymptomatic patients. For the latter purpose, public programs were organized to encourage all women over age 35 to submit to a yearly mammographic examination, in hope of discovering minimal and potentially curable lesions that would otherwise escape notice. Recently, however, not only the efficacy but also the safety of the process has been challenged. Some critics have suggested that exposure to radiation — even at the low dosage levels employed in mammography — may in itself cause a significant number of breast cancers.

The issue is far from resolution because precise information about both risks and benefits of mass screening by mammography has yet to be obtained. Indeed, it would take many years to accumulate enough data to form a definite conclusion. In many ways the mammography issue is a paradigm of the kind of "cost-benefit" problem that is stirring public and professional discussions of current medical practices. The advocates of general use of mammography are primarily those physicians convinced from professional experience that the technique can aid in early cancer detection and thereby save lives — or at least facilitate more effective treatment. On the other hand, to achieve any benefit, mammography must be applied wholesale to large populations, and

68

this process raises serious questions about costs and hazards. Such questions can be answered best by epidemiologists, economists, and experts in radiation safety—specialists who deal not with individual cases but with bloodless statistical and economic data.

Clinical trials and their inherent problems

All of the current controversies presented here have one element in common—that is, they can be resolved only through scientifically based, carefully constructed, long-term controlled clinical trials. As we have already noted such research programs are extremely costly and require long periods of time before reliable results can be obtained. Length and expense, however, are relatively minor problems, when compared with the many other difficulties inherent in the process.

First there is the problem of establishing initial comparability of the experimental subjects. This involves matching for age, sex, ethnic background, medical history, and any other factors relevant to the condition under investigation. Once the comparability of all subjects has been established, it is extremely important to ensure that all members of experimental and control groups receive consistent treatment. There are also ethical and psychological problems involved in the selection and assignment of patients to different treatment groups. Fully informed consent must of course be obtained—patients may, however, have strong personal beliefs about the type of treatment they think will be most successful. A patient who has great faith in the coronary bypass procedure, for example, may not be willing to allow his medical treatment to be determined by random assignment. Similar objections may be encountered among the attending physicians, who may be convinced that one mode of treatment is necessary for some patients but possibly dangerous for others. Finally, there is the problem of proper interpretation of test results. Even when analyzed by trained biostatisticians, these results may not always yield the hoped-for unambiguous answer. Even when a controlled prospective clinical trial has been carried out, it does not guarantee that all disagreements will be settled. Such studies may, in fact, have precisely the opposite result—they may in themselves kindle new controversy.

We must remember that underlying most, if not all, medical controversies of the day are basic biological riddles. If these could be solved, many of the dilemmas posed by contemporary medical practices would disappear. Most debates about diagnostic or therapeutic techniques, such as those we have discussed above, are concerned with "half-way" methods, that is to say, with empirical, palliative approaches that really do not get to the heart of the difficulty. Even while we attempt to bring some order and rationality into our empirical medical practices through the application of careful clinical trials, we must not neglect basic research. Only through the understanding of nature will we ultimately acquire the definitive means of preventing and treating disease.

FOR ADDITIONAL READING:

Binger, Carl. *Revolutionary Doctor: Benjamin Rush, 1746–1813.* New York: W. W. Norton and Co., 1966.

Bordley, James, and Harvey, A. McGehee. *Two Centuries of American Medicine.* Philadelphia: W. B. Saunders Co., 1976.

Culliton, Barbara J. "Cancer Institute Unilaterally Issues New Restrictions on Mammography." *Science* 196 (1977): 853–857.

Fuchs, Victor R. *Who Shall Live?* New York: Basic Books, 1975.

Ingelfinger, Franz J.; Relman, Arnold S.; and Finland, Maxwell, eds. *Controversy in Internal Medicine.* 2 vols. Philadelphia: W. B. Saunders Co., 1966–1974.

Knowles, John H., ed. "Doing Better and Feeling Worse: Health in the United States." *Daedalus* 106, no. 1 (Winter, 1977).

Kolata, Gina B. "Coronary Bypass Surgery: Debate Over Its Benefits." *Science* 194 (1976):1263–1265.

Rothstein, William G. *American Physicians in the Nineteenth Century.* Baltimore: Johns Hopkins University Press, 1972.

Shryock, Richard H. *Medicine in America.* Baltimore: Johns Hopkins Press, 1966.

The Therapeutic Relationship

by Eric J. Cassell, M.D.

After the physician had finished examining his patient (who had had a heart attack), he walked down the hospital corridor to the nurse's station to write his findings and diagnosis. Before leaving for the evening, the physician decided to go back and look in again at the patient, a man in his fifties whom the doctor had not previously known. The patient was lying propped up in the bed with his eyes closed. For one awful moment the doctor could see no sign of breathing and it flashed through his mind that the patient was dead. The quick panic subsided as the man turned in bed. Still somewhat shaken, the doctor spoke a bit about what would be done and how the breathing discomfort would ease, and saying goodnight, left.

That brief but frightening experience is known to every physician. Every parent has also had the same feeling at one time or another looking in at a sick or sleeping child. We understand why parents get so terrified—it is their child, after all. But what is the basis of the strange relationship that exists between doctor and patient, often previously strangers, that causes one to trust his life to the other, who in turn feels that what threatens that life threatens him?

Ideas about the mysterious, even mystical, bond that we call the doctor-patient relationship have evolved throughout history and vary from one culture to another. Our Western view of this relationship has changed dramatically in recent times, as physicians try to establish a balance between the role of the teacher-physician described by Plato, and that of purveyor of the 20th century's runaway technology.

The doctor-patient relationship has been little studied or appreciated by either doctors or their patients. Everyone, however, is familiar with the idealized concepts of the physician as paternal and authoritarian, tending the helpless sick. The diversity of the physician's role as healer and friend is symbolized by the pictures of a physician sitting at the patient's bedside anxiously waiting for the crisis to pass. One classic painting portrays a venerable family doctor putting his stethoscope to a doll held by his young patient, exemplifying the necessary union of science and sympathy. This is the image of the doctor that has come down to us from Hippocrates, the father of Western medicine. He expected physicians, more than most mortals, to be honest and objective as well as empathetic, trustworthy, gentle, and kind.

The pace of medical progress, however, is threatening our sentimental view of the doctor-patient relationship. It should be reexamined, that

Eric J. Cassell, M.D., *is Clinical Professor in the Department of Public Health at Cornell University Medical College, New York City.*

70

we might preserve the art of the true physician, reemphasizing his or her role on the personal level.

The basis of the therapeutic relationship lies somewhere between the traditional image of the doctor as the sage family friend tending the helpless sick, and the newer view of him as merely a purveyor of a specialized technology who is to be considered in the same market-place terms as an engineer or a carpenter. That is to say, the doctor-patient relationship can take many forms, depending on the partici-pants and the situation. Lately we have come to see the therapeutic relationship not as a thing, but rather as a social process occurring between individuals who are acted on by social norms and by biological and psychological forces often beyond their control.

Questions that both physicians and patients need to ask themselves in exploring this subject are why the relationship has fallen into disre-pute in some quarters and how it has come to be seen in such techno-logical and mechanical terms. These questions and their answers are of great significance. I phrase them as I do because to me the doctor-patient relationship remains now, as always, the essential element in the care of the sick.

The key to understanding the importance of the therapeutic relation-ship lies in understanding what it means to be sick. If the ill were not somehow different from the well in their attitudes (which not everybody seems to recognize) and in the peculiar status that society allows them, and if drugs and machines were all that were needed to make sick people better again, then there would be no need for the doctor-patient relationship at all.

What it means to be ill

The sick person finds himself different in that he has lost the sense of personal indestructibility that well people enjoy, the unconscious con-fidence that misfortune always befalls somebody else. In illness we learn the truth—that the body is a frail machine just a heartbeat from death. The depression that so often occurs after a heart attack is due in part to the sudden realization that death is possible. In long-term illness the patient often feels that the body will never be trustworthy again, and in very serious illness the reasoning may even be impaired.

The patient also finds himself "disconnected" from his usual world by his illness. Normally we are at home in our world, knowing who and where we are. We do not have to look at our feet in order to walk, nor wear a name tag to be identified. Illness changes all that. The very symptoms disconnect the patient. The problems are compounded if the patient requires hospitalization. He finds himself surrounded by strangers and living by different rules. If healthy friends avoid the sick person, the disconnection from a familiar reality can become even more striking. The loss of connection also sometimes comes from within the ill as they lose interest in the world around them.

This failure of reason, loss of the sense of indestructibility, and the disconnection from the world that occur in illness combine to reinforce

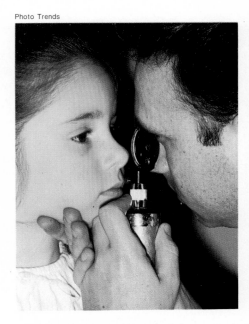

"But what is the basis of the strange relationship that exists between doctor and patient. . .?"

". . . if drugs and machines were all that were needed to make sick people better again, then there would be no need for the doctor-patient relationship at all."

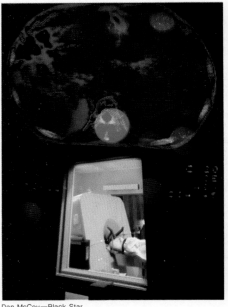

"Normally we are at home in our world, knowing who and where we are. We do not have to look at our feet in order to walk, nor wear a name tag to be identified."

perhaps the most important and frightening aspect of illness that the sick person must endure—the loss of his sense of being able to control himself, his body, and his world.

The sick do not do, they are done to. Aleksandr Solzhenitsyn's novel *Cancer Ward* can use the world of the cancer patient as a metaphor for the totalitarian state precisely because we all know that the sick are powerless. How much the sick suffer from loss of control, reasoning power, indestructibility, and connection with the world varies with the severity of the disease and the patient's perception of the illness, as well as with personality and social factors.

When symptoms of illness occur, the sick person seeks reasons and causes from his own limited knowledge or experience, or from the experience of others. From what is in fact a trivial complaint, he might well construct an idea of disease that is frightening—because it is forced to fit many other factors in the patient's life, not merely the physical facts. One patient might be convinced that pain in his joints is arthritis, because his mother had arthritis. Another, out of work and looking for a job, might be scared into thinking that severe hip pain is cancer or some crippling disease because it fits already existing fears that she will not be able to find work and support her family.

Some diseases, such as tuberculosis, stand as symbols for isolation from the healthy, and until recently the word *cancer* was avoided in polite conversation. Although some people tolerate the loss of control, or even the disconnection of illness, for many these are shattering experiences. The social setting of health care can make them better or worse. In an intensive care unit men and women are in adjacent beds and often all semblance of privacy or personal identification is lost.

It is in this context that the doctor has to interact with the patient, an interaction that is influenced by the patient's past, present, and even the possibility of future illness. Physicians have to bring their personali-

72

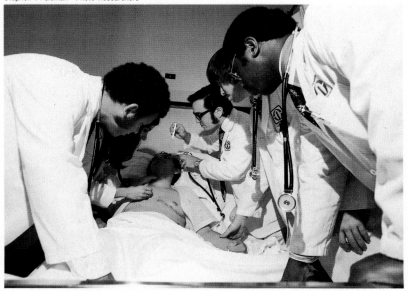

ties into the interaction, and since their abilities to relate to patients differ, so do their abilities to deal with the phenomena of illness.

"The sick do not do, they are done to."

Illness is so frightening to most people that they often pretend that serious illness can never occur, or that they will always be able to handle things just as they do when they are well. Such a viewpoint is understandable enough considering how most people deny fate, but it can lead to difficulties if it encourages the view that the physician is merely a technologist whose knowledge of diseases and their treatment is all that is needed for the care of the sick. It is obvious that some doctors will deal better, some worse with the phenomena of illness, just as their personal interactions are better with some patients than with others. Thus, in seeking a doctor, a patient is not only looking for a technically competent practitioner, but also for a physician who will deal with the person and those personal factors that are, or will be, of serious consequence to the patient in his or her illness.

"In an intensive care unit . . . men and women are in adjacent beds and often all semblance of privacy or personal identification is lost."

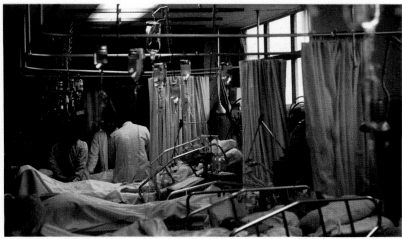

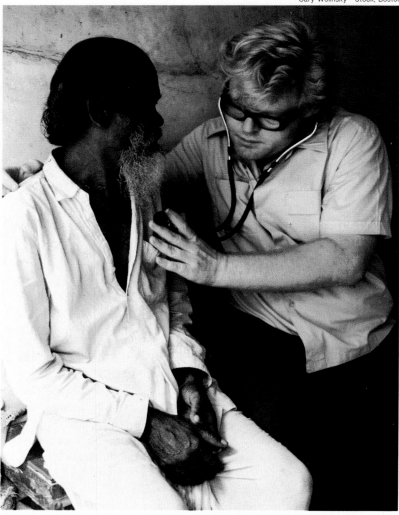

"Western-trained physicians have a lot of trouble establishing a relationship with patients in societies holding other views of illness. These patients simply do not trust a Western doctor's knowledge."

The physician in the therapeutic relationship

To better understand the relationship described, it is necessary to examine what the doctor and patient each contribute to it aside from their personalities. The physician brings technical expertise, drawn from training and experience. This knowledge includes not only the practical skills involved in the treatment of patients, but also a knowledge or perception of disease, an ability to bring order to and to remove mystery from its many manifestations.

It is important to realize that while we tend to think about our illnesses in disease terms ("my cough, fever, and chest pain come from pneumonia.") the word *pneumonia,* as with all disease names, stands for the way modern Western scientific medicine sees the world of illness. Much as the 12-tone scale is a way of slicing up the world of musical sound, but nevertheless is not the only way (witness the strangeness of Oriental music to our ears), so too the disease system which American doctors use is only one way of understanding what

74

makes people sick. The Western system, however, has been a very useful one, judging from its success in conquering many of the infectious plagues of the past and in dealing with such conditions as heart disease, cancer, and stroke, which still cause much suffering.

It is not only doctors who look at the sick using a disease system. So do most of us in this society. It is important not only that the system works, but that it is culturally acceptable. Western-trained physicians have a lot of trouble establishing a relationship with patients in societies holding other views of illness. And just as Oriental music sounds strange to our ears, so too would the explanations of a traditional Chinese doctor. We would like to believe that our scientific ideas are correct and that those of the Chinese are wrong—but that cannot be entirely true. No system of healing lasts for many centuries unless it is at least partly effective.

The basic point remains that the knowledge the doctor brings to the therapeutic relationship must be culturally consonant with his patient and not merely true, since all explanations of illness as well as role relationships between doctor (healer) and patient are related to the belief system of the culture in which they occur. This is underscored by the fact that explanations of illness for most of history and in most cultures have proven inadequate or false with the passage of time, despite the fact that they served their function while they were in vogue.

A main point, however, is that while everyone is aware that technical expertise is part of the doctor's contribution to the therapeutic relationship, the physician can also bring healing skills of which neither he nor the patient may be aware. This is particularly true in Western scientific medicine. The healing skills, which involve personal and moral concern for the patient, are necessary in dealing with the more emotional or abstract aspects of illness mentioned earlier.

The doctor's rational system of explanations helps solve the patient's problems of reasoning in illness. What is a mystery to the patient, and consequently an exacerbating factor, is not a mystery to the doctor. In this regard it is important that the patient's disease have a name, since the name of a thing is seen as containing it. To name the beasts of the field was to control them. The name serves a social function, since it allows the patient to tell friends and family the nature of his trouble. It also has institutional functions when it can be stated on insurance forms, disability forms, or simply letters of excuse.

The physician as a person, not just his or her knowledge, is essential to help the patient feel whole again. The physician's high social status, which pertains in almost all social groups, helps the patient replace lost social and physical connection. The patient connects with the doctor ("my doctor" is a generally heard phrase), who in turn is connected to the hospital—in itself a source of confusion—and to the world around.

The doctor's own, often overdeveloped, sense of indestructibility helps compensate for or repair the patient's own injured sense of body. In fact, people are often surprised when doctors become ill, as though such things are not supposed to happen to physicians. The doctor

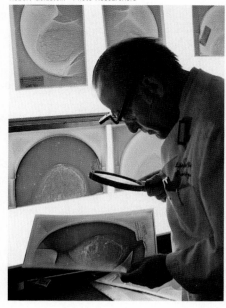

"Often the doctor's expertise is essential in protecting the patient from unnecessary technology."

75

"When we are sick, we are excused from many of our social and personal obligations. The sick are allowed to be passive and dependent."

serves as an alternative method of control for the patient, helping him once again restore some balance in his relationships with other persons, the outer world, and his body.

In all of this I have portrayed the doctor as an extension of the patient, as though the two had some strong connection with one another. I believe that to be true.

The physician also brings to the relationship access to other parts of the medical care system—such as medical specialists, drug prescriptions, diagnostic treatment facilities, hospitals, and other institutions. This function has become increasingly important in the highly technical and specialized world of medical care that exists in Western cultures.

It would be hard for a lay person even to find his way around the corridors of a modern hospital, much less through the equally baffling maze of competing technologies and specialty functions of modern medicine. Often the doctor's expertise is essential in protecting the patient from unnecessary technology.

The social and moral function of physicians has been much discussed in recent years, with special attention paid to their ability to provide access to and to legitimize the sick role. Without this cachet, the patient cannot assume the special position that is assigned to the sick in this and in other societies. When we are sick, we are excused from many of our social and personal obligations. The sick are allowed to be passive and dependent. They are allowed to talk about themselves and their illness and they do not have to work. The other side of the coin is that the sick provide an opportunity for others to give to them and to nurse them. The physician may also approve or even reinforce the reentry of the sick person into the healthy world. This function of physicians is illustrated on a larger scale by the change in status of alcoholism in recent times. Previously a moral and a legal problem that called for punishment, alcoholism is now increasingly considered to be an illness that requires care. The physical rehabilitation movement that followed World War II also illustrates how medical wisdom has made a whole group of people well again by decree. Increasingly, the permanently disabled are being considered healthy and productive members of society.

The Platonic concept of the doctor as teacher is not commonly discussed, but it is nonetheless significant. The educational process may, when extreme, apply to all aspects of the patient's life; but it certainly applies to matters connected to health or sickness. Attitudes toward drug use, exercise, and cigarette smoking are obvious examples. Less apparent to both doctor and patient, but no less important, are basic beliefs that the physician transmits about sickness and its course and about attitudes toward the body. Each episode of illness, no matter how trivial, provides an opportunity for the doctor to teach. One physician, for example, may counsel that illness must be borne in passive silence, while another may argue the opposite. One doctor may promote the attitude that the body is full of dangerous hidden mysteries that may strike at any time, while another maintains that it is a mutable friend. It is regrettable that more physicians are not aware of their role in this regard, and do not give more thought to what they teach.

In this aspect of the relationship, as in others, the patient is not merely a passive recipient. He or she may reject the lesson and the physician with it. Indeed, the patient is also the teacher. Doctors are exposed to wide variations in human behavior. They learn the depths of human suffering, but also the largeness of the human spirit. They find that there are many ways that life can be lived, some more successful than others. In other words, they are exposed to the realities of existence, great and small, inspiring and mean, and this exposure inevitably shapes their own lives, their work, and their moral beliefs.

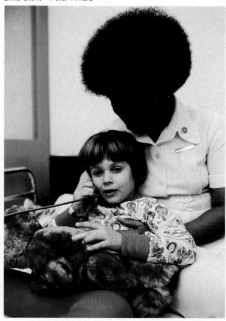

"The other side of the coin is that the sick provide an opportunity for others to give to them and to nurse them."

77

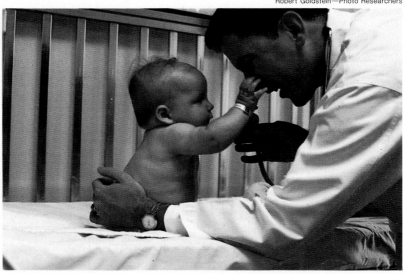

"Starting in infancy . . . all of us become aware of acceptable symptoms and ways in which symptoms must be expressed in order to warrant the care of a doctor."

The patient's contribution to the relationship

The patient brings to the therapeutic relationship a need expressed by symptoms, all of which are culturally conditioned and are part and parcel of "naming the beast." Starting in infancy, as part of socialization, all of us become aware of acceptable symptoms and ways in which symptoms must be expressed in order to warrant the care of a doctor. That is, we all soon learn what others consider illness. A child, for example, soon finds out that "My throat hurts, Mom," deserves a different kind of attention from "I don't want to go to school." Adults know that fever seems to have more respectability than many other symptoms of illness. But in whatever terms, symptoms are the expression of need. The patient usually brings to the relationship a desire to get better. That is considered part of his social responsibility. Patients are expected to be honest and trusting in the relationship, as well as providing physical access to their person in a manner not usually accorded to strangers. Finally, of course, the patient provides monetary reward to the doctor.

Again there is another side to the coin. It is the patients and their needs that validate the doctor's knowledge, his professional existence, and confirm him as a person. It is the basis of his status. In short, without patients the doctor is not a doctor.

Acting as client, the patient exercises powerful controls over both the form and substance of the physician's act. This may be done through a self-determined referral system, in which consultation is sought when the illness is perceived as beyond the competence of the primary doctor. Or the first doctor may be caused to do further diagnostic tests, to seek consultation, or even hospitalize the patient.

These demands may be explicit, but they are more often made merely by the continued presence of symptoms. Physicians as a group have often changed what is considered good medical practice primarily because of the expectations of patients. The best example of this is how rapidly the Papanicolaou cervical smear for cancer detection (Pap

"To deny a wide social view of medicine would be to deny the gains that will result from a much wider dissemination and utilization of modern medical technology."

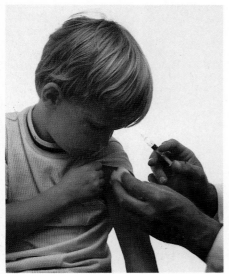

smear) became part of a proper physical examination, more because of patients' expectations than professional education.

The widespread and increasing knowledge about medicine and science among the lay public has been of great importance in changing the practice of medicine, particularly in urban societies. The modern patient simply knows more than patients ever have before and because of that is increasingly becoming an intellectual partner in his own care.

If a patient's demands are perceived as excessive, however, the bond of trust that holds the physician to the patient may be diminished. The growing fear of malpractice is the negative side of patients' desires for autonomy, and such fears also diminish the trust between physician and patient. It is virtually impossible to practice good medicine if either doctor or patient perceives the other as an adversary.

Two views of the therapeutic relationship

The doctor-patient relationship as I have described it leads to a view of this interaction that is different in emphasis from the description by social scientists of the past generation. The eminent sociologist Talcott Parsons saw the doctor-patient relationship as a perfect place to explore many other social interactions. Following his lead (or in reaction to it), social scientists have often described the therapeutic relationship in terms of social roles, role conflicts, or power conflicts within the role model. Their view of the doctor-patient relationship is that it is primarily technical and social, whereas what I have described above is primarily technical and personal. There are several reasons for the different viewpoints that are important to understanding the relationship. In the primarily social view, the sick person is seen simply as a well person with a disease, rather than as qualitatively different not only physically but also socially, emotionally, and mentally. Indeed, seeing sick people solely in the light of the diseases they have is so widely accepted that those features of the state of being ill such as the loss of the sense of indestructibility or the loss of control have not been the subject of sufficient study.

If one forgets that the doctor-patient relationship itself is an important element in caring for the sick, it is possible to make the error of believing that the physician's job is primarily the use of technology for cure. When that happens, health can be seen as merely a commodity that is purchased from doctors. In its most radical form, this view equates medical practice with any other marketplace activity. A common idea that follows from the technical-social understanding of the doctor-patient relationship is that health comes primarily from medical care. More recently, as the concept of preventive medicine has become more widely accepted and practiced, health has begun to be recognized as a result of such care. In both instances, however, access to health is seen as access to care. Such commodity views of medical practice are only true to a limited degree, since the healthy people in a population are generally those who have never been seriously ill. It is becoming increasingly obvious that health is now and has always

"The patient alone is often powerless to act against his illness, the thief of autonomy."

Edward Lettau—Peter Arnold

FOR ADDITIONAL READING:

Cassell, Eric J. *The Healer's Art*. New York: Lippincott, 1976.

Hall, Edward T. *The Hidden Dimension*. New York: Doubleday and Co., 1966.

Hippocrates. *The Genuine Works of Hippocrates*. Translated by Francis Adams. New York: William Wood and Co., 1886.

Laín Entralgo, Pedro. *Doctor and Patient*. Translated by Frances Partridge. New York: McGraw-Hill, 1969.

The Therapy of the Word in Classical Antiquity. Edited and translated by L. J. Rather and John M. Sharp. New Haven: Yale University Press, 1970.

Lévi-Strauss, Claude. *Structural Anthropology*. Garden City, New York: Doubleday and Co., 1967.

Magraw, Richard M. *Ferment in Medicine*. Philadelphia: W. B. Saunders, 1966.

Ramsey, Paul. *The Patient as Person*. New Haven: Yale University Press, 1970.

Solzhenitsyn, Aleksandr. *Cancer Ward*. New York: Bantam Books, 1969.

been related far more to behavioral, social, and environmental factors than to medical care. Like it or not, medical care is properly seen as illness care—not health care.

Therefore, the two views of the doctor-patient relationship, primarily social and primarily personal, rest on differing ideas about the nature and source of health and the function of doctors. Two developments in modern society may widen the gap between these beliefs rather than bringing them closer together into a necessary amalgam. The first, supporting the technical-social view, is the increasing use of the technology of medicine, paraprofessionals, and nonmedical personnel to spread technical advances more widely. Here involvement of physicians is often seen as unnecessary or even wasteful. The opposite trend, supporting the technical-personal view, is the increasing size of the aged population.

Here, and in dealing with the chronic and incurable complaints that increasingly make up the disease picture of modern societies, patients are better served by a medicine resting on a basic understanding of the personal nature of the therapeutic relationship. It seems important, however, that both major views of the therapeutic relationship be better understood. To deny a wide social view of medicine would be to deny the gains that will result from a much wider dissemination and utilization of modern medical technology. On the other hand, to deny the intimately personal nature of illness, and with it the healing as well as technical functions of physicians, would force medicine increasingly into a technological mold whose benefits might well be many, but whose cost in human terms would be high.

The medicine of a society can never be looked at apart from the other aspects of the society. All around us we see attempts to bring technology back under control as servant, not master. In medicine, that trend is expressed by a growing move toward a medicine of persons and not merely of diseases. The demand for patients' rights, for respect for the autonomy of patients, is an expression of that trend. But what is autonomy? The autonomous person is one who can make choices and act in a manner that reflects his or her true and authentic self. But we have already discussed the power of illness to undermine autonomy, to remove choice as well as the ability to act, and, as the result of disability and suffering, even to impair the dignity and authenticity of the patient. The concept of autonomy can show us the fundamental function of the doctor-patient relationship. The patient alone is often powerless to act against his illness, the thief of autonomy. The physician alone, without regard to the nature of the person he is treating, can act against the illness only as a deliverer of technology. But together in that unique, intimate human bond, the doctor-patient relationship, they can fulfill the basic function of medicine, which is the preservation of autonomy within the constraints of fate.

The Boundaries of Medicine

by Abraham B. Bergman, M.D.

Who are the healthiest people in the world? Though there are no official standards for judging states of health, few would dispute bestowing the title on three groups living in remote areas. The world's highest concentrations of inhabitants over the age of 100 are in the village of Vilcabamba in the Andes Mountains of Ecuador, in Hunza in the mountains of Kashmir, and in Abkhazia in the Caucasus Mountains of the Georgian Soviet Socialist Republic. Alexander Leaf of Harvard Medical School visited these Shangri-Las seeking common threads that would explain the longevity and vigor of these people.[1] In his travels he did not come across many coronary intensive care units, kidney dialysis centers, CAT-scanners, or multiphasic screening laboratories. He didn't find any health maintenance organizations, professional standards review organizations, or health systems agencies. In fact, the only physicians he mentions are a couple of scientific colleagues involved in similar studies of the aging process.

Leaf found that the centenarians shared some common features:

(1) Long-lived parents: One has little choice about one's genes, but their importance should be recognized.

(2) Physical activity: They all lived in mountainous areas and constantly were clambering up and down narrow trails.

(3) Scant diet: In the United States the average daily caloric intake is 3,300 calories. In contrast, the average intake of the group in Kashmir was 2,000 calories, in Georgia 1,800 calories, and in Ecuador only 1,200 calories. These people consumed relatively little animal fat; protein and fat were largely of vegetable origin. Leaf saw neither obesity nor undernutrition.

(4) High social status: The old people have a sense of usefulness and are esteemed for their wisdom. Even those well over 100, for the most part, continue to perform essential duties and contribute to the economy of the community. A mandatory retirement age is unknown.

(5) Sexual activity: Women pass through menopause with little effect on their libido, and the men retain potency to a very advanced age.

The point is that one's health will be affected far more by life-style than by encounters with physicians. Gordon T. Stewart of the University of Glasgow says:

It is often thought or pretended that improvement in health can be bought by expenditure upon ultra-modern hospitals and medical training. The sad fact is that modern medicine can claim only some limited advances, mainly in the relief

Abraham B. Bergman, M.D., *is Director of Outpatient Services, Children's Orthopedic Hospital and Medical Center and Professor of Pediatrics and Health Services, University of Washington, Seattle.*

81

Photographs, John Launois—Black Star

"The world's highest concentrations of inhabitants over the age of 100 are in the village of Vilcabamba in the Andes Mountains of Ecuador, in Hunza in the mountains of Kashmir, and in Abkhazia in the Caucasus Mountains of the Georgian Soviet Socialist Republic."

of suffering and prolongation of elderly life. Improvement of general health in any community comes now, as it has in the past, from relatively simple ameliorations of feeding, housing, sanitation, general education, and preventive medicine, in that order. Curative medicine and surgery, including some spectacular advances, come lower on the list and usually make no difference to vital statistics even if they do a great deal for morale and relief of sickness.[2]

Seventh-day Adventists

It is not necessary to trek to mountain ranges abroad to observe the beneficial effects of life-style on health. Studies made among California Seventh-day Adventist church members showed that risk of death from many diseases is lower for this group than for persons of corresponding age and sex in the California population as a whole. Adventists abstain from smoking, drinking alcoholic beverages, and eating meat. Not only are Adventist death rates markedly lower from diseases directly related to smoking and drinking, but they are lower from other diseases as well.

The effects of life-style on disease have long been known. The subject has received scant attention, however, because of the fatalistic belief that nothing can be done. Until recently, virtually the whole field of preventive medicine has been ceded to counterculture practitioners, who through either idealistic or profit motives tout almost any theory that is antimedicine. A multimillion-dollar health food industry capitalizes on the fears of the alienated and the abdication by the medical profession of legitimate preventive measures.

Overselling medical care

In the last year or two, more has been said about preventive medicine in respectable circles. Not surprisingly, the reason is money. Bluntly, the benefits of medical care have been oversold to the American peo-

82

*" 'Curative medicine and surgery,
including some spectacular advances,
come lower on the list and usually make
no difference to vital statistics even if
they do a great deal for morale and relief
of sickness.' "*

ple. Health programs are being cut because they cost too much and
their benefits are not apparent. General Motors says its health insurance payments exceed those to U.S. Steel, one of its largest suppliers.
In fiscal 1960 national health expenditures totalled $25.9 billion; in
1976 the figure was $139.3 billion, over 8.6% of our gross national
product. Health is now competing for dollars not only with defense,
foreign aid, and highways, but with programs of comparable social
value such as those aimed at providing housing, education, and a liv-
able environment.

Most politicians still have not caught on. Cut costs, they say. Thus,
there are more regulations, more review bodies, more alphabet soup

83

"Most afflictions of mankind . . . have not been conquered. Death, disease, and disability will always be with us, no matter what weapons, medical or otherwise, are employed against them."

like HMOs, PSROs, HSAs, producing more jobs for regulators, paper suppliers, and computer operators, but none of them making people any healthier or significantly lowering costs. Leon S. White says:

We should all like to believe that if we could just make the health-care system more efficient and effective we shall all be healthier, infant mortality will drop, and life expectancy will increase. The situation reminds me of the old story of the drunk who lost his last quarter: The drunk was searching around near a lamppost when a passerby noticed him and asked what he was doing. "Looking for a quarter I lost," replied the drunk. "Where did you lose it?" asked the passerby. "Further down the road," answered the drunk. "Then why are you looking here?" asked the passerby. "Because the light's better," replied the drunk.

There is no doubt that the light shines brightest around the health-care system, but is better health to be found there? Maybe we should begin to look elsewhere, if we are really interested in discovering ways to improve health.[3]

It is these areas away from the streetlight that need further exploration. Sanity is likely to return to the American health care scene only if the public has more realistic expectations of what medicine can and cannot provide. A corollary is that better health will result only when the public takes greater responsibility, both individually and collectively, for achieving it.

Though a more detailed examination of the physician-patient relationship appears elsewhere in the symposium, brief mention of society's changing view of the physician seems in order. A mighty change took place at the time of World War II. Emil P. Taxay puts it thus:

It is my impression, after many years in medical practice in the United States, that the following evolution has taken place. At the onset of my contact with patients we had comparatively little to offer in the way of sophisticated technology or therapeutics. Comfort, understanding and reassurance were the most effective measures available. The majority of patients appeared genuinely grateful; litigation was virtually unheard of, and doctors were considered professionals. In spite of our technical inexpertness, patients did amazingly well.

After World War II, in association with, or perhaps as a result of, the rapid increase in technology, the sociology of our country changed. With it, the technology and sociology of medicine also changed. The explosion of knowledge frequently benefited the individual patient and in some cases the nation at large. With an increase in technology and expertise, the magical elements of medicine (consolation and reassurance) lost their status. To the degree that medicine became metric, quantitative, predictive, and verifiable, it also became public, common, costly and conventional. It was but a short step in time for the doctor to lose his professional status conceptually and become a technologic representative within the health-care field.[4]

What doctors don't know

Currently the public relations machinery of the health industry deluges us with unending stories of new medical miracles. Instant cures are demanded; it now is virtually unacceptable to remain ill.

Dramatic advances *have* been made in medicine, but in most cases they involved diseases afflicting a relatively small proportion of the population. For example, several years ago at Children's Orthopedic

Hospital and Medical Center in Seattle, more children were dying from congenital heart disease than from any other cause. (The incidence of congenital heart disease is approximately 6 per 1,000 live births.) Thanks to modern surgical techniques, death from congenital heart disease is now a rarity. Thus incredible benefits for a relatively few children have been achieved. Most afflictions of mankind, however, have not been conquered. Death, disease, and disability will always be with us, no matter what weapons, medical or otherwise, are employed against them.

Physicians often find themselves spending more time with patients discussing what doctors *don't* know, than vice versa. Many are the hours, for example, spent explaining why no cure is available for the common cold. Our increasingly sophisticated patients read all about scientific miracles and expect results. To illustrate the depth of our ignorance, it need only be noted that we still don't know how the most commonly used drug, aspirin, works to reduce inflammation and pain.

How does medical care affect mortality and morbidity? About 80% of human illness is self-limited and about 10% progresses inexorably in spite of modern medicine. Thus, in only about 10% of cases is it likely that medical intervention may be dramatically successful.

Most of medicine, though, is concerned not with vital statistics, but rather with individuals—their hurts, their ills, their well-being. Franz J. Ingelfinger, the erudite former editor of the *New England Journal of Medicine,* has said:

Mankind has gone and continues to go to priests, shamans, general practitioners or ultra-certified specialists because the patient wants to feel better, not because he wants to contribute a datum point to some graph. Since the chances that the doctor will indeed provide some relief in some form are considerably better than 50–50, the patient is generally satisfied even if the doctor's ministrations do not change the statistics of health. Perhaps the role of the doctor as reliever rather than as healer should be accentuated to mitigate any disappointment that he cannot appreciably reorient mortality and morbidity trends. In brief, tremendously important as they are, health statistics appear somewhat irrelevant to the ordinary purposes of patient care, which deal with the hope of an individual human being that his troubles will be meliorated.[5]

Health care jargon

Our "new" language in this field muddies the water. "Health care" has become a commodity to be "delivered" by "vendors" to "consumers." One can pay for the services of a physician, but can health or "health care" be purchased as though it were a concrete item on a grocery shelf? Richard M. Magraw says:

We need to bear in mind that patients are not the same thing as consumers. Patients ask for help and care (derivatively "patient" means one who suffers), whereas consumers buy and use things. Sick people may describe themselves as being "sick" or "ill" or even as being "patients," but never as "consumers." Hence, he who speaks with a "consumer" in mind is probably not speaking for patients. The term "consumer" has overtones of "buying power" and economies of scale. Patients are sick. Are consumers? If they are not, how can they

"One can pay for the services of a physician, but can health or 'health care' be purchased as though it were a concrete item on a grocery shelf?"

85

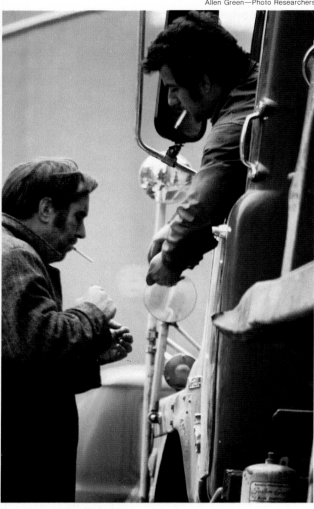

"... 'the real malpractice problem in this country today is not the one described on the front pages of daily newspapers but rather the malpractice that people are performing on themselves and on each other.' "

"consume" the medical-care part of health services? "To consume" hardly seems the right verb for that service, in any case.

Once launched, some of this jargon attains a momentum of usage, but other factors help it flourish. Some prefer this language because it helps make the awkward human complexities of personal medical care more manageably abstract—for planning, to fit economic theory and for other purposes. Others use it to belittle (unconsciously) the still rather grandiose social role of the physician. They prefer to speak of "providers and consumers" rather than "doctors and patients" or of "vendors" rather than "physicians." We have perhaps not given enough thought to elements of pretentiousness in our staked-out claims of professional expertness and responsibility, and to the effects of the residual grandeur of society's lingering image of the doctor.[6]

Put bluntly, the emperor needs his clothes, the Wizard of Oz needs his trappings, and the physician needs his aura to achieve maximum benefit for his patient. Take away the "magic" and honesty is gained, but a measure of healing power is lost. For better or worse, the trend towards egalitarianism probably will not be reversed.

Let's return to Leon White's streetlight. He says, "the real malpractice problem in this country today is not the one described on the front pages of daily newspapers but rather the malpractice that people are performing on themselves and on each other."[7] Take the matter of heart disease. We don't need a hundred more research studies to know that coronary artery disease is related to excessive weight, lack of exercise, smoking, and the consumption of animal fat. The lessons to be learned from the mountain centenarians are obvious.

Altering health behavior

If an unhealthy life-style is the enemy, how is the battle to be fought? The timeworn answer is through educating the public. That is nonsense, if we think of health education as the traditional imparting of information. There can't be an American alive who isn't aware of the harmful effects of smoking cigarettes or the beneficial effects of wearing seat belts. Altering behavior that affects health is incredibly difficult for two basic reasons. First, there is no effective leadership in this direction. The public still looks to the medical profession for guidance in matters of health, and, so far, physicians have paid only lip service to the importance of prevention.

The second factor is the incredible financial resources that are expended to promote activities that are injurious to health. The most glaring example is cigarette advertising. Currently it is estimated that over 3,000 adolescents between 12 and 18 in the U.S. take up smoking every day. Why? Cigarette ads are more sexually oriented than nude pictures. Smokers appear rugged, manly, sexy, sophisticated, etc. There is a broad implication that cigarettes provide free passage to a fantasy land where gorgeous creatures of the opposite sex gambol in a green field by a silvery stream. Who could resist?

In the area of nutrition we are dealing with a cultural bias that equates a fat baby with a healthy baby. Note the type of baby that appears in the ads; thin ones need not apply as models. We know that the tendency

Marc Lalonde, Canada's minister of national health and welfare, provides a list of the more destructive life-style habits:

Drugs

(a) alcohol addiction, leading to cirrhosis of the liver, encephalopathy, and malnutrition;
(b) excessive social use of alcohol, leading to motor vehicle accidents and obesity;
(c) cigarette smoking, causing chronic bronchitis, emphysema, and cancer of the lung, and aggravating coronary artery disease;
(d) abuse of pharmaceuticals, leading to drug dependence and drug reactions;
(e) addiction to psychotropic (mind-altering) drugs, leading to suicide, homicide, malnutrition, and accidents;
(f) social use of psychotropic drugs, sometimes leading to social withdrawal and acute anxiety attacks.

Diet and exercise

(a) overeating, leading to obesity and its consequences;
(b) high fat intake, possibly contributing to atherosclerosis and coronary artery disease;
(c) high carbohydrate intake, contributing to dental caries;
(d) fad diets, leading to malnutrition;
(e) lack of exercise, aggravating coronary artery disease, leading to obesity and causing lack of physical fitness;
(f) malnutrition, leading to numerous health problems;
(g) lack of recreation and lack of relief from work and other pressures, associated with stress diseases such as hypertension, coronary artery disease, and peptic ulcers.

Other deleterious life-style habits

(a) careless driving and failure to wear seat belts, leading to accidents and resultant deaths and injuries;
(b) sexual carelessness, contributing to venereal diseases.[8]

"Promoting breast-feeding and delaying the introduction of solids would be a simple, concrete way to attack obesity and future heart disease."

"Note the type of baby that appears in the ads; thin ones need not apply as models."

towards obesity may be determined in infancy. In the 1930s, the average infant's birth weight doubled by six months of age. Now that event occurs on the average of just under four months.

Two centuries ago children had to cope with mere survival and were victims of scurvy, rickets, growth failure, and epidemics. Today the main nutritional disorders among children are obesity and tooth decay. Whereas in the 1920s solid foods were introduced around one year of age, they are now given in the first few months of life. Promoting breast-feeding and delaying the introduction of solids would be a simple, concrete way to attack obesity and future heart disease.

We see increasing death rates from coronary artery disease, diabetes, and intestinal cancer in countries where Western-type diets are consumed. Such diets mean overconsumption of meat, animal fat, and sugar, as well as less fiber. Yet continuous efforts are made to increase the protein content of food in the American market. A major reason for not modifying the American diet is that some industries would be adversely affected.[9]

The invidious promotion of ill health is seen in other areas as well. While the public cries out against drug abuse, television commercials incessantly demonstrate how the ingestion of pills is the answer to relieving every conceivable ache, pain, and mood, or to just staying healthy. The TV networks and their advertisers too often are the pushers and our impressionable children—and we ourselves—are the junkies for junk food, junk toys, and junk medicine.

Health promotion

As usual, it is easier to identify problems than formulate solutions. The basic theme here, however, is, "patient, make *yourself* healthy." Physicians, who are chiefly responsible for overselling medicine, must begin unselling their services.

Inducements must be made available to promote more healthy lifestyles. As mentioned before, knowledge does not by itself induce changes in behavior. What about financial incentives? Everyone likes a bargain. The person who scoffs at the possibility of being thrown through the windshield of his car may fasten his seat belt if it means paying a lower insurance premium or a fine. Auto insurers provide discounts for honor students and for cars with impact-absorbing bumpers. Why not give health insurance premium discounts to people who adopt healthier life-styles?

Counter-commercials

To be effective, the attack on unhealthy life-styles must begin in childhood. Such labors should take place not in hospitals or clinics, but in homes and schools. Hitherto, health education has consisted mostly of moral preaching about what not to do. To promote healthier living, we must copy the techniques of the consummate masters, the advertisers. If a whole deodorant industry can be spawned by making people feel that they *need* perfume in all of their bodily nooks and crannies, it should be possible to get people to think twice about killing themselves. Some interesting counter-commercials have been produced by consumer and voluntary health agencies, such as the American Cancer Society, but no one is paying to have them shown. Since the public owns the airways, perhaps all licensed TV and radio stations should be required to provide more free time for creative health education.

Some people might object, arguing that such suggestions come perilously closer to "thought control" than to education and that they infringe on our civil liberties. The issue is a serious one that deserves careful consideration. Right now, though, it is the large corporations who possess the greatest capability to control thoughts and actions through advertising.

Like most arguments, those involving freedom have two sides. Motorcycle riders in several states, for example, vigorously protest the laws that require them to wear safety helmets, arguing that such laws abridge their freedom. Because taxpayers must support most of their hospitalization or their surviving children when they are injured or killed in a crash, however, it seems reasonable that the state should indeed have some control over the risks cyclists take. Beyond that, why should everyone have to pay the same health insurance premiums as an overweight, alcoholic smoker who doesn't buckle his seat belt? It all depends on one's perspective of freedom.

As a result of the energy shortage, Americans are already making life-style changes to an extent previously thought impossible. If given a fair shot at the facts, our people may opt for changes that make life healthier, and maybe even happier. Medicine has taken great strides toward finding cures for some diseases and eliminating others and toward alleviating the suffering of the sick and the handicapped. By far the greatest part of a physician's training and practice is directed at those ends. But he works within boundaries that limit what he has to offer the vast majority of people, who are seeking not cures but the means to stay healthy. For them, the medical profession can, at best, offer its advice, but they must decide for themselves whether to act on it. The ball is out of the court of the health professionals and into the court of the public.

1. Alexander Leaf, "Every Day Is a Gift When You Are Over 100," *National Geographic* 143 (January 1973): 93–118.
2. Gordon T. Stewart, "Medicine and Health: What Connection?" *Lancet* 1 (March 29, 1975): 705–708.
3. Leon S. White, "How to Improve the Public's Health," *New England Journal of Medicine* 293 (Oct. 9, 1975): 773–74.
4. Emil P. Taxay, "Social Change and Patient Ethology," *New England Journal of Medicine* 296 (Feb. 3, 1977): 280–81.
5. Franz J. Ingelfinger, "Health: A Matter of Statistics or Feeling?" *New England Journal of Medicine* 296 (Feb. 24, 1977): 448–49.
6. Richard M. Magraw, "Language of Medical Care," *New England Journal of Medicine* 279 (Aug. 15, 1968): 383–84.
7. White, p. 773.
8. Marc Lalonde, *A New Perspective on the Health of Canadians* (Ottawa, Canada: Department of National Health and Welfare, 1974).
9. D. Mark Hegsted, "Protein Needs and Possible Modifications of the American Diet," *Journal of the American Dietetic Association* 68 (April 1976): 317–20.

Paul Fusco—Magnum

"It all depends on one's perspective of freedom."

FOR ADDITIONAL READING:

Dubos, René J. *Mirage of Health; Utopias, Progress, and Biological Change.* New York: Harper and Row, 1959.

Haggerty, Robert J. (ed). "Does Comprehensive Care Make a Difference?" *American Journal of Diseases of Children* (December, 1971) 467–82.

———."The Boundaries of Health Care." *Pharos* (July 1972): 106–11.

Halberstam, Michael J. "Liberal Thought, Radical Theory, and Medical Practice." *New England Journal of Medicine* (May 27, 1971): 1180–84.

Magraw, Richard M. *Ferment in Medicine.* Philadelphia: W. B. Saunders Company, 1966.

McKeown, Thomas. *The Role of Medicine: Dream, Mirage, or Nemesis?* London: Nuffield Provincial Hospitals Trust, 1976.

Computers in Medicine

by Elemer R. Gabrieli, M.D., F.C.A.P.

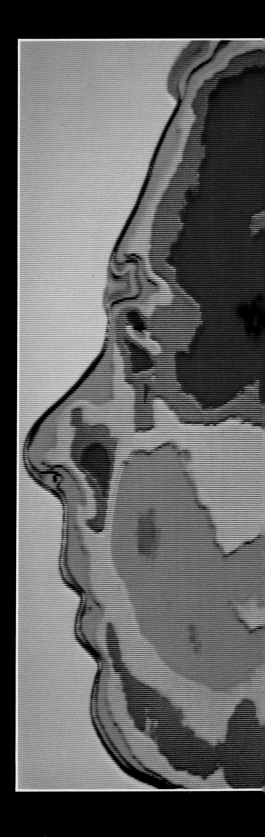

In the past many people have equated the use of computers in medicine with the replacement of the family doctor by a robot. As society has accepted the benefits of computer technology in other areas of life, however, medicine has become increasingly interested in using the computer to improve health care. When properly used, computers can help physicians offer better treatment for patients, keep down health care costs, improve the efficiency of hospitals, and allow important technological innovations.

Medicine and information

Medicine is a profession that depends on information. Making a diagnosis or prescribing therapy are examples of information processing. The patient's signs and symptoms are compared with the patterns of many diseases stored in the memory of the physician. The most fitting pattern is selected as the diagnosis, or the most effective drug is prescribed, according to the physician's knowledge and experience.

Formal medical knowledge is the sum of medicine's past experience and research findings; personal experience is the accumulation of previous data from similar clinical cases. In both areas, information is the essential common element. Information is the basic element of medical learning, thinking, and recall, the basic unit of knowledge and experience, the atomic structure of the science of medicine.

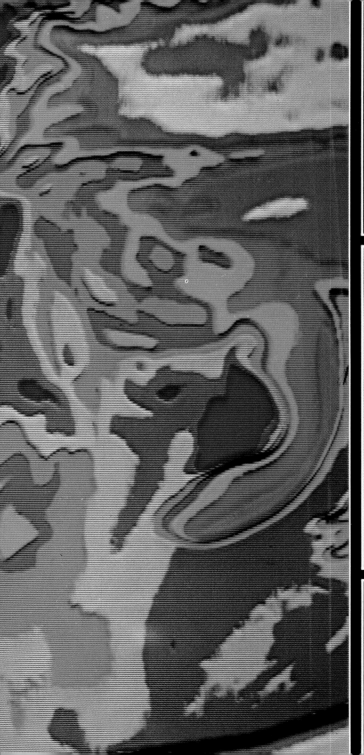
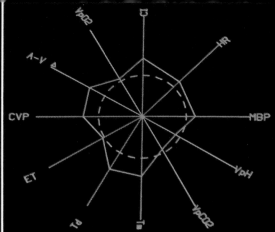
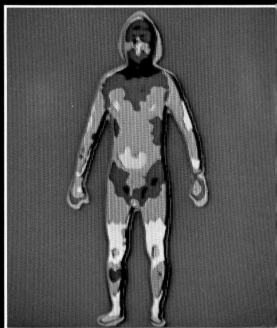

One can postulate that the "best" medical judgment would be based on full knowledge of all pertinent information, and that the "best" decision would use all pertinent information. The pride of modern medicine is the large body of knowledge that theoretically can be used for treating diseases. In practice, however, the amount of knowledge available to a physician may limit the accuracy of his decision.

Growth of medical knowledge

From the time of Hippocrates to the 1920s, a well-trained physician could master all aspects of medicine. What he learned in medical school was useful for his lifetime. In the 20th century, however, knowledge in all the sciences has grown dramatically. In medicine, after World War I, the explosive generation of new scientific information began to make it impossible for physicians to keep up with progress. It has been said that between 1945 and 1970 factual medical knowledge increased more than threefold and about elevenfold between 1930 and 1975. At the same time, the useful life of knowledge gathered during the years in medical school began to shrink.

After World War II, medicine openly admitted its inability to cope with the expansion of biomedical knowledge by establishing formal training programs for specialists such as obstetricians, surgeons, pediatricians, and psychiatrists. For these specialists, not only was the length of training doubled but the breadth of competence was also reduced. The ophthalmologist was expected to know in depth only the eye diseases, whereas the cardiologist became the expert for treating heart ailments. The avalanche of new information began to erode further the useful life-span of the medical school curriculum. For example, a graduate of a medical school in 1960 could expect that half of the rules he learned for drug treatment would be obsolete in six or seven years.

Medicine has experienced a true information revolution, since the changes outstrip physicians' ability to cope with them. As a last-ditch response to the information explosion, during the 1960s medicine encouraged the development of subspecialties such as hematology, rheumatology, urology, orthopedics, neurosurgery, and clinical genetics. It was an attempt to further narrow the scope of a specialist in order to cope with growing knowledge. At the turn of the century a good doctor knew all areas of medicine; today a subspecialist knows but a small part of clinical medicine. Many diseases, however, ignore the arbitrary borders of specialization. Diseases such as diabetes mellitus, arteriosclerosis, or cancer may require the joint opinion of several medical specialists. Consultation leads to escalation in health care costs and to inefficiency in patient care.

Moreover, academic medicine is increasingly concerned about the growing gap between existing knowledge and its use in clinical practice. There is a widening gap between optimal treatment and actual practice, because a physician can no longer keep up with the latest research that may help his patients. Forward-looking medical educators are beginning to recognize that the practice of medicine from

Elemer R. Gabrieli, M.D., F.C.A.P., *is editor of the* Journal of Clinical Computing *and Director of the Clinical Information Center, E. J. Meyer Memorial Hospital, Buffalo, N.Y.*

(Overleaf) The application of computer sciences to medicine has produced remarkable advances in both diagnosis and treatment. Thermography employs heat-sensitive devices to detect infrared radiation produced by the body. Computers transform the data into multicolored "heat maps" that enable the physician to locate tumors and inflammations. The Life Support Column (top right) is a computerized system for monitoring and displaying in graphic form a patient's vital signs; the perfect circle represents established norms for heart rate, blood pressure, and other functions, while the irregular shape maps the patient's actual condition as transmitted by electrodes attached to the body. Another computer display (bottom right) monitors cancer therapy delivered by means of a linear accelerator.

Photographs, Dan McCoy—Black Star

memory is an anachronism that results in inferior health care. There is more to know than physicians can memorize. Human memory must be extended, and computer technology has the capability of extending it. Once physicians know how to make the computer assist them, they can use computer technology to improve diagnoses and treatments.

Electronic data processing

The brief history of the computer in medicine now spans two decades. During this period, computer technology itself has advanced at a spectacular pace. The history of computers in medicine can be divided into five areas, although all five evolved nearly simultaneously.

Processing fiscal data. Initially, computers were expensive research tools for enterprising investigators seeking useful applications for the new toy. The first practical breakthrough was mechanization of billing. In a hospital a typical patient receives five to 15 different services every day—laboratory tests, X-ray studies, and other diagnostic examinations and treatments. Each item of service has to be added to the patient's bill. In a large modern hospital, recording thousands of individual services rendered every day, pricing them, and posting them on patients' accounts grew to be a monumental clerical task.

Fifteen years after computers became available, practically all large hospitals in the United States had either acquired a computer system or employed the services of a commercial computer center. The output of these fiscal data systems is a daily inpatient census (a master list of

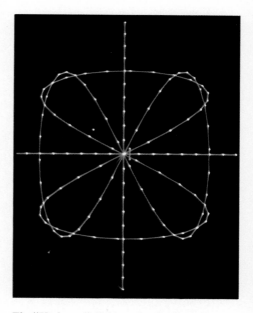

The "Utah arm" (left), under development at the University of Utah, Salt Lake City, is an example of the application of computer technology to the improvement of prosthetic devices. When perfected, the battery-operated arm will receive electrical impulses from the skin, and, with the aid of a microcomputer, will function as a normal extension of the remaining portion of the limb. Each microcomputer will be separately programmed to the unique needs of the wearer. An engineer testing the programming process (below left) works at a computer console, applying pressure to a force-sensitive handle. The image on the display screen (above) both supervises and records the subject's movements. The data obtained will be used to formulate a "prescription" for the microcomputer of the prosthesis.

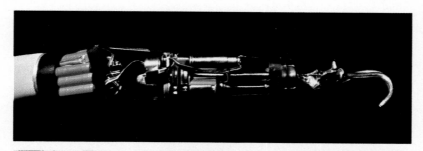

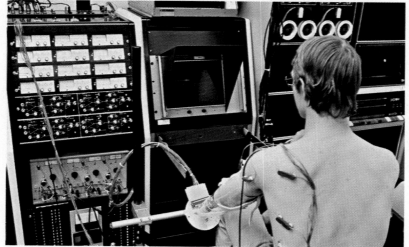

Photographs, Dan McCoy—Black Star

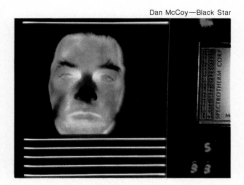

In the first stage of thermography, as shown above, the image is not fully registered; as the computer is gradually adjusted, however, the tissues with greatest blood circulation register "hot" colors—red, orange, yellow—and the areas of lesser circulation produce the "cooler" colors in the spectrum, ranging from green to dark blue and purple, as seen on pages 90 and 91.

all patients with their bed locations), daily patient billing (direct to the patient or to the insurance carrier), and various cost-accounting functions (such as overdue bills, accounts receivable, and budgeting). Numerous outpatient clinics and group practices are also using computers to schedule patient visits, which reduces patients' waiting time. The remarkable proliferation of fiscal and medical data centers indicates that computerization is a cost-effective measure. It has streamlined the growing clerical burden of billing and scheduling.

A similar clerical task is carried out by computer systems created for filing and retrieving data on vital statistics (deaths, births, and morbidity statistics). Computers can make the data readily available to health departments and to various disease registries (including cancer, hereditary disease, and psychiatric registries).

Computer communications. A somewhat more advanced use of computers is programming to disseminate information to departments in a hospital. In a large hospital, for example, when a physician admits a patient with a suspected heart attack, many hospital sites should be promptly notified of the admission. The head nurse on the ward must make arrangements for a diagnostic workup and prepare a bed. The kitchen should know the diagnosis in order to plan the proper diet. The laboratory should schedule a technician to take blood for chemical tests to determine the extent of heart muscle damage. The electrocardiograph technician should be notified so he can make a heart tracing. The information desk should know about the patient's condition so that telephone calls from relatives can be answered properly. The business office should be notified so that an account can be opened. Insurance carriers must be notified promptly so that the patient's eligibility can be quickly established.

Computers can be programmed to recognize all necessary sites and to notify them. In cases where minutes may be crucial, fast communication can save a life. As technology advances, communication by computer becomes less and less expensive; the cost-effectiveness ratio is rapidly improving.

Several blood banks also have installed computer systems to monitor the inventory of blood units. Because refrigerated blood is usable for only three weeks, it must be carefully accounted for. In addition, some programs store blood in several hospitals, others at a central blood bank. The blood type, the age, and the location of each unit must be recorded. A computer-based system can efficiently record all of these factors and maximize the use of available blood.

Business and industry have progressed much further than medicine in developing sophisticated computerized communication systems. Airline reservation systems, for example, are much more highly developed than current medical systems. Medicine is only now learning how to exploit the technology.

Rapid data processing. Perhaps the best example of rapid data processing in medicine is computerized axial tomography, a remarkable new radiological technique. In traditional radiology, both the X-ray ma-

94

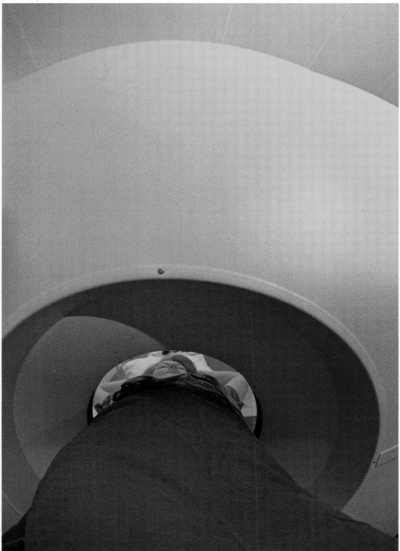

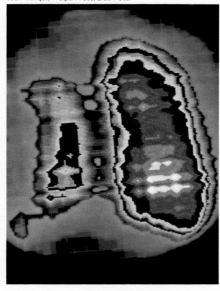

The computerized axial tomography (CAT) scanner is one of the most highly sophisticated diagnostic X-ray devices in current use. The scanner, attached to a typewriter-like keyboard computer, rotates around the patient's body, directing a thin beam of X-rays through the tissues; the computer processes the data and produces an image of a cross-sectional slice of the body. A CAT-scan of a patient's chest (above) indicates that one of the lungs has collapsed.

chine and the patient are stationary. X-rays traveling from the X-ray tube through a particular part of the human body are absorbed at varying rates by different organs and tissues before striking the X-ray film. The result is a two-dimensional "snapshot" picture in which the various tissues appear superimposed, but in which discrimination between organs and tissues with similar absorption rates is lost.

In computerized axial tomography, the X-ray tube is moving, rotating around the patient, scanning the body. During the procedure, the scanning X-ray tube continuously emits X-rays. The X-rays pass through the body and are recorded by a detector. During the scan of any part of the body, a vast number of measurements are captured by the detector. The computer transforms the detector data into numeric values and stores them. When the scanning is completed, the computer is able to reconstruct pictures by synthesizing the measurements. The light in-

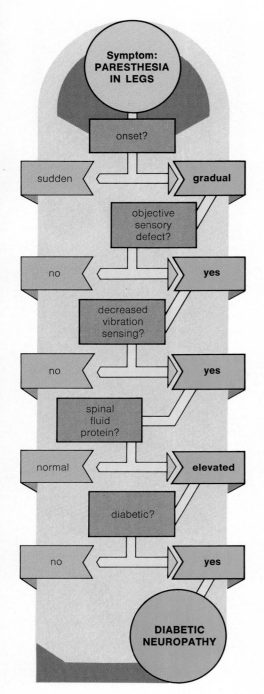

Symptom: PARESTHESIA IN LEGS

onset?

sudden ← → gradual

objective sensory defect?

no ← → yes

decreased vibration sensing?

no ← → yes

spinal fluid protein?

normal ← → elevated

diabetic?

no ← → yes

DIABETIC NEUROPATHY

tensity of each small area on the cathode-ray tube on which the X-ray absorption data are displayed represents within its matrix the intensity of X-rays at a particular point of the body, passing through the tissues scanned, at a particular time. The radiologist views a representation of a thin, detailed slice of the human body.

Because of the sensitivity of computerized tomography, its diagnostic accuracy is much greater than that afforded by traditional two-dimensional, static X-rays. The core of the technique is the computer, which accepts, processes, stores, and, under the control of the radiologist, displays the scanning results. Computerized tomography is a major advance in diagnostic radiology and a remarkable achievement of sophisticated technology.

Another interesting development is the use of computers for processing bioelectric analog signals. Such signals are the electrical current generated by the contracting heart or the electrical phenomena associated with the functions of the central nervous system. Both of these bioelectric phenomena are used extensively in medical diagnosis. An expert can recognize certain cardiac disturbances by examining the tracing recorded by an electrocardiograph machine or detect some disorders of the brain by studying electroencephalographic recordings. Computers can be programmed to convert the curves of these electrical signals into numeric values (analog-to-digital conversion) and to compare the numerical values with a set of established physiological ranges. As a result of the comparison, the computer can state any abnormal findings. In certain limited areas, such as interpreting an electrocardiogram or an electroencephalographic tracing, the computer can be programmed to carry out a large number of comparisons and to reach a diagnosis.

It must be recognized, however, that such interpretations can be made by computers only in areas with a very limited number of variables, where human reasoning can be sufficiently explicated and computerized. There are only a few areas in medicine where the exact meaning of each variable can be as clearly delineated as in the interpretation of an electrocardiogram. Although progress is constantly being made, computer-based interpretation is today still significantly less accurate than the judgment of the expert cardiologist—just one example of the current limitations of a computer compared with human ability. Computers can, nevertheless, recognize normal cases, detect the abnormal, and reduce the chore of the cardiologist by the prescreening of large numbers of electrocardiogram tracings.

Pattern recognition. In medicine, clusters of visible abnormal changes (signs) and abnormal sensations and experiences (symptoms) occur in a certain time sequence and in characteristic combinations. They are the manifestations of a disease or condition. An experienced physician combines signs and symptoms (clinical data) with diagnostic data such as laboratory findings or X-ray studies and recognizes the pattern representing a disease. If all the observed abnormalities, signs, and symptoms fit one particular disease, the physician can have a high degree of confidence in his diagnosis. If one or more findings appears uncharacteristic or unusual, the physician must assign a lesser probability value to his "working" diagnosis and begin to consider other possibilities. Diagnostic logic can be represented in the form of a tree structure (*see* p. 96).

At the end of the logical process, the physician reaches the most probable diagnosis. In this case, the logical conclusion is diabetic neuropathy. As each of the other possibilities becomes unlikely, the probability of the diagnosis increases. For example, the result of the test for spinal fluid protein level separates tumors or inflammatory diseases from metabolic diseases as the cause of the symptoms, increasing the probability of the diagnosis of diabetic neuropathy.

Using this logic, and some other mathematical models, computers have been successfully used as teaching machines. The student interacts with the computer through a keyboard terminal and tries to reach a logical conclusion—a rational diagnosis or the most logical therapeutic decision. When the student submits an incorrect answer, the computer corrects it and explains the reason for the proper answer.

Bayes's theorem is a frequently used model for constructing a diagnostic decision system. Essentially it is used to assign relative probabilities to various possible diagnoses based on signs and symptoms exhibited by the patient, and thus helps the physician establish priorities for further examination, treatment, and care. The probabilities can be represented by $P(D_1)$, $P(D_2)$, $P(D_3)$. . . $P(D_n)$, where $P(D_1)$ is the probability of the patient's having disease D_1, and so forth. The statistical model is based on two assumptions: (1) that the list D_1, D_2, D_3, . . . D_n is an exhaustive list (that all possible diseases are listed) and (2) that all diseases within the list are mutually exclusive. In the real world of clinical medicine, both requirements are often not met. There are, nevertheless, a number of computerized diagnostic programs designed for specific diseases such as thyroid diseases, congenital malformations of the heart, or radiological diagnosis of bone tumors for which a computer can match or exceed the accuracy of the best human diagnosticians.

Medical information system. At its highest level of sophistication, the computer serves as a true mental partner with a physician; each does what he or it can do best. In such a symbiotic relationship the computer provides an extension of human memory, under the full control of the thinking and deciding human. This man-machine relationship is analogous to the help given by the microscope. With the microscope, the human eye can see much smaller structures than are visible to the naked eye; in other words the microscope provides further information. With an electronic memory extending human memory, the physician is neither limited to the information stored in his memory nor is he forced to pollute his memory with thousands of trivial and perishable details. When needed, the machine can display all pertinent information, enabling the human to carry out the highest mental functions—judgments with humanitarian compassion and decisions with empathy.

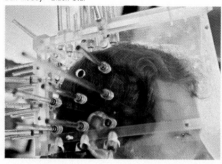

Another new application of computers in medicine is intended to aid in early detection of cerebrovascular disease by means of a three-dimensional analysis of blood flow in the brain. Still in an experimental stage, the device consists of a helmet-like apparatus that measures distribution of blood flow, thickness of scalp, and other factors, and a computer that synthesizes the data to produce a diagnosis.

Destruction of cancerous tumors by bombardment with nuclear particles is one application of the energy produced by the linear accelerator at the Clinton P. Anderson Meson Physics Facility at the Los Alamos (New Mexico) Scientific Laboratory. The Cockcroft-Walton generator (opposite) speeds particles in the first stage of the accelerator system.

The negative pi mesons, or pions, produced as protons with energies of 800 million electron volts, are shot through the half-mile long accelerator to strike a graphite target. Computers channel and shape the beam of pions, monitor the delivered dosage, and control the volume of the treatment while the Biomedical-Channel control console (above) gives the radiotherapist a continuous readout and, through a TV camera, a view of the part of the body receiving the pions. Though preliminary experiments are limited to attacking surface tumors, the goal of this treatment is to destroy deep-seated tumors with minimal damage to healthy tissue.

Only recently has medicine attempted to build an electronic cognitive memory, but the initial results have been encouraging. Medical knowledge, according to one research program, can be broken down into individual units of information. Each unit is carried by a concise statement that describes relationships between two or more terms. Each statement or relationship has a distinct truth value, and each term has a meaning. The program requires a list of formalized statements that are highly suitable for coding and computerization. The scheme seems to enable computer architects to build, step by step, an electronic cognitive network and to construct a medical knowledge bank. The system allows selective retrieval of facts and also permits "browsing" for more general medical information. Once such a system is fully developed, it is expected that physicians will routinely consult it as a part of the diagnostic and therapeutic process. Perhaps in the not too distant future, medical decisions made without checking with a computer will be allowed only in rare emergency situations.

Although the enthusiastic architects of medical information banks predict with confidence that computers will play an increasing role in tomorrow's medical practice, others warn us that computers can only mechanize what humans have fully explicated and that only lower level mental functions can be computerized. Where the true limits of technology may lie is at the moment unclear. Much current medical knowledge cannot be computerized. Usually only hard facts are suitable to definition, to explicit verbalization, and then to coding for a computer. Designers of computerized medical memories must first sort out, with great difficulties, hard facts from ambiguous assumptions and anecdotal information. It would be reckless to propose that computers at present can solve our complex human problems. The computer can learn and know only those facts explicated by a human programmer. The computer can reiterate solutions for well-defined problems, as stated by human experts.

Data banks and ethics

Traditionally, patient records were kept in the offices of physicians or at the record rooms of hospitals. The records were often nearly illegible, written as private notes about diagnoses or treatments. The only real risk to the privacy of the patient was an indiscreet remark by a doctor or a medical assistant. Computerization of medical data has introduced new problems. Data centers receive, store, and process thousands or even millions of medical records, and a single dishonest (or simply careless) computer operator can hurt many patients.

There are many people who would be interested in the medical data of others. Employers may want to know the mental stability, or simply the health status, of job applicants or employees. Police, tax authorities, insurance companies, businesses, or simply an unfriendly neighbor might like to see a person's medical record.

Another risk is that computers can exchange information by merging files. There are computers handling credit card billings, court and

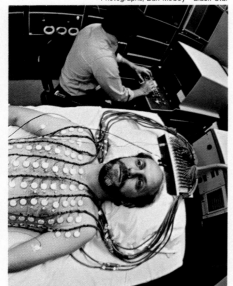

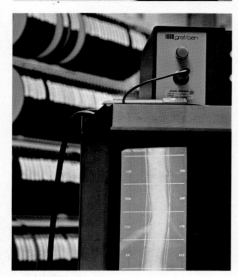

criminal records, bank and credit data, educational records, tax information, hotel accommodations, restaurant reservations, theater tickets, religious affiliation files, political activity records—information on virtually any aspect of human endeavor. By connecting data from different systems an agency could reconstruct a person's entire life pattern without any participation by the individual under scrutiny. Information on a person's health could become just another data file, potentially accessible to anyone who is willing to pay for the search, a frightening possibility. Perhaps even more important is the merciless permanence of electronic records. A machine cannot "forgive." Embarrassing records of a venereal disease or a bout with mental illness may be retrievable, after cure, for the entire life of the individual.

Medical privacy means that the patient can reveal the most confidential and sensitive information to his doctor, believing that the physician will keep it in strictest confidence. Loss of this trust would soon destroy frank communication between doctor and patient. In certain situations, fear of "creating a record" would make patients reluctant to seek medical help. The challenging task is to find the proper balance between the inalienable right of the patient to privacy and the knowledge needed by secondary users of medical data. The solution may be the development of community health data banks with strict protection regulations. Local centers would "disidentify" the data before releasing it to other users such as health departments, insurance carriers, and educational and social agencies.

Raw medical data can also be misinterpreted by laymen unfamiliar with the curability and clinical course of diseases. Currently physicians interpret medical data for laymen, for sociologists and economists, for educators, for politicians. Computerization makes medical data more directly accessible, and may prejudice laymen not equipped to understand it.

Future of medical computing

Despite the vast potential of the information sciences and computer technology and despite the information crisis in clinical medicine, progress in the use of computers is still rather slow. One reason is the widespread hesitation by academic medicine to accept the computer as a new medical tool. Having a good memory was, and still is, a major requirement for admission to medical school and for an academic career in medicine. Some people intuitively consider computers a threat. Some members of medical faculties, trained since childhood to memorize information before using it for judgment, tend to see the computer as a simplistic toy, as a new problem rather than a help. Students currently entering medical schools, however, belong to a different generation. They consider computers another technological tool like the microscope, the laser, and the X-ray. Some researchers in the field of medical computing expect explosive progress within the next decade, when the new generation of "computer-compatible" physicians begins to exploit the technology to its fullest.

100

We can only speculate about the impact of information-processing science and technology on clinical medicine and on social values. It seems reasonable, however, to expect that drastic changes will take place in selection of medical students. Today, the academic record, which favors good memorizers, is a far too important factor. A computer-assisted physician must be genuinely interested in each patient as a person, and he must be logical, capable of making rational instead of intuitive or impulsive decisions. Strict scientific reasoning combined with humanitarian interests may be the values that will be required of physicians in the future.

Another problem is that medical knowledge currently is disseminated through print. The physician reads journals and textbooks, learns the rules, and applies them to clinical problems as they are encountered. Rules are developed for intelligent readers, to be applied to a conceptual patient, suffering from a conceptual disease. In sharp contrast, in a computer-based medical system, the answers must be specific to the actual case. Factual and pertinent statements based on quantitative or probabilistic values, must be formulated by the computer. The answers must be specific. To achieve this, the entire body of knowledge, now kept according to rules in textbooks, must be reorganized, explicated, and made compatible with the computer. Instead of trying to force a patient into a set of rules, a computerized system will force the rules to fit the patient.

Medicine will benefit from computers. The social challenge is to maximize the benefits and to minimize the risks. Technology should serve people rather than enslave them.

FOR ADDITIONAL READING:

Collen, Morris F., ed. *Hospital Computer Systems.* New York: John Wiley and Sons, 1974.

Gabrieli, E. R. "Coding of Medical Data." *Journal of Clinical Computing*, 1975.

———. *Computerization of Clinical Records.* New York: Grune and Stratton, 1970.

———. "Potential of Medical Computing." *Journal of Clinical Computing*, 1975.

Giebink, Gerald A., and Hurst, Leonard L. *Computer Projects in Health Care.* Ann Arbor: University of Michigan Press, 1975.

Hemphill, Charles F., Jr., and Hemphill, John M. *Security Procedures for Computer Systems.* Homewood, Illinois: Dow Jones-Irwin, 1973.

Jacquez, John A. *Computer Diagnosis and Diagnostic Methods.* Springfield, Illinois: Charles C. Thomas, 1972.

Records, Computers, and the Rights of Citizens. U.S. Department of Health, Education, and Welfare. Advisory Committee on Automated Personal Data Systems. Washington, D.C.: U.S. Government Printing Office, 1973, stock no. 1700–00116. DHEW publication, no. (05) 73–94. Also Cambridge, Mass.: MIT Press, 1973.

A new electrocardiograph (ECG) process (opposite top), using 190 electrodes, feeds information into a computer for processing. Because of its capability for gathering more extensive data, the technique may eventually render the present ECG process obsolete. "Vascular image processing" (opposite bottom) is a diagnostic technique in which an ordinary angiogram is processed by a computer; the result, seen on the viewing screen, is a schematic representation of the interior of the artery, showing the areas of fatty deposits (irregular inner line), and the computer's calculations of the artery's normal boundaries (outer lines). The computer's ability to measure precisely the fatty buildup enables a physician to monitor the atherosclerotic process over a period of time and to assess the effectiveness of a given course of treatment.

Alcoholism: The Rand Report Debate

by Mark Bloom

As resistant to modern medicine as it was to the ancient apothecaries, alcoholism is among the oldest and most persistent of diseases. Just as medieval physicians puzzled over the roots of alcoholism, today's doctors are still trying to explain why some people drink to excess and others don't. With an infusion of federal funds, alcoholism treatment centers are starting to proliferate across the nation. But with neither the tools for rapid, successful treatment nor the patience for extended, frustrating therapy, most doctors shun the alcoholic patient as a pariah. Laymen's organizations such as Alcoholics Anonymous (AA) are the traditional refuge for the chronic alcoholic, but problem drinkers rarely seek such aid. Despite an impressive array of research findings in the past generation, alcoholism is still shrouded in a medical and scientific haze that shows little sign of clearing.

No one knows how many alcoholics there are in the United States. Some say that 10 million Americans are problem drinkers and alcoholics, while others put the figure at 20 million. The estimates are muddied by lack of agreement on whether alcoholism and problem drinking are one and the same disease or whether alcoholism is in fact several diseases. Ernest Noble, director of the National Institute on Alcohol Abuse and Alcoholism (NIAAA), says it is all largely guesswork, and that one goal of his federal agency is to determine the true scope of the problem. Also unknown is how many Americans die prematurely because of diseases brought on by drinking. It is not clear how many Americans are killed on the highways because of alcoholic drivers, nor is it known how many lives are emotionally scarred or ruined by a close relative's alcoholic behavior. What is clear, however, is that alcoholism is an enormous problem, one that grows worse every year.

Few crusaders are as zealous as the reformed drunk. Only those who have been there feel they can know truly how hard it is to return. So when, with a flare of publicity, a federally funded study suggested last year that abstinence was not the only answer for alcoholics, the reaction from the nation's reformed drunks was vitriolic. Essentially, the study of patients at the NIAAA's 44 treatment centers concluded that

Mark Bloom *is a Senior Writer on the staff of* Medical World News, *New York City.*

Illustrations by John Youssi

103

some alcoholics can and do revert to controlled social drinking. There was no indication of how to distinguish the alcoholics who can drink safely from the pool of those who should be abstinent, however, nor was there any suggestion that this be attempted. The only ethical way to conduct this kind of research, it was emphasized, would be to work only with those alcoholics who had repeatedly—and unsuccessfully—tried to quit drinking.

The Great Debate

Not since the rise and fall of Prohibition was the world of alcoholism so stirred. Taking the lead in opposition were the National Council on Alcoholism (NCA), a powerful voluntary organization with close ties to AA, and various state and local NCA constituents. AA does not enter into public debate, but its board chairman, John L. Norris of New London, N.H., predicted that alcoholics would die because of the publicity surrounding the report. "I think they have already," he added.

The study was funded by an NIAAA grant and was prepared by David J. Armor of the Rand Corporation in Santa Monica, Calif. The study quickly became known as the Rand report. In the aftermath of a debate that is still swirling around it, there emerged the story of a year-long struggle by abstinence-oriented officials of various alcoholism groups to alter the report's conclusions or to kill it altogether.

Attacks on the Rand report came from several directions both before the study was published and afterward. There were charges that the approach was scientifically unsound and that key conclusions had no statistical significance. Consequently, insisted the critics, the conclusions should be changed to fit the data. Others cried out that even if the findings were true, it was irresponsible to make them public when there is no way to forecast which alcoholics can handle moderate drinking. Still others claimed that, even if the study was valid as far as it went, these so-called controlled drinkers would inevitably go out of control, with likely tragic results. Some insisted that those who could drink moderately were not true alcoholics, but merely problem drinkers. Others felt that it simply was not fair to the alcoholic nor to his family to play such a dangerous game when abstinence, with just a little more effort, was so much surer and safer.

The great debate greeted Noble just as he took over as director of the NIAAA. He had mixed emotions. A highly respected scientist and physician in the field of alcoholism, he acknowledged that no scientist could suppress data just because it ran counter to dogma. Nevertheless, he felt it made little medical sense to treat a poisoning with the very poison that was causing the problem. And he was quite upset that the Rand Corporation chose to make this complex scientific publication known first to the press rather than through the usual scientific channels.

Charges of sensationalism

Even so, the great furor over the Rand report was perplexing because the medical literature had been filled with reports of controlled drinking

104

studies for more than a decade. Alcoholism authorities, both conservative and radical, were well aware of the research. By 1975 there were more than 400 studies of psychologically oriented alcoholism treatment, including 60 studies of controlled drinking by alcoholics. But either through oversight or because these studies were too tentative, none had been given prominent press coverage. Marvin Block, former chairman of the American Medical Association's (AMA) Committee on Alcoholism, says physicians have known for years that, for some unknown reason, alcoholics may revert to moderate drinking, sometimes spontaneously, sometimes after a period of abstinence. "But," he says, "you don't publicize it. If you do, people will stay away from treatment, thinking they are in this exceptional group. Alcoholics look for something like this to justify their continued drinking. And then it is too late." Even AA's Norris would claim only that abstinence is necessary in "a great majority" of cases—not all.

The Rand report's conclusion was moderate in tone but clearly hurled a challenge at the dogma of abstinence.

Our findings that some alcoholics appear to return to moderate drinking without serious impairment and without relapse, and that permanent abstention is relatively rare, suggest the possibility that normal drinking might be a realistic and effective goal for some alcoholics. . . . The data from this study, and other similar studies, are simply not adequate to establish, beyond question, the long-term feasibility of normal or "controlled" drinking among alcoholics; nor do the data enable us to identify those specific individuals for whom normal drinking might be appropriate. On the other hand, we have found no solid scientific evidence —only nonrigorous clinical or personal experience—for the belief that abstention is a more effective remedy than normal drinking.

The great publicity that ensued, undoubtedly with the inevitable misunderstandings that the abstinence forces had predicted, was due as much to the struggle to counteract the Rand report's impact as it was to the report's conclusions. Frank Seixas, medical director of the NCA, acknowledges that the bristling NCA response may have backfired to some degree. The day after the Rand report was released to selected members of the press, it was characterized as a "cruel hoax" at an NCA press conference in New York City. Seixas himself suggested that a proposal by Armor to study the natural remission of alcoholism was indistinguishable ethically from the recently revealed study of untreated syphilis in prison inmates.

It emerged that the publicity was an unfortunate result of mutual paranoia. Rand publicity director Paul Weeks says Rand was under the impression that the groups in California that had been trying to alter or kill the report, having failed, were planning a prepublication publicity barrage to undercut the scientific integrity of Armor's work. So Rand opted for a preemptive publicity strike.

The opposed groups were shocked when they learned that Rand was planning to issue the report to chosen science reporters at major news outlets—the *Los Angeles Times*, *The New York Times*, the *Washington Post*, the Associated Press, and United Press International. Weeks says

continual use of alcohol associated with dependency (psychological or physical) or harm in the sphere of mental, physical, or social activity."

This definition bypasses disease—the "red herring" of alcoholism—says Davies, because alcoholism does not have a steady progression as do physical ailments such as measles. Alcoholism's harmful clinical signs may emerge only when it's too late. But by this logic, hypertension might not be classified as a disease either.

In lieu of a definition satisfactory to all schools of thought, a host of disciplines and specialties do what they can for those who have trouble with drinking. Most of these patients have sought help freely; some have been forced to it by employers or the courts. Just about everything is tried, and studies show that when the alcoholic is motivated, just about everything works—for perhaps about one-third of the patients on a long-term basis. Initially, during the early phases of treatment, as many as 70% may be helped. But as with many of the "facts" about alcoholism, statistics on the long-term benefit of treatment programs are vague. Follow-up studies are next to impossible, and definitions of success vary greatly.

Despite the spread of government-sponsored multidisciplinary alcoholism centers, the growth of behavioral and family therapy to combat alcoholism, and the establishment of halfway houses and rehabilitation techniques, Alcoholics Anonymous remains the cornerstone of American efforts to help the drinker. AA, at any given time, has some 200,000 members, equal to the number of patients in all other government and private treatment programs in the country.

It is estimated that the average alcoholic has been in need of help for 10 years before he seeks it voluntarily or before serious illness or accident brought on by continual drinking forces him into a treatment program. People who can't handle alcohol are usually the last to admit that they need help. And some do, indeed, defeat their drinking problems on their own. But those who drink in the morning, anticipate the cocktail hour as the best time of the day, have alcoholic blackouts, or discover that a fifth of liquor doesn't last much more than an evening probably should consider getting outside help. Perhaps one out of every 10 alcoholics ultimately does so.

he felt these reputable reporters were unlikely to sensationalize a delicate story, and he insists that it was responsibly reported until NCA made its sensational charges. NCA and the other opposing forces elected to respond noisily because they felt the prestige of the Rand Corporation would lend inordinate weight to a study they believed was misleading at best and downright inaccurate at worst.

Abstinence versus controlled drinking

Psychologist Mary Pendery, director of the alcoholism program at the San Diego Veterans Administration (VA) Hospital, was, in Armor's opinion, the most effective opponent of the Rand report while it was under review prior to publication. Other opponents included a member of the Rand board of directors who resigned in protest against publication of the study. Pendery, chairman of the California State Alcoholism Advisory Board, says her major disagreement with the Rand report was that it included clearcut, physiologically addicted alcoholics in the group that could and did, on some occasions, revert to moderate drinking. She differentiated these people from very heavy drinkers who were not necessarily addicted. In short, she contends that those very heavy drinkers who become controlled drinkers are not necessarily alcoholics, and that the study had insufficient data to prove that they were alcoholics. She and the other opponents therefore attempted to convince Armor to alter his conclusions at least for this group. And with a member of the Rand board among them, the opponents were not without clout. "We particularly objected to the Rand group's extending its conclusions on the return to normal drinking to those who are definitely alcoholics—to those who are physically addicted," says Pendery. "If they had deleted that one phrase, I would not have fought so hard. Their data just don't support this key conclusion."

"Their position seemed to be that if we weren't going to change this report to their satisfaction, they were going to discredit us in the media," rejoins Armor.

As far as NIAAA's Noble was concerned, the most satisfying conclusion from the Rand report did not involve controlled drinking at all. It was that some 70% of those alcoholics who sought help at the NIAAA centers reported improvement, if not total abstinence, so long as they kept up the effort. This conclusion was in agreement with other studies that indicate the same level of improvement, though not necessarily cures, no matter what the treatment philosophy. The key is to get the alcoholic to admit he or she has a drinking problem, to seek treatment, and to stick with it—not an easy task.

Some believe this is where physicians have abrogated their responsibilities. "Medicine, whether it likes it or not, is very much involved in many of the consequences of excessive drinking," says Arnold M. Ludwig, a psychiatrist who directs the alcoholism research program at the University of Kentucky Medical Center at Lexington. "But physicians are certainly not doing very much about treating the causes. I am a specialist, and I have no astounding statistics to show or cures to advocate. I can't tell a general physician that if only he would do such and such, his cure rate would soar. The difference is that I am willing to work with these people. I believe I may understand a little more than the general physician what alcoholics are coping with and what their problems are.''

Ludwig is among those scientists who have been studying the possibility of controlled drinking for several years. His research has involved trying to learn which alcoholics have the physiological ability to recognize when they are getting drunk and to take this as a cue to stop drinking. In a recent study Ludwig found that about 50% of alcoholics were unable to recognize that the alcohol level in their blood was rising above the point where their drinking was socially acceptable. They were highly conditioned to internal and external cues that sharply increased their craving for more alcohol. So this study of alcoholics showed that half of them, compared with but 5% of social drinkers, could not keep their blood alcohol levels under the problem level, and that abstinence might be the proper route for them. On the other hand, 50% of the alcoholics *could* recognize and control rising blood alcohol levels. ''This indicates that these alcoholics have a capacity for social drinking if a suitable treatment program is devised to teach them how to do it.''

In several centers research is under way to devise such a program, but no one has yet reported long-term success. A notable failure was reported by John A. Ewing, a psychiatrist who directs the Center for Alcohol Studies at the University of North Carolina. Ewing's paper, which appeared within a month or so after the Rand report's publication, commented on 14 patients who had successfully learned to control their blood alcohol levels in a socially acceptable range. But, within periods ranging from 27 to 55 months after starting the program, one by one, all lost control of their drinking. ''Based on our experiences with these patients and a long-term follow-up, we have concluded that, in our hands at least, further attempts to inculcate controlled drinking by such methods are unjustified,'' Ewing concluded. ''Some of the optimistic claims made by other workers may have been premature. It should be noted that no similar treatment program has yet reported a follow-up greater than 24 months' duration.''

Ewing suggested that other groups might be better off pursuing controlled drinking among young alcoholics whose patterns were less rigid than those of people who have been alcoholics for 15 or 20 years. He also recommended that persons with any family history of alcoholism be screened out.

Peter Nathan, director of the Alcohol Behavior Research Laboratory at Rutgers University, says so many alcoholics fail time after time at abstinence that the struggle to find a way to help them drink moderately is not only ethical but urgent. ''With these alcoholics, it seems to be either controlled drinking or uncontrolled drinking,'' he says. At his laboratory and elsewhere, research is examining biofeedback and other behavioral reinforcement methods to find clues to controlling

107

An Easy Descent

EARLY STAGES:
social drinking

Drinking to calm nerves

Increase in alcohol tolerance

Uncomfortable in situation where
there is no alcohol

Occasional memory lapses after
heavy drinking

MIDDLE STAGES:
loss of control phase—
rationalization begins,
help needed

Lying about drinking

Increasing dependence on
alcohol

Feeling of guilt about drinking

Increased memory blackouts

Tremors and early morning
drinks

Grandiose and aggressive
behavior

Repeated failure to control

Neglect of food

Family and friends avoided

Drinking alone—secretly

LATE STAGES:
now thinks responsibilities
interfere with drinking

Deterioration of family
relationships

Physical deterioration

Loss of will power

Urgent need for morning drink

Onset of drunken binges

Persistent remorse

Decrease in alcohol tolerance

Successive drunken binges

Hospital or sanitarium stays

Indefinable fears

Unable to work

All alibis exhausted

Complete abandonment

CONTINUED DETERIORATION

the craving of the alcoholic. "The treatment of choice for a given alcoholic is never unequivocal," says Nathan. "Instead, its choice must reflect a painstaking analysis of the individual's life situation and its attendant relationship to problematic drinking."

Seixas, the NCA medical director, says it in another way, but with a big difference. "We aren't simplistic and we don't say that AA is the only way. We are learning a lot about the effect of alcohol on the neuro-amines, the brain's neurotransmitters, and perhaps one day that will give us some very specific answers to the problem of the disease. But in the meantime, we must mobilize the alcoholic's defenses to get him abstinent. This may be through AA, it may be through group therapy, it may be by screening out the people who are manic-depressives or schizophrenics and treating them appropriately."

But Seixas does not suggest, as would Nathan, that efforts to simply reduce an alcoholic's drinking to a socially acceptable level should be in the alcoholism armamentarium. AA's efforts notwithstanding, he says, abstinence has not been tried with sufficient vigor on a wide enough scale. He rejects any trend toward downgrading the goal of abstinence. "The fact of the matter is that nobody has been trying very hard in many areas of the country with enough people. With the increased government funding, we were just beginning to get a leg up with abstinence programs, and it is very unfortunate to have it thrown over by the publicity over this controlled drinking business."

AA's philosophy embraces the absolute surrender to alcohol, the complete acknowledgement by alcoholics of alcohol's supreme power over their lives. "We admitted we were powerless over alcohol—that our lives had become unmanageable," reads Step One of the AA program to recovery. Among younger authorities, it has become almost fashionable to criticize AA, but, as NIAAA's Noble points out, AA was there when there was nothing else. It is the least expensive, most widespread alcoholism treatment program in existence. Nevertheless, its emphasis on humility and self-castigation, combined with overtones of religiosity, make it difficult for some alcoholics to accept.

Nathan states, "AA's failure to reach more alcoholics may also be due to the mixed message it gives its members. While the organization professes a single-minded rejection of continued drinking on the part of its members, AA meetings typically reinforce members for being willing to recount in sordid detail the nature and effects of prior drinking on their lives. Moreover, AA fosters an 'in-group' feeling that disparages the nonalcoholic as someone who cannot know what it is to have been an alcoholic. As a result, the new AA recruit receives a mixed message: while it is bad to drink now, it was necessary to have done

A Steep Road Back

so before in order to gain entry to AA. Finally, AA's consistent rejection of any treatment goal for its members other than abstinence has probably removed from its potential ranks many persons who are not able to stop drinking completely as well as those who, from prior repeated experience, despair of ever finally achieving total abstinence. Both groups of alcoholics are probably substantial in number."

The limits of "safe drinking"

While treatment does not seem to have progressed far beyond the observation about drunkenness made by Sebastian Franck in 1531—"Much has been tried. . .but nothing has been achieved"—there is increasing scientific evidence of the damage that alcohol can do.

The government has issued a national health warning on the hazards of drinking during pregnancy, contending that as few as two drinks a day could affect the maturing brain of the fetus. Moreover, Noble reports that there is no longer any doubt that heavy drinking by pregnant women causes serious harm to their children, sometimes in a severe form known as fetal alcohol syndrome. In the last five years, fetal alcohol syndrome has been recognized as a frequent sequel to an alcoholic pregnancy, leaving the baby both physically and mentally stunted. There is also some indication that the effects of alcohol on the fetus are compounded by nicotine from smoking and by malnutrition, both frequent companions to alcoholism.

Noble says there is no solid evidence on whether there is a safe level of drinking for anyone. "I don't know what 'drinking responsibly' means—two drinks a day, 10 beers a day," says Noble. "We need research to find out the limits of safe drinking so that when a patient asks a doctor how much he should drink, the doctor will have some sort of a guide. As it stands now, the doctor may drink as much as the patient and think he has no problem—when they both do."

But Noble and others in the business of alcoholism research are very careful to avoid suggesting that social drinkers should stop. Block, the former head of the AMA's alcoholism committee, says, "I trust my thoughts will not be construed as being opposed to drinking. For persons who can drink without harm to themselves or others, there is no problem." Clearly, if the authority hopes for any credibility at all, he must make clear that abstinence is only for the alcoholic.

One long-standing pillar of medical belief that recently has been overturned held that cirrhosis of the liver, one of the most common causes of death among chronic problem drinkers, could be prevented if the alcoholic maintained a nutritious diet. But Charles S. Lieber of the Bronx VA Hospital and Mount Sinai School of Medicine in New

RECOVERY
Sobriety continues
Begins contentment in sobriety
Employer regains confidence
Increased interest and activity in group therapy
Increase of emotional control
New interests develop
Adjustment to family needs

Desire to escape passes
Some self-esteem returns
Natural rest and sleep
Diminishing fears and anxieties

Beginning of realistic thinking
Regular nourishment taken
Attempts at honest thinking
Care of personal appearance and hygiene begins
Starts to react to group therapy
Desire for alcohol persists
Attempts to stop drinking
Learns alcoholism is a disease
Detoxification
Meets recovered alcoholics
CALLS FOR HELP

York City showed that alcohol is indeed the culprit, not malnutrition.

Lieber accomplished this major development in alcoholism research by performing animal experimentation on baboons instead of the previously more commonly used rats. The short-lived, uncooperative rat would not consume enough alcohol nor did he live long enough to develop the cirrhotic liver. But Lieber developed a liquid diet that was nutritionally balanced and had a sufficient alcohol content to turn baboons into chronic drunks. After consuming sufficient alcohol over a long enough time, the well-nourished primates developed cirrhosis just as their human cousins do. Lieber hopes that his baboons may soon reveal why only some heavy drinkers develop cirrhosis and how to predict which ones may be susceptible.

Unsolved mysteries of alcoholism

An outgrowth of his baboon research has been the development of a blood test that can detect chronic alcoholism even if the patient has dried out for a week or more. The test measures the ratio of two amino acids in the blood, α amino-n-butyric acid and leucine. For some as yet undiscovered reason the α amino-n-butyric acid concentration is more than twice as high among chronic drinkers than among social drinkers. The concentration was unrelated to the alcoholic's state of nutrition, and it registered high regardless of the drinker's blood alcohol level. Lieber hopes that this specific test for alcoholism will have a three-fold value: aiding physicians in diagnosing alcoholism, helping them to judge objectively whether alcoholics are faithful in attempts at abstinence, and understanding the process of cirrhosis of the liver, among other degenerative diseases attributed to alcohol, once it is known why the α amino-n-butyric acid concentration is high.

Lieber's inventive animal and clinical research is more the exception than the rule, partly because money has always been scarce for alcoholism studies, and partly because alcoholism is not a fashionable field of research. NIAAA devotes only about 8% of its budget to research, most of the rest going into treatment programs. At the same time, NIAAA estimates that alcoholism costs the American economy some $25 billion annually.

As an example of what is still to be learned about the disease, scientists have no generally accepted explanation of the neurological process of intoxication. Without a definitive scientific understanding of how a person becomes drunk, the whole scientific edifice upon which efforts to explain alcoholism rest has a fundamental weakness. Concomitantly, attempts to discover drugs for detoxification of alcoholics or as antidotes to drunkenness are conducted largely on a hit-or-miss basis. So far, they all have missed.

Three other areas of health research have provided tantalizing hints about the mysteries of alcohol and alcoholism. They suggest that alcoholism runs in families and in ethnic groups and that there are relationships between alcohol and cancer and alcohol and heart disease.

For example, among Irish Americans there has long been a tradition

110

of hard drinking; among Jewish Americans, light to moderate drinking is the stereotype. Epidemiology indicates that, on the whole, both groups drink to reputation, but the unanswered question is whether alcoholism among them is cultural or hereditary. Or, as alcoholism authorities are prone to ask, is the disease caused by nature or nurture?

Pioneering studies of twins and adoptees in Denmark by Donald Goodwin of the Washington University Addiction Research Center in St. Louis, Mo., have suggested that hereditary factors may outweigh environment in alcoholism among men, at least for very severe forms of alcoholism. But Goodwin acknowledges that the study is flawed, and not at all conclusive. And Goodwin's most recent research among Danish women adoptees indicates that among women severe problem drinking is not hereditary. He studied 49 daughters of alcoholics and 48 daughters of nonalcoholics, all 97 of whom were adopted early in life by nonalcoholic nonrelatives. Only two women in each group were problem drinkers or alcoholics.

No attempt has been made to extrapolate these studies of hereditary drinking patterns among Danish adoptees to the cultural patterns among American Jews and Americans of Irish descent. Excellent sociological interpretations can explain the drinking habits of both groups without any recourse to genetics. So while there may be enough evidence for a doctor to include family drinking in his medical history of a patient, there is still no strong scientific backing for the contention that alcoholism is an inheritable disease.

With cancer and heart disease, the association is also suggestive but unproven. The complicating factor in cancer is that heavy drinkers are usually also heavy smokers. Cancers of the mouth, pharynx, larynx, and esophagus appear to be related to heavy drinking—along with heavy smoking—among Americans, the action of alcohol possibly augmenting the carcinogenicity of the tobacco. Despite the wealth of statistical indications that drinking and some cancers are related, it has been impossible to single out alcoholism as a direct cause of cancer, and alcohol has not produced cancer in laboratory animal experiments.

In heart disease, the nation's number one killer, there is some suggestion that alcoholism plays a role in cardiomyopathy, one of the lesser cardiac ills, but studies have found no link between drinking and coronary artery disease, the leading cause of heart attacks. In fact, one study of men covering a decade or more indicated that coronary artery disease incidence was lower among drinkers than among abstainers. On the other hand, points out Noble, this does not mean that drinking has a protective effect against coronary artery disease. Men classified as abstainers in the study may have been in poor health, and may have cut out drinking on a doctor's orders.

But regardless of how much physicians and scientists learn about its potential ravages, alcohol is America's drug of choice—just as it is for most other nations, just as it has been throughout recorded time, and just as it is likely to remain. And alcoholics, whose cure rate is probably little higher than it was in antiquity, are still largely on their own.

Growing Old Gracefully
by Robert Neil Butler, M.D.

Aging is an intrinsic part of the passage from birth to death. Old age, marked by the accumulation of wisdom, perspective, and judgment, is often characterized by declines and losses in biological function as well. While we know that the biological clock slows down for everyone, we do not yet know why it slows at different rates in different people, some of whom carry mental and physical vigor much further into their advanced years than others. Even defining the aging process is complicated by the difficulty of separating the deleterious changes produced by aging alone from those produced by the accompanying ravages of disease and social adversity.

The population explosion

The search for knowledge about aging is intensifying in the United States, largely as a matter of necessity. The number of people aged 65 and over is greater than ever and is increasing rapidly. The country is faced with a social and health problem of enormous proportions, made all the more urgent by the fact that until recently it had been neglected or actively avoided.

The magnitude of the problem is indicated by the data. In 1900 only 4% of the population of the United States was over 65. When the White House Conference on Aging took place in 1971, the proportion had reached 10%, and demographers predict that the percentage will increase to 12% by the end of the century and to 20% by the year 2030.

The children of the post-World War II baby boom who greened America in the 1960s will be the generation that grays America in the 21st century. In absolute numbers there are today some 23 million Americans over 65. Scientists expect that number to double between the years 2020 and 2030, reaching between 42 and 50 million. Even these estimates may be low, since they are based on medical knowledge and standards of health care that prevail today. New knowledge resulting in increased longevity could inflate the numbers dramatically.

Robert Neil Butler, M.D., *the author of* Why Survive?, *is Director of the National Institute on Aging, National Institutes of Health, Bethesda, Maryland.*

112

John Launois—Black Star

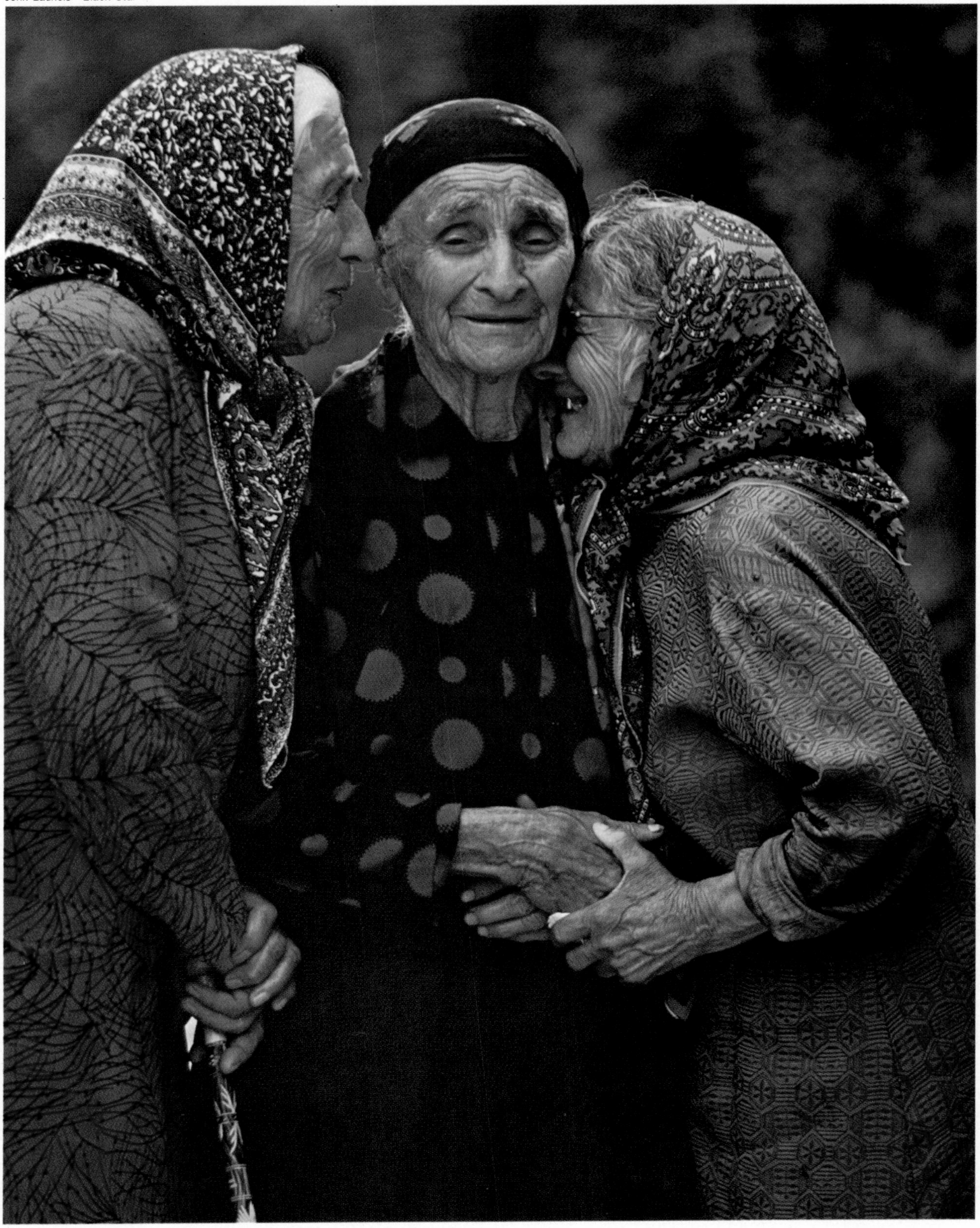

"The most serious problem in aging in the United States is monetary rather than medical. Many older people in this rich nation are living in desperate circumstances."

Whatever the actual figures, there is no avoiding the fact that the repercussions of the baby boom will be felt for several decades, and its social, economic, and personal consequences will be considerable. As a society we are going to need new policies for the social, economic, and medical well-being of the aged, policies that will reintegrate them into the community. We also need a new philosophy to eliminate cultural prejudices against old people, prejudices that are often absent in non-Western societies. Finally, there must be much more medical research into the phenomenon of aging itself.

Social and economic problems of the aged

The most serious problem in aging in the United States is monetary rather than medical. Many older people in this rich nation are living in desperate circumstances. By official standards, 20% of people over 65 are poor. This measure of poverty, however, is based on a stringent definition of emergency food needs established by the United States Department of Agriculture. A broader but more realistic definition of poverty, as an income of less than half the American median, for example, would put more than a third of our older citizens at or below the poverty line. The average single elderly American, in fact, lives on $70 a week. Bare economic survival erodes the body and the spirit, even when it is a common condition. But it is all the more humiliating in the United States, which for all its great wealth, spends only 4.2% of its gross national product (GNP) on the old. Countries with lesser resources, Great Britain and France, spend 6.7% and 7% of their GNPs on the elderly.

Passage of Medicare legislation in 1965 signaled a new era of concern about health care for older Americans. Medicare has made a vital contribution to improved health care for the aged, but it has its limits. Medicare was set up to treat old people almost as though they were still young. It does not have any provisions for some of the services that old people particularly need, such as checkups, foot care, dental care, hearing aids, glasses, or long-term care. It is a system that favors treatment over prevention. It is filled with shortcomings that illustrate a mysterious denial of the realities of old age, a blindness that is, unfortunately, common in our culture.

While poverty affects most old people, it particularly hurts widows and members of minority groups. The current life expectancy for women is almost eight years longer than that for men, and women tend to marry men who are an average of three years older. A woman is thus likely to face eleven years of widowhood, often with a percentage of her husband's social security benefits as her only income. Consequently, widowhood in old age frequently is associated with poverty, loneliness, isolation, and vulnerability to crime and the perpetrators of frauds and schemes who often victimize the elderly. Members of minority groups are especially likely to face old age in poverty. The same forces that limited achievement and financial success in their younger years still plague them in old age.

114

"While poverty affects most old people, it particularly hurts widows and members of minority groups."

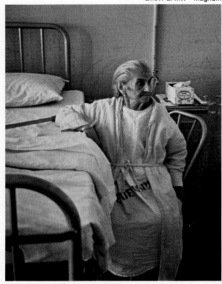

"One million people . . . live in the nation's nursing homes, which in many cases provide little more than basic custodial care."

(Opposite) "Forced retirement can be devastating to people who have the capacity, the desire, and the financial or emotional need to work."

Poverty forces some 30% of older Americans to live in substandard housing. Another one million people, 5% of the older population, live in the nation's nursing homes, which in many cases provide little more than basic custodial care. The facilities often are staffed with untrained workers, and there are serious questions about the quality of service within them. Half of all nursing homes, for example, do not even meet basic sanitation and fire standards.

Current policies seem to force old people into poverty. Mandatory retirement is a good example. The practice was introduced in the United States in the midst of the economic depression of the 1930s, in association with Social Security laws. Before then retirement was largely functional, depending on the individual's physical and mental health. Unemployment problems now make it difficult to abandon the widespread requirement that people quit working at age 65, despite the fact that forced retirement can be devastating to people who have the capacity, the desire, and the financial or emotional need to work. Aside from financial problems, some older people have great emotional difficulty in adjusting to retirement. Indications so far are that an individual's response to retirement is influenced not only by his or her personality, work history, health, and economic status—factors over which a person might not have much control—but also by the degree of mental preparation that has been made.

Many old people are forced to find work after their official retirement because they are unable to live adequately on retirement incomes. In fact, one-third of the income that old people have they earn through their own work, despite a hiring bias against them. In the competition, however, some older people are forced to labor under humiliating circumstances, without the fringe benefits offered to younger workers or for wages that they dare not report on their income tax.

The concept of aging

The term aging actually refers to the progressive changes that take place in a cell, in an organ, or in the total organism over the passage of an entire lifetime, but the study of aging is primarily concerned with the changes from maturity until death. Gerontologists are trying to identify factors that influence these changes so they can reduce the disabilities associated with aging. The most pressing question facing gerontologists is whether the changes that occur in the body are the result of aging itself, or of the diseases that accompany it. If they can answer this question, they may be able to develop effective treatment to prevent or retard degeneration.

Each person ages at a different rate and, even in the same person, aging affects each organ and body system differently. Since the probability of death increases rapidly with advancing age, researchers know that certain changes must occur that make people more vulnerable to disease. A young adult, for example, can recover easily from pneumonia, but an elderly person may die from it. Many changes occur in the body's cardiovascular, digestive, nervous, and hormonal systems.

116

The immune system's effective response to infection also declines with age, as do various other body defensive and protective reactions such as the white cell response or the feeling of pain. Doctors treating elderly patients should be aware of this.

There are several theories as to why the body ages. Some scientists believe that the life-span of the organism is either wholly genetically determined, or that certain genetic errors occur in key proteins, preventing their working properly. It may even be that the cells mutate as they divide, so that aging is due to the gradual accumulation of these abnormal mutated cells. There are also several nongenetic theories of aging; the "wear and tear" theory, for example, assumes that cells wear out with time or that waste products accumulate in the cells and interfere with their functioning. The "autoimmune" theory of aging holds that immune defenses normally directed against disease organisms or foreign tissues turn against the body's own cells with increasing age. Yet another possibility is that aging results from a breakdown in the mechanisms needed to perform complex functions.

Gerontology and geriatric medicine

The aging process itself remains essentially a medical problem, with myriad ramifications. The study of aging and the development of the specialty of geriatric medicine have been somewhat neglected by American medical schools and universities, despite the efforts of the Gerontological Society and the American Geriatric Society. Gerontologists have learned that the study of aging is a derivative science, drawing on prospective studies (following a group of people as they pass from youth to old age) and on a broad range of disciplines.

Geriatric medicine, the application to individual cases of medical knowledge about human aging, physiology, and pathophysiology, has lagged behind gerontology but is now a growing field. There is certainly room for it. As recently as 1970 more than half the medical schools in the United States had no special elective courses in geriatrics. At present there is only one endowed chair of geriatric medicine and not one medical school requires students to rotate routinely through nursing homes as part of their training, even though on any given day there are more patients in nursing home beds than in general hospital beds. Medical students need to train both in long-term care facilities and in a variety of settings where healthy elderly people congregate, so that they can see a broad spectrum of old people. Education in geriatric medicine for the medical directors of nursing homes would also result in improved diagnosis and treatment.

Seven industrialized nations—the U.S.S.R., Romania, France, The Netherlands, Israel, Japan, and the United States—have major institutes conducting research on aging. In the United States there is the National Institute on Aging, created by the Research on Aging Act of 1974. It is one of the National Institutes of Health, the biomedical research establishment of the federal government. The Research on Aging Act provides federal support of research to improve the quality of

117

*"Some older people have great emotional
difficulty in adjusting to retirement. . . .
[but] indications so far are that an
individual's response to retirement is
influenced not only by his or her
personality, work history, health, and
economic status . . . but also by the
degree of mental preparation that
has been made."*

life for older people as well as to extend the average life-span. The institute's mandate includes study of the normal processes of development. Its research plan, submitted to Congress, is entitled *Our Future Selves*. The report advises that a necessary first step in dealing with the problems of aging is to recognize that the aged are not "them," but are potentially and ultimately each one of us.

Directions in research

Among the various directions research is taking, the immune mechanism is getting a great deal of attention. In the person 65 and older the immune mechanism, by which the body musters its own resources to fight disease, is only about 10% as effective as that of the adolescent. Old people thus find it harder to fight off diseases, and that is why they frequently die of infections that young people virtually shrug off. Scientists are learning through animal studies that the immune response can be strengthened. This knowledge may do much to increase the vitality of older people.

Physicians unversed in the subtleties of geriatric medicine frequently fail to recognize a reversible brain syndrome in old people, dismissing it as senility, confusion, forgetfulness, or general problems with attention and concentration. Gerontologists now know, however, that there are some 100 causes of so-called senility, a condition that affects as many as one-fourth of all old people. The causes range from malnutrition to excessive medication, unrecognized congestive heart failure, walking pneumonia, or anemia. Breakthroughs in effective diagnosis and prompt treatment of devastating brain disorders that occur frequently in the elderly could reduce the nursing home population considerably. Likewise, development of an effective method of preventing osteoporosis, a softening of the bones that occurs after menopause, could drastically reduce the number of crippling fractures suffered by older women.

Research must also pursue the effect of medication on older people. Although there is plenty of information on the absorption, distribution, and toxicity of drugs in the body generally, their effects on older people have not been studied systematically. Doctors are learning that certain drugs show adverse or paradoxical effects in the elderly. For example, older women show a greater likelihood of bleeding when they take a certain anticoagulant. Tranquilizers that calm younger people may make older patients dangerously drowsy. Barbiturates in sleeping pills can cause an abnormal reaction in older people.

An exciting way of studying old age involves looking at the life cycle as a whole. One sees the transformation from youth to old age as a series of changes from infancy, childhood, adolescence, early adulthood, middle life, to early and late old age. There is among gerontologists a controversial "stage theory" of development, implying that movement from one stage to another requires certain preconditions. While natural human development may not be so orderly or precise, broad features do seem to characterize different periods of life. Geron-

119

"While it is difficult to establish the precise limits of the human life-span, . . . studies of long-living people indicate that the natural life-span may be somewhere between 110 and 120 years. Studies may also provide information that would lead to equalizing the life-spans of the sexes and of various racial and ethnic groups, differences which may be accounted for in part by differences in social class, occupational risks, or stress diseases. Genetic programming and individual and family life-styles may also contribute to these differences."

tologists hold two views on research on the life-span. There are those who wish to extend life beyond what we consider possible today. Others are more concerned with the quality than with the quantity of life. Much research, therefore, aims not so much at extending life beyond what may be the natural human life-span but at increasing the opportunities for more people to maintain vitality and comfort throughout that span.

While it is difficult to establish the precise limits of the human life-span, appraisals of various physiological characteristics—vision, for example—and studies of long-living people indicate that the natural life-span may be somewhere between 110 and 120 years. Studies may also provide information that would lead to equalizing the life-spans of the sexes and of various racial and ethnic groups, differences which may be accounted for in part by differences in social class, occupational risks, or stress diseases. Genetic programming and individual and family life-styles may also contribute to these differences. Controlled longitudinal studies, that is, studies of different groups of people as they are aging, may help distinguish those aspects of aging that are truly a result of the body's maturing process.

Because gerontologists themselves are only human and cannot always monitor the full life-spans of their human subjects, they must turn also to animal models. Studies range over a broad variety of animal species, from a worm that lives a mere 30 days to the cat and mouse, various farm animals, and a type of rhesus monkey that seems to be an excellent model for the study of human menopause.

There is a need, too, for research into psychological and social aspects of aging to put an end to the stigma of old age in American life. Studies of learning, memory, motivation, and creativity show that physiological, pathological, psychological, and social factors may all be involved in these cultural prejudices. Older people, for example, may feel that they are not supposed to be very capable or gifted because they are influenced by the cultural stereotypes of age. On the

Ellis Herwig—Stock, Boston

other hand, a person's memory may be damaged by a stroke or organic brain disease. It would be of great value to be able to determine whether an elderly patient's problem is pathological or attitudinal.

Gerontologists could use knowledge gained by their research to develop programs to aid older people, devising batteries of tests, scientifically sound standards that society would use to measure a person's capacity to continue working. Realistic measurements of an older person's work capability may bring an end to mandatory retirement policies which so often force the aged into a life of "leisure" they do not want and for which they have not prepared.

Research shows, too, that the family life of older people has been misunderstood. Romantic notions of a three-generation family flourished at a time when few people survived into old age. The opportunity for extended families has actually increased in recent years since more people are reaching old age. Some 40% of older parents now have great-grandchildren. The likelihood of a 10-year-old child having four living grandparents is now 1 in 14, whereas in 1920 the chances were only 1 in 90.

A modified version of the extended family does indeed exist in American life, research has shown. About 80% of older parents live within a half-hour of one or more of their children. On the other hand, approximately 25% of all older people have outlived all their other close relatives, and 50% of patients in nursing homes have no living family. The American family of the 1970s has been greatly affected by social and cultural conditions, including frequent divorce and rising unemployment. Social policies do not provide effective support to families who want to care for older relatives. In 1976, for instance, New York State paid about $15,000 per year in Medicaid funds for each nursing home patient. More imaginative social policies could help many families to keep older relatives in their own homes at far less cost than New York is paying. Some patients without close relatives could be maintained in their own or in foster care homes with the help of homemakers, health

"Gerontologists share a vision of the creation of a sense of community among young and old. They would reconcile the generations to build an effective compact that would assure every person . . . a truly decent and dignified old age."

aides, and community food programs. This would be much less expensive than institutional care.

Another important area of research is sexuality in older people. According to stereotypes, older people are supposed to lose their interest in and capacity for sexual activity, though in fact many people retain both to a very advanced age. Elderly people can benefit from sympathetic psychological assistance with their sexual problems, many of which result from disease, drugs, alcoholism, and social prejudice rather than from diminishing sexual desire.

Two other stereotypes that have been contradicted by research portray old people as politically conservative and unable to learn and change. There may well be an inherent psychological conserving tendency that comes with age, an instinct valuable not only to the individual but also to human progress. Many researchers believe, however, that the elderly hold the same wide variety of political views as the young. Many of the social, economic, and medical programs for the aged in the United States are the result of political activism by older people themselves, beginning with the Townsend movement in the 1930s. An elderly physician, Francis Townsend worked to improve the economic condition of older Americans during the Depression. Hundreds of thousands of older people and their families joined Townsend to influence the Committee on Economic Security, which had been appointed by President Franklin D. Roosevelt to develop social security legislation.

In the 1960 campaign, elderly voters organized a group called Senior Citizens for Kennedy. After John F. Kennedy's election as president, the group worked for the development of Medicare and eventually organized to become the National Council of Senior Citizens. Other groups continuing to speak for the elderly included the National Retired Teachers Association, the American Association of Retired Persons, and, since the early 1970s, a small activist group known as the Gray Panthers. Although these organizations have not had an overwhelming political impact, their efforts have paralleled the appointment of special congressional committees devoted to the problems of aging, as well as the passage of the Older Americans Act, establishing the Administration on Aging within the Department of Health, Education, and Welfare.

Studies of how people learn as they grow older might expand education throughout life. In France, for example, there is an educational program aimed at what is called the third age. In the United States, junior colleges and universities are beginning to expand opportunities for older people to continue their education, some even offering free tuition to people over 65.

A relatively new area of research is the study of death and bereavement. Gerontologists are developing a new awareness of the psychological stages people go through in coping with death, their own and that of their friends and relatives. Further study and understanding of the ways in which people face death, and a comparison of the ways in which members of a bereaved family support each other will enable

122

(Top) Ron Shuman; (bottom) Owen Franken—Stock, Boston

more people, both young and old, to deal with the final stage of life.

Geriatric medicine and gerontology are gaining importance, not only for sentimental or scientific reasons, but also because of the soaring costs of caring for the elderly. In 1976 in the United States, for example, half the $139 billion spent on health care covered the costs of chronic illnesses, conditions that constitute most of the health problems of the elderly. About 86% of all people over 65 have one or more chronic conditions, such as high blood pressure, arthritis, diabetes, heart disease, or arteriosclerosis. Even though 95% of people over 65 live in the community and are relatively independent, the elderly account for more than a quarter of the nation's health expenditure. This is due not only to their greater need for medical services, but also to the more costly nature of their illnesses. Older patients require more physician time, more frequent hospital admissions, and longer hospital stays. They are the main users of long-term care facilities and home health agencies. They consume 25% of all drugs. Medicare and Medicaid paid $25 billion in 1976 for the health care of older people. Together, the private sector and the government spent $15 billion on nursing home stays. Even if the proportion of old people in nursing homes should stay constant at 5%, that will mean there will be some 2.5 million in nursing homes by 2020 compared with 1.2 million today.

These staggering costs could be reduced by improving the health and vitality of older people and by continuing their productivity and contribution to the work force. Today's older citizens confirm that improvement is possible in that they are "younger" and healthier than previous generations. The medical profession is learning to reject the discriminatory view that one is automatically old at a certain age. The World Health Organization, in fact, has developed a spectrum of the aged to replace the arbitrary designation of everyone over 65 as "old." This spectrum compares young, healthy, and active 65-year-olds with people over 80, who are more often frail, dependent, and ill.

Ultimately society can best reduce the cost of aging and the need for services for the elderly by developing new ways of preventing the illnesses, disabilities, and social problems of old age. Until progress is made, older people can be trained to help and care for themselves, so that they have greater control of their bodies and their lives and have an enhanced quality of life.

It is not easy to predict the future. Predictions must be based on present knowledge, which is often incomplete. Unexpected discoveries can change the face of the future and romantic social visions often fall by the wayside when challenged by social and personal realities. Gerontologists share a vision of the creation of a sense of community among young and old. They would reconcile the generations to build an effective compact that would assure every person—those now old as well as their children and their children's children who must one day become old themselves—a truly decent and dignified old age.

123

Kaiser-Permanente: Prepaid Care Comes of Age

by Samuel Moffat
photographs by Ron Shuman

In 1933, during the depths of the great Depression, a young surgeon hung out his shingle in the southern California desert, among the construction workers building the dams, tunnels, and canals that would eventually make up the aqueduct that brings water from the Colorado River to sprawling Los Angeles. The doctor, Sidney R. Garfield, borrowed money against his own belongings to build and equip a small hospital and to purchase an ambulance.

But despite the presence of thousands of workmen in need of medical care, Garfield was losing money. Victims of serious on-the-job injuries were hurried to Los Angeles by the contractors' insurance companies. The workers spent their wages on other—to them, more important—things, such as Friday and Saturday nights, so he earned nothing from taking care of their off-the-job ailments, either.

The concept of prepayment

To enable him to survive, Garfield and an executive of one of the insurance companies developed a prepayment plan for medical care. Under the plan the companies would pay him five cents a day per worker, and a similar voluntary contribution from each man would cover nonindustrial care. This predictable revenue supported Garfield and a small team of doctors and nurses, eventually making it possible for him to build two more hospitals.

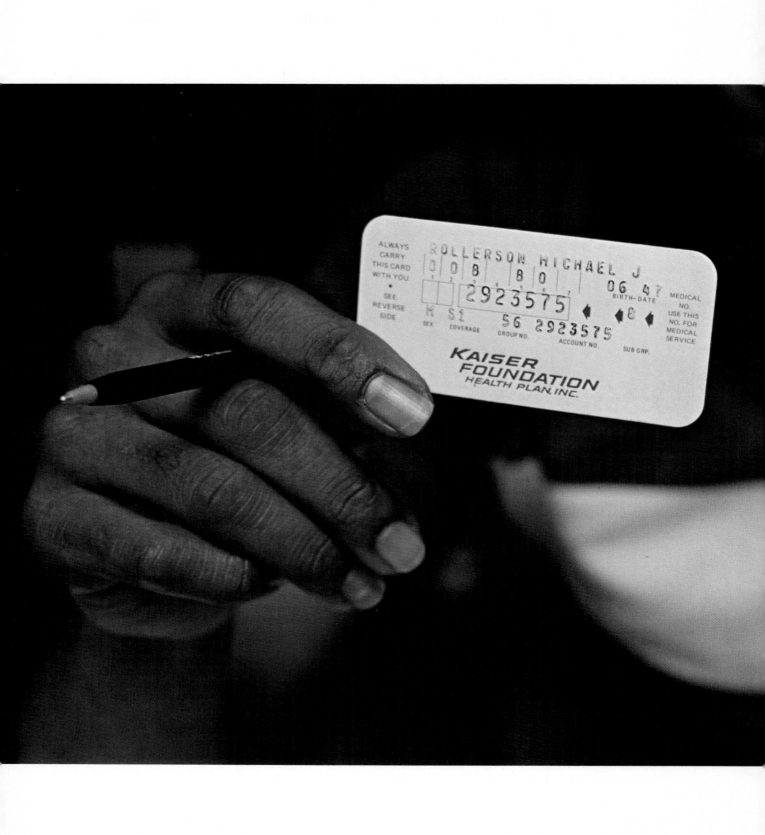

Five years later, Garfield was asked by Edgar F. Kaiser, son of industrialist Henry J. Kaiser, to provide medical and hospital services on the building site of Grand Coulee Dam in eastern Washington. There were 5,000 employees to be cared for and the workers' wives and children, too. Garfield organized a larger group of physicians to do the job. Eventually it included surgeons, internists, an obstetrician-gynecologist, and a pediatrician. At first only the workers were covered, under the same sort of prepayment arrangement used in the California desert project, but later the unions demanded that families be covered as well. Garfield and his associates had no experience judging the costs of such coverage but "took some figures out of the air."

In those days, prepaid group practice of medicine was rare in the United States. The first two pioneers in the field, the Community Hospital Association of Elk City, Okla., and the Ross-Loos Medical Group in Los Angeles, had come into being only in the late 1920s. Today, however, 40 years after the start of the Grand Coulee program under Garfield's guidance, prepayment and group practice are the federal government's chosen mechanisms for attempting to restructure the delivery of medical care and to combat the tremendous inflation of health care costs in the U.S.

Did Garfield and his associates think they were blazing a new trail for American medicine four decades ago? No, they did not, Garfield recalls today. But his boss, Henry J. Kaiser, used to ask at Grand Coulee, "Why aren't we doing this all over the country?" Henry Kaiser headed the group of construction companies building the dam, and his energy and initiative eventually spawned more than 100 industrial and commercial companies as well.

The fruits of Grand Coulee

Little did Garfield and his fellow physicians, or even the far-seeing Kaiser, imagine the fruit that their idea would ultimately bear. From Grand Coulee they went on to develop company-sponsored health plans serving Kaiser shipyard and steel workers during World War II (90,000 of them in one California location alone), and then the pioneering community plans that operate today in six states from Ohio to Hawaii. Now known as the Kaiser-Permanente Medical Care Program, this system serves more than 3 million members. Medical economist Anne R. Somers has noted that Kaiser-Permanente is "the world's largest private direct-service health care plan." (The name *Permanente* derives from one of Kaiser's early business ventures, which was located near Permanente Creek, Calif.)

Even if Garfield and his fellow physicians had been presumptuous enough — and they were not — to foresee that their prepaid group practice might someday be a model for the whole nation, they faced a formidable obstacle in the transitory nature of their enterprise: the dam would soon be finished, the patients gone, and the group disbanded. "Toward the end of the project," Garfield said, "we started dreaming of what we could do with a plan like ours in a permanent community.

Samuel Moffat *is a free-lance writer, primarily on medical subjects, whose articles have appeared in the* New York Times Magazine, Family Health, *and* Modern Medicine.

Ron Shuman, *whose books of photographs include* Portraits *and* Day by Day, *is a versatile photojournalist whose pictures have appeared in numerous consumer and professional magazines.*

But the possibilities were remote. We'd need a membership and money for permanent facilities. And we were concerned about opposition from other physicians. So when Coulee was completed, we thought we had come to the end of our journey into medical care."

The group dispersed and Garfield took a teaching job at the University of Southern California. But it did not remain dispersed for long. When Pearl Harbor was attacked and the U.S. joined World War II, Henry Kaiser needed medical services for the tens of thousands of workers building Liberty ships in his shipyards. The company asked Garfield to duplicate and expand his previous program. He was in the Army at the time, however, and scheduled to leave soon for India. This proved a small obstacle. A. B. Ordway, the insurance company executive who had worked out the prepayment plan for the aqueduct project and who had been Henry Kaiser's very first employee when he started out in the construction business in 1914, took off for Washington, D.C. He returned with a release from service for Garfield signed by none other than President Franklin D. Roosevelt.

Garfield built up a roster of 100 doctors to care for the 90,000 workers in the San Francisco Bay area. Similar groups were developed for Kaiser's shipyards in Vancouver, Wash., and a steel plant in Fontana, Calif. All told, they were responsible for medical services for 200,000 employees. Most of the workers were poor medical risks, which had prevented them from being drafted into the armed forces.

The birth of Kaiser-Permanente

At war's end most of the employees went back home, and so did many of the doctors; only 16 physicians remained in northern California, fewer in Vancouver and Fontana. But the groups wanted to continue. They had the wartime facilities and the nucleus of a membership in former Kaiser wartime employees who had stayed on near the plants and wanted the plan available for the public. So the program was opened to the community, although for a while its financial status was perilous. Money was so tight that to get a new pencil an employee had to turn in a stub no more than two inches long. Garfield prohibited the use of expensive cellophane tape for any purpose other than bandaging a patient who was sensitive to adhesive tape—it was *not* to be used on paper.

Gradually the financial picture improved. Patients were satisfied with the plan and membership grew, so that by 1949 more than 100,000 persons were enrolled. But physicians in the community were not happy. They questioned the ethics of prepayment, charging Garfield and his associates with soliciting patients. The county medical societies refused to admit new Kaiser-Permanente physicians to membership; Garfield was brought before one society's ethics committee three times; a close associate of his was dropped from the staff of a San Francisco hospital after Kaiser opened medical offices there.

Still, the program survived, largely because it already had Kaiser hospital facilities where participating physicians could admit their most

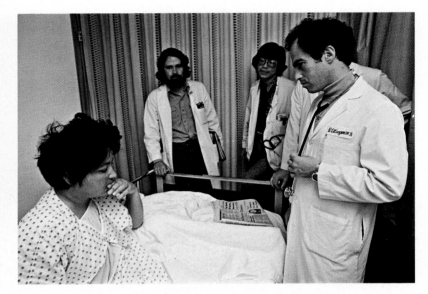

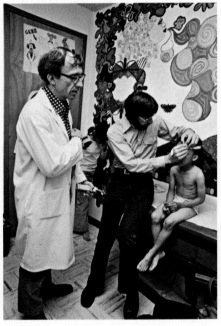

One of Kaiser-Permanente's six basic operating principles is group practice, which provides access to specialists of all types. Kaiser-Permanente Medical Center staff members in these photographs are: an internist who specializes in primary care (top left); an endocrinologist (top right), on hospital rounds; and a pediatric neurologist (bottom), seen examining a young patient with assistance from a resident.

critically ill patients. The doctors strove to meet the highest standards of care, so that Kaiser-Permanente's quality of medicine could never be questioned. "The opposition forced us to cover everything thoroughly," Garfield said. Today relations with the rest of the profession are excellent. Kaiser-Permanente physicians belong to their local medical societies and are active in state and national medical organizations.

As far back as 1932, a blue-ribbon panel called the Committee on the Costs of Medical Care recommended that medical care in the U.S. "be furnished largely by organized groups of physicians . . . and other associated personnel [organized] preferably around a hospital, for rendering complete home, office, and hospital care." The committee also urged "that the costs of medical care be placed on a group payment basis." More than a dozen years later, Garfield met the chairman of that committee, Ray Lyman Wilbur, who had once been president of the American Medical Association (AMA). They met during the period when local members of the AMA, through their county medical societies, were making difficulties for Kaiser-Permanente. "I asked him why the doctors were giving us all this trouble. 'Young man,' Wilbur said, 'nothing new or great has ever been achieved without great opposition. If you didn't have any opposition you wouldn't be doing anything worthwhile. You should be very happy with it.' "

Basic principles of the plan

Although Garfield and his associates had developed certain operating principles by necessity as early as the days of the Los Angeles aqueduct, the underlying guidelines were not formalized until the late 1940s. By that time the Kaiser plan was beginning to be accepted, and outsiders wanted to know how it worked. Eventually the plan's six basic principles became known as "the genetic code." They are: (1) *group practice;* (2) *integration of facilities,* meaning combining both outpatient and hospital facilities to get maximum utilization of equipment and personnel; (3) *prepayment;* (4) *preventive medicine,* which emphasizes keeping the patient well as much as treating the sick; (5) *voluntary enrollment,* which enables those who do not like the prepaid group practice format to choose an alternative type of plan and which provides a barometer of patient satisfaction (Kaiser-Permanente members through employer and union groups may leave the plan, if they desire to select an alternative type of plan, at annual intervals); and (6) *physician responsibility,* not only for patient care but also for other aspects of the program, including financing, planning, and allocation of resources. It is worth noting that four of these six principles are incorporated in the U.S. Health Maintenance Organization (HMO) Act of 1973. (Exceptions are numbers 2 and 6.)

Even these "genetic" principles are not immutable, however, as is fitting for any evolving organism. In Hawaii, Kaiser-Permanente has one medical office staffed by a single doctor and another with only four physicians; these doctors may refer patients to associates elsewhere who belong to the group, but this still represents a variant of the basic system. In Colorado the facilities are not integrated, since Kaiser-Permanente owns no hospitals there but relies on other community hospitals. Nonetheless, with the basic foundation of prepaid group practice, the economic and medical advantages that prevail in other Kaiser regions are still achieved.

One additional central principle—focusing on fiscal policy—has also been vital to Kaiser-Permanente: the program must be self-sustaining. In the 30 years of the program's existence, less than 1% of its capital financing has been donated by either private or governmental sources. New facilities and equipment are paid for out of funds generated by the operation itself and by means of long-term loans. In most U.S. nonprofit community hospitals, on the other hand, private philanthropy or government grants have financed most new construction.

The Kaiser-Permanente system is designed not only to deliver the best possible medical care to each patient but also to keep the cost of such care to a minimum. Toward this end, integration of facilities —the combination of clinic and hospital facilities so that equipment and personnel are used to maximum efficiency—is also incorporated into the basic principles. The technician at work above is employed by a clinical laboratory that serves several Kaiser-Permanente Medical Centers.

Introducing HMOs

The steady membership growth of one private health plan, however, even taken together with the good performances of other prepayment plans by smaller groups, would not have been enough to convince the federal government it needed a new health policy—one promoting prepaid group practice as a way of reducing health costs. What was needed was a stimulant, a catalyst. The catalyst was Paul M. Ellwood, Jr., a physician and health policy researcher who in the late 1960s conducted two studies that affected major health policy legislation. In 1970 Ellwood helped develop the policy statement that led to federal legislation establishing HMOs. According to his description an HMO is "an organization which delivers comprehensive care—including preventive services, ambulatory and inpatient physician services, hospital services, laboratory and X-ray services, and indemnity coverage for out-of-area emergency services—to voluntarily enrolled consumers, on the basis of fixed-price contracts. By its contract, the HMO guarantees the availability of quality health care services to its enrollees."

129

Prepaid group practices can qualify for federal certification as HMOs by meeting requirements of the Health Maintenance Organization Act of 1973 (amended in 1976). In addition, two other types of HMOs are permitted—one in which physicians are paid employees (staff HMOs) and another where individual physicians contract to provide services (Individual Practice Associations, or IPAs, sometimes also called medical foundations). But all HMOs are required to give specified health services for a prenegotiated fee that is paid periodically in advance. (Kaiser-Permanente groups would of course make ideal HMOs. Applications for federal qualification are pending, and two of its plans— in Ohio and Colorado—are qualified as HMOs under state laws.)

What Ellwood did in 1970 was persuade officials of the U.S. Department of Health, Education, and Welfare (HEW) that in order to head off the rapid inflation in medical care costs, the government would have to change the medical care system in which there is little economic incentive for providers to keep prices down. To foster competition, the HMO act and amendments require that employers who must pay the minimum wage and who provide health benefits for their employees must also make HMO membership an option if a qualified HMO is available in their area, and if 25 employees reside in the area served by the HMO. And what Ellwood proposed to the federal officials was that the new system incorporate certain key elements of the Kaiser-Permanente experience, particularly comprehensive medical care, delivered to a specific population for a fixed price.

In most regions, Kaiser-Permanente owns and operates its own community hospitals, which provide service to the general public as well as to plan members. Here a patient in cardiac arrest is brought into the emergency room at the plan's South San Francisco medical center.

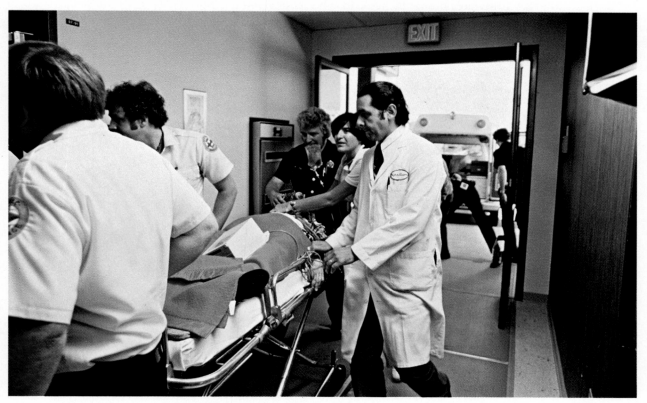

Applying the lessons of Kaiser-Permanente

"Just as soon as I had met with the people from HEW," Ellwood recalled recently, "and they said, 'let's do this and put it in a presidential health message,' I got on a plane and I went out to Oakland and sat down with the top management at Kaiser-Permanente." [The program's head-quarters are in Oakland, Calif.]

"Kaiser served a defined population and knew how much it cost to provide services to people. Much of the really fundamental information about what it takes to give medical care to a group of people was available there. Our best data about how many beds we need, how many nurses, even how many bandages, comes from that operation. The HMO concept wasn't some pipe dream, it was already being used for a couple of million people."

What Ellwood knew was that studies that had been made of the Kaiser-Permanente experience showed that the program delivered high quality care and, at the same time, reduced costs. In 1967 the National Advisory Commission on Health Manpower had concluded that Kaiser's "services are provided at significant savings by comparison with the cost for equivalent services purchased in the surrounding communities and the country at large. . . . These economies appear due almost entirely to the elimination of unnecessary health care, particularly hospitalization."

The commission had difficulty getting exact comparisons between Kaiser members and non-Kaiser populations. On the average, Kaiser-Permanente members are younger and healthier than the general population, as they consist largely of employed persons and their families; their medical care costs are paid primarily by an employer or out of union funds. Nevertheless, even allowing for a 25% increase over Kaiser costs because of differences in populations, the commission believed costs "would still be only 70–80% as large" as comparable expenses. (This part of the study compared Kaiser-Permanente Northern California data with statewide California figures.)

The special nature of the Kaiser-Permanente membership—and of memberships of other prepaid groups—used to make it possible for critics of such plans to claim that the groups' lower costs came about because they "skimmed off" patients who were healthier and therefore less expensive to care for. Recent studies, however, show this accusation to be untrue. For example, a Social Security Administration (SSA) study compared government costs for Medicare patients who belonged to seven prepaid group practice plans against the amount paid for similar Medicare recipients living in the same areas but receiving their medical care under individual fee-for-service arrangements. Overall, fee-for-service care cost 10% more than care in the prepaid plans. Where the groups controlled their own hospitals, fee-for-service costs rose to 20% more than those of prepaid group practice. The study declared that "the evidence showing that hospital utilization and overall costs are lower under group practice prepayment plans appears conclusive."

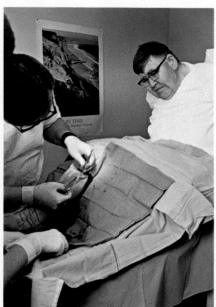

Because hospital expenses represent the single largest component —roughly 40%—of all medical costs in the U.S., eliminating unnecessary hospitalization can save a great deal of money. Another SSA study which analyzed hospital use by more than 8,000 Medicaid families illustrates the economy of prepaid group plans in this respect. Members of HMOs received 340 days of care a year per 1,000 members. In contrast, among matched patients receiving fee-for-service care in the same geographic areas, hospital utilization more than doubled—888 days per 1,000 persons.

The authors of this study found that among both categories of patients, doctors were contacted with almost the same frequency, about 3.5 visits a year for each person. And the researchers observed "no significant difference between the study groups and their controls in terms of health status perceived or number of chronic conditions." Commenting on these findings, Alain C. Enthoven, professor of public and private management at the Stanford University Graduate School of Business, said that "this would suggest that the prepaid group practice plans do not achieve their lower costs by selecting healthier persons as members, or at the expense of the health status of the members."

Prepayment and prevention

Clearly there are fundamental economic differences between fee-for-service physician and hospital care and prepaid plans providing the same services. Professor Enthoven has summarized the situation:

Most medical care is organized and financed in this country so it provides many powerful cost-increasing incentives and few restraints.

First, fee-for-service rewards physicians with more income for providing more care and more expensive care, whether or not more is necessary, effective, or beneficial to the patient. . . . Second, cost reimbursement for the hospital (or payment of cost-based charges) rewards the hospital with more revenue for providing more costly care, whether or not more costly care is necessary, effective, or beneficial to the patient. . . . And third-party insurance relieves the patient of most of the extra cost of more costly care so he has little incentive to question the need for the expenditures made on his behalf, and is in a poor position to do so in any case.

On the other hand, physicians and hospitals who are paid fixed fees to care for a given group of patients have strong incentives to keep costs down. It is to their advantage to eliminate unnecessary and unnecessarily expensive care because doing so increases the group's income per member and per patient. But it would be foolish for them to reduce services too drastically, to the point that patients did not get the care they really needed. The result of such a policy would be that patients would only seek care when their illnesses were more advanced, thus requiring more expensive care than if the ailments were detected and treated early. In other words, prepayment in a group setting fosters preventive medicine.

Kaiser-Permanente's Sidney Garfield had realized this in the 1930s when he was just beginning to care for the aqueduct builders in Southern California. Many workers came in with puncture wounds in their feet, caused by nails sticking out of boards. At first Garfield went out and pounded the nails down himself; later he got the safety department to be more active in preventing injuries. The results, of course, were healthier workers and fewer wounds for Garfield to treat.

And at Grand Coulee he learned another lesson in preventive medicine that he has never forgotten. "Before we started the family plan," he recalls, "we used to see quite a few really sick women and children in our hospital as we walked down the corridors—terminal cases of pneumonia, ruptured appendixes, things like that. After the prepayment plan for families had been operating a while, the terminal pneumonias became early pneumonias, the ruptured appendixes became early, simple appendicitis. And of course the answer was simple—with the barrier of cost removed, the people were coming in earlier for care. We were able to treat their illnesses sooner, keep them from getting complications, and I believe we kept quite a few from dying."

Prepayment and efficiency

Other advantages of the prepaid group model are that it encourages better use of medical manpower, improves quality control among physicians, and promotes innovation in the delivery of care. For example, in certain parts of the country there are too many surgeons. Not occupied full time in their specialty, they are not as proficient in the operating room as they ought to be. But a group of physicians in a prepaid plan need employ only the number of surgeons (or any other

From its inception, one of the goals of the Kaiser-Permanente plan has been to eliminate unnecessary hospitalization by encouraging preventive medicine, fostering a program of home health care nursing (opposite top) that employs registered nurses specially trained in public health, and performing minor surgery in the physician's office (opposite bottom). Another feature of the system is the maximum use of paramedical personnel. A paramedic (below) applies a full-body cast to a patient with a spinal problem.

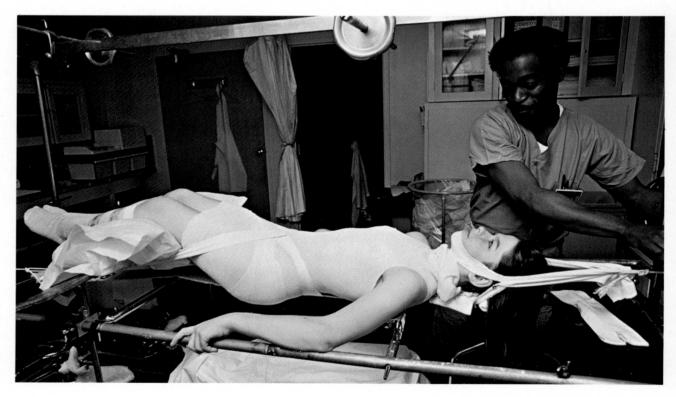

specialists, for that matter) required to render the care needed by a defined membership. Kaiser-Permanente, for example, has decided it does not yet have enough open-heart surgery cases in northern California to justify having its own surgical team; it sends these patients to community facilities such as Stanford University, where surgery is performed by the team of Norman E. Shumway, one of the world's leading heart surgeons. Kaiser-Permanente pays the bills.

A prepaid group may also use primary care physicians more effectively, since outpatient care is emphasized over hospital care, and may turn to paramedical personnel, or "physician extenders," to deliver care. In addition, group health education programs, which encourage members to adopt healthful living habits or to manage their own illnesses more capably, should be a natural part of preventive medicine and can use nonphysician personnel very effectively. Kaiser-Permanente has pioneering health education centers where members use a variety of sources from pamphlets and books to movies and film strips for learning more about many medical conditions.

Quality control among physicians is fostered in a prepaid group setting because patients are referred within the physician group. If one doctor is not giving proper patient care, others will quickly know. More importantly, inadequacy on the part of one group member will actually cost the group money, which means that corrective action is more likely to occur promptly. Finally, Ellwood's studies found that HMOs and similar structures foster the development of new organizations for the delivery of care. An example comes from the Kaiser-Permanente experience. "The head of the San Joaquin Foundation for Medical Care in Stockton, Calif., told me flat out that they created it to compete with Kaiser," he said. "Furthermore, medical delivery-system innovations tend to spread contiguously. HMOs beget HMOs."

The future of the HMO

Despite the obvious financial and medical advantages of prepaid group practice, the HMO movement has progressed quite slowly. Currently there are more than four times as many organizations active than there were in 1970, when the federal government first began promoting the idea, in advance of the HMO Act. But growth has slowed recently, partly because limited funds have been available for feasibility studies, planning, and initial development. Ellwood says the program has also run into "reluctance on the part of physicians to give up fee-for-service."

In mid 1976 there were slightly more than 6 million Americans enrolled in HMO-type plans with more than half of them—a little over 3 million—in Kaiser plans. But even with growth more rapid than that of Kaiser-Permanente, which has more than doubled its membership in the last decade, it seems unlikely that HMOs will prove as popular as anticipated a few years ago; in 1973, for example, an article in *Fortune* magazine said, "government and private sources figure that as many as 50 million people could be enrolled by the mid-1980s." Nevertheless, the HMO approach is a proven method of delivering quality care

A keystone of preventive medicine, patient education is emphasized at most Kaiser-Permanente centers. Richard Hardin, a retired anatomy professor, is a volunteer lecturer at the Kaiser-Permanente Health Education Center at Oakland, Calif.

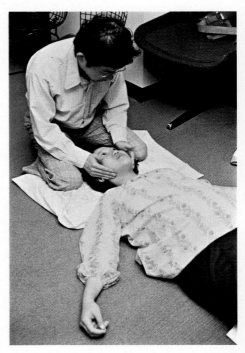

Among its numerous educational facilities, the Kaiser-Permanente Medical Center in Oakland has individual and group programs for expectant parents. A pregnant woman learns about breast-feeding from a TV cassette available in the audiovisual library (left); for couples interested in natural childbirth, the center offers classes in the Lamaze method.

for a reasonable price. It seems unlikely that its ability to contain costs will be lost on the American people and their politicians, given the obvious need to limit rising health costs.

The real future of HMOs will probably depend upon the government's long-range attitude toward them. If the HMO concept, or some form of prepaid group practice, is tied to national health insurance, the approach will undoubtedly gain wider acceptance. Ellwood is also trying to devise ways of stimulating other delivery systems that produce similar results. For instance, some multispecialty group practice clinics have very low hospital utilization rates even though they operate on a fee-for-service basis. He would encourage the development of such clinics as "essential building blocks to any cost contained health system." (Doctors practicing alone outnumber those in groups by a ratio of 5:1.) In addition, he would like to see insurance companies "organize doctors and hospitals into separately priced groups" on the basis of cost and utilization experience. This would allow consumers—the government included—to select those groups offering more benefits for the same price.

Kaiser-Permanente today: goals and obstacles

What does the future hold for Kaiser-Permanente? Certainly the existing medical program should see steady growth in membership. In addition, the fact that federal and state officials, government advisors, and industrial leaders are increasingly aware of the accomplishments of the program should lead to wider application by others of its operating principles. As just one illustration, in 1977 an advisory group from Kaiser-Permanente was engaged by Ford Motor Company to explore the feasibility of Ford's establishing a prepaid group practice plan to serve its employees and others living in and near Detroit. The advisory group also is expected to carry out similar studies for other large industrial employers.

Internally, Kaiser-Permanente is committed to improving the exem-

135

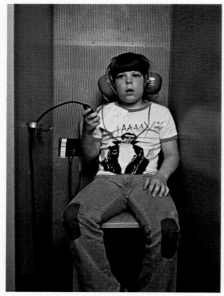

Regular checkups are another aspect of preventive medicine promoted by the Kaiser program. Young patients take routine tests at the Multiphasic Health Checkup Center in San Francisco (top left and right), and healthy infants regularly receive well-baby examinations.

plary health care delivery system that it pioneered. "I believe we do an excellent job of taking care of the ill," says Dr. Bruce J. Sams, Jr., executive director of the Permanente Medical Group in the northern California region—the largest group of physicians associated with Kaiser-Permanente. "But we have not yet fulfilled our potential when it comes to caring for the healthy."

Dr. Sams feels progress needs to be made in three interrelated areas: improved health-screening techniques, better matching of physician time to patient needs, and increased patient education. Kaiser-Permanente has been in the forefront of health-screening studies, particularly those dealing with cost-effectiveness of different types of early diagnosis and screening. "Quite frankly," says Dr. Sams, "a large part of any screening effort at the present time is aimed at reassuring the patient that nothing is wrong. A significant portion of our outpatient load has the same essential objective. There is little a doctor can do for the flu, colds, and other ailments for which there are no cures. But today's patient still desires a doctor's reassurance that there is nothing more seriously wrong. We need to develop better methods—screening systems, nurse practitioners, physicians' assistants, whatever—to minimize these demands on physician time so the physician can do what he or she was trained to do—take care of the ill."

Externally, Kaiser-Permanente and other prepaid plans must deal with problems that accompany government support and regulation of medical care in the U.S. today. As James A. Vohs and Walter K. Palmer of Kaiser-Permanente said at a 1976 University of Pittsburgh conference on capital financing of health facilities, "Basic incentives to operate effectively and efficiently are eroded and destroyed by retrospective cost reimbursement systems of payment. Payment of a fixed prospective rate would maintain and support these incentives and save substantial administrative costs for both the providers and the government." Vohs is president and Palmer financial vice-president of Kaiser Foundation Health Plan, Inc., and Kaiser Foundation Hospitals, two of the principal operating components of the Kaiser-Permanente Medical Care Program (*see* box on page 127).

Rather than support or initiate any single approach to financing and delivering health services in the United States, Kaiser-Permanente has consistently advocated a pluralistic approach to preserve such principles as innovation and consumer choice. Yet along with other cost-effective health plans, Kaiser-Permanente must contend with increasing public expectations that government will control the escalation in national health care expenditures.

Vohs emphasizes, "Basic incentives for organizers, providers, and consumers of health care must be included in any legislation or other initiatives aimed at encouraging more efficient and cost-effective health care delivery, including national health programs. Without incentives, we should not expect significant change in the way health or hospital services are currently organized and delivered under traditional approaches."

To preserve private initiative in health care economics, Vohs noted recently, "It remains for the major employers in the United States, who are already reacting to the burden of runaway health care costs, to become directly involved in the organization, financing, and delivery of health care services. They have both the resources and motivation to do so."

Kaiser-Permanente is also concerned that "certificate of need" laws, which require approval by state, regional, or local planning agencies before hospitals and other health care facilities may be built, be expanded, or acquire certain expensive equipment, could prevent organized health care systems from meeting their members' needs. This could occur even though such systems may represent the most economical way of delivering care and the most efficient use of hospital beds, according to program officials.

Despite the many problems facing Kaiser-Permanente and other forms of prepaid medical care, including HMOs, more people than ever before accept the underlying principles of such groups and see their value not only to individual patients but to society as a whole. And even though the principles are still evolving, they have brought about a radical change in the way Americans can look at health care delivery and costs. "The very fact," said Ellwood, "that the government advocated reshaping the health system and changing its organization and incentives has, to my way of thinking, reversed health policy in this country forever after. Some permanent change has been made here, so that we will never again consider financing health care in isolation."

FOR ADDITIONAL READING:

"HMOs: Are They the Answer to Your Medical Needs?" *Consumer Reports* 39 (1974): 756–762.

Crile, George, Jr. "The Surgeon's Dilemma." *Harper's Magazine* 250 (1975): 30–38.

De Kruif, Paul. *Kaiser Wakes the Doctors.* New York: Harcourt, Brace and Co., 1943.

Ellwood, Paul M., Jr., et al. "Health Maintenance Strategy." *Medical Care* 9 (1971): 291–298.

Enthoven, Alain C. "Prepaid Group Practice and National Health Policy." In *Proceedings of the 26th Annual Group Health Institute*, pp. 2–19. Washington, D.C.: Group Health Association of America, 1976.

Fuchs, Victor R. *Who Shall Live? Health, Economics, and Social Choice.* New York: Basic Books, 1975.

Rothfeld, Michael B. "Sensible Surgery for Swelling Medical Costs." *Fortune* 87 (1973): 110–119.

Somers, Anne R., ed. *The Kaiser-Permanente Medical Care Program.* New York: The Commonwealth Fund, 1971.

Medical Pioneers

The Physicians
of
Ancient China

by William K. Beatty, B.A., M.S.L.S.

Courtesy, The Metropolitan Museum of Art, New York City, anonymous gift, 1944

Between 2950 B.C. and A.D. 1560 Chinese medicine passed through four major periods. The first, from 2950 to 2600 B.C., was the time of the three medical emperors, primarily an era of myth and legend with only approximate dating of events. It was the period of the beginning of acupuncture and moxibustion, two uniquely Chinese methods of treatment. The events of the next two thousand years are obscure, but a slow growth of medical knowledge and gradual changes in medical practice can be assumed.

The second period was a mixture of legend and fact centered on the career of Pien Ch'iao—about whom anecdotal material dates to the first half of the 5th century B.C. The third period was that of the great practitioners, the physicians Chang Chung-ching and Wang Shu-ho and the surgeon Hua T'o, running from about A.D. 150 to 300. The individuals and events were real, although legends have grown up around them. The final 1,300 years, featuring the compilation of encyclopaedic works and the writing of commentaries on earlier authors, produced little that was original. In the second half of the 16th century, tenuous communication began with medical representatives from the West and the character of Chinese medicine began to change.

The three medical emperors

The legendary Five Rulers of China led their people for almost seven and a half centuries before Christ. The first three of these emperors— Fu Hsi, Shen Nung, and Huang Ti—were also medically oriented. Fu Hsi discovered the Pa Kua ("eight trigrams"), the symbolic basis for medical, philosophical, and astrological thinking. Shen Nung, called the founder of Chinese medicine, was also known as the Divine Husbandman. Huang Ti, the famed Yellow Emperor, supposedly wrote the *Nei Ching* (*The Classic of Internal Medicine*), the medical work that was to be revered for thousands of years. The three men later were worshipped together at many shrines.

Fu Hsi. The legendary founder of the Chinese people reputedly showed his subjects how to fish, raise domestic animals, and cook. Fu Hsi taught them the rules of marriage and the use of picture symbols. He also made known the Pa Kua, which he first saw written on the back of a "dragon-horse" as it rose from the waters of the Yellow River. To accomplish all of these things Fu Hsi had to have an unusual beginning and a long reign. The former was provided by his mother, who conceived the future emperor miraculously and carried him in her womb for 12 years. His reign, by good fortune, ran from 2953 to 2838 B.C.— 115 years!

The Pa Kua consists of eight trigrams, or three-line symbols, composed of continuous and broken lines. The continuous lines are called yang and basically represent all things male; the broken lines are called yin and represent female aspects of life. Yang and yin are complementary rather than antagonistic. Such is the profundity of meaning contained in these symbols that Confucius himself once stated that if he could study the Pa Kua for 50 years he might be able to obtain

William K. Beatty, B.A., M.S.L.S., *coauthor of* The Story of Medicine in America *and author of "Hippocrates, a Man, an Influence" for the* 1977 Medical and Health Annual, *is Professor of Medical Bibliography, Northwestern University Medical School, Chicago.*

(Overleaf) Chinese imperial dragon, 18th-century embroidered medallion. In the Metropolitan Museum of Art, New York City.

美君人題書
朝散大夫大和守和氣成
大日本太醫令從五位下
寬政十年吉月冬至之日
其德永不渴
千億萬年後
光明如日月
高大如天地

The three emperors of medicine, Fu Hsi (center), Shen Nung (right), and Huang Ti (left) were also the first three of the five legendary emperors during China's first seven centuries. Fu Hsi made known the Pa Kua, a basic symbol for the principles underlying health and disease. Shen Nung studied and tested medicinal plants and is generally called the Father of Chinese Medicine. Huang Ti invented acupuncture and was long thought to be the author of The Classic of Internal Medicine. *The three medical emperors shown here on a 1798 Japanese scroll painting were frequently worshipped in the same temple.*

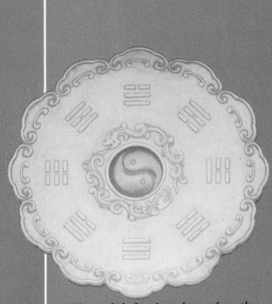

*The symbols for yin and yang form the
center of this carved white jade amulet of
the 18th century, and are surrounded by
the Pa Kua, the eight trigrams embracing
combinations of yin (broken lines) and
yang (continuous lines).*

*This 17th-century painting on silk shows
a group of sages pondering the symbols
for yin and yang.*

wisdom. Confucius did, however, study the Pa Kua long enough to write a commentary that forms part of the *I Ching* (*Classic of Changes*), one of the books revered by the Chinese people.

The ideograms for yin and yang first appeared in an appendix to the *I Ching*. In diagrammatic form, yin and yang appear as two fish in a circle, yin in black and yang in white. The fact that each yin contains a little yang and each yang a little yin is symbolized by the eye of each fish which is of the opposite color. Yin also stands for Earth, moon, night, cold, moist, death, passive, among other things, while yang represents heaven, sun, day, heat, dry, life, active, and so forth.

Medically speaking, everything could be classed either as yin or yang, and to heal diseases, the ancient Chinese physician strove to bring these two qualities back into balance. The inside of the body is yin, the surface or skin is yang; the spleen, lungs, and kidneys are yin, the heart and liver are yang; a disease is yin when it results from internal causes, yang when it comes from external causes; purgatives, bitter substances, and cold infusions are yin drugs, while resolvents, pungent substances, and hot decoctions are yang drugs. Yin and yang are present throughout the macrocosm of the world just as they are present in the microcosm of man.

Shen Nung. The second legendary emperor, Shen Nung, is said to have ruled from 2838 to 2698 B.C. and was known as the Red Emperor because his patron element was fire. His mother was a princess and his father a heavenly dragon. Shen Nung reportedly invented the plow, taught his people to be farmers, and found and tested plants that had curative or poisonous qualities. He supposedly wrote down much of this information in the *Pen-ts'ao* (*Great Herbal*), where he categorized the medicines as superior (nonpoisonous and rejuvenating), medium (having some toxicity based on the dosage and exerting tonic effects), or inferior (poisonous but able quickly to reduce fever and cure indigestion). Although most authorities now agree that the *Pen-ts'ao* was written about the time of Christ, Shen Nung is generally looked upon as the father of Chinese medicine.

Huang Ti. The third of the three medical emperors reigned from 2698 to 2598 B.C. Called the Yellow Emperor, because his patron element was earth, Huang Ti is the best known of the three early rulers. He was long supposed to have written the *Nei Ching* (*The Classic of Internal Medicine*), although the work is now believed to have been composed in the 2nd century B.C. Nevertheless, the *Nei Ching* has been the highest Chinese authority on medical matters for over 2,000 years and has appeared in many editions. The first part of the work, "Plain Questions," has been translated into English. However, the major contribution Huang Ti made to medicine must certainly be the invention of the nine needles for acupuncture.

Like his predecessors, Huang Ti had a remarkable birth and a long life. He supposedly taught his people how to print and how to make utensils of wood, pottery, and metal. A good administrator, he delegated to his aides such assignments as building boats, making the

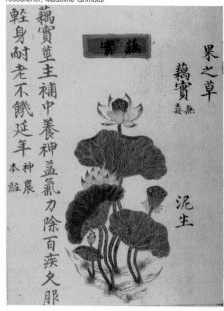

Two pages from Liou Wen-t'ai's early 16th-century compilation of the Pen-ts'ao *show arrowroot (top), used to restore inner repose, increase vitality, and cure a hundred afflictions, and azure monkshood (bottom), used for smallpox, diarrhea, fevers, and coughs.*

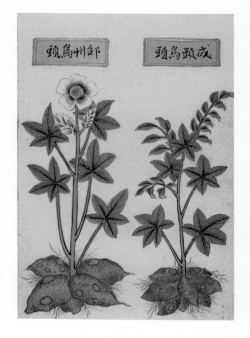

143

wheel, inventing a system of currency, composing a calendar, and many other useful tasks. Huang Ti himself allegedly visited both the Immortals and the Goddesses Scarlet and White to obtain information on diagnosis, the pulse, and other medical matters. The True Middle Emperor gave him the formula for the "nine gourd powder," while the little spirit Huang Kai presented to him the "nineteen gold and silver prescriptions." He also acquired the prescription for making the "nine tripod pills." All of these he prepared on a special stove, one of his own inventions. To keep the fire going in this busy stove, thousands of tigers and leopards came to his home to take turns helping. When the last pills had been made, a yellow dragon came down from heaven and escorted Huang Ti to paradise. Seventy of his concubines and most faithful ministers accompanied him on this final flight.

The emphasis in the *Nei Ching*, and indeed throughout most of Chinese medical history, is on the preventive rather than the curative. Physicians were rated on the basis of whether they could keep well people well. The physician who could take action only after the disease had manifested itself for all to see was looked on as an inferior practitioner. The *Nei Ching* states this concept clearly with some well-drawn analogies:

To administer medicines to diseases which have already developed and to suppress revolts which have already developed is comparable to the behavior of those persons who begin to dig a well after they have become thirsty, and of those who begin to cast weapons after they have already engaged in battle. Would these actions not be too late?[1]

The elements of anatomy in the *Nei Ching* underlie the discussion of diseases. Yin and yang are distributed throughout the body in an even balance in a healthy individual. However, a specific organ or area may have more of one than of the other. These two principles are each subdivided into three degrees: yin has a great female principle, a female principle proper, and a young female principle, while yang has the male counterparts. These subdivisions differ from each other primarily in the relative amounts of air and blood contained in them. When these principles are balanced, the individual will be healthy.

Disease can also be caused by winds, the seasons, and noxious airs. The winds, some commentators believe, played such an important part in Chinese medicine because the original Chinese came from the Yellow River area where the winds were usually active and where changes in direction and intensity often foretold difficulties or disasters. The noxious airs were usually thought of as indicating improper living habits, especially deviations from the rules of the Tao, or Way. If an individual strayed from the right way, he could expect to suffer for it, and medical problems were one type of penalty.

The organs (liver, heart, spleen, lungs, and kidneys) were thought to store materials. The viscera (gallbladder, stomach, large intestine, small intestine, bladder, and the three burning spaces—unique areas that cannot be specifically identified) were looked on as eliminators.

144

A man napping in a boat under a bamboo thicket (opposite), from a 15th-century painting, exemplifies life spent in harmony with nature. This, the Taoist ideal, was also a major requirement for a healthy life; deviation from the ideal often led to illness or death. The 12th-century painting (above) shows two herdsmen on their buffaloes fleeing before a storm. Strong winds, or changes in their direction, were believed to cause disease. The cloaks of straw might protect the herdsmen from the wind-driven rain but they could do little against the wind-carried disease.

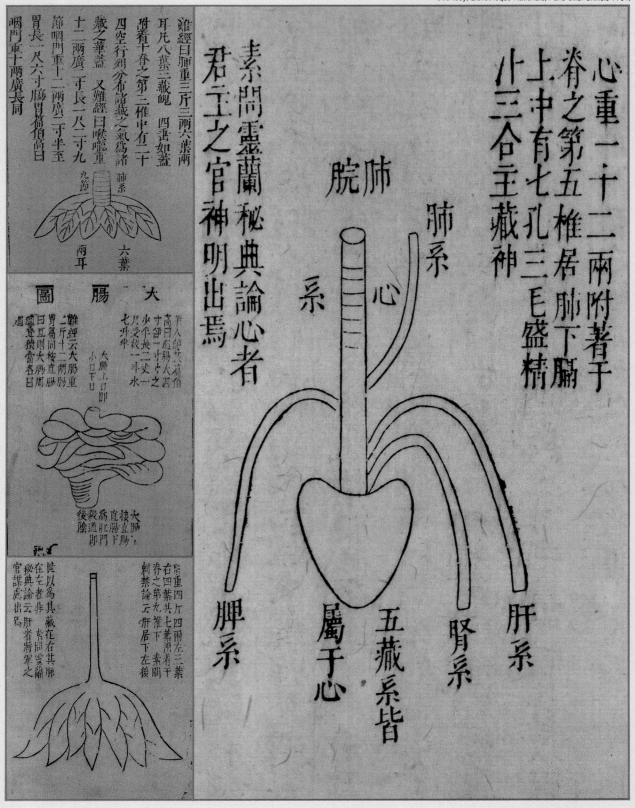

心重十二兩附著于
脊之第五椎居肺下膈
上中有七孔三毛盛精
什三合主藏神

素問靈蘭秘典論心者
君主之官神明出焉

雜經曰肺重三斤三兩六葉兩
耳凡八葉三藏魄
甜着十脊之第二椎中在于
四空行列分布諸藏之氣為者
藏之華蓋　又難經曰喉嚨重
十二兩廣二寸長一尺八寸九
節咽門重十二兩廣二寸長至
胃長一尺六寸腸胃儲伯高曰
咽門車十兩廣長同

大　腸　圖

肺系
系
脘
肺
心
肺系

脾系
屬于心
五藏系皆
腎系
肝系

The comprehensive correspondences between these organs, viscera, substances, seasons, winds, and many other qualities, concepts, and things played a major role in Chinese medicine. The doctrine of the five elements—metal, water, wood, fire, and earth—was also important. The physician strove for a balance among the elements and the items related to them.

Using volumes that 500 years before had belonged to Chang Chung-ching, Wang Ping compiled the most complete edition of the *Nei Ching* in the middle of the 8th century A.D. The governmental authorities determined that the work should be classed as a medical book. The decision meant that the *Nei Ching* was delivered into the hands of craftsmen (physicians) rather than into the hands of men of higher education who could appreciate the philosophy behind the medical teachings as well as the governmental and religious aspects. This unfortunate situation was later corrected by the Emperor Jen Tsung, a ruler in the more enlightened Sung Dynasty.

Acupuncture

When Huang Ti, the Yellow Emperor, discovered the concept of acupuncture and invented the nine needles, he began one of the unique elements of Chinese medicine. The basic idea behind acupuncture is that by using the appropriate needle in the most suitable manner, at the proper point, at the most fitting time, and under the most encouraging circumstances the physician allows the evil influence (air or blood) to escape so that the patient is once again in balance. The author of the *Nei Ching* included many references to acupuncture and the method has been used for thousands of years. The Sung Dynasty (A.D. 960–1279) saw the real flowering of the practice. An early monograph on acupuncture was published during that period, and in A.D. 1027 the emperor had two life-size bronze models of the human body made with the meridians and points along them marked.

The many possible variations in acupuncture treatment begin with the nine needles, made of various metals. The needles are designated by specific terms and are used for broadly defined purposes. For example, one needle is arrow-headed and is used primarily for skin diseases and fevers in the head. It is usually inserted shallowly. Another needle has a point as fine as a hair. It is used to remove stale air and to cure unusual tinglings, prickings, and numbnesses. Because of its small diameter, the needle can be inserted deep into bony structures.

The needles used may be either hot or cold and may be inserted and quickly removed or left in place for up to several days. Acupuncturists may push the needles in to almost any depth, quickly or slowly, twisting them in one direction or another or not twisting them at all; and they insert them at a variety of angles into normal, stretched, or pinched flesh. Often more than one needle is used at the same time.

The location of the point of insertion requires a detailed knowledge of the hundreds of points (originally 365, now many more), the twelve basic meridians, a number of specialized meridians, and the proper

(Opposite) An early 17th-century encyclopaedia, San-ts'ai t'u-hui, *shows on the left (from top to bottom) the lungs, large intestine, and liver, and on the right the windpipe and the heart. The lungs consist of lobes (there should be only five), which show the networks of bronchial tubes, and the ring-like structure of the cricoid cartilage in the larynx. The liver is also made up of lobes. The heart, shaped like a lotus flower, has tubes leading to the liver, kidney, spleen, and lungs.*

(Above) This head, from a life-size bronze model made in A.D. 1027 for Emperor Jen Tsung, shows acupuncture needles inserted at various sites.

147

measuring unit. In addition, the position of the patient, the direction and technique of the puncture, and the duration of the puncture must be determined. A short, weak insertion generally creates a tonifying effect; a longer and stronger insertion will sedate the patient. In addition, the insertion and withdrawal must coincide with the inhaling and exhaling of the patient.

The unit of measurement is the individual "inch," the distance along the middle of the second section of the middle finger. This unit makes it possible to adjust to differences in size among a wide variety of human beings. The patient is usually put in a position so that the part of his body to be punctured is resting firmly to prevent movement that might cause the needle to miss its goal or even break. The needle is generally inserted at right angles to the body for the more sensitive points or those located above thick layers of muscle. The 45° angle is used for most points on the chest. Smaller angles (12 to 15°) are used on the face, head, and neck. The typical insertion is 3 to 10 mm; some procedures call for insertions up to almost 10 inches. The twelve basic meridians or ducts along which the acupuncture points lie are deeply embedded in muscles. These channels provide links to the blood vessels, although they nowhere touch those vessels. The blood vessels are intimately connected with the organs and viscera. The organ-viscera and other standard body relationships thus play important roles in acupuncture. As might be expected, six of these meridians are yin and six are yang. The basic meridians, as well as the additional specialized ones, often extend for considerable distances from the related parts of the body so that the physician frequently inserts his needle or needles at some distance from the place on which they are to act. In the same way the successive points on a specific meridian may affect widely different areas or conditions. For example, the first six points of the yin lung meridian deal primarily with swollen joints, excessive heat in joints, bleeding of the nose, heart pains, mental depression, and inability to stretch the arm above the head.

The location of points is mastered by the use of diagrams or models. Diagrams are found in books or on posters, often carried by itinerant acupuncturists as advertising or spread out on the ground at the treatment site for information or to increase the mystique of the performance. The models, made of metal or porcelain, and ranging from four or five inches to life-size, have the points either painted on or drilled through them. In a student examination, the holes are plugged and the model filled with water and wrapped with a cover to hide the points. If the student is successful, the water coming out of the punctured hole announces his triumph.

Moxibustion

Moxibustion, the use of burning herbs, is another distinctive element of Chinese medicine. Mugwort (*Artemisia vulgaris*) has been the most frequently used substance. Other medicinal herbs such as mulberry, ginger, and aconite are also used. The crushed herb can be made into

Acupuncture points lie along the various meridians. Illustrated here (starting at upper left and moving clockwise) are the meridians for the liver (Chüeh Yin), kidney (Shao Yin), spleen (T'ai Yin), and a special meridian, the Tu, which in its lower part relates to physical energy and in its upper part to moral force.

148

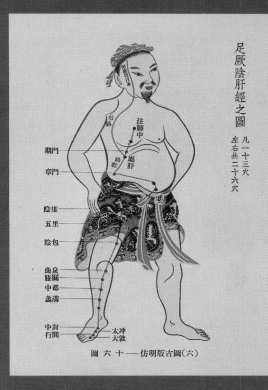

足厥陰肝經之圖

凡一十三穴　左右共二十六穴

右脇
注肺中
屬肝
期門
章門
急脈
五里
陰包
曲泉
膝關
中都
蠡溝
中封
行間
太衝
大敦

圖六十——仿明版古圖(六)

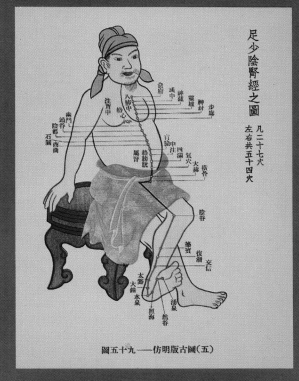

足少陰腎經之圖

凡二十七穴　左右共五十四穴

注腎中
八肺中
幽門
通谷
陰都
石關
腹通谷
四滿
中注
肓俞
屬腎
横骨
大赫
氣穴
俞府
彧中
神藏
靈墟
神封
步廊
陰谷
築賓
交信
復溜
太谿
大鐘
水泉
照海
然谷
湧泉

圖五十九——仿明版古圖(五)

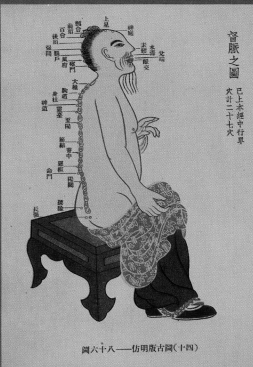

督脈之圖

巳上本經中行鼻　穴計二十七穴

上星
神庭
顖會
前頂
百會
後頂
強間
腦戶
風府
瘂門
大椎
陶道
身柱
神道
靈臺
至陽
筋縮
脊中
懸樞
命門
陽關
腰俞
長強
素髎
齦交

圖六十八——仿明版古圖(十四)

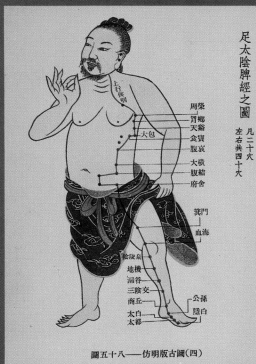

足太陰脾經之圖

凡二十穴　左右共四十穴

上行俠咽
周榮
胸鄉
天谿
食竇
大包
大橫
腹結
府舍
箕門
血海
陰陵泉
地機
漏谷
三陰交
商丘
太白
太都
公孫
隱白

圖五十八——仿明版古圖(四)

a ball or a cone called a moxa and may be placed directly on the skin or on a small base (a slice of garlic or ginger) resting on the skin. The physician can also crush these herbs, wrap them in a special paper, light the end, and then hold the stick near the prescribed point.

The modern healing goal is to build up a pleasant warmness without scorching or burning the patient. Historically, this was not the case; in ancient times direct burning was favored. Just as we sometimes believe that medicine cannot be effective if it does not taste unpleasant enough, so it was with moxa that did not produce a substantial scar.

Moxibustion is discussed at some length in the *Nei Ching*, and it has a long record of wide use in China. Occasionally, moxa even outstripped acupuncture as the most popular medical technique. The procedure was probably used in the Stone Age to quell the rheumatic pains that must have frequently bothered the early Chinese people living in the northern climate or in damp caves.

Pien Ch'iao

The first outstanding physician after the three medical emperors lived over 2,000 years later. Pien Ch'iao's birth date is uncertain, but is thought to be in the early years of the 5th century B.C. Although some facts are known about his life, Pien Ch'iao is also a somewhat mythical figure. The Herodotus of China, Ssu-ma Ch'ien, wrote a long biography of him, contemporary authors wrote about his cures, and several books are assumed to have been written by him.

According to one story, Pien Ch'iao ran an inn when he was a young man. One of the older residents of the inn, Ch'ang Sang-chun, recog-

The village doctor, in this 12th-century painting on silk, is applying moxibustion. Everyone involved is obviously suffering along with the patient.

nized Pien Ch'iao's sterling qualities and decided to make the younger man his medical heir. Ch'ang Sang-chun told Pien Ch'iao that he could have his medical secrets if he would vow not to divulge them to others. When Pien Ch'iao agreed, Ch'ang Sang-chun handed over a book and some herbs. Pien Ch'iao was to take the herbs in a special liquid for 30 days and he would then be able to understand all the secrets of nature. Immediately after giving his instructions, Ch'ang Sang-chun vanished. Pien Ch'iao followed the instructions carefully, and at the end of the 30 days discovered that he not only understood the secrets of nature but also could see through the human body. Wisely he kept this ability to himself and publicly derived his information about the patient's inner workings by carefully attending to the pulse.

Many miraculous cures and predictions were credited to Pien Ch'iao. When the great Chao Chien-tzu had been unconscious for five days, the officials sent for Pien Ch'iao, who accurately predicted that Chao would recover within three days. When this occurred, Pien Ch'iao was given 6,500 acres of land as a reward. Once when he was traveling through Kuo, Pien Ch'iao heard that the prince had died. Going immediately to the palace gate, Pien Ch'iao sought detailed information. What he heard led Pien Ch'iao to say that he could bring the prince back to life. He diagnosed catalepsy, had his assistant apply moxa and acupuncture to several points, and received the plaudits of the assembled throng when, indeed, the prince's life was restored.

Pien Ch'iao's handling of the Marquis Huan of the Kingdom of Chi serves as a cautionary tale. While dining with the Marquis, Pien Ch'iao told him that he had a latent disease that should be treated immediately. The Marquis replied that he certainly was not ill. Five days later Pien Ch'iao saw the Marquis again and informed him that the disease had entered the blood. The Marquis responded by saying that he was not only well but was also becoming rather annoyed. After another five days, Pien Ch'iao told the Marquis that the disease was in the stomach and intestines, but he received the same response. After five more days, Pien Ch'iao again came into the Marquis' presence, but this time the physician said nothing and backed out of the room. His action upset the Marquis, who immediately sent a messenger to get an explanation for this strange behavior. Pien Ch'iao replied with devastating logic:

When a disease was only skin deep it may be reached by concoctions and applications; when in the blood system by puncturing; when in the stomach and intestines by alcoholic extracts. But when it had penetrated the bone-marrow, what could a doctor do? Now that the disease has lodged in His Excellency's bone-marrow, it is useless for me to make further comments.[2]

The Marquis became ill five days later, as Pien Ch'iao had predicted, and died shortly thereafter. This story is a beautiful example of the Chinese emphasis on preventive or early treatment rather than on attempts to cure a disease in its advanced stages.

Pien Ch'iao wrote the popular *Nan Ching* (*Difficult Classic*) in which he explained 81 of the most abstruse passages in the *Nei Ching*. He also included the measurements and weights of various organs taken from

Portrait figurine of Pien Ch'iao, outstanding physician of the 5th century B.C. For centuries the highest honor a Chinese physician could be paid was to be told that he was a "living Pien Ch'iao".

151

cadavers. One of Pien Ch'iao's major struggles was against superstition. He endeavored to instruct medical men and laity alike wherever he went. One of his most frequently quoted aphorisms was, "A case is incurable if one believes in sorcerers instead of in doctors."

Pien Ch'iao was looked upon by many as the most knowledgeable user of pulse lore, although Wang Shu-ho, who lived 750 years later, is generally accepted as the chief authority on this peculiarly Chinese medical subject. Whatever may be the confusion over myth and fact in this great physician's life, the highest compliment one could pay to a Chinese physician was to call him a "living Pien Ch'iao".

The great practitioners

The Chinese Hippocrates, Chang Chung-ching, flourished toward the end of the 2nd century A.D. He wrote an important book on dietetics, but he achieved his greatest fame for a treatise on typhoid and other fevers, a work highly regarded in the Far East for as long a time as Galen's works were popular in the West. Chang described typhoid clearly and recommended the use of only a few potent drugs in treating it. The drugs were to be used one at a time, a considerable advance from the shotgun prescriptions then common. Chang stated that cool baths were also an important part of the treatment, an idea that remained unused for 1,700 years until Scottish physician James Currie promoted it in his famous treatise on fever therapy.

Chang Chung-ching paid close attention to the physical signs, symptoms, kind, and course of a disease, and carefully recorded the results obtained from any drugs that he prescribed. Chang forthrightly stood for the dignity and responsibility of the medical profession, and this attitude, coupled with his close powers of observation, make it easy to understand why he has become known by the name of his Greek medical ancestor. In the 16th and 17th centuries there was a strong revival of his teachings and practices.

Hua T'o. The Yellow Emperor's *Classic of Internal Medicine,* the *Nei Ching,* devotes only a minute amount of space to surgery. Chinese doctors in the early periods felt that surgery was a matter of last resort, and little time was spent teaching or describing surgical techniques. What surgery was done was usually carried out by a lower grade of medical worker. However, around the beginning of the third century A.D. a surgeon named Hua T'o began to change Chinese surgery. As a young man, Hua T'o traveled and read widely. He probably first became interested in medicine while trying to help the countless soldiers who had been wounded in the many wars of that violent period.

As a young surgeon Hua T'o believed in simplicity, using only a few prescriptions and a few points for acupuncture. Using a preparation of hemp and wine, he was able to make his patients insensitive to pain. Hua T'o was thus the discoverer of anesthetics, although some say that Pien Ch'iao had used them. He engaged in a wide variety of surgical procedures including laparotomy, removal of diseased tissues, and even a partial splenectomy. To treat gastrointestinal diseases Hua T'o's

The famous surgeon Hua T'o operates on military hero Kuan Kung for an infected battle wound. The general would have nothing to do with anesthetics and preferred fixing his attention on a game of go with a colleague. This Japanese print is from the early 19th century.

152

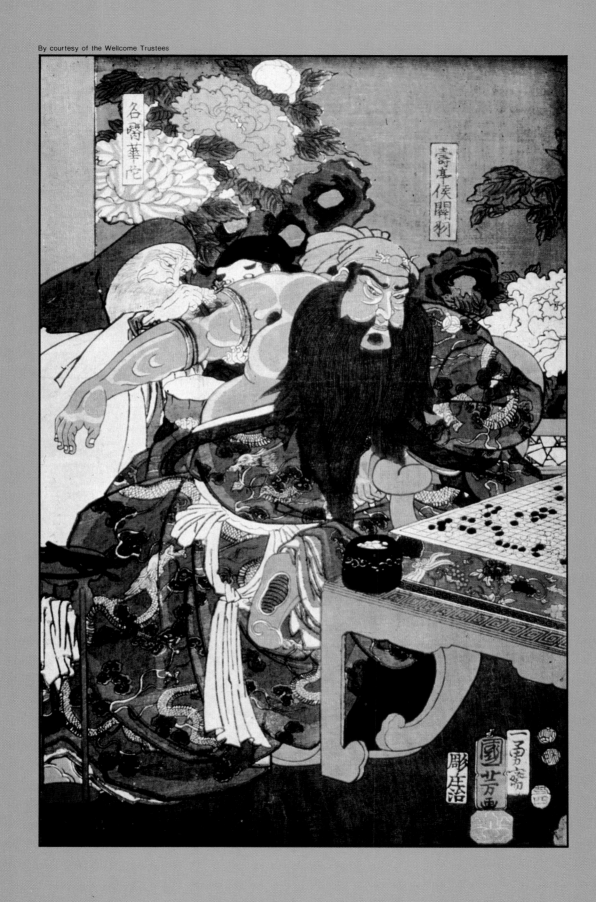

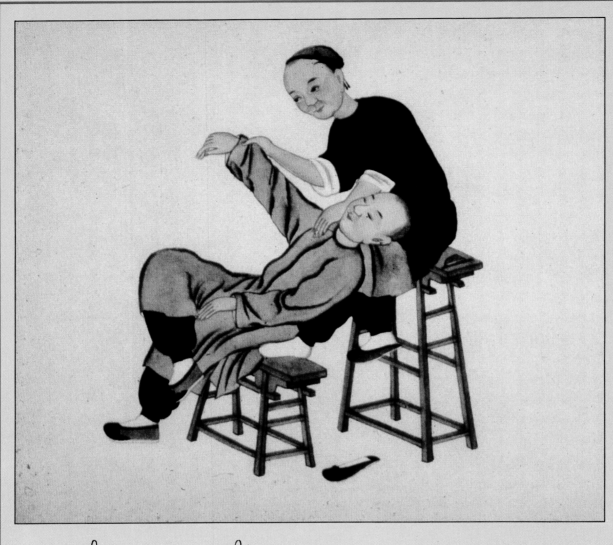

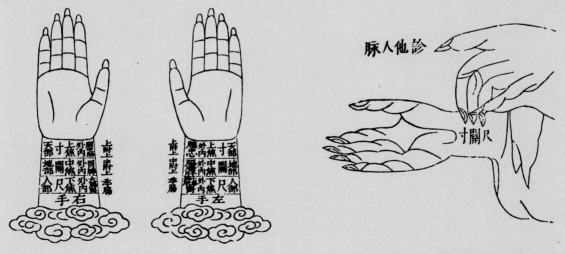

favorite procedure was to resect the viscera and wash the inside. He probably even performed end-to-end anastomoses of the intestines although it is not known what substance he used for the sutures.

Of the stories told of Hua T'o, one—possibly apocryphal—is that General Kuan Kung, one of the great military heroes of the time who eventually became the God of War, came to Hua T'o because of an arrow wound in his arm that had become badly infected. The surgeon prepared to give his patient the usual anesthetic drink, but General Kuan laughed scornfully and called for a board and stones for a game of go. While Hua T'o scraped the flesh and bone free of infection and repaired the wound, Kuan and one of his military companions proceeded calmly with their game.

Surgery, although his main interest, was only one of Hua T'o's pursuits. He pioneered in hydrotherapy, and also did innovative work in physiotherapy. His series of exercises known as the frolics of the five animals, in which the patient imitated movements of the tiger, deer, bear, ape, and bird, was well known and widely adopted.

The end of Hua T'o's life is hidden in a mist of conflicting and doubtful stories. A likely set of these has him late in life becoming court physician to Ts'ao Ts'ao, king of Wei. The surgeon temporarily relieved the ruler of his giddiness by acupuncture. When the king asked him to do something to remove this annoyance permanently, Hua T'o said he would have to cut into the royal skull. Ts'ao Ts'ao's wife was in favor of surgery as a desperate hope, but the king became suspicious that his enemies had bribed Hua T'o to kill him. In a fit of rage, perhaps triggered by these very headaches, the king had the surgeon thrown into jail and executed. Hua T'o's major book, *Ch'ing Nang Shu* (*Book of The Blue Bag*) was burned, either by the jailer who wanted to remove all traces of the prisoner or by the surgeon's wife acting in accordance with Hua T'o's wishes expressed before he was jailed.

Hua T'o earned his place as the greatest surgeon in Chinese history. Unfortunately, the destruction of his writings and the Confucian dogma against mutilation of the human body combined to prevent the growth of surgery that might have been expected to follow the life of such a remarkable pioneer.

Wang Shu-ho and the pulse. Since medicine was far more important than surgery in Chinese history, diagnosis was of considerable significance. Although the early Chinese physician examined with care the color of the patient's skin at various key points and noted any other external signs, he drew mainly on the pulse for diagnosis. Indeed, the study of the pulse was one of the major occupations of the physician, who listened for an almost endless variety of sounds and rhythms. The classic work in the field was the *Mo Ching,* written by Wang Shu-ho around A.D. 280. Wang also wrote an important commentary on the *Nei Ching,* but his labors over the pulse are what raised him to the highest rank of Chinese physician. In the *Nei Ching* itself may be found the assertion, "Nothing surpasses the examination of the pulse."

Basically, the physician had three places on each wrist at which he

The pulse was the major source for the physician's diagnosis. Wang Shu-ho, late 3rd century A.D., was the leading authority in this complicated field. The physician first made the patient comfortable and then carefully examined the pulse at each of the three areas along both right and left wrists.

155

一女三歲

雁行痘形三十三

An 18th-century miniature shows a young girl suffering from smallpox. Chinese physicians in medieval times developed the practice of inoculation against this disfiguring and often deadly disease.

must ascertain the quality and quantity of the pulse. The place closest to the hand was known as the *ts'un* ("inch"), the middle position was the *kuan* ("bar"), and the one farthest from the hand was called the *ch'ih* ("cubit"). Yin representing right and yang left, a woman's right pulse indicated disorder and her left pulse order; the opposite held for a man.

The physician not only read three different pulses on each wrist but also read each pulse at two levels. For example, on the left wrist, when the inch was lightly pressed the pulse indicated the state of the small intestines; when heavily pressed, the heart. The bar lightly pressed indicated the state of the gallbladder, and when heavily pressed, the liver; and the cubit lightly pressed indicated the state of the urinary bladder, heavily pressed, the kidneys. The right wrist had its own relationships to the body organs.

The actual pulses were further divided into seven *piao* ("superficial") and eight *li* ("sunken") pulses. What could these pulses indicate? To take just one example, the seven superficial pulses on the inch position could indicate, among other things: (1) pains and heat in the middle region of the body and in the head; (2) accumulation of blood in the chest; (3) belching and vomiting; (4) insufferable heat within the thorax; (5) severe thoracic pains; (6) headaches; and (7) heat in the chest. Although to Western minds these varieties and relationships may appear complex or ridiculous, the Chinese physician trained in pulse lore could achieve some remarkable diagnoses.

Final period

In addition to the three medical emperors, as well as physicians such as Pien Ch'iao, Chang Chung-ching, Hua T'o, and Wang Shu-ho, other individuals made single contributions of substantial importance to Chinese medicine. Ko Hung (A.D. 281–361), in a handbook of prescriptions for emergencies, gave a clear and detailed description of smallpox. Ko Hung's achievement came almost six centuries before ar-Razi (Rhazes), the great Arabic physician generally given credit for the first description of this deadly disease. About 700 years after Ko Hung, the practice of inoculation against smallpox grew out of a rather hazy background. Supposedly, a nun living on a mountain began the practice by using scabs that had been dried, ground into a powder, and inserted into the nostrils. The method spread and cut the mortality rate substantially.

From the time of Wang Shu-ho in the 3rd century to the middle of the 16th century A.D., Chinese medical men devoted much of their efforts to the compilation of massive encyclopaedias and the writing of commentaries on the classical works. In 1644 official rites for worshipping the ancient physicians were instituted at the Ching Hui Palace near the College of Imperial Physicians in Peking. These rites were celebrated in the spring and fall for many years.

When Bishop Belchior Carneiro established Saint Raphael's Hospital in the 16th century near Canton, tentative medical communication be-

156

gan between East and West. As Western medicine gradually made deeper inroads in the country, some Chinese began to believe that everything in Western medicine was scientific and good, and therefore better than the traditional medicine practiced in China. Despite the appearance once again of a physician, Sun Yat-sen, as the ruler of the country, this blind faith in Western medicine continued to grow at the expense of native medicine. Not until after the Communist revolution of the late 1940s did traditional Chinese medicine really begin to find its rightful place again. It is somehow fitting that China, the nation with the longest continuous culture, should not only practice medicine in the traditions of both East and West but should also export indigenous methods such as acupuncture to an increasingly receptive West.

1. Ilza Veith, *The Yellow Emperor's Classic of Internal Medicine* (Berkeley: University of California Press, 1966), p. 105.

2. K. Chimin Wong and Lien-Teh Wu, *History of Chinese Medicine*, 2nd ed. (Shanghai: National Quarantine Service, 1936), pp. 25–26.

FOR ADDITIONAL READING

Li, Choh-luh. "A Brief Outline of Chinese Medical History with Particular Reference to Acupuncture." *Perspectives in Biology and Medicine* 18 (1974): 132–43.

Majno, Guido. *The Healing Hand: Man and Wound in the Ancient World.* Cambridge: Harvard University Press, 1975. Chapter 6 is on "The Yang I."

Morse, William R. *Chinese Medicine.* Clio Medica Series, no. 11. New York: P. B. Hoeber, 1934.

Pálos, Stephan. *The Chinese Art of Healing.* Translated by Translagency, Ltd. New York: Herder & Herder, 1971.

Veith, Ilza. "The Supernatural in Far Eastern Concepts of Mental Disease." *Bulletin of the History of Medicine* 37 (1963): 139–58.

———. *The Yellow Emperor's Classic of Internal Medicine.* Berkeley: University of California Press, 1966. Chapters 1–34 of *Huang Ti Nei Ching Su Wen* are translated from the Chinese with an introductory study.

Wallnöfer, Heinrich, and Rottauscher, Anna von. *Chinese Folk Medicine.* Translated by Marion Palmedo. New York: Crown Publishers, 1965.

Wong, K. Chimin, and Wu, Lien-Teh. *History of Chinese Medicine.* 2nd ed. Shanghai: National Quarantine Service, 1936. Edition in 2 vols. New York: Gordon Press, 1976.

Yousuf Karsh enjoys well-deserved renown as one of the world's great portrait photographers, and as such he has captured on film the souls of hundreds of historic figures. A less well-known fact about Karsh is his life-long reverence for medicine, which gives special meaning to the fact that many of the most honored physicians of our time have sat before his camera. The following pages contain eight portraits, with commentary, from a series entitled "Healers of Our Age" that Karsh donated to the Francis A. Countway Library of Medicine in Boston. Inspired by his wife, Estrellita, Karsh gave the portfolio both to help the Countway preserve medicine's heritage and to make a partial repayment for the "great favors bestowed on me during my life."

Healers of Our Age

by Yousuf Karsh

On coming to the New World and the sunshine of freedom from troubled Armenia at the age of 15, my original desire was to be a physician. This was not to be. But I have had the supreme joy of portraying with my camera those men and women who are devoted to the art and the science of healing. I have had the privilege of being welcomed into their consultation rooms, operating theatres, and laboratories where significant advances for the benefit of human welfare were being accomplished. Although these men and women differ in outlook and personality, they are united by their common desire to relieve suffering, whether of the body or the spirit. I am proud and happy that this photographic collection "Healers of Our Age" may assist in the preservation, enhancement, and accessibility of our medical historical heritage.

Walter Clement Alvarez

"No doctor can be purely a specialist. If he is to help his patient, he must spend much of his time being a physician to the troubled mind and the bruised spirit."

(1884–   ), American physician. He received his medical training at Cooper Medical College, Harvard Medical School, and Hahnemann Medical College. He practiced in Mexico and California and held early teaching posts at Stanford and the University of California. He was Professor of Medicine at the Mayo Foundation of the University of Minnesota, and he was widely honored for his scientific and clinical work in the fields of gastroenterology and psychosomatic medicine. Alvarez was a member of leading professional societies and holder of many distinguished lectureships, as well as being an editor of clinical journals and writing for the laity.

Walter C. Alvarez had retired from the Mayo Clinic to his second career in Chicago writing a popular syndicated column when I photographed him in 1960. Lean and aristocratic, the pioneer of psychosomatic medicine loped toward me with the easy stride of a mountaineer. Behind the effortless cordiality, creating instant rapport, were the analytic, yet nonjudgmental eyes of the famous diagnostician. I could understand his success in eliciting intimate histories from patients. "I urge my residents to listen to the patients, and they will often make your diagnoses for you. I remember the sweet old lady who described her own 'little strokes.' 'Doctor,' she said, 'Death is taking little bites of me'." Dr. Alvarez did not believe doctors should rely exclusively on medical technology: "Why should a doctor order a battery of tests when his patient is dying of a broken heart?" His conversation was full of such touches of homely practicality combined with clinical wisdom. In 1915, this lucidity caused an editor to reject his paper because "Even a layman could understand it"! "We have come a long way since then," Alvarez mused. The compassionate physician told me of his long career which spanned saddlebag to space medicine, from his Victorian boyhood in Hawaii when he made calls on horseback with his physician-father, to his early practice in a Mexican mining camp. "When I studied at Harvard with my beloved teacher and friend, Dr. Walter B. Cannon, in 1913, I told him how my father would dicker with the Kahuna witch doctors. It stimulated Dr. Cannon to start his research into voodoo deaths." Alvarez mused, "I try to follow the example of my hero, Sir William Osler, and keep my friendships in constant repair." Was religion compatible with his life in science? "Not formal religion," he answered, "but as a lifelong student of Darwin and evolution it is hard not to feel wonder at what appears to be a grand design." Later, I discovered, to my not-so-great surprise, that among the "G's" in his files, was one labelled simply "God."

160

Alfred Blalock

"No satisfaction is quite like that which accompanies productive investigation, particularly if it leads to better treatment of the sick."

(1899–1964), American physician. He was educated at the University of Georgia and Johns Hopkins University and held early teaching posts at Vanderbilt Medical School. He subsequently became Professor of Surgery at Johns Hopkins University and Surgeon-in-Chief at the Hospital. A member and officer of numerous leading scholarly societies, he was the recipient of many awards, medals, and honorary degrees. He was also on the editorial boards of a number of surgical journals, and he was a pioneer and leader in surgery for the correction of congenital heart disease. He was also a leading researcher in vascular disease and shock.

In 1950, Dr. Alfred Blalock, the surgeon who with Dr. Helen Taussig perfected the operation on "blue babies," was about to perform his thousandth "blue baby operation," and his colleagues prevailed upon me to photograph him. But the surgeon could be enticed before my camera only with innocent subterfuge. I was to tell him that, in the interests of his profession, he must be included in my gallery of scientists. At dinner, by way of discovering his personality, I talked freely about doctors and remarked rather brashly that many of them were vain. He took this in good part and suggested that, if I were interested in his profession, I had better witness a "blue baby" operation for myself. I was amazed, and not a little nervous, to find myself in the operating room next morning wearing a mask and gown and standing at Blalock's left hand. Then, for two hours, he applied the magic of his mind and fingers to the body of a seven-year-old boy. I was awed by Dr. Blalock's dexterity, and still more by his calm. He proceeded easily, often talked to me with no sign of tension, and explained his methods to visiting doctors from many parts of the world who were watching in the amphitheater. He finished the surgery and removed his gloves like a man who had done an ordinary morning's work. His only thought, after the patient had been wheeled out of the operating room, was for the child's mother. Before he had even removed his gown, he went to a wall telephone and assured this anxious woman that her son's operation had been successful. His compassionate telephone conversation, even more than his technical skill, told me what sort of man I was going to photograph. I hastened to say, "Dr. Blalock, I take back everything I said last night about the vanity of doctors. If you have such a thing, which I doubt, you are more than entitled to it."

162

William Boyd

"Dissect in anatomy, experiment in physiology, follow the disease and make the autopsy in medicine. This is the three-fold path without which there can be no anatomist, no physiologist, no physician."

(1885–   ), Canadian physician. Although he was born in Scotland and educated at Edinburgh, he spent most of his professional life in Canada, at first at various Canadian schools and hospitals and finally as Professor of Pathology and Bacteriology at the University of Toronto Medical School and Chief Pathologist at the Hospital. He is known for his pathology texts and his important research into cancer. He was a leading expert on the physiology and pathology of the cerebrospinal fluid, providing physicians with a refined diagnostic tool.

"It doesn't matter what book you recommend—they will all read Boyd," is how one medical school professor put it. Visiting with William Boyd, the great pathologist and medical writer, some years after I had photographed him in 1949, the Scottish burr and gentle charm were still there, as was the trained, articulate voice and characteristic puckish twitch of the eyebrow which had engaged generations of medical audiences. We looked out at his simple garden, roses and lilies blooming in profusion: "They are such obliging perennials," Boyd mused, "and they need only kindness." On his study wall were treasured photographs—of the Matterhorn, the Scottish manse where he was born, of Lawrence of Arabia, his hero—and a beloved book of hand-copied quotations dating from Edinburgh days. In Boyd's student roster I was pleased to see the name of my physician-brother, Jamil, who had spent a landmark year with him. Boyd remained the masterful raconteur as he pointed to the straight-backed chair on which he wrote the first edition of his famed "Textbook of Pathology"—after a cold bath at 5 A.M.! How did he become a pathologist? "I was a psychiatrist for three years before the letter from Winnipeg, Canada, came inviting me to be their first professor of pathology. On the boat, I read Mallory's *Pathology* to prepare for giving one hundred lectures. I knew very little, but then, the students knew nothing. I managed to keep one day ahead of them." This from the author whose texts had enthralled millions. "I take pride in my four medical pathological museums and the library named for me at the University of Toronto, but I have never relished any part of my life better than now. Reading Shakespeare is as enjoyable to me as writing my books—which I never regarded as work. I hope this spirit has transmitted itself to my readers." Later, reading his textbook, I understood. Through the exquisite precision of his prose glowed an intense, fierce respect for all living creatures. To pathology, a hitherto traditionally dead subject, he had brought his own sense of the celebration of life.

164

Thomas Stephen Cullen

"To build a small cottage, a small foundation is sufficient. To erect a mighty structure, deep foundations are essential. Pathology is the foundation of a surgical career."

(1868–1953), Canadian and American physician. Educated in Toronto, Cullen specialized in gynecology at Johns Hopkins University under the legendary Dr. Howard A. Kelly. He wrote and taught extensively on embryology, anatomy, diagnosis, and treatment of clinical gynecological conditions. A member and officer of surgical and gynecological societies, he was the first to recognize a number of diseases and their physical signs (*e.g.*, Cullen's sign for ruptured ectopic pregnancy). His work on gynecology was the standard textbook for many years.

"A photographer's paradise," I exclaimed of Tom Cullen's bristling eyebrows when first we met at his Canadian summer retreat in 1947. His favorite younger sister had arranged for me to photograph the eminent Johns Hopkins gynecologist when he returned to Baltimore in the fall. Now I was becoming acquainted with his summer alter-ego. The elegant physician returned to the frugality of his boyhood as a Methodist minister's son; he wore patched clothes and repaired his sneakers with old rubber tires. At Ahmic Lake, he brought his meticulous attention to clinical detail to bear on his young nephews who were neglecting their canoes. With the same grave twinkling formality with which I was to see him address his gynecologic residents, he delivered a one-minute lecture on the care of boats, and presented the hapless youths each with an envelope containing a "Certificate of Demerit"—and a five-dollar bill. Cullen's relationship with his family was especially close. Early in his career, he stopped suddenly in the middle of an operation and said, "Something is happening to my kid sister!" Indeed, at that very moment, many miles away, she was drowning and was rescued only at the last moment. On many other occasions, Dr. Cullen related, he had "premonitory extrasensory feelings." At Hopkins, in the fall, I accompanied Dr. Cullen on rounds. He brought a hopeful atmosphere of warmth and reassurance into the sickroom. To a woman, apprehensive about the extent of her forthcoming surgery, he explained, "I think I know what you want me to do—as much as necessary, but as little as possible." I later learned that the payment Cullen received for her operation was his favorite—a sack of hickory nuts which appeared at his doorstep on Christmas Eve from the lady's grateful husband.

Sir Alexander Fleming

"It [penicillin] arrived nameless and numberless—all I did was to notice it."

(1881–1955), British bacteriologist. Born in Scotland, he was educated at the University of London and St. Mary's Medical School, where he subsequently became Professor of Bacteriology. He was also the Rector of the University of Edinburgh, and the Head of the Wright-Fleming Institute of Microbiology. He received numerous honors, awards, and honorary degrees, and he was knighted in 1944. Fleming discovered lysozyme in bacteria in 1922, and penicillin in 1928. In 1945 he was awarded the Nobel Prize for Physiology or Medicine (with Chain and Florey).

If Fleming were not a genius, one might have thought his choice of medicine, of bacteriology, and even his discovery of the properties of penicillin was pure chance. He went into medicine because his brother was a physician, into bacteriology because he was a good marksman for the Bacteriology Department Rifle Club; and one day, through his window floated a certain particle of mold spore. Noting and isolating the mold in September of 1928 led to the mass production in the 1940s of penicillin, the most powerful antibiotic the world had till then known. What struck me most about this Scottish gentleman when we met at St. Mary's Hospital, London, in 1954 was that simplicity I had noticed in so many other men of greatness. His microscope had a most up-to-date lens, but the stand was old-fashioned in the extreme. The modern microscope, as compared to Fleming's, was like a Cadillac beside a Model T Ford. But this suited him—and it had penetrated some profound mysteries. As we went about our work together, I plied him with some of my favorite questions. Where would medicine make its next great advance? "Cancer," he replied in his laconic style. Sir Alexander brought in from his laboratory the sealed glass tray containing the original mold of penicillin. Since it is one of the most significant exhibits of our age, and a great symbol of the healing art, I felt it must form an integral part of Fleming's portrait. Before long, Sir Alexander hoped to relinquish his administrative duties and devote himself entirely to research. What was he looking for? Nothing less, I was amazed to hear, than a vaccine which would give "total immunity to disease." "There's so much left to do," he mused, "so many problems. I just want to sit and work." Alas, that opportunity for him and for mankind was soon to be lost.

Carl Gustav Jung

"True art is creation . . . and beyond all theories. That is why I say to any beginner: Learn your theories well, but put them aside when you touch the miracle of the living soul."

(1875–1961), Swiss psychiatrist. He was educated in Zurich, where he subsequently lectured and practiced psychiatry. In 1908 he organized the First International Psychoanalytic Congress, and he was the author of many books on the psychoanalytic interpretation of man's nature and history. He defined and described the concept of introversion/extroversion, and he stressed the connection between physiological and psychological phenomena. Jung used his knowledge of mythology and yoga to explain his psychoanalytic concepts, most of which differed from the more simplistic notions perpetuated by those of his teacher and colleague, Freud.

A photographer must be an amateur psychologist of sorts; but, in the presence of Dr. Carl Jung, at his home in Zurich in 1958, I felt somewhat at a disadvantage. This "poet of the mind" turned out to be very human, and his conversation provocative. Were we overemphasizing psychology in modern society? "Quite the contrary," Jung answered with an impish little smile. Was it true that modern man had become psychologically diseased? "Modern man," he replied, "is as rational and as crazy as he ever was. Things are going too fast and too far. Science is only man's honest attempt at understanding. There's no end to the various aspects of psychology. Only their totality makes possible an approximate cognition. But no cognition has ever increased the sum total of well-being, because every Good is paid for too heavily." How, I asked, did a psychiatrist cope with his own psychological problems? "Yes, how indeed," said Jung. "He copes, like everybody else, as well as he can, that's all. And it's usually deplorably enough." He agreed with the title of James Thurber's then-new book, "Leave Your Mind Alone" but, he remarked, "Unfortunately the mind is not discreet enough to leave you alone . . . that's the trouble!" I said I would make an unsatisfactory patient for the psychiatrist because I gained my happiness through my work. "Ah," he answered, "the secret of happiness is unhappiness because man has fear, sadness, and shadow over his life. Those who seek happiness can never find it. It's extinguished when you seek it. You should wait till it comes, like the arrival of a guest late in the evening." "Many great men of science," I ventured to say, "do not believe in God." "True," blithely answered Jung, "but that doesn't injure God."

170

Albert Schweitzer

"Here, at whatever hour you come, you will find light and help and human kindness." (Inscription on the lamp outside of Schweitzer's jungle hospital at Lambaréné)

(1875–1964), Alsatian physician, medical missionary, and musicologist. He studied medicine and theology in Strasbourg, and tropical medicine in Paris and Hamburg. He was active as preacher, deacon, and curate at St. Christopher's, Strasbourg, and as acting principal and teacher at the Theological College. His musical activities included founder-membership in the Bach Society (founded in 1905), the editing of Bach's organ works, and the reintroduction of the baroque organ. He wrote numerous books on theology, philosophy, and music, and he was the founder of the world-famous jungle hospital in Lambaréné, Africa. He received the Nobel Peace Prize in 1952.

I had long admired "le Grand Docteur"—musician, philosopher, humanitarian, theologian, and writer. But I feared that the man himself might fall below his legend. But when we met in 1954 in his home town of Gunsbach, in Alsace, I felt at once the presence of a conscious and immense wisdom, the stronger for its utter simplicity. What struck me most was his power to concentrate totally; during the preparations for photography, he turned back to his writing as if he were alone in the room. Only when I was ready did he give me his full attention. While we talked, I watched Dr. Schweitzer closely, especially his hands. They are the hands of a musician and a healer. I wished to photograph him holding some significant books, preferably an album of Bach, but he protested. To use Bach's music for this purpose would be like "choucroute garnie." With a shy smile, he brought out some of his own books. Remembering his ministrations to the Africans, I asked him how he thought Christ would be received were He to appear today. In his quiet voice, Dr. Schweitzer replied, "People would not understand Him at all." Which, then, did he consider the most important of the Ten Commandments? For a long moment he thought, the granite face was illuminated, the man behind the legend suddenly visible. "Christ," he said, "gave only one Commandment, And that was Love."

Paul Dudley White

"The patient leads the way."

(1886–1973), American physician. Educated at Harvard College and Medical School, he trained at the Massachusetts General Hospital and remained on its staff until his retirement. He was also Clinical Professor of Medicine at Harvard, and he studied under Sir Thomas Lewis and James MacKenzie in England. A founder of the American Heart Association, he was a pioneer in the development of clinical electrocardiology and author of one of the greatest cardiology texts of all time. He taught distinguished students in all parts of the world, including China, which he visited in 1971. He was famous for his unabating care and concern for each of his patients, one of whom was President Eisenhower.

My talk with Dr. White in 1957 in his office in Boston was highly scientific—or so it appeared to me. To this slight, small man with a rare twinkle in his eye, my questions were doubtless elementary, but he answered them readily, simply, and cheerfully. Patience, I suspected, must be the secret of his distinguished career as an investigator of that wonderful pump, the human heart. The first book I noticed on his waiting room table was "Low Fat Diets." In heart or other diseases, White said, the amount of fat necessary in a diet depended solely on the individual. He insisted that heredity plays a larger part in a person's health than was previously supposed. Many people could be saved from premature death or crippling diseases if their doctors knew more of their family histories. Family Bibles which included a few words about illnesses, operations, and general health of each family member would be an invaluable guide in treating the young. Finally, he gave me a useful piece of advice—constant exercise at all times of life, including old age. He especially approved of walking, his own favorite exercise, the natural exercise of man. Or cycling: he had been trying to arrange for the construction of bicycle paths in his neighborhood, and he would have been gratified at the current upsurge in popularity of the bicycle. For long flights on airplanes, he advocated stationary bicycles for the passengers but as yet, the airlines had not seen fit to heed his advice. His own habits had clearly made Dr. White a perfectly healthy man, and a happy one. But he put it all down to his family medical history, remarking with a chuckle, "Mine is a pure case of heredity. My father was a family doctor."

The World of Medicine

Contents

Aging

For some people, the onset of old age is simply a step into a different portion of an active, effective, full life. Famous artists, writers, and musicians have reached the highest point of their creative lives in their sixties, seventies, or eighties. Writers Tolstoy and Goethe, artists Titian and Picasso, and musicians Casals and Milhaud lived an old age that was, as Shakespeare described it, "a lusty winter." Grandma Moses did not even begin her career as an artist until she was well past "retirement age." For these people and others like them who are not so well known, growing old simply offers another challenge.

Chronological versus actual age

Although people may be classified as "senile," a life stage reached at the chronological age of 72, active, productive individuals do not think of themselves as senile, a term that conveys inability to function normally mentally or to continue to lead useful lives. Many of these older people become involved with community service programs such as Foster Grandparents. They join clubs, travel, make new friends, develop a whole new life-style. They do not feel old or worn out, even though their bodies may not function as well as they once did.

For some people, however, old age is a time of distress and pain. Their working lives are over; their friends are growing old, dying; their bodies are becoming more susceptible to cancer, stroke, kidney and cardiac disease, and other debilitating physical disorders. Their minds are no longer quick and alert. They are often lonely and grow depressed. In short, in their old age they find life more as Plato described it, a "dreary solitude." They may grow so depressed that suicide seems to be the only solution to the problem. Indeed, 25% of the known suicides in the U.S. involve persons 65 or over, although they make up only 10% of the population. And the actual rate may be even higher, because families often feel shame or guilt and hesitate to acknowledge a death as suicide.

Why does aging affect people in such drastically different ways? Perhaps because people themselves are drastically different. Their genetic inheritance is different; their life situations are different; their ability to cope with change and stress varies; their overall health is different. All of these factors enter into the aging process that begins around the age of 30 and continues, often almost imperceptibly, for the rest of the lifetime.

For most people the aging process causes little or no difficulty. Though there is some loss of ability, the normally aging person's functions simply slow down. His brain does not cease to function. He retains his vocabulary skills, though he may have trouble forming concepts. He may not be able to cope with new input, but past learning and the ability to keep up with day-to-day events are retained. His perceptual motor skills decline, but his ability to interact socially remains intact. He may, however, have difficulty coping with multiple challenges. Because all the changes frighten him and make him feel lost and confused, he defends himself by becoming withdrawn. But this is a normal effect of aging; it is not yet pathological.

Senile dementia

When aging becomes a pathological condition, all these mental mechanisms decline further—recent memory fails; the ability to form concepts and function socially disappears; finally, orientation to time, place, and other persons is lost, and senile dementia, mental deterioration, is complete. In a recent study in Scotland, it was found that 109 of every 1,000 persons over 75 suffered from senile dementia, but only 24 per 1,000 under 75 had the same problem.

Can these behavioral changes in older persons be directly related to organic brain changes? No, say the scientists; it has traditionally been considered impossible, even using a microscope, to examine the brain of an elderly person and determine whether the aging process for that individual was normal or abnormal. Yet new knowledge suggests some exceptions to this rule. Both the normal and the abnormal brain contain arteriosclerotic vessels and so-called senile plaques, and in both there is a loss of nerve tissue.

Recent studies show that aging reduces the chemicals (neurotransmitters) that operate at nerve endings to inform an organ that it should begin, continue, or cease functioning. In one of these systems, for example, the neurotransmitter that regulates movement and thinking is depleted due to cell loss. An older person thus affected is slow-moving and slow-thinking, with trembling hands and a shuffling walk.

Scientists formerly focused on the cortex, or outer portion of the brain, as the probable locus of mental deterioration in an aging person. Now, using a recently developed computerized tomography technique, they are concentrating on the deeper recesses of the brain and are finding that mental deterioration is more likely to be associated with enlarged ventricles (brain chambers) caused by atrophy of the surrounding structure.

It has been established that the blood vessel changes that accompany narrowing of vessel diameter are not a factor in failing mental activity or in the unmistakable dementia of the old person. The circle of Willis, a network of arteries essential to

Aging is a process that affects each individual differently, both physically and psychologically. For many persons the period of senescence can be a productive and enjoyable stage of life.

blood flow in the brain, is usually free of arteriosclerosis in patients suffering senile dementia; however, the nerve cell loss accompanying this disease is 25–30%, in contrast to the 10–15% that occurs normally. Cells in the frontal and temporal regions of the brain are particularly affected.

The number of senile plaques found in the aging brain of the mentally disordered elderly person is greater than that in the normal old person. It is now known that the plaques consist of living tissue; they are made up of twisted microtubules that have enzymatic activity. In victims of the most common of the presenile dementias, Alzheimer's disease, the number of plaques is 10 to 15 times that of normal aging persons.

Can this descent into what appears to be dementia be halted? In many cases the answer is yes. Often the severe psychosocial regression that looks like dementia is really a depression that can be treated with modern techniques. External factors, too, produce a reaction that may seem to indicate dementia. This process often happens when an older person moves to a nursing home. When he is separated from people, activities, and places familiar to him, his impaired vision and hearing plus the limited ability to comprehend make it difficult for him to adjust. To counteract the problem of

the confused and sleepless nights that usually accompany these problems, he is given drugs—which only add to the difficulties of the deteriorating brain and can turn a simple dementia into a psychosis. However, 50–60% of these older persons recover and readjust if they are taken off sedatives, if nutrition and digestion are carefully watched, if they are given a simple, supportive, family-style environment, are kept occupied during the day with carefully selected activities, and are allowed to sleep in a dimly lit room to cut down the confusion or terror of waking in unfamiliar surroundings during the night.

Aging at the cellular and systemic levels

Thus, aging does not have to be a time of frustration and fear. It is not a disease but a normal, natural process that goes on throughout the body. It is the result of altered cell interaction, cell loss, or both. Some cells divide and replace themselves all through life, so there is no cell loss. Others, however, do not regenerate. When they have been damaged or destroyed, the body must get along without them.

Blood cells and cells of the gastrointestinal tract quickly replace themselves. White blood cells, for example, live about 20 minutes, then divide and

179

The loneliness and confusion produced by separation from familiar surroundings may cause an elderly person to become withdrawn or even severely depressed.

create new cells. Even liver, bone, and kidney tubule cells divide intermittently. But, of course, all these cells regenerate more slowly as the body gets older. Consequently, an injury in an older person will heal much more slowly than a similar injury in a child. Unlike most cells, nerve and muscle cells do not regenerate. Those present at birth must last throughout one's life. This is why injured cardiac muscle or brain tissue will heal only with scar tissue, with an inevitable loss of function, even in children.

Much of the process of aging is determined even before birth, as hereditary and genetic factors start an individual on his own particular program of growth, development, aging, and susceptibility to diseases leading to death. While the fetus is growing and developing, sequences of cell differentiation and growth are being programmed into it. Because of this, the organs and body of one 60-year-old may be more like those of a 40-year-old, while another's may appear similar to those of an 80-year-old. Some of the changes in the body are due to molecular errors that build up over a long period of time.

Closely linked with hereditary-genetic factors in the aging process is the activity of the brain-endocrine system. The brain integrates learning, biological drives, and emotions. The endocrine system not only regulates growth and reproductive capacity through the release of hormones but also integrates the body's responses to the environment. The pituitary gland on the lower surface of the brain and the hypothalamic area of the brain have a major effect on the way a person reacts, for example, to stress.

Because the brain-endocrine system loses some of its internal stability, or homeostasis, during aging, older people often find it difficult to cope with their environments. They are no longer as able to tolerate extremes—heat, cold, noise, confusion—as they once were. Events that they would have taken in stride in younger years are very upsetting, and the resulting stress may even be severe enough to cause death.

Changes in the skeletal, vascular, and skin systems are often more obvious than are changes in other body systems. The skin becomes wrinkled and dry; connective tissue loses some of its elasticity, joints become stiff and the body is less supple than it was; the walls of arteries become stiffer and impair blood circulation. Some changes in internal organs also show up in everyday life. Kidney and respiratory capacities, for example, drop 60% between the ages of 30 and 80. The physiological functions of organs begin to decline at about age 25 or 30, and after 30, physiological decline is linear while mortality rate increases exponentially.

The aging process, however, may not be the cause of an individual's death. Disease is often likely to be the real culprit. Currently, two-thirds of the deaths among elderly persons are caused by cardiac disease, malignancy, and stroke. Only 75 years ago, people were more likely to die from pneumonia, tuberculosis, influenza, diarrhea, or inflammation of the intestine (enteritis). Now medication or immunization can control or stop these diseases, thus reducing deaths among younger persons and at the same time ensuring a larger population of the elderly.

The introduction of mental and chronic-disease hospitals, along with medical and paramedical care, means that the cost of such care for an older person is 50% less than it would be if he were in a fully equipped general hospital. And about 50% of the chronic-disease-hospital patients are able to return to their homes. In Sweden, an innovation in care of the aged has been the establishment of "day care hospitals." Though patients are usually discharged after six months, many return once a month to "meet old friends, patients, and staff, for a social-therapeutic encounter."

Aging is not a disease. It is simply a gradual decline in the efficiency of body functions with a decreased ability to resist pathological changes. With continued research, the growth of understanding in both the medical community and the population at large, and the implementation of new programs and techniques, perhaps more and more people will be able to lead and enjoy an old age that is really "a lusty winter."

—Benjamin Boshes, M.D., Ph.D.

Allergy and Immunology

Approximately 25 million Americans (more than 10% of the population) have allergic diseases or symptoms. Each autumn many people have hay fever, with itchy eyes, a runny nose, and cough. Similar symptoms, caused by inhaling airborne pollen, may also occur in spring or summer. Other people have paroxysms of wheezing resulting from constriction of their bronchial passages after they inhale minute particles of animal dander, mold spores, or weed and grass pollens. Some allergic individuals develop a skin rash after eating strawberries, lobster, tomatoes, or other foods. Fatal reactions sometimes occur within minutes after a beesting or an injection of penicillin; each year hundreds of allergic individuals die from such anaphylaxis (hypersensitivity).

Common allergies

What causes allergic symptoms? Why do they occur in some individuals but not others? What do doctors do about them? Hay fever, a typical allergic reaction, results from excessive swelling of the nasal turbinates, spongy projections in the inner re-

cesses of the nose. In addition to its role of filtering air and detecting odors, the nose also warms and humidifies air before it reaches the bronchi and delicate air sacs in the lungs. Water vapor is added to the air stream as it passes through narrow regions between the turbinates and the nasal walls during inspiration. The turbinates act like sponges, alternately filling with and secreting water-containing mucus.

The location of the turbinates, their filling with fluid, and their discharge all render them highly sensitive to a variety of irritations. An infection may cause them to swell; a "stuffy" nose is the usual accompaniment to a common cold. Strong odors, changes in altitude, cold air, irritating dust, even strong emotional upsets can cause nasal obstruction. Such causes of nasal blockage produce vasomotor rhinitis, nonallergic in origin.

Allergies also commonly cause the nasal turbinates to swell. The medical term for obstruction caused by an allergic reaction is allergic rhinitis. Many people develop blocked nasal passages as an allergic response to a variety of different microscopic particles, *e.g.*, plant pollens, animal danders, dust, and mold spores. The important common feature of these agents is that they contain protein. Substances containing protein that lead to allergic responses in susceptible individuals are called allergens. Inhaled proteins of virtually any type can lead to an allergic reaction. Some household laundry detergents, for example, contain enzymes which, when activated in solution, digest food stains. Such enzymes are proteins and lead to chronic allergic reactions in industrial workers at the detergent-manufacturing plant.

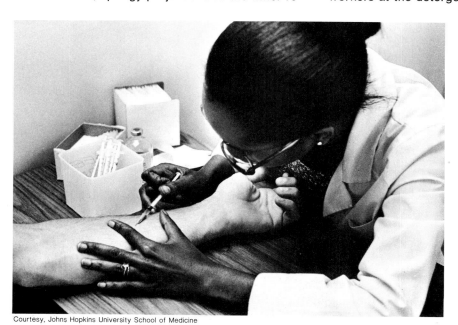

Courtesy, Johns Hopkins University School of Medicine

For a susceptible person, the allergic reaction to an insect sting may cause shock or, in some cases, death. A recently developed test that allows doctors to identify allergic patients and their specific sensitivities involves the injection of minute concentrations of pure insect venom. An allergic response is indicated by the development of small welts at the site of the injection.

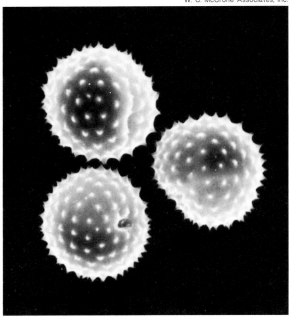

Ragweed pollen, highly magnified in this electron micrograph, is one of the most common allergens.

In asthma, another common allergy, swelling occurs in the linings of the bronchial passages. Mucoid secretions are released by the cells lining the passages. Air passes through the bronchi, which are narrowed by spasm and contain excessive amounts of thickened mucoid secretions, leading to a characteristic wheezing sound not unlike the sound of air escaping from the squeezed neck of a balloon. Skin rashes in allergic individuals caused by eating certain foods follow this same general pattern. The resultant swelling occurs in the skin rather than the nasal turbinates or the bronchi.

The children of allergic parents very often, but not invariably, are allergic themselves. What is inherited is the tendency to respond to the allergens that are present in a geographical area. Thus, the hay fever sufferer who moves to a place free of ragweed pollen may be symptom-free for a time. His symptoms are likely to return as sensitivity to local agents develops.

Although one member of a nonallergic family may have true allergies, the incidence is much less common than in the allergic family. Patients from nonallergic families whose initial symptoms occur in adulthood probably do not have allergen-induced reactions. Individuals of any age whose symptoms are nonseasonal and for whom skin tests are negative are rarely allergic.

Diagnosing allergies

How does an allergist determine if a patient's stuffy nose is caused by allergies? How does he learn which allergen may be the cause of the patient's symptoms? The best clues are often given by the patient himself. For example, allergic individuals often notice that their symptoms occur only during a particular season of the year. Patients sensitive to ragweed, for example, complain of symptoms in the late summer and fall, when ragweed plants may release literally tons of pollen into the air.

To determine which allergens cause a patient's symptoms, doctors inject a minute quantity of an extract of each of the suspected allergens into the patient's skin. A miniature reaction occurs at the injection site if an allergy exists. A small area of redness and swelling, a hive, appears within 15 to 30 minutes, indicating a positive reaction, and lasts an hour or so and then subsides. Thus the hay fever sufferer who is allergic to ragweed pollen forms a hive at the site of injection of an extract of ragweed pollen. Patients allergic only to ragweed will not form hives from injections of grass pollen, dust extract, or other agents. Multiple allergies may exist in the same patient, of course, who will react positively to the injection of each allergen to which he is sensitive.

Chemistry of allergies

Allergic reactions occur as a result of the release of chemical agents, including histamine, from special cells, causing a local increase in capillary permeability. The passage of serum through such "leaky" capillaries leads to swelling. In time, as the excess fluid is gradually reabsorbed and the capillaries return to their normal state, the swelling subsides.

Another chemical agent involved in allergic reactions is known as slow-reacting substance of anaphylaxis (SRS-A). It is distinguished from histamine by its insensitivity to antihistamines and the longer duration of its effects. The specialized cells that store histamine, SRS-A, and other chemical elements in the allergic response are called mast cells. Widely distributed throughout the body, mast cells have granules containing histamine and SRS-A that migrate upon stimulation to the peripheries of the cells. When triggered by an allergen, the cells release the content of their granules.

Mast cells are coated with Immunoglobulin E (IgE), a class of antibodies that binds almost exclusively to this type of cell. The sensitivity of different molecules of IgE to different allergens is quite precise. Thus a cell coated exclusively with molecules of IgE that are specific for the proteins of ragweed pollen will discharge its histamine and SRS-A only upon interaction with ragweed. Patients who have sensitivity to multiple allergens have individual cells coated with molecules of IgE specific for many different allergens. For example, a patient can have both ragweed and grass pollen sensitivity; mast cells in the nasal turbinates of such a person release their granules following contact with either allergen.

Fatal anaphylactic reactions that occur following beestings or injections of drugs into hypersensitive individuals result primarily from the effects of massive amounts of histamine and SRS-A released simultaneously from billions of mast cells throughout the body. The blood pressure falls precipitously as capillaries dilate, asthmatic symptoms impair vital air flow, and the swelling of the larynx leads to literal asphyxiation.

The discharge of the granules of the mast cell is not lethal to the cell itself. New granules form, and redischarge may occur on subsequent stimulation. Furthermore, the allergen sensitivity of the IgE coating the cell may change as molecules of IgE, specific for one allergen, are replaced by IgE molecules specific for a different allergen. It is a dynamic process.

Treatment

The several methods of treatment for allergies are aimed at preventing the release of histamine and SRS-A, or after release has occurred, at preventing their acting upon nearby blood vessels. Antihistamine drugs are used routinely to treat a variety of allergies, usually with success, although the drowsiness that often accompanies their use limits the amount that can be taken. Compounds such as epinephrine and theophylline prevent histamine release from cells through complex biochemical reactions. They are especially useful in treating asthma and, to a lesser extent, in treating allergy-induced skin rashes and allergic rhinitis.

Patients with allergies sometimes take a series of injections containing extracts of allergens. For example, for hay fever, weekly injections of ragweed extract may be administered. As toleration increases, the quantity of extract in each injection is increased slightly in a "hyposensitization" process. The injections usually begin several months before the season when symptoms occur, and they often effectively reduce symptoms so that less medication is required for relief. This procedure is not effective for allergies caused by foods.

The precise cellular mechanism responsible for hyposensitization is not fully understood. Another class of antibodies, IgG, appears as a result of the injections. IgG shares the binding specificity of IgE for the allergen but does not attach to mast cells. It is thought that IgG combines with the allergen before it reaches the IgE-sensitized mast cells, effectively inactivating the allergen and blocking the allergic reaction. Hyposensitization has been used in the treatment of allergies with varying and unpredictable success for at least 60 years. It is only

since the discovery of IgE and an understanding of the mechanism of the allergic reaction that scientists have come to begin to understand the process of hyposensitization.

A new agent, disodium cromoglycate, is proving to be effective in preventing asthma attacks and allergic rhinitis. The drug, obtained originally from the seeds of a Mediterranean plant and now synthesized industrially, prevents the release of histamine and SRS-A. How the drug works is not known. Disodium cromoglycate is administered as a fine, dry powder inhaled with the aid of a special device. The drug is inert, *i.e.,* it cannot be metabolized by the body, and it is excreted mainly through the urine. Patients inhale the drug before symptoms appear, relying on conventional medications if an attack occurs. Disodium cromoglycate is the first new development in the treatment of asthma in many years.

As yet, no definitive cure for allergic diseases is available. All the procedures used offer short-term benefits at best. Symptoms return in the presence of the allergen as the effectiveness of the various treatments and medications gradually diminishes. As is the case with many other illnesses for which no cure has been found, current treatment for allergies usually allows patients to lead less medically restricted and more comfortable lives.

—Edward P. Cohen, M.D., Ph.D.

Anesthesiology

The relatively young but vigorously growing medical specialty of anesthesiology continues to make progress in clinical care, research, and socioeconomic concerns. The 14,000 members of the American Society of Anesthesiologists continue their work to make surgery safe and to allay pain.

Trend to intravenous and local anesthetics

There has been a growing awareness of the physiological shortcomings of the new nonflammable, nonexplosive inhalation anesthetics that were developed to replace the classic, more explosive gases. This concern has led to a trend toward using "balanced" anesthesia—a combination of narcotic, hypnotic, and tranquilizing drugs administered intravenously along with the inhalation of a mixture of oxygen and nitrous oxide, a mild inhalation anesthetic. One added advantage of intravenous methods is that they eliminate the trace amounts of the potent inhalation anesthetics that escape into the operating room. Inhalation anesthetics have been found to be harmful to operating room personnel, particularly anesthesiologists, who are exposed to them over long periods of time. The trend away from inhalation to intravenous anesthetics could prove to be of major significance. It has already stimulated the search for safer inhalation agents, a difficult biomedical task, and for better intravenous drugs, probably less difficult.

There also has been a resurgence in recent years of the use of the classic techniques of regional or local anesthesia to produce analgesia (pain relief) in large segments of the body, usually the lower half. Development of new local anesthetics and a more extensive knowledge of their side effects have contributed to their use. Pain relief in childbirth by regional anesthesia using extradural nerve block, for example, is practiced extensively. The anesthetic is injected into the space just within the bony spinal canal through which pass the nerves that need to be anesthetized. This method has less of a depressant effect on the newborn than does a general anesthetic. (Although such depressant effects are transient and minimal in the healthy baby, they can be significant in the high-risk infant.) Indeed, there is evidence from neurobehavioral testing done immediately after birth that, when extradural nerve block is done with one of the new local anesthetics, infants tend to score as high in tests of bodily function and responsiveness as those whose mothers received no anesthesia in "natural" childbirth.

New facts about anesthetic toxicity

The knowledge that inhaled anesthetics can be toxic under certain circumstances has stimulated research into the metabolic mechanisms involved. For the most part, toxicity has been found to be a product of substances formed from the anesthetics in the course of their breakdown and transformation in the body. Most important, perhaps, have been recent studies that pinpoint the exact sites of these metabolic processes within the cells of the major metabolic organs, particularly the liver. Other studies have demonstrated that chronic exposure to minute amounts of these anesthetics, as occurs with operating room personnel, accelerates the rate at which the anesthetics are metabolized, thus causing more rapid production of their toxic breakdown products.

The studies offer a probable explanation for the increased incidence of miscarriages, birth defects, and certain types of cancer in nurses and doctors who regularly work in operating rooms. The same effects of anesthetics within the cells may also explain why some anesthetics transiently depress the body's systems of defense against such stresses as infection, allergic reactions, physical injury, and even the spread of cancer. Undoubtedly, the knowledge of the specific nature of anesthetic toxicity will contribute significantly to the development of means for preventing toxicity and for increasing anesthetic safety.

Humanizing the care of the terminally ill

Anesthesiologists, because of their major role in critical care medicine, have been widely involved in the death with dignity issue. Following the public response to the Karen Quinlan court decision and the passage of the California "right-to-die" law, anesthesiologists have participated with other members of the hospital team in several types of programs to humanize the medical care of the terminally ill. Such programs incorporate all possible safeguards to protect and serve the best interests

Local anesthetics are frequently used to relieve pain during childbirth. An anesthesiologist administers an epidural block, inserting the needle into the interspace between the third and fourth lumbar vertebrae.

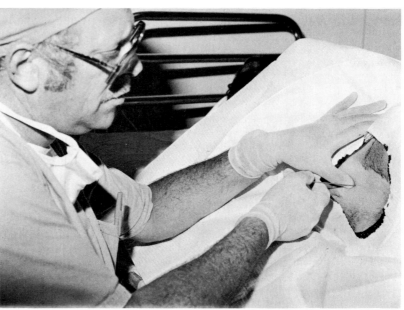

of patients and families, and all the necessary decisions are arrived at openly.

One program focuses on the diagnosis, certification, and management of brain-dead patients, and, with family approval, facilitates the procurement from such patients of healthy donor organs for transplantation. Another program is aimed at defining the steps required to make a medically justified decision not to undertake vigorous cardiopulmonary resuscitation measures when breathing or heart action spontaneously ceases in patients who are terminally ill and for whom death is imminent. In all cases, patients are made as comfortable as possible with painkilling drugs and tranquilizers. The open consideration of the futile emotional and monetary expenses of prolonging life for certain terminally ill patients has thrust the anesthesiologist into the center of the exceptionally complex medical, legal, and ethical questions involved. (*See also* Death; Medical Ethics.)

Reducing the cost of medical care

A corollary to the death with dignity issue is the serious consideration being given to the costs of intensive care as those costs relate to patient survival, degree of functional and vocational recovery, and "quality of life." Anesthesiologists have become involved in efforts to study the tremendous expense of sustaining patients, many of whom will die within a short time. The issue is not the value of a single human life but rather how much of its limited resources a community can afford to put into hopeless situations.

Studies in 1972–73 showed that, for critically ill patients admitted to intensive care units, hospital charges—not including physicians' fees—could average $15,000 per patient or $500 per day of hospitalization, more than twice the cost for other hospital patients. The grim follow-up data pose the sensitive social dilemmas of cost-effectiveness and of triage, *i.e.,* which critically ill patients should be treated, how vigorously, and for how long. Within one month approximately half of the studied intensive care patients had died. After one year, only 25% remained alive, fewer than half of whom were able to function as before their illness. The cost to society was approximately $125,000 per fully recovered patient. (Costs in 1977 were significantly higher, probably by 20%.) It is the total community —medical, legal, legislative, and public—that properly should and will have to make the ultimate decisions. The question has been raised and will continue to be an important one.

Preadmission clinics

Delayed elective surgery for hospitalized patients can also be expensive to patients and to the community. Patients are usually surgically and medically evaluated by means of laboratory tests performed on an outpatient basis. After admission to a hospital for scheduled surgery, patients frequently find that their operation must be postponed because additional preoperative tests or treatments are needed.

On a pilot basis, anesthesiologists have been establishing preadmission evaluation clinics. Patients report seven to ten days prior to their scheduled hospital admission. During the clinic visit all required treatments or further tests are completed if feasible. If necessary, the scheduled admission to the hospital is postponed pending completion of procedures necessary to ensure the optimal medical condition for surgery. It has been found that such clinics can reduce the length of hospitalization by an average of almost four days. For larger community hospitals and medical centers, the savings in 1977 amounted to as much as $800 to $1,000 per patient. Attention to this type of medical service will undoubtedly grow.

—*Solomon G. Hershey, M.D.*

Birth Control

With four billion people on earth and an additional four billion expected within 35 years, the limitation of population growth has become an urgent matter. The birthrate in industrialized countries has slowed, but the rate in developing countries has accelerated. To reduce the birthrate in all countries to a point where it approaches the death rate will require massive educational programs and the discovery of universally acceptable contraceptive techniques. To be acceptable by all people, birth control techniques must be efficient, safe, free of serious side effects, simple enough to be used by a nonliterate population, inexpensive, and readily available. A final requirement is that they must not interfere with coitus. An ideal contraceptive that fulfills all of these requirements has, unfortunately, not yet been developed.

New contraceptives

The search for better methods of birth control continues and includes projects as simple as improving the quality of condoms and as complex as the development of antipregnancy vaccines. One promising discovery that is easy to use, inexpensive, and safe is a spermicidal substance obtained from a common plant growing widely in India. The substance is extracted inexpensively and mixed with vaginal creams or jellies. Its long-term safety is still in doubt, however.

Another innovation is injection every three to six months of a progestin (medroxyprogesterone) that

Birth control

inhibits ovulation. Approximately one million women in several countries have taken the hormone with remarkable success. Advantages of the method are that it requires infrequent administration and can be given by paramedics. The hormone's disadvantages are irregular menstrual bleeding in some women and prolonged periods of amenorrhea (absence of menstruation) in others. Its use may be followed by several months of infertility and, rarely, by sterility.

Monkeys can be immunized against pregnancy with the injection of seminal or placental substances. In a recent experiment, female monkeys were immunized with an antifertility vaccine that neutralized placental hormones necessary for maintaining pregnancy in its early stages. Only one pregnancy occurred despite 28 matings in 13 vaccinated animals.

Oral contraceptives for males are being studied. One substance, cyproterone acetate, given by mouth daily for several weeks, will reduce the number and motility of spermatozoa without altering male libido. It is also known that both ovarian and testicular hormones (estrogen and testosterone) will reduce male fertility. However, the unpredictability and the side effects of chemical or hormonal therapy for males make the methods now being studied as yet unsuitable for human use.

Surgery

Surgical sterilization remains the only method of permanent birth control, and recent reports indicate that it is becoming increasingly common. According to a mid-1977 publication of the Planned Parenthood Federation of America, sterilization is currently the method of choice for couples married ten years or more or those who have completed their families. Oral contraceptives continue to be the most popular method of birth control among women married fewer than ten years. Statistics released in 1977, based on a 1975 survey, indicated that the number of married couples of childbearing age who had chosen sterilization was nearly equal to the number using oral contraceptives.

Although closing the fallopian tubes in women and the vas deferens in men can be reversed surgically, successful reversal is the exception rather than the rule. Obstructing devices such as clamps and plugs that can be removed at a later date have been developed but have not proved satisfactory. Closing the vas deferens by injecting a scar-producing solution into or about it has been successful in animals, but there are no reports of its use in humans. It is likely that this method would permanently obstruct the vas deferens.

Tubal ligation (tying) or resection (cutting) of the fallopian tubes is an accepted method for perma-

"Child spacing hasn't been a problem. I had one baby in Denver, one in Duluth and one in Waxahachie, Texas."

nently sterilizing women. It has been considered free of complications other than those associated with any relatively simple abdominal operation. There is now evidence, however, that from 15 to 40% of patients have more or less irregular menstruation and uterine bleeding following the surgery. There are no adequate explanations for these complications.

Oral contraceptives

It is generally accepted that the great majority of healthy young women can take oral contraceptives with very little risk of serious side effects. Medical investigators, however, continue to explore the possible relationship between oral contraceptives and certain medical complications. From published reports and from the experiences of physicians, it is now possible to identify patients who are most likely to suffer serious side effects from oral contraceptives.

Mental depression characterized by despondency, tension, and change in sexual desire occurs in a small number of women taking oral contraceptives. In the past it was thought that the depression might be of psychological origin because of the woman's religious or cultural attitudes toward the use of birth control. Recently it has been suggested that a possible cause is a biochemical disturbance resulting from the effect of estrogen on the concentration of certain chemicals in the brain. Whatever the cause, there is general agreement that caution should be exercised in prescribing the Pill to patients with a history of depression or anxiety. If such patients do decide to use oral contraceptives, they should receive periodic examinations, including a review of their mental state.

A history of certain conditions, notably phlebitis, thrombophlebitis, hypertension, and varicosities, predisposes women who take the Pill to blood clots in the lungs. In addition, women who have a history of marked hypertension, impaired liver function, heart disease, genital bleeding of unknown origin, cerebral vascular disease, and breast or uterine cancer should not take oral contraceptives. Women who suffer from migraine or vascular headaches likewise should use some other form of contraception. If such women do take oral contraceptives, however, they should have periodic ophthalmoscopic examinations. Any patient taking an oral contraceptive who develops eye symptoms should discontinue the drug and should be examined by a physician.

There is little evidence that oral contraceptives increase the risk of heart attacks among healthy women under the age of 35 who do not smoke. The combination of age (40 and over), smoking, and oral contraceptives multiplies the risk of myocardial infarction three- or fourfold. Because of the relationship of high blood cholesterol, high blood pressure, diabetes, and heavy smoking to heart attacks, women who have any of these predisposing factors, regardless of their age, should use another form of birth control.

The "morning after" pill is used by many women. It consists of large oral doses of an estrogen or stilbestrol started within 48 hours of coitus and continued for five days. In one report from The Netherlands, where from 45,000 to 50,000 women per year take the "morning after" pill, there were only 17 pregnancies among the 3,016 women in the study who used it. The method is relatively effective and safe but often has unpleasant side effects. Half of the patients experience nausea, one-fourth vomit, one-fourth complain of tender breasts, and many have abnormal uterine bleeding. A pregnancy in a woman who takes the "morning after" pill should be terminated by abortion because of the possible serious adverse effect on the embryo. Many physicians feel that the "morning after" pill, despite its effectiveness, should be used only in emergencies, *e.g.,* in cases of rape.

Once-a-month oral contraceptives have been in use for a number of years, but attempts to improve their effectiveness and reduce their side effects have not been very successful. The most widely used preparation, quinestrol, a synthetic estrogen, combined with a long-acting progestin and taken orally, is deposited in fatty tissue in the body and then slowly released into the blood stream. It requires only infrequent administration, but its use is associated with a relatively high incidence of abnormal genital bleeding. It is less effective than other oral contraceptives, with the same risks and contraindications.

Until new and better methods are devised, oral contraceptives continue to be the most effective means of birth control. They are safer than preg-

Because of their relative safety, economy, and effectiveness—and because they require no special effort on the part of the user—intrauterine devices, or IUDs, are particularly suited to the needs of family planning programs in developing countries.

Courtesy, the World Health Organization

nancy and more efficient than any other contraceptive. The infrequent serious complications occur, for the most part, among patients who have certain medical conditions. It is important that women and physicians be aware of predisposing causes of serious side effects and that patients who have a history of such conditions use some other type of birth control. (*See also* Diet and Nutrition.)

—*John W. Huffman, M.D.*

Blood Diseases

Just a few years ago, the prognosis for leukemia was so grave that making the diagnosis in a patient was tantamount to passing a death sentence. In recent years, however, the outlook has changed considerably. Today, there is hope that substantial advances in leukemia research not only will prolong the life of afflicted patients but also will produce cures for this dreaded malady. This change in thinking and the rationale behind altered modes of therapy for leukemia are the result of the combined efforts of clinicians and scientists working together in many different disciplines, such as biochemistry, cell kinetics, pharmacology, experimental pathology, and biostatistics. Their efforts have led to a major breakthrough in the attempt to conquer the different forms of cancer that affect the blood and the lymph organs.

Chemotherapy for leukemia

In leukemia, changes in the white blood cells result in abnormal, highly uncontrolled cell growth and behavior patterns. Frequently, but not always, large numbers of these abnormal white cells appear in the blood. (The term *leukemia* is derived from the Greek words *leukos* meaning white and *haima* meaning blood.) More importantly, large quantities of the leukemic cells also invade the body tissue responsible for the production of blood cells, the bone marrow, and impair its normal functioning.

The recognition of the abnormal growth pattern and behavior of the leukemic cells now enables doctors to use new drugs that act specifically against these abnormal cells. Such treatment with chemical agents is termed chemotherapy. Frequently, several chemicals are administered together to produce a concerted effect on the leukemic cells, each drug exerting its toxic effect on the abnormal cell at specific stages of growth in the cell's life cycle. The goal of the combined effort is to interrupt the growth of the cells, thus either killing them or preventing them from proliferating further. Courses of such treatment repeated at frequent intervals make it possible to remove most of the leukemic cells from the blood and from the bone marrow, allowing the marrow to resume its normal function. At this point, the patient is said to be in remission of the leukemia. Though the patient who is in remission appears to be in good health, remaining leukemic cells may again proliferate and multiply to large numbers unless the treatment is continued until the last leukemic cell has been destroyed. Only then can a patient be considered cured, a goal that requires many such courses of treatment given over many months. If a patient remains symptom-free for five years after the treatment is stopped, the likelihood of a cure is high.

Rates of remission and cure

At an International Congress of Hematology in September 1976, scientists reported on results in treating leukemia. According to the reports, approximately 80% of leukemic children who had achieved complete remission and who had stopped receiving further chemotherapy are enjoying long-term, leukemia-free life today. Since, with proper treatment, complete remission is expected to occur in at least 80% of patients, a child with leukemia today has a better than 60% chance of being cured. Among adults, the corresponding figures for remis-

In research and clinical treatment the continuous flow centrifugal blood cell separator has replaced earlier methods of separating blood into its component parts.

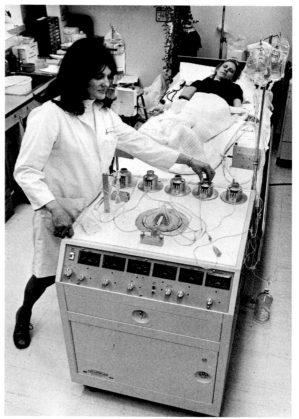

Courtesy, American Instrument Company, Travenol Laboratories, Inc.; *Aminco Laboratory News,* Spring, 1977

sion and for cures are lower—approximately 60–80% for complete remission and 70% for continued remission, providing a 40–50% chance for cure—but most scientists hope that these cure rates will continue to rise with improved supportive care.

Additional modes of treatment

Two common causes of mortality during the early phase of treatment of acute leukemia are bleeding and infection. Modern devices for procuring blood platelets from healthy donors for leukemic patients help to control the bleeding in most cases. The availability of wide-spectrum antibiotics and special isolation procedures for the patient have reduced mortality caused by infection. Patients whose resistance to infections has been reduced by the leukemic process can now be placed in a "germ-free" environment. Furthermore, the science of blood matching is now so refined that matched, healthy white blood cells can be given to help the patient fight infections.

Another new method of treatment is a systematic process of stimulation of the patient's own immune system by use of vaccines. Earlier hopes that this might help the body's immunologic defense mechanisms to eliminate any remaining leukemic cells following chemotherapy have not been borne out by clinical data, however. (*See also* Lymphatic System Diseases.)

—Hau C. Kwaan, M.D.

Cancer

Cancer is a major cause of death in the U.S. and is perhaps the single most feared disease. The American public probably regards cancer with more dread than any of the other major causes of death and disability. Through their representatives in Congress and donations to the American Cancer Society, Americans have given the highest priority to cancer research. More money is now available for research in cancer than for any other disease.

Research

A large community of cancer researchers has developed; in the last four or five years the number of investigators has probably increased three- or four-fold. New cancer centers have been established (predominantly at medical schools), and other cancer centers have expanded. The growth of research has recently slowed down, however, and probably has reached 80% or 90% of its ultimate extent. In the future the National Cancer Institute (NCI) will likely not be able to fund all of the meritorious research applications that it will receive.

The U.S. research effort is now approaching the size suggested by the NCI plan developed in 1972.

Formulated in collaboration with 250 scientists and physicians, the plan has been both criticized and praised. But if it has done nothing else, it has served as a basis for the budgeting necessary to carry out a large new national effort.

The plan for research has been developed and is now beginning to yield results. Much new information has been produced, and much more is being compiled. From development of a research idea to completion of the investigation and dissemination of the results, however, may require a minimum of 3 years; for some studies 10 to 15 years may be necessary. Thus, although researchers have produced no startling new information that will quickly eliminate cancer as a medical problem, they have begun to develop a foundation for better management of the problem. There have been no dramatic breakthroughs, only steady progress. In terms of what researchers need to know, they are still far from reaching the ultimate goal of prevention and cure. Scientists now know much more about fundamental life processes; it remains to be determined how the knowledge can be applied to prevent, diagnose, and treat cancer.

Study of the herpesvirus (seen here as the target-like spheres in a magnified cross section of a human cell) and its link with cervical cancer is one current focus in cancer research.

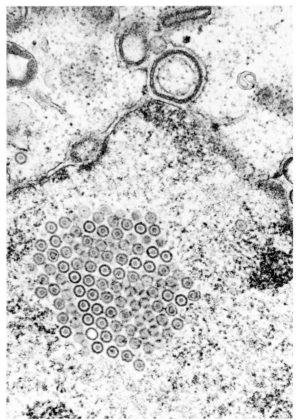

Courtesy, Stanford University Medical Center; *The Healing Arts,* Winter 1975

A technician prepares a cancer patient for treatment with the new medical linear accelerator, which provides supervoltage radiation therapy that is safer than conventional X-ray therapy.

There are three ways to approach the control of cancer: (1) to determine its cause or causes and to use the knowledge to prevent cancer; (2) to diagnose cancer at a stage favorable for treatment; and (3) to treat cancer effectively at any stage. There have recently been advances in all three areas.

Prevention

One of the principal goals of research in cancer prevention has been to find a virus or viruses that produce cancer in man. The effort began with the discovery in 1911 that one virus could cause cancer in animals. Later research discovered more than 100 viruses that cause cancer in experimental animals, including primates. But no virus has as yet been identified as a cause of cancer in humans.

There is, however, an emerging view holding that if a virus or group of viruses plays a role in causing cancer in man, they are common viruses found in many people but causing cancer in only a few. Strong evidence in favor of this view is found in the existence of a link between a herpesvirus and can-

cer of the cervix. There is also evidence linking both craniopharyngioma (a particular cancer of the head) and Burkitt's lymphoma (a cancer mainly afflicting African children) with the Epstein-Barr virus, a herpesvirus that is associated with infectious mononucleosis. As the links between cancer and common viruses are substantiated, attempts to find a single human cancer virus are being deemphasized. This shift in the orientation of research makes the development of a cancer vaccine based on a causative virus even more unlikely.

At the same time, researchers are investigating the role of chemicals in causing cancer. Certainly for cigarette smokers and for particular occupational groups chemicals are major factors. But the problem remains of determining that a given chemical causes cancer in man. In fact, it is not easy to determine that a given chemical causes cancer in experimental animals.

Radiation has long been known to cause cancer in man, and a number of steps have been taken recently to reduce exposure to X-rays. There has been widespread discussion about the use of X-ray examinations to detect breast cancer. In the Chicago area several medical groups are reexamining people who in the past had X-ray treatment of the head and neck for noncancerous conditions (principally acne and enlarged tonsils and adenoids). A disproportionate number of patients so treated have developed thyroid tumors, some of which are malignant.

Two reports linking drugs and breast cancer have generated considerable concern. A report from Detroit indicates that women given thyroid medication have had an increased incidence of breast cancer. Further confirmation of the connection will be necessary. Another report indicates that women given estrogens over a long period of time for the treatment of menopausal symptoms have had an increased incidence of breast cancer. The report has led officials to issue a warning that estrogens should be used only in women who specifically need them and that they be used for as short a period of time as possible.

Diagnosis

There is general agreement that the smaller a tumor is, the less likely it is to have metastasized and the greater the likelihood that surgical removal will effect a cure. The major difficulty in early diagnosis is that symptoms sufficient to cause the patient to go to a doctor occur late in the course of most cancers. To make a diagnosis before metastases occur, physicians must search for cancer in persons who are without symptoms but who are at risk. Such searching is called screening.

How large a part of the population should be or

can be screened depends on the age for beginning screening. There are reasons to begin at age 40, but the yield between the ages of 40 and 50 may be too low to be economically feasible. There are, on the other hand, reasons to begin Pap testing for cancer of the cervix in women in their 20s and 30s. There is no simple criterion, nor is there a combination of simple criteria, for selecting those who should be examined. Nor is there data on the extent to which mortality from cancer could be reduced by searching for frequently occurring cancers in those over a particular age who do not have symptoms.

Another difficulty is that, at present, health insurers usually do not pay for screening examinations. Blue Cross has announced that, under sponsorship of the NCI, it is developing and testing a plan for offering a cancer screening examination to its subscribers. This program has the potential to make a cancer screening examination available to a large percentage of the population that is at risk.

Such a program has major problems. What would it cost? What would be the benefit? Definitive answers will not be available for some time. In terms of present knowledge, however, the program seems justified by the evidence that mortality from cancer of the breast and cervix can be reduced by screening. There are preliminary data indicating that such a program would also reduce mortality from cancer of the lung among cigarette smokers and from cancer of the bowel and prostate. There are, however, no data on the effects on mortality of a comprehensive cancer screening program.

A study by the Health Insurance Plan of Greater New York showed a one-third reduction in mortality from breast cancer among women who were offered a series of physical examinations and X-rays of the breast. The NCI and the American Cancer Society subsequently developed 27 breast cancer detection projects, each to examine 10,000 women annually for a period of five years. More than 250,-000 women were enrolled in the program. The agencies had reviewed the two questions of public concern about the program: What is the hazard of the radiation dose used? What is the evidence for the benefit of such a program?

There are no direct data from which to calculate the hazard, so indirect data were used, based upon the development of breast cancer in three groups: (1) women exposed to atomic bomb radiation at Hiroshima and Nagasaki; (2) women who repeatedly were fluoroscoped during the treatment and management of tuberculosis; and (3) women given large doses of X-rays to treat breast infection after the delivery of a baby. From data on these women, it has been calculated that one million women given one rad (a unit of radiation dose) would develop approximately 120 additional cases of breast cancer by age 40. But it should be remembered that 70,000 cases of breast cancer will occur in this same group of women whether or not they receive radiation.

Although the hazard of radiation can only be estimated, radiologists have recently developed and are now using X-ray techniques with much lower radiation doses than were given a few years ago. In fact, doses are now sufficiently low that the potential benefit is great compared to the hazard.

Some critics pointed out that in the original New

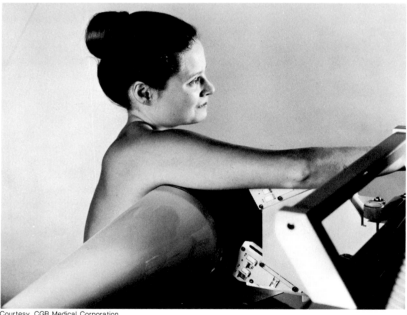

Courtesy, CGR Medical Corporation

With radiation a known carcinogen, concern has recently grown in medical circles over the safety of mammography, or X-ray examination of the breasts, for the detection of breast cancer.

Cancer

York study there was no reduction in breast cancer mortality in women under 50, leading to the recommendation that screening not be done before that age. Others have challenged the recommendation, principally because breast X-ray techniques and interpretation have improved considerably since the original study. And in contrast to the New York study, the current project is finding more women with cancer both under and over 50, by X-ray alone. The cancers that have been found in the current project are earlier (that is, smaller) and present a more favorable outlook for cure than those found in women who wait until they feel a lump in the breast before going to a physician. The debate over the hazards of such screening by X-rays will probably continue for several years until the data from the current project can be analyzed further to determine how the women who participated benefit.

Another major development in diagnosis has been the introduction of the computerized brain scanner, or CAT-scanner, a diagnostic X-ray machine originally designed for examination of the brain. The scanner produces X-ray pictures of slices of the intact living brain by measuring repeatedly the absorption of a thin X-ray beam. Although simple in concept, the scanner requires the solution of a large number of equations requiring a computer. In only a few years, the scanner has proved its value in X-ray diagnosis of the brain.

Encouragingly, current studies in Italy indicate that post-surgical injections in radical mastectomy patients of CMF, a mix of three proven anticancer drugs, appear to have greatly lowered the recurrence of cancer.

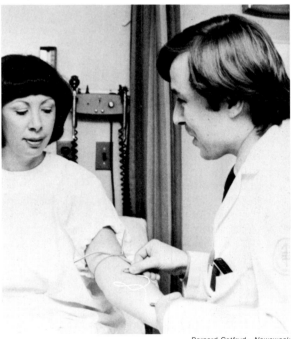

Bernard Gotfryd—*Newsweek*

In those hospitals with a brain scanner, the accuracy of diagnosis has increased remarkably. The high cost (from $300,000 to $400,000) and the large number of scanners purchased have raised questions. Should all hospitals have a brain scanner? How are they to be paid for? Scanners for the body have also been developed. Again considering the cost ($600,000 to $800,000), there are questions about the economics of body scanners.

Treatment

Surgery followed by radiation and drug therapy (chemotherapy) continues to be the pattern for treating common cancers. In the last few years there have been several studies that have added drug therapy shortly after surgery, particularly for breast, lung, and colon cancer. In each instance some benefit was seen, but as time has passed, it has become apparent that such treatment, while initially very promising, has proved to be less beneficial than originally projected.

Most patients who die of cancer after surgical removal of a tumor die because cancer has spread throughout the body by the time of the surgery. The only way to treat such patients is with drugs, but it will take additional time to determine which drugs should be used and how to use them. Initial reports on the use of L-PAM to treat women after surgery for breast cancer has shown that the drug has less effect in postmenopausal than in premenopausal women. Similarly, the CMF (cyclophosphamide, methotrexate, fluorouracil) study in Italy has shown less success with post- than with premenopausal women. The results of both studies, however, are important because they show a significant delay in recurrence and delay in the growth of metastases. The studies are an important first step, recalling the history of the development of the use of drugs to treat childhood acute leukemia. While the success with L-PAM and CMF has been less than was hoped for, the studies represent significant progress in developing drug treatment that can be begun at the time of surgery and continued for one to two years afterward.

There has also been much discussion of and interest in immunotherapy. At the present time, however, leading researchers in the field are beginning to think that the current studies using BCG (bacille Calmette-Guérin), the vaccine used to immunize for tuberculosis, will not prove to be very effective in killing tumor cells and that immunotherapists must turn to other immunological techniques.

(*See also* Blood Diseases; Diet and Nutrition; Lymphatic System Diseases; Obstetrics and Gynecology; Pediatrics Special Report: Treating Cancer in Children.)

—*Nathaniel I. Berlin, M.D.*

Special Report:
The National Cancer Program

by Nathaniel I. Berlin, M.D.

One of the new programs—and perhaps to many the most important—of the National Cancer Act of 1971 was the National Cancer Program. This legislation was the basis for coordinating federally supported cancer research, principally that within the National Cancer Institute (NCI), with the work supported by other federal agencies, the states, and private philanthropic groups and the programs carried out at U.S. universities, medical schools, hospitals, and research laboratories. While precise figures are not available, it is likely that two-thirds to three-quarters of U.S. cancer research is in fact supported by grants-in-aid and contracts from the NCI. Some of this research is performed in the institute's own laboratories in Bethesda, Md.

The National Cancer Act of 1971 resulted from a report entitled "Report of the National Panel of Consultants on the Conquest of Cancer." The panel was created by the Senate Committee on Labor and Public Welfare and was headed by then Sen. Ralph W. Yarborough (D, Tex.); co-chairmen of the panel were the late Boston physician Sidney Farber and Benno Schmidt, a New York businessman with a long and deep interest in cancer. The panel concluded that "While it is probably unrealistic at this time to talk about the total elimination of cancer within a short period of time or to expect a single vaccine or cure that will eradicate the disease completely, the progress that has been made in the past decade provides a strong basis for the belief that an accelerated and intensified assault on cancer at this time will produce extraordinary rewards. The Committee is unanimously of the view that an effective national program for the conquest of cancer should be promptly initiated and relentlessly pursued."

The 1971 act called for, among other things, 15 new cancer centers, a cancer control program, and a three-member panel to be called the "President's Panel on Cancer." Most importantly, it provided for the submission of the NCI's budget directly to the president; thus the institute's budget was not subject to the direct review of the National Institutes of Health (NIH) or the Department of Health, Education, and Welfare (HEW). HEW and NIH were to be given the opportunity to comment upon the budget but could not alter it.

It has long been recognized that cancer is a dread disease. Whether justified or not, the fear of cancer is very real. A great proportion of the population fear cancer more than anything else, and in many respects the National Cancer Act of 1971—and its renewal in 1974—recognized two issues related to this fear: (1) the belief by some cancer researchers that the time had come for a greatly increased effort and (2) the willingness of the public to give financial support to this effort. Neither among the senior staff of the NCI nor in the Congress or executive branch was this effort thought comparable to the task of "putting a man on the moon." All acknowledged it to be more difficult and less certain of success.

Financing the program

Congress has supported the commitment to increase funds for the nation's anticancer effort. The amount budgeted for fiscal year 1971 was $180 million; for fiscal 1978 it is expected to exceed $850 million. Although each year's appropriation has been somewhat less than requested, increases have been substantial. As a result, a large cancer-oriented biomedical research community has been created. It may in fact be too large—in recent years the budget has not been adequate to support more than half of the promising new programs. This limitation of funds will probably result in some decrease in the number of cancer researchers. Most of the research initiated since 1971 is still in progress, and while some new knowledge has been acquired, it will be another three to five years before much of what is being done now will be completed and ready for presentation to the medical profession and the public.

The plan

In addition to the sections calling for new cancer centers and a cancer control program, the 1971 act called for a "plan." This plan was formulated by the NCI in 1971 and 1972. Its structure was developed by the NCI staff, but the substance of the plan came from some 250 outside experts. The plan had one central objective—the elimination of cancer as a cause of death. More particularly, it included seven subobjectives calling for development of the means for (1) reducing the effectiveness of external agents that produce cancer; (2) modifying bodily

"New and better screening and diagnostic procedures [to detect cancer] are needed, and existing ones still remain to be tested adequately."

mechanisms so as to minimize the hazards of cancer-inducing agents; (3) preventing the transformation of normal cells into cells capable of causing cancer; (4) preventing the development of cancer from precancerous conditions and the spread of cancer from primary sites; (5) achieving an accurate assessment of (a) the risk of cancer development in groups and individuals and (b) the present extent and probable cause of existing cancers; (6) curing cancers and retarding the progress of those not cured; and (7) improving rehabilitation of cancer patients. These objectives were thought to be all encompassing. They did not prejudge whether prevention, diagnosis, or treatment would be the pathway to the conquest of cancer. Later a research objective in rehabilitation was added—acknowl-

edging that the ultimate objective may be in the distant future and that, until the ultimate objective is achieved, it will be necessary to care for and rehabilitate patients.

The plan, which in itself could fill a whole bookshelf, and its supplements, summary statements, and analyses represented a new approach. Perhaps the most significant aspect of the plan was not the objectives set forth by its developers, but its effect on the allocation of the resources, personnel, and facilities needed for implementation.

This type of planning was new to the biomedical research community, and although many scientists participated in its development, it has been criticized heavily—both by some who participated in its development and by others who did not. There is no evidence that the senior staff of the NCI used the plan to direct or dictate the course of research. In fact, they probably did not. Today the plan appears to be an effort of the past. It has accomplished the purpose for which it was intended, namely, to provide a scientific basis for justification by NCI staff of budget requests. It is worth noting in this connection that all of the senior staff, the director and division directors who were responsible for the development and implementation of the plan, had left the NCI by October 1976.

Cancer centers

The 1971 legislation called for the creation of 15 new cancer centers and authorized grants of up to $5 million for each center. Since that time, 16 new centers have been recognized by the NCI as "comprehensive," a designation which indicates that they meet ten requirements set by the institute. These include research, both laboratory and clinical; patient care, both diagnostic and therapeutic; and education, within both the center and in its community. The new centers are dispersed across the country. No center has been awarded a $5-million grant, nor has any received a grant as a result of its "comprehensive" designation. These centers, along with the three already in existence in 1971, make it possible for the NCI to demonstrate that it has met all the requirements of the law. Other facilities, called specialized centers, have been designated and have received grants. They vary considerably in scope, from multidisciplinary (carrying out both laboratory and clinical research coupled with patient care) to single-purpose units such as radiation therapy centers.

The control program

The 1971 act also called for a cancer control program. *Control,* in this context, has a different meaning from that usually associated with the term. It implies transfer of new knowledge from the research laboratory and research hospital to the entire medical profession and, ultimately, to the public. The basis for this element of the act was the belief that the transfer process was slow at best and that the researchers who should be in the forefront of dissemination of information were in fact not fulfilling this function. This allegation is difficult to prove. What is not widely known is that during 1971 and 1972 the senior staff of the NCI made a number of attempts to define "cancer control," to identify what new research already "proven effective" was ready for widespread application but was not being so applied. Some examples of this failure were found, and in 1972 and 1973 the initial cancer control projects began, including the establishment of the Breast Cancer Detection Demonstration Project, institution of networks of hospitals for the treatment of leukemias and lymphomas, and efforts to make the Pap test more widely available through state health departments. Today the Cancer Control Program encompasses many additional projects.

Progress in patient care

Since the 1971 act there have been no major new conceptual advances in patient care that have resulted in a significant decrease in mortality. The care rates of most common cancers are not appreciably different. The few exceptions to this statement apply to certain rather uncommon cancers. Nonetheless, while the rate of cure has not increased, new drugs and new combinations of drugs have provided some relief and made possible some prolongation of life. Today the outcome for most patients is already determined when the diagnosis of cancer is made, for the simple reason that about two-thirds of these patients have disseminated cancer (mestastases) when first diagnosed and cannot be cured by present techniques. It is theoretically possible, however, to reduce mortality by screening, that is, by searching for cancer in asymptomatic individuals. Currently screening is not being carried out on any widespread basis, primarily because it is too costly.

The future of the program

Since its inception the National Cancer Program has had its critics. They claimed that a plan was not possible or was inherently wrong, that there was not enough basic research or not enough clinical research, and that the planned or targeted programs were not necessary. For each criticism there was a response, and as of today, neither the critics nor the defenders can be proven right. What can be said is that a diversity of pathways is being explored, a direct result of lack of fundamental knowledge. We did not know then—nor do we know today—when it will be possible to conquer cancer; we certainly do not know how it will be done.

We do know that through the NCI and the National Cancer Program, the U.S. cancer research community has been significantly expanded. The program has also succeeded in establishing coordination with other federal agencies and with philanthropic organizations, although this coordination is more often informal than formal. The American Cancer Society (ACS), the largest private supporter of cancer research and public and professional education, regularly exchanges information with the NCI. The ACS has, for example, developed a joint program with the NCI for breast cancer detection. There are also exchanges with other federal agencies, *e.g.,* the Clearinghouse on Chemical Carcinogenesis. An International Cancer Research Data Bank, which provides information about worldwide cancer research, has been established. In this respect the staff of the NCI is fulfilling its congressional mandate to establish a National Cancer Program.

If financial support by Congress is continued, the system may be expected to produce new knowledge and insights into how to prevent, diagnose, and treat cancer. Patience and understanding of the complexity of the problem will be required, and progress is likely to be slow. The effort to isolate a human cancer virus similar to the viruses that produce cancer in a number of experimental animals is declining, based on the current opinion that if a virus is indeed implicated in human cancers, it is a common virus that infects many persons but produces cancer in only a few.

Effective preventive methods—other than elimination of cigarette smoking—have yet to be developed. New and better screening and diagnostic procedures are needed, and existing ones still remain to be tested adequately. New drugs and improved ways of using existing drugs are needed. Immunotherapy, a promising avenue of research, is still in its infancy. What is needed is more knowledge about the basic properties of both normal and neoplastic cells. It is hoped that increased knowledge of cell biology will provide new approaches to the control or conquest of cancer in man.

Only time will tell which of the current approaches to the conquest of cancer will ultimately be the most productive. For the moment, we must continue to pursue every likely pathway, and it is this attempt at diversity that prompts criticism. Those who have chosen one line of research have not convinced their colleagues working in alternate fields. Yet this very lack of unanimity makes it both desirable and necessary that the present multiplicity of approaches continue.

Cardiovascular System Diseases

More deaths occur annually in the United States from cardiovascular disease than from the next two leading causes of death (accidents and cancer) combined. However, the U.S. death rate from cardiovascular disorders has fallen steadily but significantly since 1968. The cause of this small but apparently meaningful decline is the subject of continued speculation and debate.

Coronary artery disease

During the past decade a number of key risk factors in coronary artery disease, the major contributor to mortality, have been identified and widely publicized. Coronary artery disease is a result of the accumulation of atheromata, or cholesterol-filled plaques, in the lining (the intima) of the large arterial blood vessels supplying oxygenated blood to the muscle of the heart. Major risk factors are age, family history (other family members known to have suffered from coronary artery disease in early middle age), cigarette smoking, hypertension, and increased concentration of serum cholesterol.

A recent study by the American Cancer Society showed a decrease in cigarette smoking among adults and a shift in the mean age of smokers to a younger population. The decline in the death rate from cardiovascular diseases has also coincided with the switch by U.S. smokers to "safer" filter cigarettes with less tar and other harmful by-products. Whether this decline in the type and quantity of tobacco consumed by the population at risk has contributed to the decrease in cardiovascular deaths is speculative, since the exact relationship of tobacco to mortality from heart disease is not known.

Some specific effects of smoking are known, however. Certain alkaloids and other substances in tobacco induce intense vasoconstriction (narrowing of blood vessels), especially in susceptible subjects. Furthermore, cigarette smokers have significantly higher concentrations of carbon monoxide in the blood than do nonsmokers. Carbon monoxide binds hemoglobin, the substance in red cells that transports oxygen from the lungs to the tissues, with an avidity many times greater than that of oxygen. An increase in the blood concentration of the chemical combination carbon monoxyhemoglobin significantly decreases the availability of oxygen to the peripheral tissues.

In the patient with preexisting coronary artery

Although smoking has been identified as a major risk factor in coronary artery disease, studies show that quitting smoking significantly reduces the risk of death from heart attack.

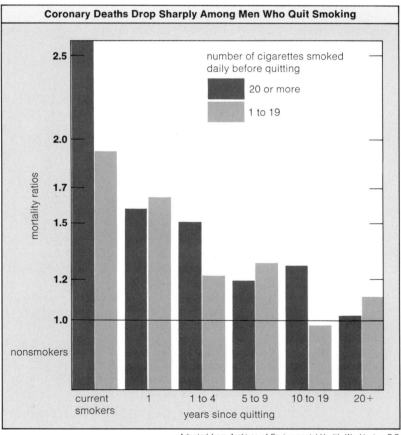

Adapted from *Archives of Environmental Health*, Washington, D.C.

"All I can say is, if polyunsaturated fats are going to do this for you, it's going to take the gilt off longevity."

Scully—© Punch/Rothco

disease, the added burden of increased carbon monoxyhemoglobin could result in reduced oxygen tension in critical portions of the heart muscle, or myocardium. For this reason, the excess carbon monoxide in the blood of smokers is thought to play an important role in the added risk of heart attack and fatal arrhythmia (alteration in force or timing of the heartbeat). This mechanism would explain the observation that the risk of fatal heart disease falls significantly over a period of several weeks after an individual stops smoking; during this same period the excess carbon monoxide in blood is slowly eliminated, returning eventually to normal levels.

In the period from 1970 to 1975 the death rate from hypertension as reported in the vital statistics of the United States dropped by 28%. Detection of more asymptomatic cases and effective treatment of mild and severe cases of hypertension may be contributing to the decline in mortality, a trend that was discernible even before effective drugs for the control of hypertension became widely available. Recent widely publicized clinical research studies have emphasized the effectiveness and safety of proper treatment for hypertension, reinforcing the value of detection and the need for early medical attention.

Diet is another factor that has long been thought to influence the incidence of coronary artery disease, and there is evidence of significant changes in the eating habits of the American public during the past decade. Saturated fat and cholesterol consumption have decreased in the U.S. The prudent diet—high in polyunsaturated fats, low in saturated fat and cholesterol, with emphasis on fish, poultry, and lean cuts of meat—has been widely publicized by such organizations as the American Heart Asso-

ciation. Many U.S. families drink skim milk and use margarine made with unsaturated fat rather than butter. Jeremiah Stamler, cardiologist and epidemiologist at Northwestern University, believes that changes in the American diet during the past several years may be an important contributing factor in the decreased rate of mortality from cardiovascular disease.

Atherosclerosis

Fundamental information continues to accumulate on the mechanism of the development of atherosclerosis (narrowing of arteries due to the accumulation of fatty deposits).

Medium-sized arteries contain three layers: an innermost layer, the intima, which surrounds the opening; a middle layer, the media, which contains elastic tissue and smooth muscle; and an outer layer, the adventitia. Normally, smooth muscle does not occur in the intima. However, when an atherosclerotic plaque, or atheroma, develops, smooth muscle proliferates in the intima and becomes laden with cholesterol deposits.

How does the smooth muscle develop in the intima? Earl P. Benditt of the University of Washington, Seattle, has suggested that the cells of an atherosclerotic plaque are the progeny of a single mutated smooth muscle cell that migrated to the intima from the nearby medial layer, perhaps as a result of injury. According to this theory, the plaque may have begun as a form of benign tumor of the arterial wall. Electron microscope studies have shown that the cellular cap covering the cholesterol-rich material in the atheroma is made up not of connective tissue cells, as was originally thought, but consists predominantly of smooth muscle cells.

Atherosclerosis occurs at branch points in large vessels. In the heart, for example, the sclerotic plaques form only in the arteries coursing over the surface of the heart; they do not occur in the smaller vessels penetrating into the myocardium. Recently, attention has focused on the site of early intimal injury. Normal wear and tear may be sufficient to initiate the atherosclerotic process, yet some individuals who have died of other causes in their eighth, ninth, or later decades have been found at autopsy to have essentially normal blood vessels. A knowledge of how these unique persons escaped the ravages of so common a disease would be a significant advance in our understanding of atherosclerosis.

In experimental preparations, the blood platelets are of critical importance in initiating the clotting process. Platelets cluster at the site of injury to the intima and release a number of biologically active substances, including a factor that promotes

197

smooth muscle proliferation. It has been postulated that this factor, when released at the site of mechanical injury of large blood vessels, could initiate a critical early step—accumulation of smooth muscle in the intima—in the development of the atherosclerotic plaque.

Recent interest has focused on the correlation of atherosclerosis with certain genetic traits. A number of antigens in white blood cells, or leukocytes, have been identified. Recently J. D. Matthews of the University of Melbourne, Australia, demonstrated a correlation between the specific antigen HL-A-8 and the death rate from heart disease for men in various countries. Finland has one of the world's highest death rates from coronary heart disease, and it has long been suggested that genetic as well as dietary and environmental factors may play a role. Of special interest is the observation by Matthews that the Finnish population has a very high frequency of HL-A-8. Why this particular antigen should be a marker for coronary artery disease is at present unknown. Many families have been recognized to have an unusually high incidence of premature heart disease in young males without identifiable risk factors. The possibility that genetic makeup influences the response of the arterial walls to injury—and the subsequent development of atherosclerotic plaque—suggests promising areas for research.

Cholesterol

The level of blood cholesterol is one of the most powerful risk factors for coronary artery disease yet to be identified. Studies from many different sources indicate that an individual's risk of developing clinical manifestations of coronary artery disease is directly related to his blood cholesterol level. But despite these well-accepted observations, heart attack victims more often exhibit normal blood cholesterol levels than elevated levels. In part this may reflect changes of blood cholesterol with time and age. But this finding also suggests that there are major, as yet unrecognized, influences at work in the development of coronary atherosclerosis.

Recent investigations have provided new insights into the relationship between lipids (fatty substances) in the blood and the development of atherosclerotic plaque. Many individuals with a history of familial hypercholesterolemia (high cholesterol level) have evidence of coronary artery disease in their third and fourth decades and suffer from premature heart attacks. Cholesterol, the major lipid component of atherosclerotic plaque, is a water-insoluble substance carried in the blood in the form of lipoprotein (a combination of lipid and protein). Lipoproteins are polar molecules; that is, they contain electric charges on their surfaces. They also vary in density, and different groups of lipoproteins can be separated by ultracentrifugation of plasma samples.

Three classes of lipoproteins can be recognized according to their density: VLDL, very low density lipoproteins; LDL, low density lipoproteins; and HDL, high density lipoproteins. LDL are the major carriers of cholesterol. HDL appear to be the major mechanism for transport of cholesterol to the liver for ultimate removal from the body. At the liver, cholesterol is excreted in the bile into the small intestine. Some of this cholesterol is resorbed in the lower portion of the ileum and recirculates through the body.

Cholesterol is a major building block of the cell wall. Recent research has shown that the surfaces of certain cells contain specific receptors for LDL. LDL are bound to the receptors on the cell membrane, which then surrounds the carrier to form a pocket that is incorporated within the cell, thus transferring the cholesterol from the plasma into the cell. Using tissue culture techniques and fibroblasts (connective tissue cells readily obtained by removing a small piece of skin) researchers have found that individuals with familial hypercholesterolemia lacked receptors for LDL—or had a lower than normal number of receptors—in their cells. These observations suggest that certain patients with genetic abnormalities of cholesterol metabolism are unable to transport cholesterol from the plasma into the cell substance.

The smooth muscle cells in the intima of human arteries are capable of taking up large quantities of LDL and VLDL and lesser amounts of HDL. Experiments with animals, however, have shown that reduction of oxygen tension in the cell decreases the ability of smooth muscle to break down LDL. If the same process occurs in humans, it could have important implications for the atherosclerotic process. The presence of smooth muscle cells in the intima could be the first step in a vicious cycle: the initial smooth muscle proliferation and accumulation of atherosclerotic plaque reduce blood flow, and oxygen tension falls downstream from the plaque, in turn allowing further cholesterol to accumulate by inhibiting the normal breakdown of LDL within the cell.

Population studies have suggested that high blood concentrations of HDL may be protective; individuals with above average amounts of HDL in plasma appear to have a reduced incidence of coronary heart disease. Presumably this reflects effective transport of cholesterol by HDL from peripheral sites to the liver for metabolism or excretion, thus maintaining low blood cholesterol levels.

Recognition that cholesterol is recycled in the

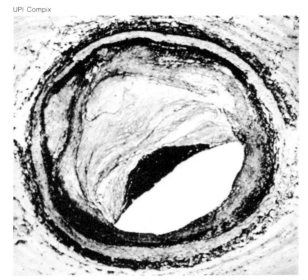

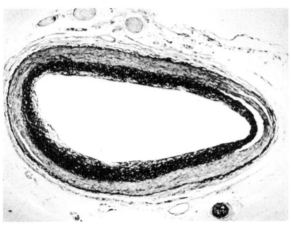

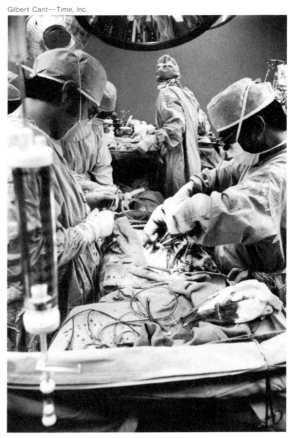

Cross sections of coronary arteries (left) compare a normal artery (bottom) from a 100-year-old patient who died of noncardiac causes to a partially occluded artery (top) from a 65-year-old heart attack victim. An open-heart team is shown above performing a coronary bypass operation.

lower part of the intestine after being excreted through bile has led to the development of a surgical procedure for patients with high blood cholesterol levels. In this procedure, termed an ileal bypass, the terminal one-third of the small intestine —the part responsible for the absorption of cholesterol—is excluded, with the preceding section of the intestine connected to the large bowel. The process thus causes bowel contents to bypass the absorptive site. Preliminary studies in man have shown that this procedure reduces serum cholesterol by 30 to 60%. The resulting change in bowel function may produce mild to moderate diarrhea, which usually can be controlled by medication. Because the bypassed site is also the area of vitamin B_{12} absorption, a deficiency of this vitamin develops unless a supplement is administered on a regular basis. An uncontrolled preliminary study of the operation suggests the possibility that this surgical bypass may retard the development of atherosclerosis in certain high-risk individuals who have

a metabolic abnormality leading to extremely high levels of serum cholesterol.

Hypertension

Elevated blood pressure, or hypertension, affects approximately 25 million persons in the United States. Initially, many victims of hypertension experience no symptoms. However, the condition is associated with an increased risk of stroke, heart attack, and kidney failure. In less than 10% of all individuals with hypertension can a recognized cause—such as a tumor of the adrenal gland or reduced blood flow to the kidney—be established. In the vast majority the elevated blood pressure is termed "essential," meaning that no cause has been identified.

Maintenance of normal blood pressure depends upon multiple factors including the volume of blood, the amount of blood that the heart pumps (cardiac output), and the resistance to flow generated in the peripheral arteries. In most patients with

199

established hypertension, blood volume and cardiac output are within normal limits, but there is marked increase in resistance to flow. Harriet Dustan and co-workers at the Cleveland Clinic have suggested that intermittent, or labile, hypertension in young individuals may initially reflect changes in cardiac output but that later alterations in peripheral resistance lead to the condition of fixed, or essential, hypertension.

The kidney plays an important role in the regulation of blood pressure. Recent studies have demonstrated that reduction of blood flow to the kidney causes a release of the enzyme renin from cells located close to the small renal arteries. Renin catalyzes the splitting of angiotensinogen, a protein circulating in blood, to form several substances, including angiotensin II, one of the most powerful vasoconstrictors known. Angiotensin II causes intense constriction of the small peripheral arterioles (the terminal portions of the arteries). Increased concentration of angiotensin II in the blood also stimulates the adrenal gland to secrete aldosterone, a hormone that acts on the kidney to enhance sodium and water retention. Thus there is a complex interplay of factors that provides an effective defense mechanism when blood pressure is reduced from dehydration or blood loss. However, in patients with hypertension, the forces involved in maintaining normal blood pressure become unbalanced, and blood volume, resistance to flow, or cardiac output are abnormally high.

John Laragh of Cornell University Medical College has suggested that classification of hypertensives according to their level of blood renin, measured with a newly developed radioimmunoassay technique, is useful for diagnosis and treatment. He has found that approximately one-sixth of patients with hypertension have high renin levels. About 60% have normal levels, but the values may be viewed as inappropriately high, since hypertension normally should suppress renin activity. Although there is considerable debate about his conclusions, Laragh believes that patients with high or normal renin are at considerable risk of vascular complications such as heart attack or stroke. In his experience about one-quarter of patients with hypertension have low renin values and high blood volumes. Patients with high renin activity are often treated with drugs that seem to have a specific antirenin effect. Patients with low renin are treated with diuretics, which often reduce blood volume and lower blood pressure.

It has long been thought that the central nervous system also plays a role in the genesis and maintenance of hypertension. The view that increased stress is associated with a tendency for elevated blood pressure is widespread, but critical proof that this applies to individuals at risk is lacking. On the other hand, several areas in the brain are important for control of blood pressure. A negative feedback system by which receptors in the aorta inhibit sympathetic vasoconstriction, thus lowering blood pressure, is well known. Experimentally, destruction of the area postrema, a way station for this reflex in the brain, leads to severe hypertension and heart failure. It is likely, therefore, that alteration of brain function may have an influence on the development or maintenance of hypertension in some individuals.

Prostaglandins, a complex family of lipidic hormone-like substances, may also influence blood pressure. It has been postulated that hypertension may in some instances reflect a deficiency of a specific prostaglandin, PGE_2. The prostaglandin system is known to interact with substances called kinins, peptides that cause vasodilatation and reduce blood pressure. As with the prostaglandins, the kinins circulate in the blood in inactive form; they are activated by the enzyme kallikrein. One of the kinins, bradykinin, also stimulates the release of PGE_2. There is suggestive evidence that some hypertensive individuals have a reduced amount of kallikrein and hence might have less PGE_2 than normal. In this case there would be a deficiency of factors functioning to counteract the hypertensive effect of the angiotensins.

Limitation of myocardial damage

One of the major manifestations of atherosclerosis is acute myocardial infarction, or heart attack. When infarction occurs, a significant portion of the heart muscle is deprived of its blood supply, and muscle cells are damaged. While full clinical recovery is possible, a portion of heart muscle is replaced by scar tissue. Recent interest among experimental and clinical cardiologists has focused on means for limiting the extent of muscle damage after the heart attack has occurred.

The heart performs continuously as a pump and requires a constant supply of oxygen and nutrients. Heart muscle has little metabolic reserve. Within seconds of reduction of blood supply, the efficiency of contraction is decreased; within minutes, recognizable cellular changes may occur. Myocardial need for oxygen is controlled by the heart rate, the degree of stretch of the myocardial fibers (tension), and the forcefulness of fiber shortening (contractility).

Experimentally, if the amount of work required from the heart can be reduced, the area of muscle damage from acute infarction can be made smaller. When blood pressure is moderately reduced in experimental animals with acute infarction, myocardial oxygen needs are lowered and the area of infarction becomes smaller, while the pumping function of the heart is maintained. Data on the effectiveness of reducing blood pressure in human heart attack victims are not yet available. In the laboratory the situation is simplified; the coronary arteries of experimental animals are normal, not diseased. Generally, the decreased blood pressure is well tolerated, and flow of blood into the coronary arteries is maintained. In the patient with acute heart attack, however, there is almost invariably extensive atherosclerosis, obstructing the coronary arteries and causing increased resistance to blood flow. While reduced blood pressure might decrease myocardial oxygen demand, unfortunately, coronary blood flow may also be lowered because the diseased vessels require a high blood pressure to maintain adequate perfusion (flow of blood through the heart tissue). Thus, the consequence of reduced blood pressure in a patient with a heart attack may not be entirely predictable, the results depending on an unknown balance between the effects of a reduction of myocardial oxygen need and too great a reduction in blood flow through the coronary arteries.

Another possible technique for preserving damaged myocardium is administration of the enzyme hyaluronidase, which may permit more ready diffusion of nutrient materials into damaged tissue. Experimental injection of the drug has been shown to limit the area of acute heart damage, and clinical trials are under way to evaluate its effectiveness. Other methods of limiting heart damage currently being investigated include the administration of the drug propranolol to reduce sympathetic nervous activity, slow heart rate, and reduce contractility. Mechanical heart support with counterpulsation techniques also shows promise. In counterpulsation, a balloon is inserted into the aorta by means of a catheter. The balloon is deflated during heart contraction and inflated during heart relaxation. When appropriately synchronized to the cardiac cycle, counterpulsation reduces cardiac work during contraction of the heart and maintains coronary blood flow during the diastolic, or relaxation, phase.

Coronary bypass surgery

Nearly ten years have passed since the technique of coronary artery bypass grafting for the treatment of symptomatic coronary atherosclerosis was first introduced. In this procedure, a vein, or in some cases a small artery, is grafted to the aorta just above the aortic valve. The other end of the graft is sewn to a coronary artery, in some cases as small as 1 mm in diameter, beyond a point of partial or complete obstruction. Thus the localized coronary obstruction is effectively bypassed. It is estimated

that more than 70,000 coronary bypass operations were performed in the United States in 1977 at a cost approaching $1 billion.

Before a coronary bypass operation can be performed, the anatomy of the coronary vessels must be visualized; this is accomplished by means of an X-ray technique known as coronary arteriography, in which a radiopaque dye is injected into the coronary artery. The films produced make it possible to visualize coronary vessels as small as 1 mm and to estimate the degree of atherosclerosis. As with all medical procedures, coronary arteriography has some risk, currently estimated as less than one death per thousand procedures. There is also a slightly higher incidence of some degree of heart damage. In "good risk" patients (those under age 65 with normal heart function, no recent heart damage, and no other significant diseases) coronary bypass surgery may be accomplished with a mortality of less than 2–3%. In skilled surgical hands some 80–90% of patients undergoing coronary artery bypass have complete or significant relief from symptoms.

Enthusiasts have suggested that the surgical procedure reduces the incidence of heart attack and prolongs life in subjects with symptomatic coronary atherosclerosis. Other physicians, mindful of the problem of evaluating new procedures, find the evidence unconvincing and believe that careful long-term evaluation of the results will be necessary to determine whether the procedure can alter the natural history of coronary artery disease.

Medical management of coronary disease

For 50 years, beginning with initial observations by Paul Dudley White and continuing through more recent studies in the late 1960s, the medical treatment of patients with coronary artery disease has changed but little. Throughout this period many clinical studies have shown that the mortality of patients with angina pectoris, a disorder characterized by intermittent chest pain during exertion and recognized as a major symptom of coronary disease, has been about 4% per year. In a number of recent studies, however, comparing effects of surgical and medical treatment, the mortality rate of patients managed medically has been considerably less than predicted. Better recognition of risk factors, improved treatment of arrhythmia, and reduction of cardiac work using the drug propranolol may all be contributing to the apparent increase in effectiveness of medical treatment.

The improvement in medical outlook for patients with coronary artery disease is important in evaluating the effects of surgery. Surgical procedures are often evaluated by the use of historical controls, that is, data reported from earlier clinical

The Parcours, a 1.4-mile track punctuated with exercise stations, is one element of a physical fitness program developed by the General Foods Corporation for its employees in the Westchester County, N.Y., area.

investigations of the natural history of a condition which do not take into account the effect of new procedures. The use of historical controls is justified, however, only when there has been no change in medical management. Current medical treatment may significantly alter the outlook for patients with coronary artery disease. Thus, the effectiveness of coronary artery surgery on longevity or incidence of myocardial infarction can be determined only by studying a random sample of patients currently being treated either medically or surgically.

Preliminary results from one such study, sponsored by the Veterans Administration (VA) suggest that the outlook is similar for most subjects whether medical or surgical treatment is chosen. Following coronary bypass, there are fewer episodes of angina pectoris and fewer symptoms reflecting intermittent myocardial ischemia (deficient blood supply), but to date neither longevity nor the frequency of heart attack has been altered. In patients with major obstruction of the main left coronary artery, a condition encountered in less than 4% of subjects in the study, a preliminary analysis of the VA data suggests that coronary artery surgery may have a significant beneficial effect. These results are only suggestive, however, and will be extended and modified as further analysis of the operative results is evaluated.

The effects of exercise

While there is no conclusive proof that regular exercise increases longevity or reduces the incidence of cardiovascular disease, several indirect studies suggest that individuals with lifelong patterns of vigorous physical activity have lower incidence of coronary artery disease and lower death rates.

Physically active individuals have lower resting heart rates, lower blood pressure, and reduced levels of certain blood lipids such as free fatty acid. Regular physical training or conditioning permits the adapted individual to respond more successfully to increased exercise loads and to perform more work with fewer signs of fatigue than can the untrained individual.

Adaption to exercise significantly improves the amount of oxygen that can be consumed during a sustained maximum effort. This function, termed oxygen consumption, is the single most reliable objective criterion for evaluating the effect of training and the ability to perform muscular work. As exercise progresses, both oxygen consumption and heart rate increase. The correlation between these two variables is sufficiently linear that heart rate generally is used as an index of the severity of the exercise or the amount of work being performed when a steady state has been reached.

The achievement or maintenance of good physical condition requires about three vigorous sessions per week in which the exercise reaches 60% of maximum oxygen consumption. Physical conditioning can decline rapidly, within three weeks of inactivity. Trained athletes have heart rates 10 to 20 beats per minute slower than those recorded prior to training. The mechanism of this slowing is not precisely known but may involve an increase in production of the neurotransmitter acetylcholine in the pacemaker cells controlling the basic heart rhythm.

Training produces cardiac enlargement, but the form is different depending upon the type of exercise. Weight lifters develop an increase in heart mass, whereas runners and swimmers develop an increase in heart volume and mass. Current evi-

202

dence suggests that the cardiac enlargement of professional athletes may persist for many years after they cease to be unusually physically active. Training also increases maximum oxygen consumption and cardiac output. In addition, changes that occur in the skeletal muscles may enhance efficiency of oxygen delivery.

Exercise testing and heart disease

Since the heart is basically a pump, designed to respond quickly to increased stress or demand, it is important to evaluate the effect of exertion on cardiovascular function in individuals suspected of having heart disease. During the past 50 years the exercise stress test has been developed from a primitive tool, in which the patient climbed up and down a few steps, to a precise analysis of the effect of walking on a treadmill or riding a stationary bicycle on such indicators as electrocardiogram, heart rate, and blood pressure. According to the current theory a "positive" exercise test reflects the development of ischemia, not present at rest but manifested as the heart rate and cardiac output are increased with exercise.

The heart action of a patient undergoing an exercise stress test is monitored continuously by an electrocardiograph.

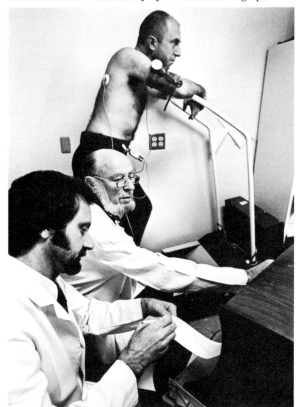

Josephus Daniels—Photo Researchers

In evaluating any test for human disease it is important to determine the sensitivity and specificity of the test. The sensitivity of a test is defined as the percentage of true positive results obtained when individuals with the disease are tested. The specificity of a test is defined as the percentage of individuals without the disease who show true negative results.

Victor F. Froelicher, Jr., of the U.S.A.F. School of Aerospace Medicine, Brooks AFB, Texas, has concluded that the exercise test has a sensitivity of about 65%. In other words, about 35% of individuals with coronary disease will be overlooked because of a false negative exercise test. On the other hand, the specificity is about 90%, which means that individuals who do not have coronary artery disease have only about a 10% chance of producing a so-called false positive result. Coronary arteriography can be correlated with the patient's electrocardiogram to further confirm a positive result on the exercise test.

Myocardial imaging with radioisotopes

When compounds containing radioisotopes are injected into the circulation they concentrate in the bloodpool or in the heart muscle. An image of the heart may be created when the surface of the chest is scanned with a radioactive detecting device. The distribution of the radioactive material is critically dependent upon coronary blood flow. Thus, the areas of myocardium with normal blood flow show uniform concentration of the injected radioactive substance. Areas of deficient blood flow have low or absent concentration. Several types of radioactive substances are currently in use, including potassium-43, cesium-129, rubidium-81, and thallium-201. These substances are rapidly cleared from the blood and distributed to the tissues. Myocardial clearance is slower, however, thus allowing an image to be detected.

Myocardial perfusion scintiphotography, as the technique is called, is performed several minutes after intravenous injection of the radioactive tracer substance. A normal myocardium appears as a homogeneous concentration of radioactive emission; areas of poor perfusion or scar tissue appear as "cold spots" due to low or absent concentration. Some substances are selectively concentrated in ischemic or infarcted heart muscle. When radionuclides such as technetium-99, coupled to tetracycline or to pyrophosphate, are injected, the scan will show a "hot spot," produced by accumulation of radionuclide in the area of infarction or ischemia.

In another technique a radioactive tracer element is injected into the circulation and an image of the heart chambers is built up by scanning the chest at certain times in the cardiac cycle. This is called a "gated scan," since the scanning mechanism is open only at the beginning or the end of ventricular contraction. The gated scan technique allows an analysis of heart size and contraction that is similar to that obtained from a left ventricular angiogram.

The radioimage techniques are especially useful and desirable because they yield information about the integrity of heart muscle or the size of chambers without the necessity of entering a catheter into the heart or injecting dye directly into the coronary vessels. Since they do not involve invasion of the heart by either catheter or needle, such techniques are called "noninvasive." These procedures offer great promise for providing repeated checks on the structure and function of the myocardium without significant danger to the patient. The body is exposed to some radiation during these techniques, but the half-life of the isotopes is generally short, and the total amount of body radiation is well within allowable limits. Improvement in the quality of the scanning images has been rapidly accomplished. Unfortunately the equipment needed to provide the image is very expensive, and radioimage techniques currently are available only in large medical centers.

A further refinement of myocardial imaging is the application of nuclear medicine to analysis of heart function during exercise. The results obtained when a radionuclide is injected for myocardial imaging just before the end of an exercise stress test are being compared with an analysis of the electrocardiogram during exercise. Coronary angiography may also be performed in the same patient. Changes in myocardial blood flow or the development of ischemic areas during exercise may be recorded and correlated with symptoms, the electrocardiogram, or the angiogram. Even from the limited results to date, it is clear that the comparison of myocardial imaging at rest and during exercise adds a new dimension to evaluating the effects of coronary artery disease on the structure and function of the heart.

— *Thomas Killip, M.D.*

Connective Tissue Diseases

Considerable information has been developed concerning the structure of the major molecular components of connective tissue. Of the proteins in connective tissue fibers, collagen is the most abundant. It is now known that there are several molecular species of collagen and that each connective tissue has its own particular collagen composition. For example, the major collagen in skin and bone is called type I. Cartilage is composed primarily of type II collagen. Type III collagen is present in skin, blood vessels, and synovium (lining of the joints).

Inheritable disorders of connective tissue

Much recent progress has been made in understanding several inheritable disorders of collagen metabolism. Many such disorders can now be defined in terms of the abnormality of collagen structure. For example, in some cases of osteogenesis imperfecta (with characteristics such as blue sclera of the eye, deafness, multiple fractures, and loose-jointedness), there is a defect in the synthesis of type I collagen in skin and possibly in bone. In one type of Ehlers-Danlos syndrome, there is insufficient formation of type III collagen, and an absence of type III collagen in the aorta, skin, lungs, and gastrointestinal tract. Another type of Ehlers-Danlos syndrome is characterized by thin and hyperextensible skin, recurrent joint dislocations, scoliosis (curved spine), and fragile connective tissue of the eyes. Several connective tissue disorders have been found to be related to the presence of a defective enzyme.

An interesting new disorder, the wrinkly skin syndrome, has recently been investigated. It is transmitted as a genetically recessive trait and is characterized by the appearance at birth of wrinkled skin about the hands and feet.

Acquired diseases of connective tissue

The connective tissue diseases usually considered as acquired include rheumatoid arthritis, rheumatic fever, progressive systemic sclerosis (scleroderma), polymyositis and dermatomyositis, and various types of vasculitis such as polyarteritis nodosa. In all of these diseases a combination of genetic, immunologic, and viral factors is believed to be involved as the cause.

One of the most significant recent developments concerning adult and juvenile rheumatoid arthritis has been the finding that each condition is associated with a different genetic marker. The genetic marker HL-A DW4 on the surface of white blood cells was found in 59% of patients with adult onset rheumatoid arthritis as compared with 16% in normal persons. In patients with juvenile rheumatoid arthritis, however, a different genetic marker, LD-TMo, was found. The risk of developing juvenile rheumatoid arthritis was 17 times greater in LD-TMo positive persons than in those who lacked the antigen. In patients with juvenile rheumatoid arthritis, the incidence of LD-TMo was 33%, compared with less than 3% in normal children. The different markers appear to characterize the two types of arthritis, suggesting that adult and juvenile rheumatoid arthritis are two distinct diseases, probably resulting from different causes.

Courtesy, Merck Sharp & Dohme and (top) Fred Sammons, Inc., (bottom) Rehabilitation Technical Components, Inc.

Rheumatoid arthritic inflammation

The persistent chronic inflammation that occurs in rheumatoid arthritis eventually causes degradation of many different joint structures including cartilage, ligaments, bones, tendons, and joint capsules. The swelling and pain that occur are produced in part by release of mediators such as prostaglandins. It has recently been shown that an enzyme, collagenase, is also released by the synovial cells in patients with rheumatoid arthritis. The release may be triggered by lymphocytes commonly present in the rheumatoid synovium. Collagenase can degrade collagen from skin, cartilage, joint capsules, tendons, and bones. Much of the collagen loss is irreversible. Other white blood cells, polymorphonuclear leukocytes, are also present in the joint fluid of rheumatoid patients. They release several enzymes, including a collagenase, an elastase that breaks down elastic fibers, and a neutral protease that breaks down protein. These enzymes can also contribute to joint destruction.

It has not been generally recognized that rheumatoid arthritis can affect most of the organs of the body. While the majority of patients have disease confined to joints, many patients have involvement of the eyes, heart, lungs, spleen, salivary glands, and blood vessels (vasculitis). A much better understanding of the basic immunologic mechanisms involved in these conditions has been gained over the past several years.

Treatment

Although salicylates (aspirin) continue to be a mainstay of therapy for rheumatoid arthritis, a number of nonsteroidal anti-inflammatory drugs have recently been introduced. They include ibuprofen, naproxen, and fenoprofen, all related derivatives, as well as tolmetin, a chemically unrelated compound. The effect of these drugs is similar to that of aspirin, but side effects, especially gastrointestinal, occur much less frequently than with aspirin. These agents offer new options for treatment of rheumatoid arthritis.

Cytotoxic drugs (acting on cells) and antimetabolites (anticancer agents) have been used with considerable success because of their suppressive effects on immunologic mechanisms. Hair loss, bladder problems, liver toxicity, and development of malignancies are possible side effects, however. Further studies are necessary before the exact application of these drugs can be determined. It has been shown in recent studies that gold salt administration is also associated with reduced inflammation and probably decreased joint destruction by X-ray. Penicillamine is another agent known to provide effective treatment although the side effects are relatively great.

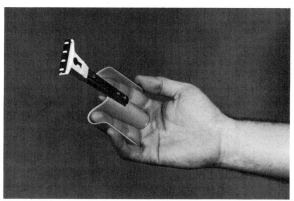

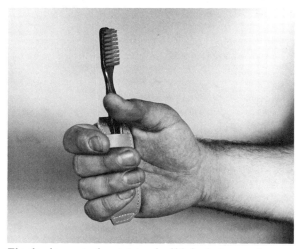

The development of a variety of self-help devices, such as the specially designed grooming implements above, help to alleviate for the arthritic patient the extreme difficulties presented by many daily activities.

Total joint replacements are being used with considerable success. Total hip replacement is a widely used procedure and has a high rate of success, especially in eliminating pain. It may also improve stability and motion of the joint. Total knee and finger joint replacements have been used with variable results. Replacements for wrist, elbows, shoulders, and ankles have recently been introduced and are being perfected.

A number of self-help devices have been created over the past several years to help arthritic patients perform daily activities. Today there are a large number of specially designed implements available to assist in grasping and holding, reaching and withdrawing, and cutting. For example, for patients whose gripping power is reduced, special cups and cup holders are available. Carefully designed implements—*e.g.,* combs, toothbrushes, nail clippers —are available to assist the patient in basic grooming tasks. One example of this type of implement is a long-handled brush or comb. Extension handles can be easily adjusted to the requirements of both left- and right-handed arthritic patients. Because handwriting is a complex activity requiring coordination and dexterity of the upper extremities, arthritis may significantly impair the ability. There are now available many devices that allow arthritics to write with greater ease. For example, special holders provide easier grasping of a pen or pencil.

Diagnosis

A number of new laboratory tests have been devised that help the clinician and researcher better diagnose connective tissue diseases and predict their courses. Discovery of one such laboratory test has provided insight into a previously unrecognized condition, the mixed connective tissue disease (MCTD) syndrome. The basic symptoms include arthritis, skin changes in the hands similar to scleroderma, and inflammation of the muscles (myositis) similar to polymyositis. Skin rash, similar to that in systemic lupus erythematosus, also may be present. The unique feature of MCTD is that all patients with the disease have identifying antibodies in their blood. Although patients may have symptoms common to several different connective tissue diseases, the prognosis for MCTD is probably better than that for individual diseases.

Within the past few years, it has become apparent that the hepatitis B virus may be related to or responsible for a substantial number of cases of polyarteritis nodosa, a form of vasculitis that affects many parts of the body, including the kidneys, intestines, skin, and muscles. In one series in which 55 cases were studied, 55% had hepatitis B antigen and 28% hepatitis B antibody. In 69%, either the antigen or antibody was present. Hepatitis B virus particles were seen in 20 of 27 cases investigated by electron microscopy. Because hepatitis B virus can be transmitted by dirty needles, drug addicts are susceptible to both hepatitis and polyarteritis nodosa. Multiple aneurysms similar to those seen in polyarteritis nodosa, especially in kidneys, have been detected by X-rays of drug addicts who also have hepatitis B antigen.

—Eric R. Hurd, M.D.

Death

Death, the termination of life, is a single phenomenon, but not a simple one to comprehend. Today new complexities about this event are beginning to appear as technical advances provide equipment to maintain vital body functions. The development of artificial life-support systems has posed a whole new set of ethical questions. Does the patient or family want any interference with the natural process? Is such interference an invasion of the patient's privacy? On the other hand, if the physician does not take advantage of all available life-sustaining measures, is he violating his own ethical code or his legal obligation?

Other issues are surfacing. May the patient refuse treatment, for example, artificial respiration if natural respiration fails? May a person with terminal cancer, severe heart disease, or crippling stroke request that no special measures be instituted if the heart stops or breathing fails? If the patient is incapable of communication, in deep coma, or incompetent, may the family or a conservator make the request? If the patient is a child or a mentally ill or mentally defective person, may the parent or conservator specify that in case of vital organ failure, no effort at resuscitation be made?

Defining death

Death, according to *Webster's Third New International Dictionary,* is: "The ending of all vital functions without possibility of recovery either in animals or plants or any parts of them; the end of life." The definition appearing in *Black's Law Dictionary* (Fourth Edition, Revised 1968) is more explicit: "The cessation of life; the ceasing to exist; defined by physicians as the total stoppage of the circulation of the blood, and a cessation of the animal and vital functions consequent thereon, such as respiration, pulsation. . . ."

What is unclear in the Webster statement is that all parts of the human body do not always die simultaneously; even when breathing and heart function have stopped, other parts, still quite alive, may be transferred, with permission, to needy human recipients. Thus the kidney, skin, bone, or cornea may be transplanted to others to continue a useful life.

What then are the criteria of death? What do we currently regard as the "vital functions"? From ancient times to the present it was evident that when respiration and heart action stopped, the brain would die within a few minutes. The heart was considered the central organ of the body, and its failure indicated the beginning of death. Therefore, cessation of the heartbeat was synonymous with death. Asphyxia, as by acute respiratory difficulties, stran-

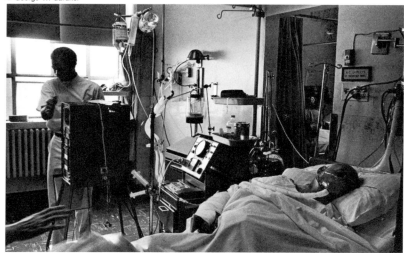

In recent years the issue of death and dying has become vastly complicated by the development of artificial life-support systems, raising for the patient, family, and doctor alike an array of ethical and legal questions hitherto absent from the deathbed scene.

gulation, drowning, open wounds of the chest, or failure of the breathing mechanism, brought about heart standstill and death. Now new techniques in respiratory and cardiac resuscitation, including life-sustaining machines, can literally "restore life" — assuming acceptance of the traditional definition of death. Current technology permits the heart and lungs to be bypassed through the use of a heart-lung machine. The patient's heart may actually be removed from the body while he is thus artificially maintained, as is done during heart transplant surgery. A more common medical phenomenon is the patient who, because of some medical condition, is totally unable to sustain respiration on his own, is completely unreceptive and unresponsive to outside stimuli, and cannot move. With the use of an artificial respirator this patient's heart may be kept beating. Yet is that person truly alive? If the respirator is turned off, how long will he remain so? Are there individuals who are totally unresponsive and completely dependent on the respirator at one time but capable of survival later when disconnected from the machine? What happens to the brain of the patient who is maintained on a respirator 24, or 48, or 96 hours; what happens after one week, three weeks, a month? These are troublesome questions that carry serious moral, ethical, religious, and legal, as well as scientific, implications. The need to redefine and update the criteria for determining death is apparent.

The concept of brain death

The train of events toward the cessation of life suggests four stages: (1) a time of impending death; (2) a period of reversibility, with or without residual damage; (3) a period of irreversibility; and (4) absolute death as set forth in the current legal definition. Many experts — physicians, legal scholars, and members of the clergy — have applied themselves to the question of when death occurs, and the state of the brain has arisen as the primary issue. The physician's obligation is to determine when this organ has ceased to function and has no possibility of restoration. Such a brain, for all practical purposes, may be declared dead. The condition has been described as irreversible coma, cerebral death, brain death, artificial survival, or coma *dépassé*. The French term *dépassé* is well chosen because it indicates that the individual is beyond coma; his state is irreversible and ahead of him, inevitably, is death.

Pope Pius XII addressed the issue when he spoke to the International Congress of Anesthesiologists on the "Medical Morals of Resuscitation (*la réanimation*)." In considering the religious and ethical questions, he pointed out that "verification of the moment of death can be determined, if at all, only by a physician." He suggested that death occurs when all circulation stops or irreparable and overwhelming brain damage occurs. The Pope added that determination of death was not within the competence of the Church, but that it was incumbent on the physician to take all reasonable, ordinary means to restore spontaneous vital functions and consciousness. The doctor was expected to employ such extraordinary means as were available to him but was not obliged to continue extraordinary means indefinitely in hopeless cases. The Pope suggested that it was the view of the Church that a time comes when resuscitative measures should stop and "death be unopposed."

The vital organs, those essential in maintaining life, are the lungs, heart, and brain. Failing respiration can be maintained by a machine, and a stopped heart can at times be restarted and stimulated to go on unaided. If the heart stops permanently, death automatically ensues. But what happens if the brain dies before the heart, and the breathing mechanism controlled by the impaired lower brain center gives out, as can occur in the case of head injury, stroke, brain tumor, or other illnesses? As the brain becomes successively affected by the disease process, the lower part, the brain stem, which regulates respiration, breathing, and heartbeat, finally turns off. Respiration may stop, and after a time, hours to days, even with the use of a respirator, the heart finally arrests. Thus two situations may be encountered. When breathing and heartbeat cease completely for more than six to eight minutes, the brain dies and total death ensues. Likewise when the brain is totally dead, first breathing and then heartbeat stop and death inevitably ensues.

While it is a simple matter to detect the cessation of respiratory or heart function, the determination of brain death is more difficult and must be made by a physician. The criteria include the combination of several factors: (1) total lack of response to any type of stimulation, sound, noise, or even pain; (2) inability to breathe unaided; (3) absent cephalic reflexes (certain reflex responses about the head including coughing, swallowing, and selected eye movement); (4) electrocerebral silence indicated by a flat brain wave (an electroencephalogram, or EEG, that shows no evidence of electrical activity coming from the brain) for at least 30 continuous minutes; and (5) a confirmatory test indicating absence of blood flow through the brain for 30 consecutive minutes.

The application of these criteria would guard against a premature diagnosis of brain death in instances of drug intoxication and illnesses where the pathological process might be reversed on treatment. Thus, sedative drug intake determined by history, evidence about the patient, or blood test must be ruled out. It is important to recognize that no single indicator, such as a flat EEG, is a determination of brain death.

According to current opinion then, two conditions can meet the criteria of death. The Task Force on Death and Dying of the Institute of Society, Ethics and the Life Sciences states the conditions as follows:

A person should be considered dead if in the announced opinion of a physician, based on ordinary standards of medical practice, he has experienced an irreversible cessation of spontaneous respiratory and circulatory function. In the event that adequate means of support preclude a determination that these functions have ceased, a person will be considered dead if in the announced opinion of a physician, based on ordinary standards of medical practice, he has experienced an irreversible cessation of spontaneous brain function. Death will have occurred at the time when relevant functions ceased.

Under this proposal, the determination of death is based on observation of certain vital bodily functions, the permanent absence of which indicates that the individual is no longer a living human being. The model statute disregards the fact that some cells or organs may continue to live after this point, just as others may have ceased functioning long before the determination of death.

Artificial life

The connection between the standards is clear. If cardiac and pulmonary function have ceased, brain function cannot continue. If there is no brain activity and respiration must be maintained artificially, the same outcome is inevitable—the heart will eventually stop. The difficulty arises when the physician must present the patient's family with the facts. If breathing and heartbeat have stopped there is no problem. However, if the brain is determined to be dead but the patient is being maintained on a respirator, the heart will continue to beat strongly. The patient will exhibit normal coloring, and the kidneys will continue to produce urine (readily visible in the plastic bedside bag). The physician must help the family understand that the patient meets the criteria to be declared dead. They must realize that this is artificial life, dependent on mechanical supports, and that death in the ordinary sense is inevitable, being postponed only through machine action.

Only the family, however, can authorize turning off the respirator. In the much publicized Karen Quinlan case, the reverse situation occurred. Two undisputed experts agreed that the patient's coma was irreversible. Her parents requested that the respirator be turned off, but the attending physicians refused on the basis that she did not meet the criteria of brain death; certain reflex activity, and an EEG which at times cycled wake and sleep, gave evidence of a brain that was maintaining some biological activity. The question was carried to the Supreme Court of New Jersey, and the decision by Chief Justice Richard J. Hughes hinged on the court's recognition of the individual's "right to privacy" in life-sustaining medical decisions. According to the court's opinion, the state's interest in preserving the sanctity of human life ultimately must yield to an individual's right to privacy "as the degree of bodily invasion increases and the prognosis dims." The court reasoned that if Karen could somehow express an opinion based on knowledge of the inevitable outcome, she would request that the respirator be discontinued. Because she was incompetent due to the deep coma, her father, named guardian, was empowered to take steps to turn off the life-sustaining machines. But despite measures in the judicial decision protecting both doctors and hospital, certain loopholes and confused issues quickly became apparent. None of the physicians caring for Karen Quinlan was willing to remove the respirator, despite the hopeless prognosis. By scientific criteria her brain was still alive, despite her essentially noncognitive state. In May 1976, some 13 months after she had lost consciousness, the respirator was gradually removed, and Karen began to breathe on her own; steps were taken to transfer her to a nursing home where she remained in a coma.

This account points up some problems that may arise around the question of death today. Other dilemmas involve the issue of optimal care for the hopelessly ill patient and the ethics of orders "not to resuscitate." Such orders may come from the patient, early in the course of the illness, or from the family when the patient can no longer make the decision. Two U.S. hospitals have established optimal care committees and classification systems to help the medical staff deal with these decisions. Others concerned with the ethical problem have suggested the utilization of the "living will" (first made legal in the state of California), which requests that the signator's life not be prolonged unduly under certain specified circumstances.

The issues surrounding death are far from settled, and coming years will find not only doctors and clergy involved but also lawyers and the courts. It is to be hoped that a precedent may be set that will allow the termination of life to be dignified and as free from all types of pain and anguish as is humanly possible, for both the patient and his loved ones.

—*Benjamin Boshes, M.D., Ph.D.*

Dentistry

The dental profession in recent years has placed increasing emphasis on the importance of prevention as one of the most economical and effective forms of treatment. Dentistry also has made new inroads in the treatment of children (pedodontics), the elderly, and handicapped patients, and in the improvement of materials and techniques for orthodontics and reconstructive surgery.

Prevention

Beyond a doubt, the increased emphasis on preventive dentistry has not only helped to slow the rapid increase in the cost of dental care but also has played an important role in upgrading the general public's dental health. One of the most significant preventive measures that the profession has promoted is the use of fluorides in community water supplies. Unfortunately, despite a wealth of studies that have demonstrated conclusively the

benefits of fluoridation, some groups still oppose the practice. The National Health Foundation, for example, recently reported data showing a higher incidence of cancer in communities with fluoridated water. The National Institute of Dental Research, the American Medical Association, and the National Cancer Institute have repudiated this connection and have endorsed the use of fluorides as a community health practice. Objections notwithstanding, studies conducted over a period of several years have demonstrated that adding fluoride to a community's water supply is not only safe but is probably the single most effective large-scale means for prevention of dental caries.

Nursing bottle syndrome

Among very young children, a common problem characterized by rampant decay of the maxillary labial tooth surfaces (the surfaces facing the lips) has been termed the "nursing bottle syndrome." In cases where a nursing bottle has been misused, there appears to be a positive correlation between the sequence in which teeth are affected and the eruption sequence for the primary teeth. Among the interacting factors are excess carbohydrates, microorganisms in the mouth, reduced salivary flow during sleep, and failure to wean the child from the bottle. Researchers found that a variety of decay-causing agents—sugared, milk-based preparations, fruit juices, syrup, and vitamin supplements—are related to the condition and that these agents are increasingly destructive in proportion to their sugar content and to the duration of nursing bottle use. Prevention involves education in the appropriate function of the nursing bottle itself, along with use of fluorides, diet counseling, and proper home prophylaxis. Early treatment of decayed teeth is mandatory.

New treatment for hemophiliacs

The hemophiliac patient's tendency to bleed uncontrollably following injury or surgical procedures has always presented a serious problem in dental treatment. Recently, however, it was reported that epsilon amino caproic acid (EACA), given orally and combined with preoperative administration of blood coagulation factor VIII, prevented intraoral bleeding following tooth extractions in hemophiliac patients. The new discovery makes possible not only extractions but other types of dental procedures that would ordinarily produce massive bleeding.

Orthodontia for adults

A recent nationwide survey by the American Association of Orthodontists indicates that one out of every ten orthodontic patients is an adult—a rec-

Dentists rank "nursing bottle syndrome" among the primary causes of tooth decay in very young children.

ord-setting statistic. Tilted and migrated teeth are the most common adult conditions, and their correction can help to prevent gum disease and tooth loss, as well as providing aid in chewing.

Depending on the severity of the malocclusion, adult teeth can be moved into proper positions in some cases in only a matter of several months, without discomfort to the patient. Both fixed and removable appliances are used for treatment. The removable appliance consists of a plastic prosthesis that uses arch wires, springs, and small hooks for elastics. Once the ideal occlusion and tooth position have been achieved, a short period of stabilization is required to allow time for the supporting tissues of the teeth to adjust and adapt to the new environment.

Success with overlay dentures

The replacement of natural teeth with artificial in a way that is efficient and comfortable for the patient is one of dentistry's most persistent problems. With the loss of teeth, the alveolar process (the part of the jaw that holds the teeth) disappears, and the sensory nerve endings located in the periodontal ligament are eliminated. Over a period of time, edentulous patients (those who have lost all natural teeth) show ridge resorption, which makes the usual full dentures—especially in the lower arch—

unsatisfactory. With the loss of sensory nerve endings necessary to signal and transmit stimuli, the patient's control over precise movement of the mandible (lower jawbone) is reduced.

Now, however, researchers have reported a significant advance in treatment, involving the use of the roots of remaining natural teeth to support, stabilize, and retain overlay complete dentures. By retaining these roots, the overlay denture allows preservation of the important bone, tissue, and nerve structures that degenerate with the use of traditional dentures.

The overlay denture is a complete denture that fits over one or more of the selected natural teeth. These teeth are first treated periodontically as necessary and root canal procedures are performed; the teeth are then restored with an alloy filling or some type of casting. In addition to preserving the residual ridges and increasing the stability of the denture, overlay dentures have the advantage of greater psychological acceptance than traditional appliances.

Other recent findings

A University of Washington research group has reported the discovery that the upper jaw does not completely unite with the frontal bone of the human skull until after an individual reaches 70 years

210

of age. Vincent G. Kokich and Benjamin C. Moffett found that the frontozygomatic sutures do not fuse between the 18th and 35th years as had been previously assumed; in fact, these bones do not unite until after age 70 and then only partially. This new knowledge makes it possible to treat adult patients who have midface problems—protrusion of the maxilla (upper jaw), and other related disfigurements—using traditional appliances instead of, or in addition to, surgery.

Progress continues in the field of dentofacial orthopedics. Particularly, new techniques in orthodontic and bone grafting procedures for cases of cleft lip and palate appear to show great promise. A successful treatment recently reported by Sheldon W. Rosenstein at Children's Memorial Hospital, Chicago, consists of inserting an intraoral prosthesis prior to or at the time of lip closure, molding of the arch segments by means of an autogenous bone graft (that is, use of bone from the patient's own body), and retention of the prosthesis until palatal closure is achieved. The early performance of this procedure affords the opportunity for more complete orthodontic treatment at a later stage of development, when the patient possesses a full permanent dentition and is ready for comprehensive treatment.

— Leon D. Rosenfeld, D.D.S., M.S.D.

Diet and Nutrition

Supplies of food and knowledge about nutrition have changed greatly over the past 150 years. The building of national rail systems, the invention of refrigerated cars, and the development of the canning industry in the late 19th century meant that more people could have a wider variety of food that was safe to eat. The passage of food and drug laws provided governments with urgently needed tools for ensuring the safety of food supplies. Food adulteration, which was rampant in the 19th century, continued into the 20th century (and unfortunately still does occur), but at least governments now have the legislation needed to control food quality and to prosecute violators.

With the exception of the knowledge that fresh citrus fruits and green vegetables contained a substance that prevented scurvy, the existence of vitamins was virtually unsuspected before the 20th century, and only a few minerals, among them calcium and iron, were recognized as important in nutrition. By 1941, many more minerals and all the vitamins known today, except vitamin B_{12}, had been discovered. A large body of knowledge about the role of these nutrients in human and animal nutrition has now been amassed and much has been learned about the cause-and-effect relationships between specific nutritional deficiencies and the development of diseases.

Today nutritionists are concerned with more subtle problems, including the critical examination of those factors in our diet that positively or negatively affect the development of disease and therefore the quality of life. There is much recent evidence of the possible relations between nutrition and diseases such as cancer, osteoporosis, and diabetes, as well as of the effects of oral contraceptives on nutritional requirements.

Food additives and cancer

Concern over the potentially carcinogenic effects of certain food additives has been widely publicized, leading the U.S. Food and Drug Administration (FDA) and agencies of other governments to reevaluate additives formerly thought to be safe. The latest round in this controversy began in March 1977 when the FDA announced its intention to ban the use of saccharin in all foods, beverages,

Studies seeking to link diet and cancer have yielded, among other data, indications of a low incidence of breast cancer among women in developing countries.

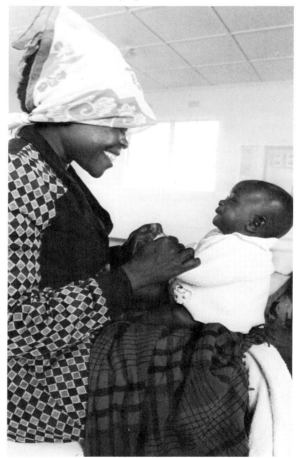

Courtesy, the World Health Organization; photograph, J. Mohr

and cosmetics. The agency's decision was based on a Canadian study in which relatively large amounts of saccharin were found to cause bladder cancer in laboratory animals. The announcement of the ban met with a torrent of criticism from manufacturers, organizations representing diabetics, the public, and many physicians, the latter contending that diabetic and obese patients would incur greater health hazards from sugar than from exposure to a potential carcinogen. The FDA, however, was bound by the so-called Delaney clause of the 1958 food additives amendments to the Federal Food, Drug, and Cosmetic Act; under the Delaney provisions, the agency is obliged to prohibit food processers from using any additive known to cause cancer in either humans or animals. Since drugs are not covered under Delaney, however, the FDA proposed that saccharin continue to be marketed in liquid or tablet form as an over-the-counter, non-prescription drug. But as in the case of other new drugs, manufacturers would be required to prove the substance's effectiveness; if the proposed rule takes effect, the FDA would require that all saccharin products carry a written warning advising consumers of possible carcinogenic effects.

Nutrition and cancer

Another concern of research, one that has received far less attention in the media, is the quest for clues that link nutrition and diet to the development of cancer. The knowledge that the incidence of cancer varies worldwide and tends to change with migration has led to the theory that environmental factors, including diet, may be important carcinogenic factors. In the U.S., one major impetus for exploring this possibility came from the National Cancer Act Amendments of 1974 that mandated the National Cancer Institute to "collect, analyze, and disseminate information respecting . . . the relationship between nutrition and cancer."

It is impossible to review all of the data that has been collected on the matter in recent years. Two important findings, however, are the possible relationship between diet and cancer of the breast and of the colon and some basic research on the possible effects of synthetic varieties, or analogs, of vitamin A in the prevention of cancer.

The excessive intake of certain nutrients appears to be related to the development of cancer of the breast. Data shows, for example, that breast cancer is uncommon in developing societies and in Japan, but increases among those populations after they emigrate to the U.S. Breast cancer is common among Jewish women in New York and in Jewish women who have emigrated from Europe, but it is uncommon in Jewish women who emigrate to Israel from Asia and Africa. There is also a higher incidence of breast cancer among Puerto Rican women living on the U.S. mainland than among those living in Puerto Rico. A comparison of data on food intake among these populations shows a general correlation between fat intake and the incidence of breast cancer.

A relationship has also been shown to exist between age at menarche (beginning of menstruation) and the incidence of breast cancer in different countries. Earlier growth spurt and earlier menarche have been associated with better nutrition, including higher levels of dietary protein. Since most high-protein foods contain considerable fat, an increased intake of protein is also accompanied by an increase in fat consumption. In Japan, for example, average daily protein intake jumped from 13.0 grams to 27.7 grams between 1948 and 1963. At the same time fat intake more than doubled from 14 to 36 grams a day.

Laboratory data also supports the idea that dietary fat may be related to the development of breast cancer. A series of studies has shown that when rats are given a carcinogen and fed a high-fat diet, the incidence of breast tumors is greater than that in studies using the carcinogen alone. It has been suggested that diets including excessive amounts of certain nutrients, especially fats, may have an effect on the body's hormonal system that contributes to the development of cancer of the breast. Whether this theory will hold up under further examination remains to be seen.

A second type of cancer that may be related to dietary fat intake is cancer of the colon. Here again much of the evidence rests on epidemiologic observations that show a low incidence of cancer of the colon among populations that consume a low-fat diet and a high incidence when the diet contains large amounts of fat. Trends in disease rates provide some particularly interesting clues. For example, among Japanese who move to the U.S., the incidence of the disease rises. In addition, the rate of occurrence of cancer of the colon seems to be rising in Japan itself, where the diet is becoming more westernized.

It has been suggested that a high-fat diet results in a greater concentration of anaerobic bacteria (those that thrive in the absence of oxygen) in the feces and also in greater production of both bile acid and cholesterol breakdown products. Some metabolic studies have shown that the feces of high-risk populations do contain greater numbers of anaerobic bacteria, which may break down bile acids to produce substances that promote carcinogenesis. The feces of individuals eating a high-fat diet do contain more end products of bile acid and cholesterol breakdown. Similar findings have been observed in patients with cancer of the colon. In the laboratory, animal studies have shown that two bile acids promote tumor development in rats previously injected with a carcinogen.

A full understanding of the interaction between bacterial flora, metabolic end products of fat and cholesterol, and the lining of the colon itself, and of the role of these factors in the production of cancer requires a great deal more research. But, as with cancer of the breast, some researchers feel that there is now enough data to suggest a reduction in dietary fat as a prudent measure.

A totally different area of basic research in the field of nutrition and cancer is concerned with the use of synthetically produced variants, or analogs, of vitamin A in the prevention of epithelial-cell cancers, the most common fatal forms of the disease. Vitamin A is necessary for the formation of the epithelial tissue that makes up the skin and the mucous membranes lining the various cavities and passages of the body. A deficiency of the vitamin has been shown to increase the susceptibility of animals to certain types of cancers. In a recent study of 8,000 Norwegian men matched for smoking habits, a low vitamin A intake correlated with a relatively high incidence of lung cancer.

Researchers have suggested the use of retinoids (naturally occurring as well as synthetic forms of vitamin A) as a possible way of preventing the growth of abnormal epithelial tissue. Natural vitamin A, however, is toxic in large amounts. In animal experiments toxic effects limited the amount of vitamin A that could be given, and it was impossible to achieve adequate tissue distribution of the vitamin. However, a synthetic retinoid has been shown to reduce the incidence of certain types of cancers in animals given a particular carcinogen. Much more research must be done before a practical application of the results can be attempted, but in the future some retinoids may be used to help prevent epithelial-cell cancers in high-risk individuals.

Calcium and osteoporosis

Demineralization of the bones, or osteoporosis, can cause pain, skeletal deformity, loss of height, and spontaneous fractures. A number of factors are thought to be responsible for the loss of minerals, particularly calcium, from bones. Two important factors are the change in hormonal balance in women at menopause and the decrease in physical activity that accompanies aging. Until recently, osteoporosis was thought to be a natural and inevitable phenomenon of aging. In carefully controlled studies conducted over an 11-year period, however, a significant number of individuals ranging from 66 to 75 years of age at the end of the study showed no loss in bone mass.

Two dietary factors are now thought to play im-

Horst Schäfer—Photo Trends

Increased consumption of so-called junk foods, high in artificial ingredients and low in nutritional value, has been linked to conditions as diverse as hyperkinesis in children and osteoporosis in adults.

portant roles in preventing osteoporosis. One is an adequate intake of calcium. Some adults excrete more calcium than they take in. Calcium stores in the bones are then continuously tapped to maintain blood calcium levels, which results in the gradual depletion of the mineral from the bones.

A second factor may be the ratio of calcium to phosphorus in the diet. Vegetarians have a higher bone density than omnivores who eat phosphorus-rich meat. And carnivorous Eskimos, eating only meat, have a lower bone density than omnivores. Moreover, animal studies have demonstrated that bone loss does not occur, even on a low-calcium diet, as long as the calcium intake is greater than the phosphorus intake.

Changes in food consumption patterns in the U.S. and in some other countries, however, have resulted in a diet containing fewer calcium-rich dairy products. At the same time, increased consumption of meat and snack foods such as potato chips, soft drinks, and crackers, as well as the commercial use of many additives that contain phosphorus, has increased phosphorus intake. Based on present evidence, recommendations for the prevention of osteoporosis include a diet that contains adequate amounts of regular or low-fat dairy products and less junk food. Regular exercise appears to be an additional preventive measure.

213

The ill effects of a high-sugar diet may include not only tooth decay and weight increase with related physical problems but also diabetes.

Sugar and diabetes

An increased intake of sugar has, of course, long been associated with a greater rate of dental decay. Recent evidence suggests that a high sugar intake may also be a precipitating factor in the development of diabetes. In a study of 12 population groups, it was found that the incidence of diabetes is generally greater where sugar consumption is higher, although the findings were not completely consistent.

Other studies have shown that the incidence of the disease changes when people migrate and alter their dietary habits. Indians who have migrated to South Africa, for example, where they eat a high-sugar diet, have ten times more diabetes than do people in India, where the diet is low in sugar. Israeli immigrants from Yemen, who consume almost no sugar, have a very low incidence of diabetes. Researchers have found that after ten years in Israel, where sugar is used generously, incidence of diabetes among the Yemeni equals that of the Israeli population.

It is, of course, true that immigration brings about other changes in life-style that may affect the incidence of the disease. Animal studies, however, have shown that sugar intake can indeed influence the development of diabetes. In laboratory experiments, a strain of rats bred to be genetically susceptible to diabetes showed decreased glucose tolerance when fed a high-sugar diet. And many of the rats on a high-sugar diet developed diabetes, while those on a high-starch diet did not. It has been suggested that in humans with a genetic tendency for diabetes, a high-sugar diet may impair the ability to metabolize sugar, resulting in diabetes.

Oral contraceptives and nutrition

It was recently estimated that about 50 million women in the world (about 10 million in the U.S.) are currently using oral contraceptives. Many reports have noted that the use of such drugs alters a woman's nutritional requirements, but that once the drug is discontinued requirements revert to normal. In general, the nutritional effects of oral contraceptives are minor. The net effect varies with the exact nature of the drug, the length of time it is used, the existence of other factors that may contribute to malnutrition, and any individual predisposition. It has been said that the nutritional effects of the Pill tend to exaggerate the nutritional problems of the population in which it is used.

Vitamin B_6 is one nutrient commonly affected by estrogens. Vitamin B_6 is necessary for the metabolism of amino acids, tryptophan in particular. When given a load dose of tryptophan, Pill users excrete abnormal amounts of xanthurenic acid, one of the breakdown products of tryptophan metabolism. Such a reaction indicates a possible lack of vitamin B_6. However, other measures of B_6 metabolism are normal in such women, and clinical B_6 deficiency has not been documented in women taking oral contraceptives. Moreover, it has been suggested that depression, a frequent side effect of oral contraceptive use, might be due to a B_6 deficiency; but reports of the effectiveness of B_6 supplementation to treat such depression have been mixed.

Folacin, or folate, is another nutrient for which the requirement seems to increase among users of the Pill. Some studies have shown reduced levels of folate in blood plasma and in red blood cells. It is thought that oral contraceptives may interfere with folate metabolism by increasing the rate of clearance of folate from plasma to the tissues. A few cases of megaloblastic anemia, an anemia associated with folate deficiency, have been attributed to use of the Pill, but in such cases the deficiency appeared to be the result of coexisting malabsorption or of a low intake of the vitamin. Long-term use of certain drugs known to impair folate utilization, as well as alcoholism and certain chronic diseases such as rheumatoid arthritis, may also result in folate deficiency in women using the Pill. Generally, a well-balanced diet including good sources of folate such as green leafy and other vegetables, liver, whole grain bread and cereals, and dried peas and beans should provide adequate amounts of folate.

Vitamin B_{12} is also affected by the use of oral contraceptives. About half the women taking the

In India and in other countries where the diet is generally low in sugar, the incidence of diabetes is very low.

Ira Kirschenbaum—Stock, Boston

drug show low serum levels of the vitamin, but levels in tissues are unaffected. Low levels of vitamin C in plasma, platelets, and leukocytes have also been associated with use of the Pill. Estrogens appear to increase the rate of vitamin C breakdown by raising levels of ceruloplasmin, a copper-containing protein known to trigger vitamin C oxidation.

Not all nutrient levels are lowered by the use of oral contraceptives. Among those that seem to rise is vitamin A. This is apparently explained by the fact that estrogen increases the concentration of a lipoprotein that binds the vitamin. While vitamin A requirements may thus be slightly reduced for women using oral contraceptives, there appears to be no risk of vitamin A overload while a normal diet is maintained.

Women on the Pill may also have a lower demand for iron. One reason is lowered blood loss as a result of reduced menstrual flow. In addition, in some studies serum levels of iron have been found to be higher and iron-binding capacity greater, with an increased capacity to absorb iron. How much effect oral contraceptives have on iron status apparently is affected by the particular drug being used, how long it is used, and by the individual intake of dietary iron. Finally, estrogens are associated with a marked rise in blood levels of serum copper and ceruloplasmin. The fact that no changes occur in urinary excretion may indicate a decreased need for copper.

A recent statement of the Committee on Nutrition of the Mother and the Preschool Child established by the Food and Nutrition Board of the National Academy of Sciences concluded that "any consequences of the many other nutritional and metabolic effects of oral contraceptives are not yet known, but the need for continuing surveillance is clear." Apparently a well-balanced diet is adequate to prevent nutritional deficiencies in women taking oral contraceptives, and no definitive recommendations for the use of nutritional supplements can be made without consideration of further information. The committee's report calls for additional long-term studies to delineate more precisely the metabolic effects of oral contraceptives and to correlate these with long-range effects. Such studies must take into account nutritional status and cultural and geographic factors, and should assess the effects of different dosages and of the different components of contraceptive drugs.

—*Jeanne P. Goldberg, M.Ed., R.D.*

Digestive System Diseases

Peptic ulcer disease is one of the world's most widespread forms of stomach disorder, and its treatment and management—special diets and

Digestive system diseases

various over-the-counter medications for relief of gastric discomfort—are among the most popular medical subjects in the lay press. Until recently, medical attempts to control the gastric acid secretion that characterizes peptic ulcers have involved the administration of large quantities of antacids or anticholinergic agents that interfere with nerve impulses controlling acid secretion. Surgical measures have traditionally included interruption of the pathway of the vagus nerve to the stomach and other viscera as well as the actual removal of the acid-producing portion of the stomach. Recent research on the nature of histamines and antihistamines, however, offers some promising new treatments for those suffering from peptic ulcers.

New concepts in peptic ulcer disease

Excessive gastric acid secretion has long been recognized as a significant factor in the causation of peptic ulcer disease. Gastric secretion can be stimulated in a number of ways, locally (intragastric) by the presence of such substances as meat extracts or nonlocally by the psychic or physiological stimulation of the vagus nerve. Vagal stimulation, for example, can be initiated when blood glucose is lowered. These stimuli act, through release of acetylcholine, either directly by stimulating the acid-secreting cells in the stomach or indirectly by release of the hormone gastrin from cells in the pyloric antrum (located between the stomach and the pyloric canal).

Histamine, an amine found in many human tissues, is thought to be released in the stomach in response to acetylcholine or gastrin and may be the final mediator for gastric secretion; it has recently been demonstrated that certain antihistamines, notably the H_2 antagonists, block the stimulation by histamine of gastric secretion. Since the first reports, which were released in 1972, a number of such compounds have been tested in the laboratory and in human subjects. One of these H_2 antagonists, metiamide, was shown to be capable of significantly reducing gastric secretion, but because of bone marrow toxicity in a few patients, metiamide was removed from clinical testing. It has since been replaced by another less toxic compound, cimetidine. This agent reduces both basal gastric acid secretion and that stimulated by food, histamine, gastrin, and caffeine in the human body. Studies in Great Britain and Europe on almost 400 patients have demonstrated that cimetidine can cause symptomatic relief and healing of peptic ulcers in a high proportion of patients. It is taken orally, in tablet form, four times per day. Fortunately, the few side effects that have been reported tend to be mild. In the U.S. a number of studies are now examining the effectiveness of cimetidine therapy in treatment of both gastric and duodenal ulcers, as well as its use in disorders of acid reflux from the stomach into the esophagus. If the results of the U.S. experiments are similar to those produced elsewhere, the introduction of cimetidine will represent a major advance in ulcer therapy, provided that long-term usage proves safe.

New findings about coffee

Caffeine is a known stimulant of acid secretion in the human body. This fact has led to the recommendation that regular—as opposed to decaffeinated—coffee should not be consumed by patients with peptic ulcer disease.

In a recent study, however, it was found that decaffeinated coffee and regular coffee had similar capacities for stimulating the secretion of gastric acid. Interestingly, if equal amounts of caffeine were tested alone and in coffee, coffee was still shown to be the more potent stimulus for acid secretion, thus suggesting that coffee may contain

"I've noticed that the point during a discussion at which you begin to worry about my ulcer is invariably the point at which I begin to turn the tide."

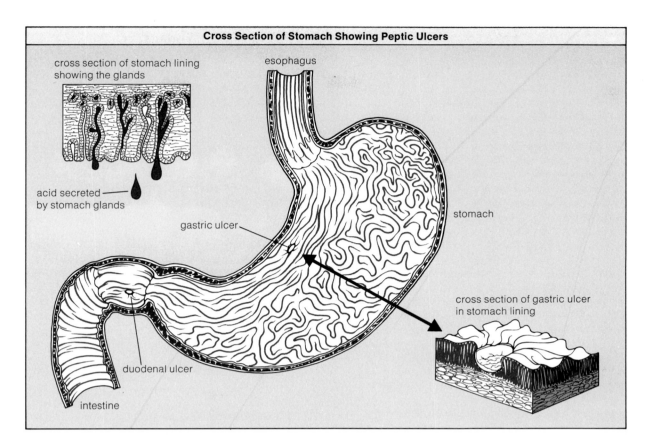

Cross Section of Stomach Showing Peptic Ulcers

cross section of stomach lining showing the glands

esophagus

acid secreted by stomach glands

gastric ulcer

stomach

cross section of gastric ulcer in stomach lining

duodenal ulcer

intestine

other substances that stimulate gastric acid secretion; findings using decaffeinated coffee supported this concept.

Crohn's disease: a possible viral etiology

Crohn's disease (also known as regional enteritis and granulomatous ileocolitis) is an inflammatory bowel disorder that can involve the entire gastrointestinal tract; other systemic manifestations may also include involvement of skin, joints, liver, kidney, and eye. The cause of Crohn's disease has always been obscure, but various recent studies have indicated that it may be caused by a virus. Researchers found that filtrates of ileum (a portion of the small intestine) from patients with Crohn's disease caused in rabbits a response that resembled Crohn's disease; the viral hypothesis has also been supported by the transmission of granulomas (a characteristic type of inflammation) to mice from human tissue extracts. More recently, viral agents have actually been isolated from diseased human tissues. Present evidence indicates that the viral agent contains RNA and is probably a member of the picornavirus group. Further studies on the virus and also on the genetic and host influences that determine the response of individual patients are being conducted throughout the world.

Liver tumors and the Pill

Another current concern in the realm of digestive system diseases involves recent developments connecting tumors of the liver and oral contraceptives. The association between such tumors and oral contraceptives was first described in 1973, in a report that described seven women with benign tumors, all of whom had been taking birth control pills. Subsequently there have been numerous reports linking long-term use of oral contraceptives with both benign and, less commonly, malignant tumors. The tumors have been diagnosed in a number of ways: some are discovered accidentally during routine physical examination, while others become manifest from recurrent upper abdominal pain or even from sudden, life-threatening intra-abdominal hemorrhage. Especially in the latter case, early recognition and surgery are vital.

The possible mechanism of tumor induction by the contraceptives is still under study, but women who have been using these drugs for more than five years should be aware of the potential implications. Nonetheless, it remains to be seen whether the risks of developing liver disease are greater than those medical and social complications of unwanted pregnancy and termination of pregnancy.

—Bernard Levin, M.D.

217

Drugs

It is a rare event when drug and disease interact in a way that is exclusively therapeutic. The functions and chemistry of the human body are complex and delicate, and their reactions to exotic chemicals are likely to be adverse. The variety of disease is enormous and the bodily changes induced by disease are often incredibly devious. Drugs may not have the same actions in diseased and normal conditions. Man did not begin to accumulate a substantial body of therapeutically useful drugs until he achieved sophisticated understanding of his own body, of his diseases, and of the effects of chemicals—which now may account for more drug-induced than drug-cured diseases.

Selective lethality

It is axiomatic that all drugs—even drugs that heal—are in some way poisonous. This contributes to the difficulty of identifying beneficial drugs. Poisons have always been easier to identify than drugs that heal. Sophisticated embalming antedated effective healing by many years, and food preservatives were probably the first drugs to benefit man. Both depend on the ability to kill microorganisms of putrefaction.

Today an unremitting search goes on for drugs that cure, but chemicals that are merely poisonous are not disregarded. There are many practical and acceptable (as well as unacceptable) uses for lethal drugs in our society. Except for the now disreputable agents of chemical warfare, most of these substances are not intended for man. Rodenticides and other pesticides are very important to our economy as well as to public health. Insecticides are critical to modern agriculture. Bactericides have many medical and nonmedical uses. There are herbicides for those who cannot tolerate dandelions in their lawns, defoliants to kill leaves on plants to increase the visibility of fruit, general disinfectants to sterilize the ground under fruit trees so that fruit brought down by trunk-shaking machines will not be contaminated by food-spoiling microorganisms. Selective lethality can be beneficial; chemicals deadly to some living things but harmless to others form the backbone of modern treatment of infectious disease.

In this epoch of visionary scientific imagination, the search for new drugs is not, as one might expect, confined to the laboratory of the synthetic chemist. Nature, still far in advance of man in synthetic know-how, seems not to recognize any limit to molecular complexity, and is not in the least checked by concern for cost-benefit ratios. The screening of traditional sources of drugs continues apace; today we investigate every pharmacologi-

Agricultural insecticide sprays represent one of the practical and acceptable uses of lethal chemicals in our society.

cally unexplored crevice of the planet as soon as it is opened up. Thousands of chemicals never before known have been extracted from natural sources on the earth's surface. Pharmaceutical manufacturers have undertaken a systematic search of the sea for biologically synthesized drugs. There is no way of knowing where our next wonder drugs will come from, but the chances seem very good that some will come from fauna or flora of the sea.

Drug-induced disease

Medicine is no longer limited to the prevention of disease and the restoration of health; it now also prescribes drugs that deliberately induce abnormal functional states in normal persons, *e.g.,* temporary sterility. We also use drugs to pacify unruly people (Mace) and to render dangerous animals and insects harmless and helpless (tranquilizing darts and smoke). Man also uses drugs to excite or depress human mental activity, and abuse of this use has mushroomed into one of society's great menaces. The total established and potential physical harm from the abuse of tobacco, alcohol, heroin, cocaine, amphetamines, barbiturates, and LSD, not to mention drugs used in other cultures (a list so long as to comprise a specialty, ethnopharmacology) is staggering.

In addition to the deliberate and voluntary use of drugs, there is the unconscious and unavoidable exposure to chemicals that alter structure and function. Our agriculture and our means of locomotion pollute our water, air, and soil with a large variety of identified and unidentified chemicals in a way that may yet add more names to the catalog of drug-induced diseases.

Occupations have been an important cause of disease since man began to specialize in his work. Older occupational diseases had names like chimney sweep's cancer (of the scrotum) and paprika-splitter's lung; the names of modern industrial diseases continue to have a medieval ring—munition worker's Monday morning headache and (one of the latest) meat-wrapper's asthma (caused by vapors released when a hot wire is used to cut the plastic meat wrapping). Today industrial disease is widespread and economically devastating, but there are no realistic data on incidence, morbidity, or mortality. Almost every kind of commercial activity produces some kind of air pollutant or irritant. If exposure is substantial and irritation is intense and continued, serious permanent effects are likely to result. Work done in an enclosed space produces very intense, unremitting exposure, making inhalation of pollutants virtually unavoidable. This is the prototype of the industrial environment. It is likely that the earliest recognized chemically induced industrial diseases occurred in miners, tunnel diggers, and metal smelters because they worked under conditions that led to intense exposures to fumes or dusts in limited air spaces. Today the situation is somewhat improved, and although sophisticated machinery for controlling unhealthy industrial environments is often required by law, the problem is far from eliminated. To complicate matters further, each new technology may lead to a disease not yet known, which cannot always be anticipated and is identified only after the damage has been done.

Great catastrophes have been caused by drugs as a result of sheer pharmacological ignorance. It is probable that the mercury used in the treatment of post-Columbian syphilis killed more people than it saved—syphilis is not a uniformly fatal disease but mercury is a lethal metal. There was an epidemic of irreversible paralysis in New Orleans called the Jakes that was traced to contamination of cheap liquor with cresol used for flavoring. More recently a drug publicly proclaimed to be the safest sedative in history proved, after it had been taken by an undetermined number of pregnant women, to have caused at least 7,000 infants to be born with severely deformed limbs (phocomelia). That drug, of course, was thalidomide. Thalidomide now has a unique use in medicine. With absolute magical speed, alone of all known drugs, it promptly relieves the terrible tortures of a complication of leprosy, the acute lepra reaction. How or why it works is not known, but it has nothing to do with its sedative or teratogenic actions.

It is a biological fact that all human beings differ, and this difference extends to the way each individual deals with and reacts to drugs. Many of these differences have been traced to inheritable characteristics, but many others remain obscure. In any event, the use of new drugs is especially hazardous in the early stages of trial, when the scope of human variability has not yet been determined. Experimental animals cannot help; this is a *human* problem.

From its inception, therapeutics created a long-unrecognized but significant category of diseases, iatrogenic, or treatment-induced, diseases. Although such diseases will undoubtedly continue to develop, their incidence is now declining, a better record than medicine could claim at any time before the turn of this century. Within this context, there is also a growing body of specific knowledge

The quest for new drugs is not confined to the laboratory. Today scientists are searching every part of the earth, including the seas, for biologically synthesized substances that may have medical applications.

Russ Kinne—Photo Researchers

about the interactions of drugs within the human body. Drugs that are innocuous in isolation may combine to induce predictable—and hence avoidable—adverse physiological effects.

To deal with all the problems, to use drugs wisely and well, and to discover still more that are useful, both researchers and prescribers must increase their knowledge of the basic biological effects of drugs at the organic, cellular, and subcellular levels. We must know how drugs affect structure and function in the presence of anatomical, physiological, and biochemical abnormalities as well as in normal states; and we must also know how the body disposes of drugs. In short, we must understand all aspects of the drug response in living organisms. We must know about the effects of drugs on the structure of the cell membrane, on nuclear material (DNA), on genes, on molecular structure, on functional stimulation and depression, on enzymes, and—conversely—the effects of enzymes on drugs before we can use these chemical agents safely and effectively. Unfortunately, there are still significant limits to our knowledge and understanding, and these make educated caution and constant vigilance a necessity.

—*Walter Modell, M.D.*

Ear Diseases and Hearing Disorders

Recent experiments have proved the feasibility of using electrical stimulation of the auditory nerve to treat profound or total hearing loss. Although the first attempts at electrical stimulation of the ear were made almost 200 years ago, it has only been during the past two decades that researchers have made serious attempts to use the technique to treat deafness. A significant recent event was the presentation of the results of an extensive study of a group of patients who had undergone electrode implantation in the cochlea. The study was especially valuable because it was carried out by independent investigators not themselves involved in cochlear implantation.

Function of the cochlea

The cochlea is the part of the inner ear that converts the mechanical energy of sound waves into electrical discharges to the auditory nerve. Sound vibrations from the air are transmitted through the tympanic membrane and ossicles to the fluid of the inner ear. The fluid wave in the cochlea stimulates the hair cells, and it is in these cochlear cells that the transformation of sound energy into a stimulus capable of "firing" the auditory nerve takes place. The auditory nerve enters the brain stem, and from there multiple connections (synapses) take place

with other nerve fibers in the auditory pathways of the brain. The impulse is relayed to the auditory cortex of the brain's temporal lobes where it is interpreted as sound.

Degeneration of the cochlear hair cells may occur because of aging, exposure to loud sounds, toxic drugs, or other causes. When hair cell loss is extensive, hearing is completely lost, and amplification of sound by a hearing aid is not a satisfactory method of treating the patient. An auditory prosthesis that uses electrical stimulation of the auditory nerve through electrodes implanted in the cochlea has been developed for patients with hair cell degeneration (so-called sensorineural hearing loss). It is important, however, that the pathologic process that caused the loss of hair cells must not also have resulted in loss of the nerve fibers needed to receive the electrical stimulation. Because nerve degeneration does accompany many types of inner ear disorders, auditory prostheses using electrical stimulation of the auditory nerve are limited to certain patients.

Historical perspective

In 1800 Italian physicist Alessandro Volta reported that he perceived a bubbling sensation when a direct current was applied to electrodes inserted into his external ear canals. The magnitude of electricity used caused discomfort, however, and there was little interest in Volta's findings.

During the 1930s American investigators discovered that *acoustic* stimulation of the cochlea produced *electrical* activity in the cochlea. The discovery revived interest in electrical stimulation of the ear, and several investigators produced "hearing" by delivering small amounts of alternating currents to the normal inner ears of human subjects through electrodes placed on the skin or in the middle ear.

In 1957 French publications reported the work of two investigators who had electrically stimulated a totally deaf patient through an electrode implanted in the cochlea. The patient could not hear, but the device seemed to help the patient recognize background sounds and read lips. The report helped stimulate further interest in cochlear implants.

In the 1960s published reports described human and animal experiments involving electrical stimulation of the auditory nerve through electrodes attached to the middle ear or auditory nerve or implanted in the cochlea. It became evident that simple electrodes could be maintained in the cochlea, but that such electrodes were not capable of delivering signals of sufficient complexity for communication of speech. Researchers began to direct their attention to the use of multiple electrode implants and to the development of circuitry capable of delivering "appropriate" signals.

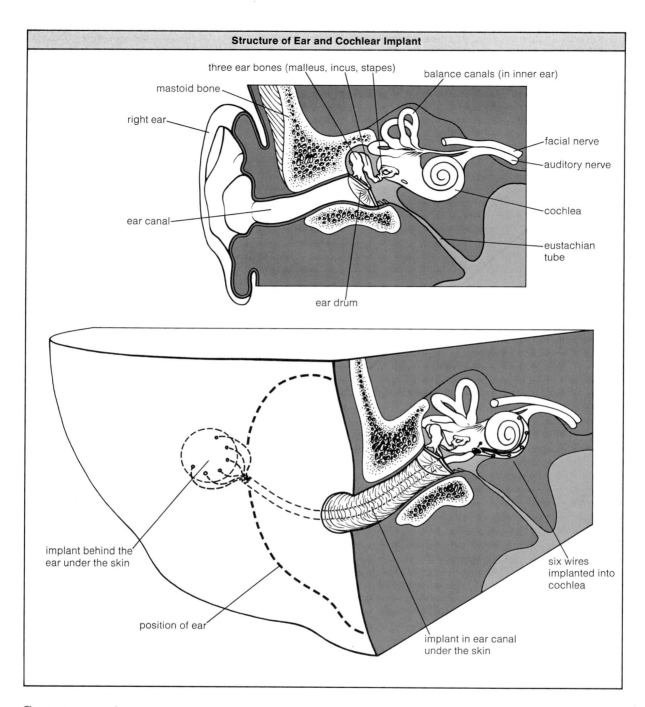

Structure of Ear and Cochlear Implant

three ear bones (malleus, incus, stapes)

balance canals (in inner ear)

mastoid bone

right ear

facial nerve

auditory nerve

cochlea

ear canal

eustachian tube

ear drum

implant behind the ear under the skin

position of ear

six wires implanted into cochlea

implant in ear canal under the skin

Current research

Several groups of investigators have continued to implant multiple electrode devices in selected patients. They have continued work to determine the most effective electrical signal to use and to find the best site for electrode placement. Researchers have implanted electrodes into the cochlea through the round window membrane and have also made direct implantation to auditory nerve fibers. They have used electronic circuitry attached to the electrodes through a coupler embedded in the skin behind the ear and, when it can be made sufficiently small and reliable, an electronic device can be surgically implanted.

Researchers have also made a few attempts to stimulate the auditory center of the brain directly. The trials have been made during brain surgery under local anesthesia or with short-term im-

221

planted electrodes following brain surgery for other reasons. An advantage of this approach is that it does not depend on an intact nerve pathway to the auditory cortex of the brain. Implantation in the brain is more difficult than in the cochlea, however, and again the design of an electrical stimulus that will allow speech perception is a problem.

At the 1976 annual meeting of the American Academy of Ophthalmology and Otolaryngology, a group of investigators from the University of Pittsburgh (Pa.) gave an extensive report on the success of cochlear implants. Their federally funded study made a detailed evaluation of thirteen patients with cochlear implants, all of whom had lost their hearing after language had developed. The investigators examined the subjects' hearing and balance, made psychoacoustic studies, evaluated their speech and communication skills, and assessed the patients' own impressions of the value of the cochlear implants.

It was found that the patients had tolerated the implants well, although a few complained of disequilibrium when the prosthesis was activated. The subjects could not understand speech with the cochlear implant alone, but the prosthesis did improve lipreading and recognition of background sounds. The patients had only a limited ability to discriminate changes in pitch or in loudness, but they could detect changes in signal duration and rhythm. If the subject's voice was intelligible without the prosthesis, it improved when the prosthesis was activated. The device did not significantly improve unintelligible voices. Although it was difficult, using standard audiometric tests, to prove that the implants improved communication for the patients, many of the subjects felt that they did.

At the present time, fewer than 35 patients have received long-term cochlear implants. The technique is still in the experimental phase, even though patients seem to benefit. Basic research needs to be done to determine more precisely the physiology of the auditory nerve and the pathways through the brain. Lack of knowledge of just what constitutes an appropriate electrical signal to the auditory nerve also is a major obstacle. Basic investigative work has been done to determine the nature of electrical activity in the auditory nerve and its individual fibers in response to sound. What type of an electrical stimulus will convey the information to the auditory nerve, allowing perception of speech to take place in the brain, is not yet known, however. With better understanding of normal function, researchers will be able to develop more accurate electrical stimuli. Cochlear implants do not yet allow the deaf to hear speech. That goal is the challenge to be met by further research.

—*Edward L. Applebaum, M.D.*

Emergency Medicine

Medical practitioners define a "true emergency" as any imminent threat to life or limb. Although this was for years the major category of problem seen in hospital emergency departments, even the earliest casualty rooms occasionally found patients seeking treatment for problems that did not, in the opinion of medical personnel, constitute real emergencies. Today such patients have become the rule rather than the exception; life-or-limb threats now represent only a small proportion of the workload of most emergency departments, which have become for many people substitutes for family doctors and points of entry into the health care delivery system.

Among the many reasons for this change in utilization patterns are a decline in the number of general or primary care physicians; the convenience of access to a medical facility that is open 24 hours a day with a physician present at all times; "third party" financial support for emergency care; a tendency among patients to seek only acute episodic medical care (crisis intervention); and the general unavailability of physicians at night, during weekends, or on holidays. The net result is that medical personnel seldom argue anymore about who should or should not be treated in an emergency department. Any patient can present himself as an emergency case. There remains, however, a need

For people who have no family physician, the emergency room functions as a source of primary medical care.

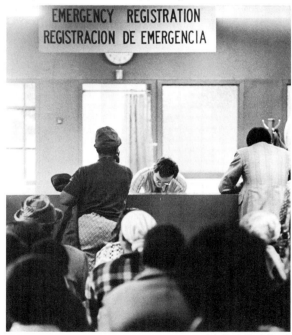

for planning a more efficient method of processing the patient's entrance into the medical care delivery system, both to lower the costs of care and to improve the quality of service. For the present, at least, the emergency department has to accept responsibility for processing and serving all varieties of patients.

While no patient is turned away, there must be a system to select the sicker patients in order to establish priorities for treatment. Most departments, therefore, use a triage system to divide their workload into three categories: true emergency; urgent (any non–life-or-limb threat that demands prompt attention to prevent degeneration into true emergency); and nonemergency, which includes all others. Categorizing patients by means of the triage system enables the emergency department to respond to all patients in a fashion that provides maximum care, especially to those who are in the most critical condition.

Although many changes in the form of emergency care have been directed toward meeting the needs of the least-ill patients, there remains an intense concern for providing high quality life-and-limb–saving care. To this end, providers of emergency care are developing a concept of the unique biology of the true emergency, separate even from the disease entity that produced the emergency.

The acute emergency

A situation becomes a true emergency when the major systems of the body begin to fail. If timely intervention does not occur during this period, the deterioration becomes irreversible and death ensues. Despite the almost infinite variety of diseases and injuries that can create emergencies, there are only a few, finite, common pathways to death. The common pathways are (1) the brain, for which almost nothing can be done directly; (2) the heart: "pump failure" is usually irreversible when it follows direct cardiac pathology but will often respond to intervention if another organ system is the primary target of the pathophysiologic process; (3) the circulatory system: loss of volume or red blood cell mass; (4) the lungs: ventilatory failure, like heart failure, is much less responsive to resuscitative efforts if it is a direct result of primary lung pathology; and (5) metabolic chaos (*e.g.,* hypoglycemia) that prevents the prior four organ systems from functioning appropriately.

Many of the current improvements in emergency care have evolved from efforts to recognize life threats, intervene, and transport patients at a stage when stabilization and restoration to a more normal physiology are still possible. This resuscitation process is the major responsibility of the emergency physician and the emergency system. Sub-

sequent specialized diagnostic, therapeutic, and maintenance programs can then be carried out, generally by members of the medical team other than those in the emergency system. It is clear (especially as one studies the statistics of trauma mortality), however, that without aggressive, expert, and high quality emergency care, few of the sophisticated and modern technologies can be applied to reverse disease processes. Emergency medicine has been criticized as being a "halfway technology." In a sense this is true: when its responsibilities have been discharged the patient frequently is still in a disordered pathophysiologic state. Without reversal of the particular life-threatening situation, however, "cure" becomes an academic problem.

The emergency department physician faced with acute, critical deteriorations of vital organ systems is under a great deal of pressure to make decisions quickly; but more than temporal pressure differentiates the decision-making process in the emergency department from that in inpatient facilities or in physicians' offices. In the latter cases, patients are approached from the point of view of individual problems or diagnoses that dictate disease-specific management and therapeutic protocols. There, the usual sequence of history-taking, physical examination, and laboratory, radiologic, and other special procedures yielding a specific diagnosis is followed by directed therapy or chronic care management. In the emergency department, however, specific diagnosis is much less important than recognition and stabilization of the degenerating homeostatic mechanisms.

Key questions that must be answered

What is the life threat? Example: A man is brought to the emergency department with a stab wound of the thigh. Shortly after arrival he develops cardiac arrest. The emergency team must restore a functional heart rhythm and replenish his diminished blood volume. Once they have succeeded, a vascular surgeon can explore the thigh wound, either diagnostically or surgically, identify the injured vessel, and effect repair. The failure of the pump (the heart) requires the emergency physician's primary attention. Were he to focus on a diagnosis of specific arterial injury, he would probably lose the patient.

What is different now? Example: A woman complains of headaches, stating that she has suffered from them for 15 years. Failure to find out that this was the worst headache she has ever had would prevent recognition of her life threat, a brain hemorrhage, and thus prevent saving her. The emergency physician must initially appraise the uniqueness of the situation in terms of systems failures

223

rather than focus on details of a disease state present for an extended time.

Does the patient need hospitalization? Example: A middle-aged man appears in the emergency department complaining of crushing chest pain accompanied by sweating. This patient needs immediate monitoring; specifically, he must be connected to an intravenous line and to an electronic cardiac monitor—before any diagnostic interventions are undertaken—to determine if he is having a myocardial infarction, or heart attack. The technology and expertise of the hospital coronary care unit must be drawn upon to protect this patient long before the physician can prove a specific etiology of his condition.

What is the most serious condition that might be present? Example: A young man complains of itching of the groin. He is dismissed as having a fungal infection only to return 18 hours later in a coma from his unrecognized diabetes. While specific diagnosis is not the first priority of the emergency physician, he must consider the most serious categories of possible problems before dismissing the patient as having a more trivial problem.

Is there enough available evidence to support the diagnosis and disposition being entertained? Example: A woman is complaining of abdominal pain, nausea, and vomiting. The emergency physician diagnoses a duodenal ulcer and treats the patient appropriately for that condition. The patient returns sometime afterward with peritonitis from a ruptured appendix. Without specific X-ray studies, the physician simply lacked sufficient information to diagnose a duodenal ulcer. Had the emergency physician recognized that he did not have enough evidence to reach a conclusion, he might have arranged for the patient to return at a slightly later time, when the infection of the appendix might have evolved to a point where it produced the clinical picture needed in order to make the appropriate interventions before the appendix ruptured.

Does the patient's chart reflect the answers to the questions? Appropriate and thorough charting is necessary not only to protect the emergency physician against malpractice claims but also to provide accurate information for the next physician who must care for the patient. Once the key questions have been answered and acted upon appropriately, the emergency physician can then revert to the more customary medical decision making. Obviously there will be many patients in the urgent and nonemergency categories for whom specific diagnosis and therapy is possible and appropriate. Nevertheless, all emergency department patients must initially be approached as though they represent true emergencies in order to prevent errors or disastrous deteriorations.

The components of good emergency systems

An innovative and important consequence of the increased attention to emergencies has been the realization that care must commence even before the patient reaches the hospital. The impetus for this has been twofold. First, it has been recognized that, while hospital coronary care units have lowered the in-hospital mortality rate for myocardial infarction to a minimal level, many deaths from myocardial infarction occur before the patient ever reaches a hospital. Second, the military medical experiences in World War II, Korea, and Vietnam have taught us that, with aggressive early care, many victims of severe trauma can be saved. Unfortunately, in civilian medical practice there are still numerous deaths that a better system of care could prevent.

The last decade has seen great strides in the development of good emergency systems, as a result of the parallel development of many components that either did not exist previously or simply had never been coordinated. One component, which has received contributions from space technology and computer science, is communications. Many communities have already developed or are in process of achieving a more effective communications network. This involves not only patient access to the system through a special, easily obtainable emergency telephone number (911 in most communities), but also free, easy, and stable access and communication between hospitals, ambulances, and fire and police departments.

A second component is the system of transportation to the place where medical care is provided. While ambulances have existed for many years, the service has been chaotic, disorganized, and diffused among volunteer, public, and private sectors. In many communities the mortician was responsible for running the ambulance service: an unhumorous potential for conflict of interest. There was minimal standardization of equipment as well as a tremendous disparity in levels of medical training for attendants.

Again drawing upon military experience, the medical profession recognized that non-M.D.s could be appropriately trained to cope with on-site emergency stabilizations. The final form of education for paramedics is still being debated, as is the question of which procedures can safely be delegated to them. State legislatures are trying to unravel the problems of introducing paramedics into the physician and nurse licensure programs. Nonetheless, many outstanding programs have been developed in both urban and rural communities, and there is a strong trend toward development of paramedic emergency squads.

The third component is the hospital emergency

department itself. The efforts of ambulance and paramedic squads will be of little avail unless they are supported by competent medical care—which, at best, is provided not only upon the patient's arrival in the emergency department, but also in telemetric communication between the emergency department and the ambulance both at the trauma scene and in transit. Moreover, an integral part of the system is the continuing education of the paramedic by the physicians with whom he or she works, so that the physicians will be willing to assume responsibility for the paramedic's field performances. Not every hospital is capable of handling all levels of emergency; nor can every emergency department afford the staff necessary to run effective telemetry. Starting with the Illinois Trauma Program, there has been an effort to categorize hospitals according to their capacity to receive and treat trauma patients. Most states are working toward developing their own system of classifying hospital trauma centers.

The fourth component is the specialist in emergency medicine. For years emergency departments have been staffed in a variety of predominantly unsatisfactory fashions. Where intern and resident physicians were used, they were generally the most junior in experience and training. Where there was no house staff, either moonlighting residents or enforced rotations of staff physicians were used to staff the emergency department. In the early 1960s

a group of physicians banded together in Alexandria, Va., to give up their inpatient practices and cover the emergency department of their community hospital full time. Subsequently, it became clear that special training and expertise were required to deal with the problems of emergency medicine. In 1970 the University of Cincinnati in Ohio began the first residency program in this field. Since then a number of other community, county, city, and university hospitals have developed training programs in emergency medicine. In 1976 the Board of Emergency Medicine was constituted. Through the energy and commitment of the American College of Emergency Physicians and the University Association for Emergency Medical Services, the physicians in the country interested in emergency medicine joined together to develop the specialty of emergency medicine. A board-certifying examination was created with the goal of processing its first candidates by late 1977. A formal application to the American Medical Association to recognize emergency medicine as an autonomous specialty also was made. It has also become apparent that the practice of good emergency medicine requires specially qualified nurses. The Emergency Department Nurses Association has been active in focusing attention on this group of dedicated and talented nurses and in providing special education for their unique field of practice.

It is obvious that the emergency department sys-

The treatment of life-threatening conditions receives priority from emergency-room personnel.

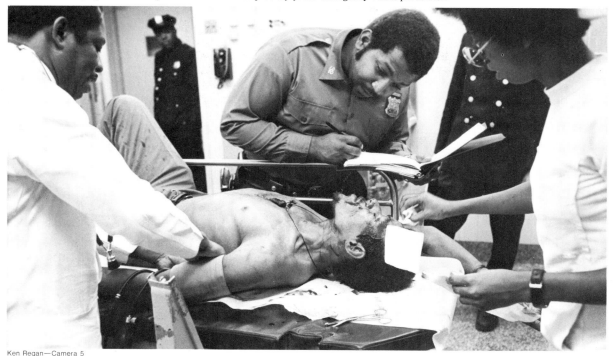

Ken Regan—Camera 5

tem cannot exist in a vacuum but requires the full support of the modern hospital and its specialists. The importance of such support to a well-organized emergency medicine system cannot be underestimated, or even the best efforts of the emergency department will not succeed.

New directions

It is clear that, once organized, a system can respond not only to individual emergency problems but also to the small and large disasters that befall each community. There must be good coordination with the police and fire departments, each of which will have its own disaster responsibilities, and also with public service agencies such as the Red Cross and the news media. While even the most politically divisive communities tend to band together under the stress of a major disaster, there can be no doubt that performance at the time of the disaster is improved by adequate planning and organization beforehand.

In many community hospitals that have no autonomous house staff, there is a tendency for the emergency department physicians to be responsible for the care of in-house emergencies and for critical care units. This seems a logical development, but there are separate critical care training programs and only time will disclose whether this is to be a continuing responsibility of emergency medicine.

The thrust of the past two decades has been to develop an improved system response to emergencies of all levels of severity. The development of this specialty is still undergoing evolution, but already great progress has been made in improving the quality of emergency care that is currently available to the public.

— Peter Rosen, M.D.

Eye Diseases and Visual Disorders

The retinas of the eyes are richly supplied with small arteries, veins, and capillaries that can be observed directly. In addition, the fact that both the retina and the optic nerve form from brain tissue means that certain diseases of the central nervous system may have manifestations that can be observed in the eyes. Finally, since the optic nerves are continuous with the brain and their ends can be seen within the eye, at least a small part of the brain also can be observed directly, without recourse to surgical procedures.

No other area of the human body affords this kind of opportunity. Increasingly sophisticated techniques for photographing the living human eye have taken advantage of this fact and have helped increase understanding not only of eye diseases but also of abnormalities in other parts of the body.

The ophthalmoscope

The instrument that is used to view the interior of a living eye, the ophthalmoscope, was invented by Hermann von Helmholtz in 1851. It aims light into the pupil of the patient's eye and provides an optical path along which the observer can view the illuminated ocular interior. The portion of the eye visible with this procedure is called the fundus.

Ophthalmoscopes have gradually improved over the years. Von Helmholtz's ophthalmoscope had no light source of its own; it merely reflected light into the eye. Subsequent instruments were equipped with electric bulbs. More recent models permit stereoscopic viewing of the fundus, creating a three-dimensional effect. All ophthalmoscopes have certain inherent problems: magnification is limited, constant movement of the patient's eye interferes with scrutiny of the fundus, and a limited number of abnormalities may be visible.

Many of these problems have been solved by photography of the fundus. A "stop-action" ophthalmoscopic picture taken using a stroboscopic light source eliminates the effects of ocular movement. Enlargements of such photographs make it possible to study the eye in detail.

Fluorescein retinal angiography

Building on this technique, H. R. Novotny and D. L. Alvis developed retinal angiography, a means of visualizing the blood vessels in the eye. They discovered that the circulation of the blood within the fundus could be studied in greater detail when they injected fluorescein, a relatively harmless dye, into the bloodstream and photographed the fundus using special light filters.

The principles underlying this technique are simple. The dye is injected into a vein, usually in the arm. It then circulates through the body to the eye. Because the dye is fluorescent, it is possible to take photographs of the blood within the vessels on a nearly black background; this produces excellent contrast and resolution. A blue filter is placed over the light source, causing the fluorescein to glow greenish-yellow. A filter that "sees" only that color is placed in front of the film. Fluorescein retinal angiography is most helpful in evaluating diseases of the blood vessels, in studying abnormalities of the optic disk, and in diagnosing ocular tumors.

Specific uses of fluorescein angiography

Diabetes mellitus is just one disease that causes alterations in the blood vessels of the retina. It produces dilatation of the veins, hemorrhages, new, fragile vessels, microaneurysms (tiny out-pouch-

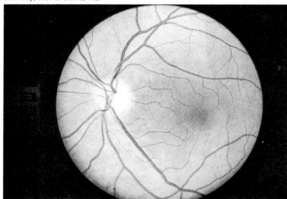

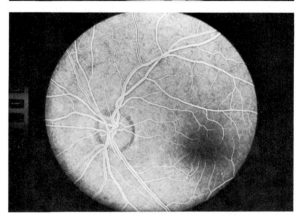

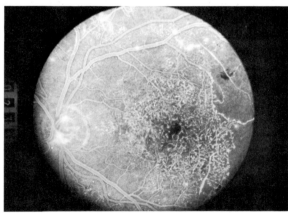

*The retinal veins and arteries radiate from the optic disk,
as seen in the normal optic fundus pictured at the top.
Two fluorescein retinal angiograms contrast a normal eye
(middle) with one in which myriad microaneurysms
are present (bottom).*

ings of the capillaries), and areas in which the capillaries are closed. All these changes can be observed easily using fluorescein angiography. Once the abnormalities have been located precisely, they can be treated by photocoagulation (the condensation of protein material by controlled use of light such as a laser).

Fluorescein angiography permits early recognition of swelling of the optic disks. Such swelling is significant because it usually indicates increased pressure within the cranium, such as results from brain tumors, brain clots, and infections of the central nervous system. It is now possible to distinguish between certain types of blood clots and tumors of the fundus with a high degree of accuracy. In fluorescein angiography, many tumors appear quite bright because they contain a large number of blood vessels; the blood clots, which contain no blood vessels, appear quite dark.

In summary, this technique permits earlier and more accurate diagnosis of a variety of disorders. Early diagnosis in turn allows for early treatment, which frequently increases the chances of successful outcome.

—Joel G. Sacks, M.D.

Family Practice

In October of 1976, for the first time in the United States, physicians originally certified by a medical specialty board were required to take a recertification examination to demonstrate that they had not lost the knowledge evidenced by their first certification and had remained current with medical advances. These physicians were qualified in the new specialty of family practice, officially recognized as a medical specialty in February 1969; it was at this time that a recertification requirement was written. Although the American Board of Family Practice (ABFP) was the first medical specialty to require recertification of its diplomates every six years, most medical specialties have now made some commitment to recertification.

Board certification is a testing procedure developed and administered within the medical profession by physicians who practice a similar type of medicine. Residency training programs are established in teaching hospitals, with approval from a committee of the American Medical Association and the American Board of Medical Specialties, to prepare medical graduates for the in-depth skills required in each specialty. Upon successful completion of the residency training program, a physician is qualified to take the appropriate board examination for certification as a specialist in that field. Physicians who pass the board examination and are so certified are called diplomates of that board; approximately 80% of the physicians taking the board examination in family practice achieve certification.

The ABFP conducts the examinations that measure the competence of physicians practicing family medicine. Five two-day examinations have been given by this board each year since 1970. In

Ted Polumbaum—*Medical World News*

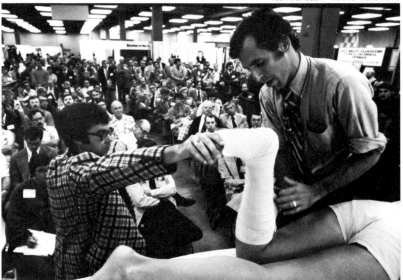

Physicians attending the 28th annual scientific assembly of the American Academy of Family Physicians, held in September 1976, took part in several continuing education programs including this demonstration on the treatment of fractures.

the first year 1,690 family physicians were certified; they were scheduled for recertification in 1976 to retain their status as diplomates of the board. A total of 8,730 diplomates have been certified in family practice since 1970.

To qualify for the recertification examination in family practice, a diplomate must first document completion of 300 hours of acceptable continuing education within the previous six years, hold an unrestricted medical license, and review 20 patient charts in problem areas designated by the board and submit written questionnaires to the board regarding this chart analysis. After these criteria have been met, the diplomate is eligible to take a half-day written examination, which is primarily a test of knowledge of new advances in family practice over the previous ten years. This thorough and somewhat complicated procedure is intended to measure physician competence by techniques that go beyond the limitations of a written examination.

Prior to the establishment of family practice as a specialty in 1969, family medical care was administered by general practitioners with no less than one year, and up to three years, of training after graduation from medical school. Because few training programs were specifically tailored to their needs as practicing family physicians, these individuals were often forced to obtain the skills and knowledge they required through experience and self-designed continuing education programs. The field was lacking in prestige, and the number of general practitioners dwindled rapidly as more and more medical graduates turned to subspecialization. The development of family practice as a specialty allowed the establishment of standards that would ensure adequate training and permit con-

cepts of family medicine to be integrated into the medical curriculum. The number of family physicians on medical school faculties rose rapidly after 1969; the proportion of medical colleges with departments or divisions of family medicine increased from virtually zero to 80% by 1976. Concurrently, a greater number of medical students were attracted to family practice, with the number of graduates entering residency training programs doubling from 8% to 16% from 1970 to 1975. At some medical schools, such as the University of Iowa and the University of Washington, 50% of the student body expressed an interest in family practice in 1975. Similarly, residency training programs specifically designed to teach the principles and concepts of family medicine have been established throughout the country. By February 1976, there were 250 three-year family practice residency programs that had been developed in teaching hospitals, and there were 3,720 residents in training and 1,300 graduate physicians already in practice.

The first specialty board, in ophthalmology, was established in 1916. Currently there are 20 primary specialties (family practice was the twentieth) and more than 50 subspecialties. This trend toward specialization has resulted in a fragmentation of the medical care delivery system and a shortage of primary care physicians, such as family physicians, who accept responsibility for the total medical care of individuals.

Family practice is defined as comprehensive medical care, with particular emphasis on the family unit. The family physician's continuing responsibility for medical care is not limited by the patient's age, sex, or a particular organ system or disease entity. Family practice is a specialty in breadth; it builds upon a core of knowledge derived from other disciplines to establish a cohesive unit that combines the behavioral sciences with traditional biological and clinical sciences. It draws most heavily on internal medicine, pediatrics, obstetrics and gynecology, surgery, and psychiatry. The core of knowledge encompassed by family practice prepares the physician for a unique role — one involving patient management, problem solving, and counseling. The family physician is also a personal physician who coordinates total medical care delivery.

The American Academy of Family Physicians (AAFP), a national association of family doctors founded in 1947, is now the second largest national medical organization, with 37,000 physician members. Until late in 1971, it was known as the American Academy of General Practice. The name was changed to reflect more accurately the evolution of the nature of primary medical care. The AAFP and the ABFP have defined primary care as:

A type of medical care delivery which emphasizes first contact care and assumes ongoing responsibility for the patient in both health maintenance and therapy of illness. It is personal care involving a unique interaction and communication between the patient and the physician. It is comprehensive in scope and includes the overall coordination of the care of the patient's health problems be they biological, behavioral, or social. The appropriate use of consultants and community resources is an important part of effective primary care.

— Robert E. Rakel, M.D.

Health Care Costs

One of the first assaults by the new administration of President Jimmy Carter was mounted against the runaway rate of inflation in the $139.3-billion health care industry. Health care costs had risen 9.5% in 1976 on top of an astonishing 12% hike in 1975 and 9.3% in 1974. Such costs, in fact, had been rising about 50% faster than the Consumer Price Index for goods and services.

In his budget message on Feb. 22, 1977, the president's first major health proposal was a limitation on payments for hospital care, expected to reduce the spending of the Department of Health, Education, and Welfare (HEW) for Medicare and Medicaid by more than $800 million in fiscal 1978. The proposal, which was designed to hold increases in hospital costs to about 10% a year (from a current rate of 15% annually), would apply to all payments for hospital care, not only those costs paid by the government.

HEW Secretary Joseph A. Califano, Jr., called a ceiling on hospital costs "an essential prerequisite to a future national health insurance program," but a national health insurance program did not appear

to be on the immediate agenda. Instead, the administration proposed creation of a new federal agency that would treat hospitals like public utilities, whose charges are subject to official scrutiny. Some 25 states already have rate review commissions, although they differ in their authority to contain or regulate costs.

Hospitals are the biggest target in an anti-inflation war against health care costs because 40% of all health dollars are spent there, making them the largest single expense in the health economy. To combat waste and rising costs, the Social Security Administration (SSA) and several state governments across the country are conducting pilot projects that introduce new ways of paying hospitals for the care they provide.

The common goal is to discourage unnecessary and overlong hospital stays. Existing financial reimbursement formulas provide hospitals with little incentive to hold costs down, since they know that the tab will be picked up by private insurers like Blue Cross or by publicly funded programs like Medicare and Medicaid. As a result, projected increases for these two federal programs alone are staggering. Some government experts predicted an increase in Medicare costs from $25 billion to $30 billion in 1977, while Medicaid costs were expected nearly to double, rising from $11 billion to $21 billion.

In an effort to arrest such increases, the Social Security Administration is funding a $2.4-million experiment in New Jersey with a prospective rate reimbursement system based on paying hospitals a year in advance for the actual kinds of cases they handle. Using computer analysis, the system would establish a hospital's annual case mix — some 383 diagnosis-related groups, ranging from false labor to open-heart surgery — with a cost-of-living adjustment and regional economic factors thrown in, then pay the hospital accordingly in one annual lump sum. The more complicated the cases, the more money a hospital would receive.

Such a system, clearly, would discourage hospitals from keeping patients longer than necessary as a means of increasing revenues. "Just pay them a flat fee for what they do and watch the beds empty out," declared one cynical health official. Multiplied across many hospitals in all the states, such a system could have an enormous impact on hospital bills. For example, health care experts say a one-day reduction in the average length of hospital stays would save nearly $2 billion annually.

Some states, faced with hospital costs they can no longer support, are trying experiments of their own. New York, where waste and inefficiency resulting from the per diem system are blamed for 10% of the state's $7-billion annual hospital bill, began on April 1 to penalize hospitals that keep patients longer than necessary. New York also involved a handful of hospitals in an experiment with diagnosis reimbursement, an approach that is strongly favored by the Social Security Administration, which is helping to finance the effort. "We believe payment by diagnosis will shorten lengths of stays," declared James Caples, chief of the program experimentation branch of SSA's division of health insurance studies. "It probably represents the best single reimbursement method being offered so far."

While all these experiments were going on, however, New York's Governor Hugh Carey struck a devastating blow to the state's hospitals when he began, Apr. 1, 1976, to cut an estimated $360 million out of the state's $3-billion annual Medicaid outlays. It was the first time any state had actually cut back on the amount of Medicaid funds allocated the previous year.

New York and New Jersey are only two of the many states getting tough with hospitals. Connecticut was one of the earliest states to attack the increasing costs of hospital care. After failing in two successive legislatures, a bill to establish a

health cost commission passed in 1973 and is probably one of the toughest and most effective restraints on hospital costs in the nation.

The Connecticut Commission on Hospitals and Health Care (CHHC) is a regulatory body, similar to those overseeing public utilities, which reviews all hospital budgets, approves or denies all rate increases in excess of 2% annually, has veto power over capital expenditures in excess of $25,000, and also has the power to review and grant or deny any additional function or service a health care facility within its jurisdiction may propose. And, in accordance with federal regulations, health facilities proposing capital outlays of $100,000 or more are subject not only to commission approval but also to a public hearing. It is a very effective deterrent.

A report of the commission's 1975 activities reveals that CHHC denied approval of $12 million in capital expenditures out of a total $63 million requested. It rejected $13 million out of a requested $51 million in capital projects for long-term care, and denied $6 million of $25 million in new facilities for the state's 35 hospitals. And the average price increase granted averaged 2.5% to 3% below the national average in both 1974 and 1975.

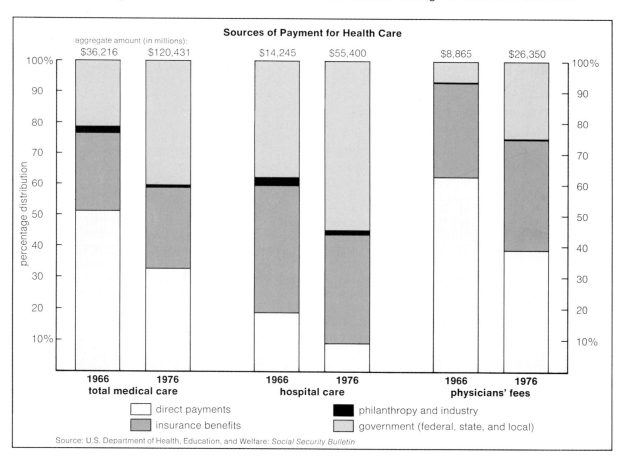

© Leo Cullum

"Why do you think they call it group insurance?"

Some form of state auditing and veto power in hospital rates and expenditures also exists in Maryland, Pennsylvania, New York, and New Jersey and is being seriously considered in several other states. Most states, however, awaited the fate of the reimbursement reforms of a bill proposed by Sen. Herman Talmadge (D, Ga.) for Medicaid and Medicare. The Talmadge reforms embody a carrot-and-stick approach that would reward efficient health care providers and exact financial penalties from inefficient ones.

Health insurance officials generally applaud the Talmadge approach, but they would like to see the same formulas applied to the private sector as well. Unless that is done, insurers fear the private sector might be forced to pick up the tab for the real or imagined shortfall in reimbursements under the federal formula.

Private health insurance, clearly, figures importantly in the nation's health care delivery system. According to the Health Insurance Institute, there were in 1976 an estimated 183 million people in the United States with some form of private health insurance, nearly 5 million more than in the previous year. Employers pay for a substantial share of this coverage. Half of the workers now covered under group medical plans have their premiums paid in full by employers, according to the Health Insurance Institute. Fewer than one in 100 pays the entire cost of his health insurance.

This means that the rapidly rising costs of health care and, subsequently, of health insurance, weigh heavily on the nation's employers and are passed along, inevitably, to consumers of that employer's

goods or services. In a rather extreme example, General Motors says its Blue Cross-Blue Shield program has now become its single largest "supplier"—surpassing U.S. Steel. By the end of 1977, GM predicted, the outlay per worker would reach $144 per month.

As measured by the Consumer Price Index, the cost of all medical care items went up 9.5% in 1976 on top of a 12% hike in 1975. Physicians' fees mirrored the tremendous increases in medical malpractice insurance premiums, as well as the normal pressures of inflation, and shot up more than 11%. And room rates for semiprivate hospital accommodations rose most of all, climbing nearly 14% over the 1975 level which, in turn, had posted a shocking 17% hike over the previous year.

Not all components of the medical care index registered such dramatic increases. Dentists' fees, prescription and over-the-counter drug costs, and the price of optometric examinations and eyeglasses rose only around 6%, in line with the national inflation rate for all consumer products during 1976. Dentists' fees, however, may be the next candidate for sharp inflation. Dentists, too, are suddenly being hit with huge increases in professional liability insurance premiums, as more and more dissatisfied patients take their toothaches to the courts.

With the public spotlight focused on them, and the threat of legislative crackdown imminent, all elements of the nation's health care delivery system are taking steps to improve the system and to arrest the serious rate of inflation in what they provide. Health insurers have invested millions of dollars in health maintenance organizations and ambulatory care facilities designed to keep more people out of hospital beds. Hospitals and doctors have embarked on vigorous programs of preventive medicine to keep patients healthy as well as to educate and alert staff members to reduce the risk of incurring malpractice claims. More and more hospitals are joining forces to share the most costly facilities, such as intensive care units, open-heart surgery units, and burn treatment centers, as well as expensive equipment like computerized tomographic scanners that can cost half a million dollars each. It is in these nonlabor areas that most hospitals have experienced their steepest cost increases in recent years.

Beyond their efforts, however, lies the increasing possibility of a federal takeover of the health care delivery system. A concerted effort by industry and labor to control medical costs is needed to avert such a takeover, which would, in the words of the President's Council on Wage and Price Stability, "result in national expenditures of truly astronomical proportions." Government, says the report of

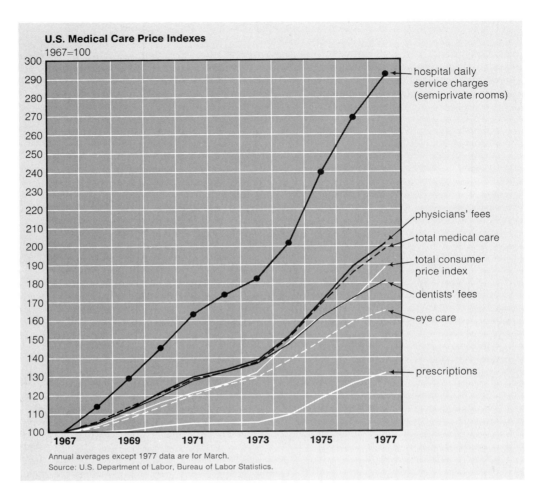

U.S. Medical Care Price Indexes

1967=100

- hospital daily service charges (semiprivate rooms)
- physicians' fees
- total medical care
- total consumer price index
- dentists' fees
- eye care
- prescriptions

1967 1969 1971 1973 1975 1977

Annual averages except 1977 data are for March.
Source: U.S. Department of Labor, Bureau of Labor Statistics.

the council, has a poor record of controlling costs. "The blizzard of rules and regulations that would accompany full federal financing and administration of the health industry would add to costs and reduce the limited incentives that now exist for efficiency and cost containment," the council said.

The report pointed to company programs that encourage employees to obtain a second medical opinion before undergoing elective surgery. Some corporations have set up in-house medical facilities because they have learned that this is a less expensive way of providing their employees with health care, says the council. In other localities, corporations and unions have become involved with hospital boards and areawide planning bodies to eliminate duplication of facilities and to introduce cost-saving efficiencies.

Meanwhile, the American Medical Association (AMA) succeeded in getting four lawmakers to introduce into the 95th Congress the AMA's own version of a national health insurance bill. Not surprisingly, the AMA plan would build on the structure of the present system.

"The bill we are introducing today would solve the problem of financing for every American," declared Senator Clifford P. Hansen (R, Wyo.), who sponsored the bill in the Senate. "It would build on our present system, rather than dismantling it and replacing it from scratch with a giant bureaucracy. It would allow everyone to choose his or her own physician, dentist, and health insurance plan, and it would be a plan we can afford." Government, of course, would provide the insurance for those unable to pay for it themselves.

Few legislators, however, gave the AMA bill much chance of passage, or even serious consideration, in the 95th Congress. Certainly, it has been weighed against the Carter Administration's own national health insurance proposal, which HEW Secretary Califano said could not yet be submitted to Congress. Speedy passage, however, is expected for measures aimed at tightening fraud provisions in the Medicare and Medicaid programs. Those, alone, should make a significant dent in the nation's health care bill.

—Resa W. King

232

Special Report:

Outpatient Health Care

by Morris F. Collen, M.D.

Medical care is now the largest "industry" in the United States, accounting for approximately 8% of the gross national product. Medical services consist of (a) outpatient, or ambulatory, medical care or medical services provided to persons who come to a physician's office or to the outpatient clinic of a medical facility; (b) inpatient medical care, or medical services provided to patients confined to hospitals or convalescent and nursing homes; and (c) home care, or medical services provided to patients confined to their place of residence. About 40% of the total expenditure for health care in the U.S. is for hospital stays and hospital services. By expanding the role of outpatient care, both public and private health care expenditures can be dramatically reduced.

Outpatient medical care encompasses both health care and sick care. Health care, or health maintenance, includes general checkups and health counseling for those who are well. Medical care, or sick care, includes preventive measures and diagnosis, treatment, and rehabilitation of the sick. Primary care is usually the concern of generalists, general practitioners, or family practice physicians who serve as a first medical contact for patients and give continuing care at the medical office. Secondary care involves consultation and specialized services, which are provided by a specialist or a medical center when technical or expensive specialized equipment is necessary for diagnosis or treatment.

Current status

It can be assumed that the average person will successfully overcome about three-fourths of his medical problems without any professional medical help. The typical man or woman in the U.S. will probably see a doctor about 100 times in his or her lifetime and, on the average, will require only five hospitalizations.

Individuals may seek outpatient care either for general health examinations or for treatment of symptoms that point to the possibility of disease (*e.g.,* fatigue, nervousness, dizziness, and abdominal, chest, muscle, or joint pain), or of some more specific condition such as an injury or a skin rash.

Most people treat themselves and seek care from physicians only when they are no longer able to cope with the problem or fear that it may become chronic or disabling.

Medical practice was at one time oriented toward care of the critically sick, and many patients seen by doctors suffered from heart disease, cancer, or stroke. Medical care was a luxury and, in contrast to the broad scope of today's public preventive care, was limited mostly to immunizations, prenatal care for pregnant women, and first-year care for infants. About 90% of the U.S. population now has some form of health insurance that pays some or all of the cost of outpatient care. Medical examinations and health maintenance are not at present typically included as benefits, however, and are usually paid for on a fee-for-service basis. In the past few years the public has begun to demand its "right" to medical care, and as a consequence, insurance plans are beginning to include medical checkups. In 1973 the U.S. Congress passed a Health Maintenance Organization (HMO) Act to encourage outpatient health care and personal preventive medical services. The act was amended in

Because of the shortage of primary care physicians and the rising costs of all medical care, nurse practitioners and physician's assistants are increasingly assuming the responsibility for providing primary patient care.

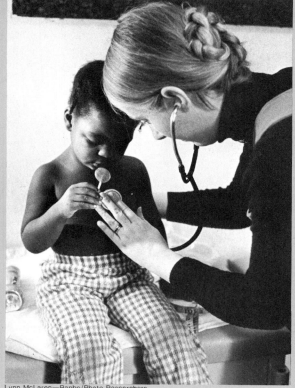

Lynn McLaren—Rapho/Photo Researchers

1976, as the concept of the HMO was reexamined and refined.

Problems in providing care

The majority of outpatients have stress symptoms that develop because the patient is unable to adjust to or cope with home, work, or social problems. Stress symptoms may generate psychosomatic illnesses that are usually difficult to treat. Many patients do not benefit from physicians' services and often seek help from such health professionals as psychologists, health counselors, or health educators. Lack of appropriate and accessible outpatient care has become a problem in the U.S. because of the insufficient number of health professionals trained to provide primary care. Most physicians are specialists, and among those who are generalists only a minority are qualified to provide primary health care.

Recent reports from mainland China suggest that the so-called barefoot doctors—native villagers who have received short training courses in medicine—have been able to fulfill primary care needs. In recent years in the U.S., new categories of health professionals have been created in an attempt to increase the number of persons trained to meet primary care needs. These include nurse practitioners, physicians' assistants, allied health personnel, paramedics, physician extenders, physician expanders, physician surrogates, and "Medex" (former army medical corpsmen).

The function of facilities called neighborhood health centers is to provide outpatient care for the community. A serious problem in providing such care is the increasing expense, due primarily to inflationary increases in physicians' fees and personnel services, the use of computerized X-rays and automated laboratory tests, and the prescription of expensive drugs.

Trends

Physician surrogates. In order to meet the increasing demands for outpatient care, more physicians will have to be trained in primary rather than specialty care, and the number of nonphysician professionals will have to increase. Neighborhood health centers have been developing "teams" or "modules" to meet primary care needs. These teams include physicians, nurses, nurse practitioners, health counselors, psychologists, social workers, and nutritionists—each of whom may see the patient and contribute to alleviating his problems.

Outpatient care protocols. The combination of too few physicians practicing primary care and increasing medical care costs has meant that physician's assistants and nurse practitioners must assume more responsibility for outpatient care services.

Nurse practitioners, for example, have expanded their primary care responsibilities to include medical examinations of adults, maternity care, treatment of such simple, acute conditions as colds and diarrhea, and continuing care for certain chronic conditions including high blood pressure, diabetes, backache, and arthritis.

In order to assure quality care by nurse practitioners and other physician substitutes, the supervising physician often prepares an extensive protocol that lists in detail the steps that are necessary for the proper care of each condition. The protocol also indicates the questions to be asked of the patient, examinations to be given, tests to be ordered, data to be collected, actions to be taken, and circumstances that indicate that the patient should see a physician. Careful studies have shown that patients managed by physician substitutes frequently receive care comparable in quality to that given physician-managed patients.

Outpatient care systems. With the emergence of regional health care planning at both the national and state level within the U.S., systems approaches to outpatient care are being developed. Neighborhood health centers staffed by one or two dozen health professionals have been established for the provision of primary care. They generally function as satellites to a large central medical facility that may contain a hospital and clinic. Within this arrangement both primary and secondary care are available.

Large outpatient centers, especially those affiliated with an HMO, can provide periodic health evaluations for individuals in the community by means of multiphasic health checkups. Multiphasic checkups make possible a comprehensive health examination in about two or three hours at a cost considerably below that incurred when a physician arranges for such tests. The term *multiphasic* refers to multiple tests completed at one location. The examination usually includes a medical history; measurements of height, weight, and blood pressure; X-rays of the chest and, in women, perhaps of the breasts; an electrocardiogram; tests for visual and hearing acuity; and analyses of blood and urine specimens. All of the test results are printed by computer and mailed to the patient's physician, who reviews them and arranges for any necessary follow-up care.

Such outpatient centers will, in the near future, store their medical records in a computer, so that health professionals will have a continuing record of each patient's medical problems, examination results, and treatments. This information will in turn help the health care team provide a more individualized approach and greater continuity of care throughout the patient's lifetime.

234

Health Care Law

Commenting on the American hospital, particularly the nonprofit community hospital, the United States Supreme Court in 1976 described changes that had taken place in the institution over the previous three decades. In its decision in *Abbott Laboratories* v. *Portland Retail Druggists Association,* the court said:

The [last few] decades have seen the hospital assume a larger community character. Some hospitals, indeed, truly have become centers for the "delivery" of health care. The nonprofit hospital no longer is a receiving facility only for the bedridden, the surgical patient, and the critical emergency. It has become a place where the community is readily inclined to turn, and—because of increasing costs, physician specialization, shortage of general practitioners, and other factors—is often compelled to turn, whenever a medical problem of import presents itself. The emergency room has become a facility for all who need it and it no longer is restricted to cases previously authorized by members of the staff. And patients that not long ago required bed care are often now treated on an ambulatory and outpatient basis.

During 1976 the New Jersey Supreme Court in its decision in *Doe* v. *Bridgeton Hospital Association, Inc.,* offered a similar view of the present nature and function of hospitals. The court noted that hospitals are nonprofit corporations organized to serve the public by operating medical facilities and that they receive substantial federal and local financial support as well as tax exemptions. The court noted that the facilities of hospitals are available to the public and concluded that the public, therefore, has an interest in hospitals, which are subject to control for the common good.

As quasi-public institutions, their actions must not contravene the public interest. They must serve the public without discrimination. Their boards of directors or trustees are managing quasi-public trusts and each has a fiduciary relationship with the public.

The court justified its jurisdiction over hospitals on the grounds that, like other institutions affecting the public interest, hospitals are subject to legislative control. Both judicial review and legislative control rest on recognition of "the quasi-public status of the hospital and its obligation to serve the public."

Such judicial statements outline some of the social, cultural, and political changes that the American hospital has undergone. Generally, these changes have taken place since the end of World War II. Most of them, however, have resulted from legislation passed since 1965, beginning with the Medicare and Medicaid programs and continuing with such recent laws as the National Health Planning and Resources Development Act, which requires hospitals to win approval of most expansion and remodeling plans from outside agencies. The injection of large sums of public money into the hospital economy has altered the system in an irrevocable way.

It is not surprising that the courts should offer such comprehensive views of the role of the hospital. While legislation has been defining what the hospital is responsible for in the community, the courts have been spelling out the ways in which the hospital, especially its governing board, is responsible for performing its task. The beginning of legislative and judicial involvement in hospital affairs can be traced to 1965, the year of Medicare and Medicaid's enactment, and of the Illinois Supreme Court's decision in *Darling* v. *Charleston Community Memorial Hospital.*

Legal decisions of the past decade have significantly altered traditional ideas about the role and liability of the American hospital. No longer simply a place where autonomous specialists provide services, the hospital is now judged to be responsible for all aspects of the care and treatment received by its patients.

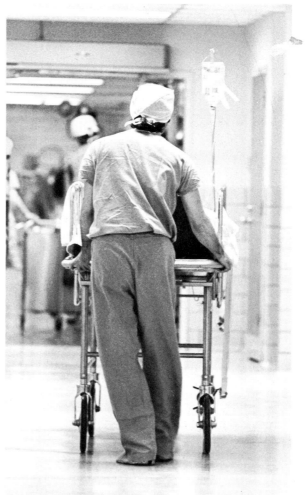

Michael D. Sullivan

The Illinois case involved a high school athlete who came to the hospital's emergency room with a broken leg suffered in a football game. The doctor on duty, not an employee of the hospital but a member of the medical staff, set the leg and applied a cast. It turned out that the cast was too tight, the leg was damaged by the treatment, and eventually amputation was necessary. The boy's father sued not only the doctor, who settled before trial, but also the hospital. He charged that the nurses on the case did not perform as they should have, particularly by failing to check for possible onset of gangrene, and that the hospital did not require consultation with specialists. Lower courts upheld the charges and awarded a large sum of money to the plaintiffs.

The hospital's defense, the Illinois Supreme Court noted, was that it should not be held responsible for the acts of physicians or for nurses who are acting on physicians' orders. Quoting another decision, the court rejected the argument.

The conception that the hospital does not undertake to treat the patient, does not undertake to act through its doctors and nurses, but undertakes instead simply to procure them to act upon their own responsibility, no longer reflects the fact. Present-day hospitals, as their manner of operation plainly demonstrates, do far more than furnish facilities for treatment. They regularly employ on a salary basis a large staff of physicians, nurses and interns, as well as administrative and manual workers, and they charge patients for medical care and treatment, collecting for such services, if necessary, by legal action. Certainly, the person who avails himself of "hospital facilities" expects that the hospital will attempt to cure him, not that its nurses or other employees will act on their own responsibility.

The court further argued that standards for hospital accreditation, state licensing regulations, and hospitals' own bylaws show that the medical profession and other authorities regard it as both desirable and feasible that a hospital assume responsibility for the care of its patients.

The meaning and significance of *Darling* were expanded by the Nevada Supreme Court in a similar decision. Following the reasoning of the Illinois ruling, the Nevada justices said that hospitals and their governing boards may be held liable for injuries resulting from poor supervision of their medical staffs. The Nevada court placed the burden of responsibility directly on the governing board, changing the hospital trustee's chair from a largely honorary position to a hot seat.

In the years since the *Darling* decision, courts in various states have extended and refined the basic judgment of the Illinois court. The concept that the hospital is responsible for the care rendered within its walls has been used in many decisions: to uphold a hospital's right to deny or rescind membership on its medical staff (*Moore* v. *Board of Trustees of Carson-Tahoe Hospital*); to give access to certain hospital records to patients who are trying to prove negligence on the part of the hospital (*Tucson Medical Center* v. *Misevch*); and to specify the supervisory responsibilities of medical staff committees in ensuring the competence of medical staff members (*Purcell & Tucson General Hospital* v. *Zimbelman*).

Perhaps the best summary of what *Darling* and its progeny have wrought is a list that was part of the Arizona Supreme Court's decision in *Tucson Medical Center* v. *Misevch.*

1. Hospitals have been given and have accepted the duty of supervising the competence of the doctors on their staffs. (*Purcell* v. *Zimbelman*)

2. The concept of corporate responsibility for the quality of medical care was clearly enunciated in *Darling* v. *Charleston Community Memorial Hospital,* when that court held that hospitals and their governing bodies may be held liable for injuries resulting from negligent supervision of members of their medical staffs. (*Moore* v. *Board of Trustees of Carson-Tahoe Hospital*)

3. The hospital has assumed certain responsibilities for the care of its patients and it must meet the standards of responsibility commensurate with this trust. (*Beeck* v. *Tucson General Hospital*)

4. If the medical staff was negligent in the exercise of its duty of supervising its members or in failing to recommend action by the hospital's governing body prior to the case in issue, then the hospital would be negligent. (*Purcell* v. *Zimbelman*)

5. When the hospital's alleged negligence is predicated on an omission to act, the hospital will not be held responsible unless it had reason to know that it should have acted within its duty to the patient to see to it that only professionally competent persons were on its staff. (*Purcell* v. *Zimbelman*)

6. Therefore, its knowledge, actual or constructive, is an essential factor in determining whether or not the hospital exercised reasonable care or was guilty of negligence. (*Purcell* v. *Zimbelman*)

In the remarkably short time of a dozen years, the courts have expressed the changing character of American hospitals and have, by their decisions, assigned the responsibility for those changes to those who work in and manage the institutions. Because judicially made changes in our society are usually evolutionary, it should be expected that assignment of responsibility and liability to hospitals by the courts will continue. (*See also* Emergency Medicine.)

*—John F. Horty, B.A., L.L.B, and
Ted Isaacman, M.S.*

Special Report:
The Laetrile Controversy

by Nancy Ethiel

How far should a government go in protecting its citizens against themselves? This is the issue at the heart of the controversy over laetrile, the name given to the chemical amygdalin by Ernst T. Krebs, Jr., the California biochemist who first turned the apricot pit extract into an injectable form in 1952. According to Krebs, the name derives from the fact that laetrile is laevorotatory (left-handed) to polarized light and because amygdalin is, chemically, a mandelonitrile. Krebs, one of the earliest promoters of laetrile, built on the work of his father, a California physician who administered an oral form of the apricot pit extract to cancer patients in the 1920s. The substance was highly toxic, however, and not until the son developed the less toxic injectable form did laetrile really begin its checkered career as a cancer cure.

The proponents of laetrile make various claims—that it can cure cancer, prevent cancer, or alleviate pain and produce a sense of well-being in terminal cancer patients—all without harm to the body. Opponents argue that there is no clinical evidence to support any of these claims and that, in fact, the chemical, which contains cyanide, may be toxic, particularly when taken orally.

The original theory behind the use of laetrile as a cancer-destroying agent rested on the premise that amygdalin, a naturally occurring chemical first isolated from bitter almonds by French chemists in 1830, can be split by an enzyme called beta-glycosidase into two substances: benzaldehyde (a mild anesthetic) and cyanide. The theory held that normal tissues contain large amounts of rhodenase, an enzyme that converts amygdalin into thiocyanate, a less toxic substance, thus rendering laetrile harmless to normal cells. Cancerous tissues, on the other hand, according to this theory, are rich in beta-glycosidase and, therefore, are destroyed by the large amounts of cyanide released by that enzyme's interaction with laetrile.

In 1953 the Cancer Commission of the California Medical Association investigated the use of laetrile in humans and in animals and declared it ineffective against cancer. Laetrile was first tested by the National Cancer Institute in 1957 and reevaluated on several subsequent occasions. None of the tests produced any evidence that laetrile has any effect on cancer. Only one study, conducted in the early 1970s at the Sloan-Kettering Institute for Cancer Research in New York City by Kanematsu Sugiura, has ever indicated that laetrile might have any efficacy against cancer. The results showed that only 17% of the test mice (of a variety that develop spontaneous mammary tumors) that were treated with laetrile developed lung metastases, in comparison with the control group in which 78% did. Subsequent repetitions of this test at Catholic Medical Center of Brooklyn and Queens and at Sloan-Kettering failed to produce the same or similar results. In fact, in some of the tests the animals receiving laetrile fared worse than those that did not. In 1977, Lewis Thomas, president of the Memorial Sloan-Kettering Cancer Center, stated, "Our conclusion is that laetrile is biologically inert—that it has no effect one way or another on cancer."

Available evidence from various experiments has shown no pronounced difference between the amount of rhodenase in comparable normal and cancerous tissue. In addition, only traces of beta-glycosidase show up in animal tissues, with even less appearing in experimental tumors. These two facts are in exact opposition to the original theoretical basis put forward by the chemical's proponents for laetrile's efficacy against cancer. Recent experiments by Harold Manner, chairman of the department of biology at Loyola University in Chicago and a strong proponent of laetrile, have also failed to show any statistically significant differences between the amounts of beta-glycosidase and rhodenase present in cancerous tissues and those in noncancerous tissues.

In 1963 an application made by laetrile's backers to the Food and Drug Administration (FDA) under the investigational provisions of the food, drug, and cosmetic act was reviewed and denied by an outside committee of cancer experts for lack of scientific proof of the drug's claims. Shortly after, Krebs renamed laetrile vitamin B_{17} and altered his original theory to hold that cancer is caused by a deficiency of the vitamin in the body. This theory is based on the idea that in the past cancers did not occur in animals and humans because they ingested plants in which amygdalin occurs naturally. The theory postulates that because of changes in our diet, especially the lack of vegetables and fruits and the introduction of synthetic substances, cancers

Ted Lau

(Bottom and right) Lester Sloan—*Newsweek*

A quarter century after its development, the unproven anticancer drug laetrile, an extract of apricot pits (left, below), has triggered a heated controversy, sharply dividing detractors and proponents—many of whom once traveled to Mexico where laetrile's manufacture (right) and injection were legal—over the drug's efficacy and the government's right to ban it.

have appeared and are increasing. Krebs now holds that the addition of laetrile to the diet can prevent cancer from occurring at all.

This claim was refuted by David M. Greenberg, a prominent California biochemist and cancer researcher and consultant, in the *Western Journal of Medicine* (122: 345–348). Greenberg pointed out that no evidence has ever been presented to prove that laetrile is a necessary nutritional compound (the definition of a vitamin). Several generations of experimental animals have been kept in good health on a synthetic diet free of laetrile, indicating that the lack of laetrile does not result in disease.

It also appears that, because there is so little beta-glycosidase in body tissues, injected laetrile is probably not broken down but is excreted more or less intact in the urine. Orally ingested laetrile, however, is broken down by the beta-glycosidase in the digestive tract, releasing cyanide into the body. This breakdown accounts for the fact that amygdalin taken orally is far more poisonous than when it is injected. And, in fact, there have been several reported cases of poisonings or near poisonings of persons who have ingested large amounts of amygdalin.

Despite the lack of proof of laetrile's efficacy as

a cancer cure and despite its potential toxicity, the chemical's proponents have engaged in a lengthy, well-publicized battle to legalize the substance. Laetrile's backing comes from numerous sources: cancer victims and their families who believe laetrile works; manufacturers of laetrile such as the McNaughton Foundation, the world's largest producer of the substance; a former Mexican army pathologist, Ernesto Contreras, whose Clinica del Mar was one of the primary sources of laetrile treatment for American patients; the John Birch Society, which rallied to the defense of one of its members, physician John Anton Richardson, who was arrested in California in 1972 for using laetrile on his patients, and which has since formed freedom-of-choice committees across the country. On the other side of the controversy is the "establishment," the FDA, the American Medical Association, the American Cancer Society, and other bastions of organized medicine and research.

One result of the controversy is that bills have been introduced in the legislatures of more than two dozen states to legalize laetrile. In twelve states—Alaska, Arizona, Delaware, Florida, Indiana, Louisiana, Nevada, New Hampshire, Oklahoma, Oregon, Texas, and Washington state—the legislation has been enacted into law. In five states—North Dakota, South Dakota, Hawaii, Maryland, and Illinois—the bills were rejected. The bills to legalize laetrile are not identical, but deal with the same issue. Because laetrile is an illegal drug under federal regulations, it cannot be transported across state lines. Therefore, laetrile will have to be manufactured within the boundaries of any state that has legalized its use. According to the FDA, this means that everything from the apricots themselves to the bottles in which the final product is sold must be produced within the state. Since there are manufacturing facilities for laetrile in only a few states—and some plants have been closed by federal court order—the new laws may be of little help to those who want to use laetrile.

However, the FDA is now in the process of reexamining its stand on laetrile. In 1975 Glen L. Rutherford, a cancer patient using laetrile, brought suit against the federal government asking that he be allowed to obtain and use laetrile legally. A federal judge, Luther Bohanon, approved his plea and ordered that he and any other cancer patient for whom no other treatment could be shown to be effective be allowed, on the recommendation of a physician, to obtain and use laetrile legally. The case was appealed, but a panel of judges upheld Bohanon's original order until the FDA could compile and present an administrative record to prove their contention that laetrile is a new drug and that it is neither safe nor effective—the standards by which the FDA decides whether or not a drug can be marketed.

One result of this court action is that cancer patients across the nation have added their names to Rutherford's petition and are now able to obtain and use laetrile legally. Another result is that the FDA held public hearings in Kansas City, Mo., in May 1977, inviting oral and written testimony from all interested parties. Over 40 persons gave oral testimony and over 12,000 pages of written testimony were accepted. The FDA was evaluating the testimony, but postponed further action. In the meantime, the Mexican ministry of health withdrew its permits for the manufacture of laetrile and ordered that criminal charges be lodged against anyone found manufacturing, distributing, or dispensing the drug. The ministry of health took the action after tests conducted in Mexico showed laetrile to be ineffective against cancer. This action will dry up one of the major sources of laetrile to the United States.

The battle over laetrile will no doubt continue to rage for a long time to come, and the issues that it raises will not go away quietly. The case of Karen Ann Quinlan has forced us to examine whether society has a responsibility to keep a body alive when there is little or no chance that the person to whom the body belongs will ever exist again. Our struggle over the legalization of marijuana has made us consider how much right we have to determine the quality and conduct of our own lives. The FDA's proposal to ban saccharin raised the same questions. May we choose our own lives? Our own deaths? If we choose to smoke cigarettes, containing a known carcinogen, should we be stopped? If we have cancer and choose to take laetrile, why may we not?

The FDA has a mandate, the Kefauver-Harris Act passed in response to the thalidomide tragedy, not to allow any drug in the marketplace unless it can be proved to be safe, effective, pure, and wholesome. The FDA must act in accordance with this mandate. But the question arises, should the FDA have such a mandate at all? If a woman who has breast cancer chooses laetrile rather than chemotherapy or surgery and later dies of cancer, who is the victim other than herself? Ought the government do any more than inform her as fully as possible about the substance she is taking? Must we not all, in the end, take responsibility for our own lives? Is it the role of government to protect us against our own ignorance? As individuals and as a society we must monitor constantly the balance between individual liberty and the well-being of society as a whole. Laetrile itself may be worthless, but the principles it forces us to examine are among the most valuable we possess.

Health Care Technology

One of the primary problems of health care professionals in the past decade has been the development of ways to deliver medical services to a growing patient population while keeping the costs of such services to a minimum. The application of electronic communications media to transmit medical data, combined with the use of computers to store and retrieve the information, is one innovation that promises a solution to both aspects of the problem.

One way to improve health care delivery is to harness the potential of telecommunications as a substitute for face-to-face treatment. The telephone is, of course, already extensively used. Technologically, we have progressed to another stage that includes both audio and video information. A combination of equipment—home television, satellites, and computers—now makes it possible for medical workers to hear and see patients who may be hundreds or thousands of miles away. The use of two-way telecommunications to make health information, skills, and services available to people to meet their health needs is called *telehealth*. Telehealth systems have already been subject to limited trial, and results thus far indicate that these systems can, in the near future, provide connections from every home television to health care facilities.

Scope of telehealth

A telehealth system has three main components: people, services, and equipment. Systems can take many forms. In all cases, however, the human component includes physicians, nurses, dentists, pharmacists, and other medical professionals as well as patients needing services.

There are at least three types of services that may be provided by a telehealth system: health educa-

tion and training, consultation, and administration and management of medical facilities.

For the health professional, educational programs maintain and increase the level of proficiency. For the patient, these programs provide the knowledge to make informed decisions about health questions or problems and to choose appropriate professional help. Videotaped and printed information on health promotion, self-care and self-help methods, and skills needed to cope with common illnesses, injuries, and emergencies are included. Education and training will in the future probably become the single most important telehealth service.

Telehealth consultation includes a wide range of services: primary care provided by a doctor or a nurse, hospital care from a specialist, speech therapy, social services, X-ray reviews, psychiatric services, and so on. All of these services can be provided from a remote location. For all consultations, with the exception of situations in which direct contact is required—surgery, blood tests, or measurement of vital signs, for example—telehealth services can substitute for traditional face-to-face treatment. Even in those situations where direct contact must be made, intermediaries such as physician's assistants or patients themselves, using standard clinical procedures and computer-based calculations, can carry out most treatments.

Telehealth can also be used to administer and manage medical facilities. A telehealth system can be used to hold meetings, provide status reviews, conduct discussions, and give reports to people at different locations. Difficult schedules and transportation arrangements need not be a problem when all that is required to carry on the day-to-day business of administering health services is an audio or video transmission. Facsimile transmission machines, computerized health records, and electronic measuring devices such as electrocardio-

A two-way telecommunications link-up allows a physician at New York City's Mount Sinai Medical Center to consult with workers at a pediatric clinic a mile and a half away.

graphs can be used to record and transmit vital information from one location to another.

Health communications equipment includes everything from the common telephone to two-way television systems that allow doctor and patient to hear, see, and make inquiries using a terminal keyboard similar to a typewriter. Included in the system are standard telephone equipment, coaxial and fiber-optic cables, and tower and satellite microwave transmission equipment. The specific equipment needed in any individual telehealth system depends on the distances involved, the terrain, and the needs of the people to be served.

History of telehealth

We have been moving towards telehealth systems since the 19th century. The process began when health agencies first used the telegraph. Since the 1930s telephone calls for appointments, consultations, and transmission of data have become commonplace. The telephone is being used today to screen patients and provide services before the patients arrive at a health facility.

The first attempt at full-fledged telehealth services began with the use of two-way video communications in Nebraska in 1959. The system was used primarily by psychiatrists working at the University of Nebraska Medical Center in Omaha who were linked with out-of-state mental hospitals. Gradually, projects involving other medical specialties were initiated across the country. Experiments were conducted in radiology, surgery, pediatrics, dermatology, and emergency and general medicine. Only medical services were offered although other services were explored. The video technology was integrated into traditional health care delivery practices. Little attempt was made to restructure the organizational and administrative patterns of health care in order to take full advantage of the new system.

During the 1970s experiments with two-way video have become less medically oriented. They have taken a more holistic view of health care and have included the use of telecommunications in speech therapy, nutrition, nursing, social services, education and training, and health management and administration.

For the most part telehealth is still a concept. One exception is a system recently implemented in Playas, New Mexico. The Playas Telehealth System includes a clinic in the town of Playas and a group practice in the town of Silver City, over 50 miles away. Playas, with a population of 800, is the home of employees of the Phelps Dodge Corporation's nearby smelter plant. Health services are provided through a clinic by a team that includes a nurse practitioner and a physician's assistant. Support is provided from Silver City, where a multispecialty group practice is located. Today this system is responding to the daily health needs of an industrial corporation's rural employees and their families. It offers an operational blueprint for the future.

Scenario for the future

The telehealth system of the future will extend into the living room and every other location that has a television set. Each home and building in the community will be wired for video communications by means of either cable or microwave transmission. To determine the availability and location of local health providers and facilities, an individual who is new to the community may "talk" to a health services directory by using a home interactive television system with an attached keyboard terminal. Once the most convenient and appropriate medical service is selected, the person makes an appointment by choosing from the available times displayed on the television screen and transmitting the choice to a centralized computer.

At this point the patient is given an option. If he

desires, most of the prescreening (which includes general patient data, medical history, the reason for the visit, and the symptoms) can be completed at home. A combination of logically developed, computer-generated questions are displayed on the television screen; these questions and the patient's responses create a medical record, which is stored in the computer. This record will be on line for use at the health facility at the time of the appointment.

The information gathered during the prescreening will determine the type of treatment to be implemented when the patient arrives at the health facility. The entire examination can be handled by a nonphysician, a physician, or by both. In either situation, especially when the examination is conducted by a nonphysician, computer-generated diagnostic routines aid and guide the procedure. Again, the collected data is immediately made a part of the patient's record.

At the clinic, the patient also has access to a computer-based console to be used for health education. The console can be used before the appointment, during waiting periods, or at the end of the visit. It is also used for staff training. The console is in essence an interactive television system that provides a far-ranging health education program. Included are programs on health promotion, prevention of illness and injury, emergency information, commonly asked questions, and other programs. The service is also available through the patient's home television set, which is connected to the information system.

If after the visit the patient needs further treatment but cannot be transported to the health facility, help is dispatched to the home. A nonphysician health worker, equipped with a miniature television camera, makes the house call. Unless the illness is serious, the patient can be treated at home. The patient's medical record is immediately available by means of his television screen. With the use of a special code to protect confidentiality, the television signs can be tied into the clinic's computer-based record system. Consultation with specialists at other locations is also possible. If a visual examination is necessary, the television camera can transmit live video data from the patient's home to the clinic or hospital.

Telehealth projections

The increasing demands of consumers and the growing supply of nonphysician medical workers will require that more emphasis be placed on health education. In addition, improvements in education and training, coupled with more efficient use of medical facilities and medical workers, will provide a more favorable setting for the development of telehealth systems. Such systems should in turn improve health services further by increasing the effectiveness of training programs and promoting even more efficient use of medical facilities.

Today the implementation of telehealth systems is limited not by technology but by lack of education on the part of those using the systems. The capacity of today's technology far outstrips the understanding of its operational capability. The task ahead is to better understand how to plan and use telehealth systems.

—Joseph T. Nocerino, M.S.

Hormones and Prostaglandins

Research in hormones and prostaglandins continues to provide some of the most exciting findings in biomedical science. These findings relate those chemical substances to fundamental aspects of brain function and to particular mechanisms in such diseases as cancer and diabetes. A full understanding of these latest developments requires some knowledge of the concept of hormone receptors, an idea that was new in endocrinology in the 1960s but now permeates many aspects of basic medical research.

Within any given cell, the first step in hormone action is the binding of the hormone to a protein molecule, called the hormone receptor. In the case of the steroid hormones, such as the sex hormones and cortisol, this receptor is in the cell sap, the more fluid portion of the cell cytoplasm; after the hormone is bound to the receptor, the receptor-hormone complex enters the cell nucleus where it activates the machinery for the manufacture of new cell products. For the protein hormones, such as insulin and the pituitary hormones, the receptor lies at the surface of the cell, on the cell membrane. When the hormone binds to this receptor, it stimulates another system to produce a second messenger within the cell, which in turn activates the appropriate mechanisms that produce the response to the hormone. Each of these hormone receptors is biologically specific, binding only to the appropriate hormone. Thus, the insulin receptor will bind only to insulin; the estrogen (female sex hormone) receptor will not bind to the male hormone.

Hormones and drug addiction

Through studies of the receptor mechanism, the fields of drug addiction and endocrinology have converged. Examination of the effects of morphine demonstrated that the first step in its action consists of binding to a specific receptor present only in certain parts of the brain. The presence of these receptors implied that there must be natural substances that interacted with them; subsequent studies led to the isolation from the brain of the

242

enkephalins, two small peptides composed of five amino acids. Furthermore, it was noted that the naturally occurring enkephalins had sedative effects. Almost immediately, researchers discovered that these enkephalins were part of a pituitary hormone, beta-lipotropin, that had been isolated and described some years earlier. Fragments of beta-lipotropin containing enkephalin were also found to have profound sedative effects.

The exact function of the enkephalins themselves is not fully known. They may serve as transmitters of the nerve impulse between groups of nerves in specific areas of the central nervous system. Although the significance of these relationships has not been defined, for the first time a relationship between brain hormones, brain function, and drug addiction has appeared. Continued research may lead to nonaddicting forms of pain relief as well as to new methods of combating drug addiction.

Hormones and cancer

Breast cancer that has spread following surgery will sometimes respond to the administration of hormones or to the removal of certain glands such as the ovaries, adrenals, or the pituitary. The rationale for these procedures is that the normal breast is dependent on hormones for its growth, and some breast cancers may therefore be similarly dependent. If hormones can alter the growth rate of a cancer, then there must be a mechanism—a receptor—for interaction of the hormone with the cell. In experimental breast tumors in rats, it was found that the presence of receptors for estrogen predicted that the tumors would regress in response to endocrine therapy; conversely, the absence of receptors determined that endocrine treatment would fail. Methods for measuring the estrogen receptor in human breast cancer have been devised, and studies from hospitals around the world have shown that when the receptor is present, two-thirds of the tumors will respond favorably to endocrine therapy. However, when the receptor is absent, less than 5% will respond. Thus, for the first time, the physician has a test procedure that guides him in making a rational decision between hormonal therapy and chemotherapy.

This is only the beginning, however, of the connection between breast cancer and hormones. The growth and function of both the normal breast cell and its cancerous counterpart are influenced by other steroid hormones such as testosterone (male hormone), progesterone (sex hormone of pregnancy), and prolactin, the protein hormone of the pituitary gland that enables the normal breast to manufacture milk. Receptors for each of these hormones are present in the breast cancer cell. Exami-

Courtesy, University of California San Francisco

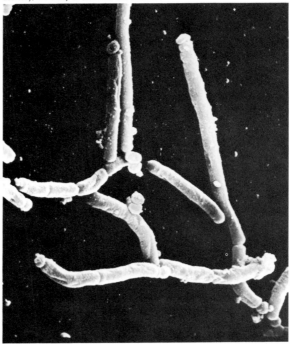

A major step toward the artificial production of human insulin, announced in 1977, was the creation of laboratory-bred bacteria capable of reproducing insulin genes transplanted from the cells of laboratory rats.

nations of the effect of relative numbers of receptors and the way hormone interactions affect cancer treatment are a part of the ongoing research program in breast cancer management.

The prostaglandins too have assumed an important role in the management of a life-threatening complication of cancer. Certain cancers affect bone metabolism, causing dissolution of bone and releasing calcium into the bloodstream. The calcium enters the blood more rapidly than it can be removed by the kidneys, so that the level of calcium in the blood rises—eventually to a lethal level—if the process is unchecked. It has now been shown that the bone disintegration is caused by a specific prostaglandin secreted by these cancers. In addition, prostaglandins are known to be one of the factors involved in causing inflammation; the discovery of compounds that decrease the synthesis of prostaglandins has been significant in the treatment of arthritis. These same compounds have now been shown to be valuable therapeutic agents for lowering the blood calcium level in the presence of particular cancers secreting prostaglandins.

Hormones and diabetes

In diabetes, the study of hormone receptors has provided insight into an unusual complication of the disease. When insulin acts on a cell, whether it

243

be a liver cell, fat cell, or white blood cell, it first binds to the insulin receptor at the cell surface. The total number of these receptors has been measured, and the factors that regulate this number are currently being studied. In some diabetic patients, the need for insulin increases so dramatically that it may be necessary to use as many as 50,000 units a day, whereas the average requirement is about 40 units. This condition has now been demonstrated to be the result of massive decreases, in either number or availability, of insulin receptors. In the case of reduced availability of receptors, the body has produced antibodies to the specific substances of the insulin receptor, which cover the receptor and prevent insulin access at the receptor site. In both cases, treatments now available are potentially capable of reversing the disease process and restoring the normal sensitivity to insulin.

Diabetes is only one of three "receptor" diseases that are currently being investigated, the others being myasthenia gravis, a disease of nerve and muscle, and hyperthyroidism. Clearly, if a cell's function depends on a hormone, and if the characteristics of the receptor for that hormone are changed, disease will result. Further exploration of the hormone-receptor complex will surely yield other examples of similar dysfunction.

—*Mortimer B. Lipsett, M.D.*

Human Sexuality

Throughout the past decade the so-called sexual revolution has received considerable attention in the media, with emphasis on the increase in sexual activity and growing tolerance for types of behavior once considered unacceptable. At the same time a quieter but more far-reaching evolution has been going on in professional circles since the time of Sigmund Freud. This evolution has seen the task of defining right and wrong in sexuality slowly shifting from the exclusive province of religious leaders into the not always competent hands of medical and health professionals.

Traditionally, medical problems touching upon sexuality primarily involved urogenital diseases and concerns about fertility, pregnancy, and birth control. Just a generation ago, doctors, the clergy, and people in general agreed that sex was sinful, dirty, and not to be discussed. Now, however, it is generally recognized and well documented that for both men and women sexual identity is an important part of total personality and enjoyment of sex an important part of life. The realization of satisfactory sexual identity in adulthood has been shown to be inextricably linked to the ability for satisfactory sexual function. Sexual satisfaction and gratification in turn exert a powerful influence on overall

Health professionals hear a talk at the Sexual Dysfunction Clinic at Loyola University Medical Center in Chicago.

health and well-being. Unfortunately, the adult sexual psyche often is scarred as a result of the strong combination of false, contradictory, and misleading values and the unmet expectations that are a part of our social mythology.

Help for sexual problems

Although a large portion of the American public still retains a puritanical attitude that denies the importance of a satisfying sex life, each year a significantly increasing number of persons are seeking help to improve their sexual functioning and enjoyment. Books and articles abound on every aspect of the subject, from general self-help books and magazines to professional clinical and medical journals; lectures, courses, and workshops are given regularly. Sexuality is one of the most widely discussed topics today; yet for many of the reasons already stated, it remains one of the least understood aspects of the human experience. For individuals and couples who find—even after reading all the books—that their sex lives are still problematic or just plain unrewarding, improvement may come through two main routes: new life-styles or therapeutic help.

A growing number of individuals and couples who are not happy with traditional monogamy or dating patterns are experimenting with and exploring alternate sexual life-styles. Formerly frowned-upon practices such as multiple sexual encounters, open marriage, bisexuality, and homosexuality are becoming increasingly acceptable. It should be noted, however, that this new freedom has created its own set of medical and emotional problems, with venereal disease and jealousy perhaps heading the list. For others, not ready to accept new values, it may also lead to accusations of being old-fashioned or "hung up." For susceptible individuals this kind of pressure amounts to a powerful psychological coercion that they will often give in to rather than risk social ostracism.

For people committed to traditional values, it is currently acceptable to seek help from one of the more than 3,000 sex clinics that have sprung up all over the country, an unknown number of which have dubious credentials and reliability. Others may take their sexual problems to a physician, social worker, or psychotherapist.

The medical profession also frequently becomes involved in sex counseling through indirect means. Jealousy, impotence, frigidity, and other sexual concerns may be reflected in a variety of physical and emotional ailments, such as anxiety, depression, headache, backache, nausea, asthma, peptic ulcer, and colitis, to name a few. Many persons who are having sexual problems will seek help from a doctor in conjunction with these related symptoms. Sometimes they are too reticent or embarrassed even to mention to the doctor that they are having sexual problems. Research has shown that physicians who routinely ask patients about their sex lives discover twice as many sexual problems as do doctors who wait for the patient to initiate such discussion.

The role of the professional

As people turn less to religious leaders and more toward the medical and health professions for help and guidance with problematic aspects of their sexuality, these professional clinicians have to assume fuller responsibility for providing advice and treatment. But for a variety of reasons, including inadequate education in areas of sexuality, personal prejudices, ignorance, moralistic value judgments, biases, and overreactions to sexual issues, too many doctors and other clinicians are not particularly well prepared to deal with these problems. The doctor who does not routinely ask about a patient's sex life, who chooses not to engage in a frank, open discussion with his or her patient about how to help alleviate the patient's sexual distress (either through intervention or by referral to a competent sex counselor) is in effect doing negative counseling by avoiding the topic and thus giving the impression that it is inappropriate to talk about sex. The doctor who jokes nervously about sexual concerns or who appears judgmental or moralistic, who embarrasses the patient, or tries to become involved personally in the patient's sex life may need more help than the patient does.

In choosing a competent professional counselor, the patient should seek a clinician who is knowledgeable about sex and comfortable talking about it. The right clinician will ask questions in such a way as to make the patient feel comfortable about answering them. The clinician should be aware that a wide variety of sexual problems exist; she or he should have an understanding and acceptance of the broad spectrum of normal sexual preferences and responses that exist in contemporary society, and should be gently, humanely, and professionally involved in understanding the patient's sexuality. Most importantly the clinician should be able to separate the biological and functional aspects of sexuality from the inner core of what it means to be a sexual being—spiritually, emotionally, and in terms of meaningful relationships.

Fortunately, one of the most significant trends of the past few years has been the emergence of comprehensive training in sexual issues in some medical school curricula and other professional education programs. In the knowledge that only an estimated 10% of reported sexual dysfunction problems are organic in nature, innovative programs such as those at the University of Minnesota Medical School and Loyola University in Chicago teach not only the physiological and medical information needed for informed diagnosis and treatment but also help the medical student reassess his or her own attitudes about sexuality, thus helping the student to understand how best to help the remaining 90% of the problems. Both Minnesota and Northwestern University medical schools, among others, offer intensive two- and three-day workshops designed to help professionals take a closer look at their feelings about the different facets of sexuality. Unfortunately there are not nearly enough competent schools offering this kind of training, and not nearly enough sound, competent practitioners to meet the growing need.

One therapeutic approach

An interesting, recently developed conceptual framework might help the clinician evaluate his own level of competence. This approach for examining the etiology and severity of a sex problem allows problems requiring brief counseling or education to be differentiated from those requiring long-term or intensive treatment. This model, as proposed by Jack Annon of the University of Hawaii, is called P-LI-SS-IT, which is an acronym for four increasingly intensive levels of intervention: (1) permission, (2) limited information, (3) specific suggestions, (4) intensive therapy.

1. At the permission-giving level the therapist simply gives himself and the patient permission to feel comfortable about their sex lives, in terms of sexual thoughts, fantasies, dreams, styles, and preferences without judgmental or moralistic interference as long as those behaviors and thoughts are not dangerous or harmful. Many persons suffer from ignorance, doubts, and fears about the safety and rightness of otherwise harmless sex practices. At this level the therapist reassures the patient that he or she is not perverted or abnormal and is not alone in these thoughts or desires. The patient is encouraged to enjoy those types of behavior he finds pleasurable. Clinicians should also be able to permit themselves to not be experts on everything. Theory, research, and practice in the sexual area is so far-ranging that no one individual could be expected to keep abreast of even a small portion of the total field.

2. If there are dangers in some sex practices, or if the patient is lacking even a rudimentary understanding of sex, the clinician, after a limited inquiry into the problem, restricts the specific factual information dispensed to the particular problem or to the general dispelling of myths and fallacies. At neither of these levels does the clinician try to alter or change the patient's behavior patterns, nor is it necessary for the doctor to know too much about the individual's personal sexual history.

3. In contrast to permission and limited information, specific suggestions are direct attempts to help patients alter behavior in order to achieve sexual satisfaction. Before doing so, the clinician should take a brief sexual history pertaining to the onset and nature of the problem. The suggestions will be individualized to the patient's unique circumstances and must conform to his personal value system. One would not, for example, suggest that a patient try oral-genital sex without first finding out whether he or she would find it disgusting or contrary to personal beliefs. Specific suggestions are usually given in conjunction with brief therapy and are aimed at helping to relieve some of the self-defeating grim determination that many patients bring to bear in trying to overcome their particular sexual problems. This level of treatment is reportedly particularly effective with problems concerning arousal, erection, ejaculation, orgasm, or painful intercourse. The well-informed clinician may also suggest specific reading matter that he knows will be of benefit to the patient.

4. Intensive therapy should be initiated only after the first three approaches have failed, and like the specific suggestions, should be tailored to the pa-

tient's needs. Some traditional therapeutic methods include psychoanalysis, rational-emotive therapy, nondirective counseling techniques, and behavioral therapy.

Treatment alternatives

The more dynamically oriented therapies such as psychoanalysis see problematic sexual functioning as part of deep-seated problems, often relating to childhood experiences. Some of the criticisms often leveled at this process are that it requires long-term, expensive treatment and that, after many years of professional help, the patient may understand the origin of the problem but has not overcome the problem itself.

Although the behavioral approach does not deny that sex is part of the totality of the individual, it simply regards sex as the presenting problem, and the therapist contracts with the individual or couple to work on improved sexual functioning without helping them relate their sex lives to other problems. Although it is the only method that documents measurable improvement, this approach is often criticized as simplistic, mechanistic, depersonalizing, and fragmenting.

Some new trends in sexual counseling are occurring in the field of humanistic psychology. This field is a positivistic one, focusing on the full growth potential of each person. It aims at maximizing and releasing physical, emotional, and spiritual energy through learning and structured experiences without focusing on the negative problematic aspects of one's sexuality. Albert Ellis is one of the earliest humanistic sexual theorists. Some pioneer workers in this promising field are exploring what they call "the new androgyny"—that is, the coexistence of feminine and masculine energies within each person—while others are looking at game theory as means to explore the ways in which aspects of sexual identity influence social relationships.

There are bold new programs in rehabilitation medicine that help the doctor and allied health professionals to look compassionately at a variety of impairments, disfigurements, and disabilities that sometimes prevent satisfactory sexual function. The growing acceptance of the universal human need for a healthy sex life is exemplified by this movement in rehabilitation, which encourages paralytics, stroke and coronary victims, chronic care and nursing home patients, victims of cerebral palsy, and others to think of themselves as sexual beings with normal needs and desires. Although such people were long regarded as nonsexual, it is now acknowledged that every member of society has the right to an enjoyable sex life.

—Marvin E. Lehrman, M.S.W.

Special Report:

Facts and Fallacies about Sex and Pregnancy

by Francois Alouf, M.D., and Peter Barglow, M.D

The study of human history shows that except for natural disasters (volcanic eruptions, earthquakes, epidemics, droughts, and famines), no situations arouse more anxiety and fear than those associated with birth, death, and illness. Furthermore a survey of ancient civilizations and of existing nonindustrialized cultures demonstrates that prescientific humanity's universal response to anxiety-producing situations was—and is—to evolve intricate mythological, philosophical, and religious constructs, as well as to develop complex social, religious, magical, and medical rituals. These practices aim at bringing to the environment more predictability and greater harmony and at allowing human beings the perception of better control over their fate. Among the many rules and regulations that every society has created are those dealing with sexual conduct. More specifically, based on complex traditions and taboos, nearly all cultures have clearly defined the extent of sexual activities during pregnancy and the postpartum period.

It has been said that the history of medicine is the history of humanity. Indeed, for many centuries, medicine maintained intimate ties with the cultures from which it stemmed, and medical practices closely reflected the customs, attitudes, value systems, interests, and beliefs of those cultures. In every known civilization, magico-religious medical practices evolved in relation to pregnancy, birth, and the postpartum period. Such an intimate historical connection between cultural attitudes and medical practice explains why innumerable myths, romantic fantasies, gross misinformation, and stern moralizations and taboos concerning sex in general, and sexual activity during pregnancy and the postpartum period in particular, have subtly dominated scientific observations throughout the long history of medicine.

Historical perspective

In the last 200 years travelers, scientists, anthropologists, and sociologists have made myriad observations of a wide variety of so-called primitive societies and have offered detailed descriptions of their attitudes towards sexual activity during pregnancy and the postpartum period. While some so-

cieties encouraged continued sexual activity, in the vast majority of the cultures sexual intercourse was prohibited from the time pregnancy was suspected up to several weeks, months, or even years after delivery. These societies believed that the violation of such taboos would result in terrible consequences for the offenders or perhaps for the tribe as a whole. The consequences ranged from a fear that the semen might destroy the fetus to a concern that intercourse during pregnancy might result in the birth of a deformed child or that famine and epidemics would threaten the existence of the

For many women pregnancy is accompanied by ambivalent feelings, often by both a sense of heightened self-esteem as well as anxiety over bodily changes and new responsibilities.

Suzanne Arms—Jeroboam

whole tribe. Therefore, those guilty of trespasses were often severely physically punished or even put to death.

The women of ancient Persia were considered sexually taboo after the fourth month of pregnancy and for 40 days after childbirth, and intercourse during the postnatal period was punishable by death for both the male and female. When they were menstruating or pregnant, the Illini Indian women were looked upon as sacred, or superhuman, and were thought to possess magical powers. The Indians insisted that the women be separated from the other tribe members so that they would not disturb the normal course of nature, and sexual activity was tabooed. The ancient Hindus, by contrast, believed the fetus to be the product of a mixture of semen and menstrual blood and thought that semen provided continued nourishment to the embryo. Intercourse during pregnancy was thus encouraged by some Hindu sects up to about two weeks of the expected date of delivery.

Incorporating some of these early beliefs, many organized religions also emphasized the necessity for sexual abstinence during pregnancy and the postpartum period. The Talmudic literature, the Old Testament, and specifically the book of Leviticus contain many regulations and stern injunctions concerning sexual activity during menstruation and after childbirth. During these times women were considered "unclean," and sexual intercourse was totally prohibited. At the end of the menstrual period, and at a prescribed interval following childbirth, the woman was required to take a ritualistic bath of purification before sexual activity could be resumed. The Islamic religion also forbade sexual intercourse during menstruation, pregnancy, and breast-feeding. Likewise, in the early Christian church specific rules of sexual abstinence prevailed. Husband and wife were supposed to abstain from intercourse for three months after conception and 40 days after birth.

More recently, anthropologist Clellan S. Ford and psychologist Frank A. Beach in *Patterns of Sexual Behavior* (1951) assembled data from 60 cultures around the world. Their survey demonstrated the existence of great variability in the taboos governing sexual activity during pregnancy. Up to the second month of pregnancy, in 70% of the societies studied, there was no prohibition against sexual intercourse. However, as the pregnancy progressed this percentage declined steadily. By the sixth month of pregnancy, in 50% of the societies sexual intercourse was prohibited, and by the ninth month, 75% of these societies forbade continued sexual activity. For the majority of cultures, the prohibition against sexual activity was related to the belief that intercourse might injure the fetus.

Many of the societies also insisted upon sexual abstinence after delivery, the duration of such abstinence varying from a few weeks to several months. In some instances, the resumption of sexual activity was closely related to the newborn's developmental stages. In a few cases intercourse was not allowed while the mother was nursing, a period often spanning two to three years.

Attitudes in modern times

In 1889, physician John Cowan wrote of sex and pregnancy in his book *The Science of a New Life*:

I will again repeat that during this full period of gestative influence as well as during the period of nursing, SEXUAL CONGRESS SHOULD NOT BE HAD BETWEEN HUSBAND AND WIFE. This is the law of nature, the law of God, and outside of Christendom it is never violated. Animals will not permit it — savages will not permit it, and in over three quarters of the world it is looked upon as infamous by our own species. A man acting out the licentiousness of his nature with his wife during gestation is worse than a brute. . . . Do not, I pray you, O parents, do this unclean thing.

This type of medical advice, highly reminiscent of exhortations that once prevailed in many primitive societies and in some organized religions, accounts at least partially for the lengthy time lapse that has existed between the emergence of objective, value-free data concerning this emotionally laden subject and the abandonment of the biases and prejudices that for years interfered with the physician's ability to provide rational medical advice in this everyday area of practice.

Throughout history after societies have established their economic power and military strength, their concerns shift from the matters of day-to-day survival to quality-of-living issues. Since the 1950s this trend has manifested itself in the United States by a prodigious thirst for knowledge and a sharp questioning of social values and priorities. Americans gradually became openly curious about a range of sexual matters and developed a wider tolerance for the rights of consenting adults to choose their own sexual life-styles out of the variety of possible behaviors and relationships. Reliable chemical and mechanical contraception rapidly replaced "moral" contraception (*i.e.,* virginity, celibacy, abstinence) and freed individuals to experiment with their bodies as well as with their thoughts. Human rights movements succeeded in redefining human sexual normality, medically as well as legally. Transsexuality, homosexuality, group sex, partner sharing, oral sex, masturbation, and extramarital sex came increasingly to be considered as life-style choices rather than as deviant behavior. Another significant factor was the emergence of the women's liberation movement. Half of the adult population who had for years been de-

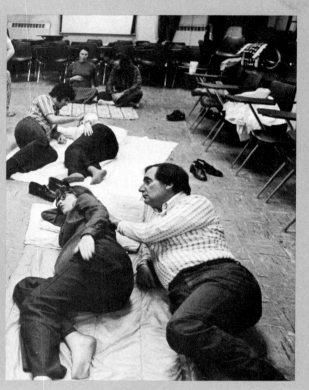

Impending parenthood can produce complex emotional conflicts for both partners which in turn can place great strain on the relationship itself. This period of stress requires that each partner develop feelings of empathy and mutuality and share in one another's concerns and pleasures from the outset of the pregnancy.

fined as passive, indifferent sex objects found themselves free to openly explore and express their interest, expectations, and involvement in their own sexuality.

These social changes provided the impetus for many scientists to attempt the collection of more accurate information concerning sexuality. As a consequence, instead of mythology, moralizations, and romantic fantasies, objective data was obtained and published. Alfred Kinsey's publications (1948–1953) surveying the sexual behaviors and attitudes prevalent among American males and females in the late 1940s and early 1950s, and the research of William H. Masters and Virginia E. Johnson on the *Human Sexual Response* (1966) and on *Human Sexual Inadequacy* (1970) reached a vast public audience. As a result, scholars from many disciplines (medicine, sociology, anthropology, psychology) became aware of the variety of sexual changes and adjustments that occur during pregnancy and the postpartum period in both sexual partners.

It also became obvious that sensitive understanding of contemporary sexual activities, attitudes, and trends would augment the physician's ability to help his patients in this area of medical practice. Several studies, published between the years 1953 and 1976, investigated details of sexual concerns and needs and sexual enjoyment during pregnancy and the postpartum period. All the studies were in general agreement. During pregnancy and the postpartum period, sexual activity tends to fluctuate. Most often the fluctuation results in a diminution of sexual desire and a decrease in the frequency of sexual interaction. It is probable that multiple factors (hormonal, cultural, and psychological) play major roles in determining the variations in the sexual responses.

The psychological factors

The psychology of sexuality for both women and men has always been altered during pregnancy. In the mid-20th century the general social impetus toward liberalization has fostered considerable revision of the psychological theories of optimal sexual functioning during pregnancy. Psychiatrists have become more sensitive to the influence on the emotional partnership exerted by typical fluctuations in self-esteem and the way in which these interfere with the mastery of negative emotions that can destroy sexual compatibility. The preceding considerations then suggest three major determinants of sexual adjustment during pregnancy: (1) maintenance of self-esteem; (2) control of negative feelings; (3) capacity for empathic comprehension of the sexual partner's feelings.

Self-esteem. Difficulties in self-esteem can arise

for both partners in a pregnancy. Most women who have doubted their femininity obviously feel reassured by the proof of fertility—culturally and psychologically pregnancy equals the essence of maturity for a woman. As a consequence, female anxiety over achieving orgasm during intercourse may diminish, and the need to reaffirm feminine identity through stereotypic feminine sexuality may disappear. But visible bodily changes in the pregnant woman nearly always create anxiety about a loss of physical attractiveness. Infrequency of sexual advances by the male may reinforce such fears and make sexuality for the woman an arena of performance and a barometer of self-esteem, rather than a source of relaxed enjoyment. The protuberant abdomen of his female partner may demolish any remnant of Don Juan "sex without responsibility," "love them and leave them" fantasies that immature males may have harbored since adolescence. But if the man is proud of his capacity to impregnate and feels his self-esteem enhanced by his partner's confidence in his ability to father and to provide for a family, his sexual functioning is improved. He may become less inclined to have to demonstrate his genital potency, and not infrequently, exhibitionistic sexual activities may become transformed into more gentle, tender, sensitive behavior as a response of gratitude for the female's "gift" to him. This attitude may intensify as the pregnancy progresses.

On the other hand, if the male has had to maintain a stereotypic, idealized sex-object image of his partner to foster sexual arousal—and to stimulate positive feelings about himself—he may find it impossible to remain sexually involved. Flirting or infidelity often result, with the accompanying guilt or shame leading to further sexual withdrawal or impotence. The pregnant woman who becomes aware of the male partner's outside sexual activities will be humiliated, feel belittled, and respond with rage and sexual rejection. (Imagine what effect this is likely to have in the formation of the mother's attitude toward the child-to-be.)

The idealized mother-woman-wife image, during pregnancy, also elicits in many men childhood taboos against incest, thereby inhibiting sexual interest. The necessity of separating the mother and the heterosexual love object accounts for the so-called madonna-maid complex, in which men choose a degraded woman to love, because she is so unlike the sacrosant, admired mother, whose pregnancies are associated with the father alone.

For the male, the presence of a healthy infant during the postpartum phase represents a confirmation of masculine prowess that is often ritualized in the father's proud phallic gift of the cigar. This increased self-love extends its positive consequences to the sexual relationship itself as well.

Negative feelings. Another problem that is faced by both partners is the control of negative feelings that arise from pregnancy and impending parenthood. In the female swelling of the breasts, gastrointestinal symptoms, unusual food proclivities, and weight change at the onset of pregnancy mimic the symptoms of physical illnesses and trigger typical psychological reactions. These phenomena usually interfere with the relaxation and comfort necessary for sexual pleasure by distracting the woman's attention from erogenous zones and, often obsessively, from the feelings of the male sex partner. Such somatic symptoms and the common metabolically induced weakness, tiredness, and mood volatility often produce in a woman the self-perception of strangeness: "I'm not myself any longer." This in turn creates a state of irritability, withdrawal, and introversion that represents a new emotional barrier between the partners, jeopardizing their habitual sexual functioning. Weight gain, the concern of "eating for two," the gastrointestinal symptoms, and feelings of helplessness and dependency can produce mental depression and conflicts about orality in the form of emotional giving or taking. Such factors may decrease the pregnant woman's pleasure in foreplay activities such as kissing, caressing, and oral-genital activity.

The fear that too vigorous sexual activity may cause abortion is a frequent preoccupation during the second three months of pregnancy, often persisting despite repeated reassurance by the obstetrician. It usually reflects an upsurge of unconscious negative or destructive wishes toward the fetus, as do fantasies that too vigorous sexual intercourse or excessive orgasmic pleasure will in some way produce a deformed or monstrous infant. Furthermore, "childhood concepts of sex as sinful or impure irreconcilable with the ideal mother" also may inhibit the pleasure of sexual intercourse. The unpleasant or unanticipated physical discomfort of the second trimester not infrequently stimulates female ambivalence toward the fetus, and the consequent resentment commonly rubs off on the other contributor to the fetus' existence—the male partner. The third trimester is generally dominated by the woman's impatience with the duration of a pregnancy that has begun to appear interminable. Her body often seems an unfamiliar burden, slow to respond and hard to manage. Routine simple activities or movements may become time-consuming or impossible. Frustration often leads the woman to be impatient with sexual activities, thus interfering with masculine sexual capacity.

Postpartum depression—or even the normal postpartum blues—sometimes delays the return of

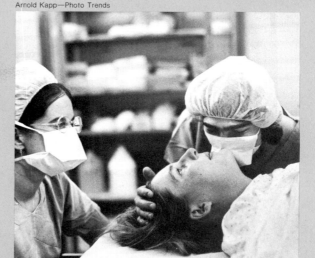

Nowadays it is not uncommon for the father to be present at the delivery of the child, sharing in, from the child's birth, the mutual bond and responsibility of parenthood.

the woman's sexual interest, even after successful delivery. Some new mothers become so totally absorbed with infant care that they temporarily lose interest in the maintenance of sexual closeness. Also, not infrequently, some women feel a conflict between their desire and need to care for their child and the necessity to return to work; such a conflict might result in sexual maladjustment. Occasionally, the woman may become preoccupied with the thought that her external genitalia or other parts of the body have been damaged by the pregnancy, the delivery, or the episiotomy. Often the male partner may have similar worries and guilt. As a consequence, both partners may become unduly disturbed by the perceived anatomical changes. Although transient, such concerns during the postnatal period can severely inhibit male and female sexual desire, responsiveness, or activity.

Empathy. In order to counteract negative and conflicted feelings, it is necessary that the partners learn to develop feelings of empathy and mutuality. All common female anxiety and depressive reactions require increased male sensitivity, protectiveness, patience, and flexibility. Male failures in this area inevitably elicit sexual withdrawal and retaliatory emotional withholding by the female partner during sexual intimacy. A woman who experiences heightened dependent helpless feelings ("I can't leave my partner when he mistreats me because of the baby") may stimulate childish and competitive wishes in the male, rather than maternal-paternal parenting attitudes. But the male's active and early

251

participation in planning for the clothing, feeding, and comfort of the expected child may bind a couple closer, enhancing sexual functioning. On the other hand, misogynist ideas resulting from a man's fear and hatred of the sexually active woman and his envy of her childbearing capacity may produce male impotence. Envious competition with the female partner often originates in a childhood injury to phallic pride created by a mother's rejection after the birth of a younger male sibling.

Some men, during the last months of pregnancy, overidentify with their partners, becoming sexually incapacitated by a *couvade* reaction. The prenatal couvade represents the imagined transfer of the pregnant woman's symptoms to the male's body, a means by which he merges with his partner's intense experience. A difficulty representing the opposite of a couvade imitation, but equally incapacitating to male genital functioning, is the hostile disidentification induced in some men by envy of the female procreative function.

The last months of pregnancy inevitably strain the empathic capacities of even the most mature men. The male's emotional strengths or weaknesses reinforce or compensate for the presence or absence of these in his partner, and the quality of the sexual relationship during the last trimester is a sensitive barometer of the emotional balance between partners. Sharing the joy, pain, and anxiety of labor, delivery, and the initial care of the newborn can reinforce feelings of emotional and sexual mutuality. The successful achievement of common, shared life goals — represented by the healthy infant — gives a couple a sense of vitality and direction, which in turn confirms the adult maturity of both partners and fosters future sexual sensitivity and cooperation.

The physician's role

The emotional course of even the optimal pregnancy and postpartum period seldom runs smoothly since intense feelings are inevitably aroused in both partners. Research indicates that pregnancy is always a time when the needs of each sexual partner for emotional support, reassurance, security, nurturance, and continued confirmation of individual sexual attractiveness are increased. Recent investigators have emphasized the importance of maintaining at least partial sexual activity and gratification during pregnancy and the postpartum period as one of the most important ways in which a couple may meet their increased need for physical and emotional intimacy.

Each couple must receive from the physician adequate information concerning the typical physiological and psychological changes that may accompany the pregnancy, so that they can better understand them and thereby increase their capacity for coping with the accompanying stress. The doctor must appreciate that each person has a unique psychological and emotional makeup and therefore requires specialized attention. In a professional atmosphere of openness, empathy, and emotional support, the physician must attempt to secure from every pregnant patient or couple factual information concerning their sexual needs and their capacity to communicate those needs to each other. It is necessary for the physician to elicit from the individual or the couple objective data about the patterns of coital and noncoital sexual activity that they have found most comfortable.

The most recent medical conclusion is that there are rarely medical reasons for sexual abstinence during normal pregnancy. The maintenance of coital and noncoital sexual activity will depend in a large measure on the physical and emotional well-being of the pregnant woman and her partner. In unusual instances, while the desire on the part of the female and her partner to maintain sexual activity is high, the male's body weight may place excess pressure on the distended uterus. The woman might find coitus in the male superior position clumsy, uncomfortable, or painful. The couple should be encouraged to experiment with other positions, especially the knee-chest, rear entry, or side by side positions, which remove excess pressure on the pregnant uterus. During the pregnancy, if sexual intercourse becomes physically too uncomfortable, or if contraindications to coital activity or to female orgasmic release exist (*i.e.,* vaginal and uterine infection, premature rupture of the membranes, severe bleeding, history of repeated abortions, incompetent cervix, and so forth), the physician should candidly explain to the couple why specific aspects of coital and noncoital sexual activity represent potential risks.

The doctor must also help his pregnant patient — and the couple as well — explore alternatives to coitus and encourage both partners to express their feelings and attitudes about noncoital activities such as masturbation, oral-genital sex, and other forms of sexual gratification. In the postpartum period, the physician should always make it a point to ask the patient and her partner about their sexual adjustment since the delivery. While it is not up to the physician to prescribe the person's or the couple's pattern of sexual activity during pregnancy or afterwards, he should help both patient and partner clarify for themselves their sexual needs and the ways in which such needs can be met. The clarification process enhances the couple's potential for maintaining, during the pregnancy and postnatally, a growth-promoting relationship that fosters sexual and emotional health.

Infectious Diseases

Although the control of infectious diseases began more than a century ago in the laboratories of such bacteriologists as Louis Pasteur, Robert Koch, and Paul Ehrlich, infectious disease continues to have considerable impact on national health programs. In addition to the problem of dealing with isolated outbreaks of disease, the possibilities of epidemics of venereal disease and influenza were of prime concern to epidemiologists throughout the world.

Venereal disease: a new threat

Venereal diseases (VD), sometimes referred to as sexually transmitted diseases (STD), were the topic of a September 1976 meeting of the World Health Organization (WHO) Regional Office for Europe, held in Vienna, Austria. Twenty countries were represented, along with members of the International Union Against the Venereal Diseases and the International Planned Parenthood Federation. The symposium noted an increase in the reported numbers of STD cases but recommended that screening programs be instituted only for high-risk groups.

Of all the STDs, gonorrhea is the most widespread, with an estimated 100 million cases per year, perhaps as many as 2 million of these in the U.S. alone. Late in 1976, epidemiologists began to express concern over increasing reports of new strains of gonorrhea that are immune to the traditional drug of choice, penicillin. Meeting in November 1976 in Geneva, the WHO Scientific Group on Neisseria and Gonococcal Infections reported that the penicillin-resistant strains had been identified in at least 11 countries, including the U.S., England, Australia, Norway, Japan, the Philippines, Ghana, and others. By spring of 1977 the new strains had been identified in 19 states in the U.S.

Called "beta" gonorrhea, the new strains are evidently a mutant of the common *Neisseria gonorrhoeae*; they produce an enzyme, beta-lactamase, that is capable of breaking down the penicillin molecule, thus destroying its antibacterial effect. Most U.S. cases were traced to military bases in the Far East, although unrelated cases appeared simultaneously in England. After some experimentation, U.S. physicians found two antibiotics, spectinomycin and tetracycline, that were effective in treating beta gonorrhea. Unfortunately, spectinomycin is considerably more expensive than penicillin, thus making its widespread use to combat a possible epidemic economically unfeasible. Perhaps the most disturbing aspect of the beta gonorrhea problem, however, is its illustration of the ingenious mechanisms by which infectious organisms can develop resistance to agents that have been able to destroy them.

Influenza

In 1918, more people died from the worldwide influenza pandemic than had died in World War I. So great was the fear of contracting the disease that people wore surgical masks in public, schools closed, and children remained indoors or were sent to the countryside, which was thought to be safer. Weddings and funerals were attended by only the closest relatives. People coughing and sneezing outdoors were subject to arrest. Known everywhere except in Spain as the "Spanish flu," the disease spread throughout the world.

More than 21 million people—about 1% of the

One of the worst outbreaks of infectious disease in history was the worldwide "Spanish flu" pandemic of 1918. Protective masks, such as those worn by these Seattle, Wash., policemen, were a common public sight.

Culver Pictures, Inc.

Infectious diseases

world's population—died from the disease during the two-year period it was rampant, 540,000 in the U.S. alone. Most of those who succumbed were young adults, otherwise healthy. The elderly and patients with chronic illnesses such as heart or kidney disease also died in large numbers. Most deaths were from the complications—pneumonia and severe bronchitis—that often followed the more acute phase of the disease.

Could so severe an influenza pandemic happen again? Flu itself is the same disease today it was in years past. In 1918, however, when the new strain of flu virus spread rapidly throughout the world, identification of the influenza virus had not been made and methods of preparing vaccines had not been developed. Effective vaccines prepared with live or killed influenza viruses are now available and widely used. Should a pandemic occur today, however, it would not be likely to lead to such widespread mortality. Antibiotics are now available to treat the secondary and life-threatening complications of flu. They are especially useful in treating pneumonia and bronchitis resulting from bacterial infections that invade influenza-damaged tissues. Antibiotics are, however, of no value in treating the acute influenza infection itself, which is caused by the virus. No drug has yet been developed to treat the acute phase of any virally caused disease.

Influenza virus. The influenza virus affects cells lining the nose, throat, and delicate air passages of the lungs. Like other viruses (*e.g.,* those causing measles, mumps, or chickenpox), the influenza virus requires living cells for growth and reproduction. The virus lacks sufficient genetic information to survive independently. The infected cell contributes to viral reproduction by subverting its own needs. The virus attaches itself to cells and is then taken inside. Part of the membrane of cells in respiratory passages consists of structures that can function as receptors for the influenza virus. The primary function of such receptors is not, of course, to provide a means for virus attachment. The virus has evolved a mechanism for entering living cells by attaching itself to structures on the cell membranes used for other purposes.

Most living things use deoxyribonucleic acid (DNA) as their chemical substance of heredity. The influenza virus, along with several other viral forms, uses ribonucleic acid (RNA) as its hereditary source. Viral RNA is reproduced in infected cells with the aid of a special enzyme formed through information associated with the virus. The enzyme is necessary in order to form new viral RNA which is discharged into the surrounding environment. Six "pieces" of RNA are present in each mature virus particle.

More than in any other viral type, mixing of in-

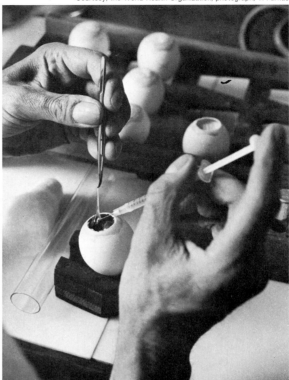

Fertilized eggs provide an ideal culture medium for influenza viruses used in research and in the production of vaccines.

fluenza viral RNA, known as genetic recombination, sometimes occurs. A fragment of one piece of viral RNA from one strain of the virus literally exchanges places with a similar but nonidentical fragment of another portion during viral reproduction. The new combinations may have properties not possessed by any influenza virus previously existent. Often, such new combinations are nonfunctional and quickly die; in some instances they reproduce mature and infectious viral particles that are killed by established bodily defense mechanisms. Rarely, a new viral structure not previously present appears and maintains itself. It is new insofar as the body's immune system is concerned and no antibodies exist to counter it.

The recombination and appearance of immunologically distinct viral strains is primarily responsible for the occurrence of periodic epidemics of influenza. Children recovering from measles and mumps are usually immune from these diseases forever after. Even though frequent exposure to such childhood illnesses occurs time after time, reinfection rarely occurs. (In the case of certain severe illnesses that reduce the functional capacity of the immune system, reinfection of adults with childhood diseases sometimes does take place.) The problem in developing persistent and lifelong natural immunity toward flu is that the number of different and immunologically distinct strains of flu viruses is quite large. New strains appear frequently, primarily following recombination of viral RNA. Thus, even though immunity toward one year's flu may be present, immunity toward another year's strain may be nonexistent. Although it is impossible to predict whether a new strain will appear in any given year, major epidemics have occurred at about 5- or 6-year intervals, as in 1957, 1962, and 1968. In those years, up to 35 percent of the population was affected. In mild years, relatively few people have the disease.

The antibodies found in the serums of elderly people indicate that the influenza virus infecting humans in the period between 1918 and 1933 was type A. In subsequent years, other strains of type A flu have been prevalent, *e.g.,* Hong Kong (the strains of influenza virus are named for their place of first discovery), Asian, London, and most recently Port Chalmers (New Zealand) flu. Three broad categories of influenza have been described, based on their antigenic structures. Types A and B are infectious for humans; type C is not. The various strains of influenza viruses are identified by using serums containing antibodies from patients who have recovered from influenza. When a new form appears, one for which population immunity is not present, it is identified and vaccine preparation begins.

Certain animals, as well as humans, are susceptible to influenza virus, experiencing many of the same symptoms. Monkeys, rodents, swine, and chickens all can have the disease. Farmers can become infected with "swine flu" from animals. In 1976, a variant of swine flu, the virus of the 1918–19 pandemic, was identified in a small number of humans. To avoid a pandemic, with the support of the

U.S. government a program of mass inoculation was begun. Approximately 40 million Americans were vaccinated before the program was discontinued. For unknown reasons, unrelated in this instance to the widespread use of the vaccine, the disease failed to spread as anticipated and seemed to disappear.

Influenza prevention. To protect people from new strains of flu that may appear, virologists throughout the world monitor prevalent flu strains, looking continually for new immunologically distinct strains of virus. WHO sponsors laboratory stations throughout the world where scientists determine through serological testing the prevalent flu strains. They report the presence of new strains, those not previously present for which immunity in the population as a whole is not likely to have been established. (Naturally, a small proportion of the population, mostly young people, are also susceptible to the established strains.) In the United States, in programs supported by the Public Health Service, vaccines for new strains are prepared soon after they are detected. Infected individuals unknowingly spread the virus, shedding it at least 24 hours before symptoms occur. Given the frequency of air travel, the virus can be widely distributed throughout the world in a short time.

To produce vaccine, new virus strains are grown on a large scale in the cells of the fetal membranes of eggs. The virus is inactivated and then separated from contaminating egg constituents so that the side effects of flu vaccination, in the past at times severe, are rarely a problem. (People allergic to eggs, however, sometimes do have a reaction.) Selection of the strains of influenza to be used for vaccine production is made throughout the year. Vaccines are administered in the late autumn, just before the time when infections are at their highest.

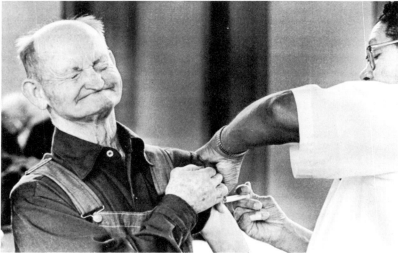

UPI Compix

Because they are at greatest risk of death or serious complications from infectious diseases, the very young and the elderly are the primary targets of large-scale public vaccination programs.

Infectious diseases

Most infections occur in the winter months, probably because people spend their time indoors, in close proximity, in poorly ventilated, and often overheated, rooms.

One might suppose that with the means of recognizing new viral forms and the preparation of effective vaccines, widespread vaccination would virtually eliminate influenza as a world health problem. Vaccination even with the appropriate strain does not, however, confer lifelong immunity, and infection with the same strain of virus used for immunization may occur later. Also, the immunity resulting from vaccination is not as effective as natural immunity following recovery from flu. Furthermore, for unknown reasons, not everyone receiving the vaccine is protected, even within the short-term immediate future. Fever, sore throat, runny nose, muscle aches and pains, and extreme fatigue sometimes occur. Usually, in otherwise healthy individuals, the symptoms last a few days and gradually disappear, and recovery is uneventful. Only

Public health officials explored every niche of Philadelphia's Bellevue-Stratford Hotel, site of the 1976 "legionnaire's" epidemic, searching for clues to the origin of the infection.

Martin Adler Levick—Black Star

about two-thirds of those receiving vaccination are fully protected. When a new strain appears, as happens every several years, a previous vaccination is, of course, no help at all. The immunity of natural infection, however, is usually lifelong.

Fortunately, in healthy adults and children influenza is not usually a life-endangering disease; several days rest in bed is usually all that is required for a full recovery. In many instances, flu goes unrecognized as a bad cold or as the "grippe." Fatal influenza is today quite unusual in otherwise healthy individuals. For people with chronic illness such as bronchitis or heart disease, influenza is a potentially serious extra burden and vaccination is strongly recommended.

Public health guidelines recommend vaccination for people with diabetes, kidney disease, asthma, emphysema, other chronic illnesses, and for the elderly and the young. In addition, people in essential community occupations, such as firemen or police, or in occupations requiring frequent exposure to patients with influenza, such as doctors and nurses, should be protected by vaccination. However, only about 10% of the at-risk population is vaccinated. Thus, many who should be vaccinated are not, either because they live in areas where the vaccine is not generally available or because of misplaced fear or simple negligence.

Research. Research scientists are working to develop effective drugs to prevent infection with influenza. In the Soviet Union, two new compounds offer promise, although both are still in experimental stages. One drug is applied as a nasal ointment during the flu season; the other is taken internally by mouth. Scientists are also evaluating amantadine hydrochloride as a preventative. Amantadine hydrochloride is recommended for use by high-risk people during the flu season. Like other preventatives it is not completely effective. Its mode of action is not established, but it may inhibit the release of viral RNA in infected cells, thereby preventing viral replication.

The body forms an antiviral substance called interferon in response to virus infection. Scientists are currently working on drugs that are safe and effective stimulants of interferon production. Interferon itself is not sensitive to any particular viral species, but prevents reproduction of many viral types. It acts indirectly, stimulating production by the cell of an antiviral protein.

Legionnaire's disease

The mystery of one of the most puzzling and frightening outbreaks of infectious disease in U.S. history was solved early in 1977 when scientists from the Center for Disease Control (CDC) in Atlanta, Ga., announced that they had isolated the organism believed responsible for the so-called legionnaire's disease, or legion fever. According to the CDC researchers, the disease was caused by a hitherto unknown or previously unidentified organism resembling a bacterium, possibly also linked to a mysterious 1965 pneumonia epidemic. Legionnaire's disease was responsible for the deaths of 29 persons who had attended or been associated with an American Legion convention held in Philadelphia, Pa., in July 1976. More than 100 others were hospitalized, suffering from a complex of symptoms that included headache, coughing, muscle pains, chills, and fevers as high as 107°F (41.7 °C). Autopsies of the victims indicated viral pneumonia. For several months researchers attempted without success to isolate the cause, ruling out viruses, food-, water-, and air-borne toxins, fungal infections, and diseases such as psittacosis, which is caused by an organism carried by birds. It was not until January 1977 that the CDC researchers, having examined lung tissue samples from one of the victims, identified the unknown bacteria-like organism as the cause of the infection. The source of the organism and its manner of transmission remained a mystery.

—Edward P. Cohen, M.D., Ph.D.

Lymphatic System Diseases

For the first time in history, some patients with acute leukemia are surviving for prolonged periods of time. In some cases, apparently cured, such patients are surviving indefinitely. Leukemia, literally meaning "white blood," had until recently been a uniformly fatal disease. In spite of the most advanced treatment, patients survived for approximately one to two years following its detection. Now, with a better understanding of the disease and its effects on the body, with new and more potent drugs and knowledge of their optimum administration, and with the use of a dramatic procedure involving massive transplantation of healthy bone marrow, many patients with leukemia are living longer.

Normal and malignant leukocytes

Leukemia is a malignant disease of leukocytes, white cells that circulate in the blood and fight off and destroy invading organisms. Usually these highly specialized cells develop and mature in the bone marrow cavity. Mature cells with special characteristics and functions enter the circulating blood. There they spend their short lifetimes, in some instances only a matter of days, seeking out and ingesting foreign organisms that have entered the body.

The steady flow of mature cells, replacing those that age normally or are destroyed fighting infections, continues with extraordinary precision. The white blood count in normal individuals is between 5,000 and 10,000 per cubic millimeter of blood. In the case of acute infections, the rate of production accelerates and the concentration of leukocytes in the blood increases, rising to 15,000 or 20,000 per cu mm or even higher. The white blood count of arctic explorers, living in a virtually germ-free environment, gradually falls to less than 5,000 per cu mm because infectious diseases are eliminated in the closed community and bacteria are virtually nonexistent. The count rises to normal levels after the explorers return home.

There are two principal types of leukocytes. Polymorphonuclear leukocytes, or granulocytes, possess granules filled with digestive enzymes. Comprising about 50% of the total, granulocytes are phagocytic cells, ingesting and destroying through enzymic means a great variety of foreign substances. Lymphocytes, or agranulocytes, which make up approximately 40% of the leukocytes in the blood, produce antibodies and engage in cell-mediated immunity. (A third type of leukocyte is the monocyte—about 7%—which also possesses granules and disposes of foreign particles.)

In leukemia the delicate balance of production, release, and death of leukocytes is disrupted. Immature malignant cells or neoplasms (new growths) appear in the blood and, capable of indefinite proliferation, gradually replace normal cells. The neoplastic cells are unable to destroy infectious agents, and patients with leukemia develop a relative deficiency of healthy disease-fighting cells. With low resistance, they often die of what would normally be trivial infections.

In one form of a similar disease, multiple myeloma, a lymphocyte undergoes a malignant transformation, proliferates in great numbers, and produces large quantities of antibodies of a single type. Normally, the total number of antibody types is extraordinarily large, reflecting the great heterogeneity of the lymphocyte population. Normal blood serum contains many thousands of different antibodies, reactive with a great variety of foreign antigens. Researchers believe that in myeloma one parent lymphocyte cell is transformed into a malignant form, beginning the process that eventually leads to the disease. It also seems likely that in leukemias of granulocytes and other cell types, individual cells are converted through an unknown process to malignant forms.

Treatment of leukemia

Traditional treatment for all malignant disease has as its primary objective the complete removal or destruction of each neoplastic cell in the body. Sur-

Lymphatic system diseases

gery, using block dissection to prevent the cancer's spreading through the lymphatic system, and chemotherapy with one or more of several cytotoxic drugs (toxic to cells) are two major modes of treatment. In some malignant diseases, and leukemia is a prime example, the neoplastic cells are disseminated throughout the body, making surgical techniques inapplicable.

A variety of drugs has been developed to treat disseminated neoplasms. Such agents ideally are more destructive of metabolically active and fast-growing cells than of normal ones. Since in most instances the rate of growth and proliferation of neoplastic cells exceeds that of normal cells, cytotoxic drugs destroy primarily neoplastic cells. There are, however, slowly growing tumors, which are less successfully treated with cytotoxic drugs. In such cases normal cells are equally affected by the drugs, limiting the total dosage that can be administered over any one period.

As yet, unique nutritional requirements that might be used as a basis for treatment of leukemia have not been discovered. If, for example, neoplastic cells required for growth a certain vitamin that they could not synthesize themselves, drugs blocking the vitamin's formation might be used as a means of treatment. In virtually every instance, however, malignant cells have the same capacity as normal cells for the formation of growth and nutritional factors, so that normal cells are also affected by such drugs.

Even under ideal therapeutic circumstances, drugs do not destroy every leukemic cell. The rate of growth and division of each cell may not be quite the same, and some survive the most vigorous treatment. Even if 99% are killed during drug therapy, the remaining cells, still numbering in the many millions, continue dividing. They quickly replace those killed and the disease progresses. Assume 10^{10} (10 billion) malignant cells at the beginning of treatment. Destruction of 99% leaves approximately 10^8 (100 million) surviving therapy. If the cells double every 24 hours, a reasonable figure, the killed cells are replaced and 10^{10} malignant cells are again present in only seven days.

To try to destroy all malignant leukemic cells, doctors have resorted to a dramatic but dangerous treatment. High doses of X-rays are administered to the patient's entire body, doses far exceeding those ever used for diagnostic purposes, *e.g.,* to determine if a bone is broken. The dosages administered in radiation therapy for leukemia are actually lethal.

The quantity of radiation received is described in rads. An X-ray to detect a broken arm requires less than one rad; few individuals can survive 600 rads of total-body radiation. To treat patients with leu-

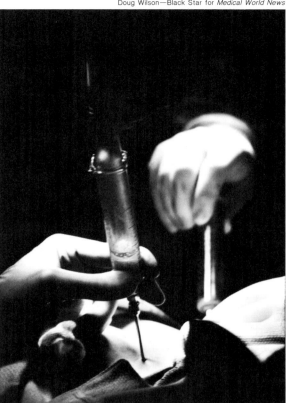

Bone marrow, collected from a healthy donor, can later be transplanted to a leukemic patient whose own blood cells have been depleted by chemo- or radiotherapy.

kemia, doctors give approximately 1,500 rads to the entire body, using machines and techniques especially designed for the purpose. Many types of cells, along with leukemic cells, are destroyed by the radiation. A large proportion of the patient's normal white and red blood cells and platelets are also destroyed by the radiation. Without additional treatment, individuals receiving such massive amounts of radiation will die, usually from anemia, bleeding, or infection.

Marrow transplantation

Patients receiving high X-ray doses can be saved, however, if they receive intact and healthy transplanted bone marrow. The marrow contains all the types of cells required to replace those destroyed, just as a blood transfusion replaces blood lost during surgery. Marrow for transplantation is obtained from the hip bones of a healthy donor, usually a member of the patient's family. Multiple needle aspirations are performed under anesthesia; the procedure is safe and does no permanent harm to the donor. Approximately 75 ml of marrow is removed, filtered under sterile conditions, and injected intravenously into the patient, usually within hours following the radiation treatment. One of the remarkable aspects of the transplanted cells is that they gradually migrate through the blood to the bone marrow and begin normal growth and proliferation. Unlike cancer cells, they do not grow in other organs or tissues of the body.

For a period of time following marrow grafting, lasting from one to several weeks, the patient is at great risk. The grafted cells do not immediately replace tissue destroyed by radiation. Until sufficient numbers of healthy marrow cells are produced, even a trivial infection may be fatal. The patient must be maintained in a carefully controlled, virtually germ-free bed, receiving antibiotic treatment and blood transfusions as required. A stream of warm, filtered, bacteria-free air is passed over his body; nurses and doctors entering the room wear surgical gloves and gowns. Gradually, cellular elements from the graft appear in the patient's blood, and the white cell count returns to normal.

It has not been determined whether or not each leukemic cell is destroyed by massive total-body radiation. In some cases the disease recurs after radiation treatment and marrow transplantation and is found in donor marrow cells, suggesting that the causative agent may be infectious. In successful treatment in which the disease does not recur, it is conceivable that immune mechanisms associated with the donor's cells eliminate any neoplastic cells not destroyed by radiation.

Problems of transplantation

Grafts of various types of tissues from one human to another are invariably rejected unless preventive measures are taken. The recipient's immune system recognizes that the donor cells are structurally different from his own and rejects the transplant. For most transplants drugs are administered to inhibit the recipient's immune system, allowing the graft to survive for longer than normal periods. In many cases, the recipient eventually becomes tolerant of the graft and lesser quantities of immune-inhibiting drugs are required. In marrow transplantation, however, the massive radiation administered to the recipient before grafting eliminates his immune system, allowing the graft to "take." The danger is that the donor marrow itself possesses all the cellular elements necessary to mount an effective immune attack upon the defenseless host, and in most cases it does so with potentially fatal results. The first indication of a "graft-versus-host" reaction is often the appearance of a widely spread skin rash, followed by enlargement of the spleen and liver. Lymphoid cells from the grafted marrow are attempting to reject the patient.

To avoid rejection, physicians carefully match the donor and recipient before the graft is attempted. Only when certain structural differences exist between the cells of the recipient and those of the donor does a graft-versus-host reaction occur. Grafts between identical twins take regularly, for just as donor and recipient are alike externally, so are they indistinguishable immunologically. Matching between nonidentical donors and recipients is done by specialized testing. Often, but not always, closely matched donors, including members of the patient's family, are suitable. By chance, approximately 25% of siblings are appropriate.

In human patients, transplant success is dependent upon identity of cell proteins and the similarity of other factors at a basic genetic level. The total number of such factors is extraordinarily large, so much so that the possibility of finding identically

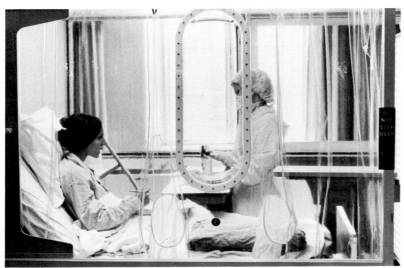

Maintenance of a germ-free environment can be crucial to the survival of an infection-prone patient. This laminar air flow unit filters all air entering the patient's room, rendering it completely sterile.

matched donors and recipients at random is virtually impossible. Thus, even within a family, graft-versus-host reactions very often occur. Fortunately, in close but nonidentical matches, transplants can be treated successfully—paradoxically with the same cytotoxic drugs used to treat leukemia. For unknown but certainly fortuitous reasons, the reaction gradually subsides as "chimerism," two genetically distinct cell types coexistent in the same host, is established.

—*Edward P. Cohen, M.D., Ph.D.*

Medical Ethics

On January 1, 1977, the Natural Death Act went into effect in the state of California. The bill, sponsored by California Assemblyman Barry Keene, is the first of what have come to be called "right to die" bills. It permits competent adults to sign a legally binding statement saying that they do not want their life prolonged artificially.

Restrictions within the law

By mid 1977 New Mexico, Idaho, and Arkansas had followed California's lead in enacting legislation. Legislation to permit stopping treatment or in some cases to permit active mercy killing upon request was considered in at least 38 states in the 1977 legislative session. There were great differences among the proposed bills; some permitted active killing for mercy; others designated guardians for patients not capable of making treatment decisions themselves. But these are difficult to write into law, and one reason the California legislation passed was that it authorizes neither of these procedures. First, it says specifically that the law should not be construed to condone, authorize, or approve mercy killing, that is, any affirmative or deliberate act to end life. Second, it applies only when a person is certified by two physicians to be terminally ill; that is, he must have an incurable condition that will, according to reasonable medical judgment, produce death, regardless of the application of life-sustaining procedures which will, in the physicians' opinion, serve only to postpone the moment of death. Furthermore, if the individual fills out the document before he becomes terminally ill, it must be renewed after five years, and it must also be reconfirmed after the terminal diagnosis is made. If the individual has already been certified terminally ill when the document is first signed, the instructions should be followed, but there must be a 14-day waiting period after the diagnosis is made. The patient may also revoke the document at any time.

These restrictions have led to as much criticism from those who think the bill does not go far enough as from those who believe that we should

Sidney Harris

"Somehow I was hoping genetic engineering would take a different turn."

not be passing any laws in this area at all. One complaint has been that the law may, by implication, deprive people of their already existing right to refuse medical treatment. It is now generally recognized that any legally competent person may refuse any medical treatment whatsoever, (unless, of course, the proposed treatment is aimed at protecting or benefiting society.) Some patients have refused to be treated with kidney machines, for example, because they found the physical and mental suffering unbearable even though the treatment would continue their lives indefinitely. This law, it is feared, could supersede the prevailing right to refuse treatment by limiting that right only to patients whose death is imminent and who will die no matter what treatment is offered.

Some people have found repugnant the idea of having to be certified as a "qualified patient" by two physicians. They, too, say the law may deprive the citizen of more rights than it establishes. In any case, the California bill is getting a great deal of attention in other state legislatures. It is the first statute that makes clear that a patient's refusal of treatment under specified conditions remains valid even if the patient becomes incompetent.

Genetic experimentation

Several other political bodies have taken on an even more complicated and far-reaching issue. With the discovery of DNA as the basic genetic material of every living organism, scientists and others have begun to experiment with techniques to remove pieces of these complex biochemicals, manipulate them, and recombine them. If DNA can be recombined by conscious human decision, we may be able to purposely change the genetic code, preventing genetic diseases in man and animals, improving agricultural crops and farm animals, and possibly even changing basic human physical and psychological characteristics.

However, it is not certain that DNA and its effects can be controlled once we begin to manipulate it. There has been fear that such manipulation might produce genetic monstrosities, or that the newly combined genetic material might join with bacteria to form a new, uncontrollably lethal strain. Since some of the living organisms being used in this research are common, such as the *E. coli* bacteria that normally live in the intestines, the effects of research could be serious. Since the research work is comparatively simple and attracts many scientists, governmental groups and the scientists themselves have heatedly debated questions about how such research should be controlled.

In 1974 a group of eleven prominent molecular biologists called for a voluntary moratorium on such research. This led to a conference in February 1975 at Asilomar in California, where an international group of approximately 140 scientists recommended that this research be continued, with certain controls governing the work they considered hazardous.

The more fundamental issue raised by the recombinant DNA debate is whether scientists should be free to set such controls themselves or whether the public should become more directly involved. While the technical and scientific questions are complex, many of the most crucial questions that need to be answered before policies of control can be determined are really not scientific at all. One of the basic issues is what to do when

there is a possibility of important benefit from research, but also the possibility of serious harm. No one can say with any certainty whether benefit or harm will result. While the risks are, for the most part, speculation, some think we should not permit research until it is certain that no serious harm will come of it. Scientists respond that it is impossible to prove that anything will be harmless, and they point out that even vaccines, common foods, and simple drugs could one day be found to be extremely harmful. The choice seems to hinge on how willing one is to take chances.

A closely related issue is how valuable one thinks the results will be. Many scientists feel that it is simply interesting and important to learn more about the basic processes of biology. At least those involved in recombinant DNA research believe there is nothing inherently immoral about manipulating the basic genetic material that controls life. In contrast, lay people may not agree that knowledge *per se* is inherently valuable; the genetic code may be one of the areas that should not be tampered with. Some argue for the freedom of scientific inquiry, while others insist that these issues are too important to be left to the scientists.

On June 23, 1976, the National Institutes of Health (NIH) issued official Guidelines for Research Involving Recombinant DNA Molecules. The guidelines recognize that there are certain experiments for which the potential hazard is so serious that they are not to be attempted at the present time. Other experiments can be undertaken provided that they can be expected to produce new knowledge or benefits to humanity that cannot readily

Cambridge, Mass., Mayor Alfred Vellucci (left) led that city's campaign for public hearings on controversial genetic experiments being carried out by Harvard University researchers. At a 1977 session of the Forum on Recombinant DNA Research, opponents of genetic experimentation staged a protest demonstration.

The Boston Globe   Paul S. Conklin

The use of prisoners as unwilling—and sometimes unknowing—subjects of medical experimentation has become a major concern of the National Commission for the Protection of Human Subjects of Biomedical and Behavioral Research.

be obtained by use of conventional methods, and provided that appropriate safeguards are incorporated into the design and execution of the experiment. Safeguards consisting of biological and physical barriers must be appropriate for the estimated potential hazard. Four levels of containment are specified, from high-level containment with specially built laboratories with airlocks and filters, biological safety cabinets, clothing changes for personnel, autoclaves within the facility, and the like, to low-level containment requiring daily decontamination of work surfaces, use of special equipment, pest control, and control of wastes leaving the laboratory.

Several state and local governments are particularly concerned that recombinant DNA research might jeopardize citizens within their jurisdictions. Actions have been taken in Bloomington, Ind., Princeton, N.J., New Haven, Conn., Ann Arbor, Mich., Cambridge, Mass., and other university towns. In Cambridge, Mayor Alfred Vellucci has long been an articulate spokesman for the interests of Cambridge residents when those interests might conflict with the interests of Harvard University. Cambridge was the first city to insist on a public, city council determination of whether the controversial experiments should be allowed. The city council called for the establishment of an advisory committee, the Cambridge Experimentation Review Board. The board was purposely made up of nonscientists and took on the job of judging whether the NIH guidelines would adequately protect the health of Cambridge citizens.

After a number of hearings the review board recommended on Jan. 5, 1977, that the research be allowed to go ahead in Cambridge, following the NIH guidelines with certain additional safeguards, including the precaution that a specially certi-

fied, weakened strain of bacteria be used in any of the experiments classified as "moderate risk" according to the guidelines. Those opposed to the research, including Mayor Vellucci, complained that the board had not been adequately critical of the NIH guidelines. Nevertheless, an important principle was established—that scientific research within a particular city is under the control of the citizens of that city, not simply of the scientists who want to conduct the research or even of the scientific community as a whole.

Human research subjects

A third major area where medical-ethical issues become a matter of public policy is in the ongoing work of the National Commission for the Protection of Human Subjects of Biomedical and Behavioral Research. This commission, appointed by the secretary of health, education, and welfare (HEW), is to review and recommend policies for protecting subjects of scientific research. Following earlier HEW regulations tightly controlling research using human fetuses, the commission, in October of 1976, issued a report recommending policies for research on prisoners. Eighty-five percent of the first tests of new drugs on humans are done in prisons. Groups of prisoners and persons concerned about protecting civil liberties have feared that prisoners may be seriously endangered by such experiments. It is felt that they cannot adequately consent to such research because they are confined; they may believe that their participation will increase the chance of getting paroled, or they may have no other way of earning money. Several states, such as Pennsylvania, have declared a moratorium on all such research because of these concerns. Yet some people, including many prisoners, have protested, saying that the risks were generally not that great, that they enjoyed the opportunity to do something interesting, and that participating gave them a chance to begin to pay their debt to society. They felt that they should have a right to participate in medical experiments and reap the benefits of participation.

The commission considered a flat ban on all prison research but rejected this alternative, concluding that research which has a reasonable probability of improving the health or well-being of the individual prisoner should be permitted. They also decided that studies of the possible causes, effects, and processes of incarceration and studies of the prisons as institutional structures or of prisoners as incarcerated persons may be conducted, provided they present minimal risks and are conducted by competent researchers and in adequate facilities. Beyond this, however, the commission has recommended that research involving prisoners should not be conducted or supported unless three requirements are met: (1) that the type of research fulfills an important social and scientific need, and the reasons for involving prisoners are compelling; (2) that the involvement of prisoners satisfies the conditions of equity; and (3) that there is a high degree of voluntariness on the part of the prospective participants and of openness on the part of the institution, including adequate living conditions, provisions for effective redress of grievances, separation of research participation from parole considerations, and public scrutiny. Detailed conditions are spelled out in the recommendations.

As in the California Natural Death Act and in the public efforts to regulate recombinant DNA research, public action to set ethical standards for biomedical actions has emerged as a central issue in the area of research on human beings. The commission calls for public scrutiny. The majority of the commission's members are, by law, people who are not researchers. The public has begun to play an increasingly important role in making ethical and policy choices about crucial medical-ethical practices. The ethical problems are ones in which the public's values may differ from those of the scientists. The issues do indeed seem to be too important to leave solely to the scientists.

—Robert M. Veatch, Ph.D.

Microbiology

Until recently knowledge of the structure of the cellular membrane of mammals was limited. Recent research has clarified details of the membrane's structure and its role in numerous functions that are important for cells and organs. What has become increasingly apparent is that the membrane is much more than simply a means of en-

veloping the contents of the cell. Through specialized molecules, mostly bound to the membrane, the internal environment of the cell is maintained. The membrane transports essential nutrient materials (*e.g.,* glucose and amino acids), ions (*e.g.,* sodium and potassium), and wastes (*e.g.,* carbon dioxide and lactic acid). The membrane maintains a precise intracellular environment for cell growth, metabolism, and many other specialized functions. Through membrane proteins, many diverse cellular roles are performed, including cell-cell recognition necessary for organization into tissues and organs, immune recognition required for antibody formation, cell-cell attachments necessary for the destruction of invading bacteria and phagocytosis (the ingestion of foreign substances).

Cell membranes

The interior of the cell itself, like its external environment, is aqueous. Virtually all internal and external substances used by the cell are water soluble. The membrane, however, exists in a water insoluble state, preserving its structural integrity, performing many diverse functions, and at the same time remaining semisolid. It has a means of "seeing" or monitoring the external environment, detecting changes as they occur and responding appropriately.

To accomplish these diverse and complicated functions, nature has evolved one basic membrane structure shared by a wide range of different animal species. As an example, the basic organization of the membranes of mosquito cells and other similar cell types are not fundamentally different from those of humans. Under special circumstances, the membranes of mosquito and mammalian cells can even be induced to fuse into a hybrid, structurally sound, functioning cell with two separate nuclei. Such hybrid cells are capable of indefinite proliferation, with the many mosquito and mammalian functions remaining identifiable. Further evidence for the similarity in membrane structure lies in the fact that after fusion of human and mosquito cells, membrane proteins of human and mosquito origin exchange places freely. Such evidence indicates that the organization and structure of cell membranes are old in an evolutionary sense and largely unchanged over many millions of years of biological development.

The membrane consists of a double layer of fatty, hydrophobic substances (not absorbing water) of small molecular size. Each molecule of the membrane has (like any laundry detergent or soap) a hydrophobic portion and a hydrophilic (water-absorbing) "head." The molecules spontaneously form double layers, with the hydrophobic portions opposed to each other and the hydrophilic heads exposed to the aqueous internal or external environments. Many millions of such molecules are required to form the membrane of a single cell.

As in many biological reactions, the components are in equilibrium, associating to form the membrane and disassociating spontaneously, forming and disrupting continuously. The individual components of the membrane exchange places with neighboring molecules approximately one million times per second, in a rapid resonance. Exchange across the double layer from the outer to the inner portion, a phenomenon known as "flip-flop," occurs very infrequently. Rapid exchange and spontaneous association and dissociation provides flexibility of the membrane and aids in its responsiveness to environmental changes affecting the function of the cell.

Membrane proteins

Approximately 50% of the membrane is composed of various types of protein molecules. It is through the diversity of these proteins that the many functions of the cells are performed. Some proteins of the membrane transport ions; some are responsible for immune recognition, and others perform many different functions. They may be thought of as the "eyes" of the cell, sensing and testing the external and internal environments. The proteins of the membrane are continually synthesized and degraded, *i.e.,* they undergo a metabolic "turnover" with a characteristic turnover rate for each type. The rate of turnover and the density or concentration of each kind of protein changes as the cell's needs change.

The membrane proteins also have a hydrophobic region, allowing spontaneous association with the hydrophobic portion of the membrane, and a hydrophilic region exposed to the aqueous environment. Thus, one portion of the protein interacts with external stimuli, and the other portion is anchored in the hydrophobic layer.

Immunoglobulin-forming cells, those that produce antibodies, have receptors on their surface

that are sensitive to particular foreign substances (antigens). A cell begins antibody formation after exposure to a specific antigen. Many different types of immunoglobulin receptors exist on many different types of antibody-forming cells so that the body can respond to the very large number of different foreign materials that are capable of acting as antigens.

The density, or concentration, of receptors per cell changes periodically, reflecting certain metabolic requirements of the cell, or as a defense following exposure to potentially lethal environmental agents. Insulin, for example, is involved in the transport of glucose, the energy-providing molecule, from the exterior to the interior of the cell. Specific receptors for insulin are present on cell surfaces, and their concentration increases at times of rapid growth and metabolism and during periods of increased glucose need. At other times, during periods of reduced metabolism, the concentration of insulin receptors decreases. It is likely that similar phenomena occur for other receptors. Hormone-stimulated cells, for example, are insensitive to excess stimulation by hormone through a decrease in receptor density.

In other more specialized examples, cell membrane proteins that are the targets of antibody attack may actually disappear from the cell in the presence of antibodies. For example, thymus leukemia (TL) antigens of certain mouse cells show this phenomenon. In the presence of TL antibodies, the TL protein antigens of the leukemia cells disappear and the cells escape destruction. The process is reversible; returned to an environment free of TL antibodies, the TL proteins of the cell are reformed. The process is one way cancer cells avoid destruction by the host's immune processes.

The number of membrane proteins of one type is about one million per cell. The metabolic turnover rate for different membrane proteins varies. The $t_{1/2}$ (the time it takes for one-half of a specific type of protein to be replaced) of TL protein antigens of invasive leukemia cells is, for example, approxi-

A fanciful diagram illustrates the organization of the major proteins in a human cell membrane. The shaded area indicates the lipid permeability barrier. Specific proteins, represented by fruit and vegetable forms, are numbered according to their order in electrophoretic analysis or identified simply as glycoproteins (GP).

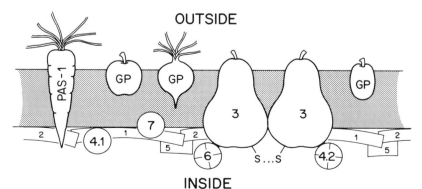

From T.L. Steck, *Journal of Cell Biology*, Vol. 62, Figure 4, pp. 1–19 (1974); reproduced with permission from the Rockefeller University Press

mately 18 hours. The $t_{1/2}$ of other proteins, for example, H-2 and a tumor-associated antigen of the same cell type, is 26 and 44 hours respectively. This turnover rate is the mechanism through which the cell regulates the quantity of membrane proteins that are exposed to the external environment. In the case of an attack on the cell by antibodies to the TL proteins, for example, the rate of removal of TL protein from the membrane accelerates. The rate of insertion of new TL protein into the membrane remains the same, leading to a reduction in the protein on the cell surface.

—*Edward P. Cohen, M.D., Ph.D.*

Muscle Diseases

Many diseases affect the skeletal muscles. Some have external causes—parasitic infections, toxins, and alcohol, to name a few—while others are hereditary. Disorders in nerve transmission may also affect muscular strength and coordination. Another category of muscle disorders appears to be the result of metabolic changes produced by endocrine malfunction, injury, or external agents such as laxatives, diuretics, or anesthetics. Among the most common muscle diseases are muscular dystrophy, the progressive muscle weakness known as myasthenia gravis, and the inflammatory condition called dermatomyositis.

Muscular dystrophy

Muscular dystrophy is actually a name for several related hereditary diseases characterized by gradual deterioration and progressive weakening of the muscles. In most types the disorder becomes evident in childhood or, occasionally, in early adolescence or young adulthood and becomes increasingly debilitating with age. Most victims eventually succumb to cardiac or respiratory failure, although there are some forms of the disease where survival to old age is known.

No cure for muscular dystrophy has yet been discovered; patients are treated with physical therapy to counteract the muscular weakness and provided with external supports and splints to aid in mobility. The so-called Duchenne type of muscular dystrophy, one of the most severe and rapidly fatal, usually affects young boys. Recent studies of this disease have shown that patients are increasingly surviving into their twenties, although the condition requires that they be confined to bed or wheelchair. Because this disorder is known to be associated with a sex-linked recessive trait, a majority of female carriers can be identified. Genetic counseling and sex determination tests early in pregnancy can help these women decide whether to have children when the disease is a likely outcome.

Disorders of nerve transmission

Various neuromuscular syndromes are associated with the inability of nerve synapses to release acetylcholine, a substance that acts in the transmission of nerve impulses. The diseases include dermatomyositis, peripheral neuropathy, and weakness similar to that in myasthenia gravis. Treatment with guanidine has proven effective in promoting the release of acetylcholine from nerve terminals and thus alleviating the muscular weakness associated with many of the diseases caused by acetylcholine blockage.

Syndromes involving acetylcholine blockage occur in 6% of persons with cancer but are particularly common in lung cancer patients. The Eaton-Lambert syndrome, usually associated with small-cell carcinoma of the lung, is characterized by muscle weakness in the shoulders, hips, and thighs and depressed or absent reflexes; other symptoms include dry mouth and numbness and tingling of the skin. The majority of male patients with Eaton-Lambert syndrome have a malignancy; among females suffering from the disorder, malignancy is less common.

Botulinum toxin (the poisonous substance produced by the bacteria that causes the food poisoning known as botulism) also interferes with the release of acetylcholine and can cause severe paralysis. A similar paralysis can be caused by the bite of the tick, through a mechanism probably involving a neurotoxin in tick saliva that interferes with acetylcholine release. The rapidly progressive paralysis, accompanied by loss of reflexes, is often confused with poliomyelitis. Although the condition can be fatal, total recovery usually occurs if the tick is removed.

The so-called restless-legs syndrome, an unusual and peculiar muscular disorder, also involves abnormalities of nerve transmission. The condition is characterized by abnormal or decreased sensation in the lower extremities, frequently accompanied by spontaneous twitching of muscles and an irresistible need to move the legs. In some recent case studies, the symptoms were found to interfere with sleep. Electromyography and muscle biopsies have suggested that this syndrome is a neurogenic disease.

Parasitic infestations and muscular disorders

Several parasitic infestations can affect the muscles. One such condition is trichinosis, caused by the nematode (roundworm) *Trichinella spiralis*. The source of infestation is usually uncooked or undercooked pork, although infestations from bear and walrus meat have been reported. Once ingested, the parasite makes its way to the host's intestines, where it reproduces; the larvae then travel through

Paul Almasy

Snails carrying the schistosomiasis-inducing flatworm are collected from a river by Sudanese workers in an effort to eradicate the degenerative muscle disease in the area.

the intestinal walls and bury themselves in the body's muscle tissue. Fever, muscular pain, and muscular weakness result. The disease is rarely fatal, although death can occur if the heart muscle is affected. Over the past several years there has been a marked reduction in trichinosis because of laws requiring cooking of garbage fed to hogs, technological advances in meat storage, and education of the public about thorough cooking of pork. Many cases currently seen result from eating uncooked blood sausage, still considered a delicacy by some people. Trichinosis can mimic other types of muscle diseases.

Toxoplasmosis is another parasitic disease that can involve muscles and cause rash, swollen lymph glands, and enlargement of the liver and spleen. The disease is caused by *Toxoplasma gondii*, a one-celled parasite widely found among mammals, especially cats and birds. The means whereby man and animals acquire *T. gondii* are unknown. Human-to-human transfer appears to occur only from mother to fetus.

In tropical countries two other parasitic diseases, trypanosomiasis and schistosomiasis, are important causes of muscle degeneration. Trypanosomiasis, also known as African sleeping sickness, is caused by the blood parasite *Trypanosoma*

gambiense. It is transmitted to man by the bite of the tsetse fly. Schistosomiasis is caused by infestation with certain blood flukes (a type of parasitic flatworm). Infection is spread by the disposal of infected human excrement into fresh water, the presence of suitable snail hosts necessary for the organism's life cycle, and the exposure of humans to infested water. Such exposure may occur from washing clothes, bathing, wading, or working in contaminated water. It is believed that about 150 million persons are currently affected by this disease, particularly in South America, Africa, and Southeast Asia.

Metabolic malfunctions

Experiments have shown that a decrease in blood potassium can produce muscle weakness. It is now recognized that there are familial patterns in certain forms of muscle weakness related to hyperkalemia (too much potassium) and hypokalemia (too little potassium). These disorders are known as periodic paralysis and usually begin in childhood or adolescence. Patients have periodic weakness brought on by cold, surgery, exercise, sleep, menses, pregnancy, or rest after stress. The hyperkalemic form may progress to quadriplegia (paralysis of arms and legs) although facial, eye, and respiratory muscles are not affected. Hypokalemic paralysis can also occur in normal individuals who make excessive use of laxatives and in patients with aldosteronism—a condition involving excessive potassium excretion—who take diuretics. Laxatives cause loss of potassium from the gastrointestinal tract, while diuretics produce increased excretion of potassium by the kidneys.

Exertional rhabdomyolysis is a form of muscle injury that occurs in healthy individuals with poor muscular conditioning who perform excessive repetitive exercises such as pushups and squatjumps. The disease is characterized by marked swelling, soreness, and weakness of muscles. Tests show an elevation of muscle enzymes in the blood, myoglobinuria (excessive amounts of the muscle protein myoglobin in the urine), and increased myoglobin in the blood. In some families, the tendency to develop the condition is believed to be due to an enzymatic defect of muscle fibers that reduces tolerance for strenuous activity. Some patients have a lifelong predisposition to attacks and must curtail strenuous physical activity.

Myoglobinuria resulting from muscle damage can also be caused by a major arterial occlusion, injury involving crushed muscles, narcotic abuse, hypokalemia due to laxative abuse, heat stroke, repeated seizures, influenza, and rare hereditary metabolic disorders. If a large amount of myoglobin is passed through the kidneys, renal failure can occur, sometimes requiring kidney dialysis.

Effects of alcohol and anesthesia

In a small percentage of patients, alcohol is responsible for muscle dysfunction. Hospitalization may be necessary to treat the acute, general muscle weakness and pain associated with excessive alcohol intake. The symptoms usually disappear within two weeks. Microscopic studies of the muscles have shown considerable but nonspecific evidence of damage to muscle fibers from alcohol. Alcoholics may become incapacitated by chronic neuropathy-myopathy in which both nerves and muscles degenerate.

An unusual and very rare complication of general anesthesia is malignant hyperpyrexia, a condition characterized by a rapid and steep rise in temperature, rapid heartbeat and respiration, prolonged muscular contraction and rigidity, and elevations of muscle enzymes in the blood. The disorder occurs particularly with halothane anesthesia, and susceptibility may be genetically determined. The condition has a 60–75% mortality rate and is apparently due to a metabolic abnormality of muscles that involves calcium. Death can result from cardiac arrhythmias or kidney failure.

In extremely rare cases, patients show an inability to metabolize succinylcholine, which is administered as a muscle relaxant for surgery. The condition is due to an enzyme deficiency. Because the patient's endocrine system is unable to inactivate the drug, prolonged paralysis may result.

—Eric R. Hurd, M.D.

Obstetrics and Gynecology

Cancer of the female reproductive organs has become an increasingly important focus for physicians in the field of obstetrics and gynecology. Of particular current interest are the causes of such cancers—with special attention to the controversial subject of postmenopausal estrogen therapy, their detection, and innovative methods of treatment. The use of amniocentesis in diagnosing fetal abnormalities is also a subject of current study.

Estrogen and cancer

In recent months physicians and patients alike have become concerned over reports of a possible link between postmenopausal estrogen therapy and cancer of the lining of the uterus (endometrial cancer). During the past decade the use of estrogen in menopausal patients has increased. Proponents of the treatment believe that postmenopausal estrogen can abolish uncomfortable and embarrassing "hot flashes," enhance the patient's emotional status, retard loss of calcium in bone, and retard aging in vaginal and breast tissue. These physicians view menopause as a deficiency disease rather than as a "physiologic" period in a woman's life. At present, however, many studies indicate that, in certain individuals, estrogen acting over a prolonged period of time will result in a condition characterized by thickening of the lining of the uterus (endometrial adenomatous hyperplasia). The most advanced degree of this condition is a surface cancer that many physicians believe precedes frankly invasive cancer.

To date, most of the information on the adverse effects of estrogen therapy is based on review of case reports and collections of retrospective results. Much more meaningful data will be available when large numbers of women are followed prospectively for a number of years. Early studies of retrospective data, however, indicate that women exposed to postmenopausal estrogen therapy are four times more likely to develop endometrial cancer than women who are not so treated. Many physicians believe that the cancer risk can be minimized by using the lowest possible effective dose of hormone, interrupting the use of the agent for 5–7 days every month, and immediately investigating any bleeding that occurs during the course of treatment. Some physicians use a combination of estrogen and a second female hormone, progesterone, to manage the menopausal symptoms. In combination, these two hormones prevent the development of endometrial hyperplasia; the drawback of this treatment is that menstrual periods continue.

Early reports indicate that the cancers found in estrogen-treated patients are less advanced, less aggressive, and respond more favorably to treatment than cancers found in women not treated with estrogen. Survival rates appear to be higher for estrogen-treated patients. Many physicians, including members of a special committee of the American College of Obstetricians and Gynecologists, continue to support the use of postmenopausal estrogen in symptomatic individuals in a well-planned program of health care. For minimum risk, estrogen administration should be cyclic, low-dose, and terminated at the earliest opportunity.

Colposcopy and cancer detection

Diagnostic colposcopy was developed in the mid-1920s by a German physician named Hans Hinselmann. The technique was slow to gain acceptance in the United States, primarily because of competi-

A gynecological oncologist uses a colposcope to examine a patient's vaginal and cervical tissues.

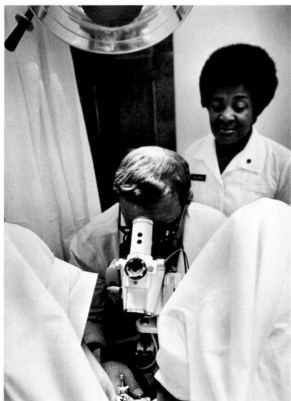

George Tames from *Contemporary OB/GYN,* September 1973

tion in diagnosis with the Pap smear (cervical vaginal cytology). In recent years, however, colposcopy has assumed a great importance, not so much as a screening process for cervical cancer but as a tool for evaluation after the Pap smear has revealed an abnormality. The colposcope is basically a binocular magnifying instrument that is inserted into the vagina for examination of vaginal and cervical tissues, magnifying an area under study approximately 13 times. Coupled with the optical instrument is a powerful light source that illuminates the area under observation.

The colposcope is used primarily to evaluate the uterine cervix (mouth of the womb). Thirty years ago cancer in this site was, in the female, the leading cause of death due to malignancy. It is widely felt that early diagnosis and treatment have contributed to the more than 50% reduction in the death rate for this cancer. The colposcope is used in the doctor's office for examination of the cervix. If it reveals any of the several characteristic patterns of abnormality, the physician will remove portions of the abnormal tissue for study in the laboratory. This procedure is called biopsy; it is almost painless to the patient and requires no anesthesia. The combined use of the Pap smear and colposcopy enables physicians to identify and treat the early precursors of cervical cancer. These precursors are called *dysplasia* or, in their most severe degree, cancer *in situ* (surface cancer). When discovered and treated in these early. stages, abnormalities of the cervix are virtually 100% curable.

Cryosurgery

The most recent method of treatment for the cancer precursor known as dysplasia is called *cryosurgery,* a freezing technique in which a refrigerant gas is administered to the disease site by means of a treatment wand. First, the wand is placed against the area to be treated. When the apparatus is turned on, the refrigerant reduces the temperature at the tip of the wand to the range of −94 to −292° F (−70 to −180° C). After the tissue is frozen it is allowed to return to normal temperature and then is frozen again for a short time. This freezing, thawing, refreezing technique causes crystallization within the diseased cells, thus destroying them. After cervical cryosurgery the patient has a profuse vaginal discharge for several weeks, during which the cervix undergoes healing. Before the advent of cryosurgery, precancerous conditions in the cervix were treated with electro- or heat coagulation or even surgical removal of the affected tissue.

Amniocentesis

Amniocentesis, the removal of a small amount of the amniotic fluid that surrounds a developing fetus, is a technique that is being increasingly relied upon for the diagnosis of numerous conditions. The technique may be used any time following the 10th week of pregnancy until just before delivery, although it is more commonly done in the 14th to 16th weeks. The obstetrician first washes the mother's abdomen with a surgical soap, then anesthetizes a small area on the abdomen over the uterus and passes a needle three to four inches long through the mother's abdominal wall and into the pregnant uterus. (The amount of amniotic fluid surrounding the fetus varies from a few drops in the early weeks of pregnancy up to a quart or more just prior to delivery.)

After the fluid sample is withdrawn, it is studied in the laboratory. In most cases the sex of the baby can be determined by examining cells in the fluid. The procedure also allows for the diagnosis of more than 40 biochemical disorders. A number of severely handicapping genetic disorders may be detected in very early stages of pregnancy, including such diseases as mongolism (Down's syndrome), gargoylism (Hurler's syndrome), Tay-Sachs disease, and Pompe's disease. Prenatal diagnosis of these conditions allows the parents to opt for early abortion or, if they decide against abortion, gives time for emotional and medical adjustment in advance of the baby's arrival. Study of the fluid can also disclose prenatal infection secondary to either bacteria or virus.

The risks of amniocentesis are relatively small. Infection and hemorrhage in the mother have been reported on rare occasions. Fetal complications are more common and include damage to the fetus from the needle itself; fetal complications resulting in miscarriage as a direct result of amniocentesis occur in less than 1% of all procedures performed. The value and advantages of amniocentesis lie in its allowance for qualitative evaluation at a time when the pregnancy can be safely terminated if such action meets with the moral and ethical standards of the pregnant patient.

— Robert E. Rogers, M.D.

Osteopathic Medicine

The osteopathic profession in early 1977 numbered 15,894 D.O.s (doctors of osteopathy), in addition to a 1977 graduating class of nearly 900. Because an estimated three-fourths of D.O.s are in general practice, and a substantial proportion of the remainder are in such specialties as internal medicine, pediatrics, and obstetrics and gynecology, osteopathic physicians continue to contribute primary health care to a larger proportion of the population than would be expected on the basis of their numbers. Surveys show that the average D.O. sees 128 patients per week, a total of 105 million patient visits per year for all D.O.s. Osteopathic hospitals also contribute significantly to public health care; in 1976 an estimated 825,000 patients spent a total of 6.3 million days in osteopathic hospitals, with another 3.1 million outpatient visits recorded.

Several factors in osteopathic philosophy seem to contribute particularly to the profession's emphasis on primary care. One factor is an emphasis on the wholeness of the patient, as opposed to seeing him as a group of loosely connected body systems, which is the danger in subspecialty medical practice. The holistic view is a natural outgrowth of several traditional osteopathic tenets: a respect for the body's own healing power; a practice that stresses the interrelationship between nerves, muscles, bones, and the internal organs; and the general inseparability of structure and function, whether of the cell or of the whole patient. Another factor is the person-to-person contact with individual patients that arises from practicing manipulative therapy. Manipulation is, of course, only part of osteopathic medical practice, as are surgery or prescription or laboratory examination. Osteopathic manipulation was for a time so closely

A highly specialized branch of osteopathy diagnoses and treats the delicate musculoskeletal system of infants.

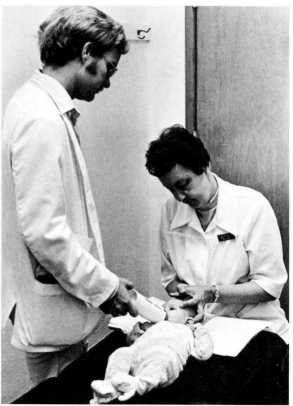

Courtesy, American Osteopathic Association

identified with the profession that many people erroneously came to think that D.O.s practiced nothing else. This emphasis on manipulation to correct faulty structure has almost certainly affected the way osteopathic physicians think about patients.

Osteopathic diagnosis and treatment

In addition to using conventional medical diagnosis and treatment, osteopathic physicians typically examine and treat the musculoskeletal system. The D.O.'s ordinary structural diagnostic methods include recording of the patient's medical history, observation, motion testing, and palpation, or manual examination. Other, less frequently employed methods include electromyography, X-ray, and various laboratory tests.

Structural examination of certain joints, for example, might yield the following findings: restriction or excess of motion; abnormality of body tissues, including tissue states of congestion, spasm, inflammation, or fibrosis; unusual asymmetry of joint structure or function; or significant patterns of pain or tenderness. A typical diagnosis would accompany such findings with a very detailed description of the abnormality as well as all related findings.

While this diagnosis can in itself provide the basis for treatment, most osteopathic physicians also wish to determine the cause of the patient's problems in order to help the patient avoid similar ailments in the future. Causes commonly found by the osteopath for musculoskeletal disorders include occupational strain, difference in leg lengths, injury, and the lack of exercise; less common causes might include disk disorders, tumors, or any of dozens of visceral diseases that would affect the musculoskeletal system.

To treat the musculoskeletal problems of motion restriction, asymmetry, pain, and tissue change—assuming, of course, no medical complications—the D.O. would probably use manipulation. However, the D.O. may also prescribe the use of heat, exercise or other physical therapy, muscle relaxants, or other suitable medications. When using manipulation to treat motion restriction, special care is given to avoid injury to the patient. The physician must know exactly how each joint normally works and the types and extent of force that can be tolerated by the body tissue of the patient in question. The D.O. must also be skilled in a variety of manual procedures that facilitate the application of force in precisely the correct manner required to reestablish the normal range of motion.

Motion restriction can be corrected either directly, by forcing the joint to resume its normal range of motion; semidirectly, by having the patient participate in resistive exercises to break down the barrier to normal motion; or indirectly, by using reflex points, soft-tissue stretching or massage, or other methods that essentially remove the obstructive barrier and allow the joint to resume its ordinary functioning.

While tissue texture abnormalities will often correct themselves when joint motion is restored, they may also be treated separately. The known effects of any soft-tissue treatment may include the relief of spasm and the improvement of local circulation and local muscle tone.

To a certain extent everyone is affected by musculoskeletal asymmetry, but most people easily compensate for this asymmetry in their normal bodily movement and functioning. When the osteopathic physician speaks of asymmetry, he or she is concerned either about the loss of compensation for asymmetry or about the temporary asymmetries that accompany motion restriction and tissue change. Asymmetry, however, is ordinarily regarded as part of the entire treatment complex rather than as a separate entity.

The same might also be said of pain as the patient's pain patterns can provide clues to the primary focus of dysfunction and would certainly affect the way in which treatment is given. Ordinarily, however, once visceral or other medical causes for pain are ruled out, pain and tenderness are considered indicators of the resolution of the musculoskeletal problem. Additionally, of course, pain is regarded as a symptom requiring temporary relief until its underlying cause can be corrected.

Growth of the field

Osteopathic diagnosis and treatment is a far more exact science than can be indicated by the brief description above. Although the profession is reluctant to call structural diagnosis and treatment a specialty, an osteopathic board was authorized in 1977 to certify those D.O.s who have displayed requisite academic and practical skills in manipulative medicine. These physicians are now identified by the letters "F.A.A.O." after their degree, representing an earned Fellowship in the American Academy of Osteopathy, the academic affiliate of the osteopathic profession that gives special attention to structural diagnosis and treatment. Many D.O.s have not yet sought certification, however, but are of course equally skilled in their profession.

The emphasis on family health care has motivated public support for new colleges of osteopathic medicine in several states in recent years. The trend began with the establishment of a new college in Michigan in 1969, with the first class admitted that fall. Classes have subsequently begun studies in new osteopathic schools in Texas (1970), West Virginia (1972), Oklahoma (1972), and Ohio

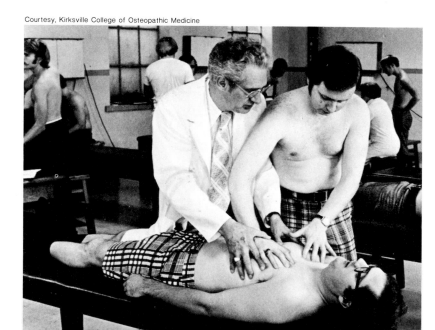

A physician shows an osteopathic student how to evaluate motion of the rib cage. This motion testing will reveal how the musculoskeletal phase of respiration is working and may also help the D.O. localize one of the kinds of pain that mimic internal disorders. Pain at the junction of a rib with the sternum, for example, is sometimes confused with pain in the heart or in the lungs.

(1976). Two new schools admitting classes in the fall of 1977 are located in New Jersey and New York, bringing the total number of active osteopathic schools to 12, with others in the planning stages. Whatever the cause, the profession is growing at an unprecedented rate, and the profession's organizational programs are designed for further expansion.

Laboratory and clinical studies in osteopathic medicine cover a full range of interests, and osteopathic specialists contribute to medical knowledge through their own and other medical journals. Among the recent studies that might be termed specifically osteopathic (that is, related directly to the structure-function question and involving the neuro-musculo-skeletal system) were some findings about the cranial structures of school children. One study suggested that learning disabilities may often have a structural component and presented some evidence that a team approach including specialized manipulative therapy can aid in correcting the problem. Another study using a standardized examination by palpation indicated that craniosacral examination findings can be used to identify children with learning disabilities, behavioral problems, and motor coordination problems.

Other studies during the year covered a wide range of topics. Among them were statistical studies pointing to the advantages of sigmoidoscopy as a cancer-detecting method for all hospital patients, showing types of cancer incidence in a group of Catholic nuns, and indicating the use of divided X-ray doses for treatment of Hodgkin's disease. Other papers suggested evidence for a musculoskeletal component in some patients diagnosed as having angina pectoris, argued against routine tonsillectomy and adenoidectomy as a dangerous and unnecessary procedure, and indicated some advantages of the newer noninvasive types of diagnostic methods, including computer-assisted tomography and echosonography.

In more basic research, one specifically osteopathic study dealt with the ability of the spine to "learn and remember" reflexes, which has implications for the continuation or recurrence of many conditions related to the spinal nerves. Another project continued study on the ability of nerve substances to actually move into muscles in some form, which relates to a variety of clinical states ranging from injury to such poorly understood diseases as the muscle-wasting disorders.

The osteopathic profession has continued to support such public health plans as national health insurance, with provisions for the patient's free choice of physician and other guarantees of individualization and efficiency. It has continued to share the concern of all health professionals about the cost and decreasing availability of professional liability insurance. Most of the profession's organizational efforts, however, have continued to be directed toward its own educational, accrediting, and regulatory programs. The profession's requirement for continuing medical education remains a major individual and organizational activity.

—*Barbara Peterson*

Special Report:
An Osteopathic Approach to Sports Medicine

by Keith D. Peterson, D.O.

With the growth of scholastic and professional sports and with the increasing numbers of individuals participating in athletics, sports has become one of the prevalent institutions in our society. A steadily increasing number of athletic programs at all levels are calling on doctors of osteopathy (D.O.s) to serve as team physicians in treating injuries and administering conditioning programs. A 1973 survey of Michigan high schools, for example, showed that a disproportionate number of D.O.s serve as physicians for athletic teams. Several professional teams in basketball, football, hockey, and other sports have employed D.O.s as team physicians. Famous individual athletes such as

Paul Steingard, D.O., team physician for the Phoenix Suns basketball team, examines former player Dick Van Arsdale. Osteopathic medicine is particularly compatible with the needs of athletes, and many doctors of osteopathy serve as amateur and professional team physicians.

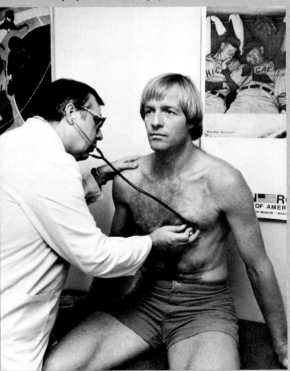

Courtesy, The Sports Medicine Clinic, Phoenix, Arizona

Muhammad Ali, Gordie Howe, Tom Seaver, and Archie Griffin have received care from D.O.s.

There is more than coincidence between the growth of sports and of osteopathic sports medicine. With its emphasis on the musculoskeletal systems, osteopathy is ideally suited to sports medicine. D.O.s use exercise and athletics as prevention and therapy for injury and disease. To the D.O. sports are more than a cause of problems; they can be treatment as well.

Osteopathic medicine was founded in the late 1800s when organized sports amounted to little. However, Viola M. Frymann, D.O., in discussing the principles of osteopathy in the 1970s, has used concepts that sound as if they might have come straight from the modern playing field. "The law of cause and effect provides the explanation for disease and health. Disease is the effect of a change in the parts of the physical body. Disease in an abnormal body is just as natural as is health when all parts are in place. Life and matter can be united, and that union cannot continue with any hindrance to free and absolute motion. Motion is the first and only evidence of life. We know life only by motion of material bodies. All motion is matter in action." When an athlete's ability to generate motion—be it the crunching lunge of a football player or the gazelle-like grace of a long-distance runner—is impaired, the physician must not only understand the disability but also be able to give the athlete the therapeutic treatment necessary to restore his skill.

The Sports Medicine Clinic and its methods

Today athletes account for about 95% of the total practice at the Sports Medicine Clinic in Seattle, Wash. The office is equipped to start patients on rehabilitation programs as soon as possible after their injuries have been treated. The methods are used on the elderly as well as on football players. Everyone is given the same basic exercises for the same types of injuries. Some of the patients can do 50 sets of an exercise; others only one. The importance of exercise in dealing with the injuries of athletes and others cannot be overemphasized.

Such an approach to the treatment of athletic injuries has in fact a long history. Written records,

The movements of an athlete such as a runner are the essence of his skill. The physician who treats the injured athlete must not only diagnose the disability but also help the athlete regain unhindered movement.

dating hundreds of years before Christ, advocate therapeutic exercise. We know that exercise and massage were used as preparation for combat as early as 1000 B.C. Greeks wrote of the value of therapeutic exercise. Hippocrates even recommended it for mental disorders.

Patients are approached aggressively. The more complete the data on patients, the more aggressive and positive the treatment can be. It is easy to be conservative, to tell the patient to put heat on the injury, rest, and come back in three weeks. Care has to be taken, of course, to avoid the risk of permanent injury. The athlete is particularly dependent on the physician as a guard against pushing himself beyond safe limits.

Some general problems in sports medicine

Of course, the medical concerns of athletes vary. When treating a high school or college athlete, the physician especially wants to prevent permanent injury. The professional athlete depends on the

physician to keep him earning his livelihood for as long as possible. But the problems are different with amateur athletes who, although they often are not in good physical condition, sometimes play with the fervor of champions. Each problem demands the best of a doctor's medical knowledge and judgment.

Many other factors influence the practice of sports medicine. It is the opinion of many physicians, for example, that one of the most common problems is withstanding coaches, and parents, who want a player to return to competition before he is ready. Such pressure puts responsibility on the physician to respect the athlete's need to live a healthy life after his playing days are over.

Studies in the U.S. in the 1970s have indicated that there are serious deficiencies in treating athletic injuries. Among other things, the study of Michigan high schools indicated that most do not provide proper care, either through D.O.s or M.D.s, for many athletes. According to the survey, less

273

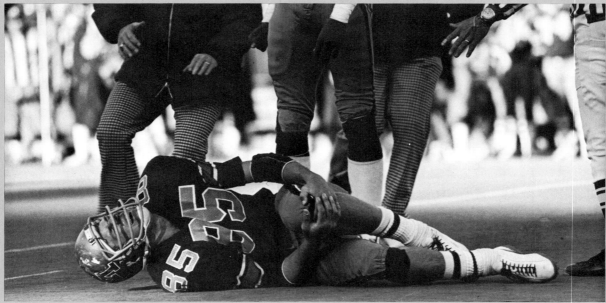

Studies have shown that many athletic injuries are not treated properly, sometimes causing permanent disabilities. Returning players to competition without adequate rehabilitation is an equally serious cause of disabilities. Although calisthenics are a part of all athletes' preparation, studies have indicated that more thorough examinations and conditioning programs would significantly reduce the number of injuries that now occur among athletes.

than 28% of the schools had a physician under contract for the care of student athletes. Less than 1% of the schools had a properly certified trainer, and only 1% of the potential athletic injuries could be treated immediately by a licensed physician.

Equally dismaying is the evidence that proper conditioning as well as treatment could reduce injuries. An osteopathic study of high school football injuries in the St. Louis, Mo., area has indicated that preseason evaluation of athletes and proper exercises would prevent a majority of the injuries that occur. The study recommends that trainers and coaches work with physicians to provide better medical care for athletes.

The rewards of practicing sports medicine have been voiced by many, but perhaps no one has expressed them as well as Raymond Forsyth, D.O.: "Thrills that include seeing a boy who was hurt badly in a game against Holy Cross University treated osteopathically all week and 'run wild' a week later to help beat the University of San Francisco; to see one of your college football stars make All-American. . . . to see one of your boys break a track record for dashes; to train a boy for the coming Olympic games; to watch a potentially great pitcher like Harold Newhouser, whose previous best record was 9 won and 17 lost, develop into a 29-game winner in his first year under osteopathic care, and repeat with 27 victories the next year, and be chosen the most valuable player both years, and then perform brilliantly in the World Series of 1945—these are all great thrills that don't come to many of us. There is room for many more osteopathic physicians in this great field, athletic therapy."

Pain

The prevention and alleviation of pain have always been among the primary goals of medicine and the healing arts. Most people have at some time experienced acute pain, usually caused by injury. But many people suffer from chronic, often incapacitating, pain, either the harbinger of a terminal illness such as cancer or the unwelcome accompaniment of a chronic condition such as arthritis. A small number of people are afflicted with a more unusual disorder—the inability to feel pain of any sort. Although some might consider this condition a blessing, those who cannot feel pain often injure themselves unknowingly and do not seek appropriate medical attention. Pain is an essential warning system, loud and insistent, that demands action. Unfortunately, even after the warning has been sounded, the pain often continues, resulting in further misery.

The very nature of the mechanism by which pain is perceived has baffled scientists for centuries. Moreover, until recently the lack of understanding of pain was reflected in the limited methods available to relieve it. Aside from a small armamentarium of potentially dangerous drugs, the physician could offer little more than sympathy to the sufferer of severe, debilitating pain. All of this began to change, however, with the announcement in the mid-1960s of a new theory of pain.

The gate theory of pain

In 1965 Ronald Melzack of McGill University, Montreal, and Patrick Wall of the Massachusetts Institute of Technology, Cambridge, announced the so-called spinal gate theory of pain perception, thus precipitating a revolution in pain research. According to the theory, millions of sensors inside the body and on its surface supply the brain with a constant stream of information. It has long been known that nerves are made up of many fibers, large and small. The larger fibers quickly conduct touch-related impulses to the brain. The smaller fibers, acting more slowly, conduct pain impulses. Both sets of nerve fibers converge at the spinal cord, where, according to the spinal gate theory, a "gatelike" mechanism ordinarily blocks out the pain impulses. However, if the large fibers become overloaded by continued or increasing stimulus, the spinal "gate" opens, allowing the pain impulses to reach the brain.

The spinal gate theory has remained controversial because it does not explain all aspects of the pain mechanism. In addition, it cannot be investigated by presently available laboratory techniques. Nonetheless, the theory has helped bring about greater understanding of many aspects of pain and has stimulated new research. The gate theory has also been invoked in explanation of acupuncture anesthesia.

Electronic pain suppressors

Shortly after the spinal gate theory was announced, surgeon C. Norman Shealy developed an electronic pain suppressor called the "dorsal column stimulator" (DCS). The device is a small radio receiver that can be surgically implanted under the skin. Tiny wires lead from the receiver into nerves that origi-

An X-ray of a patient using an electronic pain-suppressing device shows a dorsal column electrode implanted in the spine and a receiver disk in the upper chest. External components of the unit are a transmitter and antenna.

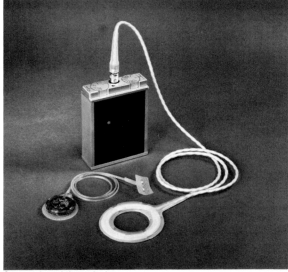

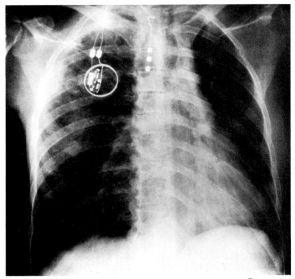

nate in the dorsal column of the spinal cord. When the patient feels pain coming on, he can activate a small pocket-sized transmitter that supplies a signal to the receiver. The receiver, in turn, sends a volley of electrical signals into the spine, thus stopping the pain impulses.

In spite of the general success of the DCS, it is not universally effective in the treatment of chronic pain and may be discovered to have negative side effects. Moreover, some patients feel embarrassment at the perpetual need to carry a transmitter in the event that pain may recur. Nonetheless, other electronic pain-suppressing devices have been developed and found to be effective for some purposes. However, the most important result of the spinal gate theory was the subsequent research that led to the discovery of the naturally occuring opiates in the brain.

Chemical pain suppression: the receptor theory

Opium was in use as an analgesic (painkiller) during classical Greek times and perhaps earlier. Even today, opium and its offspring—morphine, heroin, codeine, and others—are man's strongest painkillers. Yet until a few years ago, almost nothing was known about the mechanisms by which the opiates produced their analgesic effects or the specific sites that were affected. Some scientists believed they acted on the entire brain, overwhelming it and producing a benumbed state of painlessness. Others theorized that the opiates acted only upon specialized receptors in the brain cells. Recent findings about cell physiology have given credence to the latter theory.

For nearly 200 years, scientists believed that the

walls, or membranes, of living cells served merely to enclose the contents of the cell, acting much like a sack. In recent years, however, cell biologists have learned that cell membranes function not only to contain the cell but also to allow certain substances to enter and leave the cell while screening out others. This process is carried on at specific receptor sites located on the cell membrane. The receptor site acts much like a guard at the door of a safe deposit vault; a depositor is allowed to enter the vault only if his signature matches the one on file with the bank. In much the same way, a given substance can pass from the bloodstream into the cell only if a receptor site recognizes and admits that specific molecule.

Over the years, research findings have tended to confirm the belief that opiates act upon the cells of the brain and nervous system at the sites of specialized opiate receptors. One fact in support of this theory was that all known opiate agonists (analgesically active substances) show basic similarities in molecular structure. Just as an adept forger might fool the guard at the vault door, so some opiates might be able to fool the cell's receptor sites. In addition, researchers have produced synthetic opiate agonists that, although similar in basic structure, are considerably more potent than those occurring in nature. One notable example is etorphine, which is 5,000–10,000 times more potent than morphine. Etorphine produces euphoria and relieves pain in dosages as small as .0001 gram, making it even more powerful than LSD—often considered the most potent mind-altering substance. Researchers found the theory of action at highly selective receptor sites the most likely expla-

Molecular Structure of an Opiate Agonist and Antagonist

agonist

antagonist

morphine

nalorphine

Adapted from "Opiate Receptors and Internal Opiates," Solomon H. Snyder
© March 1977 by *Scientific American Inc.* All rights reserved.

nation for etorphine's remarkable effectiveness as an analgesic.

A third line of evidence for the receptor-site theory is that most opiates occur in at least two optical isomers (molecules that are mirror images of each other), yet only one group of isomers, the levorotatory isomers (so called because in solution they cause the plane of polarization of polarized light to rotate to the left), can create the analgesic and euphoric effects commonly associated with opiates. Again, such a stereospecificity of opiate action implies the existence of highly specific receptors that can distinguish even the "handedness" of opiate molecules.

Another crucial finding was that, with very slight molecular modification, opiate agonists can be transformed into opiate antagonists—substances that specifically block the effects of opiate agonists and yet do not produce any such effects themselves. One notable example is nalorphine, a potent opiate antagonist produced by substituting an allyl group ($CH_2-CH=CH_2$) for a methyl group (CH_3) in morphine. Nalorphine is such a potent antagonist that it can revive a victim of morphine overdose almost instantaneously—in a dosage much smaller than the amount that caused the overdose. This rapid effect again suggests a common site of action on the cell membrane. Late in 1973 this suspicion was confirmed. Solomon H. Snyder and Candace B. Pert, both of the Johns Hopkins University School of Medicine, demonstrated that opiates do indeed act upon highly specific receptors in the brain cells.

The body's own painkillers

These lines of research led inevitably to a crucial question: Why does the human brain contain receptors designed to interact with substances found, so far as is known, only in opium poppies? Seemingly, the only answer was that somewhere in the human nervous system were naturally occurring biological compounds that also bind to the receptors. In late 1975 John Hughes and Hans W. Kosterlitz of the Unit for Research on Addicting Drugs at the University of Aberdeen in Scotland announced that they had isolated such naturally occurring substances, which they named enkephalins. The enkephalins were shown to have biological effects similar to those of morphine and were neutralized by naloxone, an opiate antagonist.

The findings of Hughes and Kosterlitz were confirmed independently by Snyder and Rabi Simantov at Johns Hopkins. Both research teams found the highest concentration of opiate receptors in the limbic system of the brain, a doughnut-shaped ring of nerve tissue deep within the brain that is believed to be the seat of such emotions as joy, anger,

and remorse. In addition, researchers found that the cerebral cortex—the surrounding gray matter on the top of the brain that initiates and controls most conscious activity—was almost devoid of opiate receptors.

Further investigation revealed that enkephalin was a mixture of two short peptide chains, each composed of five amino acids in identical sequence except for the terminal amino acid. Apparently, these peptides behave like neurotransmitters (substances that carry nerve impulses). Concentrated in the terminal fibers or synaptic membranes of certain cells of the spinal cord and brain, the enkephalins inhibit the rate at which other nerve cells fire.

Medical implications of natural painkillers

Since 1975 at least five additional naturally occurring opiate agonists have been isolated. Collectively called endorphins, the enkephalins and the other opiate agonists have opened new doorways in research on pain, drug addiction, and schizophrenia. The discovery of endorphins has certainly provided the biggest step forward in the understanding of the mechanisms of pain and analgesia. Further research may not only reveal the existence of additional endorphins but also might uncover ways to control pain with great specificity at the same time avoiding the danger of drugs and drug addiction.

In addition to these important possibilities, a new understanding of pain and analgesia, combined with new insight into the mechanism of opiates and their painkilling properties, may provide essential comprehension of the mechanism of narcotic addiction and the means to counter it. Some researchers speculate that a genetically determined deficiency of natural endorphins might predispose some people to drug addiction. Even if this theory proves false, further research into the molecular mechanism of narcotic addiction could eventually produce reliable and effective treatment. The role of endorphins in human emotion is also being studied, investigating the possibility that endorphin deficiency may be a factor in mental illness.

Although research in endorphins may ultimately culminate in greater understanding of drug addiction and possibly mental illness and other aspects of the brain and nervous system, the most probable immediate result lies in the promise of new, nonaddictive, and perhaps more powerful analgesics. Preliminary studies have revealed that even natural endorphins can be addictive. Researchers hope, however, that a synthetic endorphin or even a mixture of opiate agonists and opiate antagonists may ultimately provide the future analgesia of choice.

—*James McDonald, B.S.*

A Picture Essay:
Treating Cancer in Children

text by Jordan R. Wilbur, M.D., photographs by Ron Shuman

Cancer is a word that is linked in our minds with images of illness and death. Traditionally, the notion of a child with cancer has evoked an even stronger reaction. Not only the child but the whole family is affected by the expected disruption of the family unit that is associated with long-term illness, its attendant pain, and eventual fatal outcome. As a result of improved methods of treating children with cancer, however, this image is changing, giving way to an attitude of hope and optimism.

The new philosophy of treatment

Currently cancer is the disease that causes the most deaths in U.S. children between the ages of one year and the teens. However, of patients receiving care at the major treatment centers for children with cancer, at least 50% can be expected to be alive, without evidence of disease, five years after beginning treatment. These results, markedly improved over those of only a few years ago, are a reflection of more effective anticancer drugs, new therapeutic techniques, improved supportive therapy, a cooperative, coordinated team approach, and a new philosophical approach. This new philosophical outlook is the single most important factor in the total treatment of children with cancer, for it considers the psychosocial aspects of the disease and its potentially disruptive nature.

A basic premise of the philosophical approach is that the overall treatment of the patient be conducted with the expectation that he or she is going to do well. Though such an approach must clearly recognize that some patients will not respond, all efforts should be focused on the eradication of the disease, and at the same time, the return of the patient to the most normal life-style possible, as soon as possible. This can be accomplished only with the full involvement, understanding, and support of the patient's family. Thus the patient, his parents, siblings, and other family members all become active participants, working along with the medical staff as part of the treatment team to achieve these goals.

To really be effective in providing both medical and emotional support, every member of the treatment team must become knowledgeable about the disease and its treatment. To achieve this goal, the medical and nursing staff must educate the patient and his family. And in turn, the patient and his family must educate the medical and nursing staff about the patient as a person and about how the therapy and its effects can best be managed with minimal alteration of the family's life-style.

Involvement of patient and family

Medically, the patient and his family can be involved in a number of ways: they can learn to give medications, to watch for side effects, to provide supportive treatments, to donate blood, and generally to observe and record the information that the medical staff needs to assess the results of therapy. Such involvement provides not only valuable medical assistance but an equally important, though less tangible, benefit. A knowledgeable patient and family who fully understand what is being done and why can more effectively accept a painful or uncomfortable procedure. The family can help the patient to focus on the goal of disease eradication while maintaining an atmosphere of normality—within the limits imposed by the disease.

When parents of young patients become involved as active members of the treatment team, they should be encouraged to participate only to the extent that is comfortable for them. Some parents are able to be more intensively involved than others. For instance, when a special treatment is performed in the treatment room, a parent should feel free to be present and assist, to be present and provide support, or not to be present. The patient, on the other hand, must be afforded the opportunity of having his care involve only those persons with whom he feels comfortable. Satisfying the requirements of both patient and family can pose problems. For instance, a parent may become adept at giving intravenous medications, but the child may not feel comfortable receiving an injection from the parent.

Brothers and sisters, regardless of age, should be allowed to visit and, at times, to stay in the hospital with the sibling who is ill. This provides a normal play situation for the sick child, as well as an opportunity for the brother or sister to help with care and to understand what is happening to the patient. Children generally respond well to this

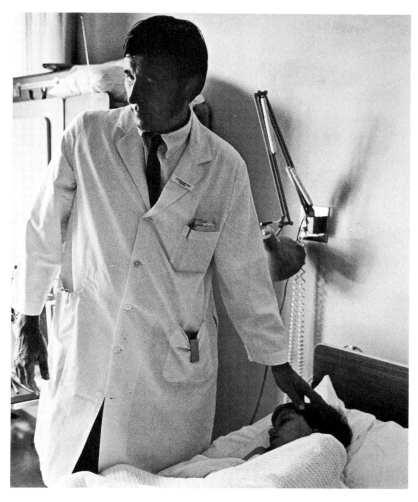

Dr. Jordan Wilbur with one of his young patients.

situation, whereas fear of the unknown, combined with active imaginations, can create difficulties for siblings who are excluded.

Children in the hospital should be encouraged to be out of bed and dressed in their regular clothes. The need for an intravenous needle in the arm should not automatically mean that the patient must be confined to the hospital or cannot carry on normal activities. Each child should be expected to continue his schoolwork and other routine activities as much as possible during the course of therapy, both in the hospital and at home. These are extremely important aspects of the patient's membership in the treatment team.

Another source of support to the child with cancer consists of fellow patients and their families. This is a group of people who understand the problem, know what it feels like, and realize what must be done in order to achieve success. Patients who are doing well provide an inspiration and a focus for those in earlier stages of treatment. They help to promote the realization that the disease can be

eradicated. Patients who are not doing well, on the other hand, promote an equally important realization—that life may continue and be enjoyable despite the problem of recurrent disease. Still other patients who provide support are those who have had recurrence and have been successfully retreated, thus demonstrating that with sufficient effort and a positive approach, it is indeed possible to eradicate the disease even when it has recurred.

Each feature of the philosophical approach is designed to contribute to the ultimate goal of successful total treatment of the child with cancer. Of course there are instances in which treatment is unsuccessful and the patient ultimately dies. In such instances, each participating member of the treatment team may experience a sense of deep satisfaction in the knowledge that he or she has contributed in every possible way. On the other hand, when treatment is successful both the child and his family may go on with the business of life with minimal emotional scars from the disease, the treatment process, and their effect on the family.

279

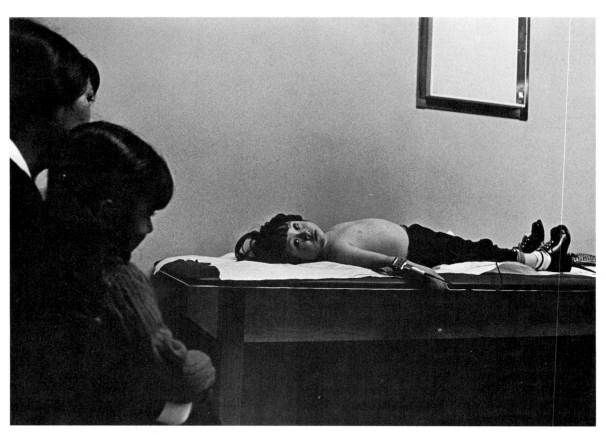

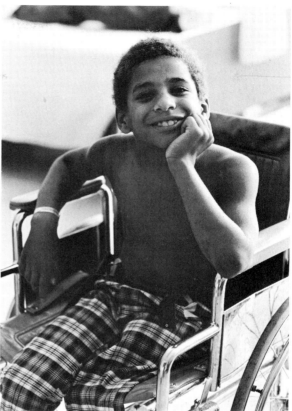

Periodontal Disease

After the age of 35, the major cause of tooth loss is periodontal disease. The bone and ligaments in which the teeth are embedded are weakened or destroyed, teeth become loose and, unless the condition is treated, they must ultimately be extracted. Treatment and prevention involve removing dental plaque (a bacterial coating on the teeth) and calculus (mineral-salt deposits on tooth surfaces) and keeping the patient's mouth free of both. While there is basic agreement that the objective of periodontal therapy is to create a healthy oral environment that the patient will be able to maintain, the best means to achieving that end is still subject to debate. Over the years, there have been advocates of both surgical and nonsurgical therapy. The basic surgical approach, which is advocated by the great majority of periodontists, has been to excise pathologic pockets (infected spaces surrounding teeth) and to correct the bony defects that are created by periodontal disease.

Nonsurgical alternatives

At a recent session of the World Dental Congress of the Fédération Dentaire Internationale, Sigurd Ramfjord of Ann Arbor, Michigan, endorsed the concept of treating periodontal pocketing by means of scaling and curettage (surgical scraping). He pointed out that the main concern in treating the condition is to make the root surface biologically acceptable to the surrounding tissue and to prevent bacterial plaque from spreading downward. On the basis of long-term study, he has concluded that surgical removal of diseased tissues provides no advantage over curettage and may even destroy the root's reattachment.

Ramfjord believes that persistent pathologic pockets that are not bleeding may be viewed merely as inactive anatomical defects. In his opinion, all groups of teeth can be treated by curettage, though results are poorer with upper molars than with other teeth.

A new method for treating intrabony defects

A method for treating the holes in the jawbone associated with periodontal disease has been developed in Denmark. These intrabony defects are characterized by a loss of vertical bone support and are classified according to the number of bony walls bordering the defect. The goal of treatment is to restore lost bone structure. After the diseased tissue has been removed and the tooth surfaces have been cleaned and smoothed, the defect can be filled with bone grafts if two or three walls of bone remain. The defect is then covered with a 2-mm-thick autogenous (self-donor) tissue trans-plant to prevent the epithelium from growing along the surface of the root. The epithelium, which is similar to the outer surface of the skin, acts as a barrier to the new attachment of the root to the surrounding bone. Although results so far have been encouraging, cases must be carefully selected for successful treatment.

New techniques in periodontal surgery

In an excellent two-year clinical study, Swedish researchers investigated the ability of periodontal tissues to heal themselves following different types of periodontal surgery. Their basic surgical procedure consists of incising and elevating a flap of gingiva (gum tissue), removing the bony defects, and then putting the tissue in a new position. They performed a similar flap procedure in which they curetted and cleaned out the bony defects, rather than removing them. They also performed flap procedures in which they treated the bony defects as described and replaced the gingiva in its former position. Finally, they performed gingivectomies (removal of infected gum tissue) in which they curetted the bony defects only.

The study's most important finding was that periodontal disease can be cured and further destruction of the periodontal tissues halted regardless of the surgical technique used for eliminating pathologic pockets. Differing techniques, however, produced different degrees of regeneration in the tissues. The most complete healing took place when the bone was not resectioned and when the tissue covering the jawbone remained intact.

Aftereffects of surgery

Periodontal surgery sometimes results in aesthetic problems and speech defects. Frequently, when the diseased tissues and pockets associated with periodontal disease have been eliminated, the patient's teeth look longer because roots have been exposed; phonetic problems arise because the spaces between the teeth have been enlarged. J. H. Jaggers has reported on a pseudogingival prosthesis that can be used to help treat these problems. The removable appliance is made of plastic and is designed to look like normal gingival tissue. It is easy to insert and remove for cleaning. Many patients have experienced the additional benefit of a reduction in thermal sensitivity related to root surface exposure.

Dilantin hyperplasia

Patients who take diphenylhydantoin (Dilantin) are prone to excessive growth of the gingiva. This is called Dilantin hyperplasia and occurs in about 60% of the individuals taking the drug. Dilantin is one of the specifics for treating epileptics; it also is used frequently for treating nervous disorders and for highly excitable children. The characteristics of hyperplasia are an overgrowth of underlying connective tissue, frequently to the point that it covers most if not all of the crowns of the teeth. The condition is a difficult one to manage.

A new appliance has been developed and used successfully in selected cases of Dilantin hyperplasia. The Kessling pressure appliance, very much like a boxer's bite guard, is fabricated from a hard, rubberlike material molded on a corrected stone model poured from impressions taken of the patient's mouth. The patient wears the appliance, except at mealtimes, for the duration of therapy. As the pressure exerted by the appliance reduces the overgrowth, new appliances are made from models of the altered tissue. It is essential that patients maintain good oral hygiene. Once the desired tissue reduction has been attained, the final appliance is worn at frequent intervals for maintenance of the altered tissue contours.

— *Leon D. Rosenfeld, D.D.S., M.S.D.*

Physical Medicine and Rehabilitation

Physical medicine and rehabilitation, also called rehabilitation medicine, became a recognized medical specialty in 1947. A physician who practices rehabilitation medicine is called a physiatrist. The physiatrist coordinates a multidisciplinary approach to disability, directing a plan of treatment designed to reach the maximum restoration possible for each patient. The other professionals on the team include a rehabilitation nurse, physical therapist, occupational therapist, speech pathologist, audiologist, prosthetist (a specialist in artificial limbs), orthotist (a specialist in braces and orthopedic devices), social worker, recreational worker, and psychologist.

Many areas of rehabilitation medicine are the subjects of new investigations: research into specific diseases and disabilities, methods of physical treatment, basic physiologic research, kinesiology (the study of the movement of body parts), electromyography (the recording of the electrical potentials developed in the muscle), orthotics (the study of orthopedic devices), prosthetics and adaptive devices, pediatric rehabilitation, rehabilitation psychology, the effect of physical disability on sexuality, and correlation of the characteristics of patients in need of rehabilitation with the best means of making health services available to them.

Research in the field has been hampered by the shortage of physicians trained in physical medicine and rehabilitation. A recent survey of 113 medical schools offering full degree programs indicates

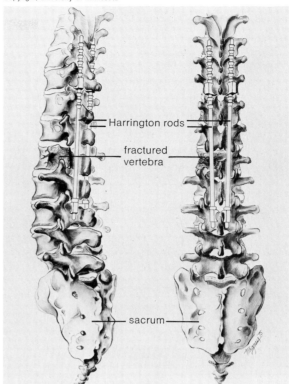

Figure 1: Metallic rods (Harrington rods) spanning and bracing an unstable vertebral fracture.

that rehabilitation medicine programs have not increased commensurately with the increase in numbers either of medical schools or of medical students. The study found that one of the major obstacles to the needed growth of research and training programs in rehabilitation medicine is the continued shortage of physician-teachers who are specialists in this field.

Diseases and disabilities

The three common disabilities considered here illustrate some of the current trends in rehabilitation medicine research and treatment.

Spinal cord injury. Traumatic transection of the spinal cord with resultant motor and sensory paralysis occurs infrequently, but is a severe, expensive-to-treat disability. An injury to the spinal cord below the first thoracic segment (approximately between the shoulder blades) produces paralysis of the legs and trunk, whereas injury to the spinal cord in the area of the neck, in addition, produces varying degrees of paralysis in the arms. If the injury is as high as the third cervical (neck) segment, it produces respiratory paralysis as well. A nationwide study is now under way to learn how to shorten the hospital stay, reduce costs, and achieve a better outcome

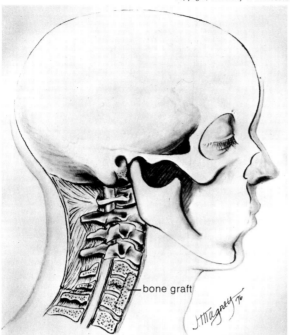

Figure 2: Spinal stabilization by means of a bone graft inserted anteriorly into three vertebrae to promote fusion.

for these patients. It has already been shown that cooperative arrangements among health care providers can effect more efficient treatment and allow the average patient to be discharged from the hospital after 100 to 120 days. Ten years ago it was common for a patient to remain in the hospital for more than a year after an injury to the spinal cord.

Better surgical techniques and management of rehabilitation have created this improvement. Surgical stabilization of the spine can shorten the period of healing that would otherwise be necessary before rehabilitation could begin. Figures 1 and 2 show methods of spinal stabilization that have been used recently. Figure 1 illustrates the surgical insertion of metal rods to stabilize the back when fracture or dislocation have made it unstable. Figure 2 shows a dowel of bone from an uninjured healthy bone that has been grafted into three adjacent vertebrae, filling the space between them and promoting bony healing, or fusion. After healing, the fusion produces a more solid neck and reduces the risk of another dislocation and further damage to the soft spinal cord.

Recent research also has resulted in improved understanding of the urinary tract after spinal cord injury. Damage to the spinal cord prevents voluntary use of skeletal muscles below the level of the injury. However, muscles so paralyzed usually become spastic, which means they contract automatically from time to time without the in-

dividual's being able to control them. Since the bladder outlet, or urethra, passes directly through the pelvic floor musculature, spasms in these muscles will pinch off the urethra and prevent urine from passing to the outside. Many patients with this condition are forced to wear a catheter (tube) in the urethra, extending from the bladder to the outside, so that the urine can be drained away (*see* Figure 3). These tubes are often a source of infection and may pose a great threat to the kidneys. Recent research has demonstrated how the function of a paralyzed bladder can be improved with special catheterization techniques. These have allowed many patients to regain automatic bladder control as well as to relax the pelvic floor muscle, reducing their dependence upon permanent catheters.

Stroke. One of the key problems resulting from stroke and its accompanying hemiplegia (*hemi,* or half, *plegia,* or paralysis) is the difficulty in walking that results when the leg on the paralyzed side of the body is weak and spastic. Researchers have studied the right and left halves of the brain for many years in an effort to determine what each part does and controls. Recent research demonstrates that a person with paralysis in the left side of the brain seems better able to learn to walk again than does one whose injury is on the right side of the brain. A recent study of 236 stroke patients shows that of patients with left-side brain damage, almost 90% were able to walk within parallel bars, and more than 80% could walk independent of parallel bars using a cane or a walker. Almost 40% became proficient in stair climbing.

Heart disease. Often after a heart attack the physician will prescribe progressive exercise programs or exercise tests, both designed to strengthen the damaged heart and the weakened body. Studies on extremely low-level exercise programs for the newly damaged heart have just been completed. First tested on volunteers free of heart disease, the measurements and exercises were then applied to patients who had recently suffered heart attacks and were still confined to bed. The result was to hasten the time when more formal cardiac rehabilitation could begin.

Rehabilitation professionals are also developing community-based programs to assist the recent heart attack victim in undertaking a long-term program of exercise to condition the body and strengthen the heart against future insult. Such programs have been shown to be not only feasible and economical but also safe.

Cardiac rehabilitation techniques have also begun to be applied to patients who have heart disease and a coexisting major physical disability. For example, the cardiac patient who also has had a leg amputated can do special exercises to condition both the body and the heart that utilize the arms rather than the legs.

Physical therapy modalities

Significant work has been done on understanding the role of exercise and fatigue in increasing the work effort of muscles. It now seems clear that fatigue, defined as the inability or unwillingness of a subject to continue a task, even with encouragement, plays a larger role in the development of the work capacity of muscle than does the amount of mechanical work actually done. The implication of this is that optimal improvement in capacity will involve an element of fatigue.

Heat is another common treatment for physical impairment. There is now reason to question whether the forms of deep heat used to treat joint pathology are helpful or harmful. Recent research indicates that the more natural, protective environment for an inflamed joint may be cool rather than warm. Thus heat applied through diathermy (the passage of high-frequency electric currents through body tissues) may contribute to the destruction of the joint cartilage, an effect exactly the opposite of that desired. The long-held belief that deep heat is beneficial because it increases local metabolic rate, dilates small arteries, increases the outpouring of white blood cells, and increases capillary permeability is now in doubt. Recent research suggests that the inflammatory process, which is characteristic of cartilage destruction in all forms of arthritis, may be enhanced by deep heat.

On the other hand, heat has been shown to be beneficial for other problems treated by rehabilitation medicine. A contracture, or shortening of tissue that crosses a joint, is a frequent accompaniment to chronic immobility. Anyone who has suffered a fractured limb and worn a cast for several weeks has experienced this kind of stiffness and loss of motion. If the limb is immobile for a long enough time the shortening of tissue crossing the joint may become severe enough to require physical therapy to stretch it out again. Here heat has been found to be useful. Collagen, the connective tissue that is largely responsible for the contracture, has been shown to yield more readily to prolonged stretching if the tissue is heated before it is stretched. Furthermore, the amount of damage to tissue being so stretched is reduced when heat is applied beforehand. In this situation heat can have a beneficial effect, reducing the amount of time necessary to restore motion and function to joints and limiting the likelihood of damage to the tissues from stretching.

Figure 3: Sagittal section of female pelvis showing relationship of bladder, spastic pelvic floor muscles, and catheter.

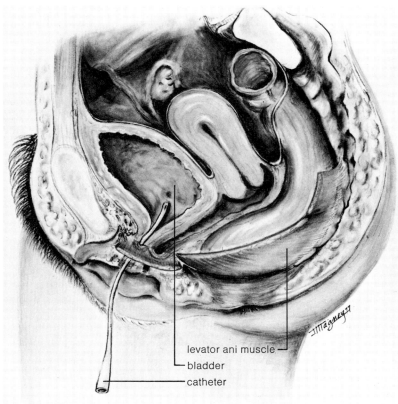

levator ani muscle
bladder
catheter

Sexuality and physical disability

In recent years awareness of human sexuality has increased steadily among lay people and health professionals and in medical schools. Since the early 1970s, this change in awareness has had a profound effect on the field of physical medicine and rehabilitation. It was first necessary to identify physical impairments that created sexual disabilities and to train professionals to recognize the sexual components of physical disability. Rehabilitation professionals are now being trained to do sexual counseling along with other kinds of disability counseling. Human sexuality is so central to the personhood of the individual (able-bodied or disabled) that failing to treat a sexual dysfunction can, in fact, foster additional disability. Like satisfying work, healthy sexuality heightens self-esteem and reduces the individual's willingness to accept the vicissitudes of life passively, with an ultimate effect on the disabled person and on society that is direct and measurable.

Target population identification and delivery of services

Rehabilitation in the United States has been heavily influenced by government expenditure. Substantial funds are distributed by the U.S. Department of Health, Education, and Welfare for the benefit of the disabled. Much of this money is channeled into state and federal systems of vocational rehabilitation. Another large portion is earmarked for medical rehabilitation.

Before 1973, the productivity of counselors in the state-federal vocational rehabilitation system was measured by the number of case closures they achieved. Agencies justified their funding requests on the basis of the number of individuals restored to employment, whose cases were closed. The result was that rehabilitation became most responsive to patients with minor impairments or those who had the greatest chance of "successful rehabilitation." In this view the person with a severe disability was less likely than the person with a minor disability to achieve an outcome that would seem to justify the effort and expense entailed.

However, in 1973, Congress changed the Rehabilitation Act. The law now mandates priority for the severely disabled. This has resulted in a significant shift in the population receiving vocational rehabilitation services and in rehabilitation research and training itself. Whereas in the past medical rehabilitation focused primarily on the health of patients and vocational rehabilitation concentrated on their livelihood, both are now being called upon to demonstrate increased concern for the quality of their patients' and clients' lives.

The consumer movement has also been partly responsible for this change in direction in rehabilitation. Indeed, the Rehabilitation Act of 1973 requires increased consumer involvement and client participation, both in decisions regarding eligibility for services and in structuring the rehabilitation treatment plan. In many cases consumers have made successful demands for social and environmental changes such as accessible transportation, removal of architectural barriers, and improved housing. They also have insisted upon a new relationship with rehabilitation care providers in which they receive treatment as equals rather than as inferiors.

How is this complex of rehabilitation resources mobilized on behalf of the millions of disabled citizens who could benefit from it? Studies strongly suggest that patients with disabilities brought on by heart disease, hypertension, stroke, hip fracture, arthritis, diabetes, and so forth, achieve better outcomes from treatment by a comprehensive rehabilitation team than do patients whose treatment is neither integrated nor comprehensive. Medical rehabilitation has demonstrated the usefulness of the coordinated interdisciplinary team in improvement of the social, intellectual, and self-care ability of disabled persons, more effective utilization of health resources, reduction of morbidity and mortality, more rapid return to employment following rehabilitation, and overall reduction in the high cost of health care.

—Theodore M. Cole, M.D.

Plastic Surgery

The specialty of plastic surgery continues to broaden its horizons in the areas of cosmetic, or aesthetic, surgery and reconstructive plastic surgery. There is actually only a fine line between cosmetic and reconstructive surgery. A procedure that may seem medically necessary to one individual, such as the reconstruction of a breast following a mastectomy, may seem purely cosmetic to another. The increasing popularity of cosmetic surgery as a purely elective procedure is due to the contemporary emphasis on youthful appearance and beauty as well as to the availability of such surgery to a wide range of individuals. Although cosmetic surgery was once reserved for the wealthy and those in public professions, many other people now have this type of operation. Some procedures, such as face-lifts, nose surgery, and chin implants, are done on both men and women. Other operations, such as breast surgery on women and hair transplants on men, are exclusive to one gender.

For those interested in achieving a more youthful appearance by eliminating lines of age and stress from the face, the rhytidectomy (face-lift) is the most common operation. Used together with a blepharoplasty (removal of wrinkles and bags around the eyes), the surgery can make a person look five to ten years younger. A chemabrasion (chemical peel) of the face, in which a special acid substance is applied to the face to smooth the skin and remove discoloration, is the procedure used to deal with fine facial wrinkling as well as scarring caused by acne.

Rhinoplasty (nasal plastic surgery or "nose job") continues to be an extremely common operation. The facial contour is taken into consideration when a plastic surgeon reshapes the nose. For the patient with a recessed chin, the procedure is sometimes done in connection with a mentoplasty (chin implant). The implant is put in place with a small incision either under the chin or in the mouth. The shape and position of the ears can also be changed. Ears are often pulled back (otoplasty) if they are protruding more than desired.

Cosmetic surgery is not now limited to the face, since recent advances allow "total body sculpturing." The most common of this type of surgery is augmentation mammaplasty (breast implant or enlargement). Not to be confused with silicone injections for breast enlargement, which are extremely dangerous and are illegal, breast implants have been perfected to make the procedure extremely safe and successful. Implants are placed beneath the breast tissue, increasing the size and contour of the breasts. When placed properly, the implants are undetectable by appearance or touch. The quick results obtained with this procedure make it very gratifying and popular. It is estimated that 125,000 women underwent this surgery in 1976.

For women with large pendulous breasts or ptotic (sagging) breasts, there are techniques available to reduce breast size (reduction mammaplasty) and give sagging breasts an uplift (mastopexy). If stretch marks or abdominal scars inhibit women from wearing brief bathing attire, an abdominoplasty can trim off abdominal marks and tighten loose skin and muscles. A similar procedure can reduce unsightly fat deposits in thighs or sagging buttocks.

There is now genuine surgical treatment for bald or balding men even though the cause of male pattern baldness is still not fully understood. Several techniques have been perfected which involve surgical repositioning of hair from the sides and back of the scalp to bald areas. The most common and well known is the hair transplant, a relatively painless procedure using punch grafts or tiny skin grafts containing hair removed from a donor site and transplanted in a bald area. A more recently developed and lesser known technique allows for the rotation of large segments of hair-bearing scalp to bald areas. Although it requires greater surgical expertise, this operation promises better and quicker results.

Another recent advance is the availability of plastic surgery on an outpatient basis. A patient may enter an outpatient facility in the morning, have surgery, spend some time in a recovery area, and

For the child below whose lower jaw had failed to develop due to a postnatal infection, plastic surgery provides a new jaw that is both cosmetic and functional, allowing him for the first time to eat solid food.

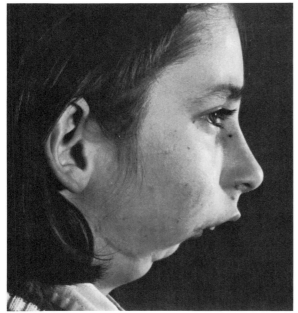
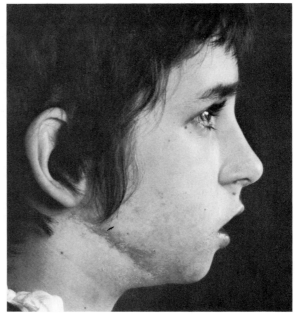

Courtesy, Institute of Reconstructive Plastic Surgery, New York University Medical Center

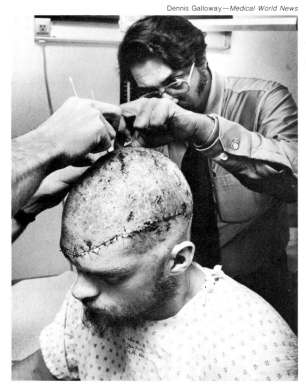

New microsurgical techniques enabled the successful reattachment of a scalp that had been completely severed.

return home the same day. The combination of rising hospital costs and greater medical expertise makes outpatient surgery both necessary and possible. Many cosmetic surgery patients who are not actually ill prefer to avoid a hospital setting.

Reconstructive plastic surgery encompasses many procedures, including cancer surgery of the head and neck, reconstruction following cancer and trauma, treatment of burns, surgery for congenital malformations, and surgery of the hand. Many advances are being made in these procedures. One particularly promising development involves recent improvements in techniques to reconstruct the breast following mastectomy for breast cancer. A breast reconstruction can offer an alternative for a mastectomy patient who does not want to use artificial devices to improve her appearance. Not all mastectomy patients are candidates for reconstruction, but many women now have reason to hope that the areas destroyed by cancer surgery can be restored. Plastic surgeons are consulted to help cancer surgeons plan their operations in order to facilitate reconstructions. A hoped-for additional benefit of this type of surgery is that knowledge of its availability will stimulate earlier visits to a doctor by women who fear mutilation from a cancer operation. It is believed that early detection may improve survival rates.

Another major advance in reconstructive surgery is the advent of microvascular surgery. Using an operating microscope, plastic surgeons can now anastomose (unite) blood vessels as small as one millimeter in diameter. The technique has particular application in rejoining amputated fingers, hands, and toes. It also allows the movement of large portions of skin from one area to another (free-flap transfer) for use in various types of reconstruction. The possibilities and applications of microvascular surgery are exciting. For the first time, refinement of operations to reconstruct congenital anomalies (birth defects) allows work to be done on craniofacial anomalies such as Apert's syndrome (a pointed shape at the top of the head).

Although the number of well-trained plastic and reconstructive surgeons is increasing, some patients unfortunately go to lay clinics and improperly trained doctors, which often leads to disastrous results. Patients should carefully choose qualified plastic and reconstructive surgeons by verifying their skills with local medical societies, medical centers, and other knowledgeable physicians.

—*David A. Ross, M.D.*

Psychiatry

The effects of drugs on the mind and on behavior are a principal concern of modern psychiatry. Current research focuses on the use of drugs in treatment of mental illnesses as well as on their "recreational" use and their abuse.

Alcoholism

The most widely used drug in the United States today is alcohol. In 1976 the Rand Corporation published a study challenging a basic tenet in the traditional treatment of alcoholism. The study, based on a questionnaire completed by 11,500 men who had attended government-run alcoholism treatment centers and followed up by in-depth interviews with 1,340 of these patients, reported that three-fourths of the "alcoholics in remission" said that they were able to drink socially without reverting to heavy drinking. The finding seemed contrary to the long-held doctrine of Alcoholics Anonymous that recovery requires total abstinence and that a single drink will precipitate uncontrollable drinking. Despite extensive research, investigators cannot yet discriminate between recovered alcoholics who can return to moderate drinking and those who cannot. Most physicians dealing with alcoholics, therefore, still recommend total abstinence.

Tranquilizers and marijuana

Prescription drugs that affect emotional behavior were brought under government regulation in

1975, when antianxiety tranquilizers such as Valium and Librium were placed under the controls of the 1970 Drug Abuse Prevention and Control Act. Valium is currently the nation's most frequently prescribed drug, and dollar sales of Valium worldwide exceed those of any other drug. Regulation under the 1970 act, which limits the number of prescription refills and requires detailed record keeping by pharmacists, was designed to restrict overuse of the drugs, especially by people addicted to alcohol and other substances. Drugs such as Valium are frequently used by heroin addicts to ease withdrawal symptoms and by people using psychedelic drugs such as LSD to "come down" from a "trip." The tranquilizers themselves appear to be only minimally addictive.

A resurrection of the medical use of marijuana or chemicals derived from it may bring about changes in the legal status of the drug. In the 19th century marijuana was used in general medical practice to relieve pain, aid sleep, and reduce anxiety. During 1976 careful studies showed that marijuana can relieve increased pressure in the eyes of patients with glaucoma, a disorder that can lead to blindness. The Food and Drug Administration granted permis-

Liaison psychiatrists help the patient adjust to the stress of illness and hospitalization.

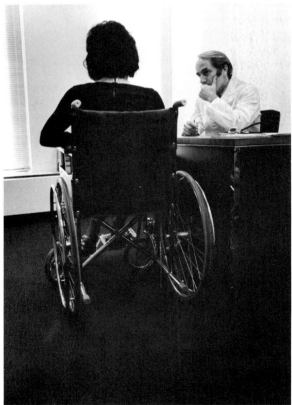

Ted Russell—*Medical World News*

sion for one patient whose glaucoma had failed to respond to other drugs to use marijuana under medical supervision. Derivatives of tetrahydrocannabinol, the active chemical ingredient of marijuana, are being used experimentally to treat anxiety as well as certain organic diseases. The low doses used do not cause intoxication.

Other developments in psychiatry

Sponsored by the National Institute of Mental Health, programs using "liaison psychiatrists" are expanding in hospitals in the United States. Liaison psychiatrists work as part of the medical team to help patients adjust to the stresses associated with illness and hospitalization and with surgery. It has been claimed that as many as 80% of all medically ill persons suffer from psychiatric problems—including fear, anxiety, and guilt—associated with being ill itself. Liaison programs have shown that the work of psychiatrists in hospitals can help patients and, by reducing the tensions of hospitalization, can also facilitate the work of the patients' physicians.

The National Commission for the Protection of Human Subjects of Biomedical and Behavioral Research recommended in 1976 that psychosurgery not be categorically prohibited. The surgery, which involves removing a part of the brain associated with disturbed behavior, is a controversial procedure. Some health officials and groups in the United States have recommended that it be prohibited. The commission reported that the procedure can be beneficial, does not involve undue risk, and does not produce significant neurological deficits. The commission did, however, recommend safeguards for psychosurgery that would include close reviews of surgeon's competence and patient's suitability for the procedure as well as restrictions to protect minors, prisoners, and confined mental patients. The commission criticized the lack of systematic research and reporting on psychosurgery and urged comprehensive testing of the procedure.

Researchers have discovered a normally occurring pain reliever, enkephalin, in the brains of animals, including humans. Enkephalins appear to be neurotransmitters, chemicals released by nerves to communicate with other nerves in the brain. Enkephalins are concentrated in areas of the brain that regulate pain perception and emotional behavior. Future research into the functioning of enkephalin neurotransmitters may be able to clarify how the brain processes information about sensations and feelings, which might lead to the development of new treatment for severe pain and emotional disturbance.

—*Solomon H. Snyder, M.D., and Lynne Lamberg, M.A.*

Special Report:
Community Psychiatry

by Albert W. Lang, M.D.

Community psychiatry is an alternative for public mental health care. Institutionalization, the traditional method of dealing with the mentally ill, simply banishes all mental health problems from the community, regardless of their nature or severity. The goal of community psychiatry, by contrast, is to provide appropriately varied solutions to mental health problems *within* the community, in the form of drug abuse programs, halfway houses, educational programs for the mentally retarded, mental health centers offering outpatient treatment, and other necessary services.

An enlightened solution to public mental health problems has been a long time coming. Until late in the 19th century, mental and emotional disturbances were attributed to such causes as demonic possession, divine retribution for wrongdoing, and the malfunction of specific organs—and were treated accordingly. Persons whose behavior could not be made to conform to accepted norms were simply incarcerated—often under appalling conditions. In spite of the work of social reformers and the emergence of a more scientific attitude toward mental illness, incarceration remained the standard solution until the middle of this century. As a result, the emotionally disturbed, the mentally retarded, the drug addicted, the criminally insane, and often the merely eccentric or misunderstood all found themselves inmates of the same large state institution, where they received undifferentiated treatment—or none at all. All patients were under the ultimate jurisdiction of the institutional psychiatrist, who was paid by and accountable to the state and community. He was the final judge of appropriate behavior and social adjustment.

The period of enlightenment

In the 1950s, when medical science succeeded in producing psychiatric wonder drugs, the psychotropic agents, society's belief in the special knowledge and expertise of the psychiatrist and other mental health professionals was reinforced. The mental health profession gained new confidence in its ability to extinguish undesirable behavior and shape the patient to the requirements of society. These drugs held out the possibility that there were alternatives to institutionalization. And, now that there were "cures," perhaps people could be-

gin to accept the mentally ill in their midst instead of banishing them from the community.

The community's acceptance of outpatient treatment of mental illness had been fostered to some extent by the writings of Sigmund Freud and the humanitarian leadership of Karl and William Menninger. The experience of the Kennedy family with a mentally handicapped child (sister of President John F. Kennedy) also contributed to public awareness. These developments, reinforced by the generally more progressive attitudes of the time, resulted in legislative action by the Kennedy administration. Massive funds were appropriated through the Department of Health, Education, and Welfare, especially through the National Institute of Mental Health. Research into the etiology and cure of mental retardation and emotional illness broadened into studies of social and environmental factors. Funding for mental health centers, drug abuse programs, educational programs stressing early intervention, and a variety of other community-based agencies encouraged innovation and community participation. Day-care programs and sheltered workshops provided critical support to many who had been living a marginal existence. The general objective was to develop and expand support sys-

Institutionalization, a traditional approach to mental illness, removes the problem from public view but may well not provide a solution for either the patient or the community.

tems within the community and to integrate into society the thousands who had been living behind locked doors.

Individual dignity versus social acceptability

Although the treatment of mental health problems had been moved out of the institution and into the community, the objective of that treatment too often remained the same: to make the patient acceptable to and assimilable by society. As a result, *care* meant effecting outward change, altering behavior, and guiding or adjusting the patient to make him conform to social norms. *Rehabilitation* meant the molding of the patient into someone who would subscribe to the work ethic and social values of a system that had alienated him. *Early intervention* in childhood disturbances meant applying a variety of forces to the child and family to achieve conformity to the social mainstream. *Sustaining care* for previously institutionalized persons meant persuading them to continue taking medications that had subdued them during their institutional experience. Only the retarded child, whose difficulties were considered purely medical (and beyond his control) was spared the overwhelming expectation of appearing normal to the community.

Not all the professionals working in community psychiatry limited themselves to this model. There were many whose humanitarian interests and code of ethics directed them to place the individual's right to self-determination ahead of his social acceptability. They recognized the person's condition as an adjustment to life experiences or factors over which he had little control and held individual dignity more important than the priorities of society.

At the end of the 1960s, when national priorities began to change, cutbacks in welfare appropriations virtually destroyed many mental health programs and seriously jeopardized others. As the funds dwindled, the governmental bureaucracies began to intensify their costly surveillance of human welfare services in an attempt to maintain standards and objectives that had been previously established. *Innovation,* the byword of the earlier community mental health movement, was crowded out by *accountability* to the governmental bureaucracy. The mental health systems could no longer afford to give priority to the emotional well-being of the individual. They focused with renewed concern on the patient's *behavior* as the index of program effectiveness.

Unrealistic goals

Under these circumstances, behavior modification was a welcome concept and was widely used to facilitate results that society could no longer allow

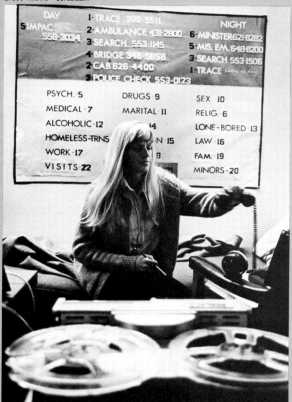

Community psychiatry responds to public mental health problems with such programs as suicide prevention centers.

the individual to achieve at his own rate. The emotional welfare of the individual was a concern only if his distress might result in a statistic (*e.g.,* suicide or the need for institutional care) that would compromise the bureaucracy. Although economic recession, unemployment, or the termination of supportive community services may have been critical factors in a patient's "regression," the community mental health center (or equivalent agency) was charged with the unrealistic responsibility of providing the "cure."

As cutbacks continued, the demand for accountability predictably increased. Monitoring programs, including additional manpower and computer systems, were implemented to meet the demand. *Management-by-objective* plans were imposed, requiring the administrator of a mental health agency to predict the program needs for the next fiscal period. He was held to these predictions in spite of the difficulties inherent in constructing a program to meet the unpredictable needs of human beings. The administrator was therefore required to expend vital energy, time, and money on bureaucratic goals rather than on services to people. A similar obligation was placed on the profes-

291

Among the alternatives to traditional institutionalization that community mental health programs might provide are educational programs for the mentally retarded, including such instruction as yoga (below), or (above) halfway houses for the emotionally disturbed that seek to reintegrate them into society, rather than lock them away from it.

sional directly rendering the service: *treatment evaluation* indicators (a variety of forms and indices, some of which are processed by computer) required the professional, on a form or checklist, to describe the patient, specify a plan of treatment related to the presenting symptoms (even though these may represent only surface manifestations of deeper and more ambiguous conflict), and anticipate the outcome within a defined period. Even more complicated surveillance techniques were advocated, all in an attempt to determine the effectiveness of programs and the attainment of goals defined by the funding agencies. While the stated purpose of these measures was to ensure the quality of service, the actual outcome was the maintenance of an alarmingly expensive superstructure that had become more important than the social need it was created to serve.

Thus, a fundamental question surfaces: How can the community mental health professional relate objectively and patiently to his clients' needs, when the system demands specific results that may have

little or nothing to do with those needs? The professional is encouraged to accept that the system knows what is best for his clients; he can be considered competent only if his clients achieve the system's goals, not their own. To the casual observer or the arbitrary statistician, the loss of humanitarian concerns may seem unimportant—but in all likelihood the same citizen would have been unconcerned about the disgraceful conditions of state institutions a half-century ago.

It follows then that unless society rearranges its priorities so that the basic rights of man have foremost consideration, the speculations of French historian Alexis de Tocqueville more than a century ago will be dangerously close to present reality: "The will of man is not shattered, but softened, bent and guided . . . power does not destroy, but it prevents existence; it does not tyrannize, but it compresses, enervates, extinguishes and stupifies a people, 'til each nation is reduced to nothing better than a flock of timid and industrious animals of which the government is the shepherd."

292

Psychosomatic Medicine

Despite its rather formidable name, psychosomatic medicine (that is, the treatment of disease symptoms for which there is no organic basis) is not new; in fact, it antedates modern scientific medicine by many centuries. The idea that pain or disease could be caused by evil forces — perhaps in the form of demons or spirits — was common in early human societies and persists today in many parts of the world. The cure was usually administered by a shaman, a healer who derived his power from divine sources. It involved the use of potent medicines and rituals that had a profound influence on both patient and family. The healing temples in ancient Greece relied on sedating medications, the use of fasting, prayer, sleep, and psychological suggestion as curing elements.

Ancient attitudes

The famous ancient Greek physician Hippocrates made detailed observations of illnesses now known as conversion reaction and delirium. He noted the psychological state of the patient and tried to relate it to what he knew of anatomy and physiology. Because he lacked modern laboratory equipment and methodology, his conclusions regarding cause were sometimes erroneous, but Hippocrates' descriptions of these mental diseases nevertheless stand as masterpieces of clinical observation and inference.

During the Dark Ages, the scientific rationalism of the ancient Greeks fell into disuse; both medicine and medical psychology regressed into mystical and magical explanations of disease or relied heavily on scholastic religious philosophy. There were, of course, islands of science and enlightenment, such as the work of the 12th-century physician Maimonides, whose treatise on asthma is highly contemporary in its recognition of the multiple factors that may influence an illness.

The period of scientific medicine

The rise of scientific medicine in the 19th century seemed to create a dichotomy between the humanistic and scientific aspects of medicine. From an extreme scientific point of view, if a disease could not be studied under the pathologist's microscope or in the test tube, it did not exist. In the 1880s and 1890s, however, the precursors of contemporary psychosomatics began with Jean-Martin Charcot, Pierre Janet, Sigmund Freud, and Josef Breuer,

Jean-Martin Charcot, conducting a medical lesson and standing at center right in this painting, was among the 19th-century pioneers in the study of psychosomatic medicine.

Psychosomatic medicine

all of whom were interested in psychological medicine and in the phenomena of conversion hysteria. The work of these men raised the study of "functional" nervous and mental illness (that is to say, illness in which no anatomic change could be observed in the brain) to the level of a descriptive and interpretative science.

The impetus of their work carried forward into the 1930s and 1940s, when pioneering psychosomatic physicians such as Howard Dunbar, Franz Alexander, and Thomas M. French made observations of the relationship between personality and illness and elucidated the connection between psychic conflict and the onset of illness. This early work stimulated the publication of many case histories illustrating the interplay between emotions and illness. Comprehensive theories emerged, for instance the specificity theory, which related unconscious conflict to illness onset in susceptible individuals. Careful studies of groups exposed to stress led to "precursor" studies, which made it possible to predict more accurately which individuals would become ill.

Recent developments

In recent years the specificity theory has been challenged by new "nonspecific" theories that point out a relationship between stress and disease but deemphasize the relationship of personality, conflict, and type of disease. Much new research has been stimulated by these ideas.

During the past decade, stress in both animals and human subjects has been studied in the laboratory. The stress of maternal deprivation during infancy has been studied extensively in the monkey by Harry F. Harlow. Monkeys "raised" by a wire and terry-cloth surrogate "mother" developed in a markedly different fashion from their normal counterparts. They developed stereotyped behaviors that represented a distorted or incomplete unfolding of the usual psychosocial development, for instance clinging to a peer or, later, displaying difficulty with instinctual patterns such as mating. In a primate colony established at Stanford University, it has been observed that chimpanzees who lose their mothers at critical ages develop behaviors analogous to depression in humans. René Spitz observed marked differences in human infants deprived of sufficient cuddling and caring during the neonatal period. Such infants appear to develop defectively and may be much more susceptible to disease than are normal babies. John Bowlby made extensive studies of psychological development in children during periods of separation and loss, such as during hospitalization.

In susceptible strains of laboratory animals stresses can be applied selectively to produce psy-

Much knowledge about the interaction of personality and disease has been learned from the study of primates.

chosomatic illness. These illnesses can then be studied by changing such variables as diet and living space, or by interfering with normal territoriality. Hans Selye has devoted his entire research career to studying the effects of stress upon the organism, particularly the psycho-endocrine response to stress. It is possible to create artificial illnesses in laboratory animals and then to study the physiological and metabolic pathways underlying the mechanisms of these diseases. Hypertension, arthritis, gastric ulcer, and heart disease are among the illnesses that can be produced in susceptible strains of animals.

Recent research describes the monkey's response to stress, which can only be characterized as "subjective emotional response." While scientists are reluctant to attribute "feelings" to animals because of concern about anthropomorphic bias, 19th-century naturalist Charles Darwin recognized emotions in animals and wrote extensively about the subject. In both animals and humans, however, it seems that the subjective response to stress may be the key factor in triggering psycho-endocrine response. A passive and undemonstrative monkey, for example, may not react to hunger with the expected stress response—an outpouring of steroid hormones in the blood and urine. By contrast, a more "spirited" monkey may respond with outrage, reflected in emotional expression, along with a profound psychosomatic response displayed in a rise in blood and urine steroids. In man it has been shown that an excitable spectator at a sports event may show endocrine changes greater than those of a participating but phlegmatic athlete.

Disease and the stress response

If more were known about these individual differences in response to stress, the data could be useful in programs of preventive screening for such stress-related illnesses as heart disease and essential hypertension. Studies that focus on large groups of people under stress support the notion that chronic occupational stress is associated with a higher rate of illness. For instance, essential hypertension and peptic ulcer occur more commonly in airport control tower operators than in other groups matched for age, sex, and other variables. Stress illnesses are also more common among the economically and culturally deprived, although other factors such as poor preventive measures and poor medical care may add to the higher incidence in this group.

Quantitative life stress scales have been developed by having large numbers of persons judge the subjective amount of distress felt in various life crises. There is a remarkable consensus among the respondents as to the degree of stress experienced in specific life setbacks such as the death of a loved one, loss of job, illness in the family, debts. Even joyous experiences can be mildly stressful, representing the need for adaptation to new circumstances. The individual who is under a great amount of stress over a period of time is measurably more vulnerable to illness, but whether he or she becomes ill also depends on other factors, particularly genetic and biochemical factors.

An important psychosocial factor is the amount of emotional support available to the individual. A person under high stress usually does not fall ill if he feels that he has emotional support from others. On the other hand, persons under high stress and having little outside emotional support are unusually vulnerable to new illness and recover more slowly than normal from established illness. This is what makes it essential that the convalescing patient have emotional backing from professionals, family, and volunteers.

There are, however, individual differences that make some persons able to resist high stress without becoming ill. These differences may be due to nurture, nature, or both—but they are certainly observable and describable. A recent study of concentration camp survivors attempted to describe and classify individuals' "coping styles," which ranged from highly successful maintenance of morale under immense stress to anticoping, maladaptive styles that were not compatible with survival. Coping and adaptational behavior may be acquired, at least partially, through processes of learning, acculturation, and identification with strong figures and values. During World War II merchant seamen were given special survival training courses that were designed to help them maintain hope if their ships were torpedoed. This training saved many lives.

More recently an experimental study of stress in humans was conducted on patients with hyperthyroidism who volunteered to allow samples of their blood to be taken periodically while they watched exciting and frightening movies. This study, and a closely related one utilizing the radioactive iodine uptake method to monitor thyroid function, have documented that the stress response in hyperthyroid patients differs from that in normal individuals. Thyroid physiology is now known to be much more complex than it was recently thought to be, and the regulatory pathways are better understood.

Air-traffic controllers, whose daily work involves them in stressful situations, suffer from higher than average incidence of such stress-related conditions as essential hypertension and peptic ulcer.

UPI Compix

Psycho-endocrine basis of behavior and psychic life

Research into the neuroendocrine basis of behavior is progressing at a rapid pace, with many new discoveries about the sites of action of neurotransmitters. This knowledge is frequently applicable in clinical situations, such as in the diagnosis and management of severe psychiatric and psychosomatic illness.

Depressive reactions, for instance, can be subclassified from a neuroendocrine point of view through an analysis of the types of hormones involved; when more fully developed, this knowledge undoubtedly will have great impact on diagnosis, prognosis, and choice of treatment. Research in the area of neuroendocrine reactions is truly "psychosomatic" in that the patient's behavior, subjective experience, and physiological signs are all interrelated. Currently the evaluation of psychotropic agents such as tranquilizers, antidepressants, and sedatives is an important focus of research. Probably the most significant change of attitude in recent years has been the acceptance of lithium carbonate as an agent for the treatment of manic-depressive illness. Many patients now on lithium therapy can be managed fairly easily and hospitalized for only short periods, whereas formerly they might have lost months or years of work and family life.

Clinical aspects of psychosomatic medicine

Many hospitals and medical centers have psychiatrists who specialize in consultation, or "liaison psychiatry." They furnish consultation to the medical practitioners, teach, and do research in psychosomatics. Patients referred to these specialists most often are suffering from an emotional response to physical illness. Such responses as rage, depression, anxiety, acting out, withdrawal, self-destructiveness, and noncompliance with the treatment plan are common reactions. A patient may respond to a medical setback with undue regression to immature, overdependent psychological patterns. The psychiatrist, social worker, psychiatric nurse, and vocational counselor all may need to interact with medical team, patient, and family in order to promote a more favorable outcome. Self-help and volunteer groups such as Reach-to-Recovery for mastectomy victims, the Ileoptimists for colostomy patients, and so forth, are very helpful in adjustment and building of morale. A recent follow-up report on breast cancer patients from Memorial Sloane-Kettering Cancer Center in New York City clearly demonstrates that an active interdisciplinary approach lessens complications and indicates that a higher percentage of patients will reach complete rehabilitation after surgery and chemotherapy.

Another clinical aspect of psychosomatics has to do with early diagnosis and the impact of publicity campaigns to fight various illnesses. The campaign against smoking, for one, seems to have had little influence on the overall population but has been effective in groups such as physicians and nurses. And even though they are taught the opposite, patients often delay seeking help when they notice one of the "seven danger signals" of cancer. Research into the successes and failures of these programs may help to design more effective means of public education.

Technological breakthroughs in medicine and surgery have also created new psychological problems and ethical dilemmas. Kidney and heart transplant procedures, renal dialysis programs, and the possibility of maintaining germfree environments all have created unusual challenges for the psychosocial specialist, at the same time raising staggering ethical and moral issues for society as a whole.

Although there is no scientific explanation for its results, acupuncture, a traditional element of Chinese medicine, has provided relief for some types of psychosomatic symptoms.

Marc Riboud—Magnum

New treatment possibilities

The usefulness of individual and group psychotherapy has been well documented for some psychosomatic illnesses. In a study at Columbia University in New York City, patients with ulcerative colitis who received at least six months psychotherapy did better on the average—in terms of easier medical management, fewer complications, and less chronicity—than did the control group. This experience has been duplicated in other disorders.

Recently there have been favorable reports on the use of family therapy in such disorders as asthma in children and appetite disturbance such as anorexia nervosa (prolonged loss of appetite accompanied by marked weight loss). Behavior modification has also been used with some success as a treatment for severe appetite disorders; this approach is relatively new, and long-term follow-up reports have not yet been published. Biofeedback training, another relatively recent technique, has yielded favorable results in treatment of various psychosomatic disorders. Migraine and tension headaches, bronchospasm, and heart rhythm disturbances have been alleviated by training the patient to control certain measurable variables such as pulse, skin temperature, or muscle tension. Some types of chronic low back pain have been helped by biofeedback relaxation training.

Furthermore, the revived interest in acupuncture has in turn renewed interest in the psychology and physiology of pain. New electronic devices have been found useful in blocking chronic pain, and several researchers are investigating naturally occurring painkillers produced by the brain itself. Several new research centers have been established for the diagnosis and treatment of patients with chronic pain problems. Usually they involve the cooperation of members of many medical disciplines—the behavioral specialists (social worker, clinical psychologist, psychiatric nurse, and psychiatrist) are important members of these teams.

Hypnotic treatment, an ancient art, is currently much underutilized by health professionals. Controlled studies of its use on patients suffering from severe burns have shown it to be of decided benefit in promoting better nutrition and greater comfort to the burn victim. Hypnosis can help in managing common health problems such as obesity and compulsive smoking and may be used for surgical anesthesia when other methods are unsuitable. One drawback of hypnosis, however, is that only a certain percentage of persons are suggestible; it is also time-consuming and requires patience for the hypnotist, who may have to spend long hours with the patient during a surgical procedure such as skin grafting.

The past decade has seen a renewed interest in psychosomatic medicine, following a dormant period in the 1950s and 1960s. Consultation-liaison services are better organized and funded than previously. But there are still many problems to face, especially the difficulty of persuading third-party insurers that such services are worthwhile as well as economical in the long run. Medical education presents still another problem. The education of medical students and nurses is continually changing and evolving, and the competition for students' attention and time is a perennial difficulty. With so much scientific and technical knowledge to acquire, the student may easily lose sight of the patient as a human being. Thus, access to someone who can conceive of the patient *in toto* can make a great difference during the formative phase of the young professional's career, and it is here, perhaps, that the psychosomatically aware physician is more needed than in any other field of medicine.

—*Edward Wasserman, M.D.*

Radiology

In 1895, while studying the flow of electrons in cathode-ray tubes, German physicist Wilhelm Röntgen discovered a previously unknown form of radiation that he called X-rays. He found that these rays penetrated certain kinds of matter and produced an image on photographic plates. With the discovery by Marie and Pierre Curie of radium and of natural radioactivity three years later and the application of radioactivity to cancer treatment soon thereafter, the foundations for medical radiology, both diagnostic and therapeutic, had been established. In the United States, an official medical structure was developed with the founding of the American Radium Society, the Radiological Society of North America, and in 1923, the American Board of Radiology, which certifies physicians as specialists in radiology. Advances in technology have since necessitated further division into three separate areas, each with its own training programs and specialty boards; these are diagnostic radiology, therapeutic radiology, and nuclear medicine.

Diagnostic radiology

Unlike light, which reflects off matter, X-rays can penetrate various substances to differing degrees; like light, they can cause changes in film. These qualities are the basis for diagnostic radiology. X-rays are produced by allowing electrons to strike a metal target within the X-ray machine itself; they are directed through the part of the patient's body to be visualized and finally strike special X-ray film. Tissue density in the area under examination deter-

A patient prepares to undergo treatment with a beam of high-energy neutrons, a promising new therapy for cancer.

mines the extent to which the X-rays are absorbed by the body, and this difference in absorption results in varying degrees of exposure on the film and in different X-ray shadows.

As the specialty has evolved, radiologists have developed increasingly sophisticated methods. Most of these techniques have enhanced contrast on the film between normal and abnormal tissue, thereby making the abnormalities more visible. Thus if a patient swallows barium (or another contrast material that will absorb many X-rays), a stomach ulcer that would be invisible on a normal X-ray will be pictured on the X-ray film. Contrast materials and techniques for their insertion have been developed for virtually every organ and part of the body; even air (which absorbs fewer X-rays than surrounding tissues) can be injected for contrast.

The most recent development in diagnostic radiology is computerized axial tomography. In this technique a thin column of precisely directed X-rays is rotated around the body; a computer processes the complex and numerous items of X-ray information and produces a three-dimensional picture of a very thin cross section of the head or body.

Each of these techniques requires expertise. It can, for example, take years for a radiologist to learn how to insert the tiny catheters used for injecting contrast materials into small blood vessels or ducts. In addition, because each new procedure creates unique patterns of shadows on the film, the radiologist must continually learn new methods of reading and interpreting X-ray pictures. Because of the many techniques available today, no one radiologist can be expert in all procedures. While most radiologists are general radiologists whose work involves interpretation of most standard X-rays, some subspecialize in fields such as angiography (outlining of blood and lymph vessels) or neuroradiology (techniques to diagnose diseases of the brain and spinal cord). It seems likely that as more accurate and advanced diagnostic procedures are developed, more subspecialists will be needed in order that medicine may take fullest advantage of technical progress.

Therapeutic radiology

The fact that high-energy X-rays can damage and even kill cells has been known almost since the discovery of radium. Led by Claudius Regaud in France and continuing even today, radiobiologists have clarified the biological processes involved in radio-induced cell death. This understanding has allowed radiation therapists to increase the efficiency of X-ray damage to cancer cells while minimizing damage to normal cells.

Most X-ray treatments are delivered by a beam of high-energy X-rays directed to the cancerous area. The course of treatment is almost always broken up into fractions (a series of treatments of calculated intensity) delivered over a period of time, thus allowing for recovery of normal tissue between treatments. Because of their relatively low energy, early X-ray beams caused a good deal of damage to non-diseased tissue. The development of cobalt-60 therapy in the early 1950s and of the linear accelerator shortly thereafter provided radiotherapists with beams of much higher energy that are more effective in destroying deep-seated tumors, while causing less damage to adjacent healthy tissues.

The job of the radiologist is to diagnose and localize tumors, to decide which cases are amenable to radiation treatment, to plan ways to deliver the beams for greatest effectiveness with least damage to healthy tissue, and to follow the patient's progress after the course of therapy is completed. The actual treatments are administered by specially trained technicians.

Radiotherapists use other forms of radiation in addition to X-ray beams. Some, such as electron beams and interstitial brachytherapy (insertion of radioactive sources into the center of a tumor) are commonly available. Others, still experimental, may improve the effectiveness of cancer radiotherapy in the near future; these forms of therapy include the combination of X-rays and heat, the use of drugs to sensitize tumors to the effect of radiation, and the application of heavy particle therapy using neutrons, protons, or pi mesons.

Nuclear medicine

Through the use of radioactive elements and radioisotopes, specialists in nuclear medicine can diagnose a variety of structural and functional abnormalities and treat diseases of particular organs and glands. Some radioisotopes are biologically active — that is, they are taken up, metabolized, and excreted by various organs of the body. If a small amount of a biologically active radioisotope is injected into a patient's bloodstream, counters and cameras focused on appropriate areas can scan the body and detect radioactive emissions. The radiologist who specializes in nuclear medicine then interprets the information provided by the scan for the patient's physician.

Using different radioisotopes for each organ of interest, specialists in nuclear medicine are able to determine abnormal structure and function of the liver, lung, brain, bones, heart, kidneys, thyroid, and many other parts of the body. Some substances actually seek out abnormal tissue such as cancer and thus can be helpful in localizing tumors. Others can be used to treat disease; radioactive iodine, for example, is used to treat disorders of the thyroid gland. Current research in this field has two major goals: first, to discover new radioisotopes that will be more sensitive to structural and functional abnormalities, and second, to find better ways to detect, count, and display data, thus increasing the accuracy of the scan and helping the attending physician make a correct diagnosis and establish proper therapy.

—Stephen L. Seagren, M.D.

Skin Diseases

In the treatment of skin diseases, new attention has been given to the therapeutic value of light. The normal effect of sunlight on psoriasis, in combination with photosensitizing drugs known as psoralens, has formed the basis for a new therapy for the disease. High-output ultraviolet light is now used, with the advantage that it is available year-round and allows controlled exposures. The treatment is called PUVA (psoralen-ultraviolet light A).

PUVA also has been reported to be useful in treating atopic dermatitis (a scaly rash often associated with hay fever), vitiligo (a pigment dis-

order), and mycosis fungoides (a form of systemic cancer that first appears on the skin). The use of light in combination with a dye to treat recurrent herpes simplex virus infections has not proven effective, however. Earlier well-publicized reports of success with the treatment were not confirmed by more extensive clinical trials.

Skin cancer

Although PUVA appears to be safe in the short run, long-term effects are unknown. Doctors are particularly concerned that the intense light exposure may cause premature wrinkling and aging of the skin. Other potentially damaging effects include cataracts and malignancies. The American Academy of Dermatology has issued a warning against the widespread use of the treatment, pending further evaluation in controlled studies at approximately 30 medical centers in the United States and Europe. The treatment has not been approved by the Food and Drug Administration (FDA) for general medical use.

A study evaluating 30 externally applied anticancer agents for the treatment of psoriasis is being conducted by investigators at the University of Miami (Fla.) under sponsorship of the National Cancer Institute. An oral anticancer drug, Triazure (azaribine), first marketed for psoriasis in 1975, was withdrawn because patients taking the drug developed blood clots.

Excessive exposure to ultraviolet light has long been linked with skin cancer, persons with fair complexions being more susceptible. Damage to the earth's stratospheric ozone layer would permit greater amounts of ultraviolet light to reach the surface of the earth and would, some scientists have contended, lead to an increase in all forms of

A study by the Food and Drug Administration has shown that many people have adverse skin reactions to the ingredients in a variety of cosmetics.

Courtesy, *FDA Consumer*

skin cancer, including malignant melanoma. A committee of the National Research Council has concluded that the release of chlorofluorocarbons from aerosol cans, refrigerating units, and other sources poses a definite hazard to the ozone layer. The FDA intends to propose a phaseout of the nonessential uses of these chemicals.

Warts and immune deficiencies

Warts, along with certain acute viral and fungal infections and some cancers, including skin cancers, have recently been associated with deficiencies in the body's immune system. More than 40% of renal transplant patients given immunosuppressive drugs develop warts within one year. The role of immunity in the control of a variety of diseases has become more evident as drugs that suppress the immune system gain greater use and as the lives of patients with immune deficiencies are prolonged. Physicians believe that even in a person without such illnesses, the presence or absence of antibodies against the wart virus and other diseases helps determine individual susceptibility as well as the likelihood of cures.

Caffeine salve for dermatitis

Dermatologists at the University of Tennessee College of Medicine in Memphis have reported that they have used a salve containing caffeine, the stimulant in coffee and tea, to treat the symptoms of atopic dermatitis. The disease, also known as eczema, is an inflammation of the skin often linked to allergies. It often causes itching that leads to infection and disfigurement. Caffeine is a naturally occurring substance and is inexpensive. Unlike other treatments, application of caffeine to the skin has no apparent side effects. Clinical trials are now under way to assess the value of caffeine as compared to other medications.

Hives

Recent research may help patients who suffer from chronic hives (urticaria). These intensely itching welts sometimes move from one site to another on the body or may come and go within a few hours. Sometimes, however, they linger for months. Exposure to certain drugs, including penicillin and aspirin, is among the more easily determined causes. Harder to pinpoint are the roles of hidden infections, intestinal parasites, and allergies, including newly recognized causes such as coloring and flavoring in ordinary foods. Recent studies have shown that cells of patients with chronic urticaria are defective in releasing a chemical thought to blunt or suppress allergic reactions. The defect may explain the persistence of symptoms in patients whose hives are chronic.

Burns

Researchers at Johns Hopkins School of Hygiene and Public Health reported in 1976 that the number of children dying from burns has decreased in recent years. The greatest decrease has been among girls, which the study attributed to the increasing popularity of long pants as clothing. Until the 1960s girls under 10 years of age had far higher death rates from burns than did boys, a unique phenomenon among injury deaths. The researchers attributed the former higher rates to loose-fitting nightgowns and dresses, then popular clothing for girls. They cited advances in medical treatment as a reason for decreasing deaths from burns among children generally.

Doctors at the Shriners Burns Institute in Cincinnati, Ohio, reported on a newly developed material used to control infections in burns. The dressing is formed on the wound itself from a solvent and a powder and forms a close-fitting film over the wound. It permits penetration by antibiotics but resists penetration by bacteria. The study conducted at the institute showed that the film alone, without use of antibacterial ointment, reduced the bacterial count in burn wounds as effectively as antibiotics used on uncovered wounds. Second-degree burns heal normally under the film. Third-degree burns still require skin grafting.

New law on cosmetic labeling

New legislation requiring the listing of the ingredients in cosmetics on package labels went into effect in 1977. Ingredients must be listed in order of predominance by weight. Claims that products are hypoallergenic (less likely to cause allergies) now must be proven. The new labeling should help physicians determine the cause of apparent allergies to cosmetics and should be useful to the consumer. The FDA now requires that each ingredient in a cosmetic and each finished cosmetic product be adequately substantiated for safety by the manufacturer prior to marketing. The cosmetics industry has organized a program for review and evaluation of the safety of cosmetic ingredients by an independent panel of scientists. The review is expected to take several years.

—Stanford I. Lamberg, M.D.,
and Lynne Lamberg, M.A.

Stress

Perhaps the most important pioneering studies of stress and its effect on the human body have been carried out by Hans Selye, an Austrian-born endocrinologist who later lived in Canada. Selye used the word to describe a phenomenon he observed while studying body reactions to injuries. He noticed that no matter what the injury, the body responded in certain standard ways. Animals that were subjected to cold shivered, but they also displayed certain other noticeable physiological changes that were the same as those produced by heat and other stimuli.

Defining stress

In the 1950s Selye defined stress as a syndrome that consists of nonspecifically induced changes within the body, a reaction characterized by a specific set of symptoms (syndrome) but caused by a variety of agents or conditions. In his book *Stress Without Distress* (1974) he updated and simplified the definition, stating that stress is the body's nonspecific response to any demand made upon it. This response is the body's mechanism of mobilizing its defenses to protect itself from harm and later to return it to normality. Walter B. Cannon, a Harvard University physiologist also interested in stress, called the stress reaction the "wisdom of the body," because its characteristic changes represent an attempt by the body to limit damage. The body's reaction to stress is a sequential process, involving specific stages of adaptation. Selye called the process the General Adaptation Syndrome, and he defined three discrete phases: (1) alarm reaction, (2) stage of resistance, and (3) stage of exhaustion.

The alarm reaction. The alarm reaction is the body's immediate response to a stressor—an agent, event, or condition that triggers the stress response. This reaction is often referred to as the

Hans Selye's studies of the body's responses to demands made on it have become a basis for understanding stress.

Karsh of Ottawa—Woodfin Camp

"fight-or-flight response." Perception by the brain of the stressor's presence is the first step; the brain then activates the sympathetic nervous system (SNS) and the pituitary. The pituitary triggers release of adrenaline (epinephrine) from the adrenal glands, which in turn further stimulates the SNS. Activation of the SNS results in dilation of the pupils, constriction of blood vessels, and increases in heart rate, blood pressure, blood glucose concentration, metabolic rate, and mental activity. These reactions prepare the organism to take action. But the kind of action undertaken depends on the individual's evaluation of the situation and his ingrained patterns of behavior. His choices in the face of a threatening situation are either to retreat, advance, or stand ground.

The stage of resistance. Once the alarm reaction has prepared the organism for action, the body begins to adjust to and resist the agent or situation that provoked the alarm response. Resistance, however, may be maintained for only a short time. Should the stressor persist beyond this time, the body automatically enters the final stage of the process, exhaustion.

The stage of exhaustion. Selye speculates that everyone has a finite amount of what he terms "adaptability energy." The body enters the stage of exhaustion when this energy is used up. Everyone experiences this protective mechanism to some extent; for example, after extreme physical work we become exhausted and must rest in order for the body to gather more energy, thus allowing work to be resumed. Unfortunately, some people ignore the signals of exhaustion that the body sends. They push themselves to the point that their reserve energy is used up; permanent damage, or even death, can result. Selye postulates that aging is caused by the gradual depletion over time of an individual's adaptability energy.

Sources of stress

Stress is everywhere! Ask a person to take note of the instances he sees as stress provoking; in a period of only a few hours, you will get a fairly lengthy list. Examples will range from a traffic jam on the way to work to one of the kids coming home late from school. Let's look at the different kinds of stress that can affect us.

One of the most common kinds of stress is the physical stress that affects individuals who are forced to draw upon previously untapped physical reserves (*e.g.,* sudden increase in exercise) or who suffer bodily trauma (*e.g.,* a broken leg). Another common variety of stress is that resulting from social situations. Some of the more convincing evidence regarding the influence on the individual of social factors comes from animal studies.

301

Stress

Investigators have shown, for example, that as the number of animals housed together increases (with other factors such as diet, temperature, and sanitation remaining constant), so also does the incidence of maternal and infant mortality. There is also an increase in the development of hardening of the arteries (arteriosclerosis). At the same time, resistance to drugs, germs, and X-rays decreases. From his animal studies, ethologist Robert Ardrey has suggested that territorialism is a crucial part of normal human functioning—that each individual needs a personal "living space" in both a physical and a psychological sense.

It has been shown that while too dense a population has its detrimental effect, so also does too little meaningful human interaction. Tuberculosis occurs more frequently in so-called marginal people —those individuals deprived of meaningful social contact. The family, the most basic unit of society, is often another source of stress. The bonds that exist among family members may serve either to strengthen or to weaken individuals within the family. The kind of stress present in the home affects how we deal with stress elsewhere; likewise, external social or physical stress on an individual member is bound to have an effect on the other members of the family, their interrelations, and their own resources for meeting stress.

Viewing stress in perspective

Lately stress has received only negative publicity. Its damaging aspects have been focused on in many recent articles, and various methods for reducing stress have been suggested. An important point to remember is that stress is a natural phenomenon and necessary for survival. The stress reaction itself is an adaptive mechanism, the body's natural method of dealing with stressors and protecting itself from harm. In an emergency situation, the stress reaction enables us to accomplish feats that would be impossible to perform under normal conditions.

Stress has been implicated in the etiology of many diseases and is believed by some to have a part in every disease. The "germ theory" has even been equated with the "stress theory." In the past, scientists such as Robert Koch and Louis Pasteur isolated specific bacteria that caused specific diseases. With the realization that every situation or condition has specific causes has come the belief that stress plays an important part in the disease process. Some have gone so far as to view stressors as the only specific cause of disease.

The role of stress in disease can be explained by comparing the disease process to the formation of a hurricane. For a hurricane to occur certain elements must be present: winds greater than 75

Both high population density and isolation are believed to be causes of stress that lowers the body's resistance to disease.

miles per hour, moving counterclockwise in the Northern Hemisphere and clockwise in the Southern Hemisphere; warm ocean waters; heavy rains; and lowered atmospheric pressure. In the absence of any one of these elements, the storm that develops is not classified as a hurricane. The disease process is also dependent on a number of variables: the host organism and its condition; the presence of germs or other agents; entry into the host by the germs; environmental conditions; and the presence of stressors. If the host can alter or eliminate any one of the elements, the disease will not be as severe or may not even develop. Since stressors cannot always be removed, the individual must learn to alter his response to them. Handling a stressful event successfully can be a strengthening process. It has long been supposed that personal growth can develop from crisis situations. The Chinese word for crisis is formed by combining the symbols for danger and opportunity. Learning to "capitalize" on stressors can make the handling of stress an opportunity for personal growth.

Methods of dealing with stress

Modern science has not yet devised one easy-to-learn plan for combating stress. Instead of one plan for one person, there are many different methods for many people. However, there are several things that can make the stress experience as meaningful as possible. Ultimately, it is up to each individual to look inward for self-knowledge and outward for available help. Maintaining the best possible physical health can be important both in dealing effectively with stress and in checking its harmful physical effects.

Several traditional treatment modalities—such as psychotherapy—may provide help in altering the emotional effects of stress. Currently, however, nontraditional means of coping with stress, such as yoga and meditation, are attracting growing numbers of followers. Eastern philosophies, in which the individual strives for the highest state of consciousness, characterized by tranquility and inner peace, are gaining popularity. Another therapy having much in common with the Eastern methods of self-regulation is biofeedback, a technique that involves the use of mechanical devices to provide a visual indication of muscle activity and relaxation and peripheral vascular efficiency. Biofeedback can help the individual who is consciously trying to relax his sympathetic nervous system. Autogenic training, which was originated in Berlin by Johannes Schultz, utilizes a combination of relaxation techniques based on a step-by-step progression first to physical relaxation and, in time, to emotional relaxation. The premise is that the body's natural abilities to deal with stress will function adequately if permitted to do so, and that decreasing the resistance of tension and anxiety will enhance that process.

Family systems therapy offers an alternative method for dealing with stress. The process involves examination of the family structure and relationships, past and present. One assumption in family systems therapy is that in order to establish and maintain meaningful one-to-one relationships with contemporaries, an individual must have done so with his family of origin, where the reactive patterns and process developed.

All of the methods discussed here—and a variety of other kinds of therapies—are available to anyone trying to cope with and adapt to stress. Each individual has the prerogative to explore for himself the methods, combinations, or adaptations that offer the most support. While the stress of modern life continues to increase, it is possible for the human mind and body to evolve in ways that promote more effective coping and adaptation.

—*M. Kathleen McIntyre, M.S.N., and Grace A. Cordts, B.S.N.*

Surgery

Minisurgery, day surgery, and outpatient surgery are all names for the same phenomenon: surgery that can be accomplished in a single day and that does not require an overnight stay in the hospital. Day surgery can be performed in a physician's or surgeon's office, in the outpatient clinic of a hospital, or—as is increasingly the case—in an ambulatory surgical facility (ASF), organized and operated especially for that purpose.

While outpatient surgery has been a familiar procedure for years, certain new developments in day surgery have attracted attention from health care experts, medical personnel, insurance and government officials, and from patients themselves. These recent developments include: (1) the increasing number and kind of operations being performed on an outpatient basis; (2) the significant reduction in costs offered to patients by day surgery; and (3) the proliferation of ASFs in various parts of the United States.

At first glance, day surgery seems a very positive, efficient, and welcome medical advance. However, great controversy has arisen over the implications of day surgery—with hospital administrators its chief detractors. They maintain that outpatient surgery removes from the hospital budget the simpler, everyday operations that have always helped to finance more ambitious, costly surgical procedures. In other words, patients undergoing tonsillectomies in hospitals have traditionally helped to underwrite costs for open-heart surgery patients. And, the hospitals argue, with the advent of day surgery complex operations may be difficult to obtain in the future because of increased costs. Who will bear these increased costs and in what form?

The growth of the ASF

Because ASFs are so new, there are no exact figures available on how many of these facilities exist, nor is there much information available on the establishment of a new facility. However, with the formation in 1974 of the Society for the Advancement of Free-Standing Ambulatory Surgical Care (SAFSASC), it was expected that more complete information about and communication among ASFs would soon exist. Estimates of the number of ASFs in the United States range from 24 to 100.

Surgicenter, established in 1970 in Phoenix, Ariz., is generally recognized as the first ASF. One of the largest in the country is Bailey Square Surgical Center in Austin, Tex., which cost more than $3 million to build and which has seven operating rooms.

Typically, an ASF is founded with investments by a group of individuals, often doctors. *Business*

303

Surgery

Week magazine reports that the return on such investments has been projected at 10% to 20% a year — varying by geographic area of the country and by the length of time the ASF has been in business.

The patient's viewpoint

Probably the chief advantage of an ASF to the surgery patient is psychological. Planners have attempted to make ASFs intimate, warm, and unforbidding. The environment is attractive, and procedures are streamlined. An emphasis is placed on personal involvement with the patient in an effort to dispel the feeling of alienation that often overwhelms people as they move through the numerous large departments of a modern hospital.

Even when a hospital tries to streamline its outpatient department, the result is seldom successful. As the patient experiences it, the result is still time-consuming, forbidding, and confusing. In *Modern Hospital* magazine, William Nick, professor of surgery at Ohio State University, states: "The delivery of outpatient surgery in a hospital tends to follow the day-to-day inpatient procedures, whereas if outpatient surgery is provided in a facility strictly for outpatient use, it can be organized for better patient flow . . . and more effective time utilization."

From a medical standpoint, the operations performed in the typical ASF are low-risk. The routine screening of prospective ASF patients eliminates those prone to complications, who are required to go to a hospital.

The approximately 300 different operations performed at Surgicenter in Phoenix bear witness to the truly impressive array of operations that can be performed on an outpatient basis. Tonsillectomies are a staple of ASFs. Other pediatric surgery is common, too, as many doctors prefer using outpatient facilities for children to avoid emotional upset. Orthopedic surgery for both children and adults is also frequently performed as are oral and plastic surgery. A number of gynecological operations, for example, abortion, sterilization, and biopsy of a tumor, are common ASF procedures. Hernia repair can also be performed expeditiously on an outpatient basis.

Most laymen would not be surprised to hear that those operations are deemed low-risk, but that some other procedures, among them ophthalmic surgery, simple mastectomies, and the stripping of varicose veins, have become one-day enterprises seems truly amazing. Many kinds of surgical procedures that formerly required from four to 14 days in the hospital are now being performed at the ASF in one day.

The cost of surgery at an ASF is always much lower than the cost at a hospital. For example, in 1975 the cost of a tonsillectomy at a typical ASF was $175 as compared to an in-hospital cost of about $500. The issue of cost is complicated, however, by the fact that not all insurance plans cover the cost of work performed at an ASF or other outpatient facility.

Insurers and the government

As of early 1976, only about one-fifth of the nation's individual Blue Cross plans paid for surgery at an ASF. Other plans maintained the traditional rule of paying only for surgery performed in an accredited hospital. Blue Cross is, of course, considered a leader among private insurers.

Another major private insurer, Metropolitan Life Insurance Co., however, has approved payments to a number of ASFs. A spokesman for the company

A child scheduled for an adenoidectomy in an ambulatory surgical facility (ASF) examines his finger as a nurse, his parents, and the surgeon watch. A wide range of low-risk surgery is now performed in ASFs, partly because of lower costs. Outpatient surgery is frequently used for children to reduce the trauma of hospital confinement.

Courtesy, Surgicenter®

extolled the ASF as economical from the view-points of patient and insurer alike.

Insurance companies are notoriously conservative, so their caution in dealing with new facilities for surgery is not unexpected. Their reluctance could be swept away, however, if the U.S. government decides to include payments to ASFs under its own benefit programs.

The U.S. Congress has authorized the Social Security Administration (SSA) to make a study of the many alternatives to the traditional hospital, including the ASF—with an eye toward the possibility of changing policy to reimburse federal aid recipients who choose such alternatives. The SSA has hired a management-study firm to prepare a detailed report on the cost factors of alternative health-care institutions, including ASFs. It would seem certain that if Medicare, for example, is authorized to reimburse patients for surgery in an ASF, then private insurers would feel confident that it is safe to do the same.

From the consumer affairs point of view, the cost difference between an ASF and a hospital is so great that some patients may save money on outpatient surgery even before ASFs are approved for insurance payments on a widespread basis. Such might be the case, for instance, for patients whose group insurance policies pay only some proportion, often around 50%, of the total bill. For a tonsillectomy costing $500 in a hospital, for example, some health insurance plans might pay only $250. If the patient can get the same surgery at an ASF for only $150, he can pay the whole bill there himself and still save $100 on what would have been his share of a hospital bill.

Until some uniformity of policy is achieved by federal and state governments, insurers, and social agencies, each patient will have to examine the specifics of his or her personal situation to determine the most advantageous course.

Sharing the cost of medical care

Hospital spokesmen maintain that someone must pay, in the end, for complex hospital procedures and equipment. They argue that it is short-sighted to examine the cost savings of one particular operation for one particular patient without considering the larger needs of other patients for expensive care. With advances in medical science, there will be a corresponding rise in demand for new, elaborate procedures and programs of treatment. Such advances are financed—so the argument goes—by the bread-and-butter operations that normally represent a profit for the hospitals.

The position of hospitals' advocates is well stated by Salvinija G. Kernaghan, writing in the journal *Hospitals,* an official publication of the

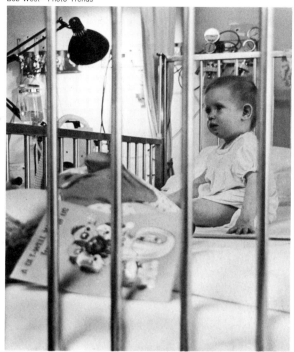

A child recuperates from open-heart surgery, one of the high-risk operations that must be performed in a hospital.

American Hospital Association: "As the source of outpatient surgery revenue is drained from hospitals by freestanding facilities, inpatient surgical costs, premiums of private insurance companies, and taxes that subsidize governmentally funded health care programs probably will rise."

The consumer is well acquainted, of course, with this informal law of economics: pay in one way today, or pay another way tomorrow. While this rule of thumb is probably true in general, and as applied to health care, it seems unfair to shift the onus for such a huge problem to the ASF—which represents just one aspect of the health care delivery system. A variety of national health insurance proposals have been introduced in Congress in recent years, and most knowledgeable observers agree that only a new national policy and a new massive financing plan on the national level will help equalize the financial burden of health care and guarantee adequate treatment for all.

—Patricia Dragisic

Taste and Smell Disorders

The mechanisms of taste and smell are poorly understood, and until recently, research in the field has been sparse. The disabling effects of these sensory disorders—unlike those of sight, hearing, and touch—are not immediately obvious. Yet such disorders can destroy the career of a restauranteur, grocer, wine taster, or perfume chemist, and they hamper the ordinary person's enjoyment of life's simple pleasures.

Indeed, persons with taste and smell disorders frequently lose interest in food and, as a result, lose weight — occasionally to the point of malnourishment. Because eating is a social experience, these disorders sometimes interfere with normal interpersonal relationships; afflicted persons frequently become depressed. They are at risk from physical dangers as well: unknowing exposure to spoiled foods, poisons, or noxious and toxic fumes from smoke or leaking gas.

There are two principal methods of measuring

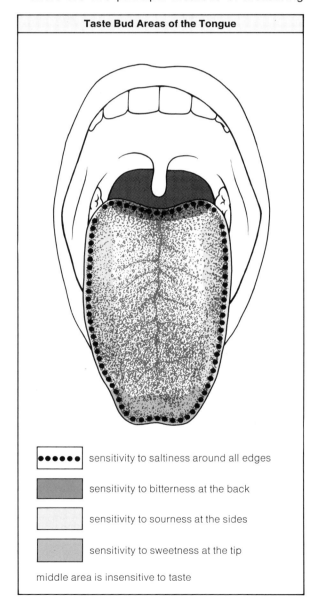

Taste Bud Areas of the Tongue

● ● ● ● ● sensitivity to saltiness around all edges

sensitivity to bitterness at the back

sensitivity to sourness at the sides

sensitivity to sweetness at the tip

middle area is insensitive to taste

taste acuity. One involves sampling various solutions in different concentrations; the other consists of the painless application of low-level electric current to specific areas of the tongue to see if taste is perceived. The ability to detect and recognize vapors can be measured by "sniff" techniques.

Classification

Taste and smell impairments fall into eight general categories. Most common are the lessened ability to taste or recognize salty, sweet, sour, or bitter substances (*hypogeusia*), and the lessened ability to detect or recognize odors (*hyposmia*). Some persons experience a distortion of normal taste or smell (*dysgeusia* or *dysosmia*). Even more discomfitting is the sensation of a foul, obnoxious taste associated with eating or drinking (*cacogeusia*), or a foul, obnoxious smell associated with the odors of substances normally considered pleasant — coffee or chocolate, for example (*cacosmia*). The total lack of ability to taste and to smell are referred to, respectively, as *ageusia* or *anosmia*.

Abnormalities of both taste and smell frequently occur together; however, the anatomy of the two senses is distinct, and disorders of either may occur independently. A disorder of the sense of smell is more common, although an individual suffering such a handicap may perceive his problem as a disorder of taste, because olfactory cues are important in taste perception.

Causative factors

While these disorders are occasionally congenital, most persons develop them after injury or illness. Researchers at the National Institutes of Health have identified a severe flulike syndrome, with fever lasting several days and fatigue lingering three or four weeks, that they believe to be a causative factor in two out of every five cases of taste and smell loss. The common cold and sinusitis may have a similar temporary effect. Even minimal head trauma may cause abnormalities in the ability to taste and smell, though the problem may not appear until several months after the injury. Problems also may appear following ear surgery and radiation therapy for head and neck cancer. The connection between surgery and patient complaints that hospital food is tasteless has only recently become a subject of medical curiosity.

Taste and smell disorders, along with severe and frequent headaches, may indicate a brain tumor. These impairments may accompany neurological and muscular disorders, diphtheria, encephalitis, hypothyroidism, pregnancy, and hormonal disturbances including menstrual irregularities and menopause. Loss of taste or smell also may be an important indication of systemic diseases, including cancer. A study to assess the clinical significance of appetite loss in cancer patients is currently under way at four U.S. medical centers under sponsorship of the National Cancer Institute. Some medications also interfere with the perception of taste and smell.

Physiological factors

Recent studies into the physiology of taste indicate that the four basic tastes—salt, sweet, sour, and bitter—are perceived quite independently of each other. Taste intensity is known to wane with age, as the number of taste buds decreases. When the sense of taste is impaired, the perception of bitter taste is usually the first to be lost, while the ability to register a sweet taste is affected least. Diminution of sour and salt taste occurs to varying degrees between these two extremes.

Persons whose ability to salivate is impaired usually suffer taste disorders. According to current hypothesis, the presence of certain zinc-containing proteins in saliva is related to the ability to taste. There has been some evidence that zinc supplements can help persons with a demonstrated zinc abnormality to regain the ability to taste. The presence of a mucous layer in the nose appears to play as critical a role for smell as saliva does for taste. Far more is known, however, about the sense of taste than about the sense of smell, and there presently is little effective therapy for olfactory disorders that have no apparent underlying physical cause.

Recent studies of taste responsiveness confirm that heredity determines some taste sensitivities. There remains the intriguing question to what extent preferences in food and drink are genetically determined and to what extent they are influenced by the more commonly considered factors such as environment, culture, and the appearance and texture of the substances in question.

— *Lynne Lamberg, M.A.*

Toxicology

Toxicology is the science that deals with poisons and their effects on living organisms. Poisons are substances capable of producing serious illness or even death and may be naturally occurring or man-made. The function of the toxicologist is to treat cases of poisoning, to search for antidotes, and to identify and eliminate toxic substances at their sources. Increasingly, however, toxicologists are being called upon to evaluate the effects of newly synthesized drugs, chemical pollutants in the environment, and chemical additives and insecticides in food and water supplies.

Acute poisoning is a relatively common medical

In 1975 two million children swallowed toxic substances; poisoning was the most common pediatric emergency.

emergency, occurring most frequently in young adults from 18 to 25 years of age. It was estimated early in 1976 that 10–15% of all emergency room visits were related to drug poisonings alone and included adverse reactions, drug interaction, and overdoses. The swallowing of toxic substances by infants and small children is also common; in 1975 about two million children were involved in such accidents, making poisoning the most frequent medical emergency encountered by pediatricians.

In 1953, in a massive preventive campaign led by the American Academy of Pediatricians, several U.S. hospitals began collecting information on poisoning in special "poison control" centers. More than 500 of these centers are now registered by the National Clearinghouse for Poison Control Centers, which was established in 1957 by the U.S. Public Health Service.

Food poisoning

Several outbreaks of food poisoning among travelers on ships and airplanes were recently reported. More than 600 passengers on two different cruise ships suffered attacks of *Vibrio parahaemolyticus;* both incidents were traced to contaminated seafood. Since all passenger liners sailing from U.S. ports now fly foreign flags, the U.S. government has no authority over shipboard sanitary facilities. Another 200 travelers aboard a flight from Tokyo to Copenhagen suffered attacks of staphylococcal food poisoning and had to be treated during a stopover in Anchorage, Alaska. The incident prompted the Public Health Service to emphasize "the importance of serving pilots different food from that of the passengers, and each other, just before and during a flight."

Higher food prices and the "back-to-nature" trend have apparently revived concern over botulism, poisoning by the toxin produced by the bacterium *Clostridium botulinum,* the most deadly food poisoning known. The toxin is found in foods that have been improperly processed. In home-canned products, the danger of botulism is present if the proper high temperature is not maintained during the canning process. The worst outbreak of botulism in U.S. history occurred in Michigan in March 1977. Forty-five persons were stricken after eating home-canned hot green peppers in a Pontiac, Mich., restaurant. There were no fatalities, but nearly all of the victims were hospitalized.

One of the most highly poisonous natural substances known is the toxin in the mushroom *Amanita phalloides,* also known as the death cap. Although the death cap has long been a common source of poisoning in Europe, it was considered rare in North America, and few cases of poisoning had been traced to it. Recently, however, the Public Health Service Center for Disease Control indicated that the death cap may be more prevalent in the U.S. than hitherto believed. The toxic properties of numerous other plants, including some common houseplants and garden flowers and shrubs, were also under scrutiny during the year. (*See* Toxicology Special Report.)

Industrial poisons

For many years it has been known that a number of chemicals and chemical products (herbicides and insecticides, asbestos and fiberglass) as well as industrial pollutants in the environment are carcinogens, or cancer-causing substances. It is only recently, however, that many industrial and agricultural chemicals have been recognized as poisons, capable of causing serious illnesses — or even death — to human beings. Identification of cases of widespread industrial poisoning has reached alarming proportions within the past year.

The dumping of toxic industrial waste products into rivers and lakes is a growing source of disease and disability. In Minamata, Japan, where the Chisso Corp. was charged with "professional negligence resulting in death" for releasing mercury-containing effluents into Minamata Bay, more than 1,000 persons have been officially recognized as victims of mercury poisoning. Some estimates said there were as many as 10,000 unrecognized victims. Although the Minamata case is probably the best known, there have been other instances of

widespread mercury poisoning through contamination of the food supply. Late in 1976 numerous cases of mercury poisoning were reported among the Indian populations in the Canadian provinces of Quebec and Ontario. Like the residents of Minamata, the Indians have traditionally depended on fish from local lakes and rivers as an important part of their diet. In the United States, mercury-based paints and fungicides are under attack by the Environmental Protection Agency as potential causes of mercury poisoning.

Kepone, a pesticide formerly manufactured by the Allied Chemical Corp., and later by the Life Science Products Company of Hopewell, Va., caused a stir of publicity when it was discovered that the substance had caused serious illness to plant workers and their families. Life Science Products was closed in 1975 and Allied's Hopewell plant was later demolished. But the damaging effects of Kepone were not limited to those who had come into direct contact with the chemical. It is estimated that 100,000 pounds of Kepone remains on the bottom of the James River, as a result of discharges from the Hopewell plant. The James flows into the Chesapeake Bay, a major fishing area, and Kepone residue has been found in fish caught as far away as the Atlantic coast of New Jersey. A fine of more than $13 million levied against Allied Chemical Corp. — the largest such penalty ever imposed on a U.S. company — was reduced in February 1977 when Allied announced that it would establish an $8-million endowment fund for cleanup of the river. But dredging the river could cost as much as $100 million, and it is possible that such an operation, by disturbing the sediment, could release even more of the poison into the environment. In the meantime, the contamination continues, and problems will persist for many years, as Kepone

A 1976 explosion in a Swiss-owned chemical plant forced many residents of nearby Seveso, Italy to flee their homes.

is a highly stable chemical that degrades very slowly in nature.

It was becoming increasingly apparent that workers in chemical and metallurgical industries were at high risk of poisoning from exposure to the toxic substances used in various manufacturing processes. A 1976 example was an outbreak of lead poisoning among employees of a Salt Lake City, Utah, smelter that had been converted from antimony processing without adequate safety precautions. In addition to plant workers, two repairmen who entered the furnace room only briefly were affected by the disease. In the goldmining region around Yellowknife in Canada's Northwest Territories, a joint report issued by a team from the United Steelworkers of America, the National Indian Brotherhood, and the University of Toronto charged that dangerously high levels of arsenic were being emitted in smoke from an ore-processing plant. In addition to being associated with certain cancers, arsenic has been linked with brain and stomach disorders and paralysis.

The danger to public health from industrial sources was dramatically illustrated in July 1976 when an explosion in a chemical plant in Meda, Italy, near Milan, caused thousands of pounds of chemicals to be vaporized. Among the chemicals released was a relatively small amount—an estimated two to ten pounds— of dioxin, one of the most toxic substances known and a suspected teratogen (substance capable of causing birth defects). The huge, foul-smelling, whitish cloud that developed over the nearby town of Seveso contained the highest concentration of dioxin ever found in the environment, and within a few days foliage in the area withered and small animals began to die. Stomach pains and skin reactions—burns and blistering—were the first symptoms experienced by the human population. Hundreds of people were evacuated and more than 200 acres of land was cordoned off with barbed wire; the Italian government prohibited consumption of any animal or vegetable products from the area. No one seemed to know how long the contaminated area would remain unsafe or how it might be detoxified, but one expert estimated that parts of the area will not be habitable for five to ten years. Because of the suspected teratogenicity of dioxin, doctors advised Seveso women to avoid becoming pregnant for three months and suggested that pregnant women who had been exposed to the poisonous fumes should have abortions.

In Michigan the most serious agricultural disaster in the history of the state resulted from the accidental mixture of PBBs (polybrominated biphenyls) with animal feed. The spread of PBBs through the Michigan food chain may turn out to pose a threat

In March 1977 more than 150 animals from one Michigan herd were killed and buried in a single afternoon because of suspected contamination by the chemical pentachlorophenol.

to human health as well. The earliest reports of PBB poisoning came in 1973, when several Michigan dairy farmers began to notice unusual disorders in milk cows. Milk production declined, animals went lame, and the death rate among newborn calves rose. It was not until 1974 that the source of the problem was identified—commercial cattle feed had somehow been contaminated with a chemical fire retardant containing PBBs; these are closely related to another class of toxic chemicals called PCBs (polychlorinated biphenyls), but are thought to be about five times as toxic. Contaminated farms were quarantined to prevent the spread of PBBs in commercial supplies of milk and meat, and thousands of head of livestock were destroyed, but these precautions did not prevent the chemical from affecting farmers and their families, who began to report mysterious illnesses. One 1977 survey examined 1,100 Michigan residents who lived on farms or bought their food directly from farms. The preliminary conclusion was that about one-third of those studied suffered an abnormally high frequency of neurological and muscular disorders. Another Michigan study reported alarmingly high levels of PBBs in the milk of some nursing mothers. In a similar, unrelated incident, also in Michigan, it was discovered that still another toxic substance, PCP (pentachlorophenol), a wood preservative that had been used to treat feed boxes, was causing cattle to sicken; again, the affected animals had to be destroyed.

—Linda Tomchuck, B.A.

Special Report:
Gardening May Be Hazardous to Your Health

by Naomi S. Suloway

Various parts of some plants grown indoors are naturally poisonous; fortunately, however, these potentially dangerous species are few in number and thus not likely to dissuade the true plant lover from his passion. But humanity, in its infinite technological wisdom, has managed to devise insecticides that can make the most innocuous of plants an object to handle with utmost caution. Perhaps more than any other consideration, the elaborate precautions necessitated by these chemical poisons could discourage even the most enthusiastic indoor gardener.

Uncommonly dangerous common plants

Among the common houseplants that have parts that are naturally toxic if eaten are azalea, croton, dieffenbachia, philodendron, English ivy, Jerusalem cherry, poinsettia, and a few bulb plants that are forced indoors—such as crocus, daffodil, hyacinth, and narcissus. Less common toxic indoor plants are the castor-bean plant (particularly the seeds) and the elephant's ear (a type of philodendron). These plants, however, require the ministrations of a horticulturally wise individual—not the kind of gardener who would be inclined to nibble his most outstanding specimens!

Parts of common plants grown outdoors and collected for indoor use are also toxic: lily-of-the-valley, foxglove, larkspur, oleander, bleeding heart, rhododendron, and laurel. In addition, the seeds or berries of mistletoe, jasmine, daphne, lantana camara, wisteria, and privet may be fatal if eaten. A full list of outdoor plants of varying toxicity would be extensive.

The concept of herbal poisons is complicated and not easy to define clearly—particularly in terms of the degree to which any given plant matter is toxic. Degree of toxicity depends on the amount of the substance involved and the susceptibility of the victim. Further, some plants are simply irritating to the skin, while others are capable of producing, on contact, allergic reactions that may even be fatal. Other plants are poisonous only when put in the mouth or when eaten. The milky, sticky juices of the croton and poinsettia and other members of the spurge, or *Euphorbia*, genus can cause inflammation of the skin of susceptible individuals; people are subject to this reaction in varying degrees. Individual tolerance to even the ingestion of certain plants may vary. Toxic plants are generally disagreeable to the taste and often to the smell, so that adults are not likely to consume them.

Thus, the greatest danger of these plants lies with children and pets. Because children automatically put things in their mouths, *all* houseplants should be positioned out of their reach. Statistics on plant poisoning in children are difficult to find. Municipal health authorities often do not know the source of the toxic substances ingested by poisoning victims, since even parents can't be certain exactly what a child may have eaten. Almost invariably, a small amount of toxic plant matter can result in death in children, whereas the same quantity would cause only various degrees of discomfort in adults. There seems to be general agreement, for example, that the ingestion of a single castor bean would be fatal to a child. The danger of plant poisoning to cats is probably less than that to dogs. Cats seem to have an instinct for knowing which plants are edible. Because pets are more agile than children and can sometimes scale even the highest shelves, pet owners might be wise to avoid all toxic plants.

The dangers of insecticides

Before the generalized use of insecticides indoors, green-thumbing was a pleasant, relaxing, and uncomplicated pastime. There is great pleasure to be had in pruning to encourage bushier foliage, snapping off a cutting to root a new plant, fingering the leaves to gauge their vigor, and poking about in the soil to see if watering is necessary. These pleasures can be disastrously curtailed, however, by the sudden appearance of uninvited guests—insect pests.

One such plague is springtails, tiny light-colored subsurface insects that live in the soil and crawl to the surface momentarily only when the plant is watered; traditional foliage sprays are not effective. These creatures have tails that act as springs with which they can flip themselves substantial distances—even into adjacent pots. The combination of such mobility and the microscopic size of

COMMON POISONOUS PLANTS

Cultivated House and Garden Plants

COMMON NAME (GENUS & SPECIES NAME)	ACTIVE PRINCIPLES	TOXIC PARTS (WHEN EATEN)	SYMPTOMS
arum family: caladium, fancy-leaf caladium *(Caladium);* elephant ear, dasheen *(Colocasia);* dumb cane, elephant ear, dieffenbachia *(Dieffenbachia);* split-leaf philodendron, ceriman *(Monstera);* philodendron, elephant ear *(Philodendron)*	calcium oxalate crystals	all parts	intense irritation to mucous membranes producing swelling of tongue, lips, and palate
castor bean, castor-oil plant, palma christi *(Ricinus communis)*	ricin	seed if chewed; if swallowed whole the hard seed coat prevents absorption and poisoning	burning sensation in the mouth, nausea, vomiting, abdominal pain, thirst, blurred vision, dizziness, convulsions
lantana *(Lantana camara)*	lantadene A	all parts, especially the green berries	vomiting, diarrhea, weakness, ataxia, visual disturbances, and lethargy
English ivy *(Hedera helix)*	steroidal saponin: hederagenin	all parts	local irritation, excess salivation, nausea, vomiting, thirst, severe diarrhea, abdominal pain
foxglove *(Digitalis)*	cardioactive glycosides: digitoxin, digoxin, gitoxin, and others	leaves, seeds, flowers	local irritation of mouth and stomach, vomiting, abdominal pain, diarrhea, cardiac disturbances
rhododendron, azalea *(Rhododendron)*	andromedotoxin	all parts	watering of eyes and mouth, nasal discharge, loss of appetite, nausea, vomiting, abdominal pain, paralysis of the limbs, and convulsions
larkspur, delphinium *(Delphinium)*	delphinine	all parts, especially the seeds	burning and inflammation of mouth, lips, and tongue followed by numbness. Paresthesia, beginning in the extremities, progressing to entire body
hydrangea *(Hydrangea macrophylla)*	cyanogenic glycoside: hydrangin or umbelliferone	leaves and buds	nausea, vomiting, abdominal pain, diarrhea, difficulty in breathing, muscular weakness, dizziness, stupor, and convulsions
apple *(Pyrus malus)*	cyanogenic glycoside	seeds	nausea, vomiting, abdominal pain, diarrhea, difficulty in breathing, muscular weakness, dizziness, stupor, and convulsions
lily of the valley *(Convallaria majalis)*	cardioactive glycosides: convallamarogenin and others	all parts	local irritation of the mouth and stomach, followed by vomiting, abdominal pain, diarrhea, persistent headache, and cardiac disturbances
sweet pea *(Lathyrus odoratus)*	beta-(gamma-L-glutamyl-amino)propionitrile	the pea or seed	slowed and weakened pulse, depressed and weakened respiration, and convulsions
morning glory *(Ipomoea violacea)*	several alkaloids which are chemically related to lysergic acid diethylamide (LSD)	seeds	hallucination-like states, nausea, loss of appetite, abdominal pain, explosive diarrhea, frequent urination, and depressed reflexes

Cultivated House and Garden Plants (continued)

COMMON NAME (GENUS & SPECIES NAME)	ACTIVE PRINCIPLES	TOXIC PARTS (WHEN EATEN)	SYMPTOMS
common garden hyacinth (*Hyacinthus orientalis*)	unidentified	bulb; leaves and flowers if eaten in large quantities	nausea, vomiting, abdominal pain, and diarrhea
holly, Christmas holly (*Ilex*)	unidentified	bright red berries	nausea, vomiting, abdominal pain, and diarrhea
yaupon, yaupon holly (*Ilex vomitoria*)	unidentified	bright red berries	nausea, vomiting, abdominal pain, and diarrhea
iris (*Iris*)	unidentified	rootstalk or rhizome	nausea, vomiting, abdominal pain, and diarrhea
ligustrum, common privet, waxed leaf ligustrum (*Ligustrum*)	unidentified	leaves and berries	nausea, vomiting, abdominal pain, and diarrhea
narcissus, daffodil, jonquil (*Narcissus*)	unidentified	bulb	nausea, vomiting, abdominal pain, and diarrhea
poinciana, bird-of-paradise (*Poinciana gilliesii*)	unidentified	green seed pods	nausea, vomiting, abdominal pain, and diarrhea
wisteria (*Wisteria*)	resin; glycoside: wisterin	whole pods or seeds	nausea, vomiting, abdominal pain, and diarrhea
oleander (*Nerium oleander*)	cardioactive glycosides: oleandroside, oleandrin, and nerioside	leaves, stems, and flowers	local irritation to mouth and stomach, vomiting, abdominal pain, diarrhea, and cardiac disturbances
Japanese yew, English yew, ground hemlock (*Taxus*)	alkaloid taxine	seeds, leaves, and bark	gastroenteritis, cardiac disturbances
European plum, wild plum (*Prunus domestica*)	cyanogenic glycosides	leaves, stems, bark, and seed pits	nausea, vomiting, abdominal pain, diarrhea, difficulty in breathing, muscular weakness, dizziness, stupor, and convulsions
apricot (*Prunus armeniaca*)	cyanogenic glycosides, cyanide	leaves, stems, bark, and seed pits	nausea, vomiting, abdominal pain, diarrhea, difficulty in breathing, muscular weakness, dizziness, stupor, and convulsions
chokecherry (*Prunus virginiana*)	cyanogenic glycosides	leaves, stems, bark, and seed pits	nausea, vomiting, abdominal pain, diarrhea, difficulty in breathing, muscular weakness, stupor, and convulsions
Jerusalem cherry, natal cherry (*Solanum pseudocapsicum*)	leaves contain cardioactive substance solanocapsine and the berries contain the glycosidal alkaloid solanine and related glycosidal alkaloids	all parts	cardiac depression
daphne (*Daphne mezereum*)	daphnin; coumarin glycosides	all parts, especially berries, bark, and leaves	local irritation to mouth and stomach, nausea, vomiting, diarrhea
rhubarb (*Rheum rhaponticum*)	oxalic acid	leaf blade	corrosive action on the gastrointestinal tract

their eggs, which poking in the soil might transfer from pot to pot, means that all plants near the infested one must be treated—requiring large quantities of insecticide. One method is to drench the soil with a solution of Malathion (0,0-dimethyl dithiophosphate of diethyl mercaptosuccinate).

This treatment, however, produces a multitude of complications. The runoff—the liquid that drains out of a well-watered pot into the saucer below—must be treated with care: the initial drenching and subsequent waterings will cause Malathion to continue to drain from the soil for several weeks. The label on Malathion reads, "Avoid breathing of spray mist. Avoid contact with skin; wash thoroughly af-

Wild Plants

COMMON NAME (GENUS & SPECIES NAME)	ACTIVE PRINCIPLES	TOXIC PARTS (WHEN EATEN)	SYMPTOMS
Jack-in-the-pulpit, Indian turnip (Arisaema triphyllum)	calcium oxalate crystals	leaves	corrosive action to gastrointestinal tract producing swelling of tongue, lips, and palate
mayapple, mandrake, ground lemon (Podophyllum peltatum)	podophyllotoxin	rootstalk, leaves, stems, and green fruit	abdominal pain, vomiting, diarrhea, pulse irregularities
water hemlock, spotted cowbane, poison parsnip (Cicuta maculata)	cicutoxin	root and rootstalk	increased salivation, abdominal pain, nausea, vomiting, tremors, muscle spasms, and convulsions
Virginia creeper, American ivy, woodbine (Parthenocissus quinquefolia)	oxalic acid	berries and leaves	corrosive action to gastrointestinal tract, nausea, vomiting, abdominal pain, diarrhea, and headache
poison hemlock, poison parsley, false parsley (Conium maculatum)	lambda-conicine, coniine, and N-methyl coniine	all parts	gastrointestinal distress, muscular weakness, convulsions, and respiratory distress
jimsonweed, Jamestown weed, thorn apple, angel's trumpet (Datura stramonium)	tropane alkaloids: atropine, hyoscyamine or daturine, scopolamine	leaves, flowers, nectar, seeds	dilated pupils, dry mouth, increased body temperature, and intense thirst, confusion, delirium, hallucinations, pulse disturbances
pokeweed, pokeroot, poke salad, inkberry (Phytolacca americana)	saponins; other unspecified	all parts, especially the root, leaves, and green berries	oral burning sensation, sore throat, nausea, vomiting, blurred vision
yellow jasmine, Carolina jasmine (Gelsemium sempervirens)	gelsemine	all parts	cardiac depression, visual disturbances, dizziness, headache, and dryness of the mouth
deadly nightshade, belladonna (Atropa belladonna)	tropane alkaloids: atropine, hyoscyamine	all parts	fever, visual disturbances, burning of mouth, thirst, hot/dry skin, headache, confusion

ter contact. Avoid contact with feed, foodstuffs, cooking utensils." Heeding such warnings is not as simple as it may seem.

Many fastidious indoor gardeners frequently wash their pot saucers—often in the dishwasher, along with kitchen utensils and tableware. But once contaminated with Malathion, the saucers must be washed in a laundry sink, touched only with rubber gloves, and dried with paper towels.

Another common plague is spider mites, best treated with Malathion in spray form. Considering the dangers of inhaling Malathion, spraying several dozen plants is simply out of the question for most apartment dwellers. The logical alternative, then, is a systemic poison.

Systemics are usually available in granular form; they are worked into the top inch or so of soil and then watered in. The insecticide is absorbed by the roots of the plant and is then carried to the stems, leaves, and flowers. An insect that eats any part of the plant will also eat the insecticide. Of course, any other living creature that eats any part of the plant also ingests the insecticide. The label on the systemic (0,0-diethyl S-[2-ethylthioethyl] phosphorodithioate) reads, "Poisoning may occur as a result of exposure. May be fatal if swallowed. May be absorbed through the skin." Runoff is not the only problem with systemics; they pose additional limitations in handling the foliage. Pinching back or pruning may leave the gardener with poison-laden sap on his fingers and under his fingernails. The result is an apartment full of plants that are potentially poisonous. Barriers must be built to keep pets and children safe, and floor plants often have to be converted to hanging plants.

Newer and more potent systemics continue to be developed and plant wholesalers and nurseries have been advised to keep plants so treated off the market for the time period required for such chemicals to dissipate. Plant experts often admonish their clients to buy only from reputable growers to ensure getting plants that will live. Perhaps this advice should also be heeded by gardeners concerned about ensuring their own personal survival.

Transplantation

The transplantation of organs and tissues from one individual to another is a relatively recent phenomenon in medical science, and one in which new knowledge and techniques are rapidly accumulating. The number of transplants performed increases annually, while the category of organs and tissues that can be successfully transplanted continues to expand. A corresponding development has been increased understanding of the body's immunosuppressive mechanisms, resulting in the creation of new means to counter rejection of foreign tissue.

Kidney transplantation

Large numbers of renal (kidney) transplantation operations continue to be performed worldwide, with more than 4,000 such procedures in the U.S. in the past year. In the U.S. alone, however, of 33,000 patients being managed by hemodialysis, more than 11,000 are awaiting transplants. Two basic factors account for this backlog. First, there have been no recent significant advances in techniques to prolong the survival of transplanted kidneys; second, a shortage of kidneys—and other transplantable organs—still exists. A major reason for the organ shortage is the legal problem of defining death: a donor must be unequivocally declared dead before the kidney (or other organs used for transplantation) can be removed. Yet the organs must be removed soon after death if they are to remain viable and useful for transplantation. Currently, more than a dozen states have passed laws that define death in terms of loss of brain function—that is, when the spontaneous electrical activity of the brain has ceased and when examination and testing indicate that the cessation is irreversible, the patient may be pronounced dead. Organs can then be removed even though the patient's heartbeat and breathing may still be sustained by artificial life-support machines.

Another reason for the shortage of cadaver kidneys is the understandable reluctance of physicians to ask permission from the bereaved relatives of prospective donors. In some European countries, physicians are not required to ask the next of kin for permission to remove organs, and the family

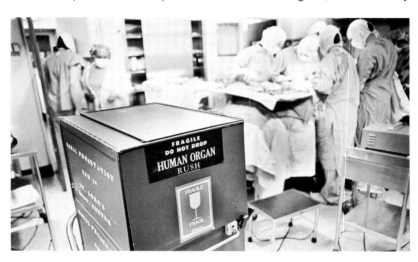

The number of patients awaiting transplants far exceeds the number of available organs, partly because many potential donors have not taken legal steps to indicate their willingness. The Uniform Anatomical Gift Act, passed by all U.S. states, makes a signed organ donor card legally binding, thus removing the burden of decision from the next of kin. Illinois provides identification stickers that can be attached to donors' driver's licenses.

ORGAN DONOR

RESTRICTION CODES

1. Corrective Eye Lenses
2. Left Outside Mirror
3. Daylight Driving Only
4. Automatic Transmission
5. Built Up Seat Cushion or Power Seat
6. Other - As indicated below

DRIVERS LICENSE CLASSIFICATIONS

Class A—Any motor vehicle through 8,000 lbs. gross weight, except class L or M.
Class B—Any motor vehicle through 16,000 lbs. gross weight, except class L or M.
Class C—Any motor vehicle except truck tractor-semitrailer combinations, stinger steered semitrailers, or class L or M.
Class D—Any motor vehicle except class L or M.
Class L—Only motor-driven cycles (less than 150 cc's).
Class M—Only motorcycle and motor-driven cycles.

DL A-51.8
REQ. MVP 738 SEPT. '74

UNIFORM DONOR CARD

OF _____
Print or type name of donor

In the hope that I may help others, I hereby make this anatomical gift, if medically acceptable, to take effect upon my death. The words and marks below indicate my desires.

I give: (a)____ any needed organs or parts
(b)____ only the following organs or parts

_____
Specify the organ(s) or part(s)
or
for the purposes of transplantation, therapy, medical research or education:
(c) — my body for anatomical study if needed.
Limitations, or
special wishes, if any: _____

(Top) Geoffrey Biddle; (bottom) courtesy, Kidney Foundation of Illinois, Inc.

may even be unaware that an organ has been used. Since this procedure is not likely to be adopted in the U.S. in the foreseeable future, pressure is being exerted on legislators to support the widest possible endorsement of brain death criteria in order to increase the number of available organs. The Uniform Anatomical Gift Act enables prospective donors, while they are still alive, to grant permission for donation upon their death of any nondiseased organs. Many states, with the aid of the National Kidney Foundation, have incorporated this form of permission on drivers' licenses.

Among adult patients the survival rate of transplanted and dialyzed patients may be similar; thus, it is usually the patient's choice that finally determines which course of treatment is to be followed. In children, however, there is a predominant need for transplantation because children in renal failure show slowing of growth, failure of sexual maturation, and development of severe bone disease. Most pediatric nephrologists therefore agree that a successful kidney transplant provides the best chance for the child in renal failure — not only because of danger to normal growth and development but also because of the psychological strains imposed on both the child and the family by long-term dialysis. After successful transplantation in the young patient, resumption of normal growth rate may occur as soon as the dose of renal cortical steroids is reduced. Rehabilitation, with return to full-time school and social activities, is often quite successful.

Other organs: heart, liver, lung, and pancreas
During 1976 heart transplants were carried out in only four countries in the world, and two-thirds of the procedures were performed in the U.S. Liver transplantation has remained at more or less the same level of activity for the past five years. In 1976 three centers reported 29 liver transplants, and of these patients, 15 survived after a year. One child has survived for nearly eight years; the outlook for liver patients may soon be comparable to that for patients receiving cadaver kidney grafts.

For treatment of diabetic patients there has been increased emphasis on transplantation of the whole pancreas or of those pancreatic cells that produce insulin. Compared to the published reports on kidney transplant surgery, there is not a great deal of available information about the procedures involved in pancreatic transplants. Any advance in this field is vitally important because diabetic patients frequently suffer complications from disease of the kidney and other organs. Thus prevention of renal failure by controlling the underlying diabetes could eliminate the need for kidney transplants in diabetic patients.

Tissue compatibility and rejection
Investigation into histocompatibility factors — those that govern the body's acceptance or rejection of foreign tissue — continues, and through electron microscopy scientists have identified the sites, or loci, of major histocompatibility factors on human chromosomes. The histocompatibility (HL-A) antigens form a system that is known to play an important role in transplantation. In most medical transplantation centers, HL-A antigens of loci A and B on human chromosome 6, for example, have been routinely matched between donor and recipient; matching of the antigens in the C locus is a relatively recent development. In addition to the matching of the A, B, and C loci, the D locus (of importance in the mixed lymphocyte culture) has significance in sibling transplants. Matching for all these factors in sibling transplants results in a high rate of success. For most patients, however, only cadaver transplants are available, and matching to this degree of complexity has not proven possible on a nationwide scale. Increasingly, regional networks have provided for available kidneys to go to the most likely recipients.

Recent advances have been made in the clinical monitoring of transplant patients, especially in the development of tests that indicate the optimum doses of the immunosuppressive agents required to prevent rejection. These tests involve the periodic testing of frozen donor cells, usually spleen cells or lymphocytes, for reactions with the cells and serum of the recipient.

An interesting change has taken place recently in the concept of blood transfusions for potential recipients of kidney transplants. For many years, most hemodialysis units did not transfuse their patients routinely unless strong clinical or medical indications were present, in order to reduce the risk of sensitization of the potential recipient to future transplantation. This approach was beneficial indirectly in that it reduced the spread of blood-borne serum hepatitis in dialysis units, but it was apparently associated with rather poor survival of transplanted kidneys. Surprisingly, it now seems possible that blood transfusion on a regular basis may produce better renal transplant results. There are promising suggestions that use of frozen blood, *i.e.,* blood that has first been washed of almost all its plasma and cells and then frozen, may improve survival of transplanted organs while at the same time reducing the risk of hepatitis.

In the therapy of transplantation, antilymphocyte and antithymocyte globulin, which is a blood fraction derived from animals (*e.g.,* goats, horses, and rabbits) that have been immunized with cells derived from human donors, is being widely tested for its beneficial effects on transplants. It seems likely that this product may, during the period of its administration, reduce the number of rejection episodes; further research is needed before long-term residual benefits can be evaluated.

—Nathan W. Levin, M.D.

Urology

Successful toilet training implies that a child can control both bladder and bowels. This ability usually occurs spontaneously as a consequence of central nervous system maturation between the ages of two and four. In spite of this natural maturation, there are many children who nevertheless fail to develop complete control over urination. Some achieve normal control, then lose this ability and lapse into daytime wetting (incontinence), nighttime wetting (enuresis), having damp pants—sporadic release of small amounts of urine. Frustration on the part of parent and child often results in the child's being brought in for a medical evaluation. The kind of urologic investigation routinely undertaken on such children in the past, including kidney X-ray studies and cystoscopy, generally failed to identify the cause of their abnormal urination. The usual course was to prescribe bladder-directed drugs, generally with unsatisfactory results. If one drug was unsuccessful, additional ones were tried. When these too failed, the children were labeled as having "psychological problems" and referred to a psychotherapist for further treatment. However, subsequent studies have determined that many of their psychological symptoms were normal reactions to the frustrations of being unable to control urination.

New diagnostic techniques

Recently, a number of studies have been made of these psychologically normal children who have a problem with abnormal urination. Newer diagnostic techniques in urology in combination with the recent recognition of certain clinical symptoms have made it possible to evaluate and treat these urinary abnormalities as physiological, rather than psychological, problems.

Several pediatric urologic centers have employed these diagnostic techniques on such children, with remarkable success. A majority of the children studied complained of changes in urination habits that ranged from almost normal control to daytime wetting, damp pants, abdominal cramps, squatting postures, sudden, unexpected urination, and nighttime wetting. These children ranged in age from 3 to 16 years, and there were equal numbers of males and females. Approximately 25% had a history of urinary tract infection. None was studied while actively infected. The uro-

logical examination included taking a detailed history, with specific emphasis on events associated with urination. The results of physical examinations generally were normal. However, 20% of the girls studied exhibited chafing and redness in the area between their thighs. These were children who frequently had damp pants. All the children had their kidneys X-rayed to eliminate the possibility of kidney pathology, such as obstruction or nonfunction. A bladder X-ray was included to see whether there was urine backing up into the kidneys during urination. Each child also had a cystoscopic examination of the bladder and urethra to discover if there was any active or chronic infection (cystitis) or a stricture or ring in the urethra.

Twenty-four hours after these tests were completed, urodynamic studies were performed. These included tests of direct bladder filling and voiding pressure and of urethral flow, volume, and pressure. Direct recordings also were made of pelvic floor and urethral sphincter muscle activity occurring during urination.

Urodynamic studies show that under normal circumstances, the bladder fills with a low, smooth pressure. When the bladder is filled and the person perceives the desire to urinate, bladder pressure will rise and by voluntary control the pelvic floor and urethral sphincter muscles will relax and open. This allows free passage of urine from the bladder through the urethra and out. By recognizing abnormalities, specific pharmacological therapy can be applied directly to suppress the sphincter spasm or the "uninhibited" contractions. By suppressing these mechanisms a clinical cure can be achieved. Drug therapy must continue for several months while the patients are symptom free (dry). Then therapy is slowly reduced and eventually discontinued. The result is a newly trained, asymptomatic, normally voiding child.

Causes and symptoms of abnormal urination

In children with abnormal urination patterns, the majority experience damp pants. This condition is created by frequent small spurts of urine escaping because of bladder muscle irritability or spasms of the urethral sphincter muscle or both. Many children with this condition will assume a squatting posture. The children take this posture in an attempt to contract their thigh, buttock, and perineal muscles enough to keep urine from leaking out. Urodynamic testing of these children clearly reveals immature bladder control or abnormal relaxation and contraction of the pelvic floor and the urethral sphincter muscles. Immature bladder control produces abdominal pain in all affected patients, and it produced damp pants with squatting postures in 55% of the children studied. Spasms of

Urination Patterns and Their Corresponding Urodynamic Tracings

NORMAL VOIDING

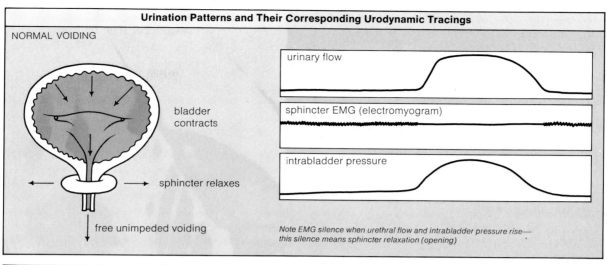

bladder contracts

sphincter relaxes

free unimpeded voiding

urinary flow

sphincter EMG (electromyogram)

intrabladder pressure

Note EMG silence when urethral flow and intrabladder pressure rise—this silence means sphincter relaxation (opening)

SPHINCTER SPASM

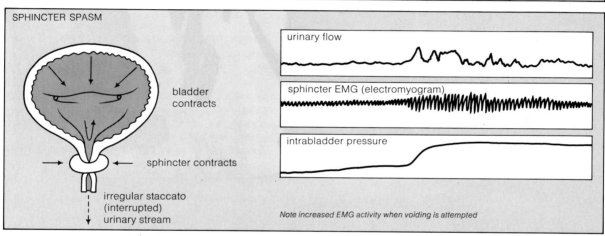

bladder contracts

sphincter contracts

irregular staccato (interrupted) urinary stream

urinary flow

sphincter EMG (electromyogram)

intrabladder pressure

Note increased EMG activity when voiding is attempted

UNINHIBITED PEDIATRIC BLADDER

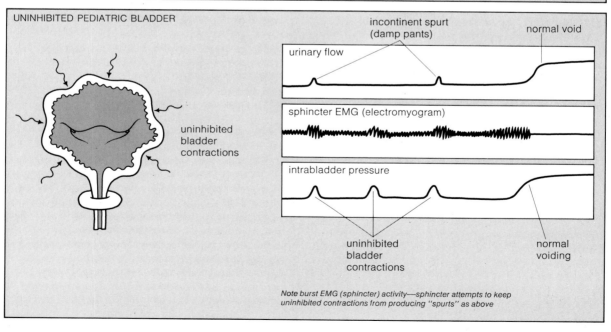

uninhibited bladder contractions

incontinent spurt (damp pants)

normal void

urinary flow

sphincter EMG (electromyogram)

intrabladder pressure

uninhibited bladder contractions

normal voiding

Note burst EMG (sphincter) activity—sphincter attempts to keep uninhibited contractions from producing "spurts" as above the urethral sphincter produced damp pants and a squatting posture without abdominal pain in nearly all the children who experienced such spasms.

New treatments for urinary abnormalities

This type of detailed, physiologic study has made it possible to discover malfunctions in bladder and pelvic floor voiding in patients who lack control over their urination. This in turn has made it possible to prescribe drugs specific to the problem: bladder relaxants such as propantheline bromide (Pro-Banthine) and urethral sphincter relaxants such as diazepam (Valium). The results are highly successful. In one study of 32 children, all were free from symptoms within two weeks after starting drug therapy. Within three to six months, 82% were clinically cured, returned to normal urination control, and off drug therapy. None of these children required psychological or surgical intervention. Those children who originally had demonstrated psychological problems were subsequently determined to be normally reactive.

Urodynamic evaluation and drug therapy to reestablish proper functioning of the bladder and pelvic floor and the urethral sphincter muscle result in normal urination. All presenting complaints, such as damp pants, squatting, and abdominal pain, disappear. The rate of success of this approach to the child with an abnormal urination pattern is one of the most exciting and practical advances in pediatric urology in recent years.

— *Casimir F. Firlit, M.D., Ph.D.*

Veterinary Medicine

The University of Florida and the University of Tennessee enrolled their first classes of veterinary students in 1976, bringing the total number of veterinary colleges in the U.S. and Canada to 24. The sexual revolution in the profession is reflected in the fact that although there were only about 1,700 women veterinarians in the U.S. and Canada in 1977, by the fall of 1976 there were 2,147 women enrolled in accredited veterinary colleges, 28% of the total student body of 7,571. Specialization in the veterinary sciences continues to be a major trend. The official recognition of the American College of Veterinary Anesthesia brings the total number of recognized veterinary specialties to 15.

Animal technicians are becoming important in veterinary medicine, performing tasks that require routine application of skill and knowledge. Technicians do blood sampling, laboratory procedures, routine vaccinations and foot trimming of cattle, artificial insemination, certain minor surgical procedures such as dehorning and castration of young animals, and, under direct supervision, ani-

Newborn pigs on U.S. swine farms are threatened by the increasing incidence of the viral disease called pseudorabies.

mal nursing and meat inspection. The American Veterinary Medical Association (AVMA) has established guidelines to accredit animal technician training programs in the U.S. By the end of 1976, 23 institutions had met the AVMA requirements, and several more schools were seeking approval for their programs.

Veterinarians from the U.S., both private practitioners and faculty from veterinary colleges, continued to share their expertise and experience with less developed countries of the world in such tasks as livestock improvement and community building. Nongovernmental approaches that engage and educate villagers were a hallmark of this work. The Institute of Cultural Affairs in Chicago and the Heifer Project International in Little Rock, Ark., were examples of nonprofit, private agencies that coordinated international programs. Local U.S. groups, as well as the United Nations Food and Agriculture Organization, also cooperated in the new missionary movement that has caught the interest of many U.S. veterinarians looking for opportunities to work in other countries.

Animal and human diseases

During the past several years there has been considerable speculation about the role of animals in the history of influenza in human beings. Many influenza viruses have been found in domestic and wild mammals and birds, and it is now known that influenza viruses of human origin have infected several animal species. On the other hand, several cases of acute respiratory disease in humans apparently have been caused by the swine influenza virus or by a virus closely related to it.

The influenza that occurred at Fort Dix, N.J., early in 1976 and that led to a national immunization program in the U.S. appeared to be caused by a virus similar to the virus that swept the world in 1918–19. At the height of the 1918–19 pandemic a government veterinarian observed an apparently new disease in Midwest swine that had signs very similar to those of the human flu. Although other human epidemics have occurred since, none has been of the 1918 type although the influenza has persisted to the present in swine.

Although the 1918 influenza virus and the virus isolated at Fort Dix have been called "swine influenza," it is not clear that the viruses originated in swine and were subsequently transmitted to man. There is, in fact, evidence that some human influenza strains, inappropriately called "swine influenza virus," can be transmitted from man to swine. The National Livestock and Meat Board has pointed out that "swine flu" should actually be called "A-New Jersey."

Some people were concerned that they could get the "swine flu" from eating pork or from contact with pigs. Humans cannot catch the flu from pork. While a very few farmers apparently caught the disease from close contact with infected swine, these were very rare occurrences. When transmission of influenza occurs, it is normally from human to human; swine and pork products pose no threat of causing an influenza epidemic. (See also Infectious Diseases.)

Another question of the possible transfer of disease from domestic animals to humans concerns the so-called bovine leukemia virus, or BLV. There is, however, no evidence to support the suspicion that human consumption of raw milk containing BLV—or human contact with BLV-infected animals —can cause human leukemia. It is known that infected cattle and sheep can transfer the disease to nursing offspring, but newborn animals that are fed pasteurized milk from the same infected animals develop no signs of leukosis. Several studies involving dairy farmers and their families, veterinarians, and laboratory researchers—all of whom had been in contact with infected animals or with the virus itself—revealed no evidence that they

had developed antibodies to BLV. A Swedish project conducted over an 11-year period also failed to show any relationship between human leukemia and BLV. Even when BLV is present in raw milk, the pasteurization process renders the virus noninfective. This finding seems to eliminate any possibility that leukemia could be transmitted in commercially distributed dairy products.

Animal diseases

Pseudorabies, a viral disease that often results in a maddening itch leading to self-mutilation, has reached epidemic proportions in Indiana, Illinois, Iowa, and South Dakota. When the disease strikes a farm, the entire crop of baby pigs can be lost through spontaneous abortions or from death soon after birth. There is no vaccine to prevent the disease, and there is no known treatment for it. Pseudorabies is a fatal disease for animals, but the virus does not affect humans. In 1976 there were confirmed cases of pseudorabies on 714 swine farms in 22 states, three times more cases than in 1975 and five times the number in 1974. If the trend continues, staggering losses can be expected for swine farmers and the cost of pork will increase substantially.

Current research into this disease has three emphases: the development of a vaccine, plans for eradication of the disease, and testing the usefulness of immune serum—which includes antibodies produced in the blood of adult pigs previously infected with the pseudorabies virus—for treatment of infected baby pigs. Illinois experiments found a 28% reduction in death in baby pigs treated with the immune serum.

The International Pig Veterinary Society Congress brought together 1,500 experts on swine diseases, health, and husbandry from 39 countries around the world in 1976. The American Association of Swine Practitioners and Iowa State University (ISU) were hosts to a conference that featured simultaneous Spanish, French, German, and English translations of research findings and progress reports from throughout the world. Advances in the prevention and treatment of enteric diseases, particularly those involving the bacterium Escherichia coli, were a major priority. The possibility of animal-to-man transfer of antibiotic-resistant strains was described and debated as a part of a larger controversy concerning the use of antibiotics fed to cattle, swine, and poultry at subtherapeutic levels to promote growth and prevent disease.

Foot-and-mouth disease (FMD) is an acute, highly contagious, and economically devastating disease that affects cattle, sheep, and swine. The disease is common in parts of Europe, Asia, Africa,

Courtesy, the World Health Organization; photographs, P. Larsen

Despite routine round-ups of cattle for vaccination, South American ranches continue to be plagued by foot-and-mouth disease. Heavy saliva and lesions around an animal's mouth are symptoms of the dreaded, highly contagious disease that attacks nearly all domestic animals and, in rare cases, humans as well.

and South and Central America. In other regions, including North America, strict measures of control and eradication have kept FMD from becoming established. Recent projections from the University of Minnesota estimate billions of dollars in potential losses to agriculture and consumers if FMD were to enter the U.S.

Despite the fact that FMD has been prevalent in South America for many decades, the disease has been nonexistent in North America since its final eradication in Mexico in 1954. One of the primary factors in preventing the reinfection of northern livestock has been the so-called Darien barrier, the underdeveloped, rugged border area between Panama—the southernmost country free of FMD—and Colombia. Composed of swamp, jungle, and mountains, the Darien barrier has effectively prevented the movement of livestock between the two countries.

The completion of the Pan-American Highway through this region, joining North and South America, would provide a convenient means of ground transportation and destroy the natural barrier against FMD. The livestock industries of Panama, Central America, Mexico, the U.S., and Canada have expressed their reservations about completing the highway. The U.S. National Security Council has recommended that there be no highway construction until effective programs can be established to prevent the spread of FMD. The U.S. Department of Transportation has been required to prepare an environmental impact statement, including FMD prevention, before contracts are awarded for completion of the highway.

Veterinarians, governments, and livestock producers and carriers are implementing a plan involving the creation of an FMD eradication zone in Colombia, a zone of compulsory FMD vaccination, rigorous monitoring, and quarantine requirements. The history of the control of FMD is one of veterinary medicine's finest examples of international cooperation to guard the world's food supplies.

Pets and humans

Problems associated with the "pet population explosion" include animal bites, transmission of diseases, automobile accidents, property damage, and the necessity of humanely destroying millions of animals annually. Few taxpayers are aware of the impact animal control has on local taxes. Many urban counties and cities have found it necessary to pass new animal control laws and to create agencies to administer and enforce them. Educational programs are being developed in several communities to discourage impulse buying of pets. The programs teach pet owners the importance of selecting pets carefully, as well as the responsibilities of pet ownership. Many veterinarians have formed associations with local humane societies to help reduce overpopulation of animal shelters and to improve the health of adopted puppies and kittens.
— *Edward R. Ames, D.V.M, Ph.D.*

World Medical News

In 1977 Australia's Medibank and Great Britain's National Health Service faced the problems of providing health care in an era of continually escalating costs. Canada utilized a fee-for-service plan with modifications within each province. South Africa emphasized health education, upgrading of hospital facilities, and control of communicable diseases.

Australia

On July 1, 1975, a new health care system called "Medibank" went into operation covering all Australian citizens. Fifteen months later, on Oct. 1, 1976, Medibank was scrapped by a new federal government in favor of "Medibank Mark II," a plan substantially different from the first. Both plans were the subject of major political controversy and the introduction of the second Medibank was heralded by a one-day national strike. On each occasion the federal government spent large sums explaining to the public how the new plans would work. And on each occasion there was substantial public bewilderment. However, people have now become accustomed to Medibank Mark II, and the system's future seems assured — at least until the next election.

Under Medibank Mark II, health insurance is compulsory, but individuals have the choice of being covered either by Medibank (the federal gov-

ernment Health Insurance Commission) or by a registered private health insurance fund. There are about 70 such funds, all voluntary, nonprofit organizations. To complicate the picture, the federal government's Medibank agency also runs a separate "private" health insurance operation in competition with the other private health insurance funds.

Persons who are covered by Medibank pay a graduated levy of 2.5% of their taxable income, which is collected with their regular tax payments. Those who pay no tax, such as pensioners and the unemployed, are automatically covered by Medibank, which means that the levies do not cover total costs, and subsidies from general tax revenues are required. There is a ceiling to the levy of $A150 a year for single persons and $A300 for families. These ceiling figures represent 2.5% of annual incomes of $A6,000 and $A12,000 respectively.

The levy ceilings have been carefully calculated to make it more economical for about half the population, the better paid half, to opt out of paying the levy and join a private health insurance fund instead. In other words, for those who want to choose the doctor who will treat them in the hospital, private health insurance at the lowest permissible level of coverage provides a more attractive alternative than payment of the levy at ceiling level. By juggling the rate of the levy and the ceiling, the federal government is able to regulate the proportion of the population for whom it accepts financial responsibility as far as medical and hospital care are concerned.

In Australia nearly all medical services provided by doctors outside the hospital — whether general practitioners or specialists — are paid for on a fee-for-service basis. An official schedule of fees, negotiated with the Australian Medical Association before an arbitrator, covers each medical service, and people are free to choose any doctor they wish, although specialist services are usually obtained on referral from a general practitioner. When a person incurs a medical expense, he takes the bill to his insurer — either Medibank or a private fund — which pays a "medical benefit" related to the scheduled fee for the service. Provided that the doctor charged the scheduled fee, the benefit paid will leave the patient with a balance of no more than $A5 to pay out of his own pocket for each service, however expensive that service may have been. For standard consultation by a general practitioner the unpaid balance is only $A1.20. Although doctors are not bound to charge scheduled fees, few charge much more.

The schedule of fees and the benefits paid are the same for Medibank and the private health insurance funds. However, Medibank offers doctors a facility called "bulk billing." Instead of billing his

Medibank patients individually, leaving them to obtain the benefit, the doctor may, if he wishes, send his bills in bulk directly to Medibank for payment at the level of the benefit. This way the patient has no cost to meet out of his own pocket and no claim to make. Bulk billing is opposed by most doctors, however, and is widely used only in billing for the elderly and other pensioners who cannot afford to pay anything out of their own pockets or who are not able to handle claims procedures. Private health funds do not accept bulk billing. Critics of bulk billing say it encourages overuse of services, since the patient has nothing to pay, and encourages fraud by enabling a few unscrupulous doctors to bill for services not performed.

The financing of care in the hospital is also covered by Medibank and the private funds, but it is considerably more complicated and is subsidized from general tax revenues. Australia has a federal type constitution, and 80% of the hospitals are owned and operated by the state governments. The federal and state governments have an agreement that they will share the net operating costs of the state's hospitals on a 50–50 basis and also that Medibank levy payers will receive free hospital accommodation when needed and free medical attention in the hospital provided by doctors employed by the hospital.

Under this arrangement the levy payer may not choose the doctor who will treat him but must accept a doctor assigned by the hospital. Choice of

doctor in the hospital — an issue about which many Australians have strong feelings — is the only substantial difference between the benefits available to Medibank levy payers and those who are privately insured.

Privately insured patients are charged for hospital accommodations, at a rate of either $A40 a day for a shared room or $A60 a day for a private room. The real cost of a hospital bed averages about $A100 a day, so there is a considerable subsidy; nonetheless, there is also a substantial charge. State hospital charges are fully covered by membership in a private health insurance fund, but, of course, the premiums for private room coverage are higher than those for shared accommodation. In addition to being charged for his hospital room, the privately insured patient is also responsible for the fees of the private doctor of his choice who treats him in the hospital. However, such fees are covered by the official fee schedule, and medical benefits to cover these charges are paid by the private health insurance funds.

About 20% of the hospital beds in Australia are in private hospitals run by charitable or religious organizations or for profit. Although they receive a federal government subsidy of $A16 a day per occupied bed, private hospitals must charge a higher rate, and an individual may pay an additional premium to a private health insurance fund to cover the increased costs of the private hospital. Other additional premiums may be paid to provide bene-

The introduction in 1976 of a revised national health program touched off what was described as the first national strike in Australia's history. About 2 million protesting workers, among them these demonstrators in Sydney, shut down the country's businesses and halted public transportation for 24 hours.

David Austen—Keystone

fits for dentistry, home nursing, physiotherapy, ambulance transport, and other ancillary services. For a family, the total cost of medical, private hospital, and ancillary service coverage—the most expensive package—is more than $A10 a week. Prescription drugs are covered by a separate federal scheme that provides virtually all drugs needed at $A2 per prescription; pensioners receive prescription drugs free. So much prized is the individual's right to choose the doctor who will treat him in the hospital that those covered by Medibank, who would normally have no such choice, can, for a small subsidized premium, buy the right to be treated in the hospital by a private doctor on a fee-for-service basis.

How does Medibank Mark II differ from Medibank Mark I? Under the first system, which was introduced by a Labor Party government, membership in the Medibank was compulsory. There was no levy, the whole cost being met out of general tax revenues. It was the imposition of a levy by the new Liberal-Country Party government that caused the one-day national strike. The first Medibank was the sole provider of medical benefits (paid on the same basis as today) and offered everyone free hospital accommodation and treatment but without choice of doctor. However, it was possible under the first Medibank to buy coverage with a private health insurance fund for preferred hospital accommodation with choice of private doctor, whose fees were covered by Medibank medical benefits. Providing this extra hospital insurance and coverage for ancillary services was, at that time, the only function of the private health insurance funds.

Prior to Medibank Mark I health insurance was not compulsory. About 80% of the population was covered by private health insurance funds for hospital and medical care, the benefits paid being partially subsidized by the federal government. There was no government health insurance program. Pensioners received free general practitioner and hospital services paid for by the federal government and the states. A disputed number of people —estimated at 6–15% of the population—had no coverage for the medical costs they incurred.

Despite its complexities, the latest system does have advantages. Everyone is covered; low-income earners pay according to their means or receive free treatment. Through insurance premiums, those in higher income brackets pay the total cost of medical care and a large part of the cost of hospital accommodation.

Although its overall cost to the nation continues to rise at an alarming rate, health care is more accessible to a greater number of people than it was before 1975. The controversies that have raged over changes in the system have centered almost entirely on money. The quality of care provided has changed little and continues at a high level.

—*Nicholas Lloyd*

Canada

The past year in Canada saw continued emphasis on preventive medicine through healthier life-styles as the ultimate answer to the steady increase in the cost of medical care. There was also new legislation affecting the way the federal and ten provincial governments will share the cost of health services. Although they may not produce any immediate changes, both of these developments could have significant long-term influence on the country's health services.

Hospital and medical care for most of Canada's 23.3 million people are provided through insurance plans operated by the provincial governments, with financial help from the federal government. In 1977, after more than five years of negotiations, the federal and provincial governments agreed on a new cost-sharing formula. Funds from the federal government will no longer be specifically earmarked for hospital or medical care or professional education. Instead, although the government will provide at least as much money as before, it will leave the allocation of funds to the provinces. The only stipulation is that provincial health programs adhere to basic guidelines.

This new system has certain advantages, for example, giving the provinces more freedom to structure health services in the ways best suited to their special needs, taking into account their wide demographic and economic differences. Freedom to use federal money for programs other than active treatment hospital care and medical care may also help bring about a shift away from hospital care—the most expensive kind of health care—to outpatient programs, such as clinics, or expanded programs for chronic, convalescent, or home care. Because hospital insurance was the first form of national medical insurance offered, the Canadian health care system has tended to emphasize hospital care. As a result, both doctors and patients often think of the hospital emergency or outpatient department as a primary source of medical treatment.

There may also be disadvantages to the new system. The Canadian medical profession fears that hospital and medical care programs will now be competing for funds with all other provincial programs, whereas before they were partly protected by the specificity of federal payments. Now the provincial governments may be deciding between highways and hospitals. And if the economic situation worsens doctors fear they may be more hard pressed, since it is politically easier—and publicly more acceptable—to squeeze doctors than to squeeze hospitals. During the past two years, provinces that tried — and failed — to close hospitals they felt were unnecessary quickly discovered the unpopularity of such action.

Rising health costs — impelled constantly upward by inflation, higher wages, and expensive new technology — have long been a primary concern of federal and provincial governments. Health costs for Canada total some $12 billion a year, rising from $118 per person in 1960 to $520 in 1976. In the 1960s and early 1970s, annual expenditure increases ran at a rate of about 9 to 10%; in 1974 and 1975 they reached 17%, according to federal government figures. Canada's health expenditure as a percentage of the 1976 gross national product is anticipated at not more than 7.5%, compared with 8.6% in the United States.

Canadian doctors are becoming increasingly unhappy, feeling they are locked into a payment system that puts them further and further behind economically. Over the past year the federal government's tough anti-inflation measures froze physicians in what they regarded as an already disadvantaged position. They are also uneasy that the fee-for-service payment method, which they see as protecting their freedom of practice, may be in jeopardy. For example, the social affairs minister of Quebec, Denis Lazure, a physician and now a member of the separatist Parti Québécois government, has warned doctors in that province that they can expect to be put on salary when their current agreement expires in 1980. The present government, however, will be close to the end of its mandate by then, so many changes are possible. Other provinces are unlikely to take such a major step: indeed, many outside the medical profession think salaried doctors might prove more expensive than those receiving fee-for-service payments. However, some modifications of the present system are probable. As G. L. Reuber, chairman of the Ontario Economic Council, noted recently, the combination of a patient who makes no direct payments with a doctor who gets a fee for every service performed is "most devoid of incentive to induce efficiency" in the delivery of health care.

While governments and patients tend to regard doctors as a major cause of rising health costs, physicians attribute the economic problem to patients who "overuse" the system, demanding services they do not need just because these services are "free." At its 1977 annual meeting the Canadian Medical Association went on record as favoring direct patient participation in paying all or part of a doctor's bill (with safeguards for the poor) as a way of simultaneously reducing demand, enabling doctors to keep up with the cost of living, and curbing doctors' fees by discouraging unnecessary tests or treatments. Despite the doctors' urgings, direct patient payments are not likely to be introduced; they tend to penalize poor patients, and governments find them politically unpopular.

Since physicians generate costs through the treatments they prescribe, reducing the number of doctors is seen as another way of holding the line. By 1976 federal immigration authorities were granting visas to foreign medical graduates only when it could be shown that no Canadian graduate was available to fill a position. Federal Health Minister Marc Lalonde, addressing the Canadian Medical Association in June 1977, predicted an annual increment of physicians of about 2.7% compared with a population increase of 1.4%, thus bringing the ratio from the present one doctor for every 570 patients to about 1:475 by 1986. Lalonde's figures have been disputed on the grounds that they in-

As a part of its program to encourage physical fitness the Canadian government recently appointed Iona Campagnolo as the country's first minister of state for fitness and amateur sport.

Canadian Press

clude many doctors not actually treating patients, so new studies are to be carried out to provide more reliable data on medical manpower. Meanwhile, the provinces, too, have been enforcing their own controls, such as cutbacks in medical school admissions and in residency training positions.

The ultimate aim of any health system is the hardest to measure: Does it make people healthier? According to Lalonde, Canadian men now rank seventh in longevity among men from 21 Western nations, while Canadian women rank third. Canadian men can expect to live two years longer than U.S. men, even though Canada spends $100 per capita less on health care. Nevertheless, the Canadian system is often described as a sickness system rather than a health system—emphasis is on treating the ill rather than on keeping people healthy. Also, degenerative diseases such as heart disease are on the rise in Canada as elsewhere in the Western world. Currently, increased emphasis is being put on health, fitness, and prevention.

Lalonde's 1974 book *A New Perspective on the Health of Canadians* urged acceptance by the individual of greater responsibility for his own well-being through changes in life-style, such as more exercise, greater attention to fitness, and less smoking, drinking, and overeating. The book has had considerable impact over the past three years. The federal government has continued its encouragement of fitness and active recreation with the appointment of the first minister of state for fitness and amateur sport, Iona Campagnolo.

Great concern has arisen in Canada—as it has in many other industrialized countries—over the impact on health of environmental and industrial materials, such as asbestos, of which Canada is one of the world's major primary producers. Workmen's compensation payments alone exceed $600 million a year in Canada. Lalonde has proposed a Canadian Centre for Occupational Health and Safety to gather information from across the country for exchange among the provinces and to stimulate and coordinate research by governments, universities, and industry. The proposal is still under consideration but is likely to be accepted by the provinces.

A Canada Health Survey is under way to explore the health status of well people, as distinct from the patterns of illness studied 25 years ago in the Canada Sickness Survey. The health survey will also be an ongoing study providing information on such subjects as physical condition and fitness, mental health, and life-style. The survey will be carried out by means of questionnaires and personal home interviews with a cross section of the population. Canadian doctors have pledged to cooperate in the survey, which, it is hoped, will provide valu-

able information for future planning of health and social services.

—*Joan Hollobon*

Great Britain

At a time when a Royal Commission on the National Health Service is examining massive evidence submitted by more than 2,000 public and private groups, the British National Health Service (NHS) stands besieged from within and without by a wide variety of ills, few of which seem to be solvable in the immediate future. The commission took as its brief a general proposal "to consider in the interests of both the patients and of those who work in the National Health Service the best use and management of the financial and manpower resources of the National Health Service." Having spent the past year gathering extensive evidence, the commission will consider the data for up to two years before making specific recommendations.

In the meantime, David Ennals, secretary of state for social services and the top man in the NHS, has pledged at least three years of stability for the NHS, despite a proliferation of problems that have led the British Medical Association (BMA) to maintain that "present conditions in the NHS have profoundly depressed the morale of all branches of the medical profession."

The events of the past year have further added to the difficulties of the beleaguered health service. The most important of these events is the continuing economic crisis being felt throughout Britain. Although the budget for the 14 NHS regions was increased by nearly 1.5% for 1977–78, the NHS has had to cut hospital construction sharply and, at the same time, close an increasing number of hospitals. An annual national inflation rate approaching 20% means that drastic belt tightening must continue; a government White Paper issued early in 1977 declared that the NHS would have to trim £31 million ($53 million) from its £5,000 million ($8.6 billion) budget in the next two years. Declared Ennals, "There is no use calling for more and more money. There is no crock of gold."

Compounded with this bleak financial outlook is a growing militancy at every level of the health service, even among the top levels of the consultants, the elite of the medical profession. At the lowest levels, hospital ancillary staff—porters and service employees, many of foreign origin—have become more eager to organize and to employ traditional trade-union methods, including strikes. In fact, strikes have been called not only to improve wages and working conditions but also to influence hospital management policies, which have traditionally been the purview of physicians and administrators. One such issue concerns the maintenance of

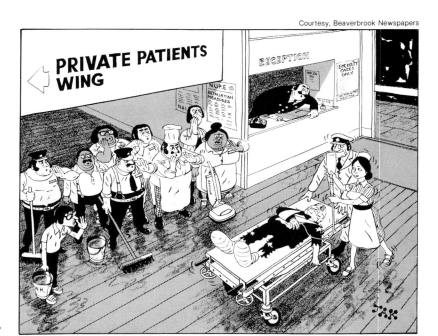

"BOOOOO!!!"

beds for private, paying patients in the no-direct-cost NHS hospitals. Militant action by hospital service employees contributed to the passage in 1976 of a new law that has thus far ordered the elimination of nearly one-third of the pay beds in NHS facilities—and further cuts are expected in the future. In addition, the NHS has increased the cost of its private beds by as much as 24% and tripled medical service costs to private patients in its hospitals. To a great extent, organized service employees in NHS hospitals are responsible for these moves against private medicine in the NHS.

But union-type militance in the NHS is far from limited to porters and other ancillary personnel. Perhaps the most successful exercise of what the BMA called "sheer power of industrial muscle" was displayed by the junior hospital doctors when they won a radical new wage agreement from the NHS that included overtime pay after 40 hours a week rather than the previous "extra-duty allowance" after 80 hours a week. Their tactics included strict adherence to all rules governing their work and the threat of a series of 24-hour national strikes. One British medical magazine credited their victory to "intelligent, adroit use of industrial tactics."

As a result of the junior hospital doctors' gains and government pay restrictions, promotion to the coveted ranks of the consultants (senior hospital doctors) can now cost a junior doctor a reduction in pay. And the consultants, long considered the most prestigious and powerful sector of the British medical profession, are studying carefully the tactics of their juniors and hoping to do as well in their current contract negotiations with the NHS. In Oc-

tober 1976 a new association of consultants and specialists called for a one-day ban on routine work to protest the suspension of one of their members. "Strikes and stoppages are no longer news in the medical service," says a BMA spokesman.

At the same time, powerful elements of the health service agree that the major reorganization of the NHS in 1974 created an unwieldy and uneconomic administrative structure, which is siphoning off money that could better be spent to provide medical treatment. Even the firm that helped to plan the 1974 reorganization wants the NHS administration simplified, agreeing with the BMA that at least one level of management—the regional health authorities—should be eliminated. The NHS has ordered a 10% cut in management costs by 1979 in an effort to trim an administration that in the past five years has grown twice as fast as overall NHS staff.

Another focus of criticism of the NHS in the past year has been the growing waiting lists for treatment of both urgent and nonurgent cases. The total number of persons waiting for treatment rose to 590,000 in 1976, an increase of nearly 12% over the previous year's total. Waiting time for nonurgent—but often incapacitating and painful—ailments can be as long as two years. In an effort toward reaching its goal of a maximum one-year waiting time for patients with nonurgent conditions and a month for urgent cases, the NHS has allocated an additional £8 million ($13.6 million) for improvement of medical facilities in 1977.

While cutting back sharply on growth, the health service is faced with the anomalous situation of a current shortage of doctors and the imminent possibility that it is producing up to a thousand more new doctors per year than the NHS will need in the near future. The problem of oversupply is in part a result of policies by the United States, Canada, Australia, and New Zealand to limit immigration of foreign physicians. At the same time, on Jan. 1, 1977, doctors in member nations of the European Economic Community (the Common Market) achieved reciprocal rights of practice within the community. With hundreds of unemployed doctors in France, Germany, and Denmark, some British officials fear that the less qualified among continental doctors will drift to Britain, while many of the best British doctors will be lured away by higher salaries on the continent. Some sources predict that the European doctor surplus may be as high as 40,000 by the early 1980s.

Also adding to the potential problem of a doctor surplus in Britain is the presence of more than 10,-000 foreign doctors in NHS hospital posts. These foreign doctors, comprising a little more than half of all junior hospital doctors, are absolutely vital to the NHS, especially in hospitals and areas less attractive to British doctors. But as many countries close their doors to foreign doctors, a greater proportion of these physicians may choose to make careers in the NHS rather than move on to other countries or return to their homelands.

The NHS admits that mental health care continues to receive short shrift, although the government has committed itself to raise expenditures for the mentally handicapped by 2.8% a year. Currently, half of the hospital beds in Britain are occupied by mental patients, but mental health care is allotted only a tiny percentage of the NHS budget. In the past year, some 5 million Britons saw their doctors for mental problems, and 600,000 used NHS psychiatric services.

Despite financial pressures, the NHS is also trying to improve community health standards and promote health education, both efforts toward preventive medicine designed to reduce the strain on hospitals. The allocation for community health facilities has been increased to £21 million ($36.7 million) from £8 million ($13.6 million), and an additional £1 million ($1.7 million) has been given to the Health Education Council for a program to combat excessive smoking and drinking. Alcohol-related hospital admissions are still rising by more than 10% a year, and smoking has not decreased appreciably despite more stringent government measures.

Thus, a little less than 30 years after its inception, the British National Health Service remains considerably short of achieving its original goals and is beset by increasing problems, the most serious being a chronic shortage of funds. But at the same time, the government, doctors, and the public wholeheartedly agree that it is not the theory behind a fully comprehensive health service that is in question, but the successful realization and perfection of such a service.

The flood of recommendations to be studied by the Royal Commission on the National Health Service will take up virtually every aspect of the chronic and acute problems facing the NHS. To a large degree, the manner in which Britain will face its growing health needs in the next generation should emerge from the proposals of the Royal Commission.

—*Charles E. Alverson*

South Africa

South Africa's pioneering cardiovascular surgeon, Christiaan Barnard, who performed the first heart transplant operation in 1967, again became the focus of worldwide attention in June 1977 when he transplanted a baboon heart into a 25-year-old woman with chronic heart disease. The animal's heart was not intended to replace the patient's but rather to supplement her failing circulation until a suitable human donor could be found. The baboon heart, however, proved incapable of maintaining adequate circulation and the patient's own heart, already irreparably damaged, deteriorated rapidly.

Dorothy Fisher of South Africa, the world's longest surviving heart transplant recipient, celebrated in 1977 the eighth anniversary of her operation, performed by Christiaan Barnard.

The Argus—Photo Trends

She died within hours of the transplant operation.

On the other hand, several of Barnard's former heart transplant patients were continuing to live relatively normal and productive lives. One such patient, Dorothy Fisher, the world's longest surviving heart transplant recipient, celebrated the eighth anniversary of her operation in April 1977. Earlier, in October 1976, Barnard met in Cape Town with Miss Fisher and four of his other surviving transplant patients.

One of the primary current focuses of health care in South Africa is the construction of new hospitals and the expansion and modernization of existing facilities. The acquisition of sophisticated diagnostic equipment and of radiological equipment for cancer therapy has been of high priority to the country's hospitals. In 1977 the Johannesburg General Hospital became the recipient of a R400,000 computer-controlled linear accelerator for use in cancer radiotherapy. The unit, housed in a specially constructed building, is the most powerful of its kind in Africa. Three other South African hospitals, Groote Schuur (Cape Town), the National Hospital (Bloemfontein), and H. F. Verwoerd Hospital (Pretoria), also installed new linear accelerators in the past year. The machines, called Linacs, are capable of treating both surface and deep-seated tumors and can provide therapy to 60–100 patients per day.

May 1977 marked the 35th anniversary of the Baragwanath Hospital, near Johannesburg, which serves the black township of Soweto and provides treatment for more than 1.5 million patients per year. Originally opened as a center for the treatment of tuberculosis, Baragwanath has become the largest hospital in Africa and one of the largest specialist hospitals in the world. A staff of 7,000 serves the facility's nearly 3,000 beds; the hospital has 23 operating theaters. The medical staff includes some 3,000 black nurses, and plans for an expansion and rebuilding program will eventually make Baragwanath the country's major postgraduate training center for black nurses. The first phase of the program includes a new maternity wing, nurses' home and doctors' quarters, medical research laboratory, mortuary, intensive care unit, and metabolic and neurosurgical research units.

Several new hospitals opened during the past year. The 350-bed Pretoria West Hospital complex boasts some of the most modern facilities and equipment in the country; for example, surveillance facilities at the nurses' stations in the pediatrics wards allow nurses to see their patients without leaving the desk. One of the most advanced hospitals in terms of design is the new 630-bed Universitas provincial hospital, Bloemfontein, which is built on the so-called racetrack principle that places essential services on an inner track and patient wards on an outer track, thus minimizing the distance between patients and services. Another notable event took place on Oct. 1, 1976, when Tygerberg Hospital, near Cape Town, was officially opened. Tygerberg is reportedly the largest hospital in the Southern Hemisphere.

South African researchers continue to make significant contributions to clinical medicine. Tropical diseases are the subject of many research studies, but new areas of concern, such as cancer and cardiovascular diseases, are beginning to receive more attention. The impact of environment and life-style on health is another subject that has come under recent scrutiny. A special research unit, the Hans Snyckers Institute, has been established within the faculty of medicine at the University of Pretoria for the specific purpose of studying the increasing susceptibility to diseases associated with Western life-style—e.g., diabetes, tooth decay, coronary artery disease—in blacks who migrate from rural to urban areas.

Tuberculosis, although controlled or nearly eliminated in many parts of the world, is still a major medical problem in South Africa. One of the more important advances of the past year was the development of an inexpensive and highly effective method of finding cases of tuberculosis, made possible by an improved technique in the collection and transportation of sputum samples. The new technique was announced by the Tuberculosis Research Institute of the South African Medical Research Council (MRC). Guidelines for the procedure were submitted to the International Union Against Tuberculosis and the World Health Organization, and a new manual explaining the technique was to be issued by the International Union.

Leprosy is another disease that is slowly being conquered in South Africa. The Rev. Reginald Ford, who retired in 1976 from his position as general secretary of the Leprosy Mission, Southern Africa, predicted that the disease would be eradicated in South Africa within the century. The number of leprosy victims was reported to have dropped from 10,000 to 1,500 during Ford's 28-year tenure with the mission.

In order to take full advantage of medical developments elsewhere in the world, the MRC, under the terms of an agreement of September 1976, recently became linked by computer to the U.S. National Library of Medicine in Bethesda, Md. A system of terminals to be established at medical libraries throughout South Africa will give local medical researchers access to the Medlars bibliographical data base, the Institute for Biostatistics, and the Institute for Electron Microscopy.

— Linda Tomchuck

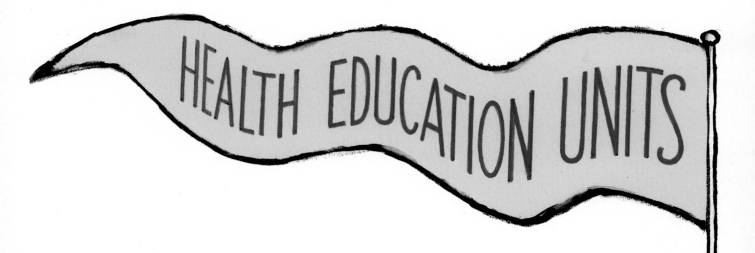

HEALTH EDUCATION UNITS

The following section contains the second in a series of Health Education Units on important medical topics. While the units emphasize the activation of the layperson's sense of responsibility for his or her own health, their purpose is to inform, not to prescribe. They offer the reader, who may be a prospective patient, a basic understanding of common health problems and of certain medical procedures. It is largely through general health education that individuals can maintain and enhance their physical well-being.

john evans

Contents

**With two exceptions, these Health Education Units
have been written under the direction and supervision of Keith W. Sehnert, M.D.,
Visiting Professor, School of Nursing, Division of Continuing Education,
Georgetown University, Washington, D.C., and Visiting Professor,
School of Applied Sciences, Case Western Reserve University, Cleveland, Ohio.**

The authors of the Health Education Units are as follows:

George Benton, M.D., St. Marys Family Practice Clinic, University of Wisconsin, Madison. Unit 4.

Joan A. Piemme, M.N.Ed., Adjunct Assistant Professor, School of Nursing, and Project Coordinator, Oncology Nursing Program, Georgetown University. Unit 16.

John H. Renner, M.D., Chairman and Professor, Department of Family Medicine and Practice, School of Medicine, Center for Health Sciences, University of Wisconsin, Madison. Unit 3 (in part).

Keith W. Sehnert, M.D., Visiting Professor, School of Nursing, Division of Continuing Education, Georgetown University, Washington, D.C., and Visiting Professor, School of Applied Sciences, Case Western Reserve University, Cleveland, Ohio. Units 1, 2, 5, 6, 7, 8, 9, 10, 11, 13, 14, 15, 18.

Claire T. Welling, R.N., Program Developer, Health Activation Network, Arlington, Va., and Health Educator, Pennsburg Schools, Fallsington, Pennsylvania. Unit 17.

Herb Young, M.A., Medical Communications Specialist, Department of Family Medicine and Practice, University of Wisconsin, Madison. Unit 3 (in Part).

Title cartoons by John Everds
Illustrations by John L. Draves

Health Education Unit 1
Health Activation and Self-care

Health activation involves enhancing people's knowledge about their bodies, their dealings with health professionals, and their understanding of the effect of environment and life-style on their health. Properly understood and practiced, health activation makes ordinary people more self-reliant and less dependent on doctors and other health care professionals for solutions to common problems. This activation provides people with new options for medical care and saves them worry, money, time, and inconvenience.

The health activation movement

Health activation is part of a self-care, self-help movement that is becoming increasingly common in the United States, Canada, and Europe. It is based on a comprehensive health education program that emphasizes staying well and that incorporates do-it-yourself techniques which are increasingly necessary for cultural, social, medical, and economic reasons.

Many observers say that health activation is a new phenomenon. Others say that medical self-care and self-help have always been practiced. Daniel K. Weiss of the University of Kentucky Medical School describes self-care as part of a dual system of health care. He has traced the system beyond ancient Greece to prehistoric times and defines it as a double track of care, offered on one level by a professional—the doctor or medicine man—and on another level by ordinary people using home remedies and folk medicine.

In nonindustrialized societies, the shaman or medicine man treats people for a fee with his incantations and secret remedies. The less affluent, when they accidentally spear themselves while hunting or are stricken with illness, have to fend for themselves or seek help from a knowledgeable older member of their tribe. This was the extent of health care in prehistoric times.

By 300 B.C., Hippocrates had helped create in ancient Greece a professional called a "physician." This new kind of medicine man used observation and logic to diagnose and treat illness and developed a training system for those who wanted to enter the healing profession. Neophyte physicians took the *Hippocratic Oath* and pledged certain ethical behavior when they began their practice. Ac-

cording to John Scarborough of the University of Kentucky, an expert on medicine in ancient Greece, the Greek physicians soon became an elite, usually the best educated people in a city. Some mixed politics with medicine as mayors of Athens, Sparta, and other city-states. Physicians' fees were high, and many people could not afford their services.

The Greeks, however, were humane and practical and it became customary for any citizen who could not afford to go to a physician to go instead to the agora, the market square. There the ailing and injured made their problems known to their fellow citizens. Self-care or self-help advice was offered and gratefully accepted. Helping those who were ailing became tradition and then part of the law. The Greek law said that if it was known that any citizen with knowledge and experience had failed to give help, the citizen could be sued for his property. With a law like that on the books, the Greeks had strong motivation to learn and practice self-care and self-help skills. It was a far cry from the dilemma facing today's Good Samaritans, who all too often avoid some situations because they fear being sued when trying to help. The dual system of health care persisted throughout the Dark and Middle Ages through such practitioners as "medical police" (precursors of today's army medics), folk healers, bone setters, and apothecaries (forerunners of today's pharmacists).

After colonial America was settled, merchants and farmers who wanted their sons to become physicians sent them abroad for training at Aberdeen or Edinburgh, Scotland, or to London. Training was expensive, and the fees the doctors charged on return to the colonies were high. Most common people, therefore, went to apothecaries for care and advice. Early American leaders such as Cotton Mather, Benjamin Franklin, and Thomas Jefferson took some training as apothecaries. A popular book was John Tennent's *Every Man His Own Doctor; or The Poor Planter's Physician.* Jefferson thought the things he learned about home care for ills and injuries so important that, as rector of the University of Virginia, he instituted a self-care and self-help course for beginning students.

In more recent times in the U.S. during the Depression, most people treated themselves and their families because they either could not afford or could not get to professional help. Older, more experienced members of the family provided counsel and help for the ill and injured with help from an always available "doctor book."

Mid 20th-century changes

At the end of World War II several factors changed the practice of medicine: higher spendable incomes, increased availability of health insurance, better communications, all-weather roads, more cars, easier access to doctors and hospitals, and other social, cultural, and economic changes. People gradually became increasingly dependent on the professional for health care. People began to believe that the doctor, with new medicines and tools, could "solve" all health problems. Patients' dependence on doctors was supported by the experience and training of doctors themselves. Military medicine during World War II, the Korean War, and later in Vietnam favored authoritarian methods: "Take your medicine . . . no questions asked and no answer expected."

America's health care system thrived. The 1950s ushered in a golden age of pharmaceuticals: immunizations to control measles, mumps, and polio; tranquilizers for mental illnesses; and the Pill for family planning. The 1960s brought space-age spin-offs and the marriage of medicine and engineering. Such developments made possible coronary care units, various types of monitoring, and the technology needed for the miracles of transplant surgery. The 1960s also saw decreasing availability of primary care—the kind of medical care provided by family doctors, pediatricians, general internists, and obstetricians and gynecologists. As older doctors died or retired, only a handful of new M.D.s stepped forth to replace them. After years of neglect, alarms were sounded for primary care.

The 1970s have seen, fortunately, a renewed interest in and emphasis on primary care. New kinds of primary care professionals—physicians' assistants, nurse practitioners, paramedics, and others—are being trained. New ways to pay for and deliver primary care such as health maintenance organizations and prepaid health insurance have been developed.

Meanwhile, something has happened to the nature of diseases treated by health professionals. In the 1950s, the killers and maimers were nature's pathogens: polio, measles, tuberculosis, meningitis, pneumonia, and other infectious diseases. In the 1970s, the primary enemy has become man-made pathogens: cigarettes, alcohol, automobiles, guns, air pollution, and other cultural and environmental factors.

The diseases of the 1950s could be controlled or vanquished by washing the hands, covering the nose and mouth, keeping things clean, receiving immunizations, taking antibiotics, and following established medical and hygienic programs. The diseases of the 1970s are, unfortunately, not as easily controlled. New types of "hygiene" are needed. People are taught by advertising to use man-made pathogens. For example, people do not inherently want or need to smoke but are "educated" to smoke—at great expense. An example of the expense is a brand of cigarettes introduced in 1977 at an initial promotional cost of $40 million. It will cost the manufacturer that much or more each year to maintain the cigarette's place in the market—all paid for by new generations of Americans taught to enjoy smoking. Similarly, people are educated to drive fast, drink alcohol, take sleeping pills, and eat rich foods—all at great cost to the consumers and to society.

Most of today's illnesses, injuries, and deaths are directly or indirectly related to life-styles. The affluence that produced better transportation and communication also produced high-cholesterol and low-fiber diets, decreased physical activity, increased air pollution, and anxiety that is assuaged with tranquilizers and alcohol. The companion changes were greatly increased hospital and medical costs, more specialists but fewer primary care professionals, an increased number of malpractice suits, more potent medicines, and increased reliance by professionals on costly high-technology equipment for diagnosis and treatment.

The result of such changes is a movement away from what professionals can do and toward what individuals can do. The self-care and self-help movement has become a force to be reckoned with, fostered by a combination of cultural, social, medical, and economic events.

Self-care and self-help

What are some of the elements, concerns, and perceptions about self-care and medical self-help? In the early 1950s many medical students were taught that every doctor-patient visit should have three distinct and equal parts: diagnosis, treatment, and education. With the understanding that such activities are equally important, every dollar spent for health care should be split equally three ways. A recent economic analysis shows, however, that less than four cents of each health dollar is spent for education and disease prevention. To put things in balance there must be substantial increases in money for education and prevention.

The overloaded primary care system could benefit from such increases. On any given day, 80% of the total demand for health care in America is for primary care. Studies show that each person requires, on an average, four such visits per year throughout life. In most communities, however, studies show that less than 50% of all health professionals are available to deliver primary care. There is a gap between supply and demand of at least 30%. In rural and inner-city areas, the gap is much greater.

There is no such overload on secondary and tertiary care. The demand for secondary level care, delivered in community and general hospitals for conditions requiring operations or more intensive medical treatment, is about 15% of the total. People need such care on an average of only once every ten years. Tertiary care is provided by university or other major medical centers where unusual, complex, or life-threatening conditions are treated. Such care is needed only once in 70 years, on the average.

Studies of the use of primary care have shown that from 30 to 40% of the visits made are either unnecessary or are inappropriate. Educational efforts could be made to help decrease such visits. People could be taught how to better use these services, decreasing some of the overload.

When people are ill or injured, there are three general resources available: professional, community, or individual. During the last three decades people have been told, "When you get sick, go to the doctor." If that is not possible, the community offers help through mental health clinics, emergency rooms, immunization services, VD clinics, various counseling and outpatient services, projects for air or water pollution control, public health offices, and other facilities and programs.

People seldom think of themselves or other non-professionals as proper resources for help. Actually, people are capable of handling perhaps a third of their common ills, injuries, and emergencies themselves. Patients can become their own paramedics. It may come as a surprise to some, but many people are aware of this possibility and are actively learning new skills. Around the United States, rapidly increasing numbers of people are signing up for classes on medical self-help and health promotion and for do-it-yourself classes on health, health care, and physical fitness.

Course for Activated Patients

One such program is the Course for Activated Patients (CAP) started in Herndon, Va., in 1970. It was established to provide people with skills that enable them to take a more active role in their own health care and that of their families. CAP has four objectives. People taking such classes learn to (1) accept more individual responsibility for their own care and that of their families; (2) develop skills of observing, describing, and handling common illnesses, injuries, and emergencies; (3) increase their basic knowledge of common health problems; and (4) use health care resources and services, insurance, and medications more economically and appropriately.

The topics covered include the following: "Your Medicine Chest: Friend or Foe?"; "Responsibility for Your Own Care"; "Listening to Your Body"; "Talking with Your Doctor: Better Communication Pays Off"; "The Dangers of Eating American Style"; "Yoga and You"; "Coping Skills"; "Tooth Tips and Dental Health"; "Self-Help Skills"; and others chosen by the participants and based on their needs.

The sessions offered in CAP are not health education lectures intended to stand alone. They are woven together in a complementary manner to encourage health promotion activities and teach self-care and self-help methods. They emphasize the benefits of staying well: more energy, greater independence, and increased fitness. The teachers use a strategy called "whole person learning," which includes demonstrations, experiments, and emotional involvement by the participants. They are helped to function actively for themselves and their families in preventing illness and in detecting and treating common illnesses, injuries, and emergencies. Participants learn to supplement professional care and, if necessary, to substitute self-care. Participants learn to look at health not as an absence of disease but as a way to achieve the energy needed to set and meet life's goals. Health thus becomes a necessary resource to achieve what is wanted in life.

Health activation and self-care

One resource for CAP participants is a spin-off of computer technology: a step-by-step health decision maker called the clinical algorithm. This new resource is based on research done at Harvard, Duke, Dartmouth, and Georgetown that was developed for training allied health professionals. The procedure was further refined by U.S. Army researchers who used computer calculations to determine whether a case was so urgent that it had to be seen immediately or could wait until the next day, and whether a patient should be seen by a doctor or could be seen by an army medic. From using algorithms to train medics about an illness to training lay people about the same illness was an obvious step. Self-help medical guides have been developed that people from many educational backgrounds have successfully learned to use. Another resource for those taking CAP has been professional medical equipment, which helps them to become better observers of common problems. The "black bag" used in CAP contains a blood pressure cuff, stethoscope, high-intensity penlight, thermometer, and an instrument for examining the ear (otoscope). Such equipment helps people become "medical reporters," able to tell more about the details of common health problems.

CAP emphasizes the role life-style plays in illness. The health hazards associated with stress, smoking, alcohol, fatty and sugary foods, high blood pressure, sedentary work, and other factors are explored. Participants learn the "Seven Golden Rules of Health" formulated by Lester Breslow at the University of California at Los Angeles. Several studies have found that the rules are commonly followed by active, healthy older people. The rules include: (1) sleeping seven to eight hours per day; (2) eating breakfast every day; (3) avoiding snacks between meals; (4) staying slender (slightly below normal weight); (5) being active in planned exercise, sports, walking, or vigorous work; (6) using alcohol only moderately; (7) avoiding smoking.

The research into the usefulness of the rules has shown that people who practice all seven generally have better health than those who practice only a few. Another interesting finding has been that active old people who follow all or most of the rules have greater life expectancies than people ten or even 15 years younger who practice only some.

The impact of CAP on the knowledge, attitudes, and behavior of individuals has been evaluated in careful studies. The results help mollify some of the critics who say past health education efforts have been disappointing, and have done little to change negative health behavior.

A controlled CAP study on Medicaid and Medicare recipients done by researchers at Georgetown University and supported by the U.S. Department of Health, Education, and Welfare showed distinct differences between those who had taken CAP and similar persons (matched for age, sex, education, and other factors) who had not. The results of the study, done in metropolitan Washington, D.C., showed that CAP people used professional services more appropriately; practiced more self-care activities; were more willing to use allied health professionals, not insisting on care by a physician; had greater knowledge about proper diet and health affairs and put this knowledge into action; successfully learned and applied clinical skills; and had greater confidence about using self-care methods for themselves and their families. The study produced surprising findings for critics who predicted that CAP would more likely produce "agitated" than "activated" patients. People who had taken the course actually were more satisfied with their professional care than were the control group.

The economic findings of the study were less clear. Efforts to determine drug, laboratory, and X-ray costs and the number of primary care visits showed somewhat lower costs with the CAP group on Medicaid. Another CAP group on Medicare, however, had higher costs. The reason for the discrepancy is not clear. The follow-up time was short —only six months—and seasonal variations affected the results. The Medicare follow-up was done in the winter and early spring when illness and injury are naturally more frequent.

The educational experience offered by CAP has been so encouraging that many health professionals are adopting it for their communities. Versions of CAP are now offered in 37 states and in some provinces in Canada. An organization called the Health Activation Network has been established to help interested people start and evaluate programs. The motto of the network is "Towards a Health Partnership: Individual and Professional Working Together." Information about a quarterly newspaper and educational materials and services can be obtained by writing to the headquarters at Box 7268, Arlington, Va. 22207.

As noted earlier in this article, Thomas Jefferson was interested in health affairs. Inside the Jefferson Memorial in Washington, D.C., is one of his best-known quotations: "The secret strength of America will be its informed citizenry." Some historians say the quote was meant in a political sense. Perhaps Jefferson could also have meant it in a medical sense as well; an informed citizenry is really what self-care, medical self-help, and health activation are all about.

—Keith W. Sehnert, M.D.

Talking with the Doctor

As the patient walked out of his doctor's examining room with the prescription in his hand, his wife asked, "What did the doctor say was wrong?"

He shrugged his shoulders and replied in a perplexed voice, "He didn't say."

She looked surprised. "What do you mean, 'he didn't say'? Did you ask him? Did he give you any instructions?"

He could see the anger in his wife's face. "Well, the doctor seemed to be in a big hurry and I didn't want to bother him. I'll call him back and ask after I've taken these pills for a couple of days."

His wife had the last word. "I'm mad at the doctor and disgusted with you. For $22, the least the doctor could do is tell you what's wrong and what you're to do other than just go to the drugstore."

Such a situation is not unusual. It represents an all too common experience in today's overloaded primary health care system, with the resultant failure in everyday communication. It is not just the disgruntled patient who suffers from such poor communication. The doctor also suffers.

In this case, poor communication will mean at least one extra telephone call for the doctor and a trip to the medical records file by his office aides when the patient inquires, "Doc, what did you say was wrong with me?" A single question is no big deal, but one question will require five or ten minutes that can have an impact on the doctor's already busy schedule. With better communication, the problem could have been handled in much less time and to the better satisfaction of all concerned.

At worst, the patient could take the new pills, not knowing that they would react with explosive fury with another prescription he takes regularly but forgot to tell the doctor about. The combination could produce a severe adverse drug reaction that could, in turn, put the patient in the hospital. His already angry wife might well seek legal counsel. The scene is set for an expensive malpractice suit. Such an incident is by no means farfetched or out of touch with reality.

Noncompliance

Usually, however, the results are somewhat less extreme. Most often we find another problem, "noncompliance," resulting from faulty communication between doctor and patient. Noncompli-

ance is a doctor's way of saying that "patients do not follow orders."

One of the great mysteries of medical practice is the large number of patients who take the trouble to see a physician but then apparently ignore his advice. The result is half-empty containers of prescriptions gathering dust in the medicine chest, diabetics sneaking sweets, convalescing patients overexerting themselves, students returning to school before they are well and suffering recurrences of their illnesses, and patients failing to make follow-up visits. All are common examples of patients seeming to flout their doctors' orders.

One expert on such problems, Milton S. Davis of the University of California School of Medicine, has reported that 35% of all patients generally fail to follow their doctors' advice. Another study by the American Academy of Family Physicians showed similar findings. Family doctors were asked, "What is the single most annoying thing patients do?" Their answer—reported by 33%—was failure to follow instructions on matters such as diet, medication, and bed rest.

How do we explain such noncompliance? Are one-third of all people who seek medical advice contrary, perverse, or just plain ignorant? The avail-

335

able evidence does not bear out such a conclusion. Noncompliance usually indicates something far different. When I first conducted a program called a Course for Activated Patients (CAP), we had one session entitled "Why Patients Don't Follow Orders." What soon became painfully evident was that we had the wrong title. The session should have been called "Why Doctors Don't Give Clear Orders." Later we called this session "Talking With Your Doctor: Better Communication Pays Off."

In most situations, noncompliance is due to poor communication. The patient does not ask for explanations and the doctor does not give any. The result is that patients do not realize why certain actions are important for health or how a treatment program in addition to medicine pays off. Many people assume that all that is needed for treatment is a magic pill. Actually, diet, bed rest, a plan to stop smoking, or other treatment is of equal or even greater importance than a prescription.

The consequences of this failure to understand the reason behind the advice are unfounded fears, confusion, wasted dollars for medicines, unnecessary absenteeism from work, time-consuming telephone calls to the doctor's office, inappropriate or misused follow-up visits, expensive visits to emergency rooms or hospitals for matters that could be well-handled at home, and last, but not least, that bogeyman, malpractice suits.

Communication in hospitals

Failure in communication occurs most often on the first level of medical care (primary care), that which is usually given by family doctors, general internists, pediatricians, general practitioners, and obstetrician-gynecologists in private offices and clinics. Primary care visits occur on an average of four times per year per person. In a family of five there may be 20 primary care visits in one year!

More complex or serious illnesses that require care in a general or community hospital (secondary care) occur less frequently, on an average of once every ten years per person. If an illness is even more rare and difficult to treat, it may require care in a medical center, usually part of a university medical school (tertiary care). The odds are that such an illness will occur only once every 70 years or once in a lifetime.

How should a hospitalized patient talk to the doctor? What kind of information does such a patient need? Consider, for example, a patient being released from the coronary care unit (CCU) of a community hospital. He had entered the CCU from the emergency room with chest pain a few days before because of a suspected myocardial infarction. The patient's doctor said, "We've been keeping you here a few days as a precaution, and we're going to send you down to the medical ward for a couple of tests and some instructions. You can plan to go home soon." Both the patient and his family were relieved at the news. "You've got some 'rust' accumulating in your arteries, but everything looks all right for now," the doctor said as he wrote the discharge orders and scribbled a prescription.

The patient looked at the mysterious scribbles on the prescription slip and inquired, "Is there anything else?"

The doctor said, "No, don't worry about anything else. We'll go over that when I see you in two weeks. Call my office for an appointment about the middle of the month."

As his physician strode out of the room, the patient had a score of questions running through his mind. Looking somewhat abashed, he turned to the head nurse. "What does my doctor like his patients to do about diet, exercise, and so on?"

The nurse gave no clues whatsoever. "You'll have to ask the doctor."

The patient was alone with his unanswered questions:

"What is the purpose of the medication?"

"Do I follow a diet?"

"Is there some exercise I should do, or shall I rest?"

"Am I supposed to stop smoking?"

"What does the doctor mean by 'rust'?"

"Is there a book I should read?"

"Why couldn't I think of some decent questions to ask?"

"Am I to look out for some symptoms?"

"If he said 'don't worry' there must not have been much wrong; but if that's so, why have I been in the $400-a-day coronary care unit?"

A hospital scene that had begun on an upbeat note had ended on an unnecessarily sour note. A conversation that could have led to a perfect "teachable moment" led instead to confusion and disappointment for the patient. What went wrong? What should have happened to make the hospital discharge a valuable learning situation?

There were, first of all, two put-downs. The doctor said, in effect, "Don't worry about it," and the nurse said, "Ask the doctor." Such answers belittled the role of the patient and cast him in a passive, dependent role that did little to enhance a "health partnership" between the patient and medical professional.

There was also a meaningless reassurance by the doctor when he told the patient, "There's nothing wrong." Such a response portrayed a certain lack of sensitivity about the anxiety and worry experienced by the patient and his family. Perhaps an honest "I don't know, but we'll keep looking" would have been better.

The Activated Patient's
Ask-the-Doctor Checklist

Before the visit (complete this part yourself)

1. Why am I going to the doctor?
*(the main reason)*_____
_____
_____

2. Is there some other reason or anything else that worries me about my health?
☐ no   ☐ yes (please list)_____
_____
_____
_____

3. What do I expect the doctor to do today?
_____
_____
_____

4. Do I need my Medicare, Medicaid, Blue Cross or other insurance cards or forms today?
☐ no   ☐ yes

5. The symptoms that bother me *most* (describe them—as a "medical reporter" asking: when? where? what? why?)._____
_____
_____
_____
_____

6. What medicines or "pills" am I taking regularly now? (please list)_____
_____
_____

During the visit (complete with help of doctor)

1. What is wrong with me?_____
_____
_____

2. When will I recover?_____
3. Why did I get it and how can I prevent it next time?
_____
_____

4. Is it catching or will it spread?
☐ no   ☐ yes (describe protective measures)

5. Are there any lab reports or diagnostic findings I should know about?
☐ no   ☐ yes (list)_____

6. Is there any medicine?
☐ no   ☐ yes (list)_____
_____

(If yes, is it available in a less expensive "generic" form?)_____

7. Are there special instructions, concerns, or side effects I should understand about the medicine?
☐ no   ☐ yes (describe)_____
_____
_____
_____
_____

After the visit (complete with help of doctor or office aide)

1. Am I to return for another visit?
☐ no   ☐ yes (when)_____

2. What should I do at home?

a) diet_____
b) activity_____
c) treatments_____
d) precautions_____

3. Am I to phone in for lab reports?
☐ no   ☐ yes (when)_____

4. Should I report back to the doctor for any reason?
☐ no   ☐ yes (reason)_____
_____

There must have been symptoms suggestive of coronary artery disease, which is commonly acknowledged to be caused by "life-style" (what we eat, how we exercise, the amount of stress we experience and how we handle it, and so forth). Most people know that cardiovascular disease requires more than pills for treatment. An educational plan for the patient and family under such circumstances is absolutely necessary. How the family can work together to reduce fats, sweets, and salt in the diet; manage stress; plan specific exercise; get information about the heart and its function and about the purpose of medication and its possible benefits and side effects is vital in a successful course of treatment.

Even though hospitalization is less common than treatment in an office or clinic, secondary care usually does involve more serious illnesses. It is, therefore, very important that there be adequate communication between the doctor and the hospitalized patient. Many doctors—and other hospital personnel—undoubtedly do not voluntarily give the patient sufficient information. The patient should insist on his need to know about his illness and about specific actions he can take to regain and maintain his health.

A checklist

If poor communication creates such a variety of problems, it should be tackled head on. One solution is "The Activated Patient's Ask-The-Doctor Checklist." I use this list in all CAP courses. It has been extensively tested by thousands of people and found to be a useful tool that enhances doctor-patient and patient-doctor communication. Perhaps it will be useful to you.

In CAP we talk about the health partnership. Our sessions emphasize the need for patients and medical professionals to establish a partnership for better health care. Both parties benefit when patients supply the doctor with as much information as possible. At the same time, patients must receive —and understand—instructions, medicines, and information provided by the doctor. When this exchange is coupled with various other skills, a patient sets the stage for a true health partnership with the doctor.

How will you benefit from the checklist? It will help you organize your thoughts and be more confident in visits with your doctor. An example of this was related to me by a patient who had used the list when she went to see her new family doctor. She told me that as she completed the list, she realized

that, in addition to her own illness, she also wanted to talk to the doctor about her husband's excessive drinking. The list also reminded her to give the doctor some other information he probably needed— including the fact that she had had a reaction when given penicillin.

Will such a checklist help your doctor? In my own experience, when a patient has used the list, I have found that it also served as a convenient checklist for myself. By covering all the essential points, the list has saved me unnecessary phone calls from patients. It has also reminded me when it was necessary to give a patient an educational brochure or a diet sheet, or to schedule a follow-up visit.

The checklist can also help a doctor improve his public relations. He will find that his office procedure becomes more orderly (and record-keeping easier) and that he may be able to shorten office visits and patients' waiting time. Occasionally the list will enable him to please patients by reminding him that he can prescribe less expensive generic drugs rather than brand-name medications.

Of course, some doctors may not see the benefits as I do. What do you do if your doctor says, "I'm too busy to complete a list like that" or "Don't worry about all that; just call me if you have any questions"?

I would counter these or similar objections by pointing out the advantages of the list to the doctor. Here are some possible answers:

1. "Your time is limited, doctor, and the list would help me use it more efficiently. All in all, I think it would cut down on the length of my visits."

2. "You know we have only one car, so when I get sick my husband has to take the day off to bring me to your office and the family loses one day of income, which means it will take us longer to pay the doctor's bill."

3. "I've got several other kids at home, and if this illness is contagious or likely to spread, the checklist can give me some tips on what to look for and I won't have to drag them in unnecessarily. I don't want to bother you when I don't have to."

I predict, however, that objections to the list will be few. The doctors I have worked with find that it offers benefits for both doctor and patient, increasing the chances of successful health partnership. So look over the list, copy it, and use it for your next doctor's visit. I am sure you will find that it is a truly healthy development.

—*Keith W. Sehnert, M.D.*

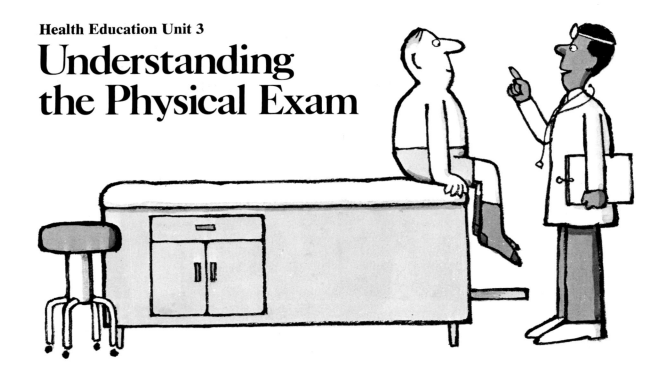

Health Education Unit 3
Understanding the Physical Exam

There is no standard physical examination. Exams vary with such factors as the doctor's training and special interests, the design of his office, the equipment he has available, his familiarity with the patient, the amount of time available, the patient's family history, age, sex, and general state of health.

Exams also vary according to what the physician may find in the course of the exam. If a routine neurological screening test for gait and posture, which involves watching the patient walk, shows a problem, then the physician will branch out to do additional testing.

Nevertheless, there are enough similarities that one can describe a rather thorough routine physical exam, the sort that the average patient might receive during an initial visit to a physician. The order in which procedures are done may vary, and your physician may delete some of these tests and observations or include others not described here, including laboratory tests and X-rays.

In many doctors' offices, the first step in the exam is to record the patient's weight and height. When compared with certain normal ratios for height to weight, these data give the physician information on obesity, malnourishment, and development. Among children, for example, abnormal height may indicate hormonal problems.

Vital signs

A likely second step in the exam is measurement of "vital signs": pulse rate, respiratory rate (number of times one breathes per minute), blood pressure, and, if necessary, temperature.

Whoever takes your pulse, be it the physician or a nurse, checks not only the rate per minute but also the volume (or strength), rhythm, and contour. Most adults have a pulse rate of from 68 to 72 beats per minute while at rest. Athletes at rest may have rates of from 50 to 60; infants may have rates of about 100. The pulse varies with exertion, emotional state, and temperature. For every degree of increase above normal body temperature, the pulse rises about ten beats per minute.

Pulse contour is checked at the same time as pulse rate. A normal pulse is not simply an on/off beat. Rather, it consists of a swift increase in pressure followed by a gradual decline. Sometimes, however, the pulse pressure rises and falls very sharply. When exaggerated, this "bounding" or "collapsing" pulse is suggestive of such diseases as essential hypertension or aortic regurgitation—a condition in which blood flows back into the heart through a faulty valve from the aorta, the large artery leading from the heart to the body. The pulse may also have a gradual upstroke and a prolonged downstroke, which may indicate a narrowing of the aorta.

Measurement of the respiratory rate is usually done surreptitiously, since your breath rate tends to change if you know you are being observed. The average adult breathes 16 to 20 times per minute. Children breathe faster.

Understanding the physical exam

A patient who feels ill will certainly have his temperature taken. A fever usually means that the body is fighting an infection, although you can have an elevated temperature from wearing too many clothes or from exertion. "Normal" body temperature is 98.6° F (37.0° C) but can actually vary slightly in a healthy person.

Blood pressure

The blood pressure is usually taken in the right arm. It is a measure of the pressure the blood exerts on the arteries. It is the heart, of course, that initiates this pressure, but the pressure also is influenced by the elasticity of the arteries, the resistance to the blood flow in the smaller vessels, the volume of blood in the system, and its viscosity. The pressure ranges between two points: the systolic, or highest, pressure and the diastolic, or lowest, pressure. The first represents the pressure as the heart pumps and the second when the heart is at rest, between beats.

When your blood pressure is being taken, you should be relaxed and breathing normally. First, an inflatable cuff is placed around your arm above the elbow. The doctor or nurse feels for a pulse in the crook of the elbow, then pumps the cuff full of air, causing it to squeeze the arm. Eventually, the cuff shuts off the blood flow in the artery, at which point the pulse disappears. While watching a pressure gauge connected to the cuff, the person taking the measurement slowly releases the pressure until the pulse can be felt (or heard) again. At this point, the pressure the cuff exerts against the arm—as measured on the pressure gauge—is exactly equal to the pressure of the blood against the arterial wall as the heart pumps. This is the systolic pressure.

As the pressure in the cuff continues to drop, more blood is able to squirt through the artery with each beat of the heart, giving rise to turbulent sounds. Finally this rushing turns to a tapping sound, which disappears as the cuff pressure falls. At the last audible tap, the pressure gauge indicates the blood pressure between heartbeats—the diastolic pressure. Blood pressure is listed with the systolic over the diastolic, such as 120/80.

Blood pressure readings can give a physician important information about the state of your heart, vascular system, kidneys, and emotions. A raised systolic pressure in the presence of a normal diastolic pressure may indicate hardening of the arteries or a malfunctioning valve between the heart and aorta. Elevation of both systolic and diastolic pressures may indicate a hyperactive adrenal gland, kidney disease, or essential hypertension. ("Essential" in this case means of unknown cause.) Among the factors that temporarily raise the blood pressure are caffeine, smoking, and exercise.

Overall assessment of health

A physical exam starts the moment the physician sees you. Immediately, the doctor starts assessing your state of health, looking for signs of distress, difficulty in breathing, coughing, or signs of pain through facial expressions or through favoring any particular portion of the body. He notes if you appear anxious or fearful.

The physician watches you move, noting any motor problems. He pays attention to gait and posture, looking for nerve damage or joint problems. He observes dress and grooming—looking not for the latest styles, but for signs of neglect that may foreshadow a mental problem. He is sensitive to unusual odors, such as the acetone smell of the breath of someone with diabetes or the smell of an infection of the mouth or respiratory system. The doctor will listen to your voice and speech—is the voice hoarse or raspy? The physician makes many of these observations without conscious effort. After years of training, he assesses your overall health automatically, catching what is out of kilter quickly and passing over the normal without a second thought. He is able to keep up a casual conversation while he listens and observes.

At this point, a history is taken, if that hasn't been done already. During the history-taking, the physician will ask more detailed or branching questions about what has been said earlier. If you have complained of any ailments, the physician will ask additional questions about the severity of the problem, the time of onset, the nature of the symptoms, and what factors seem to influence it.

The physician also starts making mental notes as to what he will focus on during the course of the exam. Did the patient say that there was a history of glaucoma in the family? The doctor will be sure to check the internal pressure of the eye, and so forth.

The eyes

When the questions are done, the doctor proceeds with the physical examination. While there is no set place to begin, many physicians start with the eyes. The physician is interested both in how well they function as sense organs and in what ocular changes are occurring that may indicate problems elsewhere in the body.

Often the first test is to have you read an eye chart, which usually is located 20 feet away. This distance is the numerator of the fraction used to express visual acuity. The denominator designates the smallest line of figures that can be read. A line is considered read successfully if half the letters are identified correctly. If one has a visual acuity of 20/40, it means that at 20 feet one can read a line of figures marked 40. This number, in turn, comes from the fact that the same line could be read by a person with "normal" eyesight at a distance of 40 feet. Each eye is tested separately. Some physicians have special charts for children that use stars, flags, circles, and other symbols instead of letters. There also are desk-mounted viewers that are used instead of charts.

After testing your vision, the physician observes the eyes to see if they are in proper alignment. Then the doctor will probably examine the lids, sclera (whites), and conjunctiva (covering of the eye), looking for, among other things, the yellow sclerae of jaundice or the redness of acute conjunctivitis. He then will look, using a light aimed at the side of your eye, at the cornea and lens for any cloudiness or obstructions. He will also look at the pupils to see if they are of normal size and equal.

Darkening the room, the physician will next check pupillary reactions. He will have you look at a spot across the room while shining a bright light first in one eye and then the other. As the light falls on the eye, he looks for two things: for constriction of the pupil in the eye being illuminated (the direct pupillary reaction) and the constriction of the pupil in the other eye (the consensual light reflex). By checking both eyes in the same manner, the physician is able to assess the integrity of the motor and sensory nerves of the eye.

Next, the physician tests the eyes' ability to accommodate—that is, to shift from a distant to a close object and still remain in focus. He will have you look at a place on the far wall and then shift your gaze to some other object that is straight ahead but close to your eyes. The doctor will look for the eyes to converge as the focus changes from the distant to the close object. He will also look for the pupils to constrict. This again gives the physician information about the state of the nerves controlling the eyes.

The physician then will ask you to follow his finger or other object as he tests the eyes' extraocular movements, moving the object to the side, upwards, and downwards. This allows him to test the condition of six eye muscles and three of the twelve cranial nerves. As the physician directs your eyes through these movements, he will look for a rapid oscillation of the eyes, called nystagmus. As the eye moves from an upward to a downward glance, the physician looks for lid lag—a failure of the lid to overlap the iris as the eye moves downward. This occurs in some types of hyperthyroidism. Having tested the movement and function of the eye, the physician next looks into the eye, using an instrument called an ophthalmoscope—an illuminating, adjustable magnifying device. Before looking into the eye, he may drop some liquid medication into the eyes to dilate the pupils. The physician shines the ophthalmoscope's light into the eye while re-

maining about 12 inches in front of the eye. He looks for an orange reflection from the eye, much like that from a dog's or cat's eyes. This is called the red reflex. If it is absent, the physician will look for obstructions in the eye, such as cataracts.

Then the physician moves toward the eye until he can look through the clear eyeball to the point at the back of the eye where the optic nerve and blood vessels enter. This area is called the optic disk, a red-orange circular area. By adjusting the ophthalmoscope, he can bring it into focus.

The physician looks for damage to the optic nerve which can result from increased intracranial pressure or from glaucoma. He also examines the tiny arteries and veins for signs of hypertension, which are signalled by changes in their shape and color. He also looks for damage in the retina—red spots, hemorrhages, etc.—that can indicate diabetes or hypertension.

If you have a family history of glaucoma or severe nearsightedness or if you are over about 40 years of age, the physician may measure the intraocular pressure with a tonometer.

The ears

After the eye exam, the physician turns his attention to the ears. He will examine the outside, often pulling on the pinna, or outer ear, and pushing on the tragus—the flap that can be pushed in to cover the canal. These movements will cause pain in external ear infections, but not in middle ear infections. As the physician does this, he looks for any discharges.

The physician next uses an instrument called an otoscope to look into the ear. The otoscope is similar to the ophthalmoscope in that it both magnifies and provides light. It is fitted with a speculum—a funnel, which is just slightly smaller than the ear canal—allowing the physician to direct the light and look into the ear. The physician looks into the ear canal and at the eardrum. He looks for signs of infection and examines the drum to see if it has become retracted due to a blocked eustachian tube or if vessels are visible, which happens in early acute suppurative otitis media (middle ear infection). As the infection progresses, the eardrum bulges outward.

After looking at the ear, the physician tests its function, perhaps by talking softly. If a hearing problem shows up, a "branching test" may be done —that is, the physician, based on what he has found, branches out to make further tests that allow him to determine where in the hearing circuit the problem exists.

First he touches the base of a vibrating tuning fork to your head, on the midline, so that it is equidistant from both ears. If the problem is in the external or middle ear, the sound will seem to come from the ear with the hearing problem. If there is a problem with the inner ear or with the nerve carrying the sound impulse to the brain, the sound will seem to come from the good ear.

Next, as a part of the branching test, the physician will compare hearing through the air with hearing through the bone — that is, conductance of sound through air compared to bone. The base of a vibrating tuning fork is placed against the mastoid bone below the ear. You will hear the tuning fork. When the sound fades away and can no longer be heard through the bone, you tell the physician, who quickly moves the tuning fork off the bone and places it close to the ear. Normally, you will still be able to hear the tuning fork through the air. If you have a problem in the external or middle ear, you will no longer hear the tuning fork after it has been removed from the mastoid. If the problem is in the inner ear or nerve, you will still hear the air-conducted sound.

The nose, mouth, throat, and neck

The physician turns next to the nose and sinuses. He still uses the otoscope, but changes to a shorter, wider speculum. He first looks at the front part of the nose and then tilts your head back a bit so that he can look deeper into the nose. He looks for growths, bleeding, swelling, and at the condition of the mucosa that line the nose. In acute rhinitis the nasal mucosa is red and swollen and gives off at first a watery, then later a sticky, pus-containing discharge. In allergic rhinitis the mucosa is also swollen, but is pale in color. The physician may push upwards just above each eye and at the level of the nostrils on each cheek to check for tenderness in the frontal and maxillary sinuses.

Next the physician examines your mouth. He looks at the buccal mucosa, the inside of the cheeks. He looks at the lips, teeth, gums, roof of the mouth, and tongue, looking for growths, the color, damage, etc. He asks you to stick out your tongue, which he inspects to see if it is symmetrical. Lack of symmetry may mean tumor, infection, or damage to the hypoglossal cranial nerve. Continuing to examine the mouth, he looks further back. He uses a tongue depressor to obtain a better view of the pharynx, the back of the throat. He asks you to say ''ah'' so that he can check the rising of the uvula as a test of the vagus nerve, the tenth cranial nerve.

Having completed the examination of the head, the physician turns to the neck. He uses his fingers to palpate (feel) the lymph nodes in up to nine areas of each side of the neck. You can help the physician in this examination by relaxing as much as possible and by bending your neck slightly forward and toward the side the physician is examining. The physician is looking for enlarged or tender lymph nodes, which could indicate an infection. Nodes that are hard or do not move may indicate a malignancy. Since each group of lymph nodes drains different parts of the head, face, neck, arm, thorax, etc., the physician can gain an idea of where an infection may be occurring by noting which group is enlarged.

The physician then palpates the trachea and thyroid, checking these structures while you swallow. The doctor may do this twice — first from a position in front of you, then from behind. At this time, the physician may also observe the arteries and veins of the neck for distension.

The lungs and heart

Next you will be asked to remove your shirt or to rearrange the examination gown so that the physician can examine your chest. The doctor first checks the back, observing it for its shape, symmetry, and proportions. The slope of the ribs and their movement can indicate lung problems such as emphysema, asthma, and obstructions of the windpipe. He will also observe your breathing rate. A normal breathing rate for an adult is 16 to 20 breaths per minute.

Using his palm, the physician may compare the vibrations at various points on your back while you repeat a word over and over again. In this way the doctor can check the condition of the pleural space and can check for obstructions of the airways of the lungs. This procedure can also be used to determine the position of the diaphragm.

Additional information about a patient's internal organs can be obtained by percussion — tapping on the chest (or any part of the body). The physician places his hand, with fingers spread, over the area he is testing. Using the second finger of the other hand, he strikes the second finger of the hand resting on the body. This sets up a vibration in the chest wall and tissues. He notes the relative volume, pitch, and duration of the vibration as he works down the back comparing several positions on each side. Air-containing space produces a hollower thud than do fluid- or tissue-filled areas.

Using a stethoscope, the physician auscultates (listens to) your chest while you breathe deeply. He listens for different types of breath sounds that vary in pitch, intensity, and relative duration as you inhale and exhale. He also listens for abnormal sounds called rales, rhonchi, and friction rubs, which can indicate moisture in the airways, obstructions of the airways, or inflamed pleural tissue. Although textbooks usually suggest examining the front of the chest while the patient is lying on his or her back, many physicians examine this part of the anatomy while the patient still is seated.

The physician will observe, palpate, percuss, and auscultate the front of the chest as he did the back, while he examines the lungs.

Having completed his examination of the lungs, the physician turns his attention to the heart. He observes, and perhaps palpates, the chest to the left of the sternum for pulsations that can be a sign of an aortic aneurysm—a bulging of the aorta. He also looks for thrills, a purring vibration that can indicate a narrowing of the aorta. He will make similar observations and palpations in several areas of the chest, looking for vibrations and pulsing that can indicate other arterial aneurysms, narrowings, or heart valve defects.

The physician uses his stethoscope to listen to the heart. The closing of the heart valves normally generates what are called the first and second heart sounds. The first of these sounds is caused by the closing of the valves separating the atrium from the ventricle on each side of the heart. These valves, the mitral and tricuspid, close with a "lub" sound as the heart begins to contract. The second heart sound is caused by the closing of the two valves leading from the left and right ventricles to the aorta and pulmonary artery, respectively. These valves create a "dub" sound as they close at the end of contraction.

Each of these valves is heard best in a different part of the chest. This is why the physician moves his stethoscope around to several different locations. While he listens for the normal sounds, he also looks for abnormal ones indicating a variety of functional or structural problems.

In addition to these heart sounds, the physician listens to cardiac rate and rhythm. He also notes the pitch, intensity, and quality of the sounds. All this information helps him determine how well the heart is functioning and can indicate what, if anything, is going wrong. The physician also listens for murmurs, which usually last longer than the heart sounds discussed above. They can indicate that the blood is flowing backward through the valves (regurgitation), through narrowed channels (stenosis), or they can indicate increased flow volume.

At this time the physician may check the pulse in the carotid artery of the neck and note the condition of the jugular veins. Observations of the latter can give information on venous pressure and possible congestive heart failure.

The breasts

If the patient is a woman, the physician will examine her breasts, first inspecting them for abnormalities such as dimpling, flattening, or bulging. This is done both while the patient sits with arms raised, and while she places her hands on her hips. These positions help the physician to see abnormal-

ities that may indicate cancer. With the patient lying on her back, he then palpates the breasts for masses. Women should learn to do a breast self-examination to perform at home between visits. In a very thorough physical examination, the male breasts would also be examined.

The abdomen

The physician next will ask you to lie on your back (the supine position) for an examination of the abdomen. (It is of great help to the physician if you are relaxed.) The physician observes the abdomen looking for signs of hernia, scars, dilated veins, pulsations, and masses. He may then listen to the abdomen using his stethoscope. He listens for the gurgling sounds that the bowels make as food is moved by muscle action (peristalsis) through the intestines. These sounds are markedly increased with diarrhea, as well as in the early stages of pyloric and intestinal obstruction. The absence of the bowel sounds occurs with advanced intestinal obstruction and peritonitis. The physician also listens for sounds, called bruits, caused by turbulent or partially obstructed blood flow in the arteries.

Next the physician percusses and palpates the abdomen. He may begin by percussing several places on the abdomen to obtain a general idea of the distribution of the hollow and dull sounds. Then he percusses the right side in order to determine the size of the liver. He does the same on the left side to check the spleen.

Light palpation is performed next. The physician places the palm of his hand on the abdomen and uses his fingers to press gently as he looks for muscle rigidity that may be an indication of an inflammation. He looks for rebound tenderness — pain that occurs as he removes his fingers suddenly from the abdomen.

Then the physician uses deep palpation to examine for an enlarged liver. To do this, he places his left hand palm up under your back. Encouraging you to relax, he places his right hand on the right side of the upper abdomen. He asks you to take a deep breath as he gently pulls up on the back with his left hand and pushes up and in with his right hand, trying to feel the liver as it moves downward. This examination is facilitated if you breathe deeply, using your diaphragm. An enlarged, non-tender liver may mean cirrhosis while an enlarged, tender one may indicate hepatitis or early congestive cardiac failure.

The spleen is palpated in a similar manner on the

344

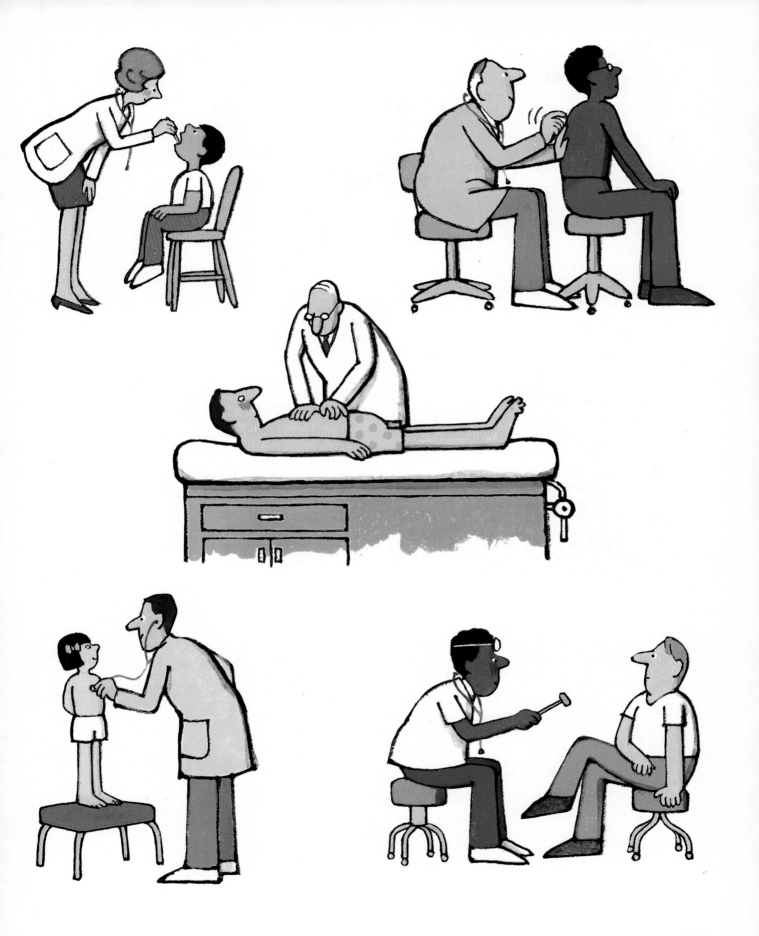

left side, except that the physician uses his left hand to move the lower rib cage rather than to lift the back. The spleen cannot usually be felt unless it has become enlarged as a result of disease. The kidneys are not usually palpable unless enlarged.

Finally, the physician will have a male patient stand as he examines for hernias. He views the lower abdomen for signs of bulges. He then uses his index finger to push upwards through the skin of the scrotum into the inguinal canal. With his finger in place, he has the patient cough or bear down as he feels for any intestine that may be palpable. This is done on both sides. He finishes his examination of the lower abdomen by examining the extreme upper thighs for hernia.

The examination of the female genitalia should be a part of any thorough examination. This type of examination is often done separately as part of a gynecological checkup.

The rectum

The rectum and anus are usually examined while a woman patient is still positioned for a pelvic exam, whereas a male patient normally lies on his side for this exam. (Though he may be on his knees and chest or bent over the examining table.) The physician, wearing a glove, spreads the buttocks to view the anus. He may have you bear down as he examines the anus for abnormalities. Then, as you relax, the physician inserts his lubricated index finger into the anus, checking for tenderness or abnormalities such as growths. Pushing his finger in further, the doctor twists the finger to palpate the prostate gland of the male patient.

After removing his gloved finger, the physician may test any fecal material it carries, using a chemical that can indicate the presence of blood. Individuals over the age of 30 may be given a proctoscopic examination.

The arms, legs, and feet

During the course of the examination, the physician examines the extremities. This may be done before or after the abdominal and rectal exams. Unless there is reason to do more, the inspection of the arms will be limited to watching you move them during the course of the examination, and perhaps to making a brief inspection for rashes, bruises, and so forth.

The legs and feet are usually examined both while you are seated on the exam table and later while you are standing. Among the things the physician looks for are symmetry, skin problems, and vein problems. He probably also will palpate the lymph nodes in the thigh. While examining the feet, the physician looks for edema (swelling caused by fluid leaving the circulatory system and entering the tissue), which can indicate problems with the venous or lymphatic systems. This examination is accomplished by pushing in on the skin and watching how quickly the impression disappears. While you are standing, the physician checks for varicose veins, which result from the stretching of those leg veins lying close to the skin. This stretching can result from failure of the valves in these veins or from obstruction of the deeper veins, which in turn forces more blood than normal through the surface veins.

Also during the examination of the extremities, the physician is likely to test one or more neurological reflexes. The knee reflex is one of the most common tests. The patient sits, relaxed, with his or her legs hanging over the edge of the examination table. The physician taps the patellar tendon with a small rubber hammer, looking for the appropriate muscle contractions. Similar tests may be done at the elbow, wrist, and ankle. If the results of any of these tests suggest the existence of problems, the physician may do additional neurological testing.

At the end of your examination, the physician may order laboratory tests, including blood and urine analyses. Some physicians routinely include electrocardiograms and chest X-rays as a part of their first or periodic examination of a patient.

Finally, the physician may sit down and discuss his findings with the patient. You should take this opportunity to ask any questions that occur about what the physician says. If the doctor prescribes therapies that seem inappropriate, costly, or difficult for you to undertake, you should clarify the issue and work out possible alternate plans with the physician's help.

*—John H. Renner, M.D., and
Herb Young, M.D.*

Blood and Urine Analysis

As an addition to an accurate, thorough medical history and physical examination, laboratory testing is an invaluable aid to the physician who must evaluate a patient's condition, or state of homeostasis (internal equilibrium). Two body fluids, blood and urine, are the most often used in testing because their chemical and cellular composition reflect what is happening in the body at a given time, and because samples of the fluids are relatively easily obtained.

Blood is an excellent source of information about an individual's homeostatic state. The many blood tests that are used provide relatively accurate numerical values for a wide variety of chemicals and cells, thus enabling a comparison of the patient's status with established "normal" tolerances.

Blood

Most people are understandably uncomfortable when they are told they need to have their blood drawn. The very idea of having someone deliberately thrust a needle into one's body seems threatening. However, an understanding of the process involved and of the reasons for doing it can allay much of the anxiety a patient experiences. It is the professional's duty to explain why any test is indicated; the patient has the responsibility to obtain enough information to be satisfied that any test is in fact necessary.

Typically, blood is obtained by one of two methods. In capillary puncture, the skin of a fingertip, earlobe or, in infants, a heel, is cleaned with an antiseptic such as 70% isopropyl alcohol. A sharpened metal strip is then used to make a surgically clean cut in the skin and cause bleeding. The blood so collected is then processed according to the dictates of the procedure. Obviously, the quantity of blood obtained by using this technique is limited because mechanisms involved in clotting blood and healing skin injuries are called into play as soon as the capillary puncture is made.

In the second method for drawing blood, venipuncture, a hole is made in the vein using an extremely sharp hypodermic needle of small caliber or gauge. The usual site for venipuncture is the antecubital fossa—that is, the crook of the elbow—where most people have large, easily felt, and easily seen veins. It is obviously much easier for the phlebotomist, or blood drawer, if the blood vessel is both visible and easily felt; therefore, a constricting band is placed around the upper arm to impede venous return, thus distending the veins without impairing arterial flow. The skin is prepared in the same fashion as for a capillary puncture, with 70% alcohol or some other antiseptic. Sometimes a needle and a syringe are used to collect the blood. More commonly today, a special double-pointed needle and plastic holder are used to transfer the blood from a vein directly into a glass tube with a rubber stopper. The tube has a vacuum that draws the blood into the tube until the negative pressure of the vacuum has been equalized by the volume of the blood filling the container.

There are some precautions regarding the procedures outlined above. Clearly, anyone who knows his or her skin is sensitive to alcohol, iodine, or whatever is being used to cleanse the skin should so inform the technician or whoever is to draw the

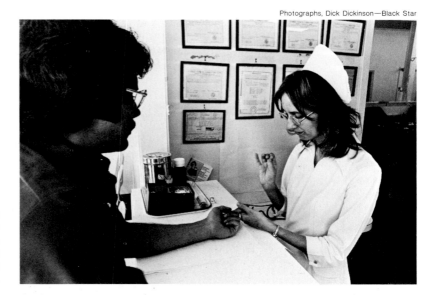

If only a small amount of blood is needed for analysis, the capillary puncture technique is commonly used. With a sharpened metal strip, the blood drawer punctures the skin of the patient's fingertip.

blood. It is also essential to tell the technician of any type of bleeding problem before any attempt to draw blood has been made.

After blood has been drawn, the patient should apply firm pressure over the puncture site in order to stop the bleeding and to prevent a hematoma from developing when the needle is removed from the vein. A hematoma results from the leakage of blood from blood vessels into the surrounding tissues. During phlebotomy, or blood drawing, a hole is made in a blood vessel. If the hole is not closed over with direct pressure, some blood will leak out. Another problem with specimen collection is the anxiety and apprehension that most people have as they think about having blood drawn. It is usually quite simple, quick, and safe to have a specimen of blood drawn. Being overly concerned and anxious about the process in advance undoubtedly aggravates the situation. It is particularly important to allay the fears of children by providing facts and by not implanting false expectations. Their imaginations are quite active enough without half-truths to feed on.

The amount of blood being taken almost always causes concern for the patient. It is frequently difficult to understand why so many tubes of different colors and sizes have to be filled when all the doctor said was, "Have this blood test done." All too often a singular word was used when in reality several tests were ordered. These different tests may require different components of blood.

What are the different components? Whole blood is a mixture of plasma and cells. Plasma is the liquid portion of the blood before coagulation or clotting takes place. Clotted blood can be separated into a liquid portion (called serum) and the "glued together" cells, or blood clot. Serum is plasma

without any of the coagulation factors (at least thirteen are known). The blood clot is the mass of red and white cells trapped in a network of fibrin strands created by the coagulation factor cascade that is set off whenever the body senses a break in blood vessel integrity.

What does all of the above have to do with the "gallon of blood that vampire took from me in the lab"? It all depends on what is to be evaluated. Your doctor may tell you only that he wants a blood count drawn, while he tells the lab that he wants a complete blood count (CBC), a fasting blood sugar test (FBS), and a serum cholesterol test. Blood that is to be used in a CBC for evaluating the quantity and quality of blood cells must be anticoagulated with one of several special chemicals in order to maintain all its elements in suspension and randomly distributed. A blood sample for an FBS also is frequently collected in an anticoagulant tube, but of a different kind and with sodium floride added. This chemical poisons the red blood cells' respiratory system and prevents a lowering of the blood glucose level over time after removal of the blood specimen from the body. The blood sample for the serum cholesterol obviously must be collected in a way that allows the blood to clot, for separation of the serum. All three tests require blood in varied quantities and in different storage containers.

Virtually every organ and tissue—seemingly almost every cell type—can be assessed through one blood test or another. A CBC evaluates the number of circulating white blood cells, red blood cells, and platelets in a given amount of blood at a given time. It also provides information about the relative percentages of the various kinds of white cells. A patient may have heard the terms *hemoglobin* or *hematocrit*. Hemoglobin is the oxygen-carrying

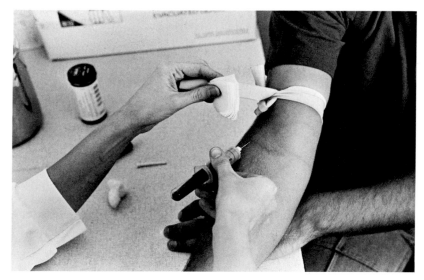

Venipuncture is used when blood is needed for several different tests. Choosing a site where a vein is easily located, usually in the crook of the elbow, the phlebotomist inserts a sharp hypodermic needle directly into the vessel. The rubber band tied around the patient's upper arm causes the veins to become distended, making them easier to see and feel.

chemical in red blood cells that allows oxygen to be taken in through the lungs and eventually to be supplied throughout the body. At the same time, hemoglobin helps eliminate waste gases such as carbon dioxide by binding them as the hemoglobin molecules release oxygen at the cellular level. *Lysis* is the rupturing or disintegration of cells, and *hemolysis* is the rupturing of red blood cells to free *heme,* an iron-rich component of hemoglobin. Hemoglobin is measured by breaking the red cells down and comparing the color provided by a measured amount of blood with a known amount of hemoglobin. The hematocrit is an easier test to understand. It is the ratio of the volume of "packed" red cells compared with a given volume of whole blood. It is obtained by centrifuging a small amount of blood in a small tube. When all the cells have been packed at one end, the percentage volume (height) of red cells is calculated against the total volume (height) of the blood column.

White blood cells are also counted after hemolysis has occurred, usually as a result of the addition of an acid. In most doctors' offices, a white blood cell count would be done by hand, using a hemacytometer—*hema* meaning blood, *cyto* having to do with cells, and *meter* having to do with measurement—and a microscope. In larger clinics and hospital laboratories, most cell counting has become automated as technology is increasingly applied to problems of health care systems.

The fourth common component test within the data supplied by a CBC is a differential white cell count and red blood cell morphology evaluation. In addition, platelets (thrombocytes) are usually assessed at this time for quantity, even if they have been counted on an automated counter. White blood cells can be subdivided into two major categories, and they can be further classified according to staining characteristics and microscopic configuration. The additional classifications are important laboratory descriptive tools, but more important is the differentiation of cells according to function.

The two major divisions of white blood cells are granulocytes (cells with granules) and agranulocytes (cells without granules). Granulocytes are further divided into three groups: (1) neutrophils, which are essential to the body's defense against bacterial infections; (2) eosinophils, whose function is not clearly understood but has to do with the body's response to allergy and parasite infection; and (3) basophils, which are present in very small numbers and whose function is not clearly understood. Agranulocytes are divided into two groups: (1) lymphocytes, which are essential in the body's immune defenses; (2) monocytes, which are involved in fighting infections and cleaning up healing areas of inflammation.

Microscopic red blood cell morphology (size and shape) is an important element in the evaluation of anemia, as are the hematocrit and hemoglobin values. Under the microscope, iron deficiency anemia looks quite different from pernicious anemia or from folate deficiency.

Other organ system functions or status can be assessed in somewhat similar fashions. The thyroid gland can be evaluated by using several different blood tests. Chest pain can frequently be differentiated from heart pain on the basis of serum enzyme levels as well as electrocardiographic changes over time. Liver function, kidney function, and lung function can be evaluated, at least in part, by blood tests. Vital information about bone and muscle can also be obtained.

349

Urine

The kidneys filter the total blood volume many times a day. With normal kidney function, this filtration process removes waste chemicals from the bloodstream and helps maintain homeostasis. As with the blood, there are many, many tests that can be done on urine specimens to provide a physician with additional data in evaluating human disease. Again, testing for a given chemical in the urine may require special collection techniques. Taking a urine culture to check for a urinary tract infection is a much different procedure from collecting a 24-hour urine specimen for total protein. As a matter of fact, collection of a urine sample for culture, practically speaking, differs significantly between men and women. This is a relatively important topic that deserves a little extra consideration.

Normally, urine is sterile. Collecting a urine specimen under sterile conditions can be difficult. However, if one pays attention, it can be done and the information obtained is valuable in helping a physician recommend specific therapy.

Suppose, for a moment, that a patient has noticed that he or she is urinating more frequently, that it burns a little, that occasionally a few drops of urine are lost unexpectedly, and recently there has been an urge to void but, when the patient tries, little or nothing happens. The patient seeks medical advice and is told to collect a clean catch, midstream urine specimen for culture and sensitivity.

What on earth is that? Let's deal with the midstream part first, because that is still basically asexual—this example applies equally to both sexes so far. Midstream collection means what it says: start voiding without collecting, stop, start again, only now collect some urine in the sterile container provided, stop again, remove the container and empty the bladder. It is essential that the sterile container contents be handled carefully. It is appropriate to handle only the outside of the container. It is necessary to leave the cap on until just before collection and the cover should be put on as soon as collection is completed. So far so good! Now, what does clean catch mean? Clean catch refers to washing the appropriate area before taking the specimen. A male should expose the glans, or head of the penis, and wash it off, starting at the opening and moving back. A female should open the labia and wash from front to back, using a separate gauze or sponge for each cleansing stroke. If there is any vaginal discharge, care must be taken to avoid contaminating the urine specimen. Urine is normally sterile, but the vagina is not. If vaginal secretions contaminate a urine specimen for culture and sensitivities, then it is hard for the doctor—and ultimately for the patient—to know what represents infection and what represents contamination.

Another way of obtaining urine for culture is catheterization. This is a procedure in which a sterile flexible rubber or plastic tube is passed through the urethra into the bladder. Urine is collected in a sterile container and the catheter is removed. Such a procedure might be indicated if previous specimens have been contaminated or if the patient cannot cooperate in collection.

Routine urinalysis provides information quickly. Data is provided about hydration, acid-base balance, kidney function as it relates to protein filtration, liver function, carbohydrate metabolism—especially glucose—as well as the presence of blood. And all of that can be derived from semiquantitative physical and chemical tests. In addition, a routine urinalysis should include a microscopic evaluation of the urinary sediment after centrifugation. This procedure provides further information about formed elements—that is, white cells and red cells as well as formed protein called casts. In addition, the presence of bacteria can be noted, and that of different crystals that reflect the body's metabolism at the time the urine was formed in the kidney.

Urine tests are frequently better than blood tests for assessing what is happening inside the patient's body. Drug screens for toxicology are more accurately run on urine than on blood. Many endocrine functions can be tested best in 24-hour urine collections. These procedures test for known breakdown products of given hormones. Certainly collection of urine specimens is easier than blood collection from the point of view of anticipatory anxiety on the part of the patient.

The technology involved in extracting information about a given element's concentration in blood and urine is quite similar. Technology has automated much of the procedural work of blood and urine analysis but the end point is still the same—data feedback for clinical assessment of a given individual's condition at a given time. The results of any one lab test or any one physical exam represent the state of a particular part of the patient's body at one point. It is important that an ongoing health care relationship be established with a primary care provider so that multiple evaluations over time are accumulated and trends can then be assessed. Such assessments should enhance health by enabling the physician to anticipate disease and thus adjust minor homeostatic disequilibriums before they become major maladjustments.

—*George Benton, M.D.*

Health Education Unit 5
Backache

There are many opinions about the causes of and treatments for backache. Treatments include massaging, heating, spraying, cooling, stretching, straightening, injecting, and using yoga, manipulation, mustard plasters, and even Oriental back rollers. This wide array of suggestions ranging from current orthopedic methods to the ancient Chinese implement represent what some of the estimated 28 million people in the U.S. with backaches believe will cure their troubles.

Causes

While there is a wide variety of causes of backaches, many people attribute their backaches to a "disk." They call it such diverse names as sciatica, lumbago, ruptured disk, and slipped disk. However, a protruding and defective intervertebral disk is in fact a relatively uncommon cause of bad backs. A recent report from Columbia and New York universities showed defective disks to be the exceptional rather than the usual cause of backache. In 5,000 case studies, 81% of the backaches were caused by muscle weakness or spinal stiffness. Other causes, including defective intervertebral disks, tumors, arthritis, and bone abnormality, made up the remaining 19%.

Although not the major cause of backaches, disks are a common problem. Located between the vertebrae, the intervertebral disks are semicartilaginous "shock absorbers." They absorb the shocks and the bumps of everyday walking, jumping, and slumping. This absorption of impact is somewhat like that offered by the shock absorbers in an automobile. After 20 years or more of use, it is normal for the disks to begin to degenerate. The degree and rate of degeneration are related to the amount of injury and general wear that the spine receives. Wear and tear can result from athletic and work injuries, careless lifting habits, slumping, bad posture, improper seating, excess weight and greater than average height, and other factors. Regular physical exercises that keep the back strong and supple may minimize trouble.

Normally the vertebrae have sliding movements in six directions: forward, backward, laterally to the right and left, and a rotary motion clockwise or counterclockwise. In most adults the ligaments that attach the vertebrae to each other become stiffened and lose their normal elasticity. However, dancers, acrobats, and some people who practice yoga-like exercises can maintain an amazing

amount of spinal flexibility. Unfortunately such vertebral health is uncommon in most of the Western world and disk degeneration and damage to the paravertebral ligaments occur frequently. With them come the symptoms of pain in the lumbosacral area and the leg and varying amounts of disability associated with "disk trouble."

If a person has a faulty disk, one of the first clues is pain down the leg, commonly called sciatica. Pain is usually experienced down the back of the leg, but it is occasionally also felt on the front or side. Depending on the degree of degeneration, the inner core of the disk pushes out and irritates a nearby spinal nerve. The protrusion causes tingling, numbness, or pain, depending on the amount of pressure it creates.

This distress is provoked by certain positions, particularly by certain types of seating. Certain sitting positions exert powerful wedging forces against the disk and cause protrusion of the inner core. If people with defective disks "listen" to their bodies and avoid troublesome positions, pain and disability can be eased or even avoided.

The worst sitting positions are associated with poor seat design—exemplified by deep, soft sofas,

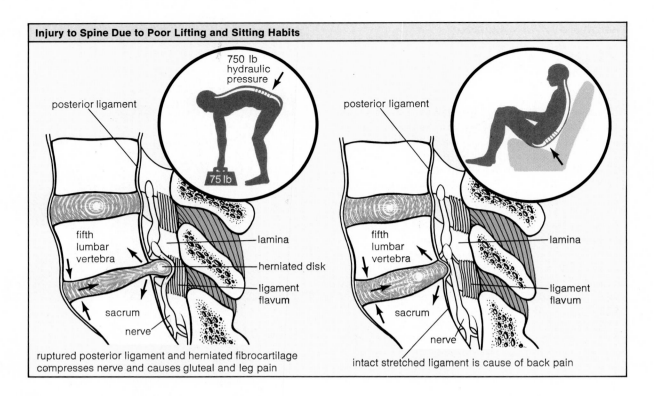

Injury to Spine Due to Poor Lifting and Sitting Habits

750 lb
hydraulic
pressure

posterior ligament

75 lb

fifth
lumbar
vertebra

lamina

herniated disk

ligament
flavum

sacrum

nerve

ruptured posterior ligament and herniated fibrocartilage
compresses nerve and causes gluteal and leg pain

posterior ligament

fifth
lumbar
vertebra

lamina

ligament
flavum

sacrum

nerve

intact stretched ligament is cause of back pain

modern low chairs, and low bucket seats. Good seating design includes several features: (1) seat height 16 inches from the floor (*e.g.,* a typical kitchen chair); (2) seat length 16 inches long; (3) back tilted at least 105° (most tilt only 90°) to allow for the curve of the lower spine; (4) moderately hard, not soft, seat cushioning; (5) open space beneath the seat to allow legs to curve inward (again as with kitchen chairs); (6) bulge in the chair back to give support to the lower lumbar region of the spine.

Relieving the symptoms

What if bad lifting practices, poor sitting habits, and injuries have already taken their toll? What if a person hurts his back by slipping on ice or wrenches it while carrying a heavy object? What if pain is present in the lower back or radiates down the leg? If such pain is present, there are certain helpful treatments. (1) Lie on a firm mattress or thick rug in a position of comfort and move around to find a position in which pain is minimized. (2) Limit activity, and rest as much as possible for 24 to 48 hours until the pain has subsided. (3) Take aspirin in recommended doses every three to four hours. (4) Splint the lower back with tape after shaving it if necessary and applying a layer of tincture of benzoin to the skin. A lumbosacral splint will give some support and can be applied on the second or third day. (5) Massage the lower back to relax muscles.

(6) Apply heat. This will also help relax some muscles, but will not be of much help in treating a defective disk, since the disk is an internal bony structure and injury to it is primarily a mechanical, not a muscular, problem.

Once the pain has been relieved, a program of follow-up and rehabilitation should begin. (1) Adopt beneficial sitting habits during recovery, sitting only on a kitchen-type chair. (2) Start daily exercises to improve the mobility of vertebrae and increase the strength of abdominal muscles. Yoga-like exercizes that stretch muscles and ligaments and help maintain vertebral motion are useful. (3) Establish a general physical fitness program including a sport that can be done on one's own time and at one's own speed, such as biking, hiking, or swimming. (4) Sleep on a firm mattress. (5) Engage in moderate activity but avoid heavy work that involves lifting. (6) Maintain good posture. (7) Get extra rest at night and if possible, take a 20-minute rest period at noon on a floor or firm couch.

There are danger signals that indicate the need for professional medical help. Call a doctor if pain or numbness in the leg persists despite treatment, or if there is a history of previous frequent and repeated incidences of disk trouble.

—Keith W. Sehnert, M.D.

Asthma

Bronchial asthma is a distressing and, at times, frightening respiratory disease associated with allergies. An attack may be caused by dust, pollen, infection, smoke, food, medication, exertion, cold and damp weather, emotional upsets, or fatigue. The severity and duration of an attack depend on the patient's general health, age, and attitude as well as on early treatment. The surroundings offered by family and home are also important.

Bronchial asthma occurs when the bronchial tubes go into spasm and the mucous membrane of their inner lining becomes inflamed, swollen, and choked with sticky mucus. When this occurs, it becomes difficult to move air in and out of the lungs. An asthmatic attack is typified by labored breathing (wheezing) and shortness of breath (dyspnea). Associated symptoms may include a runny and stuffy nose, coughing, sinus problems, fever, and muscle pains in the neck and chest. Acute attacks usually require treatment in a doctor's office or a hospital. Because asthma frequently leads to emphysema, the number of attacks must be kept to a minimum. In emphysema the lung tissue is damaged and normal respiration may be severely impaired.

Prevention

After a person has an attack, it is essential to review the probable cause and consider the things that can be done to reduce the frequency and severity of future attacks. Was the attack caused by irritating smoke from cigars, cigarettes, fires, or car fumes, or was it caused by a particular food or an emotional stress?

Prevention of wheezing is possible if certain rules are strictly followed. Create an allergy-free bedroom and install an electronic precipitator or room air-cleaning machine. Central units can be purchased from electric appliance dealers and air-conditioning and heating service firms. Room units can be purchased or rented from medical and hospital supply stores and some department stores. There are several steps required to prepare an allergy-free bedroom.

Bed: Wipe the bed and springs. Cover the box springs, pillows, and mattress with plastic covers. Do not use feather pillows. Bedspreads should be plain and easily washed (no chenille, corduroy, or ruffles). Do not use quilts or comforters. Blankets must be cotton, orlon, or acrylic material that can be washed every two weeks.

Closet: Clean the closet carefully and use it only for currently worn clothing. Do not use the closet for storage.

Floor: Do not use carpets or rugs. If the existing carpet is old, remove it. Tile, wood, and new linoleum are dust free.

Furniture: Use only wood or plastic, not upholstered, chairs. Do not use a bookcase. Use the dresser only for current clothing, not for storage.

Walls: Remove all old, torn wallpaper, repair the plaster, and paint with a water-based paint. Do not use wall decorations or bulletin boards.

Windows: Use shades but never shutters or venetian blinds. Curtains that can be washed every two weeks and plastic material that can be wiped off weekly are preferred. Keep the windows closed as much as possible.

This plan eliminates dust collectors and dust makers from the bedroom. A general rule is to strip the room of all clutter and junk. (The room should look like one that would make a Marine drill instructor happy!) Vacuum the floor daily. Keep the door shut. Pets must not be allowed in the room. Allow only nonallergenic toys in the room; stuffed toys must not be allowed on the bed.

There are other general tips to prevent asthmatic attacks.

1. Do not lie on any carpet unless separated from it by a clean blanket, plastic sheet, linoleum, or masonite panel.

2. If certain events (playing or running hard, the excitement of holidays or birthdays) always cause an asthma attack, take asthma medicine before the event.

3. Treat all colds, sore throats, and infections promptly. Ask a doctor for the following prescriptions so that you have them on hand: an antihistamine or decongestant for the nose, and an asthma medicine for wheezing. The physician may also choose to prescribe an antibiotic for infection.

4. Maintain a good level of physical fitness, including daily exercise as a part of your life.

5. Drink a lot of liquids, which will reduce the thickness of the bronchial secretions and keep them watery.

6. Stop smoking and avoid situations in which smoking occurs.

7. Keep windows closed in cars and at home and use air conditioning as much as possible.

8. Consider allergy shots (skin testing followed by regular desensitization injections). Discuss the procedure with your doctor.

Treatment

There are a half dozen treatment tips that can be followed by asthmatic people at the first sign of symptoms:

1. Get away from and stay away from whatever makes you wheeze.

2. Retire to an allergy-free room as soon as wheezing starts.

3. Begin taking medicine as soon as possible and continue until the squeaking or wheezing has stopped for at least 24 hours.

4. Drink one glass of warm liquid (tea, soup, lemonade, or liquid gelatin).

5. Do not let anyone smoke in your home or car during recovery.

6. Try to relax, lie flat, and sleep.

Treatment for children should be the same as for adults, with some exceptions. Children should not be allowed to use asthma medicine in spray form, which may even make the asthma worse. Because it is more difficult for children to cough up the sticky, irritating mucus associated with asthma, they often swallow it. Frequently, the first complaint they report is a stomachache or cramps. Children may get relief only by vomiting to rid them of the irritating mucus they have swallowed.

Because of the chronic nature of asthma, working closely with a physician is of the utmost importance. Yet many asthmatics are reluctant to consult a doctor for minor attacks. There are, however, some signals that indicate that the attack has become complicated with infection or is more severe than usual, and that a physician must be consulted. The signals are: (1) inability to talk, eat, or lie flat in bed and sleep; (2) painful breathing—wheezing can produce a dull ache in the chest, but pain caused by breathing is a danger sign; (3) vomiting more than twice in several hours, particularly if the patient is a child; (4) change in sputum color from clear white to yellow, green, or gray; (5) blood in the sputum; (6) fever present several times daily.

If the individual and family understand asthma, and are aware of practical preventive and treatment tips, they may not experience the fear and helplessness so often associated with asthma attacks.

—*Keith W. Sehnert, M.D.*

Depression

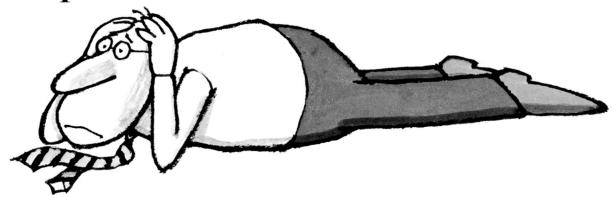

It is difficult for most people to understand depression or its most dramatic and tragic ending—suicide. People often read about the suicides of the famous and successful in the newspaper. Depression and suicide are not limited to such notables but affect all kinds of people. Are there characteristics in common between the depressions of well-known people and those of many others who suffer from the same disorder? What are the most common symptoms? Is there a link between the everyday "blues" and major depressions?

All people, great and small, who are depressed experience some similar symptoms. Classification of the depression as profound, perhaps even life-threatening, or merely as a case of everyday blues is a matter of degree. A good way to express the differences in degree is to rate any depression on a scale from one to 100. A case of the blues caused by an accumulation of fatigue and several of minor disappointments in personal or family affairs might get a rating of 20. The reactive depression experienced by a woman widowed at 55 and faced with financial uncertainty in addition to her personal grief could be rated 75 or 80. If her situation were compounded by poor health or impending major surgery, the rating could rise to 90 or higher.

The symptoms commonly reported in depression include: sleep disturbances, loss of energy and appetite, inability to concentrate, guilt feelings, inability to feel pleasure, and all too often, alcohol abuse. Sleep disturbances are the most frequent symptom. Two-thirds of all depressed persons report insomnia. It is usually characterized by early morning awakening and difficulty in returning to sleep. A typical story is: "I woke at 2 A.M. and every problem in the world passed through my mind as I tossed and turned. Then when I finally fell asleep, the alarm clock went off and it was time to get up!"

Sleeping pills or other sedatives usually do not provide relief in such cases. Another variety of sleep disturbance, too much sleep (hypersomnia), may be experienced by a depressed teenager. Parents will report, "Ever since that trouble in school, Kevin has slept *all* the time, something most unusual for him. Usually I have to fuss at him to get to bed at 11:00. Now, he's in bed at 9:00 and even takes a nap after school!"

Feelings of loss of energy and appetite are expressed by statements such as "I just can't get my house cleaned any more"; or "I'm worn out at the office by noon and then I just drag around the rest of the day"; or "I used to just love a good breakfast, but I haven't had any appetite for so long." The end result of such appetite loss and lack of energy is weight loss. Although such symptoms may conjure up the possibility of serious diseases such as cancer or tuberculosis or thyroid disorder, depression is, in fact, a much more frequent cause.

Another symptom commonly reported is inability to concentrate: the student finds that he can't study; the worker can't keep his mind on his job; and the executive expresses inability to get things done on time. All are distracted by their state of depression. Associated with distraction at work is an inability to feel pleasure. Of a once favorite recreation like bowling, the depressed patient may say, "I don't care for that much nowadays." A gourmet cook says, "Everything I make tastes like a brown paper sack." Pleasure and elation are missing. The world is flat.

Feelings of guilt or self-depreciation are commonly voiced about events long past: "If only I'd been a better wife then"; "I wish I had been a more understanding father." Old decisions return to haunt the depressed individual and are rehashed in minute detail.

Alcohol abuse by an individual who drank only in moderation in the past can be a frequently overlooked and important symptom of depression. "I don't know what has gotten into Fred lately. Last night I found him in his TV chair with an empty whiskey bottle. He couldn't even walk to bed!" People readily identify depression and "hangover" as a *result* of alcohol abuse when, more often, the alcohol abuse is the result of depression. Drinking, however, is a dangerous and ineffective coping method: alcohol only makes the depression worse.

Many experts on the subject believe that depression is a metabolic disorder. They believe that, at least in endogenous depression (not caused by outside events), there is a pharmacologic disorder, a shortage of neurotransmitter substances—chemicals at the nerve connections in the brain. Such an explanation is far different from former assumptions, still held by some, that depression is a weakness of will or self-indulgence in feeling sorry for oneself. Most people fortunately now have a more enlightened view of depression, but it is still not an "honorable" disease.

Medical experts classify depressions into these major categories:

(1) Reactive depression (normal grief and responses to loss). This syndrome can result from loss of a loved one through death, divorce, or separation. It can also occur as a result of a move to a distant place. Reactive depression is frequently accompanied by sadness, brooding, loss of appetite, and insomnia.

(2) Psychoneurotic depression (presumed *normal* brain physiology, neurotic personality defect with poor coping methods for interpersonal relations). Persons suffering from this type of depression have a history of maladaptive behavior and often resort to alcohol or stimulant or sedative abuse. Commonly labelled hypochondriacs, they frequently parade their symptoms like a badge. Although they report being sad, they don't look sad.

(3) Endogenous depression (presumed *abnormal* brain physiology of uncertain cause but probably biochemical in nature). Although they appear sad, these individuals frequently deny feeling sad. They dislike admitting symptoms but may privately worry about them and wonder if they represent some dire disease.

Only a few people, perhaps 5% of the population, are afflicted with these major types of depression, but nearly all of us suffer mild forms of depression periodically. These mild forms range from the "blahs" that last a day or two to the "blues," which may last for several days. The causes include common anxieties, fluctuations in the normal bodily cycles (premenstrual tension is one such example), and disturbances in normal physiology that may

have been caused by stress, illness, or injury.

Insight into the common causes of depression and knowledge of how to alleviate or prevent it are helpful. Being able to recognize more serious forms of depression so that they get prompt medical attention is also important.

A certain kind of person is likely to get depressed. Frequently, people susceptible to depression are highly motivated, self-denying people who are very productive when not depressed. They are often, almost to a fault, perfectionists and conscientious people; some are overachievers.

Because more women than men go to doctors' offices for treatment of depression, it might seem that depression occurs more often among women. Actually, the incidence is the same for males and females. The difference is that men do not seek help as often or as early as women. Men are taught early in life that "big boys don't cry," an attitude that is hard to get over.

What are the ages at which depression most commonly occurs? From the information one reads in popular magazines, it might seem that depression is limited to women going through menopause or to lonely old people. Actually, depression is quite evenly distributed among all age groups. It is frequently not suspected in young people, who just do not show depression as clearly as do older adults. In older people depression is overlooked or assumed to be senility. But there also is grim proof that depression is common among the young: in the United States suicide is the second leading cause of death among white males and females aged 15 to 29 and is among the top five causes of death for young black Americans.

One aspect of depression that is often overlooked is its effect on other members of the family. When a family member is under stress because of a death, loss of a job, prolonged illness, or other problem, there is what is called a "rotation effect." For example, if a wife and mother is underfunctioning while depressed, it is necessary for other members of the family to overfunction. If she does not feel that she has enough energy to do her daily chores, the husband may pitch in to help. When she begins to recover, the husband may become symptomatic because of a process called "emotional fusion." Later, when the parents are recovering, the children may show depression through poor schoolwork or other symptoms. Such unconscious psychological sharing of emotions in families is quite common.

Causes of mild depression

What are the causes of mild, everyday kinds of depression? Some have a biochemical cause. One kind of depression in some women, for example,

"Melancholia," an engraving by 16th-century German artist Albrecht Dürer, symbolizes the mental state now called depression.

occurs before menstrual periods. Called premenstrual tension, it is associated with water retention. Women afflicted with it notice that they suddenly gain several pounds. In addition to symptoms such as swollen ankles, many women experience irritability and depression.

Premenstrual water retention is associated with excess sodium intake from food and excess secretion of aldosterone from the adrenal glands and estrogen and progesterone from the ovaries. The same hormones also play a role in the depression sometimes associated with menopausal and premenopausal years. Birth control pills may also cause fluid retention and depression in some women.

The other kinds of depression are psychogenic. Interpersonal relations and life-style frequently result in a chronic anxiety state that leads to depression. Stress is a common bond among the psychogenic factors causing depression. When people suffer inconveniences and annoyances, the body responds to stress by overstimulating the adrenal glands where adrenaline and aldosterone are made. When worked overtime, the brain and central nervous system may deplete or alter the supplies of norepinephrine and serotonin at the level of the nerve connections. Stress is the common factor that can begin a cycle of depression.

With the stage set for depression, the body begins to "talk" with symptoms. Initially, the symptoms are minor, affecting attitudes and feelings. These are what many people call the blahs. Irritability, a complaining attitude about things in general, lower energy levels, and becoming easily fatigued are common symptoms. If the condition persists, with feelings of sadness, brooding, self-pity, helplessness, and loss of self-esteem, it is frequently called the blues.

When a person cannot "hear" this body talk and does nothing about it, interference with bodily functions eventually develops. Loss of sleep, poor appetite, weight loss, stomach and bowel upsets,

357

headaches (commonly at the back of the head), and even diffuse backaches are common symptoms of a depressed person. Eventually, as depression deepens, there are in some people obvious changes in behavior. A classic picture emerges: frequent weeping, sad face, slower speech, lessened body movement, and in some, suicidal thoughts.

People suffering from severe depression seldom will say that they are considering suicide. But questions from a friend, family member, or medical worker like "Do things seem too hard to bear anymore?" or "Have you thought about harming yourself?" may elicit a "yes." When this happens, the danger signal is present that an emergency exists. Prompt medical care is needed. Medicine or treatment is absolutely necessary to help prevent a suicide attempt.

What can one do to cope with depression before it becomes a medical emergency? There are some tips that help many people minimize anxiety, the frequent forerunner of depression. The advice is also useful for those who are not depressed because it can help maintain a high level of mental fitness.

Get enough sleep and rest, including a daily nap. A nap at noon is best, but if that is not possible one after work is satisfactory. Avoid those life-styles that alter patterns of eating, sleeping, working, and recreation. Follow a ritual that provides a regular hour for bedtime and avoid sleeping pills, which can cause further depression.

Get regular exercise because physical activity counters depression. Considering age and life-style, choose whatever exercise is realistic—hiking, biking, walking, jogging, golf, tennis, calisthenics—and exercise on a daily basis.

Listen to the body. A person under stress becomes anxious. Hear warning signals such as tension in neck muscles or a gnawing feeling in the pit of the stomach. When stress gives these signals, back off and ease up.

Limit the amount of salt in the diet. Avoid common table salt and salty snack foods. Limit the amount of cold cuts, hot dogs, bacon, ham, and other cured meats in the diet because they contain large amounts of sodium nitrates and nitrites.

Avoid using alcohol to cope. Drinking when anxious and faced with problems often worsens depression and helps set the stage for alcoholism.

Identify fears, even list them. A person should talk problems over with himself and with others who will listen. Try to think of ways to cope with problems. Seek information about things that are feared; knowledge can bring runaway fears down to earth.

Make decisions, right or wrong, and act on them. Anxiety results from sitting in the middle of a decision with fears tugging from opposite directions.

Avoid disruption. Try to maintain a balance in the face of disruptive elements. Reestablish calm after unavoidable upsets by following comfortable routines. Disorganization produces anxiety, confusion, and anger.

Love more. Most people need to learn to love people and use things instead of loving things and using people. Avoid loneliness by reaching out to take the initiative in friendship. Treat people as though they were already friends. Pray or meditate on a regular, preferrably daily, basis. This helps sort out what is important and unimportant in life. Laugh more, for laughter is a good tension breaker. A person should laugh at himself and not take himself too seriously. Avoid self-pity, which is a waste of time and energy.

—Keith W. Sehnert, M.D.

Common Sense About Common Injuries

Most cuts, lacerations, and abrasions have some general treatment procedures: (1) the victim should keep calm, sitting quietly or lying down; (2) bleeding should be promptly controlled; (3) the wound should be cleansed if needed; (4) skin edges should be closed if the cut is gaping; and (5) a dressing should be applied to hasten healing and prevent or minimize infection.

Most people learn such rules from first aid courses. What people frequently do not learn, however, are the "why's" of the rules. Most people, for example, have not learned the commonsense reasons for keeping a victim calm. It is important to remain calm because cuts and other injuries bleed more when a person is excited. With excitement, the heart beats faster and blood pressure goes up, which in turn causes more bleeding. The sight of the additional bleeding is alarming and leads to a vicious cycle for the victim: more excitement, more bleeding, and so on.

Sitting or lying down counters excessive bleeding by slowing the pulse rate and lowering the blood pressure. You can verify this fact with a simple experiment. Take your pulse while sitting. Typically the pulse for a person sitting is about 70. Then stand up and walk around the room twice. Again check your pulse, which will go up to 80 or 85, an increase of almost 20% in a normal situation. Excitement can quickly increase the pulse rate 50 or 60%. Now take the pulse while lying down. Usually the pulse is about 60 after a few minutes of rest, a reduction of about 15% from sitting. This test shows the result of keeping yourself or a victim calm, quiet, and resting. The rule makes sense.

All first aid courses teach how to control bleeding. The quickest way is to apply direct, firm pressure at the injured site. Use a clean handkerchief, cloth, or gauze pad. Pressure will control bleeding in 80% of cuts one inch or more, the length of most cuts, within five minutes. Many people are not taught, however, why stopping bleeding is important. Prompt control means that the healing process begins sooner. With the blood flow stopped, a clot forms, and the healing elements in the blood can start the repair process.

Cleansing a wound to remove dirt or other material is sometimes necessary and can be done

in a minute or so. Prolonged washing, however, by preventing clot formation and washing away the white blood cells, delays healing. If a wound has dirt or sand in it, less than five minutes of cleansing with soap and water is usually all that is required.

After bleeding is controlled, the cut should be closed. Such closure decreases the chances of infection and poor healing. Surgical closure with catgut or nylon sutures is needed if the wound is one inch or more and gaping. Why is this so? Gaping means that the deeper layers of the skin have been cut. In such wounds the chances of poor healing are greater because the distance between the sides of the cut is simply too great for a healing bridge to be built. With such a gap, healing must start from the bottom and progress up—a much slower process. Sutures bring the sides of the laceration together and make healing faster. If, however, the cut is not gaping but the skin is still not evenly closed, an adhesive tape closure can be used.

After the closure is made or sutures applied, the area should be splinted to keep it immobilized. It is easy to understand why this is important. During the healing process as the cut is "glued" back together, new tissue is manufactured to take the place of the old, lacerated tissue. For a while new tissue is weak. An analogy can be made between healing tissue and a broken chair seat that has been glued. If you sit on a repaired chair before the glue becomes hard, the chair breaks again. Then you must put glue over glue. A second attempt to glue a chair is not as likely to produce as strong a bond. The same is true when you reopen a cut before it is completely healed. Not only is a weaker repair likely, but the chances of infection and delay in healing increase.

Sprains

Common sense is necessary in treating sprains, another common injury. Sprains occur when the soft tissue around a joint (the ligaments, tendons, and blood vessels) become torn or stretched. Sprains result in pain, swelling, redness, and, within a day or so after the injury, black-and-blue discoloration around the area.

Prevention can play a key role in all sprains, especially of the ankle. Prevention means wearing ankle-supporting sport shoes, hiking boots, or work shoes if you are on rough terrain or in situations that make your ankles vulnerable to sprains. If an accident does occur, immediately apply ice or cold packs, which reduce the swelling and stop bleeding in the joint. Keep the injured part covered with cold applications for about an hour.

Why are cold applications so helpful? How can you remember whether the first application should be cold or hot? Common sense and experience can teach you how. Again, the best way to understand is to try a simple experiment on yourself. Fill a pan with hot water and another with cold water and a few ice cubes. Put your hand in the ice-cold water for two minutes. When you examine your hand you will see that it is paler than normal. The lack of color is the result of the blood vessels shrinking (constricting), which greatly diminishes the blood flow in an injured area (hemorrhage). If there is less bleeding in an injured area, there is less swelling, which means less blood to be absorbed in the healing process. Healing is simpler and takes less time.

Then place your hand in the hot water for two minutes. On examination you will see that your palm is both warm and pink. Heat has caused the tiny blood vessels to expand (dilate). The greater size causes more blood flow to your hand. Extra blood flow with an increased number of healing

cells carried to an injured area is helpful, particularly when accompanied by massage, after a sprain has begun to heal. Heat and massage can then speed healing and help return a sprained joint to normal function.

In addition to immediate application of cold, elevate a sprained joint on two to three blankets or pillows for the rest of the day. Cold, wet applications should be applied continuously. Rest is essential to limit further damage to a sprained joint. If the victim must be moved, splints or wraps should be used. The victim should not be allowed to bear weight on the joint. Sprains tend to be under-diagnosed and under-treated. All sprains should be seen by a doctor, particularly if swelling and pain last more than a few days.

Burns

Common sense is also important in treating burns. Mild burns (first-degree burns) result in redness and slight swelling. Second-degree burns cause deeper injury to the skin, with blistering and more intense swelling. The most severe, third-degree burns, cause charring and destruction of all the skin layers. Third-degree burns are always classed as emergencies and require prompt medical help. With such burns, it is better for the inexperienced first-aider to risk doing too little than too much.

First- and second-degree burns can be treated with a simple "miracle drug" — ice or ice-cold water —which reduces pain and minimizes swelling. Keep the cold applications on for at least an hour. Why does cold help burns? The rationale is the same as for sprains: cold constricts the arteries, reducing swelling and blistering of burned areas.

Methods similar to treatment for sprains are used after burns: the injured part should be elevated on pillows or blankets to reduce swelling, and the area should be kept at rest to help healing. The burned area should be protected from further injury by covering it with a dry dressing. You may use an ointment like sterile petroleum jelly on the dressing, which makes it easier to remove later.

In the treatment of common injuries like cuts, sprains, and burns, there are certain procedures to follow. It is important to know what steps to take to treat these injuries. It is also useful to understand the commonsense reasons for these procedures, and why they are the right steps to take.

—Keith W. Sehnert, M.D.

Health Education Unit 9
Arthritis

Whether a person has the most common of rheumatic diseases, called osteoarthrosis, or a more serious type called rheumatoid arthritis, or other diseases such as bursitis, fibrositis, or gout, the key to control and treatment can lie in the patient's own efforts. There are useful treatments that can be performed by the patient at home.

Osteoarthrosis, or degenerative joint disease (DJD)—sometimes mistakenly termed osteoarthritis—is found to some extent in most people over the age of 50. It is mild in most cases, but about 5% of those afflicted do develop serious and disabling symptoms. The joints that get the most wear—knees, back, hips, neck, and fingers—are the joints usually affected. Rheumatoid arthritis, which afflicts hundreds of thousands in the U.S. alone, usually starts earlier in life than does DJD. Most people with rheumatoid arthritis learn to control its symptoms so that it has little effect on their lives, but about 20% of patients do become severely crippled by the disease.

Connective tissue diseases

Arthritis is only one of several illnesses characterized by abnormalities in connective tissue. Other connective tissue diseases (CTD) include: (1) systemic lupus erythematosus ("lupus"); (2) scleroderma and systemic sclerosis; (3) polyarteritis; and (4) polymyositis and dermatomyositis. The Arthritis Foundation's "Primer on Rheumatic Diseases" lists these four diseases together with rheumatoid arthritis in the group of disorders termed "connective tissue diseases (acquired)."

Connective tissue exists throughout the body in many forms; it includes bone, bone covering (periosteum), cartilage, tendons and tendon sheaths, ligaments, the tough covering (fascia) around muscles, joints, the saclike spaces (bursa) where muscles pass over each other near joints, the tissue (dermis) directly under the skin, and the blood vessels. Older medical books referred to connective tissue as "collagen," and in the past many diseases affecting the connective tissues were designated as "collagen diseases." However, the term collagen is now used to designate one element of the connective tissue, a specific protein.

The most prevalent connective tissue disease is the degenerative condition known as osteoarthrosis. Experts in arthritis (rheumatologists) estimate that it occurs in the U.S. at the rate of 500 new cases per year per million persons in the population. Os-

teoarthrosis, or DJD, is believed to result both from the natural degenerative processes of aging and from chronic physical stress or repeated trauma. Although it may occur at an early age—sometimes in individuals as young as 17—DJD is a condition that generally begins in the fourth decade of life or later.

The next most frequent form of CTD, rheumatoid arthritis, is found at a rate of 250 persons per million. The incidence of the remaining connective tissue disorders is much lower: lupus (35), scleroderma (20), and polymyositis and dermatomyositis (10–15 per million persons.)

Arthritis generally is a disease of the joints that affects the cellophanelike membrane (synovium) covering the working surfaces of the joints. In rheumatoid arthritis especially, the synovium becomes swollen or inflamed and fluid collects in the joint, causing swelling, pain, and stiffness. With limitation of joint motion, muscles near the joints are used less, and in time they become weakened and stiff. Treatment tries to keep muscles strong and stretched and joints as movable as possible.

The joint pain and stiffness associated with osteoarthrosis result from destruction of cartilage, a

361

Exercises

shoulder

Lie on your back with your legs straight and your arms at your side. Raise your arm upward and as far back as it will go, swing it out to the side, then bring it back down to your side. Next, with your arms resting at your sides and your palms toward your body, raise your arm sideways as far as possible from your body, then bring it back to your side. Now raise your arm forward and as far upward as it will go, then return it to your side. Finally, stand or sit with your arm extended to the side and make increasingly larger circles with your hand, keeping your elbow stiff. Repeat for other shoulder.

elbow

Bend your elbow, then straighten it out and turn your wrist back and forth, as illustrated. Make sure to turn your wrist slowly back and forth, as though you were turning a door knob. Repeat for the other elbow.

ankle

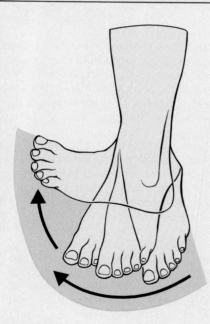

Sit on edge of bed or table and bend your foot up and down slowly. Alternately turn your foot in and out slowly, as shown. Next move your ankle in circular fashion.

knee

Sit on a bed or table and slowly straighten your leg, then slowly return it to its original position. Next, lie on your stomach. Bend your knee as far as you can, then straighten it. Finally, lying on your back with your hips raised and supported by your hands, move your legs in bicycle action.

smooth, elastic tissue that covers and protects the bones in areas where they articulate, or fit together. The disease progresses in stages, beginning with a softening and roughening of the cartilage; gradually the cartilage degenerates, becoming thinner and affording less insulation to the ends of the bones. The joint space narrows, and the newly exposed bone thickens. Bony spurs begin to form, protruding into the margins of the joint space. These spurs may even fuse across the joint, rendering it immobile. Stiffness and reduced mobility of the affected joint are the primary symptoms.

The key to control and treatment is in the control of the person afflicted by arthritis and, to a varying degree, in that of other members of the family, friends, and medical professionals. A regular program of exercise, heat, rest, and medication practiced by the patient, with guidance and advice by the professional, is the best treatment for arthritis. There are, unfortunately, no shortcuts.

There is no known cure for either degenerative or rheumatoid arthritis. Realistic treatment aims at control. Most reported "cures" can be ascribed to periods of spontaneous improvement (remission), which almost inevitably will be followed by recurrences (exacerbation). Remission and exacerbation characterize the normal course for arthritis.

Successful home treatment programs become as much a part of the arthritic's life as sleeping and eating. There are some general facts and rules that should be understood by a person trying to control arthritis. (1) Pain in a joint may result from overuse, but frequently it is caused by nothing more than changes in the weather or a drop in barometric pressure. (2) Pain from stiffness is common in the morning, before and just after getting out of bed. Such pain is relieved by movement and heat. It usually lasts about 10 minutes and seldom longer than 30 minutes. (3) Pain will usually travel from one joint to another. (4) Rest goes hand in hand with an exercise program and is equally important. Several short rest periods during the day are preferable to a few long ones. (5) Plan work so as to accomplish the most important tasks early in the day. (6) Spend no more than eight or nine hours a night in bed. The longer a person stays in bed, the stiffer the joints are likely to feel. Sleep flat on the back as much as possible, using a firm mattress with a half-inch plywood board under it. (7) The arthritic should have good posture whether standing or sitting. Pull the stomach in, and when walking, tighten the buttocks, which helps posture. (8) Do not sit or remain immobile for more than 20 minutes.

Exercise program

Exercise should move the affected joints as far as possible in all directions. Normal daily activities,

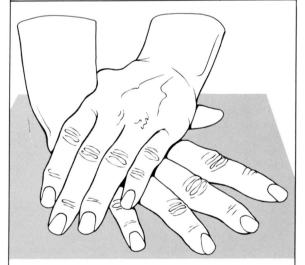

Exercises

wrist

Hold your hand with thumb upward, then move your hand up and down, as shown. Next, bend your wrist forward and backward as far as possible.

fingers and thumb

Stretch your fingers as straight as possible. If your fingers remain bent, rest your palm on the table, hold your other hand firmly on back of your resting hand, then raise your forearm to flatten your fingers as shown. Now make a fist, then straighten your fingers. Spread your straightened fingers apart, then bring them together. Touch the tip of each finger, one at a time, to the end of your thumb, making an "O". Now keep your fingers straight and bend your hand at the knuckles. Next bend your thumb, place it against your palm, and move it across the palm toward your little finger. Finally touch the tip of your thumb to the tip of your little finger.

even for people without arthritis, do not offer full range of motion. The arthritic should watch the spine, hip, leg, foot, arm, and hand movements of a child and try to match their mobility with his joints. If an arthritic is free of pain, he should be as active as possible; activity helps both psychologically and physically.

An exercise plan to strengthen muscles should be practiced three or four times daily. Start slowly and do each exercise three times; then increase to full tolerance, perhaps ten times each. It is reasonable to expect to have some pain when exercising. If the joints are red or swollen, the arthritic should ease up; rest in bed or in an easy chair for 30 minutes every four hours. Specific exercises for the hand and wrist, shoulder and elbow, and the lower extremities are shown in the figures on the preceding pages.

Heat

Applying heat increases the flow of blood and helps heal the joints and muscles. It is not a substitute for exercises. There are methods for applying both moist and dry heat.

A large towel wet thoroughly in warm water, wrung out well, and folded into thirds lengthwise can be wrapped around the joint or laid across the back. The towel should be completely covered with two layers of plastic wrap or waxed paper. A heating pad with the dial set at medium for 20 or 30 minutes should be placed over the plastic cover, making sure there is no contact between the pad and the wet towel. This method provides significant help in reducing acute chronic pain in back, arms, or legs. The heat should be applied twice daily for best results. A second method is to take hot tub and shower baths, which are convenient and comfortable forms of moist heat. The ideal bath temperature is 92–95° F.

One common method of applying dry heat to the hands and wrists is the paraffin bath. A pound of paraffin or other canning wax (available at most grocery stores) should be melted in a deep saucepan that is large enough to allow the hand to rest in it comfortably. As soon as the wax starts to melt, in about 15 minutes over medium heat, the heat should be reduced to low. Unmelted wax about the size of a half dollar should float on top at all times, an indication that the wax is cool enough to prevent burning. It will take about 45 minutes for the wax to melt initially. Great care should be taken to avoid setting the paraffin on fire. The patient submerges the hand carefully in the wax five or six times, or until a thick coating has formed around the hand. Five minutes after the first dip, he should simply peel the coating off and repeat the process. One should follow this procedure once or twice a day for 20 or 30 minutes. A second method of applying dry heat is to use an infrared bulb (250 w applied from a distance of 30 in.) or a heating pad twice daily for 20 minutes.

Medication

The medication that most physicians recommend is aspirin. Because aspirin is common and inexpensive, one should not suppose it is not effective. Aspirin is still the principal drug for arthritis even if newer, more potent, and more expensive drugs are sometimes needed for patients with more severe types of arthritis. Frequently aspirin is the only medicine needed. Aspirin's main effect is not relieving pain but minimizing inflammation and swelling in the joints. Aspirin, of course, will give some pain relief, but pain relief is a bonus.

The usual dose is two to three five-grain tablets with each meal and two to three at bedtime with milk. More tablets may be taken during the night if needed. It is important to maintain the schedule even in the absence of pain.

Ringing in the ears or acid indigestion are signs of too much aspirin. If such symptoms occur, the physician should be consulted so that adjustments can be made in the dose or schedule. Some people, for example, those with ulcers, cannot tolerate aspirin and may benefit from other analgesics.

Other treatment

There are other home treatments that may be useful. An elastic bandage in a figure eight across a painful knee provides support and helps ease pain. Knitted wool cylinders (eight inches long) worn over arthritic knees in the winter provide extra warmth. Windproof nylon or synthetic fiber gloves for the hands are also beneficial and should be worn under mittens or woolen gloves. Massaging the muscles surrounding a joint may be helpful, but rubbing the joint itself is of little value. Weight loss helps by decreasing the wear and tear on the joints. A variety of home aids, devices, and suggestions are available from a doctor or physical therapist.

Arthritis, uncontrolled and untreated, can and does cripple many people. Crippling, however, is not the inevitable end of arthritis. Many arthritics who develop an active program of exercise to strengthen and stretch muscles and mobilize joints, who apply heat to increase local circulation, and who use aspirin to minimize inflammation will have minimal deformity and will be able to maintain nearly normal functions.

—Keith W. Sehnert, M.D.

Listening to the Body's Language— Symptoms

Listen to your body talk. It is giving you symptoms all the time, telling you how it feels. Usually we do not listen even though listening would be the wiser thing to do. But sometimes our bodies force us to listen.

Consider the case of one woman, a nurse who worked in the cardiac care unit of a hospital. Even though she was afraid of flying, she flew home for a holiday vacation with her family. There, in the excitement of holiday activities, she smoked more cigarettes and drank more coffee than usual. On New Year's Day, the end of a busy day and a busy week, she had joined her family to watch television and relax. Suddenly she screamed. She felt a very fast and irregular heartbeat and had the sensation of something tightening on both sides of her neck. She was frightened and dizzy. Imagining the worst, she thought that she had only minutes to live. Someone called for help. An ambulance arrived in minutes and the doctor soon afterward.

What was happening? Her body was making her listen. The symptom of unusually rapid heartbeat (tachycardia) was the result of continued over-stimulation—coffee, smoking, stress. After taking some deep breaths and after being questioned by the doctor, she was able to tell about two previous similar episodes. Both had occurred following the combination of flying, fatigue, and overstimulation. Her mother was also able to recall a family history of tachycardia. Everything added up to a serious warning that her stressed body had given her. The warning was not, as she had feared, an indication of the type of medical emergency experienced by patients she cared for in the cardiac care unit. She had not had a heart attack.

The woman had ignored her body talk—symptoms, messages, and early warnings. Because she was young, she recovered quickly, but had she been older, it could have been a different story. Because she was able to understand that she had ignored earlier messages her body had been sending her, the crisis produced a "teachable moment." Her doctor took time to explain the symptoms so

that she understood what the danger signals had meant. Today she reports that she drinks decaffeinated coffee on a regular basis and is trying to smoke less. She has learned how to make use of the information her body gave her.

Another woman seemed to be tired all the time. No matter how much sleep she got, she never felt rested. She thought her fatigue was nothing that she would not get over, and she took extra vitamins as well as iron tablets a doctor had once given her. Vitamins and iron did not help, and she lost four pounds. Her best friend said that she looked terrible. Her message was fatigue. As she ignored the fatigue, the symptom became more and more insistent until she had to listen. Having awakened one night at 2:30 in a cold sweat, feeling completely depressed, she finally called the doctor the next day.

This woman had kept pushing despite her fatigue. Her flurried life-style had given her no time to herself for months. Although she could have had high blood pressure, she was fortunate in that all she needed was rest. An examination and some tests showed no other medical problems. Reassurance by the doctor and a relaxing week's vacation at the beach brought relief.

Another patient, a man, had had more stomach trouble than usual for several months. An economic recession had hurt his sales territory. Although he had wanted to get married for a year, he did not get an expected bonus and had to postpone marriage. He had other financial problems. As he bought a pack of cigarettes and a roll of antacid tablets at a stop on a turnpike, he felt an intense burning pain in his stomach, followed by a wave of nausea. He hurried to the rest room with not a second to spare and stared in disbelief as he saw the blood-streaked vomitus in the toilet.

The symptoms he had been hiding with tablets were caused by excessive acid secretion, stimulated by emotional distress, spicy food, and irritants such as alcohol and coffee. The result of repeated damage to his stomach lining was a peptic ulcer. He went to a doctor who put him on a strict diet to give his stomach a rest. As do many other people, this man had allowed mild symptoms to build up until they sent a message he could not ignore: pain and blood.

The symptoms most commonly felt by people under stress are specific. They are physical signs involving certain organs: the stomach, the heart, or the head, for example. Most of us are susceptible to at least one such "target" organ because something in our early life sensitized us toward this response. Sometimes the response is learned from parents. Headaches tend to "run in the family," for example, because a little girl learns that when her mother becomes too busy and tired she has a sick headache.

Some symptoms are more general and nonspecific in nature. Examples are the symptoms of menopause and premenstrual tension and the depression associated with them. Such symptoms may be only partly due to stress and partly due to physiological conditions.

One significant factor in the production of such depression is the normal physiological levels of circulating hormones. Aldosterone from the adrenal glands and estrogen and progesterone from the ovaries are the hormones most directly involved. The latter two are the female hormones directly connected with childbearing functions. In the early years of her childbearing years, a woman reaches a plateau of hormonal balance and is not particularly sensitive to environmental factors. But excesses of aldosterone may make her retain salt, which increases her weight. An increase in weight causes depression in many women because it produces puffiness in the legs and the head.

When women reach the premenopausal and menopausal years, the aldosterone level is more susceptible to emotional and environmental factors, and the accumulation of fluids can produce symptoms. A key environmental factor that plays a role in these events is salt in the diet. The salts responsible are not only table salt but also the nitrates and nitrites found in cold cuts, sausage, bacon, ham, hot dogs, and other foods. Women who suffer from depression, whether associated with premenstrual tension or the menopause, would benefit from avoiding such items in the diet. They must also pay special attention to keeping the body at a high level of health with adequate sleep, regular exercise, and a well-balanced diet.

Messages indicating that the body is not well occur in varying degrees, but all of them are warnings that require some kind of action. These messages are what we call symptoms. Some common examples are (1) localized pain (such as a headache); (2) a generally below-par feeling (fatigue); (3) a change in body appearance (for example, a rash); or (4) a change in body function (such as diarrhea).

We have to learn the language of symptoms. Consider, for example, the headache. Although 20,000 tons of aspirin were consumed last year in the United States, not all headaches require aspirin. Proper treatment for a common symptom like a headache depends on its cause. Is a headache due to hunger? If so, the action required is to eat. If fatigue, rest. If muscle tension, use heat. If eyestrain, rest your eyes and make an appointment to have your vision checked. Headache is only one of thousands of possible symptoms.

Of course, there are symptoms that cannot be ignored. Everyone understands these messages, for they are severe, persistent, and unusual and leave no doubt that you must see a doctor.

We can learn to listen to our bodies and to become accurate "medical reporters." To practice being a good medical reporter, think of an incident when your body "talked" to you. Try to give the doctor specific information about the message.

1. What was the symptom? Was it pain, nausea, bleeding?

2. Where or in what part of your body did it occur? Was it in the head, stomach, leg?

3. When did it occur? Was it after eating, upon rising, late in the day?

4. Why did it occur? Did it fit a pattern, or had it occurred under similar circumstances?

It is important to be able to describe a symptom and to be specific. The information should always include the duration of the symptom. For instance, "I haven't felt well the last month" will not do. "About a month ago I started feeling weak and tired" is more appropriate. Other guidelines to follow are to be concrete and to describe the symptom

Interpreting a Symptom: Chest Pain

Parameters	Heart Pain (Angina)	Gall Bladder Spasm	Hiatal Hernia	Anxiety
location of pain	chest midline, often spreading across the chest	upper abdomen, often spreading; chest midline	upper abdomen, spreading across the chest, but often no symptoms	over left chest or variable
radiation of pain	to either arm or both arms, or to neck or jaw, or any combination thereof	lower ribs to back and beneath right shoulder, sometimes to left region and shoulder	to either arm or both arms, neck, or jaw, often combinations	generally none
duration of pain	usually subsides in one to five minutes	usually steady for hours, sometimes intermittent (colic)	a few minutes to an hour	from less than a minute to several hours
character of pain	pressure or heavy discomfort	severe, intensifying rapidly	dull or heavy discomfort	sharp, stabbing pain or dull
associated symptoms	usually none, but occasionally indigestion	bloating, belching, upper abdominal discomfort, nausea and vomiting, dark urine later	hiccup, belching, or heartburn	vague, floating worries; fluttering sensations
causative factors	exertion, emotion, eating, cold weather	fried foods and various vegetables, large meals	lying down, exertion after heavy meals, bending over	tiredness or emotion but often none
relief factors	stop effort, take medication	watch diet, drink fluids	antacids, drinking liquids, sitting or standing upright	lying down, sedatives

A single symptom, in this case chest pain, can be a signal of a variety of problems. By closely noting characteristics of the pain such as its precise location, duration, and nature, the perceptive patient will be able both to relieve the symptom and to avoid its recurrence. In addition, a patient who is observant and in tune with his body is a great help to his physician in making an accurate diagnosis.

in your own words. Do not try to use diagnostic terms or names of diseases. Do not try to diagnose your illness.

It is helpful to know some specific instances in which the body transmits varying degrees of messages. Some messages are mild and can be easily answered by simple actions. Other messages are more serious. Some are severe and may indicate a threat to life and require professional help.

Not all symptoms are danger signals, for the body also transmits messages when it feels good. A person who is feeling good has a spring to his step and his body leans forward as he walks. Consider an enthusiastic, energetic woman who enjoys walking. She purposely parks her car six blocks from her place of work so that she has the opportunity to walk every day. As she walks she likes to look at the sky, the trees, the flowers, the birds, for she enjoys seeing all these things in the world around her. Rain and snow do not interfere with her pleasure because she dresses appropriately and comfortably. The increased circulation and breathing stimulated by the exercise of walking add to her feeling of well-being. She also enjoys hiking and seeing the beauty of the mountains. When she is feeling drained of energy, she enjoys sleeping out of doors, going to bed when the stars come out and watching them until she falls asleep. She says the experience makes her problems seem small, and after the restful sleep she returns from these overnight outings with a great feeling of well-being, "just as if I'd been restored."

Another patient practices yoga to make her body feel good. She says that her body responds positively to yoga exercises with increased flexibility and vitality. Breathing is a very important part of yoga training, and the increase in oxygen so vitally needed by the body adds to her feeling of well-being.

Most of all, feeling good is feeling in harmony with the world around you. Your body is always trying to achieve this feeling of harmony, and it is up to you to choose actions that make you feel good. Think of times when you felt refreshed upon awakening after a comfortable night's sleep. Recall how relaxed you felt at the close of a yoga session after the tension had been released from your body. Remember your exhilaration after swimming because of the increased circulation and your feeling of accomplishment. Think of the satisfaction after renewing a friendship. How are you feeling right now? How could you feel better? It is up to you to choose those activities that make you feel good.

Become aware of your body by developing the ability to interpret messages your body sends you about the way it is feeling. Develop the ability to respond appropriately to your body. Become skillful in the specific description of body messages. Trust your own body. Listen to it carefully when it gives you advice, and you too can experience a "teachable moment."

—Claire T. Welling, R.N.

Health Education Unit 11

Health Tips for Travelers

Being sick at home is bad enough, but falling victim to illness or injury while traveling can be far worse. All too frequently the misery of illness is compounded by the difficulty of finding medical care in distant and unfamiliar places. Travelers should be knowledgeable about procedures that will avoid or help solve problems that can mar travel and adversely affect their health.

If a person has a medical problem, he should see his doctor before traveling and obtain an extra copy of prescriptions in case his medicine is lost or damaged. The doctor should know where his patient is going. He may be able to recommend another physician in the area of his patient's destination. Such a reference is especially important for a person who has diabetes, severe allergies, or other chronic problems. If the physician cannot recommend anyone, the traveler can check local sources when he arrives. Many campsites run by government agencies or private corporations post the names and telephone numbers of local clinics or doctors who handle emergencies. If such information is not posted, a nearby hospital can give advice about local services.

Some physicians recommend that travelers carry a medical card or record that lists basic information about medical or surgical problems. The card should list the telephone number of the traveler's personal physician and dentist, the name and number of the hospital insurance policy, foods or medicines that the traveler is allergic to, and other pertinent information.

Gastroenteritis

What is the most common illness for travelers? The disease named most often is gastroenteritis, or "stomach flu," with symptoms of nausea, vomiting, and diarrhea. People attribute the symptoms to "something they ate." Food is often to blame because travelers eat in many different restaurants and try a greater variety of foods. New dishes or unusual seasonings that the digestive system is not used to can be irritating. Along with indiscretion in drinking alcohol that also can irritate the intestinal system, food can indeed cause gastroenteritis.

When foods or liquids are put into our mouths and stomachs there is a sequence of events that occurs called "digestion." Food is chewed and broken into smaller and smaller pieces by digestive "juices," or enzymes and chemicals whose purpose is to dissolve the proteins, fats, and carbohydrates that are ingested. Liquids are absorbed directly or acted upon by the same juices at work on the solid food.

If the food and liquids are familiar to the digestive tract and basically "friendly," the process is smooth and without event. However, if the foods are spicy, irritating, or contain bacteria or viruses that are irritating, or if liquids contain irritants such as alcohol or minerals, the gastrointestinal (GI) tract may respond protectively with greatly increased activity forward (diarrhea) or backwards (vomiting). The digestive system can adjust to new foods and drinks over the course of time as it becomes accustomed to the substances.

The most common general cause of gastroenteritis, however, is a virus, and viral gastroenteritis does occur among travelers. The disease is caught from viruses passed from other persons. Another likely cause for travelers, particularly campers, is

369

Travel Kit	
antacid	50 tablets
decongestant	24 tablets
cough medicine	4 ounces
astringent wet dressing for itching	12 tablets
aspirin	100 tablets
aspirin substitute	100 tablets
medication for motion sickness	12 tablets
bulk laxative	30 packets
antibacterial ointment	1 ounce
nose drops	1 ounce
petroleum jelly	small jar
adhesive bandages (regular and nonsticking)	mixed sizes
adhesive tape	½–inch and 2–inch sizes
gauze dressings	mixed sizes

A medical travel kit is a good idea for both foreign and domestic travelers. Most necessary items can be purchased at a local pharmacy without a prescription.

bacteria in food left unrefrigerated or in food prepared in unsanitary conditions. Parasites are the cause of digestive illness in some foreign travel, and they can cause debilitating diarrhea.

The best treatment for gastroenteritis is prevention. When camping or when eating in unfamiliar restaurants a traveler should avoid foods made with eggs or containing custards or mayonnaise. Such foods spoil quickly and make good breeding grounds for bacteria. Campers should take a portable ice chest and keep all foods cool until mealtime. Leftovers should be used as quickly as possible or, if there is any doubt about their freshness, thrown away.

Should gastroenteritis strike despite the best preventive efforts, there are some specific things to know. Diarrhea is uncomfortable but not necessarily bad; in fact, it may be protective. Through the cleansing action of diarrhea, the offending viral particles or bacteria are sped through the bowels before they can penetrate the mucous lining of the digestive tract and do more harm. It is usually best not to take antidiarrheal medication of any kind during the first six to eight hours. Diarrhea usually runs its course in 24 to 48 hours if properly treated. If not, however, it can last for a week or more.

There are several recommendations for treating gastroenteritis.

(1) The victim should have bed rest, staying horizontal until the nausea, vomiting, and diarrhea are gone. The position of bed rest helps to minimize symptoms.

(2) A strict diet is necessary. On the first day one should have only ice chips (made from purified water, of course, if there is any question about the safety of the local water supply), until the vomiting and nausea stop. On the second day clear liquids such as tea, ginger ale, or broth may be drunk. Milk is not a clear liquid. On the third day one can have a soft diet of gelatin, custard, or pudding. On the fourth to fifth day return to a normal diet, but avoid fresh fruits, salads, alcohol, and highly seasoned foods.

(3) Diarrhea may recur if the schedule is not followed. People who say "I was getting well but caught the flu again" are usually admitting that they ate normal food before their digestive system was ready for it.

(4) Medication is seldom needed, and some experts specifically recommend avoiding diphenoxylate hydrochloride or iodochlorhydroxyquin, both formerly widely used. These strong medicines should be taken only by patients under direct medical care. Even then, according to some sources, they may not be beneficial though they do relieve symptoms. However, in a 1976 field trial in Mexico, researchers from the University of Texas Health Science Center in Houston discovered that Pepto-Bismol, a widely available over-the-counter liquid medication, was an effective treatment for traveler's diarrhea.

There are certain danger signals to look for if a person has gastroenteritis: (1) black or bloody stools; (2) symptoms for more than four days; (3) diarrhea of more than eight stools per day; (4) a fever consistently over 101° F; (5) persistent pain in abdomen or rectum; (6) illness in an infant, a young child, an elderly person, or one suffering from diabetes or any other chronic illness. In such cases a doctor should be called.

Cuts, abrasions, and burns

The second most common malady to beset travelers is cuts and abrasions. They require control of bleeding, cleansing of the wound, closure of gaping edges, and application of a dressing to promote healing and to prevent or minimize infection. An antibacterial ointment is recommended.

Burns are another common hazard for campers and many other vacationers. A mild, or first degree, burn produces redness and slight swelling and pain. An intermediate, or second degree, burn causes blistering and more intense swelling and pain. Treatment of these common burns should begin with the application of ice or the coldest water available to reduce pain and minimize swelling. Apply the cold water or ice for one-half to one hour.

Campers may fall victim to any number of health hazards and diseases, from cuts, burns, and snakebites to food poisoning from improperly stored provisions.

Then gently wash the skin with mild soap and water and apply a dry gauze dressing and petroleum jelly, which makes it easier to remove the dressing later. When someone has a third degree burn with charring and destruction of all the skin layers, medical help must always be sought. For severe burns, the individual inexperienced in first aid is better off doing too little than too much.

Foreign travel

For a person traveling in a foreign country some special precautions are necessary. If a person has an allergy (*e.g.,* to penicillin) or a chronic condition such as diabetes, he should wear a bracelet that identifies the problem. A person with a heart problem should carry a photocopy of a recent electrocardiogram and an explanatory letter from his personal physician.

If regular medication is needed, a traveler should take an adequate supply. A traveler can avoid delays at customs by having each bottle carefully labeled and accompanied by a written prescription carried in the purse or wallet. An extra prescription for each medication is an additional safeguard, but one should not assume that the particular drug will be available in other countries. Drugs in foreign countries may be sold under names slightly or completely different from those used in the United States. Quality and quantity of ingredients may vary even for common products such as aspirin. The foreign traveler should read all labels carefully.

Foreign travelers should exercise caution in eating and drinking. The tap water in most hotels in large foreign cities frequented by American tourists is safe, but elsewhere bottled water, soda, beer, wine, or hot tea and coffee made with boiling water are preferable. It is even recommended that travelers heat water (to 160° F [71° C] or higher) for brushing their teeth. Bottled water can also be used. They should not use ice cubes made from tap water. All meat and fish should be well cooked and eaten while still hot. The same advice holds for vegetables, particularly those grown underground, which may be contaminated with bacteria or parasites. Lettuce and salads are risky and like milk and milk products are best avoided. Fruits that can be peeled are usually safe.

Jet lag can also be a medical problem. Fast travel causes a disruption in the schedule of normal bodily functions (circadian rhythm). It alters sleep, hunger, and bowel habits with results that can be quite upsetting to some people or merely annoying to others. Layover stops along the way can help ease distress for trips that last six to ten hours. Airline personnel can make suggestions on how to minimize jet lag.

In planning for a trip it takes at least two (and three or four for many people) days for the "inner (biological) clock" to adjust to a major trip. For example, if you leave the U.S. at 6:00 P.M. Eastern Standard Time and arrive in Europe five or six travel hours later, you'll find it is 5:00 A.M. local time.

Fatigue, caused by jet lag or too much sightseeing, and intestinal infections and upsets are among the most common causes of illness for those traveling in foreign countries.

However, your body says it is 11:00 P.M. and time to go to bed—not eat breakfast!

Jet lag begins when you decide to stay up and see the sights because it is too noisy and bright to sleep. After a busy day, when the local citizens are going to bed at midnight their time, your "inner clock" reads 7 P.M.—and the dilemma begins: it's time for dinner, not bed. This lack of synchronization causes many people to feel out of sorts, fatigued and irritable.

One way to handle this is to keep your watch set on "back home time" for two or three days. Follow your regular eating and sleeping schedule as closely as possible. Don't try to do too much sightseeing or business for a couple of days until you can convert to local time.

Business executives who travel to Europe, for example, schedule their arrival on Saturday morning and use the weekend to take it easy while converting to local time. By Monday noon, the transition is fairly well along and they schedule their first appointment that afternoon.

Immunization recommendations change frequently but there is a trend toward fewer required shots. No vaccinations are needed for direct travel from the U.S. to Canada and Europe. Several countries require smallpox or yellow fever vaccination, particularly if tourists do not arrive directly from the U.S., but most countries have dropped requirements for cholera immunization. The U.S. requires vaccination against smallpox for travelers going to Bangladesh, India, Pakistan, and Ethiopia, and the vaccination must be repeated within 14 days before return to the U.S. Yellow fever vaccination is no longer required for U.S. travelers, but the Public Health Service recommends it for travel to certain endemic zones in Africa, South America, and Panama. Vaccination against yellow fever must be done at a center designated by the Public Health Service and is usually available only by appointment on certain days. Immunization certificates correctly completed and validated must be carried with the traveler's passport. Up-to-date information on immunization requirements throughout the world can be obtained by writing the U.S. Public Health Service, Center for Disease Control, Atlanta, Ga. 30333.

—*Keith W. Sehnert, M.D.*

Health Education Unit 12
Stroke

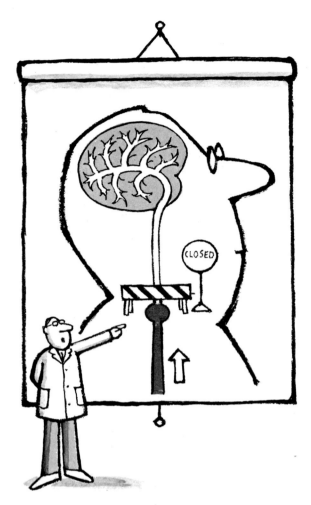

In the U.S. today stroke is the third leading cause of death. Even when a victim recovers, as is usually the case, a stroke can leave an expensive pile of hospital and nursing home bills. A stroke can also leave a burden of fatigue, stress, incapacity, and personal anguish for everyone involved.

People do recover from strokes. One famous example is Louis Pasteur, who had a stroke at age 46 but lived for 27 more years. He did much of his most famous work after the stroke, developing the treatment for rabies and establishing the Pasteur Institute. With recovery a greater likelihood now than in former times and prevention possible in many cases, the outlook for stroke victims has greatly improved.

Physiology of strokes

A stroke is a spontaneous rupture of a blood vessel or formation of a clot in a vessel, which interferes with the blood circulation to a part of the brain. A major stroke (cerebrovascular accident or CVA) causes paralysis or weakness along one entire side of the body. The most minor stroke (transient ischemic attack or TIA) causes only temporary numbness, double or blurred vision, or other fleeting symptoms.

Each half of the brain controls the opposite side of the body. A major cerebrovascular accident that affects the left arm and leg involves circulation damage to the right side of the brain. If the damage is in the left side of the brain, besides paralysis of the right side of the body there is also injury to the speech center and the victim is often unable to speak or may speak incoherently.

What is at the root of a major stroke? Most likely, especially in elderly persons, it is the result of atherosclerosis affecting the arteries that supply blood to the brain. The term *atherosclerosis* describes a condition in which fatty deposits, or plaques, also called *atheromata,* build up in the interior of an artery, narrowing the vessel and decreasing the amount of blood that is able to flow through it. Exactly how and why these fatty deposits form is a subject of intensive current medical research and debate.

Atheroma have been strongly linked with cholesterol, a lipid (a type of fat) found in the cell walls and carried in circulating blood. The amount of cholesterol in the blood — known as the serum cholesterol level — is probably the single most impor-

tant risk factor in the development of atherosclerosis. Some people have higher than normal serum cholesterol levels, a condition known as hypercholesterolemia. This condition is thought to be related to a number of variables, including diet, smoking, hormones, and hereditary factors governing such processes as metabolism and immune responses.

Diets that are high in saturated fats have been associated with stroke and other cardiovascular problems, and it has been demonstrated that the serum cholesterol level can be lowered and controlled by changes in eating habits. The incidence of cardiovascular diseases is lower among people whose diets consist of lean meats, fish, and high proportions of vegetables and grains.

There is evidence that the amount of cholesterol in the blood is also influenced by physiological processes that govern the ability of cell membranes to bind cholesterol molecules, thereby removing them from circulating blood and incorporating them into the cells themselves. Researchers have discovered that people who have family histories of hypercholesterolemia are deficient in the chemical receptors that bind cholesterol to the cells.

373

Another theory holds that an atherosclerotic plaque congregates within an artery at a site of previous injury to the arterial lining. According to this theory, trauma causes smooth muscle cells to migrate from the middle layer, or media, of the artery into the intima, the interior layer that surrounds the open cavity of the vessel. The accumulation of smooth muscle cells in the intima leads, through a complex process, to the buildup of atheromata.

Whatever their origin, these fatty deposits within the arteries eventually result in the collection of blood cells on the rough edges of the plaques. In time these cells form a clot, and eventually the clot becomes large enough to plug the blood vessel; a portion of the clot may break loose and plug a smaller vessel. Once this occurs, the circulation of fresh blood stops and the brain tissue supplied by the affected vessel is seriously damaged or dies. About 80% of all major strokes are due to such a process. The degree of damage depends on the size of the artery that is plugged and its location.

The remaining 20% of cerebrovascular accidents are caused by blowouts (hemorrhages) frequently associated with high blood pressure (hypertension) or with weak spots (aneurysms) that may have been present since birth. At times such aneurysms cause the premature and unexpected deaths of young persons in apparently good health.

Warnings and prevention

What type of symptom may be present if a person has a transient ischemic attack? Probably only the most fleeting numbness, dizziness, or interference with vision. Researchers at the Mayo Clinic in Rochester, Minn., have found, however, that such advance warnings have probably occurred in 40% of all people who later have serious strokes. Reports from some medical centers show early symptoms at a frequency of 10%; others find them as high as 75%. Other illnesses can produce similar symptoms, however.

Besides numbness, dizziness (vertigo) is one of the most common danger signals. It must, however, be distinguished from lightheadedness, which is much more frequent. Dizziness means an actual change in the ability to walk. A person may stagger and have to stop and hold on to something. Objects may seem to whirl about, and the individual may feel as if he is walking on a moving train. Lightheadedness, on the other hand, is less severe. It involves being a little unsteady for two or three seconds when changing position quickly while getting up from a bed or jumping up from a chair.

If potential serious stroke victims know that their bodies are warning them with such symptoms, can they do anything? Is prevention possible? In general, experts know that there are four predisposing factors for strokes: (1) high amounts of blood fats (hyperlipidemia); (2) hypertension; (3) heart disease; and (4) diabetes.

Assume a person's history reveals two of these four factors: hyperlipidemia and hypertension. His cholesterol has been high for years. He is taking medication for high blood pressure and is 35 pounds overweight. How do such health problems come about and then cause a transient ischemic attack? Like many others, such a person probably eats far too much food that is high in animal fats. He knows about cholesterol but finds excuses for not changing his diet. In such a person blood cholesterol is high. Over the years the fat in the food becomes deposited in the vessels of the brain, and a large plaque begins to form.

The patient's blood pressure is high, and he takes medication regularly. But he does not lose the weight his doctor orders and finds it difficult to stay away from salty snacks. He needs to limit the salt in his diet but does not realize that most Americans eat ten times more salt than they need. Excessive salt retains water in the tissues and is an important forerunner of hypertension.

The patient's blood pressure is, however, a signal in another important way; it may show he is under unresolved stress. He probably needs more than medicine to keep his body in harmony with the world around him. He needs regular exercise, preferably daily hiking or jogging. He might learn a form of meditation, yoga, or another method of relaxing. All are helpful skills that teach how to minimize the tension common in people with high blood pressure.

Why does such a person have a transient ischemic attack and not a serious stroke? The best guess is that the degree of plugging that occurs in the vessel is small enough that complete blocking does not occur. His blood pressure is not high enough to cause a blowout. Such a person may well have a stroke, and its attendant miseries, however, unless something is done.

What can such a patient do to prevent a major stroke? There are studies that can be done by nerve specialists (neurologists) and X-ray specialists (radiologists) that may help in evaluating the illness. A standard workup by his personal physician or by a specialist might include tests for sedimentation rate, fasting blood sugar, cholesterol, triglycerides, and prothrombin time. He should have a physical examination and might have other studies such as a brain wave test (an electroencephalogram), X-rays of the skull and of the arteries of the neck and the head, and possibly a remarkable new test, a brain scan by computerized axial tomography. Such tests frequently help in establishing a diagnosis and proposing treatment for patients.

Normal Arterial Circulation to the Brain

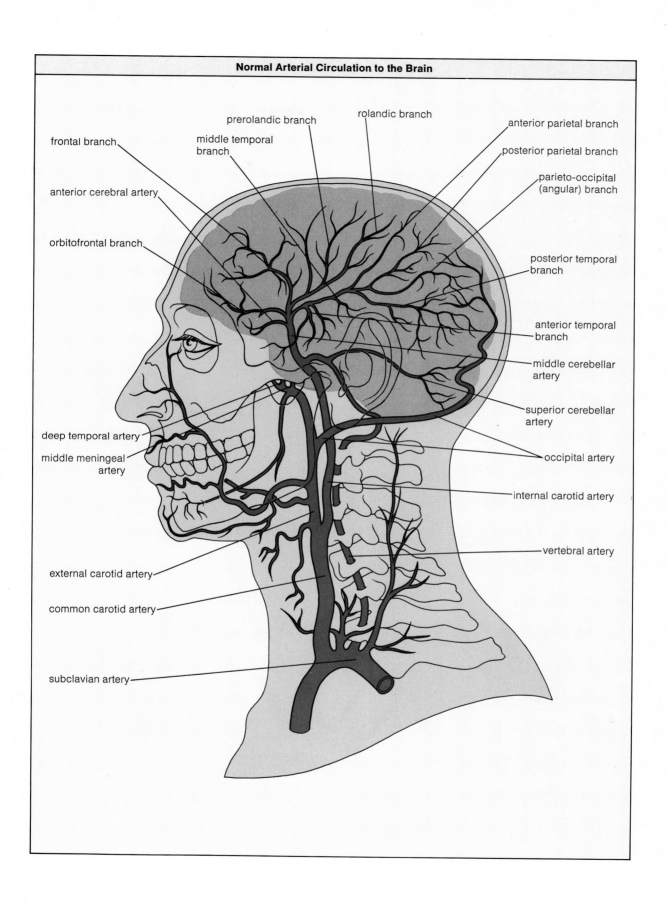

frontal branch

anterior cerebral artery

orbitofrontal branch

prerolandic branch

middle temporal branch

rolandic branch

anterior parietal branch

posterior parietal branch

parieto-occipital (angular) branch

posterior temporal branch

anterior temporal branch

middle cerebellar artery

superior cerebellar artery

deep temporal artery

middle meningeal artery

occipital artery

internal carotid artery

vertebral artery

external carotid artery

common carotid artery

subclavian artery

Stroke

The treatment could include special diets, blood thinners (anticoagulants), vessel expanders (vasodilators), or perhaps surgery to replace a blood vessel. Each treatment depends on the location and extent of involvement, the age of the patient, and the history of the condition.

Treatment

What if a stroke occurs? It is absolutely necessary that the victim be hospitalized for observation and appropriate treatment. It is necessary to call an ambulance or rescue squad because all patients with strokes should be carefully evaluated by a specialist. If a stroke occurs at home, there are necessary steps to take. If the stroke seems to be a major one, maintain an open airway and place the patient on his side so that secretions will drain from his mouth; give mouth-to-mouth resuscitation if necessary. Do not give the victim fluids by mouth unless he is conscious and able to swallow normally. Keep the victim at rest. If the stroke seems to be a minor one, protect the victim against accident or physical exertion and keep the victim at rest.

For the person who recovers from a major stroke, there may be a stay of several days or more in a hospital followed by a few months of convalescence, including physical therapy. Rehabilitation can allow some patients to be mobile again, perhaps with the aid of a walker or other device, and to take care of their daily needs. Many people survive serious strokes and are able to live independently afterward.

— *Keith W. Sehnert, M.D.*

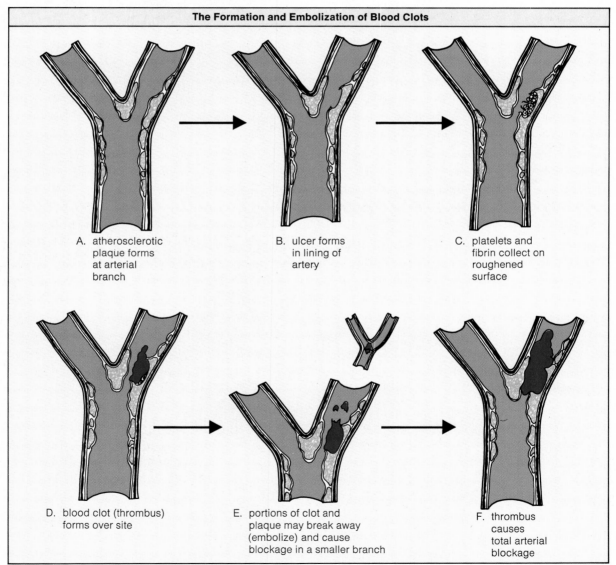

The Formation and Embolization of Blood Clots

A. atherosclerotic plaque forms at arterial branch

B. ulcer forms in lining of artery

C. platelets and fibrin collect on roughened surface

D. blood clot (thrombus) forms over site

E. portions of clot and plaque may break away (embolize) and cause blockage in a smaller branch

F. thrombus causes total arterial blockage

Adapted with permission from an original painting by Frank H. Netter, M.D., from *Clinical Symposia*, © CIBA Pharmaceutical Company, Division of CIBA-GEIGY Corporation

Health Education Unit 13

Abdominal Pain

Abdominal pain can be a symptom of one of three problems: (1) an acute abdominal condition, potentially an emergency that requires immediate action; (2) a chronic organic condition; or (3) a nervous stomach (a functional disorder).

Categorizing abdominal pain would be much simpler if pain and tenderness were always felt over or at the site of the trouble, but such is not usually the case. Pain may start at one site but then shift (radiate) elsewhere through complex pain pathways, making it difficult not only for the patient but also for the physician to unravel the cause.

Referred pain—originating in one part of the abdomen but felt in another, more distant site—follows complicated patterns. It is necessary to understand the origin of the various organs (embryologic development) in order to explain the pathways involved. Referred pain patterns are based in part on the similar origins of some of the surface skin and certain internal organs.

All of the complex parts of the adult body originate from three simple layers of cells in the embryo: the ectoderm (outer layer), the mesoderm (middle layer), and the endoderm (inner layer). Most of the ectoderm cells end up in the adult body's outermost tissues, the skin, hair, and nails, but some are found in the brain and the nervous system. The mesoderm cells develop into the skeleton, bone marrow, muscles, heart, blood cells, blood vessels, kidneys, and sexual organs. The endoderm cells form the linings of nearly all of the internal organs such as the lungs, trachea, pharynx, and digestive tract, including the pancreas, liver, and gallbladder.

Two common examples of referred pain are those related to the gallbladder and the heart. Understanding the embryologic origins of these two organs helps explain why the pain is "referred" to a seemingly distant area. When, for example, a person has a gallstone in the tube leading from the gallbladder (an organ in the right front of the abdominal cavity under the ribs), he feels pain in the back on the right side of the chest. Gallbladder pain is referred to the rear chest because that part of the chest wall and the gallbladder originated from endodermal cells quite close to each other. Only as embryonic growth occurred did the chest wall and gallbladder become more distant.

In heart disease, particularly disease associated with a heart attack (myocardial infarction), pain is felt in the left shoulder and arm, although the heart

is in the front of the chest. The explanation is that both areas originated from mesodermal cells that in the early days of the development of the embryo were adjacent to each other but with growth ended up relatively far apart.

The type of abdominal pain one is experiencing can be a helpful guide to understanding its origin, and probably gives more information than the location of the pain. The general burning pain of a perforated peptic ulcer contrasts with the sharp, breathtaking pain of gallbladder (biliary) colic that comes for a while and then subsides in a regular pattern. The gripping pain of intestinal obstruction differs from the tearing sensation of a ballooning of the wall of the abdominal aorta (aneurysm). The increasingly severe right lower abdominal ache of acute appendicitis can be distinguished from the constant ache of kidney infection (pyelonephritis).

The origin of abdominal pain is complex. In the walls and linings of the stomach, intestines, and various organs in the abdomen, there is no sensation of touch as there is in the skin. It is possible to

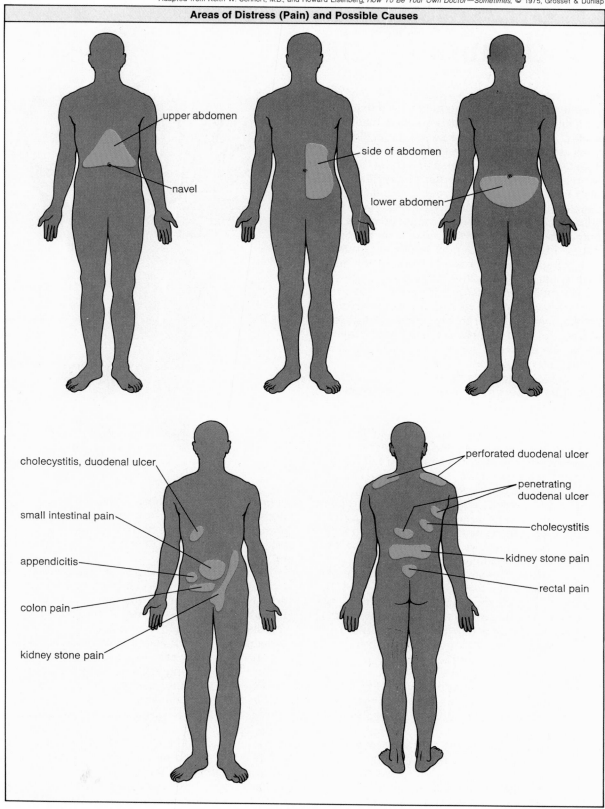

Adapted from Keith W. Sehnert, M.D., and Howard Eisenberg, *How To Be Your Own Doctor—Sometimes,* © 1975, Grosset & Dunlap

Areas of Distress (Pain) and Possible Causes

upper abdomen

navel

side of abdomen

lower abdomen

cholecystitis, duodenal ulcer

small intestinal pain

appendicitis

colon pain

kidney stone pain

perforated duodenal ulcer

penetrating duodenal ulcer

cholecystitis

kidney stone pain

rectal pain

Patterns of Pain	
type	visualization
cramps	
constant ache	
intermittent colic	
constant colic	

crush, tear, or cut intestine without causing pain; but if intestines stretch or balloon up (distend), they produce severe pain.

In evaluating abdominal pain, the history and details of the pain are most important. Laboratory tests and X-rays can be helpful, but the story you tell your doctor is usually the key to his decision as to whether the pain may require immediate hospitalization—and perhaps surgery—or whether it is symptomatic of a less serious disorder. The following self-help instructions for analyzing abdominal pain will give you a plan. With such a plan there is less reason to panic.

Analyzing abdominal pain

Describing pain is difficult. Pain scares people and usually hurts enough to make it difficult to describe. If a pain has never occurred before, there is nothing to compare it with. Ability to describe pain also depends on your physical self-awareness, degree of articulateness, and pain threshold. Although it may be difficult under the misery of the situation, an exact description is often vital. Your goal should be better than that frequent complaint, "Oh, Doctor, it just hurts all over!" It is important to be able to tell where. There are some helpful locations for most cases of abdominal pain that every person should know.

There are four types of pain: cramps, constant ache, intermittent colicky pain, and constant colicky pain. Cramps are short term, poorly localized,

and episodic. When mild, they are probably insignificant. The most common cause is stomach flu (gastroenteritis). Cramps may be associated with nausea, vomiting, faintness, or even mild panic, which may be more upsetting than the pain itself.

Constant ache is pain that steadily rises in intensity. It is comparable to a toothache. An example is the pain caused by a swollen, inflamed gallbladder. Constant ache may also suggest a condition of chronic swelling, as occurs in pancreatic disease.

Intermittent colicky pain increases to a maximum and then relents. After an entirely pain-free interval that may be short or long, the cycle is repeated. It may be associated with mechanical obstruction of the intestine.

Constant colicky pain has a variable degree of intensity, but there is always some pain present. It comes in waves and is typically observed in obstruction secondary to kidney or gallbladder stones. There are also several factors that can cause pain or make it worse. They include eating, problems with specific foods, bowel movements, breathing, physical activity, and nervousness.

Eating. Probably the most significant feature of the pain associated with peptic ulcer is its tendency to occur one to four hours after meals. The pain can be present day after day for weeks and months. Distress three to five hours after eating, once or twice monthly, may be caused by gallbladder disease. Pain within minutes after eating may be caused by reduced size of the stomach. Diseases to

379

be considered are cancer of the stomach, hernia of the stomach (hiatal hernia), inflammation of the stomach wall (gastritis), and similar problems.

Specific food problems. Fatty foods such as butter, salad dressing, and rich pork can cause gallbladder tenderness and pain by stimulating the flow of bile from the liver. Foods high in fat cause release of hormones in the mucous surface of the stomach and upper small bowel (duodenum) that in turn cause the muscle of the gallbladder wall to contract and empty. If the gallbladder and its emptying tube (duct) are normal, the bile moves smoothly on its way. A gallstone in the duct, however, can block the flow, and the pressure of the bile trying to move through the duct causes pain. Roughage from fresh vegetables or fruit can cause or aggravate lower abdominal pain in people with diverticulitis or irritable colon. Food allergies also may trigger gastrointestinal irritation.

Bowel movement or passage of gas. If lower abdominal pain is relieved by a bowel movement, a functional disorder such as nervous or irritable colon may be present. Some painful conditions, one classic example being appendicitis, may be started by excessive use of laxatives.

Breathing. Pain that is aggravated by deep breathing suggests disease of the diaphragm muscles separating the chest from the abdomen. Examples are inflammation of the gallbladder (cholecystitis) or a rupturing (perforating) stomach ulcer.

Physical effort. Definite relationships between position and pain exist with a sliding hiatal hernia. This type of hernia develops when there is an enlarged hole (hernia) in the umbrella-like muscle (diaphragm) that plays a key role in breathing and also serves as a divider between the chest and the abdominal cavities. The diaphragm is normally penetrated by a small hole in its middle through which the gullet (esophagus) passes into the upper stomach. If an injury (such as a blow to the abdomen in a car accident which forces the body against the steering wheel) or a normal event (such as pregnancy or labor) creates pressure that enlarges the hole, a hiatal hernia develops. Pain occurs when a person lies down at night and is relieved when he gets up and moves about.

Nervousness. Intense pain is more frequently caused by serious organic disease while milder pain is commonly due to nervous (functional) disorders. Nervousness can cause pain by increasing the frequency and the force of normal muscle contractions. Certain types of people, particularly tall slender people (ectomorphs), are more often bothered by functional disorders than are others. Stressful situations that make such people nervous are likely to cause nausea, vomiting, or diarrhea. Even mild stress may cause minor forms of gastro-intestinal symptoms such as cramping and the distresses of excess stomach acid, bloating, and other discomforts. If pain is closely related to emotional distress, there is a strong likelihood that the classification is functional. The final diagnosis of functional gastrointestinal disease must be based on the exclusion of organic illness and requires careful evaluation by a doctor.

Consulting a physician

You should contact a physician after you have noted the pattern and intensity of abdominal pain and have recorded the history of possible causes. Other information that may be useful to a doctor, such as a record of temperature and pulse taken on several occasions, should also be noted.

During an attack of abdominal pain, and while you are following the above plan, you should (1) limit all fluid intake to ice chips or small sips of water; (2) assume a position of comfort and rest quietly, in bed if possible; (3) avoid any laxatives or enemas.

With insight into the possible causes of abdominal pain and a better understanding of how to observe and describe the symptoms and signs, you have a plan. It is the first step in avoiding panic and perhaps an unnecessary visit to an emergency room or a surgeon's office.

—Keith W. Sehnert, M.D.

Your Medicine Chest: Friend or Foe?

For many years, I used a strategy that my new patients must have thought quite strange. Following our get-acquainted visit, I would make this request: "Before you come in for your next appointment, empty your home medicine chest, put everything in a sturdy shopping bag, and bring it to my office. I want to examine the medications and supplies you keep there."

I learned a great deal about my patients this way, and I think they learned a lot, too. The medicine bottles they toted in gave me many insights into their medical history: the number of doctors they had seen in the past few years, the kind of compliance I might expect—and most interestingly, the kind of person I had sitting across the desk from me. Likewise, my patients discovered what I thought about medications in general and learned something about my prescribing habits. Of course, they also had an opportunity to clean out their medicine chests, something far too few of us get around to doing.

About half of the patients had accumulated the usual mix of aspirin, antacid tablets, cold tablets, sleeping pills, mouthwashes, adhesive bandages, corn plasters, over-the-counter (OTC) cough medicines, and a few half-finished antibiotic prescriptions. The other half varied widely in their habits, and I came to group them into four classes: (1) those with too much medicine; (2) those with too little medicine; (3) those who keep all their medicines too long; and (4) those with a middle-ground attitude toward drugs who simply want instructions about what they should keep in the medicine chest and how to store and use medicine properly.

The people in the first category usually have at least five varieties of vitamin E, a large bottle of vitamin C tablets, iron and yeast preparations, miscellaneous tonics, and an array of antacids and laxatives. In addition to the OTC preparations, they have a hefty assortment of prescription drugs. A close examination of the labels on their prescription medications reveals that they tend to be "doctor hoppers" and go from one physician to another.

Individuals who just don't like taking medicine at all will often become offended if I ask them to bring in the contents of their medicine cabinet. Some have a deep-seated fear of any illness. I try to persuade them that both regular checkups and the proper use of medicines, when needed, are an integral part of restoring good health.

With patients who keep their medicines too long, I ask why they save everything. They confide that although they know the medications are not as fresh as they once were, if, by some chance, we have a sudden disaster, war, or general holocaust, and all the drugstores are destroyed, then slightly stale antibiotics will be better than none at all!

I use such occasions to explain that most antibiotics rapidly lose their potency after a month or so at room temperature (the moisture present in the bathroom contributes to the medication's chemical breakdown). Then I spend a few minutes explaining what should be kept in the medicine chest at home and what should be thrown away. This way, if someone needs help in the middle of a cold winter's night or on a long Fourth of July weekend when all the drugstores are closed, at least the medicine chest will be a friend, not a foe.

Some guidelines to follow

Many patients want rules about storing and using current medications and discarding old or un-

381

necessary ones. Unfortunately, even when medications are clearly and correctly labeled by name, there remain many questions about exactly how and when they should be taken. Some drugs should be taken with meals, for instance, while others lose their effectiveness unless taken on an empty stomach. Most antibiotics, to cite an example, are best taken at least an hour before meals; many should not be taken with milk or fruit juice and should never be taken in combination with antacid preparations. Blood-building medications and iron supplements may be taken immediately before, with, or just after meals but also should not be combined with antacids. Anticholinergic preparations, as a general rule, are taken within 30 minutes before eating.

Many different classes of drugs, including analgesics (painkillers), antihistamines, and tranquilizers, can cause drowsiness. The patient taking such medications should avoid alcohol and other substances that act as central nervous system depressants and should exercise extra care in activities (driving a car, operating machinery) that require alertness and good coordination. Alcohol should also be avoided by anyone taking sedatives, insulin, or nitroglycerin; certain antidepressants—the MAO (monoamine oxidase) inhibitors, in particular—do not mix with alcohol.

Some patients are in the habit of keeping unused portions of medications long after the need for the drugs has passed. They keep a few remaining pills, a half-used tube of ointment for months or even years, unaware that many drugs lose their effectiveness within a relatively short time. The liquid forms of several common antibiotics, for example, lose their potency in about two weeks. Certain antibiotic drops and ointments retain their effectiveness for only about ten days. Nitroglycerin, commonly used in treatment of angina pectoris, is an extremely unstable substance; to prevent nitroglycerin tablets from decomposing, the patient should store them in the original container and take care to close the container tightly immediately after each use.

These are only general guidelines to the kinds of rules and precautions to be followed by anyone taking prescription drugs. For specific advice about any medication you may be taking, you should, of course, consult your own physician.

To keep or not to keep

Let's run down a few tips for cleaning out your cabinets. This process should eliminate some dangerous products that you have accumulated over the years. Then there will be enough room to stock your medicine chest with basic supplies and medications. Follow the step-by-step procedure outlined here. First, sort the medications into two

---

Basic Items for Your Medicine Chest

Medications

antihistamine, oral-nasal decongestant tablets
24 tablets

nasal decongestant drops or spray
1 fluid oz each in child and adult strengths

expectorant·cough preparation
4 oz

aspirin or buffered aspirin
100 tablets

acetaminophen (analgesic, aspirin substitute)
100 tablets

mouthwash and gargle
14 fluid oz

ear wax softener
½ fluid oz

antibacterial skin ointment
1 oz

calamine lotion (for itchy conditions)
4 fluid oz

antacid
12 fluid oz

motion sickness remedy
12 tablets

bulk laxatives
30 packets

petroleum jelly
7½ oz

Supplies

adhesive strips for small wounds
mixed sizes

adhesive tape
½-inch and 2-inch sizes

anti-infective skin cleanser
1 fluid oz

gauze dressing
mixed sizes

bandages (regular and nonadhesive)
mixed sizes

groups: prescription drugs (those bearing drug labels with your doctor's name) and nonprescription, OTC products. Then, beginning with the prescription medications, examine each container and ask these questions:

1. Is the name of the drug included on the label —for example, Benadryl, Lomotil, Achromycin?

2. Are instructions for frequency of use and correct dosage clearly typed on the label?

3. If the product is applied with a medicine dropper, does the label give exact directions for administration?

4. If you have small children in the house, does the medication have a child-proof top?

5. If you are a senior citizen or if your vision is poor, can you read the label in dim light? Has the typing faded?

6. Have any special warnings that the doctor gave you verbally been transferred to the label in writing (e.g., "Do not take blue tabs if you have had alcohol," "Don't drive while taking the speckled capsules.")?

7. Do you still suffer from the medical condition for which the drug was originally prescribed?

If the answer to any of these questions is "no," throw away the medication or have it checked by your pharmacist or doctor. Make sure each container is properly labeled before you put it back in the medicine chest.

Now look at the OTC products and ask these questions:

1. Has your doctor checked your blood and told you that you need this iron supplement?

2. If the product is for sleep, have you honestly explored ways to improve your sleeping habits—by getting more exercise or planning a better bedtime ritual—so that you don't need sleeping pills? Have you talked to your doctor about why you can't get to sleep?

3. Have you read the fine print on the label so that you understand the warnings and precautions?

4. If the product is an antacid, do you know which foods or beverages cause the indigestion? Have you tried to control the problem by avoiding the offending substances instead of resorting to pills?

5. If you are in the habit of taking a laxative every day, have you tried going without it and, instead, supplementing your diet with bulk foods that contain fiber and also with more juices and other fluids? Are you exercising daily?

6. If you have a sizable stock of cold and cough remedies, have you given up smoking and continued to avoid other irritating smoke and fumes that can contribute to postnasal drip and cough? Is there a history of allergies in your family, and if so, have you consulted a doctor about your condition to rule out the possibility that something other than the common cold is causing your symptoms?

In any case where the answer to these questions is "no," you should discard the drug or seek professional help for your problems.

The remaining medications may be put back in the chest, with all container tops secure. Get a small box for miscellaneous first-aid supplies, and put it in the medicine chest for easy access. Never throw away a bottle or container of unused drugs. Instead, discard your excess medications by flushing them down the toilet or putting them in the garbage-disposal unit; bottles or containers should be empty when they go into the wastebasket. By following this clean-out, shape-up program for your medicine chest, you and your family will have a "friend" the next time there's a need.

—*Keith W. Sehnert, M.D.*

Yoga
for Health and Happiness

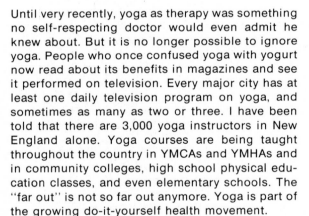

Until very recently, yoga as therapy was something no self-respecting doctor would even admit he knew about. But it is no longer possible to ignore yoga. People who once confused yoga with yogurt now read about its benefits in magazines and see it performed on television. Every major city has at least one daily television program on yoga, and sometimes as many as two or three. I have been told that there are 3,000 yoga instructors in New England alone. Yoga courses are being taught throughout the country in YMCAs and YMHAs and in community colleges, high school physical education classes, and even elementary schools. The "far out" is not so far out anymore. Yoga is part of the growing do-it-yourself health movement.

A good many physicians, including myself, have taken yoga courses. Although we do not understand exactly why and how yoga works, we do find a lot of body wisdom in it. Unlike exercises that aim at producing muscle strength or bulk, yoga seeks to stretch muscles and keep joints mobile. People who have tried yoga find that it works. If something is therapeutic, it is foolish to dismiss it as without merit simply because of its nonmedical origins.

Yoga is a Sanskrit word meaning "union." In his book *Yoga and Medicine,* Stephen F. Brena explains that yoga has religious implications but that it "stands first for the correction of human dysharmonies into a harmonious unity." The philosophical system called yoga, one of the three great systems of Hindu philosophy, is said to seek glorification of God in man. Karma Yoga is the

"yoga of action"; Mahatma Gandhi was its greatest modern disciple. Raja Yoga, the "yoga of self-realization," involves superior psychophysical training. Hatha Yoga, the "yoga of health," is the most popular form of yoga in the Western world.

My reasons for signing up for a Hatha Yoga course at a YMCA were twofold. When patients of mine who had heard of yoga or tried it wanted my medical opinion, it was embarrassing not to have one. They would say things like "Doctor, when I do the Lotus position, I get a little pain in my back. Could yoga be bad for me, or am I just doing it wrong?" or "You know, ever since I started yoga, I don't have that nervous stomach I used to have." I had a personal interest as well. Since falling off a 20-foot obstacle course wall while in the Navy in World War II, I have had back problems. I had considered surgery twice, but rejected it because of possible bad results. So I took the course not just to answer my patients' questions but also to see if there was something in it for me.

Like others, I had been suspicious of yoga. I thought it was part of an exotic foreign religion. Actually, yoga has two identities. One is the physical; the other is spiritual and philosophical.

A few words here about this spiritual dimension are necessary. In all the Eastern philosophies and religions, including Buddhism, Taoism, and Hinduism—and it is within Hinduism that yoga developed—there is a common theme of "spiritual hardiness." This comes from practicing self-reliance, personal hardiness, and self-sufficiency. Such

385

spiritual hardiness is gained from long periods of meditation, prayer, and living close to earth, living more simply and more responsibly. It involves union or "oneness" between nature and individual. (It should be noted that such spiritual dimensions are not limited to Eastern philosophies but are essential parts of those practiced by American Indians such as the Hopi, Shoshone, and others.) The methods used in Hatha Yoga that help individuals learn body control (and spiritual insight) involve deep, slow breathing exercises in rhythm with certain body postures.

Do not let the names of the postures put you off. What I might call a rocking exercise, practitioners of yoga (yogi) label the Locust. What I describe as lying on your back, they identify as the Corpse. What I might call arching my back, yogi call the Cobra. The names are a bit dramatic, but they are useful. The names paint images for people to duplicate. What could be more fluid or graceful than the movements of a cobra?

Right now, for example, what are you doing? You are sitting in a chair. Maybe your legs are crossed, cutting off circulation. Your knees and elbow are bent. If you were in an office or ironing, your back would be bent too, over a desk or table. This is your position whether you are driving a car or working at a hobby. Though relaxing, you are not relaxed. Many yoga exercises are the anatomic opposites to these positions we live our lives in.

How yoga works

Yoga encourages spinal mobility. Your spine is unique, the only sliding joint in the body. It can slide in five directions: to the front, to the back, to the left, to the right, and twist like a corkscrew.

To demonstrate the examples of movement in these five different directions, try these exercises:

To the front: Assume the Cobra position as shown in Figure 1. This causes hyperextension of your spine and the lumbar vertebrae slide forward a bit.

To the back: Now sit on the floor with your legs outstretched in front of you. As you reach out and touch your toes, lumbar vertebrae move backward.

To the left: Stand upright with your hands on your hips. Now bend your upper body sideways to the right. The bones of your spine slide to the left.

To the right: Reverse the above exercise and there is movement to the right.

Twist like a corkscrew: Assume the spinal twist position as seen in Figure 2. As your arms encircle your body to the left or to the right, your vertebrae have twisted like a corkscrew.

By our 20th birthday, most of us have stopped using the spine except to bend forward to tie our shoelaces. Many yoga exercises loosen up the ligaments and muscles in the back, giving us greater flexibility and preventing the stiffness that results from lack of stretching and exercise. If children took up yoga and used it all their lives, they would be more limber adults, not predestined to the stooped shoulders and potbellies we automatically associate with the middle-aged and elderly.

Breathing—the simplest, most natural process in the world—is another thing yoga focuses on. People do not breathe very well anymore. It may just be an urban defense mechanism, but I find that patients, particularly women, who tend to take little shallow breaths, have forgotten how to breathe. Yoga gets you to lie down on the floor and gradually elevate your arms until your hands are held over your head, while you do nothing more demanding than inhale slowly for, say, 30 seconds. By the time you are at the top of your breath, your belly is pushed out to look like you are six months pregnant. Then as you exhale, you slowly lower your arms, sucking in your abdominal wall until it almost touches your spine. Simple? Sure. But it moves the diaphragm and whole respiratory system almost 100%. It blows out the old air and draws in the new.

Is yoga medically sound? Well, we know, for instance, that if muscles are tense, we not only get fatigued but also our blood vessels become con-

Figure 1. The position known as the Cobra, which extends the neck and spine and opens the muscles of the chest, is especially beneficial in correcting poor posture.

Figure 2. The spinal twist is an exercise for maintaining flexibility of the spine.

stricted. Learn to relax them and your blood pressure goes down. The heart does not have to work as hard pumping blood through relaxed arteries, and with the whole vascular system less tense, the pulse slows. Western physicians are beginning to see this yoga wisdom.

I have seen yoga help people relax tensions, tone up physiques, and reduce smoking and drinking. I find patients with gastrointestinal problems, nervous stomach, peptic ulcer, headaches, and backaches getting dramatic relief from yoga. I know this sounds like a television commercial and I know it is only anecdotal evidence with no clinical trials to cite to support it, but the results of yoga are positive. There are, of course, no instant medical or metaphysical miracles. And if any yogi promises them, he is not a yogi but just an exploitative promoter. Yoga has to be learned, however, like swimming or painting. You simply do not take a yoga lesson or two. It takes weeks and even months of learning to do yoga well.

Once my patients have learned to do the relaxing exercises, I prescribe yoga for convenient periods. I may instruct a businessman with a nervous stomach to take 15 or 20 minutes off his lunch hour for deep breathing exercises and a shoulder stand at the office. Later in the afternoon, say at 4 P.M. when he is tight and tense and mad at the world, I tell him to turn off the lights, lie down on the floor in the Corpse position and practice stretching his arms, neck, and back muscles. Some patients have been able to stop using tranquilizers and get rid of stomach and headache complaints. I practice what I prescribe. When an executive tells me how busy he is, I can look him right in the eye and say, "I'll match your schedule with mine any day for being busy. I find time at noon, and I set aside a half-hour before I go to bed too." Then what can he say? Only, "Okay, I'll give it a try."

Some cases

One patient with back problems is a good example of what yoga can accomplish. She had been to family doctors, orthopedic surgeons, osteopaths, and chiropractors. She had gotten all kinds of laymen's advice too. But she was having persistent pain in the back, and nothing seemed to help it. Back pain is bad enough for someone in his sixties; for a 21-year-old, it is a disaster.

Because someone had told her that I taught my patients to do yoga for their back conditions, she came to see me. I immediately put her through my regular medical tests to check her muscle strength and range of motion—things like bending to each side, touching the toes, doing push-ups, and raising and lowering the legs from the prone position. She was weak and tight on every test. I found that one of her legs was slightly shorter than the other, something that students of yoga are acquainted with and refer to when discussing spinal health. I ordered a quarter-inch heel lift for one shoe and gave her some simple exercise instructions. She did not get overnight results, but each week she felt a little better. And, after 18 months of pain before coming to see me, in about 18 weeks she was well. She is getting along fine, doing yoga exercises for her back every night, and could not be happier.

Tension headaches can be helped by yoga too. Another of my patients is the busy wife of a foreign diplomat and is on the Washington, D.C., social merry-go-round. It is her national obligation, almost a patriotic duty, to attend formal, often dull, diplomatic dinners and parties and to entertain and engage in small talk no matter how bad she feels. At my suggestion, she took a yoga course. Now, whenever she feels a headache coming on, she lies down and breathes deeply to relax. She then sits up and does neck exercises—putting her chin on her right shoulder, then moving it to her left shoulder, then onto her chest, then arching it back to look at the ceiling—followed by a shoulder stand. Before, her only option was to take a very strong pain medication, grit her teeth, and smile painfully through a headache. Now she is able to control the headaches.

387

Yoga for health and happiness

Insomnia is another problem that can be treated by yoga. One of my patients is an elderly lady who was living on sleeping pills and other potions she had picked up over the sleepless years. Part of her problem was that she did not understand that the body loves ritual. After I had evaluated her, I decided that, first, she did not get enough exercise. Second, the longer she thought about going to bed, knowing she was just going to toss and turn, the tenser she got. I gave her a different kind of medication, getting her to follow a strict yoga ritual at a time of day when interruptions or phone calls were unlikely.

Her bedtime is usually 10:30 or so. She takes a relaxing bath around 9:30, and goes down to her front room around 10:00 for yoga exercises. The television and radio are turned off; there is a dim light in the next room. She lies down on a towel on the rug and begins her ritual: (1) the Corpse—lying on the floor with her mind turned off, just breathing deeply, thinking of nothing; (2) straight leg raising; (3) the Twist; (4) the Cobra; and (5) a shoulder stand—which, by the way, even an older person can learn to do. By the time she has finished, she is relaxed, able to read 15 minutes and slide off to sleep. She has not touched a bottle of sleeping pills for more than a year.

Yoga has helped some of my hypertensive patients too. I have one patient who has been on medication for high blood pressure for some time. Now, when he is uptight—gritting his teeth, clenching his fists, tightening the muscles in the back of his neck—he just breathes slowly, relaxes from his toes up to his ears, and lowers his blood pressure. He does yoga exercises regularly, has substantially reduced his salt intake, and gets regular sleep. The combination of common sense and yoga has enabled him to significantly reduce his hypertension medication.

Americans, beset with bad habits, insomnia, financial worries, physical neglect, complain "I don't have time to think." Yet we consistently deprive ourselves of that time when it is available, plugging ourselves into newspapers on commuter trains and television sets in our living rooms. A recent study astounded me with the statistic that in 50 hours of work a week the average business executive spends only 19 minutes thinking. I believe that chauffeuring, housekeeping, and babysitting wives do not do much better. A session of yoga allows you time to think. It provides another psychological plus as well, for I am convinced personally that some of the depression we see today is related to poor circulation. I am persuaded that regular yoga exercises like shoulder stands, with their increase of blood flow to the brain, are likely to have some very positive therapeutic effects.

There is a lot more to yoga and other Eastern health theories than I have been able to explain briefly—much more than I, who only dabble in it, have taken the time to learn. There is, for example, transcendental meditation (TM), which induces a state of alert wakefulness that appears to be beneficial to the body. Studies exploring these positive benefits are now underway in several medical centers. Do-In, a Chinese system of self-massage based on acupuncture points, seems to be growing in popularity.

A considerable amount of religious fervor can accompany an interest in yoga—serious study of the *Yoga-sūtras* of Patañjali for the quest of the soul and the cultivation of *maitrī* ("friendliness") and *sukha* ("virtue"). I find that I have gotten all I need from practical, healthful yoga. But a book on yoga philosophy will show that it has a great deal ethically in common with Judeo-Christian ethics and morality. The heavily illustrated *Light on Yoga,* by B. K. S. Iyengar, is considered by many to be a thoughtful and comprehensive introductory text.

There are so many hardcover and pocket books available on yoga now that it is difficult to recommend any one in particular. Richard Hittleman, who produces a California television series called *Yoga and Health,* has written several. *Yoga and Medicine* by Stephen F. Brena merges yoga concepts with modern medical knowledge. A short book written for the general public, it presents physiological concepts and everyday examples that can be used in yoga. Lilias Folan has written a book called *Lilias, Yoga and You* that women seem to enjoy, with recommended exercises for 30 minutes a day.

Expect no miracles, but do not be surprised if you feel a lot better for practicing yoga, particularly if you have been taking tranquilizers for years. Many people get into yoga as a last resort. They say, "What am I doing to myself? Going to psychiatrists, paying $50 an hour, spending $10 a week for medicine, and I still feel terrible." I have known several patients who have turned all of that around.

Yoga is something different. I heartily recommend it—after competent instructions. You can even do it if you aren't in good shape. There are some hazards, though. Do not try any of the advanced positions before you are ready for them. And when you are ready for advanced positions, avoid distractions and other interruptions.

Some of the early hippie yogi of the 1960s seemed quite far out. But of late, yoga has stepped out of the counterculture and been embraced by many others. There may be something in it for you too.

—Keith W. Sehnert, M.D.

Health Education Unit 16
Basic Facts About Cancer

Until recent years, talking about cancer was almost taboo. The word *cancer* continues to cause fear, but today people are more willing to discuss the disease. The public has become better informed. Because there is no single cause of cancer, knowing about it and getting early diagnosis and treatment are essential. In the United States, cancer is second only to heart disease as a cause of death.

Who gets cancer?

In 1978, nearly 700,000 people will be diagnosed as having cancer—this figure excludes certain non-spreading diseases such as skin cancers and carcinoma *in situ* of the cervix. One-third of those presently afflicted with cancer will be alive in 1983. Fifty years ago, fewer than one-fifth of those with cancer would survive five years. With current medical knowledge and technology, the five-year survival rate will soon be increased to one-half.

Although cancer affects every age group from birth through old age, it is predominantly a disease of middle and old age. It affects both sexes, all races, and can involve all parts of the body. Skin cancer is the most common type of cancer for both men and women and most people with this type of cancer are successfully treated. Cancer is the second cause of death in children ages one to 14 years. Among women, common types of cancer include breast, colon/rectal, uterine, lung, and pancreatic cancers, and leukemia, while in men, common types are lung, prostate, colon/rectal, stomach, pancreatic, and bladder, and leukemia.

Traditionally, age-adjusted cancer mortality rates have been higher for whites than for blacks. The death rate from cancer of black males, however, has been rising more rapidly than that of white males. The rates for black women have remained constant, while those for white women have fallen slightly. The increase in cancer mortality statistics among the black population is due in part to improvements in diagnosis; it may also reflect increased exposure to environmental pollutants and changes in occupation and life-style.

What is cancer?

People think of cancer as a single disease, but it is really many diseases with a common characteristic: uncontrolled cell growth and spread of abnormal

cells. Usually these cells build up into tumors which press upon, invade, and destroy normal tissues. If the spread of cancerous cells is not treated and controlled, it usually leads to death.

Malignant tumors generally share some common characteristics that include: (1) a higher rate of cell growth than that of the normal tissues from which the cancer originated; (2) failure to maintain the boundaries of normal tissues and organs; (3) microscopic appearance that resembles immature rather than mature tissues; and (4) tendency to spread to parts of the body distant from the site of the original cancer.

Despite these similarities, there are significant differences among the various forms of cancer. Proper diagnosis, correct treatment, and favorable outcome require the consideration of other important factors, *e.g.,* the location of the original tumor, the type of cell involved, the severity of the illness, the causes or situations that may have contributed to the abnormal cell growth, and the age and sex of the patient. At the present time, at least 100 different types of cancer have been classified.

389

What causes cancer?

There is no single cause of cancer. A focus of current research is the correlation between certain population groups and certain types of cancer. Risk factors under study—in addition to age, sex, and race, which have already been mentioned—are occupation, family history, personal habits, and environmental factors.

Occupation. The relationship of occupation to cancer was first observed in England in 1775 when scrotal cancer was found in higher than expected rates among chimney sweeps. Since then, many human cancers have been shown to be related to occupational exposure: bladder cancer in workers exposed to aniline dye; bone cancer in painters of radium luminous dials; lung cancers among certain industrial workers, caused by inhalation of chromium compounds, radioactive ores, asbestos, arsenic, and iron; skin cancer in persons who regularly handle certain products of coal, oil, shale, lignite, and petroleum; skin cancer, due to ultraviolet exposure, among farmers, sailors, and others with outdoor occupations; skin cancer and leukemia in workers exposed to radium and X-rays.

Family history. There is increased familial risk of cancer in some particular tissues. Women who have a family history of breast and ovarian cancers are at greater risk of these forms of the disease. For men, prostate cancer and colon/rectal cancers are more common if close relatives have familial polyposis (a condition characterized by multiple polyps) or if there is a long-standing history of ulcerative colitis. The risk of gastric cancer is also increased if there is a positive family history. Siblings of children with brain tumors and sarcomas are at greater risk of developing these tumors. Similarly, if one identical twin develops leukemia, the risk factors for the other twin increase.

Personal habits. The most prevalent habit associated with cancer is smoking. The association between cigarette smoking and lung cancer is so close that many people consider cigarette smoking a *cause* of lung cancer. Studies demonstrate, however, that smoking is a risk factor in the development of lung cancer and that the risk increases with the number of cigarettes smoked per day, the age at which the person started smoking, and the period of time that the habit has been continued. The recent increase in lung cancer among women is believed to be directly related to the increase in the number of women smokers over the past 25 years. Among pipe and cigar smokers, the risk of developing lung cancer is higher than for nonsmokers but significantly lower than for cigarette smokers. Death rates from lung cancer are lower among ex-cigarette smokers than among continuing smokers.

Smoking is also a significant factor in cancer of the larynx. The risk among pipe, cigar, and cigarette smokers is higher than among nonsmokers. Smoking is a factor in cancer of the mouth, and pipe smoking is related to cancer of the lip. Cigarette smoking is associated with the development of cancer of the esophagus. The combination of heavy alcohol consumption and cigarette smoking is associated with especially high rates of esophageal cancer. In addition, there is an association between cigarette smoking and cancer of the bladder in both men and women. Although many questions remain, it is clear that smoking has been identified as an important factor in several types of cancer, and that a significant reduction in smoking would result in a marked decrease in the death rate from these diseases.

Some forms of cancer can be linked with diet: iodine deficiency, for example, may be related to cancer of the thyroid. The highly refined Western diet, rich in starches and low in bulk, may be related to bowel cancer. Food additives or substitutes are evaluated by the U.S. Food and Drug Administration (FDA) and are ordered to be removed from the market if they are associated with a cancer risk. Recently certain food colorings and artificial sweeteners have been the targets of FDA bans, following reports linking these substances with tumors in laboratory animals. The connection between excessive alcohol consumption and cancer of the oral cavity, throat, larynx, and esophagus is an accepted fact.

Environmental factors. Air pollution from industrial wastes represents an important source of cancer-causing agents. Automobile exhausts and certain pesticides also may be carcinogens. Densely populated and industrialized areas are known to have higher cancer mortality rates than rural areas. This excess risk is probably related to a variety of factors including life-style (urban dwellers use more tobacco and alcohol), occupation (industrial pollutants), environment (air and water pollution), and, perhaps, other factors not yet identified.

Radiation is another cause of cancer in human beings. The connection has been demonstrated by the disproportionate incidence of cancer in populations exposed to radioactive substances in industry and medicine and fallout from tests of nuclear weapons. Patients treated with X-rays for noncancerous conditions have increased cancer risks. The survivors of the atomic bombs in Hiroshima and Nagasaki show a higher than average incidence of acute leukemia and malignant tumors.

The association between viruses and cancer remains somewhat mysterious. A number of animal tumors have been linked to infection by viruses, and a great deal of research is being done to dis-

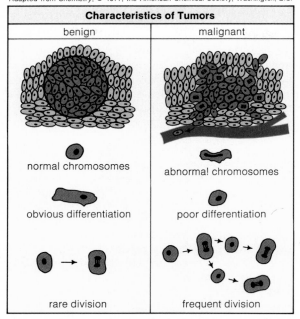

Characteristics of Tumors	
benign	malignant
normal chromosomes	abnormal chromosomes
obvious differentiation	poor differentiation
rare division	frequent division

cover if viruses can cause cancer in human beings. Discovery of a relationship between human cancers and particular viruses could lead to the development of protective vaccines. But it must be remembered that cancer is *not* contagious.

How is cancer detected?

Most cancers are diagnosed because an individual becomes aware of symptoms and seeks medical help. The American Cancer Society emphasizes the Seven Warning Signals. The signs do not necessarily mean that cancer is present, but they do indicate a need for medical attention. If you experience any of these signs or symptoms for more than two weeks, you should consult a physician: (1) a change in bowel or bladder habits; (2) a sore that does not heal; (3) unusual bleeding or discharge; (4) a thickening or lump in the breast or elsewhere; (5) indigestion or difficulty in swallowing; (6) an obvious change in a wart or a mole; and (7) nagging cough or hoarseness.

An important part of good health care practices is the individual's knowledge of what is usual for him. Periodic examinations of the skin, breasts, and mouth allow for the observation of potentially dangerous changes. Women over the age of 25 are advised to perform monthly self-examinations of their breasts and have an annual Pap smear taken from the cervix.

A diagnosis of cancer is confirmed with a biopsy, a procedure in which a small piece of tissue is removed from the patient's body and examined under a microscope. This is the only sure way of making an accurate diagnosis. There are other methods

of cancer detection. During the course of a physical examination, symptoms can be investigated and changes noted. At this time individuals having a family history of cancer should report this history to the physician. Special laboratory studies performed on blood and other body fluids may indicate the existence of cancer. There are also a number of X-ray procedures that aid in diagnosis, and many new instruments that allow a direct view of the insides of the various cavities. All of these tests help to determine if a tumor is present.

How is cancer treated?

Successful treatment of cancer involves removal or destruction of the tumor either by surgery, radiation, drugs, or a combination of techniques. These techniques are not equally effective for all forms of cancer. Some tumors can be destroyed only by radiation doses so high that healthy tissues would also be damaged; some cannot be entirely removed by surgery without destroying a vital organ. When no single technique suffices, combinations of surgery, radiation, and drugs offer a greater chance of complete destruction of the tumor and increase the term of survival.

Surgery. A great number of cancer patients are treated surgically. Because of increased knowledge and improved technology, patients who have surgery following early diagnosis have a better chance now than ever before for complete recovery and a return to normal activity. There are three categories of cancer surgery: specific, supportive, and preventive.

Specific surgery is the primary form of treatment to remove the entire tumor in cases of colon/rectal cancer and cancers of the breast, lung, stomach, bladder, prostate, cervix, and uterus. Supportive surgery is used to prolong life or to control pain or discomfort resulting directly or indirectly from the disease. Preventive surgery is performed to preclude the development of cancer by removing precancerous lesions such as polyps or moles. Currently research is being conducted to determine whether chemotherapy or radiation treatment given before, during, or after surgery will increase survival.

Radiation. Soon after radiation was discovered, scientists found that it was capable of damaging body tissue. Later it was discovered that radiation which could be tolerated by normal tissue was capable of causing considerable damage to cancer tissue, sometimes totally destroying the tumor. The radiation dose required to cure cancer must be large enough to destroy cancer cells but not so great as to permanently damage normal tissue around the cancer.

Radiotherapy for cancer may employ X-rays, ra-

391

Adapted from *Chemistry*, © 1977, the American Chemical Society, Washington, D.C.

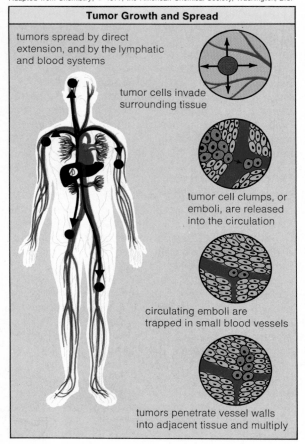

Tumor Growth and Spread

tumors spread by direct extension, and by the lymphatic and blood systems

tumor cells invade surrounding tissue

tumor cell clumps, or emboli, are released into the circulation

circulating emboli are trapped in small blood vessels

tumors penetrate vessel walls into adjacent tissue and multiply

dioactive isotopes, or atomic particles derived from radioactive materials. These forms of treatment are used for the cure of cancer or, when cure is not possible, for palliation. Radiotherapy may cure the following types of cancer: early and advanced cancer of the cervix; cancers of the head and neck, particularly those of the tongue and larynx; early stages of Hodgkin's disease (a disease of the lymph nodes); Ewing's sarcoma (a bone tumor); medulloblastoma (a brain tumor common in children); seminoma (a form of cancer of the testicle); and dysgerminoma (a cancer of the ovary). Palliative radiotherapy may reduce the size and delay the spread of cancers, heal ulcerating tumors, relieve obstruction or pain, and prevent tumor-caused bone fractures.

Chemotherapy. More than 40 drugs useful in the treatment of cancer have now been developed. Drugs can produce cures in about 15% of the cases; in the other 85%, drugs can temporarily stop the growth of the cancer, relieve pain, and allow the patient to live a longer, more comfortable life.

Several different types of drugs are used in chemotherapy. The purpose of all anticancer drugs is to interfere with the growth of the abnormal cell.

Unfortunately, anticancer drugs affect cells that normally divide rapidly, as well as tumor cells; normal cells, however, have a tremendous capacity to repair themselves and return to a normal state. Anticancer drugs can be given individually or in combination. Research studies have shown better results—and no increase in the injury to normal tissue—when several drugs are combined. Anticancer drugs are also used in conjunction with radiation therapy and surgery.

The success of chemotherapy in producing cures or prolonging survival was first noted in treatment of leukemia, Hodgkin's disease, and lymphosarcoma. Anticancer drugs are now used to treat many forms of cancer: Wilms's tumor (a childhood cancer of the kidney); neuroblastoma (a tumor of the nervous system); and some cancers of the lung, ovary, breast, colon, and testis. The length of time and the frequency of a course of chemotherapy depends upon the nature of the cancer, the types of drugs taken, body response, and side effects. Common side effects include decreased production of blood cells, temporary loss of hair, weakness, nausea, vomiting, and diarrhea. The patient must be watched closely so that the drugs can be stopped temporarily if these effects are too severe.

What can you do about cancer?

The best protection against cancer is knowledge about your body. Changes that occur and persist beyond two weeks should be reported to a knowledgeable health professional. It is important that you know your pertinent family medical history and that you pass this information on to your physician. People who work in occupations associated with increased cancer risk must follow designated safety precautions and should act to get such precautions instituted where they are not yet in effect. Nonsmokers should not start; cigarette smokers should stop, change to a pipe or cigar, or smoke less than a pack a day. Sun worshippers should keep in mind the danger of skin cancer from exposure to ultraviolet rays. Women need to learn to examine their breasts every month and remember to have Pap smears taken yearly.

The public has the right and responsibility to receive information about cancer. Patients with cancer have the right to any medically proven treatment available, as well as the right to discontinue or refuse treatment as long as they know the possible consequences of their actions. Cancer remains a dreaded disease, but with today's knowledge and technology, patients who cannot be cured are still living long, productive, and comfortable lives.

—Joan A. Piemme, M.N.Ed.

Health Education Unit 17
Health Testing at Home

In the 1950s it was quite common for patients to go to a physician's office even to have their temperatures taken. It was not common practice for people to take temperatures at home. Although that may sound surprising today, it was not until the late 1940s or early 1950s that a manufacturer first decided to sell thermometers to the general public. Prior to this time, sales had been limited to medical professionals for use in offices and in hospitals.

In the 1970s companies are no longer reluctant to sell medical products to the general public, and the United States is now seeing a major boom in products previously restricted to professionals. An ad in a popular woman's magazine appeals to the growing market, portraying a product that will enable the reader to: "Know Your Blood Pressure Twice a Day!" It urges the reader to buy a "professional blood pressure machine" for "only $15.95." A modern era in health testing at home has apparently begun.

Many doctors were surprised and some were upset by the ad, but I was not. I had been teaching patients to take their vital signs (temperature, blood pressure, pulse, and breathing rate) since 1970 in the Course for Activated Patients (CAP). Such skills were, and continue to be, a popular feature of CAP. People can learn how to make better and more accurate observations about common illnesses and injuries. They can learn not only how to take vital signs but also how to check eyes, ears, noses, and throats, how to record their medical histories, and even how to do urine and stool tests.

Many such tests are now available for home use because of improved manufacturing know-how and dramatically lower costs. Equally important, however, is that an increasingly sophisticated and well-informed general public has created a consumer demand for such products. At the same time, a more open attitude on the part of doctors and other health professionals toward self-testing has evolved. Some of the change in attitude has come about through health education campaigns conducted by the American Heart Association, American Cancer Society, and similar voluntary health associations.

The greater openness on the part of the professionals is made evident by a perusal of medical magazines and newspapers. Recent examples include a report of a research group from Rush Medical College in Chicago that with the aid of local people in rural Mississippi did 6,000 blood pressure readings. The pilot program uncovered 1,000 cases of high blood pressure and included a program of treatment and education.

Another report described a do-it-yourself throat culture plan used for five years by pediatricians with the Columbia (Maryland) Medical Plan. One thousand patients were trained to take throat cultures at home to help identify dangerous strep infections of the throat and tonsils in children. Nearly 3,500 citizens of Mercer County in New Jersey learned to take a blood test for colon and rectal cancer. More than 2,600 returned slides as part of Cancer Detection Day.

Do-it-yourself medical testing equipment is available at an increasing number of surgical and hospital supply stores, drug stores, and mail-order firms. One such mail-order firm sells only certified and professionally approved and tested products. Other mail-order firms offer low-priced products at varying levels of quality. As yet, there is no government agency at the federal level monitoring these new consumer products, and there is a great variation in the quality and warranties available.

During the years since I started teaching CAP, I have made a collection of equipment and do-it-yourself tests. This article reviews some of the tests and equipment in the hope that if you are planning to buy a "blood pressure machine" or other items or are interested in some tests that can be done at home, you can buy them with greater understanding and confidence.

The following are currently available for home use: blood pressure units, stethoscopes, high intensity penlights, urine tests, stool (or fecal) tests, and self-administered medical histories.

Blood pressure units

The products that get the most attention these days are blood pressure units. Part of the reason for this attention is the widespread publicity associated with National High Blood Pressure Month which was first instituted in May 1975.

Health professionals and government and volunteer groups have united in nationwide efforts to identify and obtain treatment for the estimated 30 million people in the United States with high blood pressure (hypertension). The medical value of knowing your blood pressure—whether taken by yourself, a family member, your doctor, or another health professional—is that it offers one important look at the condition of your heart and blood vessels (the cardiovascular system).

One of the most common disorders of this vital system is hypertension. In its earliest stages, the disease's only symptom may be an elevated blood pressure. Hypertension has been correctly named the "silent disease." Normal readings in adults range from 100/80 up to 150/90. If readings are consistently over 150/90, however, hypertension is present and should be promptly evaluated by your doctor. High blood pressure can be treated and controlled if caught early enough.

There are three kinds of blood pressure units (sphygmomanometers): gauge (aneroid), mercury column, and electronic. Each unit has three parts: a cuff which is a flat, inflatable balloon in a cloth cover; a rubber bulb pump with a valve; and a gauge, dial, or column. The unit, with a stethoscope—or in the case of electronic units, a sound sensor—makes it possible to observe the pressure of the blood as it is forced through the arteries by the action of the heart.

The entire process of testing involves the dynamics of the flow of liquids: blood coursing through the artery at the bend in your elbow is similar to the flow of water in a garden hose. There is no noise while the flow of water is smooth, but if you step on the hose with your foot or kink it with your hands and alter the flow of water, you hear sounds of turbulence. When the hose is released to its normal diameter, the sounds disappear and the water runs smoothly.

In somewhat the same manner, by pumping up the balloon in the cuff to 180 or more—the first step in taking blood pressure—you shut off the artery. When you then apply the stethoscope over the area, at first you hear no sound. Then, as you loosen the valve on the bulb and let the air slowly come out of the balloon, blood flow begins and you hear turbulence. When sounds are first heard, the reading obtained is called the *systolic* pressure. A normal example would be 125. When the cuff is loosened even more and there is no turbulence at all, the sound disappears. This lower level is called the *diastolic* pressure. A normal reading would be 80. The blood pressure would be recorded as 125/80.

The cost of a good home-model sphygmomanometer ranges from about $25 for aneroid units to $90 for mercury and electronic units. Professional models carry a 10-year warranty and are accurate for up to 30,000 tests. They are sturdier and cost around $40–$50. Low-cost units, particularly those sold for less than $20, may have a warranty for only one year (or not even that long). Because gauges and pumps do wear out or become defective, a service warranty is important. Check warranties before buying any unit; remember that it is part of the price.

Several reputable firms market blood pressure units for home use. Reliable models are also available from some department stores, retail drug stores, pharmacies, and surgical and hospital supply houses.

The most common complaint about home model blood pressure units is that the instruction booklets are poorly written. Some manufacturers do, however, provide good booklets. A good instruction booklet, "Recommendations for Human Blood Pressure Determination by Sphygmomanometers," is also available from your local chapter of the American Heart Association. Your local chapter of the American Red Cross has a valuable booklet, "Vital Signs Module II Blood Pressure Workbook." If you do not understand the directions that come with your cuff, ask your doctor or one of his office aides to show you how to use it.

Another frequent complaint is that some cuff bands are too short for large arms, a common problem because many people who have hypertension are overweight. The cuff should be tested for length before purchase. The cuff must also fit snugly, especially on a large upper arm. When the balloon inside is inflated, it must apply even pressure to the arm. Otherwise the sounds are hard to hear and an inaccurate reading may be obtained.

People with poor vision may find it difficult to

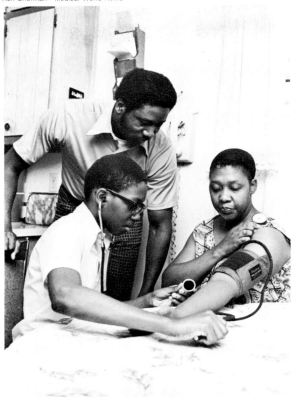

Ron Sherman—*Medical World News*

A home blood pressure unit provides a hypertensive patient with a means of monitoring her condition.

read the numbers on an aneroid gauge. Such people should try reading the dial before they buy the cuff. Others with hearing defects may have trouble with standard blood pressure units. Some electronic units have a flashing light and beeper sound for people with poor vision or hearing.

It is quite difficult to take your *own* blood pressure, and it is recommended that your spouse, friend, or neighbor take it for you. If that is not feasible, however, and you must take it without assistance, there are "palm type" and new wraparound cuffs that are more convenient for doing so. If you have questions about accuracy, the best test is to have your model checked against a mercury unit that may be found at your doctor's office.

A final caution: the gauge and inflation bulb are the parts that become defective. See if they can be easily detached and replaced on your unit should they fail to work properly.

Stethoscopes

To take blood pressure, you need a stethoscope to listen to the sounds of the changing blood flow in the artery. There is also another important use: checking the rate of the heartbeat in the chest. If

the heart rate (pulse) is so rapid or irregular that it can't be counted at the wrist—as may be the case with a young child with a fever or an elderly patient with heart problems—you may use the stethoscope to determine the rate. Listen with it on the chest area just under the left nipple and above the line of the lower edge of the ribs.

A stethoscope consists of three main parts: head, tubing, and ear pieces. There are many variations of heads, but in general they can be classified as diaphragm and bell type. The preferred head for use in taking blood pressure is the diaphragm type, the kind usually found in kits that include both cuff and stethoscope.

The biggest complaint about stethoscopes is that the ear pieces may hurt when in place. The tips of low-cost products are made of hard rubber and are uncomfortable for some people. If this is your problem after several trials, you may need a model that comes with soft plastic or rubber tips. Try it before you buy it.

Another complaint is that the length of the tubing is too short for convenient use. In some stethoscopes that have a plastic Y tube this is a serious problem. In others, with a metal Y piece, additional rubber tubing may be obtained from a laboratory supply house and cut to the proper length.

Another serious problem reported by people with a moderate hearing loss is that the blood pressure sounds are too faint. The problem is greatest with stethoscopes that have tubing of small caliber (an inner caliber of less than ¼ inch). A tubing of at least ⅝-inch inner caliber increases the transmission of sounds markedly so that they are much easier to hear.

High-intensity penlights

A high-intensity, narrow focus penlight is a valuable item to have in your family's "black bag." It can be used to examine throats, noses, eyes, and ears. The ordinary flashlight is too large and the beam of light is too diffuse for the examinations.

Disposable penlights cost $1 or less and last for many months. They are safe and accurate. The lights will have a far greater life expectancy if they are stored on the bottom shelf of your refrigerator when not in use. They are sealed and waterproof, and such storage increases battery life.

Urine tests

One pharmaceutical company has developed an inexpensive urine test, available in many retail drug stores, that can be used at home. Another company has established public service programs that are available to service clubs, schools, and other agencies interested in programs to detect urinary tract infections.

Health testing at home

These tests are safe and accurate but must be used only for *screening* of disease. Interpretation of results and recommendations for treatment or further diagnostic testing must be done by your physician.

Stool or fecal tests for blood

This test is used to detect colon/rectal cancer or other asymptomatic gastrointestinal conditions in which there may be bleeding. It is based on the guaiac paper test for occult (hidden) blood. The test is simple, inexpensive, and accurate and has been used in physician's offices and hospitals for many years. The cost is about $25 for a box of 100.

After the stool has been collected, it must be taken to a doctor's office for a 30-second test. The result is then interpreted by a physician, nurse, or laboratory technician.

Self-administered medical history

The cornerstone for all medical diagnosis is a careful history. Until relatively recent times this was done in a traditional (but time-consuming) dialogue between doctor and patient. With increasingly heavy patient loads, in the past few years many physicians have depended more and more on laboratory data and less and less on medical history data.

Depending on laboratory data has usually increased medical costs without a corresponding increase in diagnostic information. In an effort to stem this trend, some researchers have used the computer to take better histories. Others use self-administered medical histories to do a similar job without the cost of a computer system.

There are several commercial companies and medical clinics that have developed their own versions of the self-administered medical history. All must be interpreted by a physician, nurse, or other health professional when completed by the patient. The professional must then pursue the clues of trouble provided in the history.

All the health tests for home use described here are possible because of technical advancements in medical care. But it cannot be stressed too strongly that they are to be used to *supplement* the services your doctor offers, not *supplant* them.

—Keith W. Sehnert, M.D.

Health Education Unit 18
Physical Fitness

There are physically active octogenarians whose spirit and vitality seem to constitute living proof of the positive rewards of a program of regular exercise. Unhappily, there are also instances of people dropping dead while exercising. The widespread interest in physical fitness that has prompted publication of countless books and articles is thus tempered by a concern about the benefit and safety of exercise. Will a regimen of physical workouts enhance and prolong one's life, or end it?

Physician-author Kenneth H. Cooper has said that "Exercise is the medicine that keeps countless people alive. But like all medicine, it must be taken according to prescription." To provide maximum benefits with minimal risk, therefore, an exercise program must be tailored to meet individual needs and abilities. But how does one decide which program is best for oneself? Should a person see a doctor to be tested for physical fitness? Can one exercise if one has a physical or mental handicap? Should women do the same exercises as men? Should the elderly exercise at all?

Developing an exercise program

Who can develop a physical fitness program and who cannot? The American Medical Association's (AMA) Committee on Physical Fitness and Exercise has established rules for people with heart, lung, and blood vessel problems, for whom vigorous exercise can be dangerous. A vigorous exercise program is *strictly prohibited* for persons with any of the following: (1) moderate to severe coronary heart disease that causes chest pain (angina pectoris) with minimal exercise; (2) recent heart attack — a person must wait three months after an attack before starting a medically supervised exercise program; (3) severe disease of the heart valves; (4) certain types of congenital heart disease in which the skin turns blue during exercise; (5) a greatly enlarged heart due to high blood pressure or progressive heart disease; (6) severe irregularities of the heart rate and pulse requiring medication and medical supervision; (7) severe, uncontrolled diabetes; (8) hypertension not well controlled (pressures exceeding 180/110) even with medicines; (9) excessive obesity — more than 35 pounds overweight; and (10) infectious disease with fever present during its acute stage.

There are several conditions that the AMA committee calls "relative contraindications," which permit programs of exercise under medical super-

vision: (1) infectious disease in convalescent or chronic stages; (2) diabetes controlled by insulin; (3) recent or recurrent internal bleeding; (4) kidney disease (chronic or acute); (5) anemia of less than 10 grams of hemoglobin; (6) lung disease (chronic or acute) that results in breathing difficulty with even light exercise; (7) hypertension that can be lowered only to 150/90; (8) blood vessel disease of the legs in which there is pain associated with walking; (9) arthritis of the back, legs, or feet that requires medication for pain; and (10) convulsive disease not completely controlled by medicine. These conditions do not rule out physical fitness programs. Exercise may in fact benefit diabetics, arthritics, and people with other illnesses, but they should seek medical advice when starting such a program.

There are some questions occasionally raised about exercise for women and the elderly. Some are based on attitudes that are not in line with current medical knowledge. Traditionally women have been assigned passive roles and have been discouraged from participating in vigorous exercise and competitive sports, especially after the teen-

Photographs, Ralph Morse

After a vigorous workout, these men in a YMCA physical fitness program have their pulse rates checked. The pulse rate provides a measurement of the strenuousness of the exercise.

age years. Consequently, obesity is more common among women than among men. Many women's attitudes about vigorous exercise are based on half-truths and myths about childbearing. Vigorous exercise actually improves a woman's capability for bearing children, maintains good gynecologic health, and improves appearance and stamina.

Physical fitness is especially important for people over 60 when the natural aging process of the body accelerates. Good physical fitness can help retard the degenerative diseases associated with aging. Fitness can give the strength and endurance to continue to enjoy social, civic, cultural, and recreational interests and can provide physical reserves to help meet unusual demands and emergencies. Many people mistakenly think that old age is a time to take it easy, slow down, and do less. Facts indicate that the reverse is true. With inactivity, bones lose their calcium, joints stiffen, clots form in blood vessels, and glands lose their functions. An active exercise program is essential for the promotion of good health for old and young, female and male alike.

For persons who are generally healthy, and the vast majority of people are, the AMA has set guidelines. People under 30 can start exercising if they

have had a checkup within the previous year and the doctor found nothing wrong. Between the ages of 30 and 39 people should have a checkup within three months before beginning an exercise program. The examination should include an electrocardiogram (ECG) taken at rest. People between ages 40 and 59 should have a similar checkup but with one important difference—the doctor should administer an exercise ECG while the pulse is approaching levels that would be reached during workouts. For people over 59 the examination should be performed immediately before entering an exercise program. After examination a person can develop a personalized exercise program, and write his own "prescription."

Vigorous exercise programs

Without considering team sports, there are many possibilities for individual or competitive exercises. People under age 30 can enter into any exercise program that they enjoy—running, jogging, walking, swimming, biking, tennis, and so forth—choosing one that is readily available. Choosing an enjoyable activity is important. For people between ages 30 and 50 all choices are open. People between the ages of 50 and 59 should add a regular walking program and continue those activities in which they have maintained good skills and a high level of fitness. They may want to add less arduous exercises such as golf or stationary cycling. Most people over 59 are advised to avoid jogging, running, and vigorous competitive sports such as handball and singles tennis. Regular brisk walking, swimming, running in place, jumping rope, and stationary cycling are suggested for them.

When starting a program, a person should not rush. Start slowly, set goals, and work up to them. A person choosing jogging, for example, should begin with a week or two of walking; if choosing running, first develop stamina with jogging. The heart should get accustomed to the new demands, and muscles and tendons should stretch out and gain strength. Before any daily program begins, warm up properly, starting with a five- or ten-minute routine of stretching arms, legs, and trunk, followed by sit-ups and pushups. After walking rapidly for a minute or so, start running or jogging slowly, gradually increasing the speed. At the end of exercise, don't slump into complete relaxation or lie down, but allow a few minutes for the body to cool down.

As a personal program progresses, set goals for fitness. A wide variety of point systems are available. Points are made by setting and achieving goals such as running one mile in less than eight minutes, swimming 600 yards in less than eight minutes, cycling five miles in less than 30 minutes, and stationary running for 12½ minutes. Many books on exercise explain point systems.

How do people know if they have has been over-zealous in their exercise? One signal is overexertion, a symptom that occurs during exercise. Signs are tightness or pain in the chest, severe breathlessness, light-headedness, dizziness, loss of muscle control, or nausea. Anyone experiencing any of these signals should stop exercising immediately. A second signal is heart rate recovery.

A good way to assess the effect of an exercise program is to record the heart rate (pulse). It can be checked at the wrist or at the neck at the angle of the jaw below the ear. Five minutes after exercising a person should take his pulse. If it is over 120, it is a signal that the exercise is too strenuous for his condition. Ten minutes after exercise, the pulse should be below 100. If it is not, ease up on the program. A third signal is the breathing rate recovery. If you are still puffing and short of breath ten minutes after stopping exercise you are doing too much. The normal resting breathing rate should be 12 to 16 breaths per minute.

In addition to improving physical condition, exercise provides a feeling of energy, tranquility, and well-being.

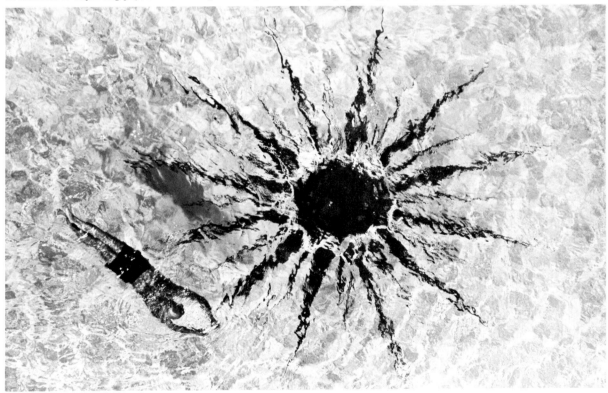

© George W. Gardner

Moderate exercise programs

Some people may choose, because of limitations of time, money, facilities, or other factors, to develop a more moderate exercise program. A moderate program should have certain characteristics for the necessary benefits. It should be: (1) easily available; (2) leisurely (taking at least 30 minutes); (3) regular (at least four times a week); (4) capable of increasing the pulse and breathing rates to at least double the resting rate; and (5) able to give a feeling of relaxation after the exercise.

Exercise can include jogging, swimming, biking, running, and other activities. There should also be a deliberate plan of walking that includes climbing from 5 to 15 flights of stairs daily (or ½ to 1½ miles of walking) up to 15 to 20 flights of stairs (or at least 1½ miles of walking).

Minimal exercise programs

If there are medical or other reasons that limit participation in more rigorous programs, people can prescribe their own minimal plan. People with major disabilities have received benefits by taking up all types of exercise programs. Examples include cross-country skiing for the blind, canoeing and horseback riding for double amputees, wheelchair basketball for paraplegics, modified ball games and folk dancing for the orthopedically handicapped.

Elderly people, even those confined to wheelchairs, can learn to do yoga-like stretching and strengthening postures, body exercises, deep breathing, and self-massage of hands and feet. They benefit from increased vigor and a sense of well-being. Such individuals should adapt modified moderate or vigorous exercise programs, choosing exercise that is enjoyable and available.

Great expectations

The first thing to expect from exercise is pleasure. It feels good to run and stretch, and the body seems to work better. Every cell in the body needs oxygen to live, and oxygen comes in with the air we breathe. Exercise strengthens the breathing muscles and makes possible deeper and more effective breathing. In the lungs, oxygen is picked up by red blood cells.

As exercise increases the heart rate, a greater volume of blood goes to every organ and tissue in the body. Blood supplies food and oxygen, resulting in increased general efficiency of all body systems. The blood vessels of vital organs stay healthy, and if injured, the organs have improved chances for quick recovery. The heart, a highly complex muscle, must have its own healthy supply of blood vessels. Exercise increases vascularization and keeps the heart strong. The exercised heart has built-in protection and extra reserves of power when stress is imposed on it.

Exercise provides beneficial effects on the digestive system. Exercise has a tranquilizing effect on digestion because it relaxes the body in general. Because exercise lets off excess energy, there is less nervous energy to stimulate stomach acid and spasms. Exercise is also a natural cathartic, aiding the muscles of the bowel in moving waste materials. Inactivity breeds constipation; exercise maintains regularity.

The most apparent changes associated with exercise are slimmer waistlines, better shaped legs and arms, and improved posture. They are by-products of exercise programs. In addition, there is less fatigue at work, more speed and grace in movement, and enhanced self-confidence.

Exercise also has beneficial effects on sleep patterns. Active people have normal, sound sleep of from eight to ten hours. People who are relatively inactive frequently sleep erratically and can develop insomnia. By relaxing the body, exercise induces sound, refreshing sleep, which, in turn, provides alertness and ability to concentrate on problem solving. A high level of fitness makes it possible for students to learn more.

Physical fitness, not surprisingly, improves mental outlook. A recent study at the University of Wisconsin showed that jogging is a better treatment for depression than psychotherapy. A ten-week program of jogging gave a cure rate of 75%, substantially better than the recovery rate of depressed persons who were treated by most traditional methods of psychiatry.

If taken according to prescription, exercise is the medicine that keeps countless people alive. There is no product at the local drugstore that provides greater lung efficiency, enlarged blood vessels, healthier tissues, stronger heart muscle, improved digestion, better elimination, more attractive and youthful-looking bodies, sound sleep, and improved peace of mind. Exercise may not be a panacea, but its obvious benefits should encourage everyone to start a program for physical fitness by "writing" their own prescriptions.

—Keith W. Sehnert, M.D.

FIRST-AID HANDBOOK

FIRST-AID HANDBOOK

Produced in cooperation with the Educational Materials Committee
of the American College of Emergency Physicians,
B. Ken Gray, M.D., Chairman.

Authors

Roy D. Beebe, M.D., and G. Richard Braen, M.D.

ACEP Educational Materials Committee

G. Richard Braen, M.D.
Philip M. Buttaravoli, M.D.
Desmond P. Colohan, M.D.
B. Ken Gray, M.D.
Robert M. Stryker, M.D.
Roger S. Taylor, M.D.

Contents

Illustrations by John Youssi

Emergency Care and First Aid

Properly administered first aid can make the difference between life and death, between temporary and permanent disability, or between rapid recovery and long hospitalization. First aid is most frequently employed to help a family member, a close friend, or an associate, and everyone should be familiar with first aid techniques and should know how best to use the emergency care system.

Public education and public awareness of potential roles in first aid have lagged behind the development of the emergency care system, which includes emergency medicine as a special area of medicine, better equipped and better staffed emergency facilities, paramedical care, communications, and transportation. The concept of first aid as simply the immediate care of the injured person is obsolete. Today a person administering first aid must be able to establish priorities in care and must understand and implement *basic life support* in an attempt to maintain vital functions. Education will reduce the chances of error and the possibly harmful results of well-meant but misdirected efforts.

Accidents are the leading cause of death among persons one to 38 years of age. In addition, over 800,000 Americans die annually of heart attacks, and a great majority of these die before they reach a hospital. The annual cost of medical attention and loss of earning ability amounts to billions of dollars, not to mention the toll in pain, suffering, disability, and personal tragedy. Thus, the delivery of quality emergency care and public education in basic life support and first aid must be accorded a high priority.

Use of This Handbook

The purpose of this handbook is both to educate and to serve as resource material for commonly encountered emergencies. It is arranged in three sections. The first deals with basic life support and the treatment of immediately life-threatening emergencies. One must understand these concepts *before* an emergency arises, since the necessary techniques must be employed immediately, almost by reflex, if the victim is to be saved.

The second section deals with emergencies that are not immediately life-threatening. It covers the common emergencies in alphabetical order.

The final section covers prevention, preparation, and use of the emergency care system. Prevention is still the least expensive medicine, and several of its most important principles will be discussed. Each home should be prepared for an emergency by having a readily accessible first aid kit, appropriate telephone numbers, etc. This section also discusses what to do and what to expect at the emergency department.

Section One:
Basic Life Support—Treatment of Immediately Life-Threatening Emergencies

Cardiopulmonary Arrest (Heart and Respiratory Failure)

Cardiac arrest is the most life-threatening of all emergencies. If circulation and breathing are not reestablished within minutes, the brain will suffer irreparable damage. Cardiopulmonary resuscitation (CPR), or basic life support, can be begun by *any person* who has taken time to learn the technique, and there is no need for special equipment. (In addition to reading the description of CPR technique that follows, one would be well advised to undertake formal training in the procedure, available through either the Red Cross or the American Heart Association.)

What Is Cardiopulmonary Arrest?

There are two absolutely vital systems in the body that must function if life is to continue: the *respiratory* system (lungs and respiratory tree) and the *circulatory* system (heart and blood vessels). The overall function of these two systems is to get oxygen from the air into the blood and then to all parts of the body. If either of these systems fails, or "arrests," death occurs very quickly unless the function is restored by CPR.

0-4 MIN.	CLINICAL DEATH	BRAIN DAMAGE not likely
4-6 MIN.		BRAIN DAMAGE probable
6-10 MIN.	BIOLOGICAL DEATH	BRAIN DAMAGE probable
OVER 10 MIN.		BRAIN DAMAGE almost certain

Phases of brain damage and death following cardiac arrest.

Respiratory or breathing failure has two basic causes: 1) obstruction of the intake of air or of the exchange of oxygen into the blood, and 2) impairment of the part of the brain that controls the rate and depth of breathing. Obstruction can result from several factors, including the presence of large pieces of foreign material (such as food) in the upper airway, swelling and closure of the airway (as in severe acute allergic reactions), and damage to the oxygen-exchanging membranes in the lung (from drowning and smoke inhalation). The most common sources of interference with the brain's ability to control breathing are drugs (narcotics, sedatives, alcohol), and carbon monoxide, electric shock, and an interrupted supply of oxygen to the brain, as when the heart has stopped.

If the heart stops pumping, or arrests, the tissues of the body do not receive the blood and oxygen they need. When this happens to the brain, there is an almost immediate loss of consciousness and breathing stops.

What To Look For

If a cardiopulmonary arrest has occurred, the victim *always:* is unconscious; has no pulse in the neck (carotid pulse); is not breathing. The carotid pulse can be checked by feeling with the thumb and index finger on either side of the windpipe (trachea). If a pulse is present, it will be felt here.

What To Consider

Any person who suddenly collapses (becomes unconscious), has no detectable pulse in the neck, and is not breathing has suffered a cardiopulmonary arrest. (A person who collapses while eating and is unable to breathe may well have a large piece of food caught in his windpipe. This is not purely a cardiac arrest, but has been called a "café coronary" and will be discussed below.)

What To Do: The ABCs of CPR

If a person suddenly collapses and loses consciousness, it must be decided immediately whether a cardiopulmonary arrest has occurred. Any delay can result in permanent brain damage or death. Try to arouse the victim. If he cannot be awakened, begin the ABCs of cardiopulmonary resuscitation.

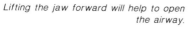

Lifting the jaw forward will help to open the airway.

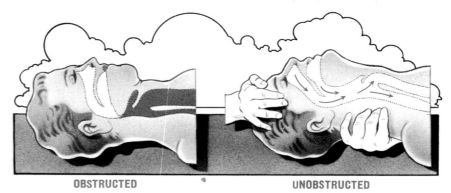

OBSTRUCTED   UNOBSTRUCTED

The back of the tongue may obstruct the airway. Lifting the victim's neck and tilting the head backward will open the airway.

(A) Airway. The first requirement is to assure a clear, unobstructed airway.
1. Place the victim on his back.
2. Hyperextend the neck (lift the victim's neck and tilt his head backward); this lifts the tongue away from the back of the throat and helps to enlarge the airway.
3. Listen for breathing by placing your ear near the victim's mouth, and watch the victim's chest for signs of breathing.
4. If there is no evidence of breathing, open the victim's mouth and remove any obvious foreign materials—false teeth, food, vomitus.

(B) Breathing (Mouth-to-Mouth Resuscitation). If opening and clearing the airway do not produce spontaneous breathing, it will be necessary to breathe for the victim.
1. With the victim's head in the hyperextended position, pinch his nostrils closed, take a deep breath, and place your mouth tightly over his mouth.

2. Exhale quickly and deeply, four times in rapid succession, each time removing your mouth and letting air escape passively from the victim's mouth.
3. If there is great resistance to your breath, no rise in the victim's chest, and no escape of air from his mouth, the airway may still be obstructed.
    a) Further hyperextend the victim's neck and lift his jaw.
    b) Look again for foreign objects in the mouth and throat.
    c) If none are found, you will have to try a different approach. Roll the victim on his side and deliver four firm slaps between the shoulder blades. With the victim on his back, place your fist just above his navel and forcefully push once. Combined, these may force air out of his lungs and dislodge any foreign body that is trapped deeper in the airway; if so, the material should be removed from the victim's mouth.
4. If the mouth cannot be opened or is severely damaged, mouth-to-nose resuscitation may be used.

(C) Chest Compression. After assuring an open airway and delivering four breaths, check for carotid pulse in the neck, on either side of the windpipe. If there is no pulse, perform chest compression, or external cardiac massage.

1. Kneel beside the victim.
2. Place the heel of your hand just below the middle of the victim's breastbone and your other hand on top of the first. Do not let your fingers touch the victim's ribs; you may compress the wrong part of the chest.
3. Leaning directly over the patient, give a firm thrust straight downward. Let the weight of your shoulders do the work.
4. The breastbone should be pushed downward about two inches in the adult, and the compressions should be repeated 60 to 80 times each minute. (Note: Use of this procedure may crack some of the victim's ribs; proceed carefully, but do not stop CPR, since the alternative is death.
5. CHEST COMPRESSION OR EXTERNAL CARDIAC MASSAGE SHOULD ALWAYS BE ACCOMPANIED BY ARTIFICIAL RESPIRATION!
    a) If there are *two rescuers:* one ventilation should be interposed between every five compressions at a compression rate of 60 per minute.
    b) If there is only *one rescuer:* one ventilation should be interposed between every 15 compressions at a compression rate of 80 per minute.
6. If the victim is a child, the ABCs of CPR are the same except:
    a) Foreign bodies are more common in the airway.
    b) The person administering CPR puts his mouth over both the mouth and the nose of the victim.
    c) If an infant's head is flexed back too much, further obstruction of the airway can occur.

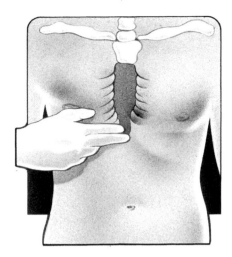

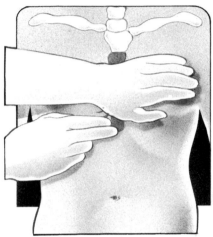

Find the tip of the sternum. The correct hand position for cardiac compression is two finger breadths above the tip of the sternum.

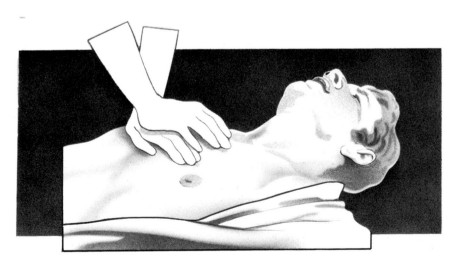

Place the heel of one hand on the sternum, and the heel of the other hand on the back of the first. Compressions of the chest should be done without placing the fingers on the chest wall.

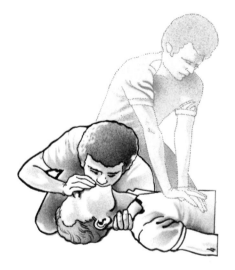

In "two-man" resuscitation, give one breath between compressions at the ratio of one breath for every five compressions.

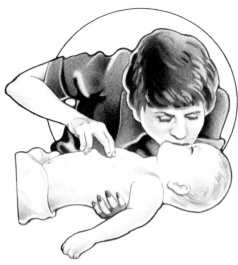

One person can resuscitate an infant by giving quick breaths while compressing the chest with the fingers of one hand.

d) Shallower breaths (puffs) should be used at a rate of 25 to 30 per minute.
e) Exert pressure over the center of the breastbone, as the heart chambers (ventricles) to be compressed are higher in a child's body.
f) Using only your fingertips, compress the chest ¾ to 1½ inches at a rate of 100 to 125 compressions each minute.

What Not To Do

1. Do not try to use CPR on any person who is alert and awake, or on any person who is unconscious but is breathing and has pulses.
2. Never compress the upper or lower ends of the breastbone; CPR is effective only when the flexible part of the breastbone that lies directly over the heart is compressed.
3. Do not interrupt CPR for more than 15 seconds, even to transport the victim.
4. Unless completely exhausted, do not stop CPR either until the victim is breathing adequately on his own and has a pulse, or until the care of the victim is taken over by more experienced medical personnel.
5. If the victim is revived, do not leave him unattended, because he may arrest again and require further CPR.

"Café Coronary" or Severe Choking While Eating

Anyone who collapses while eating may well have had a heart attack, but he may be choking on a large piece of food (usually meat). This most frequently occurs in older people, usually those who have poor teeth or false teeth, and frequently it is associated with some alcohol intake.

What To Look For

1. Before collapsing and losing consciousness, a victim who has been eating, possibly while also talking or laughing, may suddenly stand up and walk from the table, clutch his throat, or exhibit violent motions.
2. *He will not be able to talk.*
3. He may become blue.

What To Consider

The victim may be having a heart attack, but heart attack victims usually are able to talk prior to collapsing; they usually do not display quick violent motions, but collapse suddenly.

What To Do

The person will soon become unconscious and die if the obstructed airway is not cleared.

If the person is still standing:

1. Ask the victim to nod if he has food stuck in his throat.
2. Stand behind him and place one clenched fist in the middle, upper abdomen just below the ribs. Place your other hand on top of the first hand.
3. Give a very forceful pull of the clenched fist directly backward and upward under the rib cage (a bear hug from behind).
4. This will, ideally, act like a plunger and force the diaphragm upward, pushing any air left in the lungs out the windpipe and expelling or loosening the trapped object. The procedure may be repeated several times.
5. Once loosened, the foreign object can be pulled out.

If the victim has already collapsed:

1. Place him on his back, open his mouth and look for and remove any visible foreign material.
2. If none is seen, place the heel of your hand on the victim's mid-upper abdomen and give a forceful push.
3. This should dislodge the foreign material into the mouth, from which it can be removed. Repeat the procedure as often as necessary.
4. If, after the object has been cleared, the victim still is not breathing, is unconscious, and is without a pulse, begin CPR.

What Not To Do

Do not stop CPR efforts until the victim revives or more experienced personnel arrive.

Food obstructing the airway in a "café coronary" may be loosened or expelled by an upper abdominal thrust or hug; using the fist of one hand placed in the abdomen just below the rib cage, give a forceful jerk upward.

What To Expect

If the problem is noted early and foreign material is removed, the chances for the victim's survival are excellent.

Drowning

Drowning and near drowning are common occurrences. Like cardiac arrest and "café coronary," drowning requires immediate action and basic life support.

What Is It?

Many more people nearly drown than actually drown (suffer cardiac arrest). The near drowning victim may have no symptoms or he may need help because of severe respiratory distress and confusion. The drowned victim will be unconscious, will have no pulse, and will not be breathing.

What To Consider

1. The water may damage the lining of the lungs, resulting in a decreased ability to exchange oxygen from the air into the blood. Following a near drowning the victim may suffer a cardiac arrest.
2. Always consider the possibility of an associated injury—for example, a broken neck, which is likely if the victim has dived into the water.

What To Do

1. Begin mouth-to-mouth resuscitation if the victim is unconscious, is not breathing, and is without pulse, even while he is still in the water.

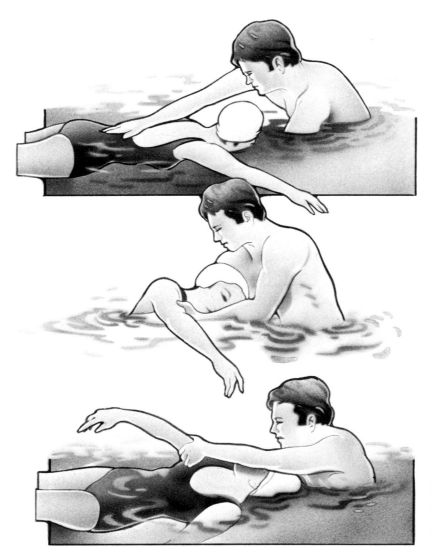

If there is a chance that a drowning victim has also injured his neck, particular care should be taken to protect the neck from further injury. The victim may be floated onto a board for removal from the water (see following page).

2. Give four quick breaths, followed by one breath every five to ten seconds.
3. Remove the victim from the water without interrupting artificial respiration except for a few seconds (one minute at most). Once he is out of the water begin CPR.
4. If the victim has a suspected spinal injury, he should be placed on his back on a flat board for removal.
5. The victim of near drowning should be taken to the hospital *immediately*. If oxygen is available it should be used, and the victim should be watched closely for the possibility of cardiac arrest.
6. The distressed victim who has difficulty breathing, has blue color, and is semiconscious may require only artificial respiration, but be sure.

What Not To Do

1. Do not use the manual (arm lift) method of artificial respiration; it doesn't work.
2. Do not try to drain water from the victim's lungs.
3. Do not fail to take near drowning victims to the hospital immediately; such victims may quickly develop respiratory difficulty.
4. Do not stop CPR until more experienced medical personnel take over, or until you are completely exhausted.

Electric Shock

What Is It?

Even the relatively low voltages of electrical appliances that are used around the home can cause fatal electrocution. Death results from paralysis of the breathing center in the brain, from paralysis of the heart, or from uncontrolled, extremely rapid twitching (fibrillation) of the heart muscle.

What To Look For

1. The possibility of electrocution should be considered whenever an unconscious victim is found near an electric wire, a socket, or an appliance.
2. Electrical burns may or may not be apparent.

What To Consider

1. There are other possible reasons for unconsciousness, such as a head injury, a cardiac arrest, or a seizure.
2. Think of possible associated injuries (head injury, neck injury) before moving the victim.

What To Do

1. Disconnect the victim from the electrical source as quickly and safely as possible. This can be done by disconnecting the plug or appliance or by shutting off the main switch in the fuse box.
2. Alternately, use a dry, nonconductive, nonmetallic stick or pole to move the wire or victim. DO NOT TOUCH THE VICTIM UNTIL HE IS DISCONNECTED OR YOU MAY BECOME ANOTHER VICTIM.

3. If the victim remains unconscious and shows no pulse or respiration, begin CPR immediately. Continue until the victim revives or until more experienced medical personnel take over.
4. If there is an associated head, neck, or back injury, let trained medical personnel transport the victim.
5. Upon awakening, victims of electric shock often are confused and agitated, and, for a short time, they may need protection from falls and additional injuries.

What Not To Do

1. Do Not Touch The Victim Until He Is Disconnected.
2. Do Not Move The Victim If There Is A Head, Neck, Or Back Injury, Except To Remove Him From Danger.

What To Expect

Even with adequate CPR the victim may need more advanced life support such as electric heart shock. However, he generally can be managed with basic CPR until more advanced life support becomes available.

Drug Overdose and Carbon Monoxide Poisoning

What Is It?

Although deaths from drug overdose and carbon monoxide poisoning may be associated with suicide attempts, such deaths do occur in other settings. An unsuspecting heroin addict may inject an exceptionally pure cut of the narcotic. A child may explore the medicine cabinet and ingest some sleeping pills, pain pills, or even antidiarrheal pills. Carbon monoxide poisoning occurs frequently in automobiles with faulty exhaust systems, in industry, and in burning buildings. These poisons all suppress the breathing center in the brain.

What To Do

1. If the person who has ingested pills is unconscious and without pulse or breathing, begin CPR.
2. If the victim is unconscious and is not breathing, but *has* pulses, perform mouth-to-mouth resuscitation only. Respiratory arrest is common in drug overdoses.
3. When transferring the victim to the hospital, take along any bottles and pills that may be associated with the poisoning.
4. Remove the victim from the carbon monoxide exposure and begin CPR.

What To Expect

Following a large drug overdose, even with adequate CPR the victim may not begin to breathe on his own or may not wake up for many hours, and he may need extended life support at the hospital in an intensive care unit.

Massive Hemorrhage (Bleeding)

Following the control of a victim's cardiorespiratory function, the next most urgent priority for the person giving first aid is to control hemorrhaging.

What Is It?

If major bleeding occurs, a large vessel (artery or vein) may be involved. Lacerated arteries tend to produce a pulsating stream of blood, signifying an injury that needs immediate first aid.

What To Consider

If the victim is bleeding massively, shock or inadequate blood circulation may develop and the victim may become unconscious or may have a cardiopulmonary arrest.

What To Do

1. Have the victim lie down to prevent fainting.
2. If he already has fainted, raise his feet higher than his head.
3. If the victim is unconscious, and there are no pulses or breathing, begin CPR.
4. With a clean cloth or sterile dressing, apply *direct pressure* over the wound to halt the bleeding. Most major bleeding (even arterial) will stop in a few

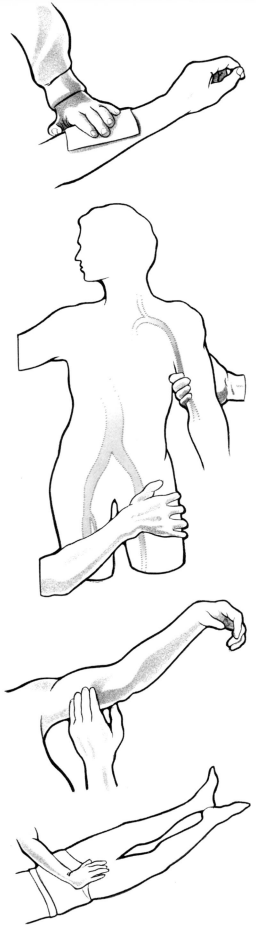

minutes if this method is used.

5. Maintain the pressure until better trained medical personnel take over.
6. If severe bleeding of an arm or leg does not stop after several minutes of direct pressure, try to stop the circulation in the artery supplying the blood by pressing firmly against it with your hand or fingers. There are three points on each side of the body where arterial pressure can be used to stop bleeding. (There are also pressure points in the head and neck, but they should *not* be used because of the danger of interrupting the supply of blood to the brain or the intake of air.)
7. Tourniquets are used only as a last resort, when all else has failed and the victim continues to hemorrhage profusely. Once a tourniquet has been applied, note the exact time and transport the victim to a hospital immediately.
8. When the bleeding stops, tie the dressing firmly in place.

What Not To Do

1. Do Not Try To Use Arterial Pressure Points In The Head Or Neck.
2. Do Not Use A Tourniquet Until You Are Absolutely Certain That Nothing Else Will Work. If the limb around which a tourniquet is applied is deprived of oxygen long enough, it may have to be amputated.
3. If the injury has been caused by a large foreign object that is protruding from the victim's body, do not remove it, or you may further aggravate the injury.

What To Expect

1. Most bleeding can be controlled by direct pressure.
2. Lacerations of the scalp bleed profusely but are rarely associated with massive blood loss.
3. Lacerations of the torso may have penetrated into the chest or abdomen and must be evaluated by a physician.

Section Two:
Common, Not Immediately Life-Threatening Emergencies

Animal Bites

All animal bites (dog, cat, and wild animal, as well as human) are dangerous and need medical attention. In addition to the injury itself, there is a chance of infection, including tetanus and rabies.

Bites from wild animals, particularly skunks, foxes, raccoons, and bats, always should be evaluated by a physician.

What To Do

1. Thoroughly scrub the wound with soap and water to flush out the animal saliva. This should be done for at least ten minutes.
2. Cover the wound with a dry, clean cloth or dressing.
3. Consult a physician immediately for further cleansing, infection control, repair, and possibly for tetanus and rabies prevention.
4. If possible the animal should be caught or identified and reported to the local authorities for observation.

What Not To Do

Do not mutilate the animal, particularly its head. (If it is a wild animal and is killed, tests can be run by the local authorities to determine if it was rabid.)

Automobile Accidents

Even with the slower, safer speeds on U.S. highways, automobile accidents still account for the largest number of the nation's accidental deaths, as well as for numerous fatalities elsewhere. Automobile accidents may cause complex or multiple injuries, and priorities must be considered for the care of the injured.

What To Do

1. Turn the car's engine off if it is still running.
2. Do as much first aid as possible *in* the car.
3. Move the victim only under the following circumstances.

a) The car is on fire.

b) Gasoline has spilled and there is a *danger* of fire.

c) The area is congested, unsafe, and presents the danger of a second accident.

4. Check the patient for breathing and pulses.

5. Control any hemorrhaging.

6. If there is a head and neck injury or fracture of an extremity, wait for medical help before moving the victim, except to insure breathing or to stop significant bleeding.

7. If the victim must be moved to a medical facility, splint any fractures and support his head and neck on a board.

What Not To Do

Do not move unnecessarily a victim who is unconscious or who has a head or neck injury. It may be necessary to move a victim who has no pulse and is not breathing, or who is bleeding severely.

Backache, Acute

Most frequently, back pain is of recent onset and follows some type of acute exertion or unusual activity, such as the lifting of a heavy object. The pain usually results from muscular strain and is not of great significance. However, back pain that is associated with acute injury or with pain radiating down the legs may be important and demands immediate medical evaluation. In addition backache accompanied by blood in the urine might indicate injury to the kidney or the presence of a kidney stone, while backache with fever or urinary pain might signify a urinary tract infection.

What To Do

1. If a backache is nagging, mild, of recent onset, and is associated with recent activity, and if there is no pain radiating into the hip or leg, and if there is no bowel or urinary problem, it may be treated with:

a) Absolute bed rest for 24–72 hours.

b) A firm, nonsagging bed—a bed board might be used.

c) Local heat or warm tub baths.

d) Two aspirin every four hours.

2. If the back pain is severe, with pain radiating into the hip or legs, or if it is associated with bowel or urinary problems, the victim should see a physician as soon as possible.

3. If the back pain follows an accident, it should be evaluated by a physician.

4. Back pain that does not improve within 48 hours should be evaluated by a physician.

Bleeding from the Rectum

The acute onset of bright red bleeding from the rectum may be caused by bleeding *hemorrhoidal* veins. The usual history includes constipation and straining to defecate, leading to bright red blood dripping into the toilet bowl and onto the toilet paper, frequently with associated rectal pain. The problem is common among pregnant women.

If rectal bleeding is not due to hemorrhoids, it needs medical evaluation. If the stools are black and tarry, it is imperative to get a medical evaluation as soon as possible. The possibility that the bleeding originates higher in the intestinal tract must be considered, since rectal bleeding may be a sign of an ulcer, tumor, or inflammation.

What To Do

1. If the bleeding is due to hemorrhoids:

a) Warm tub baths three or four times daily may promote healing.

b) Lubricating ointment such as petrolatum may decrease irritation to the hemorrhoids during bowel movements.

c) Drinking plenty of fluids will soften the stool, as will bran cereals or stool softeners available from drug stores.

2. If bleeding persists, see a physician.

Direct, firm pressure is frequently the best way to stop bleeding. If bleeding is too extensive to stop with direct pressure, locate the brachial or femoral arteries and apply pressure to stop bleeding distal to those points.

3. Get a physician's evaluation for black, tarry stools or for bright red rectal bleeding that is not known to be from hemorrhoids.

Blisters

Blisters are generally caused either by burns or by friction on the skin. Burn-related blisters can result from contact with flame or hot objects or with certain chemicals, and from severe sunburn or scalds. Blisters represent injuries to only a partial thickness of the skin. When a blister breaks, there is a loss of the natural protective insulation of the skin. Open, broken blisters are vulnerable to infection and tend to promote the loss of body fluids by evaporation. If blisters are very large, evaporation may be severe and may result in dehydration.

What To Do

1. Small blisters should not be opened. They should be protected with dry, soft dressings to prevent rupture.
2. Blisters resulting from contact with chemicals should be immediately and copiously washed with tap water to dilute the offending agent.
3. If a blister ruptures, the area should be washed gently but thoroughly with mild soap and water. The skin that covered the blister should be carefully removed, and the wound should be covered with a dry, sterile dressing.
4. Blisters of large areas of the body should be treated by a physician.

What To Expect

1. The pain from blisters usually subsides after one to two days.
2. Almost all blisters break and slough after four or five days, and the wound heals in about two weeks.
3. Ruptured blisters often become infected. Note any increased redness, pain, swelling, or heat about the wound, and be particularly aware of any red streaking up the extremity, pus from the wound, or fever.

Boils, Pimples, and Styes

When sweat glands of the skin become plugged, there may be bacterial growth and an accumulation of infected material (pus) inside the gland. Frequently, the accumulation of pus is absorbed by the body's natural defense processes. Occasionally, the area of infection expands, forming an abscess or boil (called a stye when on the eyelid). These are painful swellings that are red, warm, and can vary from less than a half inch to several inches in size. When these infections have reached this stage, the only way that the body can heal itself is to let the pus out through the skin.

What To Do

1. Apply warm, moist compresses as often as possible throughout the day (for 15 minutes every four hours).
2. When the boil or stye "points" and then ruptures, wipe the pus away gently with a dry, sterile cloth and cover it with a dressing. Continue to use warm, moist compresses.
3. If there are multiple boils or if the infection seems to be large, contact a physician.

What Not To Do

Do not attempt to squeeze or puncture boils, pimples, or styes. If hot compresses are used, early boils and styes may resolve. Most will "point" and rupture in two or three days and will then rapidly heal.

Broken Bones (Fractures)

A broken bone should be suspected whenever a person complains of pain with the loss of the normal use of an extremity. Fractures are seldom in and of themselves life-threatening emergencies, and one must make sure that the victim is safe from further harm and has good respiration and pulses before making any attempt to immobilize or move an injured person. Any victim suspected of having a broken neck or broken back should be handled in a special manner. (*See* Broken Neck or Back, below.)

There are two types of fractures that are important to recognize. Most frac-

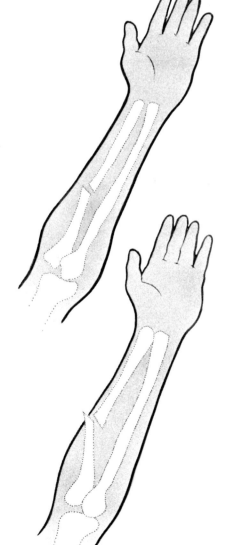

Simple fracture.

Compound fracture.

tures are "simple" or "closed," and the broken bone does not protrude through the skin. There are times, however, when the broken bone does pierce the skin; such breaks are known as "compound" or "open" fractures.

A word about sprains is in order here. Sprains may be managed at home if they are very mild. Aspirin, rest, elevation of the affected extremity, and local ice packs are the best treatment. If a sprain is severe, however, it should be treated like a fracture, and medical attention should be sought.

What To Do

1. Make certain that the victim is breathing adequately and has pulses before even considering first aid for the fracture.
2. When there is reason to suspect multiple broken bones, or when the neck, back, pelvis, or thigh might be broken, it would be best to let trained emergency personnel transport the victim to the hospital.
3. If the broken bone protrudes through the skin, cover it with a dry sterile dressing, but do not try to push it back in. If there is excessive bleeding, use direct pressure to stop it. (*See* Massive Hemorrhage, above.)

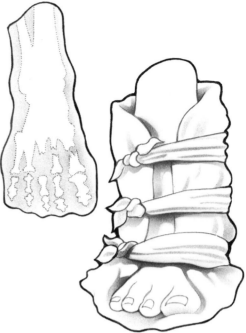

A simple splint for a broken ankle or foot may be made with a pillow or folded blanket or jacket and secured with roller bandages, tape, and so forth.

A broken forearm bone should be splinted, and a sling should be applied. If a splint is not available, the sling itself will reduce the pain.

A broken bone in the lower leg should be splinted before transporting the victim.

4. If the victim must be moved, the fracture should be immobilized with splints to prevent further damage and to make the victim more comfortable (the pain of a fracture is caused by the two ends of the broken bone rubbing together.) The basic principle of splinting is to immobilize the broken bone by securing the affected limb to some firm object (a piece of wood, broom handle, ski pole, several newspapers or magazines, or even an injured leg to the uninjured leg). Both ends of the splint must extend beyond the area of suspected fracture; the splint may be secured with bandages, belts, sheets, or neckties. Most injuries of the arm, wrist, or hand can be stabilized simply with a sling.

What Not To Do

1. Do not try to transport any accident victim who has an obviously unstable (floppy) extremity without stabilizing or splinting it first. Even though fractures can be disturbingly displaced, deformed, and very painful in themselves, they rarely represent life-threatening emergencies. If fractures are immobilized adequately, there frequently is a marked reduction in pain.
2. Do not attempt to move a victim with a suspected broken neck or back without trained medical personnel, unless it is absolutely necessary to do so.

Broken Neck or Back

The possibility of injury to the spine (neck and back) must be considered whenever a person is:

A broken collarbone can be splinted by first applying a sling to the arm, and then applying a wrap around the arm and chest, to reduce movement of the arm.

1. Involved in an accident of any type and subsequently complains of back or neck pain, has any degree of paralysis or weakness of an extremity, or has numbness or tingling of an extremity or part of his body.
2. Injured about the face or head in an accident, or is rendered unconscious.

What To Do

1. Make certain the victim is breathing and has pulses.
2. Unless it is absolutely necessary, do not move the victim, but let trained medical personnel do it.
3. Unless he is unconscious, the victim is safest on his back; avoid attempts to pick up his head or to move his neck.
4. If the victim is unconscious, convulsive, or vomiting, he should be rolled—carefully, and preferably by two people—onto his side, and his head should be supported very carefully on a pillow or coat.
5. If it is absolutely necessary to move the victim, he should be placed on a firm board. This should be done cautiously, with several people supporting the whole spine and the head. The neck or back should not be flexed (chin moved toward the chest or head dropped back).

What Not To Do

1. Do not allow any accident victim who complains of neck or back pain to sit or stand.
2. Do not give the victim anything to eat or drink.

Bruises and Black Eyes

Any direct trauma to the soft tissues (skin, muscles, etc.) of the body may injure the blood vessels as well. The damaged blood vessels then leak blood which, when it accumulates under the skin, at first looks black, in a few days looks yellow-brown, and then is reabsorbed. Also, direct trauma may cause swelling or fluid collection under the skin. The area about the eye, because of the loose tissue present, is particularly prone to this swelling, and when blood collects the result is a "black eye".

Bruises are frequent problems and are usually benign in that they represent minimal injury and get better by themselves. However, if the force is adequate, associated injuries can occur, including fractures, ruptured abdominal organs, collapsed lungs, and injuries to the eyeball. If there is an obvious deformity, severe pain, or impaired motion of an extremity, or if there is impaired vision, blindness, severe pain in the eye itself, or double vision, a physician should evaluate the injury.

What To Do

1. As soon as possible, place a cold compress or an ice bag (a towel soaked in ice water or a towel-covered plastic bag of ice) on the bruise. This will reduce the pain and swelling and should be continued for several hours.
2. Restrict any movement of the injured part, because the less it is used during the first few hours, the less it will swell. Elevation of the bruised part above the level of the heart also decreases swelling.

If the injury is only a bruise, the victim should be able to use the extremity. Most bruises and black eyes will enlarge and worsen in appearance for up to 48 hours after the injury, after which they will gradually shrink. The blue-black color becomes yellow-brown and then disappears in 10–14 days. If multiple bruises that are not associated with trauma appear over the body, a physician should be contacted, because this may indicate a blood clotting disorder.

Burns

The skin can be burned by flames, hot objects, hot liquids (scalds), excessive sun exposure, chemicals, and contact with electricity. There are three degrees or depths of burns:

First degree—reddened, hot, very painful, no blisters. Heals spontaneously.
Second degree—painful, red, blistered. Usually heals spontaneously.
Third degree—deep burns can be white or black and are always painless. These may require skin grafts.

414

Many burns that appear to be first degree may later develop blisters and may actually be second degree. Second-degree and third-degree burns frequently become infected and need more attention and care than do first-degree burns. Electrical burns frequently look small but may be much deeper than suspected. Burns in children and older people are more serious.

What To Do

1. For sunburn see below.
2. For flash burns, scalds, and small burns, towels or sheets soaked in cool water should be applied immediately for comfort.
3. If it is a chemical burn, the area should be washed copiously and continuously (under a running faucet if possible) for 15–30 minutes.
4. The burn should be dressed with sterile, dry, soft dressings.
5. If burns involve large areas of the hands or face, they should be examined by a physician.
6. Electrical burns should be treated by a physician.
7. Burns, like cuts, require tetanus prevention.

What Not To Do

1. Do not apply ointments, sprays, or greases to large wounds.
2. Never use butter on any burn.
3. Do not break blisters.
4. Do not pull off any clothing that adheres to the burn.

If a small burn becomes encrusted, has pus, or shows red streaking, it may be infected and should be seen by a physician. If large areas of the body have second- or third-degree burns, there may be an excessive water loss from the body with consequent shock. People with extensive burns, especially young children and old people, are very likely to go into shock, and they should be transported to a hospital emergency department as soon as possible. "Shock," in this case, refers to a low level of circulating bodily fluids, not to a psychological state.

Chest Pain

It is well established now that most heart attack deaths result from *treatable* disturbances of the heartbeat. The overall emphasis must be to get the person with a heart attack into an intensive care unit as soon as possible. To accomplish this there must be:

1. Equipped and staffed emergency departments.
2. Better prehospital care and transportation.
3. Public education on the signs and symptoms of a heart attack.
4. Public education on the techniques of basic life support—CPR. (*See* Cardiopulmonary Arrest, above.)

Denial of the pain and its significance, ascribing it to other causes (heartburn, gas, or pulled muscles), and trying different remedies (antacids or antiflatulence medications) often lead to fatal delays in proper medical treatment. Everyone must be aware of the significance of chest pain and heart attack.

Severe chest pain must always be considered a medical emergency. A correct diagnosis can only be made by a *physician*, using an appropriate medical history, an examination, and sometimes several laboratory tests—an electrocardiogram, chest X-ray, and blood tests.

There are several aspects of chest pain that are important. Heart attack pain is often described as a *dull* ache, tightness, squeezing, or as a heavy feeling that is usually diffusely located over the front of the chest. It is often associated with aching in the shoulders, neck, arms, or jaw. Many people become short of breath, sweaty, nauseated, and may vomit. If any of these symptoms occurs in an adult, he must be transported immediately to the nearest physician or emergency department.

What To Do

1. Chest pain, especially with the symptoms listed above, demands *immediate* medical attention. An ambulance should be called immediately.
2. While waiting, make the person comfortable and reassure him.

3. Do not give him anything by mouth except what a physician has prescribed.
4. Do not make him lie down if he is more comfortable sitting.
5. Do not leave him unattended. He may suffer a cardiac arrest and may require basic life support (CPR).

There are many other causes of chest pain that may need medical attention. Chest pain associated with fever and cough could be a symptom of pneumonia. Chest pain associated with coughing up blood or associated with thrombophlebitis (pain in the calf or thigh) might represent a blood clot in the lungs. A collapsed lung might cause chest pain and sudden shortness of breath.

There are numerous causes of chest pain, such as severe heartburn, viral pneumonia, inflammation of the cartilages of the ribs, and pulled muscles, that are not life-threatening, but a physician must make these diagnoses.

Childbirth, Emergency

Childbirth is a natural and normal phenomenon, and it rarely requires advanced medical training to carry out a safe delivery. For a variety of reasons (inadequate transportation, very short labor, etc.) many babies are born unexpectedly, outside of the hospital.

Labor is the cyclical contraction of the uterus (womb) which helps to open up the end of the uterus (cervix) to allow passage of the baby. These contractions usually are painful and occur with increasing frequency and duration until the delivery. The overall duration of labor is different for every woman. Frequently labor lasts for 12 or more hours for a woman's first baby, but the time may be reduced to a few hours or less for the woman who has borne several children.

Delivery is the passage of the baby through the birth canal and the vagina. The mother will usually experience *rectal* pressure and will know that the child is being born. The reflex action is to push or "bear down." The child's head and hair will be visible at the opening of the vagina. If the woman is "pushing" and the infant is visible, the birth is imminent. If a foot, an arm, the buttocks, or the umbilical cord is first to appear, take the mother to a hospital immediately.

What To Do

1. Let nature take its course. Do not try to hurry the birth or interfere with it.
2. Wash your hands and keep the surroundings (sheets, etc.) as clean as possible. (Fresh newspaper is often sterile, if sheets or blankets are unavailable.)
3. Support the emerging baby and let it slide out.
4. Once the baby is delivered, support him with both hands, keeping his head lower than the rest of his body. This will allow the fluid to drain from his mouth.
5. Place the infant on a dry towel or sheet and cover him immediately. Heat loss is a problem for newborn babies.
6. Aluminum foil wrapped around the baby will retard heat loss.
7. If the baby is not breathing begin mouth-to-mouth resuscitation, very gently, using puffs of air from your cheeks.
8. It is not necessary to cut the umbilical cord, and one may choose to have this done at the hospital. If medical care will be significantly delayed, however, use the following procedure to cut the cord: using a clean (boiled) ribbon, cord, or string, tie the cord tightly at two points, one that is four inches from the baby and the other at least eight inches from the baby. Cut the cord with clean, boiled scissors between the two ties.
9. Do not wash the white material from the baby (this is protective).
10. Warmly wrap the infant and transport it to the hospital.
11. Knead the womb after the child has been delivered.
12. The mother should remain supine until the bleeding stops and the placenta has been expelled.
13. When the placenta is expelled, minutes after the birth of the child, it should be retained and taken to the hospital for examination.

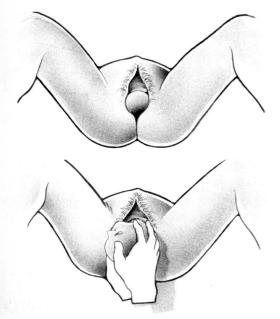

If childbirth is imminent, the top of the baby's head will begin to bulge through the mother's labia. Support the head with one hand on each side (not over the baby's face), and ease the shoulders out. The baby will be quite slippery, so be careful not to drop it.

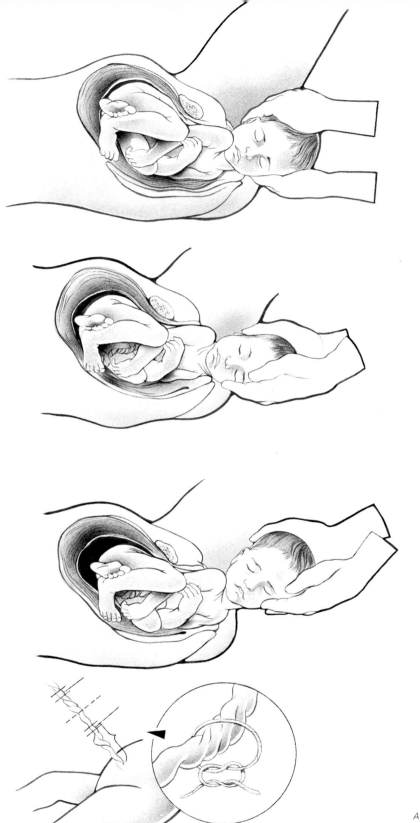

After delivery, the umbilical cord may be tied using a sterilized cord. Tie the cords at four and eight inches from the baby.

Cold, Overexposure, and Frostbite

Overexposure. Each year many people die from cold exposure resulting in *hypothermia*. The people who are particularly at risk include elderly persons with poor circulation, individuals who unpreparedly become exposed to low temperatures and high winds, and people who are intoxicated with alcohol.

CORE TEMPERATURE	SYMPTOMS
94°	CONFUSION
90°	HEARTBEAT BECOMES IRREGULAR
86°	LOSS OF MUSCLE STRENGTH DROWSINESS AND UNCONSCIOUSNESS
77°	CARDIAC ARREST AND DEATH

As the body's core (central) temperature drops, the victim becomes confused and ultimately may die.

Poor circulation, poor protection from the elements, and alcohol dilate blood vessels in the skin and allow heat loss that lowers the body core (central) temperature. Malfunction of the brain, heart, and lungs may then occur.

What To Do

1. Remove the person from cold exposure and place him in the warmest place possible.
2. Use hot water bottles or warm blankets to warm the victim as quickly as possible.
3. If the victim is awake and able to swallow, give him *warm, nonalcoholic* drinks.
4. Watch for a cardiac arrest and be prepared to carry out CPR.

What Not To Do

1. Do not give alcoholic beverages.
2. Do not leave the person unattended.
3. Do not place a hot water bottle directly against the victim's skin; wrap it in a sheet or towel.

Frostbite. Frostbite is a common injury in winter weather, particularly when low temperatures are combined with wind. Exposed, small parts of the body are the most susceptible (nose, ears, fingers, toes, and face). Again, the elderly and the intoxicated are the most susceptible. Initially, the involved part begins to tingle and then becomes numb. Frozen tissue usually is dead white in color.

What To Do

1. Remove the person from the cold as soon as possible.
2. Every effort should be made to protect the frozen part. If there is a chance that the part might refreeze before reaching medical care, it may be more harmful to thaw it and let it refreeze than to await arrival at the treatment area for thawing.
3. Rapid rewarming is essential. Use lukewarm (not hot) water between 100° and 110° F (37–43° C) or use warmed blankets. Within about 30 minutes, sensation may return to the part, which may become red and swollen. At first the rewarmed part will tingle, but it will begin to be painful and tender to the touch.
4. When the part is warm, keep it *dry* and clean. If blisters appear, use sterile dressings.
5. See a physician as soon as possible.

What Not To Do

1. Do not give alcoholic beverages.
2. Take care not to burn the person by using water that is too hot.
3. Do not let the part refreeze.
4. Do not rub the injured part; friction may cause further damage.

Convulsions

Convulsions and epileptic attacks are frightening to watch. The victim's lips may become blue, he may make a crying noise, his eyes may roll back, and his body may be jerked by uncontrollable spasms. Many seizures occur in people with known seizure disorders who have forgotten their medications, in alcohol abusers who have recently stopped drinking, and in children with an acute febrile illness (febrile seizures). *Febrile convulsions* are quite common among children aged six months to three years. They result from an abrupt rise in the child's temperature and are generally of short duration (usually ending by the time the victim arrives at the emergency department). The victim usually awakens soon after the seizure.

What To Do

1. Turn the victim onto his side so that saliva is able to drain out without being inhaled into the victim's lungs.
2. If it can be done safely, place a rolled handkerchief in the victim's mouth between his teeth to prevent him from biting his tongue. Do not force a spoon or other object into the victim's mouth.

418

3. Most people who have had a seizure need prompt medical attention at the nearest emergency department.
4. The child with febrile convulsions is treated by reducing the fever. Cool towels or sponge baths may help to lower the child's temperature.
5. If the victim has fallen or shows evidence of head trauma, he should be assumed to have a broken neck and should be treated accordingly. (*See* Broken Neck or Back, above.)

What Not To Do

1. Do not force objects into the mouth of the convulsing person.
2. Do not get bitten by the convulsing person.
3. Do not try to restrain the convulsive movements. Protect the victim from further injury.

Following the seizure (most last less than ten minutes) the person will usually fall asleep or will be confused.

Do not assume that the seizure is "just a seizure" in either a child or an adult, since seizures may be signs of other problems such as head injury, meningitis, or tumor.

Croup

What Is It?

In the fall and winter months, when houses are dry and warm, young children (usually younger than three years) may develop a "croupy," barking cough. This condition usually is caused by a viral inflammation of the trachea (windpipe) and of the larger airways, and the infection may cause severe respiratory distress.

What To Do

1. For mild cases (most cases), lowering the temperature in the room and using a humidifier will quickly help the croupy breathing. A bathroom filled with steam from a running shower may be helpful.
2. Aspirin and liquids may be used to combat low-grade fever.
3. If there is a high fever, difficulty in swallowing or talking, or respiratory distress, the child should be seen by a physician as soon as possible.

Most cases of croup are mild, and they will usually clear up after two or three days if corrective measures are taken.

Cuts, Scratches, Abrasions

Small cuts, abrasions, and scratches are common occurrences and generally require only thorough cleansing and bandaging for protection. Some cuts are larger and may require stitches for closure to minimize scarring, to reduce the chance of infection, and to restore function. Deeper cuts may involve blood vessels, and they may cause extensive bleeding or may damage muscles, tendons, or nerves.

What To Do

1. All minor wounds and abrasions should be *thoroughly* washed. There should be no dirt, glass, or foreign material left in the wound. Mild soap and water are all that are necessary.
2. Bleeding can be stopped by direct pressure that is applied over the wound with a sterile, dry dressing, and by elevating the injured part.
3. Most wounds should be covered with a dressing to protect them from further harm and contamination.
4. All bites (human or animal) should be treated by a physician because of the likelihood of infection. (*See* Animal Bites, above.)
5. If there is any question about the need for sutures, the wound should be examined by a physician.
6. If the wound is dirty or extensive, or if the victim's tetanus immunization is not up to date, there may be the need for a booster immunization.
7. Watch carefully for signs of infection (usually they do not appear for several days). The signs are:
   a) a reddened, hot, painful area surrounding the wound,
   b) red streaks radiating from the wound,

c) swelling around the wound, with fever and chills.

If an infection appears, see a doctor at once.

Diabetic Coma and Insulin Reaction

Diabetics have difficulty using the sugar in their blood. *Insulin* lowers the blood sugar level. As would be expected, it may be difficult to adjust the daily insulin requirement to the intake of sugar-containing foods and to the individual's activity level. Because of this, some diabetics occasionally suffer either from *insulin reaction* (which is a blood sugar level that is too low) or from *diabetic coma* (which can be thought of as a blood sugar level that is too high).

Insulin reaction, or acute hypoglycemia, may cause the person to become acutely confused, incoherent, sweaty, or shaky. Eventually, the person may lose consciousness.

What To Do

1. Determine if the victim is a diabetic.
2. If he is *conscious*, give him some form of sugar (a lump of sugar, candy, sweets, or soft drinks that are not artificially sweetened).
3. If recovery is prompt, take the victim to the nearest physician.

What Not To Do

Do not try to give sugar to someone who is unconscious.

Diabetic coma with hyperglycemia (a high blood sugar level) is quite different. The onset is more gradual, taking several hours or longer. The victim may have warm, flushed skin, with a very dry mouth and tongue. He frequently may be drowsy but rarely is unconscious. His breath may smell fruity (like nail polish remover), and he may be dehydrated.

What To Do

A person in a diabetic coma needs prompt treatment by a physician.

Diarrhea (in a small child)

Diarrhea may be caused by many factors, ranging from simple nondigestion of eaten foods to such conditions as bacterial or viral infections of the intestinal tract. In a small child, acute prolonged diarrhea may rapidly cause dehydration and death. The younger the child and the more prolonged the diarrhea, the more dangerous is the threat to health. Maintenance of adequate hydration is the main goal of therapy.

The signs of dehydration are: lethargy, dryness of the mouth and armpits, sunken eyes, weight loss, and the absence of urination. A child who continues regularly to wet his diapers generally is not dehydrated.

What To Do

1. Small children with acute diarrhea should be given water, liquid Jell-O, or pediatric salt solutions. Milk and whole foods should be withheld for the first 24–48 hours of the diarrhea. In acute diarrhea, the bowel is unable to digest and absorb some of the sugars in milk, which worsens the diarrhea.
2. If the diarrhea persists for more than 48 hours, a physician should be contacted.
3. If the diarrhea causes signs of dehydration, or if the child stops taking in fluids, a physician should be contacted immediately.
4. Almost all diarrheal states in children are well on the road to recovery within 48 hours. For the bottle-fed child, half-strength formula can be substituted for regular formula for one or two days before resuming full-strength formula. If the diarrhea persists, a physician should be consulted.

What Not To Do

1. Do not continue milk and whole food during an acute diarrheal state.
2. Do not use adult antidiarrheal medications for children.

Dislocated Joints

It is frequently impossible to tell the difference between dislocated joints and broken bones until X-rays have been taken.

What To Do

1. Probable dislocations in the hand, arm, shoulder, or jaw usually do not require an ambulance for transportation to the hospital. Victims should, however, be transported safely and comfortably.
2. If there is a dislocation of the hip or knee, ambulance transportation will be needed.
3. Slings or splints may be helpful. (*See* Broken Bones, above.)

What Not To Do

Do not attempt to move or manipulate the joint, or to set a dislocation yourself; the bone may be broken if these procedures are done improperly.

Eye Pain (something in the eye)

Even a small speck of dirt in the eye can cause intense pain. The covering of the eye is quite sensitive and, even after the foreign material is removed, there may be a feeling of irritation. Redness and tears are frequently present.

What To Do

1. Examine the eye by pulling the lower lid down while lifting the upper lid off the eyeball. Most specks will be visible.
2. Gently attempt to wipe the speck off with a moistened corner of a clean cloth, handkerchief, or cotton swab.
3. If the speck does not come off *easily*, or if there is persistent discomfort, a physician should be seen as soon as possible.
4. If irritating liquids are splashed into the eye, irrigate the eye with cool tap water for 30 minutes.

Fainting — Dizziness

Fainting is a sudden but momentary loss of consciousness. There are a variety of causes for it, including fatigue, hunger, sudden emotional upset, poor ventilation, etc. The person who has fainted looks pale and limp but is breathing and has a normal pulse. Simple fainting is not associated with chest pain or seizures, and the unconsciousness does not last for more than one or two minutes.

If a person faints, place him on his back or side and elevate the legs above the head.

What To Do

1. Place the victim on his back or side, with his legs higher than his head.
2. Check his airway, breathing, and pulses.
3. Apply cold compresses to the victim's forehead, and have him inhale aromatic spirits of ammonia.
4. If fainting is associated with chest pains, seizures, or severe headache, or if it lasts more than one or two minutes, the victim should be transported by ambulance to a physician.
5. If a person reports that he feels faint, have him sit with his face in his lap or stretch out on his back until he feels better.

Fainting is a relatively common problem and almost always quickly resolves in one or two minutes. Nevertheless, other causes should be considered—heart attack, stroke, internal bleeding, and insulin reaction.

Fever

Fever is an elevated oral temperature above 98.6° Fahrenheit or above 37° Celsius. Fever is a manifestation of the body's response to infection (viral or bacterial) or to foreign substances that the body is attempting to reject. People with fever frequently report muscle and bone pains, headaches, chills, and a hot feeling. Viral infections (colds, influenza, and even viral gastroenteritis) almost invariably are associated with low-grade fevers and are the most common causes of such fevers.

In susceptible children younger than three years of age, a *rapidly* rising fever may induce febrile seizures. (*See* Convulsions, above.)

What To Do—Adults

1. Aspirin and acetaminophen (aspirin substitute) are the two most effective antifever medicines available. If used appropriately, they not only effectively lower the temperature but also will provide some relief for the bone and muscle aches.
2. The person with fever should take a lot of fluids, as higher temperatures increase evaporation of water and thus accelerate dehydration.
3. Bed rest helps.
4. If the fever is very high (102° or more) and persistent (most fevers last less than 24 hours), a physician should be consulted.
5. Fever associated with chest pains, shortness of breath, cough, or with the production of sputum, or with confusion, headache, a stiff neck, abdominal pain, or earache should be evaluated by a physician as soon as possible.

What To Do—Children

1. Fever of 100° or more in an infant (less than 30 days old) is always an emergency, and the child should be seen immediately by a physician. Every household should have a thermometer for taking children's temperatures.
2. In addition to fluids and bed rest, children with temperatures over 100° may be given aspirin or acetaminophen (aspirin substitute) every four hours in doses of not more than 60 mg for each year of life.
3. The child *should not be* overly dressed but should be dressed lightly (T-shirt and diapers are enough).
4. If a child develops a temperature of 103° or more, and the fever does not respond to aspirin or acetaminophen, the child should be placed in a tub of lukewarm water (not cold) and should be sponged for at least 30 minutes.
5. If the fever still does not respond, a physician should be contacted.
6. Any child with a febrile seizure, lethargy, signs of dehydration, or excess irritability should be seen by a physician.

What Not To Do

Do not sponge a child with alcohol; it is potentially toxic and is flammable. The sudden cold is often frightening to a child.

Food Poisoning

Food poisoning is a term applied to the combination of nausea, vomiting, or diarrhea that is attributed to contaminated food. The symptoms may be identical to those of viral gastroenteritis (stomach flu), but with the lack of an associated fever. Some other causes of the same symptoms include emotional stress, viral infections, inorganic or organic poisons, or food intolerance. Food poisoning itself is caused by toxins produced by bacteria growing in the food. The most common organism causing food poisoning is the *Staphylococcus*. In *Staphylococcus* food poisoning, vomiting and diarrhea generally develop within one to 18 hours following ingestion of the contaminated food.

What To Do

1. Generally, food poisoning resolves spontaneously within a few hours. Clear liquids should be offered as tolerated.

2. If vomiting or diarrhea is prolonged, dehydration may develop. In some cases, medical attention should be sought.

What Not To Do
1. Do not take antibiotics. They are useless in this type of poisoning.
2. Do not force the victim of food poisoning to drink fluids if he has any respiratory difficulty. Victims who develop respiratory difficulty should be seen immediately by a physician.

Foreign Objects in the Nose, Ear, Throat

Nose
1. If the object cannot be withdrawn or teased out easily, consult a physician at once.
2. Do not allow violent nose-blowing.
3. Do not deeply probe the nose yourself. You may push the object deeper into the nostril or you may cause harm to the nasal tissues.

Ear
1. If the object cannot be withdrawn easily, consult a physician.
2. The tissues of the ear are very delicate and can easily be damaged. Pushing the object in further may even rupture the eardrum.

Throat
1. Large objects caught in the throat can cause severe difficulty in breathing (*see* Café Coronary, above). This requires immediate care.
2. Small objects can be swallowed—coins, fishbones, etc. Such smaller objects that get caught or that irritate the throat and that cause no difficulty in swallowing or breathing should be given a chance to pass. Drinks of water followed by eating soft foods—such as bread—may help. If the object remains caught or if irritation persists for more than two or three hours a physician should be notified.
3. Someone who has an irregular object—such as a pull tab from a beverage can, a piece of wire, or glass—caught in his throat needs immediate medical attention.

Head Injury

Injuries to the head may include lacerations and contusions of the scalp, fractures of the skull, or brain injuries. Whenever someone has suffered a serious injury to his head, one must always consider whether there might have been an associated injury to the neck. If there is a possibility of an associated neck injury, the victim should not be moved except by skilled personnel unless there is a chance that he might inhale secretions or vomitus. In that case, the victim may be very carefully rolled onto his side.

What To Do
1. Severe, deep lacerations should not be cleansed or irrigated. Instead, sterile dressings should be placed over the wound and should be secured snugly with a roller bandage. Heavy pressure should not be applied to severe lacerations because there may be an associated fracture of the skull and too much pressure may drive a fragment of bone into the brain.
2. Note any loss of consciousness or altered mental status. An examining physician will need this information.
3. Make sure that the victim's pulse and respiration are normal. If the victim might inhale his secretions or stomach contents, very carefully turn him onto his side. Note the size of the victim's pupils. If the victim is unconscious or confused and his pupils become unequally dilated, this is a medical emergency and he should be seen immediately by a physician.
4. Keep the victim lying down, but do not place a pillow under his head since doing so may cause further damage to the neck if it also has been injured.
5. Make sure that the victim's airway remains open. At times, CPR or artificial respiration (see above) may be needed.

Any head injury accompanied by a loss of consciousness should be evaluated

If there is an open head injury, apply a sterile dressing and secure it with a roller bandage. If there is significant bleeding, apply the roller bandage firmly.

by a physician. This evaluation should be done as soon as possible after the injury. Even though the victim may regain consciousness, further brain damage may develop.

Heatstroke (sunstroke), Heat Exhaustion (heat prostration), and Heat Cramps

Heat exhaustion and heat cramps result from salt depletion generally in association with dehydration. Heat cramps are characterized by muscle spasms in the extremities and in the abdomen. Heat exhaustion is manifested by shock (low blood pressure), mental confusion, and muscular incoordination. Other symptoms may include weakness, dizziness, or headaches.

Heatstroke is rare and generally affects the elderly, persons with heart disease, persons who are physically exhausted, or persons who have been consuming alcohol to excess. In this condition and in sunstroke there is a failure of the heat-regulating mechanisms in the body. The victim has a high fever and dry skin. The pulse generally is rapid and irregular and the blood pressure is low. The victim's temperature may reach 107° to 111° F (41.7° to 44° C). First aid is the same for heatstroke and sunstroke.

What To Do

1. For heat exhaustion, move the victim to a cool place and elevate his legs. If he can take fluids by mouth, give him salt water (½ teaspoon of salt in a glass of water).
2. Heat cramps may also be treated with salt solutions taken orally.
3. Heatstroke, manifested primarily by a very high temperature, should be treated by placing the patient in a cool place, by removing his clothing, and by applying cool water or ice packs to his body. The victim's extremities should be massaged vigorously to aid circulation.
4. If the victim has suffered from heatstroke, heat exhaustion, or prolonged heat cramps, medical attention should be sought.

What Not To Do

1. Avoid giving water without added salt, because this may further deplete the body's salt concentration.
2. Avoid the immediate reexposure of the victim to the heat, because he may be very sensitive to high temperatures for a time.

Nosebleeds

Nosebleeds are generally caused by trauma to the nose, which can result from nose-picking, from colds when there is hard nose-blowing, or from drying of the nasal mucosa. Most commonly, nosebleeds originate from the area of the nasal septum. Nosebleeds may also be associated with hypertension, bleeding disorders, or nasal tumors.

What To Do

1. To prevent the inhalation or swallowing of blood, have the person sit up and lean forward.
2. Gently squeeze the affected side of the nose closed for 10 to 15 minutes.
3. If the bleeding stops have the victim rest quietly for a few hours. During this time there should be no stooping, lifting, or vigorous nose blowing. Seek medical attention if the nosebleed is profuse or prolonged. The blood loss from a nosebleed can be considerable, and some people even go into hemorrhagic shock following a nosebleed.

What Not To Do

Do not allow the victim to resume normal activities for a few hours after the nosebleed has subsided.

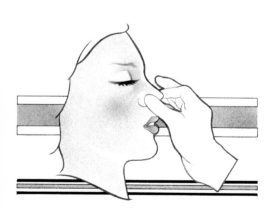

A nosebleed frequently can be stopped by firmly pinching the nose closed.

Poisoning

Poisoning is a common occurrence, particularly in households in which there are children. For the most part poisoning is accidental, but occasionally someone will ingest a poison during a suicide attempt. Households should be equipped to handle poisoning, and syrup of ipecac should be available.

Generally there are five kinds of poisons that might be ingested: a) pesticides, b) drugs, c) strong alkalies and acids, d) petroleum products, e) poisonous plants.

Two of these, petroleum products and strong alkalies and acids, are worthy of special note, because vomiting should *never* be induced if they have been ingested. Examples of petroleum products include turpentine, paint thinner, furniture polish, gasoline, and liquid shoe polish. Examples of strong alkalies include drain cleaner, lye, and some bleaches. In the case of strong alkalies or other strong substances that may cause chemical burns, the mouth and esophagus are burned when the poison is swallowed. If the person is made to vomit, he will be burned a second time as the chemical is passed up the esophagus and out the mouth again. In the case of petroleum products, vomiting may lead to inhalation of the poison, with a resulting chemical pneumonia.

The best way to handle poisons is to take precautions against their ingestion, particularly when small children are present. Medicines, detergents, and cleaning products should all be placed on a high shelf, not under the sink where children can easily find them. In addition, poisons should be kept in appropriate containers. It is dangerous to keep gasoline or furniture polish in a soft drink bottle because a child may drink from that bottle, thinking that it contains a soft drink.

What To Do

1. Initially, give ½ glass of water or milk to anyone who has ingested a poison, unless the victim is *unconscious* or is having convulsions.
2. Decide whether or not to induce vomiting. Look in the victim's mouth for burns that might indicate the ingestion of an acid or alkali. Also, smell the victim's breath to see if it smells like a petroleum product. If either sign is present, do not induce vomiting. If the poisoning has been caused by pesticides, drugs, or poisonous plants, vomiting may be induced by putting one's fingers into the back of the victim's throat to induce gagging and vomiting, or by using syrup of ipecac. Children should be given approximately one teaspoon to one tablespoon of syrup of ipecac, and adults should be given two tablespoons. Vomiting should occur within 20 to 30 minutes.
3. Contact your local physician or emergency department for further instructions. A Poison Control Center may recommend specific antidotes. Antidotes that are listed on the packaging of poisonous products may not be correct or the procedure for their administration may be faulty. It may be better to contact a Poison Control Center for specific, step-by-step instructions.
4. If respiratory difficulty or shock develop, they should be treated appropriately.

What Not To Do

1. Do not allow poisons to be within the reach of children.
2. Do not induce vomiting if alkalies, acids, or petroleum products have been ingested.
3. If the victim is unconscious or is having convulsions, do not give him water, and do not induce vomiting.
4. Do not store poisonous materials in food bottles or jars.

Poison Ivy, Poison Oak, and Poison Sumac

Contact with poisonous plants such as poison ivy, oak, or sumac frequently produces local itching and redness in allergic individuals. In some people the rash that develops is characterized by vesicles (small blisters). More severe reactions include headache, fever, and malaise.

What To Do

1. Contaminated clothing should be removed and all exposed areas of the body should be washed with soap and water.
2. Once the rash has developed, soothing lotions may be applied to the skin. Many of these lotions are available without prescription at a pharmacy. Cool, moist compresses also are valuable for relieving itching.
3. If blisters appear and begin to ooze, they may be treated with wet dressings —sterile gauze pads saturated with a solution of baking soda and water

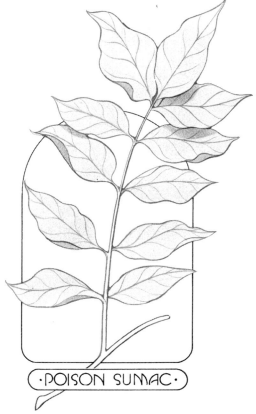

·POISON SUMAC·

·POISON IVY·

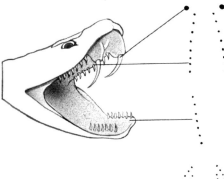

Objects stuck deep through the skin (or into the eye) should not be removed. If the object is too large to be secured in place by simply using a dressing, a paper cup taped over it may reduce further injury.

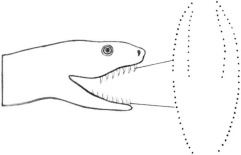

Pit vipers generally produce conspicuous fang marks. Nonpoisonous snakes and coral snakes will not leave fang marks.

(one tablespoon of baking soda to one pint of water).

4. If a severe reaction occurs, if there is a fever, or if a large area of the body is involved, seek medical advice.

Puncture Wounds

Puncture wounds are created by penetrating objects such as nails, knives, sticks, and needles. Puncture wounds do not bleed as readily as lacerations and thus there is less natural cleansing of the wound and a higher rate of infection.

What To Do

1. The site of the puncture wound should be cleansed with soap and water, after which a clean dressing should be applied.
2. For severe puncture wounds, seek medical attention for tetanus prophylaxis and for consideration of antibiotic therapy.

What Not To Do

Do not remove any foreign object that is protruding from the wound. As moving the object may cause further damage, the physician should attend to such wounds.

Rape

Rape is the unlawful carnal knowledge of a woman by a man, forcibly and against the woman's will. In the United States, rape is common, and friends or relatives are frequently called on to render assistance to rape victims.

What To Do

1. The rape victim should be protected from further harm and should be assured that she is safe.
2. If she is injured and is bleeding, direct pressure should be applied to the bleeding points. Never, however, apply hard pressure to the rectal or vaginal areas.
3. If she has a broken extremity, it should be treated appropriately.
4. Always remember that a rape victim has an absolute right to refuse medical, legal, or psychological help; however, she should be encouraged to see a physician as soon as possible.

What Not To Do

1. Even though the victim may feel unclean, she should be advised not to bathe, douche, or urinate, because doing so may destroy some evidence needed by the medical examiner.
2. The scene of the crime should not be touched, because this may invalidate existing evidence that would lead to the conviction of the attacker.
3. The victim should be advised not to change her clothing until she has been examined medically, because some evidence may be lost.

The trauma of the rape victim does not end with the rape itself. She may develop psychological problems or have marital difficulties for days or even years following the incident. In many communities, counseling services have been established specifically for the benefit of these victims.

Snakebite

In the United States there are two groups of poisonous snakes: the coral snakes and the pit vipers. The coral snake is found from North Carolina to Florida, through Louisiana to central Texas. The Sonoran coral snake is found in Arizona and southwestern New Mexico. The pit vipers include the copperhead, water moccasin, and rattlesnake. Rattlesnakes and other pit vipers account for the greatest number of the venomous snakebites in the United States, while coral snakes account for a very small number. Coral snakes produce relatively inconspicuous fang marks. Pit vipers produce a more conspicuous injury, with fang marks surrounded by swelling and blood-filled blisters.

The effect of a poisonous snake's bite depends on the size of the victim, the location of the bite, the amount of venom injected, the speed of absorption of the venom into the victim's circulation, and the amount of time between the bite and the application of specific antivenom therapy.

copperhead

water moccasin

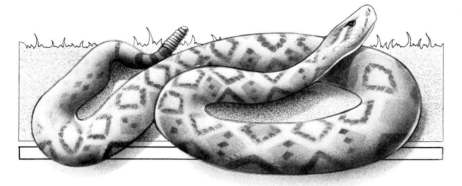

diamondback rattler

coral snake

What To Do
1. First aid begins with reassuring and calming the victim.
2. The victim should be transferred to a physician as soon as possible. Even if the bite was inflicted by a nonpoisonous snake, a physician may want to give tetanus prophylaxis and antibiotic therapy.
3. Immobilization of the bitten extremity will help retard absorption of the toxin.
4. Application of an ice pack at the site of the fang mark may also slow absorption.

What Not To Do
1. Incisions over the fang marks are not recommended, nor are constricting tourniquets.
2. Do not give the victim alcohol in any form.

Spider Bites and Scorpion Stings

The reaction to the toxins of spiders and scorpions varies from mild, with resulting local pain, redness, and swelling, to severe, with convulsion, nausea, vomiting, muscular pain, and even shock. In the United States the two spiders that are generally the most harmful are the black widow spider (*Latrodectus mactans*) and the brown recluse (*Loxosceles reclusa*).

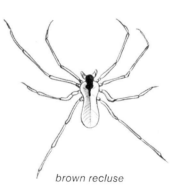

brown recluse

What To Do
1. The two best first aid measures for spider bites and scorpion stings are the immobilization of the affected part and the application of ice packs to the site of the bite or sting.
2. A medication like aspirin may help relieve the pain.
3. For brown recluse bites, black widow bites, and some scorpion bites, a physician's attention should be sought.
4. If the spider or scorpion has been killed, don't discard it. A physician may be able to further identify the species if he sees it.

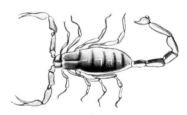

scorpion

Stings (Wasp, Bee, Yellow Jacket, and Hornet)

The stings from these insects are relatively common, and they rarely cause death except in highly sensitive individuals. The sting may be painful, but the symptoms are usually mild and are of short duration.

black widow

Some people are highly sensitive to insect stings and may develop an allergic reaction, possibly with anaphylaxis (a massive allergic reaction) and subsequent death.

What To Do

1. Most people have no problem from an insect sting if they apply local cool compresses or a solution of water and baking soda.
2. Aspirin sometimes helps.
3. If the person is highly sensitive to insect bites and has developed allergic reactions in the past, seek immediate medical attention. If medical attention will be delayed more than a few minutes, attempt to remove and discard the stinger and attached venom sac if present, being careful not to squeeze it.

wasp

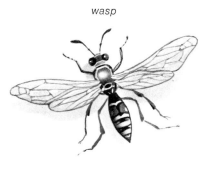

yellow jacket

honeybee

bumblebee

hornet

Stroke

Strokes are often referred to as cerebral vascular accidents. "Cerebral vascular" refers to the blood vessels in the brain, which are affected either by a clot or by rupture with subsequent hemorrhage. Major strokes may be accompanied by facial weakness, an inability to talk, the slurring of speech, loss of bladder and bowel control, unconsciousness, paralysis or weakness (particularly on one side of the body), or difficulty in breathing and swallowing. Sometimes strokes are associated with vomiting, convulsions, or headaches.

The most important things to watch are breathing and vomiting. Recovery from strokes is quite variable.

What To Do

1. If the victim is having difficulty breathing, his airway should be opened. (*See* Cardiopulmonary Arrest, above.)
2. The victim should be positioned on his side so that his secretions will drain out of his mouth and not into his airway.
3. If vomiting occurs, the victim should be kept on his side and his mouth should be wiped clean of vomitus.
4. Get prompt medical attention for all stroke victims.

What Not To Do

1. Fluids should never be administered by mouth unless the victim is fully conscious.
2. The victim should not be left alone for any length of time because of the chance of his vomiting and then inhaling the vomitus.

428

Sunburn

Ordinary sunburn is caused by overexposure to the sun's ultraviolet rays. The initial symptoms may begin as early as one hour after exposure and are manifested in painful redness and swelling of the area, and, in more severe cases, in the formation of blisters over the sun-exposed areas. When very large areas of skin are involved, fever, gastrointestinal upset, and weakness may occur.

Fair-skinned people and people taking certain medications should avoid exposure to the sun. Even dark-skinned people should initially avoid being in the bright midday sun for longer than 30 minutes. For added protection there are many good sun-screening ointments, creams, and lotions available. The most common and most effective ingredient in these is para-aminobenzoic acid (PABA), which screens out the ultraviolet rays that cause sunburn.

What To Do

1. Mild sunburn can be treated at home with cool compresses.
2. If there is an accompanying fever, aspirin may help.
3. Commercially available lotions often have a soothing effect on the skin.
4. For more severe cases, it may be necessary to consult a physician.

What Not To Do

1. Avoid further exposure to the sun until the acute reactions have subsided.
2. Avoid greasy preparations.

Sunburns usually resolve themselves, but occasionally the blisters become infected. If much of the skin has peeled off, the underlying skin will be quite sensitive to reexposure to the sun for several days or weeks.

Unconsciousness

Unconsciousness is a sleeplike state from which one may or may not be arousable. A person in "stupor" may be aroused with stimulation and only then with difficulty, while a person in coma cannot be aroused even by the most powerful stimuli.

The most common causes of unconsciousness are fainting, intoxication with alcohol, head trauma, strokes, poisoning or drug overdoses, seizures, diabetic acidosis, hypoglycemia, various types of shock, and hypoxia. Elderly, poorly nourished, or otherwise debilitated people are more prone to unconsciousness regardless of the nature of their illness.

The cause of unconsciousness is often difficult for even a physician to diagnose, and laymen should be careful not to ascribe a patient's unconscious state to something like intoxication. Alcoholics are of course not immune to other more serious causes of unconsciousness.

What To Do

1. Any unconscious person should be checked for an open airway and for palpable carotid pulses (*see* Cardiopulmonary Arrest, above).
2. If the person is not arousable but is breathing well and has good carotid pulses, he should be placed on his side so that he will not inhale any stomach contents if he vomits.
3. Anyone who is comatose should be evaluated by a physician. If drug ingestion or poison is suspected, the containers from the suspected toxin should be brought to the emergency department. Observations made about the person before his lapse into unconsciousness also will be of great help to the examining physician.

What Not To Do

1. Unconscious persons should not be left alone for any length of time, except for summoning help.
2. Fluids should never be administered by mouth and vomiting should never be induced.
3. Do not unnecessarily move an unconscious person unless you are certain he does not have a neck injury.

If unconsciousness resulted from a fainting attack, the victim may awaken within a few minutes. If unconsciousness recurs or if the person remains unconscious for several minutes, an evaluation by a physician should be sought.

Vomiting

Vomiting is the action by which the stomach rids itself of its contents. Vomiting can be caused by disturbances in either the abdomen or the head.

Causes of vomiting arising in the abdomen include: irritation or mechanical obstruction at any level of the intestinal tract, or irritation of abdominal organs like the gallbladder.

Causes of vomiting that originates in the vomiting centers in the head include: emetics (drugs), various toxins (poisons), increased pressure inside the head, decreased oxygen content of the blood in the head, disturbances of the semicircular canals of the ear (as occurs with seasickness), and, occasionally, psychological factors.

Severe or prolonged vomiting may lead to dehydration. When vomiting is associated with respiratory difficulty it may indicate that some of the vomitus was inhaled, and this is a medical emergency.

Simple acute vomiting may be caused by the effects of alcohol on the stomach lining, by dietary indiscretions, by viral gastroenteritis, or by the morning sickness of pregnancy. Severe or prolonged vomiting may reflect more severe gastrointestinal or systemic disease.

What To Do

1. Care should be taken to turn bedridden people onto their sides, so that they do not inhale any vomited stomach contents.
2. If a comatose person vomits, he should be turned onto his side and the vomitus should be cleared from his mouth.
3. After the initial episode of vomiting, solid food should be withheld temporarily and clear liquids should be given. (A clear liquid is one through which it is possible to read a newspaper.)
4. If the person goes twelve hours without vomiting, solid foods may be resumed, beginning with dry foods such as crackers.
5. If vomiting is prolonged or associated with severe abdominal pain, seek medical attention.

What Not To Do

1. Milk or formula should not be given to infants until the vomiting has subsided.
2. Solid foods should not be given to adults and children until the vomiting has subsided.

Section Three:

The Emergency Care System

To be most effective, emergency care must begin as soon as possible at the scene of an accident. In the home—one of the most common accident sites—there are two important steps that should be taken *before* an accident occurs: prevention and preparation.

The cheapest and most effective medicine is prevention. Every attempt to make the home as safe as possible is mandatory. Accidents in the home may be prevented by keeping stairways well lit and entryways unobstructed, by the careful placement of loose rugs, by proper care and maintenance of electrical appliances and cords, and by the proper shielding and use of power tools.

Particular care should be taken in the home to prevent poisoning. All prescription and over-the-counter drugs (including aspirin, cold remedies, and vitamins) should be stored in "child-proof" containers. In addition, old medications should be flushed down the toilet. The passage of time may cause drugs either to lose their potency or, through evaporation, to increase in potency. All medicine should be stored out of the sight and reach of children.

All cleaning solutions, drain and oven cleaners, solvents, and petroleum products (kerosene, gasoline, turpentine, charcoal lighter), insect spray, roach tablets and roach powder should be stored on high or locked shelves where children can't get at them. Never put any of these substances in a beverage or food container. Beverage bottles look particularly inviting to toddlers.

FIRST-AID HANDBOOK

Every home should have a separate box (not just the medicine cabinet)
containing at least the following supplies

First Aid Tools
Thermometer, oral
Thermometer, rectal
Flashlight
Hot water bag
Pair of scissors
Pair of tweezers
Packet of needles
Safety matches
Ice bag

First Aid Material
Aspirin, adult
Aspirin, children's, or aspirin substitute
Bottle of ipecac syrup (2 to 3 oz)
Bottle of aromatic spirits of ammonia
Antiseptic cream for burns
Sunscreen medication (para-aminobenzoic acid)

First Aid Dressings
Sterile 4″ × 4″ dressings
Gauze (2″ wide) for bandaging
Box of assorted adhesive dressings
1″ adhesive tape

Appropriate List of Telephone Numbers
911 (the universal emergency call number in some communities)
Local hospital emergency department
Ambulance or rescue squad
Police department
Family physician
Poison Control Center (if one is available in the area)
Fire department

Prehospital Care

Wherever there is a serious accident, or when there is any question of serious injury, it is best to call an experienced ambulance or rescue squad. Many services are upgrading their capabilities with better equipment and training. Most ambulance drivers and attendants are at least basic Emergency Medical Technicians (EMTs). The EMTs have received 81 hours of intensive first aid training, have passed a minimal proficiency test, and are certified by a state health agency. Many communities also have advanced EMTs (paramedics) available for emergency care. These individuals are basic EMTs but have had an additional 500 to 1,000 hours of intensive training in advanced life support (defibrillation, use of intravenous medications, advanced airway management, etc.). They generally function through radiocommunications with a hospital-based physician.

To Summon Emergency Aid

Have the telephone numbers of an ambulance service or, if none is available, the local police or fire department readily accessible. When you call, be as calm as possible. *Do not* hang up until all of the following information has been given: a) your name; b) your location (how to get there); c) your telephone number; d) the type of emergency (number of people involved, etc.).

The Emergency Department

The emergency department of the local hospital is the best facility to evaluate and treat true emergencies. Because many people may be seeking emergency care at the same time for different degrees of emergencies, the emergency department might seem to be a very confusing place. Most emergency departments, however, are organized to quickly establish priorities for care, and to provide appropriate treatment for each individual as soon as possible within the limits of those priorities.

The system starts with the nurse, who usually sees the victim first and, by means of a few basic medical questions or tests (temperature, blood pressure, pulse, etc.), attempts to determine the nature of the victim's problem. This nurse is trained to recognize life-threatening problems and to assure that they are seen and evaluated first. In an emergency department patients are not seen on a first-come, first-served basis. For example, a person with a sprained ankle would have to wait to be seen until a man with severe chest pains had been treated.

Better hospital emergency departments have physicians present around the clock to see and treat emergencies. These physicians are specialists in the treatment of emergency problems. Their availability in the hospital and their special training make them the physicians best suited to initially evaluate and stabilize any true emergency. The emergency physician's practice frequently is confined to the emergency department, and he should not be assumed to be in competition with one's regular physician.

Index